Nanostructured Materials

Nanostructured Materials
PHYSICOCHEMICAL FUNDAMENTALS FOR ENERGY AND ENVIRONMENTAL APPLICATIONS

ZESHENG LI

College of Chemistry, Guangdong University of Petrochemical Technology, Maoming, China

CHANGLIN YU

College of Chemistry, Guangdong University of Petrochemical Technology, Maoming, China

ELSEVIER

Elsevier
Radarweg 29, PO Box 211, 1000 AE Amsterdam, Netherlands
The Boulevard, Langford Lane, Kidlington, Oxford OX5 1GB, United Kingdom
50 Hampshire Street, 5th Floor, Cambridge, MA 02139, United States

Notices

Knowledge and best practice in this field are constantly changing. As new research and experience broaden our understanding, changes in research methods, professional practices, or medical treatment may become necessary.

Practitioners and researchers must always rely on their own experience and knowledge in evaluating and using any information, methods, compounds, or experiments described herein. In using such information or methods they should be mindful of their own safety and the safety of others, including parties for whom they have a professional responsibility.

To the fullest extent of the law, neither the Publisher nor the authors, contributors, or editors, assume any liability for any injury and/or damage to persons or property as a matter of products liability, negligence or otherwise, or from any use or operation of any methods, products, instructions, or ideas contained in the material herein.

ISBN: 978-0-443-19256-2

For information on all Elsevier Science publications visit our website at https://www.elsevier.com/books-and-journals

Publisher: Candice Janco
Acquisitions Editor: Charles Bath
Editorial Project Manager: Anthony Marvullo
Production Project Manager: Paul Prasad Chandramohan
Cover Designer: Greg Harris

Typeset by TNQ Technologies

Working together to grow libraries in developing countries

www.elsevier.com • www.bookaid.org

Contents

PART 2 Application types of nanomaterials in energy and environment fields

PART 4 Opportunities, challenges, and future outlooks

PART 1

Physicochemical fundamentals of nanomaterials

CHAPTER 1

Introduction

1.1 Introduction of nanostructured materials

The scientific and technological revolution has provided new tools that are profoundly changing the relationship between man and nature. Research has shown that, since the 21st century, about 90% of the world's 960 most significant scientific research directions are related to nanotechnology. Xue-Sen Qian, a famous scientist from China, early pointed out that: "Nanotechnology is the focus of scientific and technological development in the 21st century, which will be a technological revolution and an industrial revolution." To date, the subject scopes of nanotechnology have included nanoenergy, nanoenvironment, nanobiology, nanoelectronics, nanomechanics, nanomaterial, nanochemistry, and other technical fields. As a frontier and interdisciplinary platform science, nanoscience provides an innovative driving force for seven basic disciplines: physics, materials, chemistry, energy, environment, life, as well as engineering. Nanoscience has become one of the most innovative scientific research fields of mankind and an important source of transformative industrial manufacturing technology [1–3].

Nanostructured materials or nanomaterials refer to the materials composed of crystalline or amorphous ultrafine structural units within the nanoscale (1–100 nm). Due to the unique surface electronic properties and crystal structure effects of nanomaterials, there are usually four effects that macromaterials do not have, namely, small-size effect, quantum effect, surface effect, and boundary effect. Nanoscience takes nanoscale substances as the research object to explore their unique physicochemical properties and functions; nanotechnology is to manipulate atoms and molecules at the nanoscale, process materials, and manufacture nanodevices with specific functions. Therefore, the research of nanomaterials includes two main directions: one is the basic theoretical research, that is, the formation mechanism and structure–function relationship of nanomaterials; the second is engineering application research, which takes the physical scale and nano dimensionality as the starting point to develop the applied technologies such as the preparation, processing, measurement, and application of nanomaterials [4–6].

The sustainable development of energy and environment are two important strategies of human society in the world. With the development of global economy, people's demand for energy is growing, and the development of new energy is imperative; At the same time, it is urgent to strengthen environmental protection and ecological restoration in the technological development process [7,8]. Nanomaterials exhibit unusual mechanical, electrical, magnetic, optical, chemical, and catalytic properties, opening up new

Nanostructured Materials
ISBN 978-0-443-19256-2, https://doi.org/10.1016/B978-0-443-19256-2.00003-X

fields of research and application for energy development and environmental protection. At present, a variety of metallic or nonmetallic nanomaterials play an important role in energy (energy storage and conversion) and environmental (environmental protection and purification)-related technology applications [9,10]. The energy and environmental applications often involve the physicochemical reaction process (e.g., electrochemical, photochemical, or thermochemical reactions) of nanomaterials. Most nano nonmetallic materials (such as carbon and phosphorus) and nano metal materials (including transition metals, noble metals, and their alloys, oxides, nitrides, carbides, sulfides, phosphides, etc.) can strengthen the reactive or catalytic efficiency in the above reaction process [11,12]. It is important to elucidate the relationship between the structural characteristics of nanomaterials and their reaction or catalytic activity in energy development and environmental remediation. The structure—activity relationship often depends on the surface properties of nanomaterials and the structural effects, such as size effect, electron effect, geometrical effect, dimensional effect, crystal effect, confined effect, interface effect, synergistic effect, and so on [13—15]. In particular, how to correlate these effects with physical and chemical properties through electronic structure is the ultimate way to reveal the structure—activity relationships of nanosystems. Therefore, an in-depth understanding of the physicochemical basis of nanomaterials is very important for the rational design of efficient and practical nanomaterials. It is an urgent and core scientific issue in the fields of nano energy and environmental science (see Fig. 1.1 for details).

1.2 Introduction of physicochemical principles

Physical chemistry is a science to explore the basic laws of chemical changes and related physical changes from the relationship between physical phenomena and chemical principles. It is an important branch of chemical science. Physical chemistry often presents the

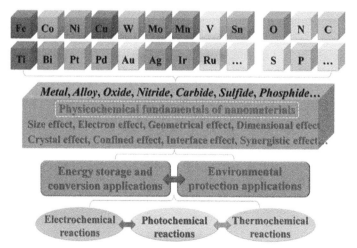

Figure 1.1 Categories and structural effects of nanomaterials for energy and environmental applications.

principles and methods of chemical science with the help of the theories and experimental means of basic sciences such as mathematics and physics. It is a sub-discipline of chemistry to illuminate the macrophenomena, microlaws and basic theories of the chemical reaction system, and also the theoretical basis for connecting nanomaterials to chemical principles [16—18]. Physical chemistry can include eight research directions and discipline branches: thermodynamics, kinetics, phase equilibrium, chemical equilibrium, electrochemistry, interface chemistry, colloidal chemistry, and theoretical chemistry. The principles and theories from the eight branches of physical chemistry are closely related to the synthesis, characterization, and application of nanomaterials [19,20].

Thereinto, the physicochemical principles of chemical equilibrium, phase equilibrium, and colloidal chemistry play significant roles in the controllable synthesis (including solid-phase, liquid-phase, and gas-phase synthetics) and structural regulation (including crystal structure, dimensional structure, and assembly form) of nanomaterials. The theories of electrochemistry and surface chemistry can guide the two key applications of electrochemical energy storage/conversion and photocatalytic/adsorption environmental remediation for the nanomaterials. In particular, from the perspective of physical chemistry (such as thermodynamics, kinetics, and theoretical chemistry), one can deeply understand the essential properties, internal laws, and mutual relationships of nanomaterials, and construct physical or chemical theoretical models based on empirical facts, which is very conducive to obtaining more accurate structure—activity relations and general scientific laws [21—23]. Meanwhile, the thermochemistry (or catalysis), photochemistry (or catalysis), or electrochemistry (or catalysis) of nanomaterials are closely related to the principles of physical chemistry (including interfacial chemistry and electrochemistry) and their industrial applications (including energy and environmental fields) (see Fig. 1.1) [24,25]. Therefore, it is of great significance to elucidate and summarize the relationship between the physicochemical principles and nanomaterial's physicochemical properties for promoting the practical application of nanomaterials and accelerating the progress of nanotechnology.

In terms of teaching and scientific research, "Physical Chemistry" is a basic theoretical course in the undergraduate stage, while "Nanomaterials" is often a professional content in the graduate stage. The research of nanomaterials (such as energy and environmental applications) is a specialized and detailed research field in the field of physics or chemistry. After repeated and long-time precipitation, the important physicochemical principles (such as Gibbs free energy theory, Langmuir adsorption theory, reaction kinetic equation, Nernst equation, Tafel equation, and Laplace equation) are directly related to the thermal- or photo- or electro-chemical or catalytic application of nanomaterials. As long as a teacher has a good grasp of the basics of each subfield of physical chemistry, he or she can often find unexpected joy in guiding students in scientific activities: "Undergraduates are creative, inquisitive, and can come up with new ideas when they collide with their ideas". For example, Professor Ye-Xiang Tong of Sun Yat-sen University, when talking about the role of light energy and heat energy in the catalysis of solar energy, quoted the statement "the combination of two swords" of Yang Guo and Xiao Longnv in Chinese martial arts novels to vividly explain the complementary and joint relationship between light and heat. The new idea was put forward by the undergraduate students under the guidance of Tong [26]. Finally, two nanomaterial's results about the idea of light and heat synergistic catalysis were published in two important international academic journals: Angewandte Chemie-Int. Ed. and Journal of the American Chemical Society [27,28]. Recently, by rationally linking the "physicochemical principles" and "design of nano-structured materials," two undergraduates in our research group also completed an aca-demic research paper about the photocatalysis of nanomaterials in the Journal of Hazardous Materials [29] and a critical review paper about the thermocatalysis of sub−nanomaterials on the Green Chemistry [30]. The results from "Nanomaterials" and "Physical Chemistry" collisions are likely to serve as demonstration cases for undergrad-uate and graduate education in chemistry and material-related fields.

1.3 Introduction of energy applications

With the depletion of traditional fossil energy and the increasingly severe environmental problems, people's demand for sustainable clean energy (including gas energy, solar en-ergy, wind energy, water energy, and electric energy) is increasing rapidly. The develop-ment of sustainable electrochemical energy storage and conversion technology is considered as one of the most promising methods to solve this series of problems [31,32]. In addition, gas energy is efficient, clean, economic, and safe, which is an ideal quality energy and can be widely used in power generation, heating, transportation (gas vehicles), and other fields [33]. Accelerating the development of gas energy has become an important choice for the United States and other developed countries to achieve a sus-tainable development strategy [34]. Based on these, in this book, the energy-related ap-plications of nanostructured materials mainly include three parts: (1) electrochemical energy storage (such as supercapacitor, metal-ion battery, and metal-sulfur battery); (2) electrochemical energy conversion (such as solar cell, fuel cell, and metal-air battery); (3) production of energy gases (such as hydrogen, methane, ethene, carbon monoxide, ammonia gas, etc.) via the electrocatalytic, photocatalytic or thermocatalytic routes.

Because at least one dimension of the three-dimensional spatial scale of nanomaterials is in the nanometer scale (<100 nm), and its size is between atoms, molecules, and macro-systems. Nanomaterials have many characteristics, which makes the system composed of nanoparticles have many special properties different from the bulk macro material system. These properties can greatly change the common carrier physical transport and chemical reaction process in electrochemical energy storage and conversion, which shows the op-portunity to improve the efficiency of electrochemical energy storage and conversion de-vices. Recently, Lei, Sun, and Zhang [35] jointly clarified that: the highly controllable nanomaterials can further optimize the performances of related electrochemical devices and realize efficient utilization of materials by changing their structural parameters (size, morphology, heterostructure, and spatial arrangement). In general, the use of nanomaterials to enhance electrochemical energy conversion and storage includes four important research directions: (1) the size controlling of nanostructures, (2) the morphology controlling of nanostructures, (3) the design of nanostructure heterojunctions, and (4) the design of spatial arrangement of nanostructures (see Fig. 1.2A for details) [35].

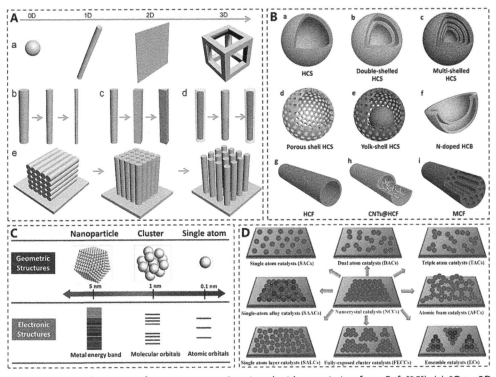

Figure 1.2 (A) Schematics of nanostructures (reprinted with permission from Ref. [35]): (a) 0D to 3D nanostructures, variable structure parameters of (b) size, (c) morphology, (d) heterojunction, (d) spatial arrangement; (B) Schematics of nanostructures (reprinted with permission from Ref. [36]): (a–c) different-shell hollow nanospheres, (d and e) porous nanocages, (f) nanobowls, (g–i) hollow or porous nanowires; (C) Schematics of geometric and electronic structures (reprinted with permission from Ref. [37]); (D) Schematics of atomically dispersed sub–nanostructures (reprinted with permission from Ref. [38]).

Highly controllable nanomaterials show advantages in electrochemical energy storage and conversion by changing the structural parameters (size, morphology, heterostructure, spatial arrangement) due to the enhancement of two aspects: physical transport of carriers and chemical reactions [35]. For example, the controlled surface atom ratios increase the surface area per unit mass of material, and the ordered spatial arrangements provide fast carrier transport channels, which improve the related electrochemical reactivity. The controllable size, morphology, and heterojunction of nanostructures provide huge spaces for regulating their properties (such as changing band gap, carrier transport, and chemical potential) and causing nanoscale confined effect and interface synergistic effect. On the other hand, the hollow nanostructures have wide application prospects in energy storage and conversion due to their functional nano-shells and sufficient internal space. These hollow nanostructures mainly include hollow nanospheres with microporous or mesoporous shells (including single shell and multiple shells) and hollow nanowires (or porous nanowires) (see Fig. 1.2B for details) [36]. By adjusting their external geometry, chemical composition, shell structure, porous structure, and internal space structure, the hollow nanostructures can effectively improve the electrochemical properties of nanomaterials (including dynamics, power/energy density, and electrochemical reactivity).

With the rapid growth of world energy demand, the development and utilization of diversified energy systems are imperative. At present, about a quarter of the global energy conversion process is directly or indirectly related to metal catalysis reaction [39]. Compared with traditional metal nanoparticle catalysts (generally larger than 5 nm), the active components in sub−nanometal catalysts ($\sim$ 1 nm) or single-atom metal catalysts (0.1 nm) are almost completely exposed to the reactant with an atomic utilization rate of nearly 100%. At the same time, the low coordination unsaturated state of the metal active site and the unique electronic structure (molecular orbitals and atomic orbitals) can greatly improve the intrinsic activity of atomically dispersed sub−nanostructured metal catalytic materials (see Fig. 1.2C for details) [37]. The initial concept of single-atom catalysts (SACs) was proposed by Zhang et al. in 2011 [40], and several different atomic nanostructured catalysts were later defined, including single-atom alloy catalysts (SAACs), dual-atom catalysts (DACs), triple-atom catalysts (TACs), fully exposed cluster catalysts (FECCs), single-atom layer catalysts (SALCs), atomic-site ensemble catalysts (ECs) and ultra-high-density atomic foam catalysts (AFCs) (see Fig. 1.2D for details) [38]. Whether it is synthesis, characterization, or application, the concept of atomic-structured materials is a great progress in the field of nanostructured materials. These atomically dispersed sub−nanostructured materials will become important research branches in fields of energy-related nanoscience in the coming years or even decades.

1.4 Introduction of environmental applications

With the rapid development of industry, a large number of pollutants are discharged into the environment, causing many environmental problems, such as soil, water, and air pollution, which pose a great threat to the ecological environment and human health. There is no time to delay in dealing with the problem of the environment. In order to alleviate environmental pollution, people are now making scientific development toward green environmental protection [41]. In recent years, with the rise and development of nanotechnology, various nanomaterials have been widely used in the treatment of environmental pollutants, where the nanoremediation technology has become a research hotspot in the field of environmental science [42]. The scientific reports of nanomaterial in air purification, wastewater treatment, soil remediation, and other aspects emerge in endlessly, and there are also successful application examples in practical environmental treatment projects [43]. In the remediation of air and water pollution, the advantages of nanomaterial can be brought into full play. And the main factors restricting its application are cost and social factors. Soil remediation is more difficult than air and water remediation. It is necessary to transfer pollutants from the solid phase to liquid phase in order to play the role of nanomaterials. In a word, three waste management (waste residue, waste gas, waste water) is the three major environmental problems.

Compared with traditional materials, nanomaterials have the advantages of large specific surface area, many active sites, and high repair efficiency. They are considered as excellent materials for treating many pollutants by means of adsorption, photocatalysis, and advanced oxidation. By controlling the size, morphology, and chemical structure, the catalytic, adsorption, optical, quantum, electrical, and/or redox properties of nanomaterials can be optimized, so as to improve the efficiency of environmental remediation [44]. For example: (1) nanomaterials can enhance the selectivity of adsorbents and photocatalysts to reduce the obstacles of interfering compounds and improve efficiency; (2) separation and desalination technology based on nanomembrane may continue to be a key tool for water treatment; (3) nanotechnology will help overcome operational barriers, such as poor selectivity in the separation of specific ions or molecules [45]. Because the low dimensional structures (0D, 1D, 2D, 3D, and their composite dimensions) can effectively enhance light absorption, promote charge transfer and accelerate surface reaction; and the nanostructured hybrid dimension heterojunction photocatalysts are especially beneficial for the separation of photogenerated carriers and adsorption and activation of substrates due to geometric compensation and hetero interface interaction [46] (see Fig. 1.3A for details). Low dimensional cocatalysts play an important role in providing photocatalytic properties [47] (see Fig. 1.3B). After the size diminishing of cocatalyst, more low-coordinated surface atoms can be exposed and the total number of active centers on cocatalysts can be greatly increased [48] (see Fig. 1.3C). The design of heterojunction can effectively improve the performances, and the design of nano interface (including two semiconductor interface and main catalyst—cocatalyst interface) is particularly important [49,50] (see Fig. 1.3D and E).

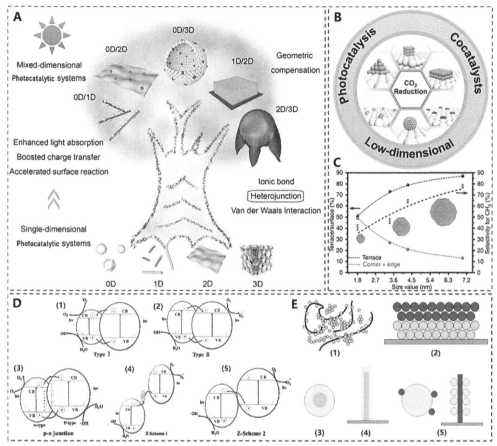

Figure 1.3 (A) Schematics of nanostructured photocatalysts (reprinted with permission from Ref. [46]); (B) Schematics of nanostructured cocatalysts (reprinted with permission from Ref. [47]); (C) Schematics of size diminishing of cocatalyst (reprinted with permission from Ref. [48]); (D) Schematics of heterojunction charge transfer (reprinted with permission from Ref. [49]); (E) Schematics of heterojunction dimension structure (reprinted with permission from Ref. [50]).

In addition, electroadsorption, electrocatalytic reduction/oxidation, and other processes can also play a role in metal ion enrichment, metal ion reduction, and degradation of organic pollutants. These electrical-related technologies (especially based on nanomaterials) can also be regarded as efficient environmental remediation technologies [51].

Based on the above analysis, in this book, the environment-related applications of nano-materials mainly include three parts: (1) electrocatalysis in the environment (such as elec-trocatalytic oxidation and reduction technology); (2) photocatalysis in the environment (such as photocatalytic oxidation and reduction); (3) adsorption in the environment (such as physical, chemical and electrical adsorption); (4) Advanced oxidation in the environ-ment (such as persulfate activation and Fenton oxidation).

1.5 The core contents of this book

The book of "Nanostructured Materials: Physicochemical Fundamentals for Energy and Environmental Applications" is based on the authors' years of accumulation in the fields of nanomaterials, physical chemistry, and electrochemistry/photocatalysis. This book con-sists of four parts: physicochemical fundamentals of nanomaterials (Chapters 1—6), appli-cation types of nanomaterials (Chapters 7—18), typical cases of nanomaterials (Chapters 19—32) in energy and environment fields, and summary section (opportunities, challenges, and future outlooks) (Chapters 33—35). The structure, properties, and mechanism of nanomaterials are deepened layer by layer. The detailed classification, controllable prepa-ration, energy, and environmental application' rules and mechanisms of nanomaterials are mainly introduced; The physical and chemical characterization and structure—performance relationship regulation of nanomaterials are also discussed in detail. It aims to provide comprehensive thermodynamics, dynamics, surface, and interface regulation laws in the preparation and application of nanomaterials, as well as the characterization and control technologies of material/structure changes, and provide multidimensional in-formation (including electrochemical, photochemical, and thermochemical information) for the study of nanomaterials in energy and environmental applications.

The book of "Nanostructured Materials: Physicochemical Fundamentals for Energy and Environmental Applications" can be used as a reference book for scientific re-searchers, postgraduates and teachers engaged in nanoscience, material chemistry, elec-trochemistry, photocatalysis, and related fields in teaching and scientific research, as well as for undergraduates in chemistry, chemical engineering, environment, biology, energy, and materials in learning physical chemistry. Nanomaterials have always been the focus of scientific researchers. A timely understanding of the latest nanomaterials and their characteristics is of great benefit to enlighten research ideas, and also accelerate the application of nanomaterials in energy, environment, physics, chemistry, and so on. This book can help researchers and industrial technicians to understand the development status and specific applications of nanomaterials and provide an important reference for students to choose and understand the research direction in this field. It also looks at future prospects related to current breakthrough nanotechnology, studies the energy and environmental applications of nanomaterials in an interdisciplinary way (e.g., chem-istry, materials, physics, energy, and environment sciences), and informs readers on how to effectively use nanomaterials to provide solutions to the public focus.

Acknowledgments

This book was supported by National Natural Science Foundation of China (22078071, 22272034), Natural Science Foundation of Guangdong Province (2021A1515010125, 2020A1515010344), Maoming Science and Technology Project (mmkj2020032), Guangdong Province Universities and Colleges Pearl River Scholar Funded Scheme (2019), Guangdong Basic and Applied Basic Research Foundation (2019A1515011249, 2021A1515010305), Key Research Project of Natural Science of Guangdong Provincial Department of Education (2019KZDXM010), Environment and Energy Green Catalysis Innovation Team of Colleges and Universities of Guangdong Province (2022KCXTD019), the program for Innovative Research Team of Guangdong University of Petrochemical Technology.

References

[1]   Y. Zhao, Nanotechnology 'Fights Big with Small', 20th ed, People's Daily, 2020.
[2]   L. Yan, F. Zhao, J. Wang, Y. Zu, Z. Gu, Y. Zhao, A safe-by-design strategy towards safer nanomaterials in nanomedicines, Advanced Materials 31 (45) (2019) 1805391.
[3]   W. Zhu, P.J. Bartos, A. Porro, Application of nanotechnology in construction, Materials and Structures 37 (9) (2004) 649−658.
[4]   V. Balzani, Nanoscience and nanotechnology: a personal view of a chemist, Small 1 (3) (2005) 278−283.
[5]   G.M. Whitesides, Nanoscience, nanotechnology, and chemistry, Small 1 (2) (2005) 172−179.
[6]   J. Jeevanandam, A. Barhoum, Y.S. Chan, A. Dufresne, M.K. Danquah, Review on nanoparticles and nanostructured materials: history, sources, toxicity and regulations, Beilstein Journal of Nanotechnology 9 (1) (2018) 1050−1074.
[7]   I. Dincer, M.A. Rosen, Energy, environment and sustainable development, Applied Energy 64 (1−4) (1999) 427−440.
[8]   A.G. Olabi, Developments in sustainable energy and environmental protection, Energy 39 (1) (2012) 2−5.
[9]   F. Li, X. Jiang, J. Zhao, S. Zhang, Graphene oxide: a promising nanomaterial for energy and environmental applications, Nano Energy 16 (2015) 488−515.
[10] X. Chen, C. Li, M. Grätzel, R. Kostecki, S.S. Mao, Nanomaterials for renewable energy production and storage, Chemical Society Reviews 41 (23) (2012) 7909−7937.
[11] A. Ali, P.K. Shen, Nonprecious metal's graphene-supported electrocatalysts for hydrogen evolution reaction: fundamentals to applications, Carbon Energy 2 (1) (2020) 99−121.
[12] Y. Sun, T. Zhang, C. Li, K. Xu, Y. Li, Compositional engineering of sulfides, phosphides, carbides, nitrides, oxides, and hydroxides for water splitting, Journal of Materials Chemistry A 8 (27) (2020) 13415−13436.
[13] P. Potasz, A.D. Güçlü, A. Wójs, P. Hawrylak, Electronic properties of gated triangular graphene quantum dots: magnetism, correlations, and geometrical effects, Physical Review B 85 (7) (2012) 075431.
[14] F. Meng, C. Donnelly, C. Abert, L. Skoric, S. Holmes, Z. Xiao, et al., Non-planar geometrical effects on the magnetoelectrical signal in a three-dimensional nanomagnetic circuit, ACS Nano 15 (4) (2021) 6765−6773.
[15] Q. Shao, P. Wang, T. Zhu, X. Huang, Low dimensional platinum-based bimetallic nanostructures for advanced catalysis, Accounts of Chemical Research 52 (12) (2019) 3384−3396.
[16] P.M. Monk, Physical Chemistry: Understanding Our Chemical World, John Wiley and Sons, England, 2008.
[17] M. Ramanathan, L.K. Shrestha, T. Mori, Q. Ji, J.P. Hill, K. Ariga, Amphiphile nanoarchitectonics: from basic physical chemistry to advanced applications, Physical Chemistry Chemical Physics 15 (26) (2013) 10580−10611.
[18] Y. Dai, P. Lu, Z. Cao, C.T. Campbell, Y. Xia, The physical chemistry and materials science behind sinter-resistant catalysts, Chemical Society Reviews 47 (12) (2018) 4314−4331.
[19] E.A. Moelwyn-Hughes, Physical Chemistry, Cambridge University Press, 2015.

[20] X. Fu, W. Shen, T. Yao, Physical Chemistry, 4th ed, Higher Education Press, Beijing, 1992.

[21] E.Y.X. Chen, T.J. Marks, Cocatalysts for metal-catalyzed olefin polymerization: activators, activation processes, and structure- activity relationships, Chemical Reviews 100 (4) (2000) 1391−1434.

[22] A.S. Rosen, J.M. Notestein, R.Q. Snurr, Structure−activity relationships that identify metal-organic framework catalysts for methane activation, ACS Catalysis 9 (4) (2019) 3576−3587.

[23] X.Y. Li, B. Zhu, Y. Gao, Exploration of dynamic structure−activity relationship of a platinum nanoparticle in the CO oxidation reaction, The Journal of Physical Chemistry C 125 (36) (2021) 19756−19762.

[24] T. Krauskopf, F.H. Richter, W.G. Zeier, J. Janek, Physicochemical concepts of the lithium metal anode in solid-state batteries, Chemical Reviews 120 (15) (2020) 7745−7794.

[25] L. Chen, Z. Liu, Z. Guo, X.J. Huang, Regulation of intrinsic physicochemical properties of metal oxide nanomaterials for energy conversion and environmental detection applications, Journal of Materials Chemistry A 8 (34) (2020) 17326−17359.

[26] https://www.sohu.com/a/290203275_286128.

[27] H. Yang, L.Q. He, Y.W. Hu, X. Lu, G.R. Li, B. Liu, et al., Quantitative detection of photothermal and photoelectrocatalytic effects induced by SPR from Au@ Pt nanoparticles, Angewandte Chemie International Edition 54 (39) (2015) 11462−11466.

[28] H. Yang, Z.H. Wang, Y.Y. Zheng, L.Q. He, C. Zhan, X. Lu, et al., Tunable wavelength enhanced photoelectrochemical cells from surface plasmon resonance, Journal of the American Chemical Society 138 (50) (2016) 16204−16207.

[29] D. Chen, B. Li, Q. Pu, X. Chen, G. Wen, Z. Li, Preparation of Ag-AgVO$_3$/g-C$_3$N$_4$ composite photo-catalyst and degradation characteristics of antibiotics, Journal of Hazardous Materials 373 (2019) 303−312.

[30] Y. Hu, H. Li, Z.S. Li, B. Li, S. Wang, Y. Yao, Progress in batch preparation of single-atom catalysts and application in sustainable synthesis of fine chemicals, Green Chemistry 23 (2021) 8754−8794.

[31] Z. Li, J. Lin, B. Li, C. Yu, H. Wang, Q. Li, Construction of heteroatom-doped and three-dimensional graphene materials for the applications in supercapacitors: a review, Journal of Energy Storage 44 (2021) 103437.

[32] Z. Li, K. Xiao, C. Yu, H. Wang, Q. Li, Three-dimensional graphene-like carbon nanosheets coupled with MnCo-layered double hydroxides nanoflowers as efficient bifunctional oxygen electrocatalyst, International Journal of Hydrogen Energy 46 (69) (2021) 34239−34251.

[33] F. Fei, Z. Wen, D. De Clercq, Spatio-temporal estimation of landfill gas energy potential: a case study in China, Renewable and Sustainable Energy Reviews 103 (2019) 217−226.

[34] M. Xie, J. Min, X. Fang, C. Sun, Z. Zhang, Policy selection based on China's natural gas security evaluation and comparison, Energy 247 (2022) 123460.

[35] R. Xu, L. Du, D. Adekoya, G. Zhang, S. Zhang, S. Sun, et al., Well-defined nanostructures for electrochemical energy conversion and storage, Advanced Energy Materials 11 (15) (2021) 2001537.

[36] Z. Li, H.B. Wu, X.W.D. Lou, Rational designs and engineering of hollow micro-/nanostructures as sulfur hosts for advanced lithium−sulfur batteries, Energy & Environmental Science 9 (10) (2016) 3061−3070.

[37] L. Liu, A. Corma, Metal catalysts for heterogeneous catalysis: from single atoms to nanoclusters and nanoparticles, Chemical Reviews 118 (10) (2018) 4981−5079.

[38] Z. Li, B. Li, Y. Hu, X. Liao, H. Yu, C. Yu, Emerging ultrahigh density single-atom catalysts for versatile heterogeneous catalysis applications: redefinition, recent progress, and challenges, Small Structures 3 (6) (2022) 2200041.

[39] S. Ding, M.J. Hülsey, J. Pérez-Ramírez, N. Yan, Transforming energy with single-atom catalysts, Joule 3 (12) (2019) 2897−2929.

[40] B. Qiao, A. Wang, X. Yang, L.F. Allard, Z. Jiang, Y. Cui, et al., Single-atom catalysis of CO oxidation using Pt$_1$/FeO$_x$, Nature Chemistry 3 (8) (2011) 634−641.

[41] Y. Liu, A. Wang, Y. Wu, Environmental regulation and green innovation: evidence from China's new environmental protection law, Journal of Cleaner Production 297 (2021) 126698.

[42] S. Das, B. Sen, N. Debnath, Recent trends in nanomaterials applications in environmental monitoring and remediation, Environmental Science and Pollution Research 22 (23) (2015) 18333−18344.

[43] R.K. Ibrahim, M. Hayyan, M.A. AlSaadi, A. Hayyan, S. Ibrahim, Environmental application of nano-technology: air, soil, and water, Environmental Science and Pollution Research 23 (14) (2016) 13754—13788.

[44] F. Pulizzi, W. Sun, Treating water with nano, Nature Nanotechnology 13 (8) (2018) 633.

[45] G. Zhang, C.D. Sewell, P. Zhang, H. Mi, Z. Lin, Nanostructured photocatalysts for nitrogen fixation, Nano Energy 71 (2020) 104645.

[46] X. Zhang, Y. Wei, R. Yu, Multidimensional tungsten oxides for efficient solar energy conversion, Small Structures 3 (2) (2022) 2100130.

[47] J. Di, B. Lin, B. Tang, S. Guo, J. Zhou, Z. Liu, Engineering cocatalysts onto low-dimensional photocatalysts for CO_2 reduction, Small Structures 2 (10) (2021) 2100046.

[48] C. Dong, C. Lian, S. Hu, Z. Deng, J. Gong, M. Li, et al., Size-dependent activity and selectivity of carbon dioxide photocatalytic reduction over platinum nanoparticles, Nature Communications 9 (1) (2018) 1—11.

[49] K. Yang, X. Li, C. Yu, D. Zeng, F. Chen, K. Zhang, et al., Review on heterophase/homophase junctions for efficient photocatalysis: the case of phase transition construction, Chinese Journal of Catalysis 40 (6) (2019) 796—818.

[50] H.S. Yu, X. Quan, Nano-heterojunction photocatalytic materials in environmental pollution controlling, Progress in Chemistry 21 (0203) (2009) 406—418.

[51] E. Brillas, Recent development of electrochemical advanced oxidation of herbicides. A review on its application to wastewater treatment and soil remediation, Journal of Cleaner Production 290 (2021) 125841.

CHAPTER 2

Structure types and characteristics of nanomaterials

2.1 Introduction

In recent years, with the expansion of the types of low-dimensional nanomaterials and the improvement of their properties, their applications in the fields of energy, environment, biomedicine, and so on continue to develop, which has brought great convenience to our lives. Low-dimensional nanomaterials refer to a new class of functional materials in which at least one dimension of solid materials (metal or nonmetal materials) is reduced to the nanometer scale (within 100 nm). Because its characteristic size is similar to the de Broglie wavelength of electrons, the movement of electrons in such materials is limited, and its energy changes from continuous state to discontinuous energy level, which leads to many new physical and chemical properties, and has attracted extensive attention in the scientific and industrial circles [1]. According to their dimensions, low-dimensional nanomaterials can be divided into zero-dimensional (0D) nanomaterials (such as subnanometer metal clusters, semiconductor quantum dots, fullerenes, and metal nanoparticles), one-dimensional (1D) nanomaterials (such as nanowires, nanorods, and nanotubes), two-dimensional (2D) nanomaterials (such as graphene, metallene, and metal nanosheets), and macroscale three-dimensional (3D) micro-nano assemblies derived from multiple dimensional nano-structured combinations [2–5].

In this chapter, we are going to comprehensively introduce the basic definition, structural characteristics, typical cases, and advantages of multidimensional nanostructures (including 0D, 1D, 2D, and 3D nanostructures) toward the energy and environment-related applications. At the same time, the fundamental connotations of porous nanostructures, hollow nanostructures, composite nanostructures, and newly developed atomically dispersed subnanostructures are also systematically described and summarized. Because their scale is between macromatters and microparticles, multiple low-dimensional nanomaterials have some unique physical essences and chemical properties and have very significant research significance and application value in the fields of materials, electronics, energy, and environment science [6–8]. In particular, in order to better describe the differences and connections between nanostructures with different dimensions, we selected 23 works as typical case studies (including 0D, 1D, 2D, 3D, porous, hollow, composite, and atomic structures) from the recent work of our group or cooperative groups (see Fig. 2.1) [9–31].

Nanostructured Materials
ISBN 978-0-443-19256-2, https://doi.org/10.1016/B978-0-443-19256-2.00004-1

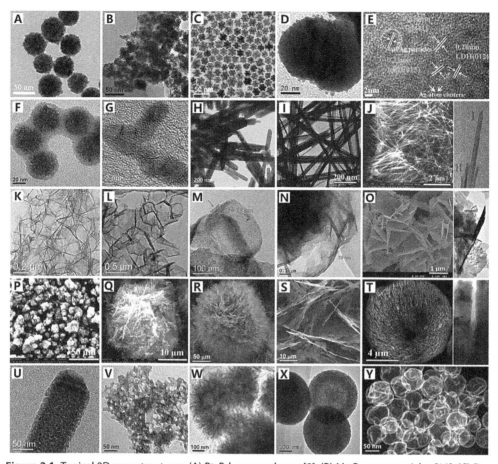

Figure 2.1 Typical 0D nanostructures: (A) Pt_3Pd_1 nanospheres [9], (B) MnO_2 nanoparticles [10], (C) Pt–Ni–Cu dodecahedrons [11], (D) $g\text{-}C_3N_4$ quantum dots on $BiPO_4$ [12], (E) Ag atom clusters/particles on NiCo-LDHs [13]; Typical 1D nanostructures: (F) SnO_2@carbon core-shell nanochains [14], (G) polycrystalline PdPt nanowires [15], (H) MnO_2 nanorods [16], (I) MnO_2 nanowires [17], (J) MnO_2 nanoneedles [18]; Typical 2D nanostructures: (K) Graphene nanosheets network [19], (L) graphene nanosheets polyhedron [20], (M) graphene nanosheets shovel [21], (N) NiCo-LDHs nanosheets [22], (O) Bi_2WO_6 nanosheets [23]; Typical 3D nanostructures: (P and Q) MnO_2 nanowires microspheres [24], (R and S) Cu_3P nanosheets microspheres [25], (T) $ZnGa_2O_4$ nanorods microarrays [26]; Typical porous nanostructures: (U) Porous SnS nanorods [27], (V) porous $g\text{-}C_3N_4$ nanosheets [28], (W) porous $NiCo_2O_4$ nanoflowers [29], (X) hollow $NiCo_2O_4$ nanospheres [30], (Y) hollow IrCo nanospheres [31] (these nanostructures are mainly obtained from the work of Zesheng Li's group and cooperative groups in recent years).

2.2 Zero-dimensional nanostructures

As an important part of low–dimensional nanomaterial system, 0D nanostructure is also the foundation of building other low-dimensional nanomaterials, and plays an important role in the development of nanomaterials science. The 0D nanomaterials usually mean that the three dimensions of materials are within the nano scale range (<100 nm), such as nanospheres of about 100 nm, nanoparticles of 5−100 nm, quantum dots of 1−5 nm, single atoms or atomic clusters of 0.2−1 nm, etc. (see Fig. 2.1A−E) [9−13]. These 0D nanomaterials, (A) Pt_3Pd_1 nanospheres [9], (B) MnO_2 nanoparticles [10], (C) Pt−Ni−Cu dodecahedrons [11], (D) g-C_3N_4 quantum dots on $BiPO_4$ [12], (E) Ag atom clusters/particles on NiCo-LDHs [13] are mainly from the work of Zesheng Li's group or cooperative groups in recent years.

Carbon nanospheres or metal nanospheres with diameters less than 100 nm are the most classical 0D nanostructured materials. Recently, Shen et al. successfully designed noble metal alloy Pt_3Pd_1 nanospheres (polycrystalline spherical structure) with a diameter of about 50 nm (see Fig. 2.1A) [9]. Thanks to the unique spherical nanostructure and abundant crystal plane structure, this 0D nanostructured material shows excellent characteristics in electrocatalysis applications. Previously, our group also synthesized a quasi-spherical 0D MnO_2 nanoparticle material, which has low crystallinity structure and rich pore structure, and shows excellent performance for electrochemical energy storage of supercapacitors (see Fig. 2.1B) [10]. Polyhedral nanoparticles are a special class of 0D nanostructured materials, whose abundant crystal structures and highly exposed atoms play a key role in the regulation of their surface chemistry or catalytic properties (such as the Pt−Ni−Cu dodecahedrons in Fig. 2.1C) [11]. The unique property of 0D quantum dot is based on its own quantum effect. When the particle size reaches the quantum level (~ 5 nm), quantum dot will cause size effect, quantum confinement effect, macroscopic quantum tunneling effect, and surface effect. Our group also committed to quantum structure design and developed a semiconductor quantum dot (g-C_3N_4 quantum dots supported on $BiPO_4$ nanospheres), which has achieved a good application effect in the field of photocatalysis and attracted extensive attention from other scientists (see Fig. 2.1D) [12]. Metal atomic clusters structure of 0.2−1 nm is a limit mode of 0D nanostructure (subnanostructure), which can also be regarded as the transitional zone from nanostructure to single atom structure. In particular, the combination between metal atomic clusters and metal nanoparticles can reveal a synergistic effect involving scale and electronic structures, showing desirable characteristics and reliable application prospects in a wide range of heterogeneous catalysis (such as the Ag atom clusters/particles supported on NiCo-LDHs in Fig. 2.1E) [13].

Zero-dimensional nanostructures (including nanospheres, nanoparticles, and quantum dots) have obvious structure characteristics: the surface atoms are amorphous layers with disordered arrangements (the state of the surface atoms is closer to the gas state), while the internal atoms are orderly arranged. Because the particle size is small and the surface curvature is large, a very high Gilibs' pressure ($dG = \sigma \times dA$, $\triangle P = 2\sigma/r$) is generated inside, which can lead to deformation of the internal structure. Therefore, these structural features of 0D nanostructures make them have unique physicochemical properties and remarkable catalytic performances [32]. In particular, by adjusting the radius (r) of 0D nanoparticles, the geometric curvature can be effectively adjusted κ (κ = 1/r). The surface properties of small-size nanoparticles with large curvature and large-size nanoparticles with small curvature are obviously different. By changing the basic properties of spherical nanoparticles (such as size and curvature), the 0D nanostructures can have different interfacial interactions and self-assembly functionalities (largely determines the catalytic properties of the 0D nanostructured materials) [33].

In addition to the radius of curvature, the activity of the 0D nanostructured catalyst depends to a greater extent on the density of metal particles or atomic sites [34]. Therefore, it is of great significance to develop 0D nanostructured catalyst with high metal loading (high particle density or high atom density). In order to better clarify the relationship between metal particle density (or atomic site density) and catalyst performance, in a recent review paper, we proposed two methods to determine the metal density or site density on the carrier surface: (I) the relative distance of metal particles or atomic sites (i.e., the ratio of the actual distance to the particle diameter or atomic diameter) and (II) the average number of particles or atoms per unit area (i.e., the number of particles per 100 nm^2 and the number of atoms per 1 nm^2) (see the schematic diagram in Fig. 2.2A for details) [34].

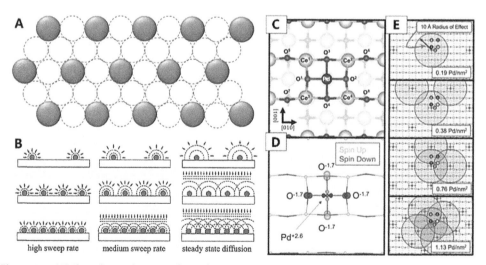

Figure 2.2 (A) The relative distance of metal particles or atomic sites, (B) the diffusion models of nanoparticle arrays under different potential sweep rates, (C–E) schematic diagram of atomic site electrostatic interaction (these images are obtained from a review paper of Zesheng Li's group [34], where the image (B) originates from Ref. [35] And the images (C–E) originate from Ref. [36]).

(I) Significance of high-density 0D particle system: In the general electrochemical process, the 0D electrocatalyst with high particle density can produce unique ion diffusion characteristics and interface interaction (see Fig. 2.2B) [35]. From this surface density-dependent diffusion model of the nanoparticle array, it can be seen that at high scanning rate, the thickness of the diffusion layer is much smaller than the average distance of these adjacent particles. At medium scanning rate, the diffusion layers of adjacent particles overlap due to their high particle density, while at low scanning rate, all the particle arrays in different densities can reach steady-state diffusion. These characteristics can promote the design of high-density 0D particle electrocatalysts, and the diffusion layer-overlapping effect of adjacent particles may have a positive electrocatalysis synergistic effect on high-density 0D particle structures.

(II) Significance of high-density 0D atomic system: The subnano 0D electrocatalysts with high atomic density can also produce unique electronic properties and catalytic activity (see Fig. 2.2C−E) [36]. It is shown that in the structural model of CeO_2-supported Pd atom catalyst the electrostatic interaction of atom is depended on the surface atom density. Due to the cumulative enhancement of the reducibility of the carrier, the activity of Pd sites increased linearly with the increase of Pd atomic density. With the increase of Pd atomic density, the long-range electrostatic footprints around each Pd atom overlap with each other, resulting in a different catalytic activity (that is the catalytic activity can be adjusted by changing the surface density of a single metal atom). These theoretical models provide positive help for the development of 0D atomic catalysts with high specific activity and high atomic density.

Although 0D nanostructures have many superior properties due to the 3D confinement effect, for single 0D materials, their components, structures, and limited functions limit their wide application in interdisciplinary fields. Therefore, the development of advanced 0D nanostructures (such as core-shell, alloy, hollow or porous 0D structures, or atom-particle hybrid 0D structures) is conducive to further improve the catalytic performance of nanomaterial systems [37]. On the other hand, in order to fully improve the material properties, we can also strengthen the correlation and interaction between 0D nanostructures and other dimensional nano-systems (such as designing 0D and other dimensional composites).

2.3 One-dimensional nanostructures

Among many nanodimensions, 1D nanostructures are one of the most concerned nanostructures as excellent anisotropic nanomaterials. 1D nanomaterials are defined as follows: there are two dimensions in the three space dimensions of materials within the nanometer scale (~ 100 nm), such as nanorods, nanowires, nanobelts, and nanotubes. Thereinto, nanowires are a kind of special 1D nanostructures, which are limited to less than 100 nm in the transverse direction, while there is no maximum limit in the longitudinal direction. The typical aspect ratio of nanowires is between 10 and 1000 (defined as nano-rods if the aspect ratio is less than 10). Nanobelts are long and thin flat-type structures. Generally, the aspect ratio is greater than 10 and the width-thickness ratio is greater than 3. Nanobelts have a certain scale in width, that is, they have some 2D characteristics. Nanotubes can be seen as hollow nanorods or hollow nanowires (including circular nanotubes and square nanotubes).

For 1D metallic crystalline nanomaterials, there are two growth modes: (I) the intrinsic crystal structure guides the crystal growth to form a single-crystal 1D nanostructure (or a specific covering agent induces a specific crystal plane to grow into a single-crystal 1D nanostructure); (II) surface ligands induce crystal growth to form integrated polycrystalline 1D nanostructures (or 1D polycrystalline nanostructures connected by surface coating). In these two growth modes, the adsorption/desorption process of surface ligands on the crystal surface has an important impact on the growth and dimensional control of nanocrystals [38]. In terms of dynamics, the competitive adsorption of ligands will change the adsorption/desorption rate, and determine the crystal growth rate to a certain extent, thus affecting the final size of 1D nanocrystals. In terms of thermodynamics, the competitive adsorption of ligands changes the adsorption components on crystal surface, which will affect the thermodynamic stability of the crystal surface, resulting in the change of the final morphology of 1D nanocrystals.

Previously, our research group (Zesheng Li) and Yueping Fang's research group jointly developed a carbon layer coating and assembly technology, successfully prepared a unique polycrystalline 1D nanostructure, SnO_2@carbon core-shell nanochains, and applied it in the field of lithium-ion batteries as a high-performance cathode material (see Fig. 2.1F) [14]. The well-shaped polycrystalline SnO_2 nanospheres are coated by amorphous carbon layer and assembled into graceful 1D nanochains. Besides, Zesheng Li and Peikang Shen recently designed polycrystalline PdPt nanowires on active graphene nanosheets for electrocatalysis, where the closely-contacted 0D PdPt nanoparticles are assembled into a 1D structure on a specific region of graphene nanosheet (see Fig. 2.1G) [15]. Usually, polycrystalline nanowires have abundant grain boundary or mesoporous structure, which endow with high surface activity and catalytic efficiency. We also focus on the design and application of single-crystal 1D nanostructures, such as the preparation of manganese oxide 1D nanostructures and energy storage application (e.g., MnO_2 nanorods (Fig. 2.1H) [16], MnO_2 nanowires (Fig. 2.1I) [17], MnO_2 nano-needles (Fig. 2.1J) [18]). These single-crystal 1D nanostructures have high crystal plane orientation and large aspect ratio, exhibiting excellent crystallographic and electrochemical properties.

At present, there are two kinds of controllable preparation methods for 1D nano-wires: (1) gas-phase synthesis method and (2) liquid-phase synthesis method. The gas-phase synthesis methods include gas-solid (VS) growth method and gas-liquid-solid

(VLS) growth method. The VS method is a preparation method that one or several re-actants are heated to form steam in the high-temperature region, and then transported to the substrate in the low-temperature region or deposited by rapid cooling to grow into 1D nanowires [39]. The VLS method is a special VS growth method based on metal droplet catalyst, where the small droplets eventually remain at one end of nanowires as solid particles. Liquid-phase synthesis methods include low temperature hydrothermal method (such as solution-liquid-solid (SLS) method) and electrochemical method (such as template electrochemical deposition). In the SLS low-temperature hydrothermal treatment, the precursor in the solution will be thermally decomposed into metal droplets as the liquid core for nanowire growth, and the reaction products will continue to dissolve into the droplets. When the solution is saturated, the solid phase products will precipitate, resulting in undersaturation of the droplet, and then continue to dissolve into the reaction product, resulting in oversaturation precipitation. In this way, 1D the nanowires can be formed repeatedly [40].

Previously, our research group (Zesheng Li) and Yueping Fang's research group jointly developed a simple solution–liquid–solid (SLS) method under hydrothermal condition for the one-pot synthesis of Ga-doped/self-supported aligned 1D ZnO nanostructures (see Fig. 2.3A for details) [41]. Fig. 2.3A illustrates a formation process of the Ga-doped ZnO nanorods with the SLS synthesis route. In brief, this process consists of four steps: (i) formation of the liquid Ga droplets in hydrothermal solution (1); (ii) production of ZnO by $ZnSt_2$ hydrolyzation and its diffusion to liquid Ga droplet to form liquid-solid interface (2); (iii) 1D growth of the Ga-doped ZnO nanorods at the liquid-solid interface (3); (iv) continuous 1D growth of ZnO consumes the liquid Ga droplet, thus completing the SLS assembly of the Ga-doped ZnO nanorods (4). As a result, self-supported aligned ZnO nanorods were obtained by this simple substrate-free Ga-mediated SLS hydrother-mal route [41]. It should be noted that this is a new and universal mechanism for growing doping-type oriented nanorods. By selecting different metal droplets, reactants, and reac-tion conditions, it should be possible to produce diversified 1D nanomaterials with different compositions, sizes, and heterogeneous structures.

In addition, Zesheng Li and Peikang Shen recently further exploited a new solid-liquid-gas-solid (SLGS) growth route to prepare carbon-supported porous SnS nanorods via a convenient pyrolysis strategy from sulfur-containing resin (S-resin)-supported SnO_2 nanoparticles hybrid precursors (see Fig. 2.3B for details) [27]. Fig. 2.3B illustrates a for-mation process of the porous SnS nanorods with the SLGS synthesis route. In brief, the 1D growth process consists of two main steps: (i) intermediate state and (ii) nanorods developing state. The intermediate state includes the formation of the Sn liquid droplets resulting from SnO_2 carbothermal reduction and the production of SO_2 gas by thermal decomposition of S-resin during the pyrolysis. Then, the SO_2 gas first diffuses into Sn liquid droplet to form SnS liquid—solid interface and the 1D growth of the SnS nanorods initiates at the liquid—solid interface, and then the continuous 1D growth of SnS

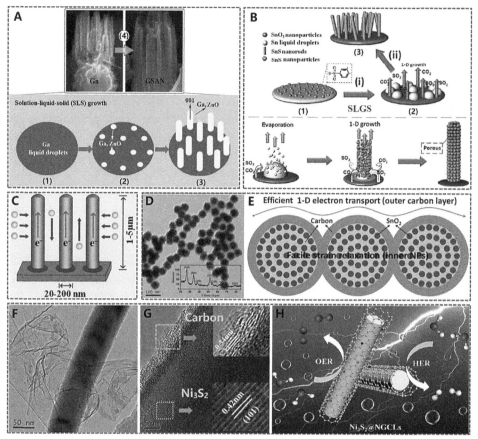

Figure 2.3 (A) The SLS formation process of Ga-doped ZnO nanorods [41], (B) the SLGS formation process of carbon-supported porous SnS nanorods [27], (C) schematic of ordinary oriented 1D nanostructures [18], (D–E) SnO$_2$@carbon core-shell nanochains [42], and (F–H) Ni$_3$S$_2$@carbon core-shell nanowires [43] (these 1D nanostructures are obtained from the work of Zesheng Li's group or cooperative groups in recent years).

nanorods which consumes the Sn liquid droplet, leading to the completion of the SnS nanorods assembly. Particularly, the produced CO$_2$ gas from thermal decomposition of resin could easily penetrate into the generated liquid-solid interface in the developing state of SnS nanorods, which provides appropriate cavities responding to their porous textures (see the bottom in Fig. 2.3B) [27]. As a result, the porous SnS nanorods/carbon hybrid materials are obtained by this simple pyrolysis-induced solid-liquid-gas-solid (SLGS) synthesis.

In recent years, our research group (Zesheng Li) and collaborators have designed a great deal of 1D nanostructures, such as nanorods [16,27], nanowires [15,17,43], nanoneedles [18], and nanochains [14,42], for various energy storage and conversion applications. In contrast to nanoparticles, these 1D nanostructures usually exhibit additional advantages due to their anisotropy, unique structure, or surface properties. Expressly, oriented 1D nanostructures (e.g., 1D MnO_2, V_2O_5, TiO_2, and PANI) grown on conductive substrates (e.g., graphene and other carbon materials) by different synthetic routes were approved to be a promising candidate electrode for high-performance energy storage. A schematic of this oriented 1D architecture is depicted in Fig. 2.3C [18]. Typically, these 1D nanowires have a diameter of 20−200 nm and a length of 1−5 mm and are grown on conductive substrates in oriented 1D nanostructures. The advantages of these oriented 1D nanostructures in electrochemical energy storage include five main aspects: (I) 1D nanowires have high electrode/electrolyte contact area and easy ion diffusion leading to higher charge-discharge rate (high capacity and high power), (II) 1D nanowires can provide an efficient continuous path for the electron transmission (electrons are transported along the long axis and have a constraint effect on radial direction), (III) 1D nanowires show good contact with conductive substrates that allows operation at high power (1D nanowires can be grown on/from the porous structures of carbon substrates), (IV) 1D nanowires can adapt to volume expansion, inhibit mechanical degradation and prolong cycle life, (V) 1D nanowires exhibit excellent mechanical flexibility and Young's modulus, which is of great significance for the manufacture of flexible electronic components [18,44,45].

Previously, our research group (Zesheng Li) and Yueping Fang's research group jointly proposed a novel SnO_2@carbon core-shell 1D nanochains integrate most of the above design advantages [42]. Experiments show that the anode composed of this core-shell super structure has a very high lithium storage capacity and excellent cycling performance. Generally, these SnO_2 nanoparticles with a size of about 40 nm as the core, are uniformly coated with a carbon layer of about 10 nm to form a perfect core-shell nanochain structure (with 3D branching structure) (see Fig. 2.3D and E for details) [42]. This geometry has several advantages and leads to improved performance of these materials as anode materials for lithium-ion battery: (I) the smaller SnO_2 can better adapt to larger volume changes and easily relieve the stress in bulk materials. (II) This ultrathin 1D nanochains provide very high electrochemical activity region, which improves the storage capacity of lithium. (III) The uniform carbon layer coated on SnO_2 can withstand the large strain during the lithium process, so the problem of pulverization is successfully avoided. (IV) The continuous carbon layer nanostructures provide a direct 1D electron conduction path, allowing effective charge transfer and good dynamics [42].

More recently, our group (Li) and Pang's group jointly designed a novel Ni_3S_2@N-doped graphene-like carbon layers (core-shell nanowires) on nickel foam (i.e., Ni_3S_2@NGCLs/NF), as high-performance electrocatalyst for oxygen evolution reaction (OER), hydrogen evolution reaction (HER), and overall water splitting (see Fig. 2.3F—H for details) [43]. The well-defined Ni_3S_2 nanowires are coated with an extremely thin graphene-like carbon layer (<10 layers of graphene). As a guiding growth layer, the NGCLs play a key role in the formation of 1D Ni_3S_2 nanostructures (see Fig. 2.3F and G). The as-prepared Ni_3S_2@NGCLs/NF composite electrocatalyst affords several advantages: (I) As the combination of tubular NGCLs and Ni_3S_2 nanowires, the high conductivity of NGCLs allows electrons to shuttle easily to Ni_3S_2 nanowires. (II) The great chemical and mechanical stability of NGCLs improves the stability of Ni_3S_2 nanowires in long-term operation. (III) The core-shell cable-like nanostructure of Ni_3S_2 nanowires@NGCLs slows down the dissolution of Ni_3S_2 in the electrolyte, providing confined space for the continuous transformation of Ni_3S_2 into highly active NiOOH species [43]. Therefore, Ni_3S_2@NGCLs/NF 1D core-shell nanowires showed excellent electrocatalytic activity for water splitting.

At present, environmental pollution has become urgent problem in the world. The development of semiconductor photocatalysis technology has opened up a new path to solve this global problem. Ultrathin 1D nanomaterials (less than 20 nm in diameter) can be used as a highly active nanostructured photocatalyst due to their ultra-high specific surface area, direct electron transfer path, and large quantum confinement effect [46]. Ultrathin 1D nanomaterials can further improve the photocatalytic activity of 1D semiconductors and efficiently degrade organic pollutants (enhancing the transport and separation of photo-charged carriers), which is of great significance for environmental remediation and efficient utilization of sunlight by saving energy. However, due to their dimensional and size dependent physicochemical properties (such as electrical transport, heat transport, and mechanical properties), the photo-catalytic performances of ultrathin 1D nanomaterials in practical applications are heavily dependent on their aspect ratio and atomic arrangement [47]. Although there are many methods to prepare ultrathin 1D nanomaterials, it is still a great challenge to accurately control the size and atomic structure of these materials, especially for ultra-fine and ultra-long nanowires.

2.4 Two-dimensional nanostructures

2D nanomaterials refer to the one dimension of three space dimensions of materials is in the nano scale range (0.2—100 nm), such as nanosheets, nanofilms, and nanoplates. In 2004, the successful preparation of graphene opened a new era in the exploration of single-atom-layer 2D materials. In addition to graphene, researchers have also successfully prepared a considerable number of 2D materials in recent years, such as black phosphorus, transition metal disulfide, layered double hydroxides, hexagonal boron nitride, metal carbides, and carbon nanosheets [48]. These 2D nanomaterials have shown great application potential in both electrochemical energy-related fields and photocatalytic environment fields. Among the reported 2D materials, different from traditional activated carbon and conventional ultra-thin carbon nanosheets, graphene-like porous carbon nanosheet materials combine graphene-like nanostructures with porous characteristics, showing unique physical, chemical, and electronic properties, and become very attractive 2D novel electrode material [49].

For nearly a decade, our group (Zesheng Li) and Shen's group have been devoted to the development of high-performance graphene-like porous carbon nanosheets 2D material and their electrochemical energy storage and conversion applications (see Fig. 2.1K−M) [19−21]. In 2013, we proposed synchronous catalysis and activation technology for the first time, and successfully prepared three-dimensional graphene-like porous carbon nanosheet network materials. Its ultra-high specific surface area and hierarchical porous structure have established the foundation for the design of high-capacity or high-power supercapacitors (see Fig. 2.1K) [19]. By optimizing the catalytic synthesis parameters, we further obtained the polyhedral porous carbon network in 2017, which can be used as electrocatalyst support for new applications (see Fig. 2.1L) [20]. At the same time, we also designed the nitrogen-doped porous carbon nanosheets as pseudo-capacitive materials to explore their potential application prospects (see Fig. 2.1M) [21]. In 2021, we further designed 2D ultrathin materials based on metallic NiCo-LDHs nanosheets and systematically studied them as water electrolysis catalysts (see Fig. 2.1N) [22]. As recently as 2022, the new-style Bi_2WO_6 nanosheets with controllable thickness were successfully designed for photocatalytic degradation application by Li and Yu (the two authors of this book) (see Fig. 2.1O) [23].

Particularly, in the past 5 years, Li and Yu have been committed to designing high-performance 2D nanostructure and heterojunction photocatalysts, including 2D nonmetallic semiconductor (graphitic carbon nitride (g-C_3N_4) nanosheets) and 2D metal semiconductor (BiOCl, Bi_2MoO_6, $Zn_3(OH)_2V_2O_7$ nanosheets) materials [50−54]. As a typical metal-free photocatalyst, 2D g-C_3N_4 nanosheets have attracted extensive attention for the photocatalytic degradation of various organic pollutants [50] and the photocatalytic water splitting to produce hydrogen [51]. The 2D g-C_3N_4 nanosheets are a typical multifunctional nano-structured material in the fields of energy and environment. The Bi-based nanosheets [52,53] and Zn or V-based nanosheets [54] are also the most popular 2D nanostructured photocatalysts for different areas of photocatalytic purification. Generally, the physicochemical properties and photocatalytic performances of these semiconductor nanosheets can be controlled through nano dimension regulation, doping regulation, and heterojunction design.

The physicochemical properties of 2D nanomaterials are closely related to their thickness and width. Due to their unique physical, electronic, and chemical properties, the ultra-thin 2D nanomaterials (~ 5 nm) have attracted extensive attention in the fields of sustainable energy and environmental remediation [55]. The unfolding width of ultra-thin 2D nanomaterials with only a few atoms thickness can be as high as hundreds of nanometers or even several microns, thus having an ultra-high specific surface area, and increased percentage of atoms exposed to the surface. These special 2D nanostructures can confine electrons to the ultra-thin region and electrons can easily move along the "*ab*-plane" of 2D sheets. However, the intrinsic electronic properties and chemical composition limit the application of pristine ultra-thin 2D nanomaterials. Surface modulation and functionalization can be achieved through element doping or defect or strain or phase engineering. In the field of energy or environmental catalysis, the vacancy defect regulation can directly affect the intrinsic active sites of ultra-thin 2D nanomaterials [55].

2.5 Three-dimensional nanostructures

3D nanomaterials refer to the powders or blocks with hierarchical structures composed of the single-dimensional nanomaterials (such as nanoparticles, nanowires, or nanosheets), such as the microflowers assembled from nanowires (see Fig. 2.1P and Q, MnO_2 nanowires microspheres [24]) or nanosheets (see Fig. 2.1R and S, Cu_3P nanosheets microspheres [25]), hollow microarrays assembled from nanorods (see Fig. 2.1T, $ZnGa_2O_4$ nanorods microarrays [26]), and super-micro-structures constructed from nanoparticles [56]. In addition, porous macroscopic bulk materials (e.g., graphene foams and aerogels) constructed with low-dimensional nanostructures are also of immediate concern as a particular 3D material. Due to their unique morphology and complex structure, 3D nanomaterials have the advantages of large surface area, high reactivity, less agglomeration, etc., showing great application prospects in the fields of light, electricity, magnetism, catalysis, and energy [49,50,57].

Among many nanomaterials, 3D nanomaterials are considered as one of the ideal basic materials for constructing high-performance devices and have attracted extensive attention. In the field of electrochemical energy storage and conversion, various 3D nanomaterials have been designed to improve the energy storage and conversion efficiency of electrochemical energy devices, and significant research progress has been made [58]. At present, 3D nanomaterials based on micro/nano assembly have the characteristics of high thermal stability and rapid dynamics in the electrochemical reaction process and are widely constructed and applied as unique 3D composite electrode materials [59]. 3D nanostructures are often combined with the advantages of other low-dimensional nanostructures (0D, 1D, or 2D nanostructures). At the same time, 3D nanostructures can also be compatible with the characteristics of porous materials and interface materials, giving the electrode materials optimal electrochemical activity and stability.

Previous studies of our group (Zesheng Li) confirmed that, for electrocatalysis reactions, especially for catalytic reactions involving gases (such as oxygen reduction reaction and water splitting reaction), 3D nanostructures have unique advantages in building a good three-phase interface and accelerating ion diffusion and gas evolution [20,22]. Recently, Li further designed a 3D porous $NiCo_2O_4$ nanoflowers supported on 3D graphene nanosheets (3D GNs) by a simple solvothermal synthesis method as high-performance electrocatalysts for oxygen evolution reaction (OER) (see Fig. 2.1W) [29]. The excellent electrocatalytic activity and stability of $NiCo_2O_4$/GNs composite samples can be attributed to the following reasons: (I) the $NiCo_2O_4$ nanosheets assembled by nanoparticles have rich porous structure and high specific surface area, which endows the material with high effective active area and rich catalytic active sites; (II) the hierarchical architecture of stereoscopic $NiCo_2O_4$ nanoflowers constructed from 3D $NiCo_2O_4$ nanosheets provides a short path for the rapid transfer of electrolyte ions; (III) graphene nanosheets (GNs) are excellent electronic conductive materials, which make up for the poor conductivity of bimetallic oxide $NiCo_2O_4$. In addition, the enhanced stability may benefit from the high strength and chemical stability provided by 3D GNs and their inhibition on the aggregation and collapse of $NiCo_2O_4$ nanoparticles (see Fig. 2.4A and B) [29].

In the field of electrochemical storages, various 3D nanostructured materials (including 3D nanopowders, 3D micron films, and 3D macroblocks) have been widely designed and prepared to improve electrochemical energy and storage efficiency. Previously, we reported on an ion-exchange/activation-graphitization combination method by using ion-exchange resin as a carbon precursor to prepare a novel 3D hierarchical porous graphene-like (3D HPG) network (see Fig. 2.1K) [19]. As a supercapacitor material, the 3D porous graphene network has the following advantages: (I) the rich micropores and mesopores can provide a high specific surface area and generate considerable double-layer capacitance, (II) the hundreds of nanometers of macropores can form an ion buffer tank effect and provide a short diffusion distance to the inner surface of the graphene, (III) the interconnected micropores, mesopores and macropores can provide efficient ion channels and promote rapid ion transport, (IV) the graphene-like carbon nanosheets can provide excellent electronic conductivity and high electrochemical stability, resulting in high rate capability and high electrochemical stability. This 3D carbon structure is useful not only for supercapacitors, but also for many other energy storage (lithium ion, lithium sulfur and lead-acid batteries) and catalytic conversion applications (fuel cells) [19].

Compared to 3D graphene nanosheets, 3D ultrathin-activated carbon nanosheets prepared by template pyrolysis and chemical activation have a wider range of applications, because they can be prepared from a wide range of biomass or molecular precursors (see Fig. 2.4C) [20]. In the recent 3 years, Zesheng Li's group has developed two high-performance 3D activated carbon nanosheet materials by KOH activation, starting from the inexpensive Twain [20] and Spane [63] organic molecules. These activated carbon materials have well-shape 3D sheet-like nanostructure and rich microporous structure, which contribute to the formation of high double electric layer capacitance and rate capacitance (see the insets in Fig. 2.4C). Through doping of foreign elements or composite structure design, these 3D activated carbon nanoplates also have a good application prospect in pseudo-capacitor electrochemical energy storage (this is detailed in one of our recent review papers [49]).

No matter 3D graphene or 3D carbon nanosheets, the 3D nanostructured materials may be compressed in the manufacturing process of energy storage electrodes, thus losing the unique advantages of 3D nanomaterials. In order to avoid the disadvantages brought by the traditional technology, in a recent review paper, we propose the construction of

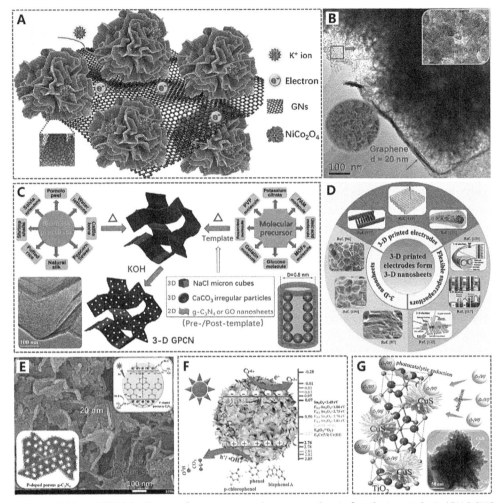

Figure 2.4 (A and B) $NiCo_2O_4$ nanoflowers on graphene nanosheets for electrocatalysis (GNs) [29], (C) schematic for the formation of 3D GPCN from different precursors for supercapacitors [20], (D) schematic of 3D nanosheets for flexible supercapacitors by 3D printing [60], (E) P-doped porous g-C_3N_4 3D nanosheets for photocatalysis [50], (F) schematic of F-doped Sn_3O_4 3D nanosheets for photocatalysis [61], and (G) schematic of 3D CuS nanorods/TiO_2 for photocatalysis [62] (these 3D nanostructures are obtained from the work of Zesheng Li's group and Changlin Yu's group in recent years).

3D nanosheets-based electrodes or devices by new-fashioned 3D printing technology for high-performance flexible all-solid-state supercapacitors (see Fig. 2.4D) [60]. Through 3D printing technology, the as-prepared 3D nanosheets-built electrodes (including inter-digital, woodpile, and fiber electrodes) are highly porous and have well 3D structures, so the advantages of 3D nanosheets are retained. This review provides new concepts and theoretical guidance for the 3D nanosheets-based flexible supercapacitors in the future, as well as new ideas for the design, preparation, and performance optimization of 3D printing nanostructured materials [60].

Recently, Li and Yu also proved that, in the field of photocatalysis, the semiconductor photocatalysts with 3D hierarchical micronano structures (3-HMNSs, such as flower-like and spherical structures) assembled by nanoparticles, nanorods, or nanosheets, can significantly improve their quantum efficiency and enhance their photocatalytic activity [50,56,61,62]. The band change caused by the quantum effect will change the absorption of light and the oxidation ability of 3D semiconductor materials [56]. For example, the lately proposed P-doped porous g-C_3N_4 3D nanosheets by Li have extremely high photocatalytic performance for rhodamine B degradation applications (see Fig. 2.4E) [50]. Especially in the hierarchical nanostructures, the 3D path of electrons is not only beneficial to the effective space separation of photogenerated electron-hole pair but also gives the 3D semiconductor material a strong redox ability. Yu also reported that the F-doped Sn_3O_4 3D nanosheets are promising for the synergistic treatment of industrial wastewater with organic pollutants (phenols) and Cr (VI) by strengthening the redox potential (utilization of photoinduced h^+/•OH and e^-) (see Fig. 2.4F) [61]. The nanosheets-built petal-like microspheres have numerous interstitial pores and secondary mesopores in nanoscale, which is conducive to the rapid transport of small molecules in the photocatalytic reaction. In addition, Yu reported that the urchin-like CuS nanorod microspheres with hierarchical porous structure and unique electrical structure also provided a strong capturing ability to the Cr (VI) ions in water. Once CuS microspheres were combined with TiO_2 crystals (P25), a surprised high removal efficiency for Cr (VI) was easily obtained (see Fig. 2.4G) [62]. In general, the semiconductor materials with 3-HMNSs can show excellent photocatalytic ability and high degradation efficiency, which could open up a new design philosophy for the construction of efficient photocatalytic system for environmental purification.

2.6 Porous nanostructures

Porous nanostructured material is a kind of material with network structure composed of open, interconnected, or closed holes. According to different dimensional structures of materials, porous materials can be divided into 0D porous materials (porous nanospheres, porous nanoparticles, etc.), 1D porous materials (porous nanowires, porous nanorods, etc.), 2D porous materials (porous nanosheets, porous films), and 3D porous materials (porous nanoflowers, porous aerogels, macrofoam materials, etc.). According to different dimensions, the channels in porous materials can also be divided into 1D, 2D, and 3D channels. The 1D nanotubes, 2D layered materials, and 3D foam materials are the most widely used 1D, 2D, and 3D channel materials, respectively. According to different pore sizes of materials, porous materials can be divided into microporous (pore size less than 2 nm), mesoporous (pore size 2−50 nm) and macroporous (pore size greater than 50 nm) materials (Classification standard source: International Union of Pure and Applied Chemistry (IUPAC) [63]). In this book, another noun of "nanoporous materials" will be appeared, which are defined as those porous materials with pore diameters less than 100 nm (such as porous carbon foam with micron dimension, mesoscopic graphene aerogel and so on).

Mesoporous nanomaterials have attracted much attention in adsorption, catalysis, and energy storage fields, because of their unique properties, such as high specific surface area, large pore volume, adjustable pore structure, controllable morphology and composition, and rich forms of composites [64]. In the past decades, there has been an increasing interest in the construction of advanced mesoporous nanomaterials with short and open channels, high-quality diffusion capacity and rich electrochemical energy conversion and storage active centers (or rich photocatalytic reaction active centers). Generally, high specific surface area can increase the reactive sites, large pore size can improve the transport efficiency of reactants and products, and the nanopore walls show small-size and quantum effects [65]. In addition, mesoporous materials provide good models for many basic energy storage and conversion (or photocatalysis) fields, such as micro- and nanoscale mass transfer kinetics, charge transfer/separation/storage mechanism, and interfacial chemical reactions in mesoporous and confined space [50]. It should be noted that mesoporous materials with different dimensions show different characteristics and advantages in energy and environmental-related applications.

The advantages of 1D mesoporous nanostructures in electrochemical energy storage and conversion (or photocatalysis) include: shortening the ion/electron/gas transmission path, improving the electrode material electrolyte contact area, buffering the volume expansion during charge and discharge, inhibiting the shuttle effect, and the mutual synergy between multi-dimensional materials [66]. In the early stage, we designed a mesoporous metal sulfide nanorods on carbon (see Fig. 2.1U, mesoporous SnS nanorods [27]), which has been well applied in the field of lithium-ion batteries (high capacity and long life). The advantages 2D mesoporous nanostructures include excellent mechanical strength and flexibility, high water permeability, high ion and molecular retention, and significant nano sieve effect [67]. We also designed a mesoporous 2D nanosheet material (see Fig. 2.1V, mesoporous g-C_3N_4 nanosheets [28]), which has been applied in solution phase photocatalysis with high efficiency and stability. The advantages 3D mesoporous nanostructures include the highly ordered or hierarchical mesoporous structure and 3D spatial structure give the materials higher adsorption capacity and energy capacity, as well considerable number of catalytically active sites [68]. We lately designed a mesoporous 3D nanoflowers material (see Fig. 2.1W, hierarchical mesoporous $NiCo_2O_4$ nanoflowers [29]), which showed excellent electrocatalytic properties. In particular, the 3D block porous materials provide rich gas—solid—liquid three-phase active interface regions and solution/gas product diffusion channels for electrocatalysis (or photocatalysis) reactions, avoid the polarization and active surface area loss caused by the use of adhesives, and can be directly applied to various efficient and stable catalytic applications [69].

2.7 Hollow nanostructures

Hollow nanostructures refer to the hollow materials with internal voids and thin-walled structures. Generally, the dimensions of hollow materials are not limited (ranging from a few nanometers to hundreds of nanometers), but the wall thickness is required to be within 100 nm. According to the morphology of materials, hollow nanostructures include hollow spheres, hollow polyhedrons, hollow tubes, hollow capsules, etc. According to the pore structure of the wall, hollow nanostructures can be divided into microporous hollow structures and mesoporous hollow structures. Hollow nanostructures with high specific surface area and high pore capacity can be designed by the double controlling of pore size and wall thickness (such as mesoporous hollow carbon spheres or mesoporous carbon cages) [70,71]. Our research group is also committed to the design and application of hollow nanostructures, such as hollow carbon nanocages with mesoporous walls [72] and metal oxide $NiCo_2O_4$ hollow spheres with 0D particles (see Fig. 2.1X) [30]. Our colleagues Shen and Tian also reported a new type of ultra-thin wall metal IrCo alloy hollow sphere (see Fig. 2.1Y) [31]. Thanks to their unique geometric and electronic structures, these hollow nanostructures exhibited excellent reactivity and stability in the field of electrochemical energy storage or electrocatalysis.

Hollow nanostructures with controllable dimensions and porous structures show unique electrochemical energy storage advantages due to the properties of nanostructure units, large specific surface area, and stable skeleton structure. The low-dimensional hollow nanostructures can reduce the ion/electron transmission distance and improve the reaction kinetics and the utilization of active substances. Large specific surface area provides abundant electrochemical active sites and hollow structures can store more active substances and relieve the structural stress during electrochemical reaction. Therefore, excellent electrochemical properties can be obtained by constructing reasonable low dimensional hollow nanostructures [73].

On the other hand, the porous hollow nanostructures are favorable for light entering the interior and multiple refraction in the cavity, so as to improve the utilization of light energy and the induced luminescence thermal effect [74]. In particular, the well-designed hollow structure and the control of size and composition help to ease the stress relaxation, so as to maintain the integrity of nanomaterials and achieve long service life (including electrochemical and photochemical applications) [75]. By exploring the correlation between hollow nanostructures (such as composition and geometric structures) and performances in energy or environment-related application, high-performance hollow nanostructures can be better designed to meet the requirements of specific applications [76]. It is believed that in the future, one can focus on the component design, batch synthesis, and practical application of hollow nanostructures to further promote the development of energy- and environment-related fields.

2.8 Composite nanostructures

Composite nanomaterials usually refer to multiphase system hybrid materials composed of different components (there are close phase interfaces or transition layers between different components). According to the number of components, composite nanomaterials can be divided into two-component composite nanomaterials, three-component composite nanomaterials, or more-component composite nanomaterials. According to different nanodimensions, common structures of composite nanomaterials include 0D-1D composite nanostructure, 0D-2D composite nanostructure, 1D-2D composite nanostructure, 2D-2D composite nanostructure (such as van der Waals 2D-2D heterostructure), and 0D-1D-2D composite nanostructure. According to different composite forms, composite nanomaterials can be divided into three categories: core-shell 0D composite nanostructures, coaxial 1D composite nanostructures, and sandwich 2D composite nanostructures. Through the intersection and superposition of different components or different dimensions, composite nanomaterials can show unique 3D network structures and distinctive physicochemical properties relative to single component or single structure [77].

In the last decade, our research groups (Zesheng Li and Changlin Yu) have designed and prepared several two-component or three-component composite interface materials, which have been applied in the fields of electrochemistry or photochemistry [12,18,46,78−82]. Due to their unique multidimensional (or multicomponent) factors and potential interface (or synergistic) effects, these composite nanomaterials show higher energy storage capacity or higher catalytic activity than single-component materials. For example, 1D CdS nanorods supported on 2D g-C_3N_4 nanosheets (1D-2D composite structure) exhibited excellent photoelectrochemical properties (see Fig. 2.5A−C) [78]. Porous carbon microspheres supported 1D MnO_2 nanoneedles (1D-3D composite structure) had very high pseudo-capacitance storage capacity and high ion diffusion rate (see Fig. 2.5D−F) [18]. SnO_2@carbon nanochains loaded Pt−Ru alloy nanoparticles (0D-0D-1D composite structure) had obvious synergistic electrocatalysis effect (via the electronic effect between SnO_2 and Pt Ru) (see Fig. 2.5G and H) [79]. Graphite carbon sheets supported Co_3W_3C and Pd nanoparticles (0D-0D-2D composite structure) also

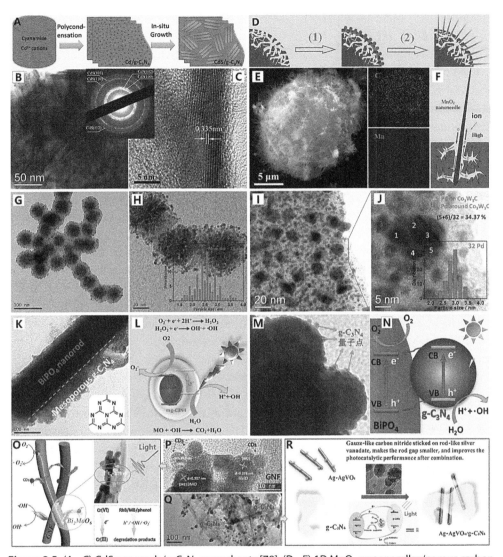

Figure 2.5 (A–C) CdS nanorods/g-C_3N_4 nanosheets [78], (D–F) 1D MnO_2 nanoneedles/porous carbon microspheres [18], (G, H) SnO_2@carbon nanochains loaded Pt–Ru alloy nanoparticles [79], (I, J) Graphite carbon sheets supported Co_3W_3C and Pd nanoparticles [80], (K, L) mesoporous g-C_3N_4 coated $BiPO_4$ nanorods [81], (M, N) $BiPO_4$ nanoparticles supported g-C_3N_4 quantum dots [12], (O, P) carbon quantum dots/Bi_2MoO_6 nanosheets/graphitic nanofibers [82], (Q, R) Ag quantum dots/$AgVO_4$ nanorods/g-C_3N_4 nanosheets [46] (these composite nanostructures are obtained from the work of Zesheng Li's group and Changlin Yu's group in the last decade).

demonstrated significant synergistic electrocatalytic effect (via the electronic effect between Co_3W_3C and Pd) (see Fig. 2.5I and J) [80]. In a word, for electrochemical energy
storage, the composite materials can improve the conductivity and stability of electrodes,
while for electrochemical conversion, the composite materials can induce an interface effect and synergistic electrocatalytic effect.

For photocatalysis, the purpose of designing composite nanostructures is to construct
heterojunctions, that is, composite nanostructures with special interface charge transfer
function. Constructing a heterojunction system is an effective approach to accelerate
the separation of photogenerated electrons and holes produced by photocatalytic materials. Recently, we have successfully prepared a heterojunction photocatalyst composed
of mesoporous $g-C_3N_4$ and $BiPO_4$ nanorods through a two-step design strategy of "template synthesis-interface assembly" (see Fig. 2.5K and L) [81]. Through the "ultrasound-
assisted-interface synthesis" strategy, we further prepared a heterojunction photocatalyst
composed of $g-C_3N_4$ quantum dots and $BiPO_4$ nanospheres (see Fig. 2.5M and N) [12].
Thanks to the rationality and progressiveness of the composite nanomaterials, the two
heterojunction systems have achieved ideal results in the degradation of corresponding
organic dyes, especially the visible light degradation performance of the quantum dot-
based heterojunction system has been significantly (3.3 times) improved. In addition,
we have lately designed two three-component heterojunction photocatalytic systems,
namely, carbon quantum dots/Bi_2MoO_6 nanosheets/graphitic nanofibers (see
Fig. 2.5O and P) [82], and Ag quantum dots/$AgVO_4$ nanorods/$g-C_3N_4$ nanosheets
(see Fig. 2.5Q and R) [46]. Thanks to the high visible light response capacity and favorable Z-scheme heterojunction, the two composite catalysts exhibit extremely high
oxidation and/or reduction capacities. In brief, using appropriate components to
construct composite photocatalysts can not only expand the light absorption range but
also improve the separation of light energy carriers. The interfacial bonding of heterojunction is an important parameter to control the photocatalytic performance, which
will affect the transfer of photogenerated carriers in the composite.

2.9 Atomically dispersed structures

Recently, atomically dispersed sub-one-nano structured catalysts, including single-atom
catalysts (SACs) [83], dual atom catalysts (DACs) [84], and atomic cluster catalysts (ACCs)
[85], have received extensive attention, and their atomic utilization efficiency and catalytic efficiency have been improved by a quantitative level compared with nanocrystal
catalysts (NCCs). In particular, when the catalyst support has enough coordination atoms
or groups, the single atom loading with ultra-high atomic density (5—15 atoms nm^{-2})
and very close distance to the metal atom site (0.2—0.5 nm) can be achieved through
appropriate synthesis strategies. These ultra-high density metal atoms usually do not

form metal bonds. They form a 3D foam-like site distribution through oxygen bridging or spatial accumulation. For the first time, we define these ultra-high-density SACs supported on some specific substrates as atomic foam catalysts (AFCs) (see Fig. 2.6A) [86]. The AFCs can be regarded as the intermediate form of SACs to NCCs, combining the advantages of both and producing new catalytic properties.

At present, the hot research and development directions of atomically dispersed catalysts include coordination environment (first coordination and adjacent environment), molecular engineering (precursor molecular design and molecular catalyst grafting), support engineering (nanostructure design and defect structure regulation), thermodynamic stability (thermal atomization in preparation and stability in application), dynamic catalytic structure evolution (dynamic change of metal atom distribution during catalytic

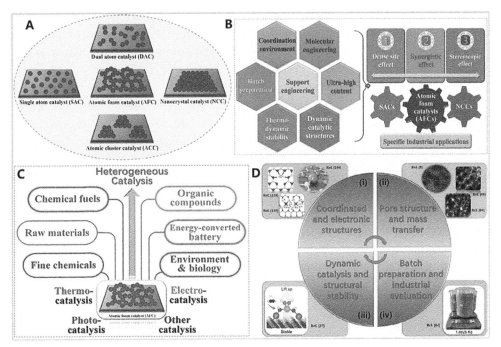

Figure 2.6 (A) schematic diagram of AFCs and other types of catalysts, (B) hotspot research directions of SACs and structural functionalities of AFCs, (C) application fields and target products of AFCs in versatile heterogeneous catalysis, (D) scientific and technological challenges of AFCs (these images are acquired from a review paper of Zesheng Li's group [86]).

reaction), large-scale preparation (such as gram level and kilogram level preparation) and promotion of ultra-high metal content (limited loading on different carriers and site density-distance effect of single atoms) (see Fig. 2.6B left). The structural function effects of AFCs include (I) dense site effect, (II) synergistic effect, and (III) stereoscopic effect (see Fig. 2.6B right) [86]. These effects make the AFCs shine brightly in a variety of industrial applications (heterogeneous catalysis).

The application of AFCs in heterogeneous catalysis mainly focuses on (1) chemical fuel production: hydrogen fuel, hydrocarbon (such as methane, ethanol, etc.), and oxide fuel (such as formic acid, acetic acid, etc.); (2) preparation of chemical raw materials: ethylene, ammonia, carbon monoxide, etc.; (3) preparation of fine chemicals: drugs, pesticides, etc.; (4) synthesis of complex cyclic organic compounds (COCs): aromatic compounds, heterocyclic compounds, etc; (5) batteries: hydrogen-oxygen fuel cell, metal air cell, etc.; (6) biology and environment: nano-enzyme antibacterial and persulfate activation (see Fig. 2.6C) [86]. For thermo-, photo-, electro-, and other catalytic applications, the catalytic activity of AFCs will increase with the increase in metal atom density. In particular, the ultra-high density transition metal AFCs show very high catalytic performances for complex catalytic reactions.

Although AFCs have many advantages, they still face quite a few scientific and technical challenges in controllable preparation and catalytic applications, including (1) coordination and electronic structure (further control of coordination structures and exploration of electronic effects are needed); (2) pore structure and mass transfer (specific pore structures need to be designed to enhance catalytic dynamics); (3) dynamic catalysis and structural stability (further identification of dynamic catalytic active sites and improvement of stability are needed); (4) batch preparation and industrial evaluation (the developing batch preparation technology and promoting industrial application is necessary) (see Fig. 2.6D) [86]. At the same time, it is also an important research direction to explore the synergistic effect of atomic-structured catalysts and nano-structured catalysts. Promoting the atomization of nanostructures and utilizing the nano-atom interface effect is an ultimate goal of monatomic research.

2.10 Summary

In this chapter, we comprehensively summarize the definitions, classifications, advantages, and application values of nanostructures with different dimensions (0, 1, 2, 3D nanostructures) and nanostructures with different characteristics (porous nanostructures, hollow nanostructures, composite nanostructures, and single-atom dispersed sub-one-nano structures). These nanostructures have shown their own value and unique contributions in electrochemical energy storage and conversion or photocatalytic environment applications. In particular, at present, it is the transition period from nano-structured age to atomic-structured age. Many new concepts and physicochemical properties of nanomaterials or subnanomaterials will be discovered, and they will shine brightly in the fields of energy and environment (including science and technology aspects).

Acknowledgments

This book was supported by National Natural Science Foundation of China (22078071, 22272034), Natural Science Foundation of Guangdong Province (2021A1515010125, 2020A1515010344), Maoming Science and Technology Project (mmkj2020032), Guangdong Province Universities and Colleges Pearl River Scholar Funded Scheme (2019), Guangdong Basic and Applied Basic Research Foundation (2019A1515011249, 2021A1515010305), Key Research Project of Natural Science of Guangdong Provincial Department of Education (2019KZDXM010), Environment and Energy Green Catalysis Innovation Team of Colleges and Universities of Guangdong Province (2022KCXTD019), the program for Innovative Research Team of Guangdong University of Petrochemical Technology.

References

[1] S. Yu, Low Dimensional Nano Materials: Preparation Methodology, 2019, ISBN 978-7-03-060644-0.

[2] Z. He, J.L. Wang, S.M. Chen, J.W. Liu, S.H. Yu, Self-assembly of nanowires: from dynamic monitoring to precision control, Accounts of Chemical Research (2022) 8130−8134.

[3] C. Gu, H.M. Xu, S.K. Han, M.R. Gao, S.H. Yu, Soft chemistry of metastable metal chalcogenide nanomaterials, Chemical Society Reviews 50 (12) (2021) 6671−6683.

[4] L. Sun, Y. Liu, R. Shao, J. Wu, R. Jiang, Z. Jin, Recent progress and future perspective on practical silicon anode-based lithium ion batteries, Energy Storage Materials 46 (2022) 482−502.

[5] P. Prabhu, J.M. Lee, Metallenes as functional materials in electrocatalysis, Chemical Society Reviews 50 (12) (2021) 6700−6719.

[6] J. Lu, Z. Chen, Z. Ma, F. Pan, L.A. Curtiss, K. Amine, The role of nanotechnology in the development of battery materials for electric vehicles, Nature Nanotechnology 11 (12) (2016) 1031−1038.

[7] B.C. Hodges, E.L. Cates, J.H. Kim, Challenges and prospects of advanced oxidation water treatment processes using catalytic nanomaterials, Nature Nanotechnology 13 (8) (2018) 642−650.

[8] H. Jin, C. Guo, X. Liu, J. Liu, A. Vasileff, Y. Jiao, S.Z. Qiao, Emerging two-dimensional nanomaterials for electrocatalysis, Chemical Reviews 118 (13) (2018) 6337−6408.

[9] R. Wu, Y. Li, W. Gong, P.K. Shen, One-pot synthesis of Pt−Pd bimetallic nanodendrites with enhanced electrocatalytic activity for oxygen reduction reaction, ACS Sustainable Chemistry and Engineering 7 (9) (2019) 8419−8428.

[10] H.Q. Wang, G.F. Yang, Q.Y. Li, X.X. Zhong, F.P. Wang, Z.S. Li, Y.H. Li, Porous nano-MnO_2: large scale synthesis via a facile quick-redox procedure and application in a supercapacitor, New Journal of Chemistry 35 (2) (2011) 469−475.

[11] M. Tang, S. Luo, K. Wang, H. Du, R. Sriphathoorat, P. Shen, Simultaneous formation of trimetallic Pt-Ni-Cu excavated rhombic dodecahedrons with enhanced catalytic performance for the methanol oxidation reaction, Nano Research 11 (9) (2018) 4786−4795.

[12] Z. Li, B. Li, S. Peng, D. Li, S. Yang, Y. Fang, Novel visible light-induced g-C_3N_4 quantum dot/ $BiPO_4$ nanocrystal composite photocatalysts for efficient degradation of methyl orange, RSC Advances 4 (66) (2014) 35144−35148.

[13] B. Chu, Q. Ma, Z. Li, B. Li, F. Huang, Q. Pang, J.Z. Zhang, Design and preparation of three-dimensional hetero-electrocatalysts of NiCo-layered double hydroxide nanosheets incorporated with silver nanoclusters for enhanced oxygen evolution reactions, Nanoscale 13 (25) (2021) 11150−11160.

[14] B. Zhang, X. Yu, C. Ge, X. Dong, Y. Fang, Z. Li, H. Wang, Novel 3-D superstructures made up of SnO_2@C core-shell nanochains for energy storage applications, Chemical Communications 46 (48) (2010) 9188−9190.

[15] Z. Li, Y. Li, G. He, P.K. Shen, Novel graphene-like nanosheet supported highly active electrocatalysts with ultralow Pt loadings for oxygen reduction reaction, Journal of Materials Chemistry A 2 (40) (2014) 16898−16904.

[16] Z. Li, Z. Liu, B. Li, D. Li, Z. Liu, H. Wang, Q. Li, Large area synthesis of well-dispersed β-MnO$_2$ nanorods and their electrochemical supercapacitive performances, Journal of the Taiwan Institute of Chemical Engineers 65 (2016) 544–551.

[17] Z. Li, Z. Liu, D. Li, B. Li, Q. Li, Y. Huang, H. Wang, Facile synthesis of α-MnO$_2$ nanowires/spherical activated carbon composite for supercapacitor application in neutral electrolyte, Journal of Materials Science: Materials in Electronics 26 (1) (2015) 353–359.

[18] Z. Li, Q. Li, Y. Fang, H. Wang, Y. Li, X. Wang, Unique mesoporous carbon microsphere/1-D MnO$_2$-built composite architecture and their enhanced electrochemical capacitance performance, Journal of Materials Chemistry 21 (43) (2011) 17185–17192.

[19] Y. Li, Z. Li, P.K. Shen, Simultaneous formation of ultrahigh surface area and three-dimensional hierarchical porous graphene-like networks for fast and highly stable supercapacitors, Advanced Materials 25 (17) (2013) 2474–2480.

[20] Z. Li, L. Zhang, X. Chen, B. Li, H. Wang, Q. Li, Three-dimensional graphene-like porous carbon nanosheets derived from molecular precursor for high-performance supercapacitor application, Electrochimica Acta 296 (2019) 8–17.

[21] Z. Li, B. Li, Z. Liu, D. Li, H. Wang, Q. Li, One-pot construction of 3-D nitrogen-doped activated graphene-like nanosheets for high-performance supercapacitors, Electrochimica Acta 190 (2016) 378–387.

[22] Z. Li, K. Xiao, C. Yu, H. Wang, Q. Li, Three-dimensional graphene-like carbon nanosheets coupled with MnCo-layered double hydroxides nanoflowers as efficient bifunctional oxygen electrocatalyst, International Journal of Hydrogen Energy 46 (69) (2021) 34239–34251.

[23] M. Yu, Q. Pu, X. Liao, H. Yu, S. Lin, Z. Li, X. Zhong, Controllable synthesis of bismuth tungstate photocatalysts with different morphologies for degradation of antibiotics under visible-light irradiation, Journal of Materials Science: Materials in Electronics 32 (13) (2021) 17848–17864.

[24] H.Q. Wang, Z.S. Li, Y.G. Huang, Q.Y. Li, X.Y. Wang, A novel hybrid supercapacitor based on spherical activated carbon and spherical MnO$_2$ in a non-aqueous electrolyte, Journal of Materials Chemistry 20 (19) (2010) 3883–3889.

[25] J. Zhu, Q. Wu, J. Key, M. Wu, P.K. Shen, Self-assembled superstructure of carbon-wrapped, single-crystalline Cu3P porous nanosheets: one-step synthesis and enhanced Li-ion battery anode performance, Energy Storage Materials 15 (2018) 75–81.

[26] Z. Li, B. Li, Z. Liu, D. Li, C. Ge, Y. Fang, Controlled synthesis of ZnGa$_2$O$_4$ nanorod arrays from hexagonal ZnO microdishes and their photocatalytic activity on the degradation of RhB, RSC Advances 4 (89) (2014) 48590–48595.

[27] J. Cai, Z. Li, P.K. Shen, Porous SnS nanorods/carbon hybrid materials as highly stable and high capacity anode for Li-ion batteries, ACS Applied Materials and Interfaces 4 (8) (2012) 4093–4098.

[28] S. Yang, W. Zhou, C. Ge, X. Liu, Y. Fang, Z. Li, Mesoporous polymeric semiconductor materials of graphitic-C$_3$N$_4$: general and efficient synthesis and their integration with synergistic AgBr NPs for enhanced photocatalytic performances, RSC Advances 3 (16) (2013) 5631–5638.

[29] Z. Li, B. Li, J. Chen, Q. Pang, P. Shen, Spinel NiCo$_2$O$_4$ 3-D nanoflowers supported on graphene nanosheets as efficient electrocatalyst for oxygen evolution reaction, International Journal of Hydrogen Energy 44 (31) (2019) 16120–16131.

[30] Z. Li, R. Yang, B. Li, M. Yu, D. Li, H. Wang, Q. Li, Controllable synthesis of graphene/NiCo$_2$O$_4$ three-dimensional mesoporous electrocatalysts for efficient methanol oxidation reaction, Electrochimica Acta 252 (2017) 180–191.

[31] J. Zhu, M. Wei, Q. Meng, Z. Chen, Y. Fan, S.W. Hasan, P.K. Shen, Ultrathin-shell IrCo hollow nanospheres as highly efficient electrocatalysts towards the oxygen evolution reaction in acidic media, Nanoscale 12 (47) (2020) 24070–24078.

[32] Y. Gong, Z. Cao, Z. Zhang, R. Liu, F. Zhang, J. Wei, Z. Yang, Chirality inversion in self-assembled nanocomposites directed by curvature mediated interactions, Angewandte Chemie 134 (10) (2022) e202117406.

[33] D. Liu, X. Li, S. Chen, H. Yan, C. Wang, C. Wu, L. Song, Atomically dispersed platinum supported on curved carbon supports for efficient electrocatalytic hydrogen evolution, Nature Energy 4 (6) (2019) 512–518.

[34] Z. Li, B. Li, Y. Hu, S. Wang, C. Yu, Highly-dispersed and high-metal-density electrocatalysts on carbon supports for the oxygen reduction reaction: from nanoparticles to atomic-level architectures, Materials Advances 3 (2) (2022) 779—809.

[35] P. Diao, M. Guo, Q. Zhang, How does the particle density affect the electrochemical behavior of gold nanoparticle assembly? The Journal of Physical Chemistry C 112 (17) (2008) 7036—7046.

[36] Y. Kim, G. Collinge, M.S. Lee, K. Khivantsev, S.J. Cho, V.A. Glezakou, J.H. Kwak, Surface density dependent catalytic activity of single palladium atoms supported on Ceria, Angewandte Chemie International Edition 60 (42) (2021) 22769—22775.

[37] X. Tian, X.F. Lu, B.Y. Xia, X.W.D. Lou, Advanced electrocatalysts for the oxygen reduction reaction in energy conversion technologies, Joule 4 (1) (2020) 45—68.

[38] L. Xu, G. Wang, X. Zheng, H. Pan, J. Zhu, Z. Li, S.H. Yu, Competitive adsorption between a polymer and its monomeric analog enables precise modulation of nanowire synthesis, Chem 4 (10) (2018) 2451—2462.

[39] X. Zhao, Q. Li, L. Xu, Z. Zhang, Z. Kang, Q. Liao, Y. Zhang, Interface engineering in 1D ZnO-based heterostructures for photoelectrical devices, Advanced Functional Materials 32 (11) (2022) 2106887.

[40] F. Wang, A. Dong, J. Sun, R. Tang, H. Yu, W.E. Buhro, Solution-liquid-solid growth of semiconductor nanowires, Inorganic Chemistry 45 (19) (2006) 7511—7521.

[41] S. Yang, C. Ge, Z. Liu, Y. Fang, Z. Li, D. Kuang, C. Su, Novel Ga-doped, self-supported, independent aligned ZnO nanorods: one-pot hydrothermal synthesis and structurally enhanced photocatalytic performance, RSC Advances 1 (9) (2011) 1691—1694.

[42] X. Yu, S. Yang, B. Zhang, D. Shao, X. Dong, Y. Fang, H. Wang, Controlled synthesis of $SnO_2@$ carbon core-shell nanochains as high-performance anodes for lithium-ion batteries, Journal of Materials Chemistry 21 (33) (2011) 12295—12302.

[43] B. Li, Z. Li, Q. Pang, J.Z. Zhang, Core/shell cable-like Ni_3S_2 nanowires/N-doped graphene-like carbon layers as composite electrocatalyst for overall electrocatalytic water splitting, Chemical Engineering Journal 401 (2020) 126045.

[44] K. Yu, X. Pan, G. Zhang, X. Liao, X. Zhou, M. Yan, L. Mai, Nanowires in energy storage devices: structures, synthesis, and applications, Advanced Energy Materials 8 (32) (2018) 1802369.

[45] G. Zhou, L. Xu, G. Hu, L. Mai, Y. Cui, Nanowires for electrochemical energy storage, Chemical Reviews 119 (20) (2019) 11042—11109.

[46] D. Chen, B. Li, Q. Pu, X. Chen, G. Wen, Z. Li, Preparation of Ag-AgVO3/g-C3N4 composite photo-catalyst and degradation characteristics of antibiotics, Journal of Hazardous Materials 373 (2019) 303—312.

[47] Y.P. Zhu, J. Yin, E. Abou-Hamad, X. Liu, W. Chen, T. Yao, H.N. Alshareef, Highly stable phosphonate-based MOFs with engineered bandgaps for efficient photocatalytic hydrogen production, Advanced Materials 32 (16) (2020) 1906368.

[48] Y. He, X. Zhuang, C. Lei, L. Lei, Y. Hou, Y. Mai, X. Feng, Porous carbon nanosheets: synthetic strategies and electrochemical energy related applications, Nano Today 24 (2019) 103—119.

[49] Z. Li, J. Lin, B. Li, C. Yu, H. Wang, Q. Li, Construction of heteroatom-doped and three-dimensional graphene materials for the applications in supercapacitors: a review, Journal of Energy Storage 44 (2021) 103437.

[50] Z. Li, Q. Chen, Q. Lin, Y. Chen, X. Liao, H. Yu, C. Yu, Three-dimensional P-doped porous g-C_3N_4 nanosheets as an efficient metal-free photocatalyst for visible-light photocatalytic degradation of Rhodamine B model pollutant, Journal of the Taiwan Institute of Chemical Engineers 114 (2020) 249—262.

[51] Q. Lin, Z. Li, T. Lin, B. Li, X. Liao, H. Yu, C. Yu, Controlled preparation of P-doped g-C_3N_4 nanosheets for efficient photocatalytic hydrogen production, Chinese Journal of Chemical Engineering 28 (10) (2020) 2677—2688.

[52] C. Yu, H. He, Q. Fan, W. Xie, Z. Liu, H. Ji, Novel B-doped BiOCl nanosheets with exposed (001) facets and photocatalytic mechanism of enhanced degradation efficiency for organic pollutants, Science of the Total Environment 694 (2019) 133727.

[53] X. Liu, W. Zhou, F. Li, C. Yu, Eu^{3+} doped Bi_2MoO_6 nanosheets fabricated via hydrothermal-calcination route and their superior performance for aqueous volatile phenols removal, Journal of the Taiwan Institute of Chemical Engineers 125 (2021) 276–284.

[54] D. Zeng, K. Yang, C. Yu, F. Chen, X. Li, Z. Wu, H. Liu, Phase transformation and microwave hydrothermal guided a novel double Z-scheme ternary vanadate heterojunction with highly efficient photocatalytic performance, Applied Catalysis B: Environmental 237 (2018) 449–463.

[55] F. Bai, L. Xu, X. Zhai, X. Chen, W. Yang, Vacancy in ultrathin 2D nanomaterials toward sustainable energy application, Advanced Energy Materials 10 (11) (2020) 1902107.

[56] Z. Li, M. Luo, B. Li, Q. Lin, X. Liao, H. Yu, C. Yu, 3-D hierarchical micro/nano-structures of porous Bi_2WO_6: controlled hydrothermal synthesis and enhanced photocatalytic performances, Microporous and Mesoporous Materials 313 (2021) 110830.

[57] Z. Li, B. Li, L. Du, W. Wang, X. Liao, H. Yu, Q. Li, Three-dimensional oxygen-doped porous graphene: sodium chloride-template preparation, structural characterization and supercapacitor performances, Chinese Journal of Chemical Engineering 40 (2021) 304–314.

[58] H. Zhao, Y. Lei, 3D nanostructures for the next generation of high-performance nanodevices for electrochemical energy conversion and storage, Advanced Energy Materials 10 (28) (2020) 2001460.

[59] F. Li, Z. Zhou, Micro. Nanostructured materials for sodium ion batteries and capacitors, Small 14 (6) (2018) 1702961.

[60] B. Li, M. Yu, Z. Li, C. Yu, H. Wang, Q. Li, Constructing flexible all-solid-state supercapacitors from 3D nanosheets active bricks via 3D manufacturing technology: a perspective review, Advanced Functional Materials (2022) 2201166.

[61] D. Zeng, C. Yu, Q. Fan, J. Zeng, L. Wei, Z. Li, H. Ji, Theoretical and experimental research of novel fluorine doped hierarchical Sn_3O_4 microspheres with excellent photocatalytic performance for removal of Cr (VI) and organic pollutants, Chemical Engineering Journal 391 (2020) 123607.

[62] Z. Wu, X. Liu, C. Yu, F. Li, W. Zhou, L. Wei, Construct interesting CuS/TiO_2 architectures for effective removal of Cr (VI) in simulated wastewater via the strong synergistic adsorption and photocatalytic process, Science of The Total Environment 796 (2021) 148941.

[63] B. Li, M. Yu, Z. Li, C. Yu, Q. Li, H. Wang, Three-dimensional activated carbon nanosheets modified by graphitized carbon dots: one-step alkali pyrolysis preparation and supercapacitor applications, Journal of Energy Storage 51 (2022) 104515.

[64] Y. Yan, G. Chen, P. She, G. Zhong, W. Yan, B.Y. Guan, Y. Yamauchi, Mesoporous nanoarchitectures for electrochemical energy conversion and storage, Advanced Materials 32 (44) (2020) 2004654.

[65] L. Zu, W. Zhang, L. Qu, L. Liu, W. Li, A. Yu, D. Zhao, Mesoporous materials for electrochemical energy storage and conversion, Advanced Energy Materials 10 (38) (2020) 2002152.

[66] Q. Wei, F. Xiong, S. Tan, L. Huang, E.H. Lan, B. Dunn, L. Mai, Porous one-dimensional nanomaterials: design, fabrication and applications in electrochemical energy storage, Advanced Materials 29 (20) (2017) 1602300.

[67] Y. Yang, X. Yang, L. Liang, Y. Gao, H. Cheng, X. Li, X. Duan, Large-area graphene-nanomesh/carbon-nanotube hybrid membranes for ionic and molecular nanofiltration, Science 364 (6445) (2019) 1057–1062.

[68] Z. Li, X. Hu, D. Xiong, B. Li, H. Wang, Q. Li, Facile synthesis of bicontinuous microporous/mesoporous carbon foam with ultrahigh specific surface area for supercapacitor application, Electrochimica Acta 219 (2016) 339–349.

[69] D. Xu, H. Lv, B. Liu, Encapsulation of metal nanoparticle catalysts within mesoporous zeolites and their enhanced catalytic performances: a review, Frontiers in Chemistry (2018) 550.

[70] H. Zhang, O. Noonan, X. Huang, Y. Yang, C. Xu, L. Zhou, C. Yu, Surfactant-free assembly of mesoporous carbon hollow spheres with large tunable pore sizes, ACS Nano 10 (4) (2016) 4579–4586.

[71] X.K. Wan, H.B. Wu, B.Y. Guan, D. Luan, X.W. Lou, Confining sub-nanometer Pt clusters in hollow mesoporous carbon spheres for boosting hydrogen evolution activity, Advanced Materials 32 (7) (2020) 1901349.

[72] Z. Li, L. Zhang, B. Li, Z. Liu, Z. Liu, H. Wang, Q. Li, Convenient and large-scale synthesis of hollow graphene-like nanocages for electrochemical supercapacitor application, Chemical Engineering Journal 313 (2017) 1242–1250.

[73] Y. Fang, D. Luan, S. Gao, X.W. Lou, Rational design and engineering of one-dimensional hollow nanostructures for efficient electrochemical energy storage, Angewandte Chemie 133 (37) (2021) 20262–20278.

[74] M. Cai, Z. Wu, Z. Li, L. Wang, W. Sun, A.A. Tountas, X. Zhang, Greenhouse-inspired supra-photothermal CO_2 catalysis, Nature Energy 6 (8) (2021) 807–814.

[75] M. Xiao, Z. Wang, M. Lyu, B. Luo, S. Wang, G. Liu, L. Wang, Hollow nanostructures for photocatalysis: advantages and challenges, Advanced Materials 31 (38) (2019) 1801369.

[76] J. Wang, Y. Cui, D. Wang, Design of hollow nanostructures for energy storage, conversion and production, Advanced Materials 31 (38) (2019) 1801993.

[77] M. Ha, J.H. Kim, M. You, Q. Li, C. Fan, J.M. Nam, Multicomponent plasmonic nanoparticles: from heterostructured nanoparticles to colloidal composite nanostructures, Chemical Reviews 119 (24) (2019) 12208–12278.

[78] Z. Li, Z. Liu, B. Li, D. Li, C. Ge, Y. Fang, Novel CdS nanorods/g-C_3N_4 nanosheets 1-D/2-D hybrid architectures: an in situ growth route and excellent visible light photoelectrochemical performances, Journal of Materials Science: Materials in Electronics 27 (3) (2016) 2904–2913.

[79] S. Yang, C. Zhao, C. Ge, X. Dong, X. Liu, Y. Liu, Z. Li, Ternary Pt–Ru–SnO_2 hybrid architectures: unique carbon-mediated 1-D configuration and their electrocatalytic activity to methanol oxidation, Journal of Materials Chemistry 22 (15) (2012) 7104–7107.

[80] Z. Li, S. Ji, B.G. Pollet, P.K. Shen, A Co 3 W 3 C promoted Pd catalyst exhibiting competitive performance over Pt/C catalysts towards the oxygen reduction reaction, Chemical Communications 50 (5) (2014) 566–568.

[81] Z. Li, S. Yang, J. Zhou, D. Li, X. Zhou, C. Ge, Y. Fang, Novel mesoporous g-C_3N_4 and $BiPO_4$ nanorods hybrid architectures and their enhanced visible-light-driven photocatalytic performances, Chemical Engineering Journal 241 (2014) 344–351.

[82] W. Huang, S. Wang, Q. Zhou, X. Liu, X. Chen, K. Yang, D. Li, Constructing novel ternary composites of carbon quantum dots/Bi_2MoO_6/graphitic nanofibers with tunable band structure and boosted photocatalytic activity, Separation and Purification Technology 217 (2019) 195–205.

[83] A. Wang, J. Li, T. Zhang, Heterogeneous single-atom catalysis, Nature Reviews Chemistry 2 (6) (2018) 65–81.

[84] J. Zhang, Q.A. Huang, J. Wang, J. Wang, J. Zhang, Y. Zhao, Supported dual-atom catalysts: preparation, characterization, and potential applications, Chinese Journal of Catalysis 41 (5) (2020) 783–798.

[85] L. Li, Y.F. Jiang, T. Zhang, H. Cai, Y. Zhou, B. Lin, J. Li, Size sensitivity of supported Ru catalysts for ammonia synthesis: from nanoparticles to subnanometric clusters and atomic clusters, Chem 8 (3) (2022) 749–768.

[86] Z. Li, B. Li, Y. Hu, X. Liao, H. Yu, C. Yu, Emerging ultrahigh-density single-atom catalysts for versatile heterogeneous catalysis applications: redefinition, recent progress, and challenges, Small Structures (2022) 2200041.

CHAPTER 3

Structure—performance relationship of nanomaterials

3.1 Introduction

From macroscopic to mesoscopic, the reduction in size leads to a series of changes in physical and chemical properties of materials and also leads to the establishment and development of an interdisciplinary nanoscience covering physics, energy, chemistry, biology, materials, microelectronics, and other disciplines. Due to the small size, large surface area, and high percentage of disordered atoms on the surface, nanomaterials have many special basic properties, such as small size effect, surface effect, quantum size effect, macroscopic quantum tunneling effect, and dielectric domain effect [1—3]. Therefore, nanomaterials have significant physical and chemical properties, such as high surface activity, strong oxidation, superparamagnetism, and obvious blue or red shift in absorption spectra. In particular, in electrochemical energy and environmental catalysis applications, nanomaterials also have special electrical/optical properties, electrocatalytic properties, photocatalytic properties, photoelectrochemical properties, chemical reaction properties, chemical reaction kinetics properties, and special physicomechanical properties [4,5]. Nanomaterials provide many ideal properties for electrochemical energy storage devices due to their nanometer size effect. The limited size plays an important role in determining the properties of nanomaterials, such as ion diffusion dynamics, strain/stress effect, and utilization of active sites [4]. Nanomaterials are also expected to play a key role in many highly efficient and highly selective heterogeneous photocatalytic systems. The physical and chemical properties of nano-photocatalysts, such as electronic structure, geometric morphology, and surface microchemical environment, can affect the key processes, such as photon capture, separation and migration of photocarriers, and surface catalytic reaction process [5]. The regulation of nanostructures is crucial to the selectivity and photocatalytic activity of the target catalytic products.

It is generally believed that the physical origin of nanoeffect and the essential principle of structure—activity relationship can be summarized into the following aspects (from exterior to interior): (1) the reduction in size and dimension of geometric level leads to the sharp increase of specific surface area, (2) the amorphization leads to the increase in surface defect density or bulk defect density at atomic level, (3) the reduction in nanosize leads to the increase in the proportion of edge, angle, and edge sites, or the decrease in coordination number (CN) of active sites, (4) the increase in atomic defect density and the decrease in site CN lead to the change of electronic structure of nanomaterials [6]. Although the

Nanostructured Materials
ISBN 978-0-443-19256-2, https://doi.org/10.1016/B978-0-443-19256-2.00006-5

different dimension, topography, and surface/interface configurations of nanosystems, the most direct reason for the origin of the nanoeffect lies in nanoscale, deeper reason is the atomic coordination environment, and the essential reason is the electronic structure, this is common characteristics for all nanosystems in fields of energy and environment [7—12]. Therefore, how to correlate nanoscale with physicochemical properties through electronic structure is the ultimate way to reveal the various structure-activity relationships of nanostructured materials (such as size, electron, geometry, dimension, confinement, crystal, interface, and synergy effects) (see Fig. 3.1 for details).

3.2 Size effect

The core scientific question in the field of surface chemistry of nanomaterials is why and how size reduction generally enhances the surface chemical activity of nanomaterials. In the past 40 years, the top scientists in the field of nanomaterials and catalysis have made a lot of experimental and theoretical explorations to answer this basic question, trying to reveal the mechanism of the surface activity of different nanomaterials enhanced by the reduction in size. By summarizing the important literature, we can obtain the following key size effects and scientific principles: small size effect, quantum size effect, and size-dependent surface effect. The size-dependent surface effect includes size-dependent surface CN, size-dependent surface adsorption energy, and size-dependent surface electron state triplex effects.

3.2.1 Small size effect

Because of the extremely small size of the nanoparticle material, the number of atoms is very small, and the corresponding mass is very small. Thus, many physical phenomena cannot be applied to the properties of a block matter that normally has an infinite number of atoms. This particular physical phenomenon is often called the small-size effect. Specifically, when the size of the nanoparticles is equal to or smaller than the physical characteristics such as the wavelength of light, de Broglie wavelength, and the coherence length or transmission depth of the superconducting state, the periodic boundary conditions of the crystals will be destroyed, and the atomic density near the surface layer of the amorphous nanoparticles will be reduced. These parameter changes result in new physical properties in acoustic, optical, electrical, magnetic, thermal, and mechanical fields which are called the small size effects [13]. For example, when metal or nonmetal is prepared into powder smaller than a certain scale (1—100 nm), its physical properties have undergone fundamental changes, with high strength, high toughness, high specific heat, high conductivity, high diffusion, and strong absorption of electromagnetic waves and other physical properties [14].

3.2.2 Quantum size effect

According to the degree of electron motion limitation, nanomaterials can be divided into zero-dimensional quantum dots, one-dimensional quantum wires, two-dimensional

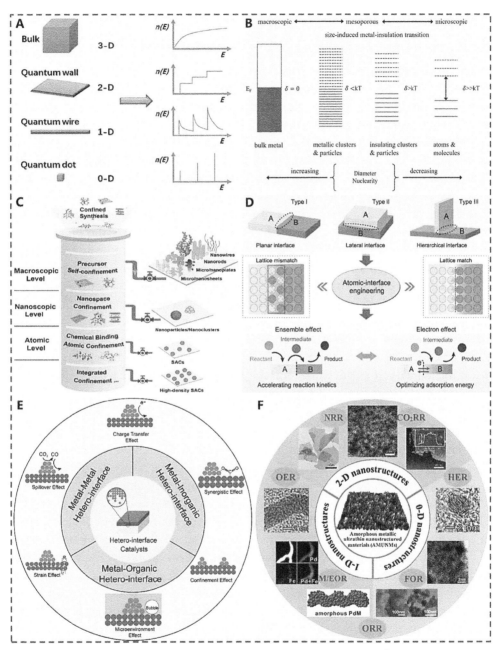

Figure 3.1 (A) Quantum confinement effect [7], (B) size/electron/geometry effect [8], (C) nano/atom confinement effect [9], (D) nano/atom interface effect [10], (E) charge transfer/synergistic effect [11], (F) crystal/dimension effect [12].

quantum wells, and three-dimensional bulk materials. Zero-dimensional quantum dot refers to a material in which the movement of electrons in the three dimensions is restricted, that is, electrons cannot move freely in the three dimensions. One-dimensional quantum wire means that the movement of electrons in two dimensions is limited, that is, electrons can move freely in one dimension. Two-dimensional quantum well means that the movement of electrons in one dimension is limited, that is, electrons can move freely in two dimensions. Three-dimensional bulk materials mean that the movement of electrons in the zero dimension is limited, that is, electrons can move freely in the three dimensions (see Fig. 3.1A for details) [7]. The difference between zero-dimensional, one-dimensional, two-dimensional, and three-dimensional materials can be further understood by solving Schrodinger equation. If a material has a small scale in a certain direction, the ground state energy and the energy of the first excited state differ greatly in this direction (the smaller the scale is, the more severely the electrons are restricted, and the greater the energy difference). At low temperature, almost all electrons are concentrated in the ground state, so the dimension in this direction can be ignored in the analysis. For example, the Schrodinger equation satisfied by the electron is solved by separating variables (see Eq. 3.1), and the wave function in the z direction is $\Phi_0(z)$, $\Phi_1(z)$ ..., the corresponding intrinsic energies are E_{z0}, E_{z1} ..., if the energy difference between E_{z0} and E_{z1} is very large, most of the electrons are concentrated in the ground state at low temperature, and the wave function can be written as $\Psi(x, y)$ $\Phi_0(z)$, the dimension in the z direction can be ignored (see Fig. 3.1A) [7].

$$\left(-\frac{\partial^2}{\partial z^2} + V(z) \right) \Phi(z) = E_z \Phi(z) \tag{3.1}$$

Generally, the smaller the scale in a certain direction, the more severely restricted the electron is, and the larger the energy difference is, the easier it is to meet the above conditions. These effects are usually called quantum confinement effects [15].

When the size of one dimension of nanomaterials is small enough to be equivalent to the de Broglie wave or exciton Bohr radius of electrons, the movement of electrons and holes in this direction is limited. Compared with bulk materials, electrons lose the degree of freedom in this direction, and the electronic states show quantized distribution. Such systems are called low-dimensional quantum systems (such as quantum dot, quantum wire, and quantum well). In addition to the quantum confinement effect, the quantum size effect is also the basic feature of these quantum systems. Quantum size effect refers to the phenomenon that when the size of nanoparticles decreases to a certain value, the electronic energy level near the Fermi level changes from quasi-continuous to discrete energy level, that is, energy level splitting or energy gap widening (generally, nano semiconductor particles have discontinuous highest occupied molecular orbital and lowest unoccupied molecular orbital energy levels) [16].

As early as in the 1960s, Kubo used an electron model to calculate the gap of energy levels (δ) of metal nanoparticles: $\delta = 4E_f/3N$, where E_f is Fermi potential energy and N is the total number of electrons in the nanoparticles. The formula states that the average gap of energy levels is inversely proportional to the total number of free electrons in the constituent nanoparticles. Band theory states that the energy levels of electrons near the Fermi level of metals are generally continuous, which is true only at high temperatures or macroscopic sizes. For ultrafine nanoparticles with only a limited number of conducting electrons, the energy levels are discrete at low temperature. For macroscopic substances containing infinite atoms (i.e., the number of conducting electrons $N \rightarrow \infty$), the energy level spacing $\delta \rightarrow 0$ can be obtained from the above formula, that is, for large particles or macroscopic objects, the energy level spacing is almost zero. However, for nanoparticles, the number of atoms contained is limited and the N value is very small, which leads to a certain value of δ, that is, the energy level spacing is split (see Fig. 3.1B for details) [8].

Due to the restriction of electron waves in metal particles and the change of band structure caused by finite size effect, the continuous band structure of infinite-size solid crystal is decomposed into discrete energy levels (the geometrical configuration of metal atoms also determines the energy levels of its bonding electrons). More importantly, the smaller the nanoparticles, the larger the Kubo gap (δ). Accordingly, reducing the size of the metal species will significantly adjust the work function, band gap, surface oxidation state, and other electronic state properties of the metal [17]. The quantum size effect must be considered when the δ of nanomaterials is greater than the heat energy, magnetic energy, magnetostatic energy, electrostatic energy, photon energy, or the condensing energy of superconducting states. The quantum size effect results in significant differences between the magnetic, optical, acoustic, thermal, electrical, and superconductivity properties of nanoparticles and their macroscopic properties. At the same time, the fluctuation of electrons in discrete quantized energy levels brings a series of special properties to nanoparticles, such as high optical nonlinearity, specific catalysis and photocatalysis, and strong oxidation and reduction properties [18].

3.2.3 Size-dependent surface effect

Surface effect of nanomaterials: the surface area of a spherical particle is proportional to the square of its diameter, and its volume is proportional to the cubic of its diameter, so its specific surface area (surface area to volume ratio) is inversely proportional to its diameter. As the particle diameter becomes smaller, the specific surface area will increase significantly, and the number of atoms on the particle surface will increase relatively, which makes these surface atoms highly active and unstable, resulting in different characteristics of the particles, which is called the surface effect. As the particle size decreases, the specific surface area of the particles increases greatly, and the number of atoms on the surface will account for a large proportion [19]. For example, when the particle size is 10 nm, the proportion of surface atoms reaches 50%; When the particle size was 5 nm, the proportion of surface atoms increased to 80%; When the particle size is 1 nm, the proportion of surface atoms reaches 99%, and almost all atoms are in the surface state. The huge surface makes the surface free energy, residual valence, and residual bond force of nanoparticles increase greatly. The chemical properties of nanoparticles are very different from those of the chemical equilibrium system because of the serious mismatch of bond states, the appearance of many active centers, the increase of surface steps and roughness, and the appearance of nonchemical equilibrium and noninteger coordination chemical valence on the surface, which generates the surface effects of nanoparticles [20]. In this book, we subdivide the size-dependent surface effects of nanoparticles into three categories: the size-dependent surface CN, size-dependent surface adsorption energy, and size-dependent surface electron state triplex effects (see Fig. 3.2 for details) [21−25].

3.2.3.1 Size-dependent surface coordination number

In recent years, one of the important scientific insights obtained by the surface science community is that people have put forward the importance of undercoordinated atoms (coordination unsaturated atoms) on the surface of catalysts [26]. With the decrease in the size of metal nanoparticles, the proportion of corner and edge atoms with lower CN is increasing (i.e., the surface unsaturation is increasing), which eventually leads to the dominant catalysis of unsaturated coordination atoms [27]. For example, the atomic ratio diagram of truncated octahedral Au particles with different diameters shows that the fraction of metal atoms at the corner, surface, and edge with CN of 6, 8 (or 9) and 7 shows a strong dependence on the size of nanoparticles (see Fig. 3.2A) [21]. Among them, when the particle size is less than 2 nm, the proportion of low coordination corner atoms increases sharply, which leads to size-dependent catalytic performance. There are four types of atoms on the surface of the regular octahedral Rh nanoparticles, which can be represented by symbols C5 (angular atom), C7 (edge atom), C8 (atom on (100) face), and C9 (atom on (111) face) according to the CN (see Fig. 3.2B) [22]. Obviously, with the increase in size, the ratio between face atoms C8 and C9 and total surface atoms (Cs) also increases, while the ratio of C5:Cs and C7:Cs decreases. The high coordination atom fraction at the face decreases continuously when the particle size decreases. The low coordination atom fraction at the edges and corners increases gradually and becomes dominant when the size is reduced to about 2.5 nm.

3.2.3.2 Size-dependent surface adsorption energy

In general, the adsorption of reactant molecules, dissociated species, intermediates and even product molecules are the elementary steps in catalytic reactions. These adsorption processes are molecular behavior on the metal atoms of a catalyst. The strong adsorption of reactant molecules on the catalyst atoms is a necessary condition for their dissociation.

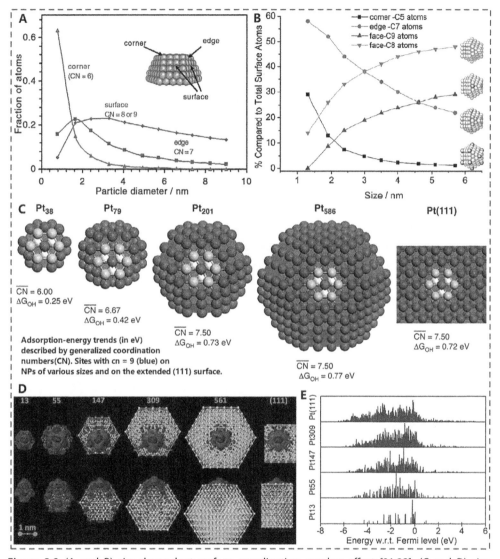

Figure 3.2 (A and B) size-dependent surface coordination number effect [21,22], (C and D) size-dependent surface adsorption energy effect [23,24], (E) size-dependent surface electron state effect [25].

The dissociated species of reactant molecules can be coupled with the molecule of another reactant or its dissociated substance to form intermediate species, and thus to form the product molecules [26,27]. The adsorption energy of reactant molecules is closely related to the coordination environment of metal atoms, and the size-dependent adsorption energy can be attributed to the CN of unsaturated-coordination metal atoms (see Fig. 3.2C) [23]. Typically, catalyst atoms with low CNs have a stronger adsorption capacity (i.e., a smaller adsorption Gibbs free energy) for a given molecule (OH) than those with high CNs. The differential charge density diagram (adsorption of O atoms) shows that, although the range of electron gain and loss is about 1 nm for both the nanoclusters and the infinite surface model, for the nanoclusters with size equal to or less than 2.7 nm (309), this range just covers the boundary of the (111) crystal plane region, while other larger catalysts only cover part of the (111) crystal plane region (see Fig. 3.2D) [24]. Blue (red) shows the regions where electrons were gained (lost). It is this range change of electron gain and loss in the local coordination environment that enhances the adsorption of O atoms on small nanoclusters.

3.2.3.3 Size-dependent surface electron state

Changing the particle size of the catalyst also results in a change in the local electronic structure of the catalyst, and the band structure of the ultra-small metal nanoparticles is more like a molecule than a metal. When the size of nanoparticles is smaller than the threshold of quantum size effect (1–2 nm), the state density of metal particles will change from continuous energy level to discrete energy level, resulting in metal-nonmetal transition and HOMO-LUMO gap increase [26,27]. According to theoretical calculations, this metal-nonmetal transition occurs when Pt is smaller than 147 atoms (1.6 nm) in size. The density of D-electron state (DOS) of Pt clusters is discrete when it is smaller than 1.6 nm, but more continuous state bands are formed when it is higher than 1.6 nm (see Fig. 3.2D) [24]. The molecule-like electronic state of a metal nanoparticle at 1–2 nm could exhibit intrinsically different catalytic performance (due to stronger adsorption capacity) in contrast to a nanoparticle with a larger size. Secondly, the stronger binding of oxygen-containing substances at low coordination sites results in a size-dependent difference in surface oxidation states. For example, the type of Pt oxide in small nanoparticles is more than that in large nanoparticles. For nanoparticles with a size of 1 nm, nearly 96% of Pt is in an oxidation state [28].

3.2.4 Size-dependent electronic and geometric combined effects

The catalytic properties of nanomaterials are mainly determined by the particle size, morphology, and interface, i.e., the size, electronic, and geometric combined effects of the active sites. The synthesis of nano-catalytic materials with controllable size and morphology and the study of their reaction properties, that is, the structure–activity relationship of catalysts, have been a hot research topic in the field of catalysis

[29]. The regulation of size on the surface chemical activity of nanomaterials has two effects: one is to weaken the constraint strength of solid energy bands on surface valence orbitals and improve the tendency and strength of surface atoms to form surface coordination bonds. The other is to amplify the effect of other structural factors, such as defects and CNs, by weakening band strength [30]. The same defect active sites contributed more to the improvement of the reaction activity on the nanoparticle than on the bulk crystal surface. The activity amplification effect is inversely proportional to the size, and the smaller the size, the more obvious the amplification effect. For electrochemical or photoelectrochemical energy applications, controllable nanosize presents two advantages. For physical transport: (1) shorten the transport length of the carrier in the electrode; (2) extend electrode interface with electrolyte; (3) move the band edge of the electrode material; (4) change the carrier transport characteristics. For chemical reactions (1) increase active sites; (2) regulate chemical potential; (3) provide new energy conversion and storage mechanisms; (4) change band gap affects light absorption [31]. The size, electronic structure, geometric morphology, and surface microchemical environment combined effects of low-dimensional nanostructured photocatalysts can also influence the photon capturing, photocarrier separation and migration, and surface catalytic reaction process [32].

The size effect of metal nanomaterials has an important effect on the catalytic activity and selectivity for thermos-catalytic reaction. In terms of geometric structure, with the decrease in particle size, the low coordination atoms are gradually exposed and the proportion gradually increases, which significantly changes the coordination structure and proportion of catalytic material active center. In terms of electronic structure, the electron energy level of metal particles also changes significantly due to the quantum size effect, which greatly affects the orbital hybridization and charge transfer between catalytic materials and reactants [33]. Since the geometrical and electronic structures of metal nanomaterials change synchronously with their size, it is difficult to distinguish the contribution of the two structural effects to the catalytic activity and selectivity and the size dependence. How to reveal the intrinsic nature of the size effect of metal catalysts, break the strong correlation between geometric structure effect and electronic structure effect and particle size, and then optimize the design of catalysts with better performance is a major challenge in the field of heterogeneous catalysis [34].

3.3 Electronic effect

Among all nano effects, the electronic effect is the most essential effect. We will discuss the electronic effect from four aspects: Charge transfer effect, d-band center theory, electron metal-support interaction (EMSI), and orbital potential theory (see Fig. 3.3 for details) [35—40].

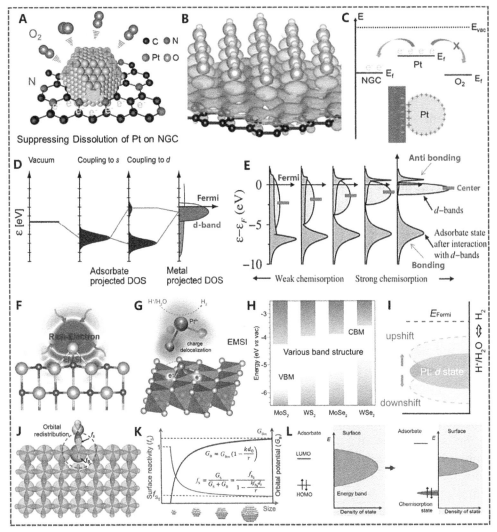

Figure 3.3 (A—C) Charge transfer effect [35], (D and E) d-band center theory [36,37], (F—I) electron metal-support interaction (EMSI) [38,39], (J—L) orbital potential theory [40].

3.3.1 Charge transfer effect

Charge transfer effect, also known as electron-gain and electron-loss effect, is based on the interface charge transfer between different components to achieve directional regulation of charge density or specific electron pump function, and ultimately achieve the adsorption and activation mechanism regulation of reactants on catalyst [41]. The physical and chemical properties of nanomaterials depend greatly on their electronic structures. When the size of the nanomaterials is reduced to the sub—nanometer scale, the electronic structure of the material will have a significant change, with strong size dependence. The overall electronic properties of nanomaterials are derived from the superposition of all atomic orbitals. The coordination or adsorption of ligands and solvents on the surface will also have a significant impact on the electronic structure and properties of nanomaterials. For supported catalysts, electron transfer occurs near the interface atoms due to the difference in Fermi energy (E_f) levels between the active site and the substrate, which have a significant effect on the catalytic properties [41].

For example, the researchers used charge analysis to show that electrons were transferred from metal atoms to carriers on nitrogen-doped carbon, while the electron transfer direction is opposite on the boron-doped carbon [42]. As a result, the metal atoms exhibit different valence states, which directly lead to different adsorption mechanisms with reactants (carbon monoxide and oxygen) molecules. The interaction between metal atoms and carbon monoxide is larger on the nitrogen-doped carbon. The interaction between metal atoms and oxygen is stronger on the boron-doped carbon. Different forces with reactant molecules lead to different reaction mechanisms of carbon monoxide oxidation on different carriers [42]. In addition, it has been found that iridium aggregates in the complexes bonded on the weak electron donor carrier SiO_2 and the medium electron donor carrier γ-Al_2O_3 to form nanoparticles and clusters, respectively. Site dispersion of iridium can be achieved when the carrier is a strong electron donor MgO. The density functional theory (DFT) theoretical calculation results confirm the dependence of iridium-carrier bond strength on the characteristics of carrier electron donor [43].

Inhibition of platinum (Pt) dissolution in electrochemical energy conversion remains a major challenge in improving the long-term stability of platinum-based catalysts. Recently, scholars from the Chinese Academy of Sciences successfully inhibited the dissolution of Pt nanoparticles by adjusting the electronic structure of Pt atoms on the surface and weakening the Pt—O dipole (see Fig. 3.3A—C for details) [35]. The Pt nanoparticles anchored by graphite nitrogen-doped carbon nanosheets with balanced nitrogen content and graphitization degree and fewer defects can significantly enhance the electron interaction between metal and carrier. The interfacial structure can accelerate the electron transfer of Pt to the substrate, reduce the surface electron density of Pt, weaken the Pt—O interaction, reduce the dissolution rate of Pt in oxygen reduction reaction, and improve the stability of the catalyst. Theoretical simulations show that the inhibition of surface Pt dissolution is due to the enhancement of the barrier during initial relaxation [35]. More recently, researchers from the National University of Singapore proposed to use the charge transfer effect to construct an optimal pore chemistry environment matching CO_2 and reducing the force on C_2H_2 in a metal-organic frameworks (MOFs) to realize efficient reverse adsorption separation of CO_2/C_2H_2 [44]. In general, the charge transfer effect can effectively regulate the adsorption or catalysis of reaction substrates by regulating the charge density in the fields of chemisorption and heterogeneous catalysis.

3.3.2 d-band center theory

In the process of heterogeneous catalytic reaction, the chemical reaction activity is affected by various complicated factors such as the element composition, chemical state, size, and crystal surface structure of catalyst. It is very difficult to control the performance of metal catalysts because of the huge performance changes caused by very small structural changes. However, there is a magical theory, d-band center theory, which proposes that the activity of metal catalysts can be effectively judged by studying a single variable [45−47].

For transition metals, the total band can be broken down into sp, d, and other bands. Only sp and d bands are analyzed here. The movement region of the electrons outside the nucleus of an atom can be divided into many electron shells from the inside out, named K, L, M, N … layers. The angular momentum of moving electrons in each shell is different, which can be divided into different electron sublayers: s, p, d, f … sublayers. The energy levels of s and p layers easily interact with each other to form sp energy levels. When many atoms gather together, sp energy levels are superposed to form sp energy bands, while d energy levels are superposed to form d energy bands. Since sp energy band is formed by s-p interaction, its energy range is very wide. The d energy band range is relatively narrow, generally near Fermi level. For O atom adsorption process, the 2p orbital and sp band interact to form a bonding band with energy close to the bottom of sp band, which is called reforming band. The d band and the reforming band are coupled to form a bonding energy level lower than the reforming band and an antibonding energy band higher than the d level [45].

The essence of adsorption in catalysis is the formation of chemical bonds between molecules (adsorbents) and metal catalyst surface. From an energy point of view, the total energy of the adsorbent and the metal catalyst surface is reduced after the adsorption, that is, the chemical bond is formed. Specifically, when adsorbed molecules interact with metal surfaces, new bonding orbitals and antibonding orbitals are formed, and if electrons fill the bonding orbitals, the overall energy of the system decreases. How much the system energy drops (that is, whether the adsorption is stable) depends on the splitting energy, which is approximately proportional to the overlap integral of the two segments (numerator) and inversely proportional to the energy difference between the two orbitals (denominator) [46]. The famous "d-band center theory" proposed by Hammer and Nor-skov is analyzed from the perspective of this denominator [36,37,47]. When the adsorption molecule is close to the metal surface, the orbital of the adsorption molecule will interact with the s and d orbitals of the metal, where the interaction between adsorption molecular orbital and metal d orbital will lead to energy level splitting, and the position of the generated antibonding orbital is very important for the stability of the system (see Fig. 3.3D for details) [36].

After adsorption, if the antibonding state is higher than the Fermi level, it is favorable for adsorption, because there are no electrons filled in the high-energy orbital. If the resulting antibonding state is lower than the Fermi level, it's not good for adsorption, because the higher energy orbital is filled with electrons. According to Norskov's work in 1995 [47], we can see whether the adsorption of metal to molecules is stable by looking at the energy level position of the newly formed antibonding state. With this in mind, we can see from the graph below (Fig. 3.3E from Norskov work in 2000 [37]) that the higher the energy levels of the d-bands (light gray), the higher the new antibonding states (dark gray) will be, making the system as a whole more stable. Since these antibonding states are above the Fermi level (they are empty), and the bond becomes increasingly stronger as the number of empty antibonding states increases. The model illustrates the variation of "weak" and "strong" chemisorption. It also illustrates a general principle about bonding at the catalysis surface: Strong bonding occurs if antibonding states are shifted up through the Fermi level (become empty); while is true if bonding states are shifted down through the Fermi level (become filled) (see Fig. 3.3E for details) [37].

It is generally believed that the binding energy between the catalyst surface and the reaction intermediate determines the reaction rate and catalytic activity. Too strong or too weak binding energy will lead to products difficult to desorb or reactants difficult to adsorb, with low reaction activity. Recent theoretical studies show that the binding energy is related to the position of the d-band center of surface atoms. The upward shift of the d-band center reinforces the binding energy (and vice versa). For transition metals with more than half-filled d-bands, band narrowing causes the d-band center to shift upward to maintain the degree of d-band filling [48]. The d-band center of metal catalyst has been widely used in qualitative evaluation of adsorption energy, activation energy, and desorption energy of active intermediates in reaction. The d-band center value directly depends on the geometrical structure of atoms in the metal, including atomic distance, atomic stacking mode, strain effect, and coordination effect [49]. It is also found that doping different transition metal in catalyst structure can cause a change in the electronic structure, such as the location of the d-band center and the number of the Eg electron filling [50]. In conclusion, if the d-band center of the same element changes, the width of the d orbital will change. When the bandwidth becomes narrow and Fermi energy level remains unchanged, d-band center must rise. The higher the CN is, the stronger the d orbital interaction is, the wider the d orbital is, the lower the d-band center is, and the smaller the adsorption energy is. By adjusting the lattice strain and changing the interatomic distance, the larger the interatomic distance, the weaker the interaction, the narrower the d-band bandwidth, and the higher the position of d-Band center (see Fig. 3.3E for details).

3.3.3 Electron metal-support interaction (EMSI)

In industrial heterogeneous catalysis, metal nanoparticles are fixed on the support, and the electronic structure of the active site of the metal catalyst can be effectively regulated by the strong interaction between the metal and the support. This is visually called as EMSI proposed by Rodriguez and colleagues [51]. EMSI is associated with orbital rehybridization and charge transfer at the metal-support interface, leading to the formation of new chemical bonds and rearrangement of molecular energy levels. Electron transfer adjusts the d-band structure of the metal catalyst and enhances the adsorption of the reaction intermediates, thus reducing the energy barrier and promoting the rate-limiting step. The concept of EMSI is similar to the concept of electron transfer effect. EMSI emphasizes the interaction between active metal and support, while electron transfer effect is more focused on describing the electron interaction between different active components. Recently, EMSI has been widely used to describe the characteristics of supported metal single-atom catalysts (SACs). Many reports suggest that the tunable electronic structure and unoccupied d-band of a metal single atom give it the potential to interact with oxide support, which is thought to be key to stabilizing atoms in catalysts and regulating their properties [38,39,52,53].

For example, Wang and Li, academicians of Tsinghua University, have proposed the use of EMSI to design high-performance single-atom electrocatalysts. Specifically, the M_1-M_2-X (X = C, N, O) model was used to explore the optimal EMSI of hydrogen evolution reaction (HER) single-atom electrocatalysts through DFT calculation. Among the selected catalysts, Rh_1-TiC with $Rh_1-Ti_2C_2$ active site was found to have the best EMSI. According to theoretical analysis, during the electrochemical reaction, electrons are transferred from the adjacent Ti atoms to the isolated Rh center through the EMSI between Rh and TiC support, so that Rh is in an electron-rich environment (see Fig. 3.3F for details) [38]. Recently, Shi et al. constructed four Pt single-atom electrocatalysts on different two-dimensional TMDs carriers (MoS_2, WS_2, $MoSe_2$, and WSe_2) using fixed point electrodeposition as model systems. It was also revealed that fine regulation of the oxidation state of the single-atom Pt catalyst by EMSI can significantly regulate the catalytic activity of acidic or alkaline HER (see Fig. 3.3G−I for details) [39]. The conduction band minimum and valence-band maximum (VBM) band edges of TMDs and the band structure show that the electron affinity and ionization potential of various TMDs provides a guideline for rationalizing the EMSI modulation of single-atom Pt. The d-state shift of single-atom Pt induced by EMSI regulates the catalytic performance of HER.

By regulating the 5d electron energy level of metal single atoms via EMSIs, SACs with high activity and stability can be designed. For example, EMSIs induced a significant increase of Pt_1 atoms in Pt_1/Co_3O_4 that did not take up the 5d state, regulating the adsorption of ammoniborane and accelerating hydrogen desorption, thus significantly enhancing the activity and stability of the catalyst in ammoniborane hydrolytic hydrogen production reaction [52]. It can be seen from the partial density analysis that the platinum single atom anchored in the boron vacancy has more d vacant orbitals above the Fermi level. The promotion effect of EMSIs on SACs is universal in many catalytic reactions, which provides a basis for the rational design of diversified advanced SACs with high activity and stability [53].

3.3.4 Orbital potential theory

Although the reduction of the size of nanomaterials is the direct structural factor leading to various nano effects, the purely geometric parameters such as size reduction and specific surface area increase cannot fundamentally reveal the intrinsic physical and chemical nature that determines the origin of the phenomenon. In addition, there has been a lack of universally applicable physical models and theories for the last 40 years to reveal strange effects at the nanoscale, so the physical nature of phenomena such as size effect, surface effect, and small size effect remains unclear [6]. The core process of surface catalysis is the formation of surface coordination bonds (chemisorption), and the formation of chemical bonds must be old and new, and its basic physical model is the redistribution of orbitals (see Fig. 3.3J for details) [40]. In this theory, the distribution of atomic orbitals on the surface is divided into two parts: one is the expansion of lattice to participate in the formation of solid energy band states, denoted by f_B, and the degree of stability; Second, surface coordination bonds are locally formed on the surface, denoted by f_S, and the size reflects the surface reactivity. All orbitals must conform to the wave function normalization principle, so $f_S + f_B = 1$, while $0 \leq f_S, f_B \leq 1$. This normalization principle determines the unity of opposites between activity and stability.

The core process of surface chemistry is the distribution of surface valence orbitals in two states. The amount of distribution on the surface or volume phase is related to the strength of adsorbed molecules and the surface as a whole to attract the valence orbital of the surface-active center. This competitiveness is a basic physical quantity reflecting the difficulty and strength of bonding. Recently, Xiang at Beijing University of Chemical Technology has defined a new term orbital potential (G) to describe this capability (see Fig. 3.3K for details) [40]. In essence, the influence of all structural parameters on the surface reactivity and chemisorption strength can be attributed to the relationship with G. G is a key intrinsic physical quantity to analyze the electronic structure mechanism of surface chemical interaction, which directly determines the surface reactivity of a site. The intrinsic relation of structure-activity relation can be clarified through function relation in an equality mathematical model (see the inset in Fig. 3.3K). The two Eqs show the dependence of orbital potential and surface reactivity on particle size. The general orbital picture of chemisorption and the weakening effect on energy bands at the nanoscale is also demonstrated (see Fig. 3.3L for details) [40]. It is proved that this orbital potential theory provides a new way to further understand the principle of chemical electronic structure and energy band structure on the surface of nanomaterials.

3.4 Geometric effect

The synthesis of nano-catalytic materials with controllable size, morphology, and structure and the investigation of their reaction properties, that is, the exploration of structure—activity relationship of catalysts, has been a hot topic in the field of catalysis [54,55]. The properties of nanomaterials are mainly determined by some important parameters such as particle size, morphology, and interface. Systematically changing these parameters provides a direct method for studying structurally sensitive reactions. The size-dependent catalytic effect can be attributed to geometric and electronic effects, and the catalytic performance is ultimately determined by the geometric and electronic structure of the active sites [29]. The rational regulation toward geometric effect (including atomic-level geometric effect, nanolevel geometric effect, and sub—micron-level geometric effect) is a direct and effective strategy to regulate the surface reaction or catalytic properties of nanomaterials (see Fig. 3.4 for details) [26,56—60].

3.4.1 Atomic-level geometric effect

When the particle size of nanomaterials decreases, the ratio of the atomic number on the surface to the total atomic number increases, and the degree of coordination unsaturation increases, leading to a sharp change in catalytic properties. The geometrical arrangement and coordination environment of atoms on the surface of a metal catalyst affect the binding strength of the reaction intermediates on the catalyst surface. Geometrically, metal atoms with different coordination structures on the catalyst surface greatly affect the breaking of chemical bonds and catalysis. Different atomic-level structures can provide a tunable electronic structure and geometry environment for molecular adsorption and surface catalysis, thus achieving the regulation of catalytic properties (this is the atomic-level geometric effect) [61].

The atomic packings of metal nanocrystals on basal (111), (100), and (110) planes are intrinsically different, which led to the different geometrical and electronic properties, such as the coverage of surface atoms on the topmost layer, the distance of adjacent atoms, the CN of surface atoms, and d-band centers (namely, shape-dependent geometric and electronic structure of metal surface atoms) [27]. Fig. 3.4A show the schematic

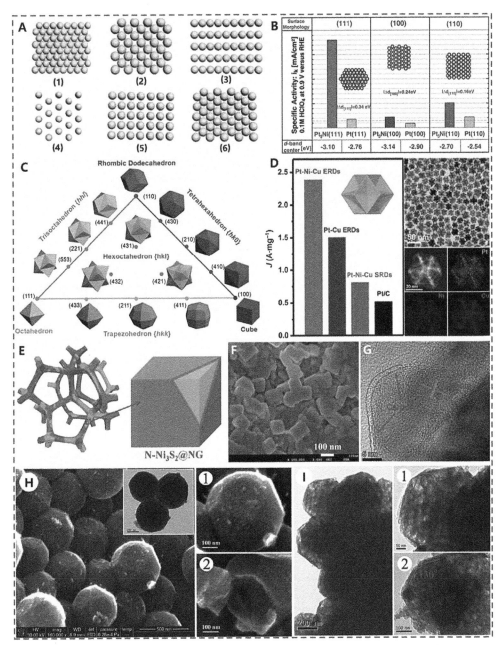

Figure 3.4 (A and B) atomic-level geometric effect [26,56], (C—G) nano-level geometric effect [57—59], (H and I) sub—micron-level geometric effect [60].

diagrams of different surfaces in face-centered cubic (FCC) and body-centered cubic (BCC) lattices (where (1) (111) of FCC, (2) (100) of FCC, (3) (110) of FCC, (4) (111) of BCC, (5) (100) of BCC, (6) (110) of BCC) [26]. The metal atoms have different electron density, CN, adjacent atom distance, and surface adsorption energy of a molecule or intermediate. These different structural and chemical factors stem from the intrinsic differences in the packing of atoms on nanocrystal surfaces. The main difference among (111), (100), and (110) planes is surface coverage in terms of occupancy by atoms of the topmost layer. The surface occupancy of surface atoms for FCC structure is in the following order: (111) > (100) > (110) (Fig. 3.4A, 1−3), while the order is (110) > (100) > (111) for BCC structure (Fig. 3.4A, 4−6).

In 2007, Nen Adm. Markovic's group reported in Science that the catalytic activity of {111} surface of Pt_3Ni alloy in electrocatalytic oxygen reduction (ORR) is 10 times that of Pt{111}, and 90 times that of commercial Pt carbon catalyst (see Fig. 3.4B for details) [56]. The results show that the high catalytic activity of Pt_3Ni{111} is mainly due to the synergistic effect of surface geometry and surface electronic structure of the catalyst. As the adsorption of $-OH_{ad}$ on the surface of the catalyst is geometrically sensitive, the geometric structure of catalyst directly affects the adsorption of $-OH_{ad}$, while the adsorption of $-OH_{ad}$ hinders the adsorption of O_2, resulting in the following relationship of catalytic activity: Pt_3Ni(100)-skin < Pt_3Ni(110)-skin <<< Pt_3Ni(111)-skin. Particularly, the addition of transition-metal Ni makes the d−Band center of Pt_3Ni move to the negative direction by 0.34 eV, and the catalytic activity of Pt_3Ni{111} is 10 times higher than that of Pt{111} [56]. In general, the atomic-level geometric effect is crucial in regulating the electronic structure and catalytic properties of ultrafine metal nanocatalysts or few atomic-structure sub−nanocatalysts.

3.4.2 Nanolevel geometric effect

The geometry of nanostructured catalyst has great influence on the mass transfer of reactants, intermediates, and products, which can make the reaction have ideal selectivity. For example, geometer-dependent local electric fields can affect the mass transfer and adsorption of intermediates, thus changing the product selectivity. Curvature can affect the stress and electric bilayer and then affect the adsorption behavior. In addition, surface and interface with rich crystal face and curvature may also cause polarization. Therefore, nanoscale geometric design should also be regarded as an important method for regulating catalytic performance (namely, the so-called nano-level geometric effect) [62].

Controlled synthesis of metal nanocrystals with specific shapes can not only change their physical and chemical properties but also broaden their applications in many fields. In particular, because the atomic structure presented on the nanocrystalline surface ultimately depends on its geometry, control by geometry and surface properties (such as crystal shape, twin defects, and surface strain) is expected to improve the potential of such nanocrystalline materials for multiple catalytic systems (via the nanolevel geometric effect) [63]. Fig. 3.4C shows the typical nanolevel geometric structure (in triangular diagram displaying) of FCC metal polyhedral configurations with different crystallographic plane exposure [57]. These configurations mainly involve low-indexed polyhedral architectures (such as cube, octahedron, and dodecahedron) and high-indexed polyhedral architectures (such as tetrahexahedron ($24\{hk0\}$ facets, $h > k > 0$), trapezohedron ($24\{hkk\}$, $h > k > 0$), trisoctahedron ($24\{hhl\}$, $h > l > 0$) and hexoctahedron ($48\{hkl\}$, $h > k > l > 0$)). Essentially, it is imperative to understand the relationship between crystal plane index and its physicochemical property (that is, the nano-level geometric effect based on the crystal plane construction). Thus, the first task is to understand the identification principles and methods of Miller indices of crystallographic plane (or crystal plane index). In crystallography, the determination methods of Miller indices of crystallographic plane include as follows: the law of conservation of plane Angle, selected area electron diffraction, and transmission electron microscopy techniques [64].

Multimetallic Pt-based alloys with excavated structures have attracted great interest owing to their compositional and morphological tunability, high specific surface areas, and impressive electro-catalytic activities. Recently, Shen and coworkers reported a new-style trimetallic Pt—Ni—Cu excavated rhombic dodecahedrons (ERDs) highly uniform nanocrystals with 3-D accessible excavated surfaces and abundant stepped atoms (see Fig. 3.4D) [58]. Benefiting from the highly excavated rhombic dodecahedral structures, electronic and synergistic effects within the trimetallic alloy, and abundant stepped atoms, the as-prepared Pt—Ni—Cu ERDs exhibit an enhanced electro-catalytic performance for the electro-oxidation of methanol. Recently, Li and Pang reported an N-doped graphene coated N-doped Ni_3S_2 nanocubes for effective overall water splitting in alkaline medium (see Fig. 3.4E—G) [59]. The core-shell structure of carbon-coated polyhedral nanocrystals can not only induce high catalytic activity (regulated by the electron density at the metal—carbon interface) but also greatly improve electrochemical stability (by the antidissolution effect of carbon coating).

3.4.3 Sub—micron-level geometric effect

The controllable synthesis and properties of nano topologies (or submicron topologies) is one of the emerging fields in recent years. The combination of sub—micron-level geometric effect and submicron topologies will expand the structure regulation of nanomaterials and is expected to generate new phenomena, and discover new effects and new applications. A research team led by Prof. Xiongwen Lou of Nanyang Technological University in Singapore has successfully synthesized a submicron (300 nm) hollow structure of a single crystal Prussian blue analog (PBA) through self-epitaxy growth [65]. By adjusting the ratio of additives in the synthesis reaction, the crystal growth kinetics is controlled, and the submicron geometric topology of the material is regulated, including three types of nanoboxes, nanocages, and nanoframes. The structure—activity relationship in electrocatalytic reaction on these topological hollow structures was found to be due to differences in electrochemical active area and ion diffusion kinetics of these submicron structures (sub—micron-level geometric effect).

Previously, Li and Fang presented a new class of submicron (400 nm) mesoporous carbon polyhedrons (MCPs) with a facet-to-facet close-packed model as electrode materials for electrochemical capacitors (ECs) (see Fig. 3.4H and I) [60]. The MCPs were evolved directly from the colloidal carbon microspheres by a new silica-free approach, the top-down carbonate (Li$_2$CO$_3$) site-occupying strategy. The obtained polyhedral materials consist of a desirable mesoporous structure with mesopores with a mean size of about 30 nm. The unique close-packed sub—micron-level geometric construction with large-size mesopores can provide a more favorable pathway for electrolyte penetration and transportation, as well as good electronic conductivity for electrochemical energy storage applications. In general, submicron materials are widely used in electrochemical energy storage (such as lithium-ion batteries) [66], where the sub—micron-level geometric effect can be well reflected in this field.

3.5 Dimensional effect

Due to the limitation of electronic freedom, the dimension of nanomaterials greatly affects their optical properties, electrical properties, and energy/matter transport capacity. Therefore, the study from the dimension of nanomaterials is of great significance to profoundly reveal the structure—activity relationship in multiple application scopes (including the electrochemical or photochemical applications). Just as the different shapes of materials enrich our daily lives, the different dimensions of nanomaterials give researchers the dream of nanoarchitects (see Fig. 3.1F) [12]. In particular, the mixed-dimensional nanoheterostructures constructed by combining diverse nanomaterials in different dimensions have been extensively studied, which can provide synergistically enhanced physicochemical properties and rich application functions [67].

3.5.1 Single-dimensional effect

Generally, the nanomaterial can be included zero-dimensional (nanoparticles, atomic clusters), one-dimensional (nanorods, nanowires, nanotubes), two-dimensional (superlattice, ultra-thin film), three-dimensional (materials composed of the first three materials as basic units) system. At present, the main effects of nanomaterials include (1) small size effect; (2) surface effect; (3) quantum size effect; (4) macroscopic quantum tunneling. These effects have been well demonstrated in single zero-dimensional nanomaterials, especially for those quantum dot nanomaterials less than 10 nm. For a single two-dimensional nanomaterial, its unique wide plane structure and ultrathin thickness structure (even atomic thickness) enable it to exhibit unique effects in energy and environmental applications, such as the Janus effect, ab positive and negative dual function, and van der Waals interlayer interaction between two thin layers. For the one-dimensional nanomaterials, the most discussed are the functions of one-dimensional conductive nanowires and the continuous directional transport effects in the fields of electrochemical energy storage and catalysis. For the three-dimensional nanomaterials, the emphasis is placed on their overall coordination function and stereoscopic space effect.

3.5.2 Double-dimensional effect

Hybrid dimensional heterostructures constructed by combining two different dimensional nanomaterials have been widely studied in the fields of energy and environment. This double-dimensional effect strategy can not only make up for the shortcomings of single-dimensional structure but also play a synergistic role between specific dimensions, which has obvious effects in enhancing the interface electrochemical storage, improving the ability of light capture, realizing the effective separation of photogenerated carriers, and improving the surface reaction kinetics. However, dimension is a subtle and key parameter in material design. It is very important to alleviate the intrinsic defects of materials with different dimensions by constructing mixed-dimensional heterojunctions and to give full play to the advantages of materials as much as possible. We should think deeply about energy transfer and charge transfer in mixed dimensional nanomaterials and explore the mechanism of apparent property enhancement, so as to provide a theoretical basis for the development of high-performance energy and environmental materials with breakthrough macro properties [67].

3.5.3 Multi-dimensional effect

Compared with single- or double-dimensional nanomaterials, the multidimensional collaborative nanostructures are easier to realize the simultaneous application of composite materials in energy storage and electrocatalysis. Yu et al. [68] proposed the idea of a multidimensional structural composite material, namely, "2 + 1 + 0" multidimensional effect. The "2" refers to the two-dimensional titanium dioxide nanosheet structure, which plays a role of providing stable substrate support. The "1" refers to that nickel cobalate nanorods are active materials in both energy storage and catalysis; The "0" refers to copper nanodots, which can reduce the activation energy of composite materials in both fields, increase ionic conductivity and improve stability. The applications of composite materials in energy storage and electrocatalysis are also studied. The work in this paper also provides new guidance for the preparation of new composite materials and has a wide application prospect [68].

Tan et al. [69] synthesized an ultra-fine V_2O_3 nanoparticles embedded in one-dimensional carbon nanotubes (V_2O_3-CNTs), which were further assembled into a three-dimensional reduced graphene oxide framework (V_2O_3-CNT-RGO). The multidimensional assembled nanostructures show unique advantages over the zero-dimensional/ two-dimensional and zero-dimensional/one-dimensional nanocomposite structures. One-dimensional carbon nanotubes can effectively limit the self-aggregation and volume expansion of active nanoparticles, and three-dimensional graphene framework can buffer the expansion stress of one-dimensional carbon nanotubes, so that one-dimensional carbon nanotubes can play a stable confined effect and alleviate the rupture of SEI film. On the other hand, the three-dimensional graphene framework and one-dimensional carbon nanotubes provide excellent electron transport capacity, and the ultra-fine zero-dimensional nanoparticles unit has a greatly shortened ion transport distance, which guarantees fast electron/ion transfer by multidimensional effect [69].

3.6 Crystal effect

Over the past few decades, great progress has been made in the regulation of various structures of nanomaterials, resulting in many unique mechanical, electronic, optical, magnetic, and catalytic properties. Different from conventional regulation strategies for structural parameters such as composition, morphology, size and dimension, crystal structure regulation of nanomaterials (including crystal phase, crystal plane, crystal boundary, crystal defect, lattice mismatch, and stress) provides an effective strategy to regulate their physical and chemical properties and functions [70]. It is well known that exposing specific crystal planes and surface atomic vacancies are two effective means to improve the activity of metal nanocrystals. However, the performance of electrocatalysts is not only related to the surface structure of the crystals, but also to the internal crystal structure. In recent years, regulating the internal crystal structure and atomic arrangement of nanocrystalline catalysts, such as atomic ordering and interlayer atom stacking, has also become an effective way to regulate the catalytic performance of metal nanocrystals [48]. Herein, we will focus on the following four modules for discussing the crystal effect: atomic arrangement and amorphization, crystal plane and crystal boundary, lattice mismatch and lattice strain, crystal defects and atomic vacancies, and crystal phase and phase transformation (see Fig. 3.5) [48,71−77].

3.6.1 Atomic arrangement and amorphization

The crystal structure regulation based on atomic arrangement can effectively improve the performance of metal nano-electrocatalysts. The atomic arrangement regulation can be divided into atomic distribution ordering and atomic layer stacking, which are mainly applied to metal nanocrystalline electrocatalysts such as platinum, palladium, gold, and ruthenium. The catalytic activity of Pt atom can be controlled to a higher level by alloying effect and stress effect. However, in the actual working environment, such as high temperature and strong acid conditions, the transition metal is easy to dissolve, resulting in a decrease in catalyst activity Compared with the disordered alloy, the atomic ordered $L1_0$ Pt-based alloy catalyst can induce the strong interaction of d orbital electrons

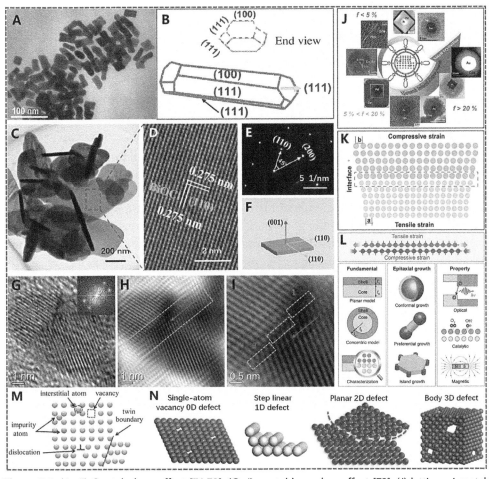

Figure 3.5 (A—F) Crystal plane effect [71,72], (G—I) crystal boundary effect [73], (J) lattice mismatch effect [74], (K and L) lattice strain effect [48,75], (M and N) crystal defect effect [76,77].

between the transition metal and Pt, thus improving the corrosion resistance of the transition metal under high voltage and acidic environment, and thus greatly improving the stability of the catalyst. In addition, the electron structure can be changed by regulating the stacking sequence of atomic layers. Therefore, atomic layer stacking regulation has become a new performance control method in recent years [48].

The crystal structure regulation based on amorphization strategy can also effectively improve the performance of metal nano-electrocatalysts. The emerging amorphous metallic ultrathin nanostructured materials (AMUNMs) usually have single or few-atom-layer thickness, disordered metal atom arrangement, abundant vacancy (or micropores), and intensively exposed atomic construction (see Fig. 3.1F) [12]. A new notion of ultra-high-density atomic-level catalysts (UHD ALCs) is proposed by Li and Shen to describe the AMUNMs with optimized atomic exposure ratio. Particularly, the AMUNMs can be regarded as a unique free-standing atomic-level catalyst system without support. The design philosophy of AMUNMs (including 0-D, 1-D, and 2-D ultrathin nanostructures) is systematically summarized in a latest review of our group for the electrocatalysis applications [12]. Obviously, the AMUNMs can provide a lot of structural advantages: (i) the ultrathin amorphous catalysts can expose more vacancy defects and unsaturated coordination bonds, which are often considered to be effective active sites for catalytic reactions (in maximum atomic efficiency); (ii) the ultrathin amorphous catalysts have abundant sub—nano microporous structures, which may realize the synergistic catalysis of surface and volume at the same time (inside-outside catalytic effect); (iii) due to its very large electrolyte-catalyst interface, the ultrathin amorphous catalyst can realize rapid electrochemical full reconstruction (rapid electrochemical activation) [12].

3.6.2 Crystal plane and crystal boundary

Crystal plane effect usually includes specific exposed crystal plane effect and high index crystal plane effect. Studies on single-crystal surfaces show that different crystal surfaces have different catalytic properties in many cases. For example, the reaction rate of ammonia synthesis varies by orders of magnitude at different Fe single-crystal planes. The ammonia production rate of Fe (111) crystal plane is the highest, which is 418 times of (110) crystal plane and 16 times of (100) crystal plane, respectively [78]. With the development of synthetic chemistry, nanocrystals exposed by specific crystal surfaces have been used to reveal the relationship between catalyst morphology and catalytic performance, and considerable progress has been made. In recent years, our research group (Changlin Yu) has also made some achievements in the crystal plane regulation of Au nanocatalysts (see Fig. 3.5A and B) [71]. From the structural model of single crystalline Au nanorods, these Au nanorods are fcc crystalline with [79] as the growth direction (i.e., the long axis). The side faces consist of four {111} facets and two {100} facets; note that the two {100} facets are formed due to longitudinal truncation of the {111} (otherwise, the four {111} planes form a parallel-ogonal radial cross section of the rod); this truncation is better observed from the end view of the rod [71]. Lattice doping engineering for specific exposed crystal planes of metal catalysts is critical for improving catalytic activity. Yu also reported a novel B-doped BiOCl nanosheet with exposed (001) facets for enhanced photocatalytic degradation of organic pollutants (see Fig. 3.5C—F) [72]. The results indicated that doping B into BiOCl could regulate and control the growth of (001) crystal facet, increase the specific surface areas and enhance the efficiency of charge separation. In addition, some studies have proved that high index crystal plane has a higher area-specific activity than single crystal plane, generalized CN can reasonably describe the local structure and coordination environment of the site, and more accurately describe the structure—activity relationship of single crystal plane and nanomaterials [80].

Crystal boundary effect can effectively improve catalytic activity and significance by optimizing adsorption and improving reactivity. Recently, it has been proved that the Faraday efficiency of ethylene and ethanol for electrocatalytic carbon dioxide reduction using Cu catalysts rich in crystal boundaries can reach 70%, which is better than that of metal Cu catalysts previously reported [81]. In situ infrared characterization and DFT showed that Cu grain boundaries can enhance the adsorption of key intermediates, thus promoting the C—C coupling reaction, and thus clarifying the special role of boundaries in electroreduction reaction. In addition, the catalytic activity of Pd catalyst with increased boundary density by crystal twins is greatly improved, where the C—H activation reaction rate of methane oxidation is 12 times higher than that of conventional Pd catalyst [82]. Recently, our research group (Zesheng Li) also made some advances in the crystal boundary regulation of $Pd_{10}Pt_1$ nanocatalysts for electrocatalytic application (see Fig. 3.5G—I) [73]. Fig. 3.5G reveals that the two nanocrystals have the same lattice spacing between (111) planes of 0.225 nm. Fig. 3.5H shows an evident crystal dislocation (see the arrow) on the boundary. As a result, a distinct three-step twin boundary is readily observed from Fig. 3.5I for the two nanocrystals. This multistep boundary structures of crystallographic plane are predicted to be of affinity with the superior catalytic properties of metallic nanocrystals catalysts [73].

3.6.3 Lattice mismatch and lattice strain

Based on the results of core@shell nanocrystals under large lattice mismatch in recent years, the research team of Jiatao Zhang of Beijing Institute of Technology systematically elaborated the influence and key role of lattice mismatch in the synthesis of heterogeneous nanocrystals and analyzed the synthesis strategies of heterogeneous nanocrystals under different lattice mismatch (see Fig. 3.5J) [74]. This review paper discusses how to adjust the lattice structure and electronic properties of heterogeneous nanocrystalline interfaces based on lattice mismatch, so as to improve their application performance in many fields. The control methods for the synthesis and performance of metal @ metal, semiconductor @ semiconductor, metal @ semiconductor heterogeneous nanocrystalline in small lattice mismatch degrees (<5%), a moderate degree of lattice mismatch (5% 20%), large lattice mismatch degree (>20%) are were systematically analyzed.

Particularly, the interfacial strain caused by lattice mismatch can effectively regulate the electronic structure of these core@shell heterogeneous nanocrystals, thus changing their catalytic performance in different catalytic applications (such as oxygen reduction, methanol oxidation, and olefin hydrogenation) [74].

Lattice strain effects (including tensile strain and compression strain effects) are often caused by core-shell lattice mismatch due to differences in crystal structure or lattice parameters of different metal components (see Fig. 3.5K) [48]. The lattice strain of the heterojunction can lead to the change of the d band center of the metal catalyst, and thus the catalytic performance can be regulated. The strain relaxation caused by interfacial mismatches (in planar or concentric models) of different metal components is also an important factor for controlling the growth and performance optimization of composites (see Fig. 3.5L) [75]. Strain relaxation reduces strain energy by introducing dislocation growth and 3D island growth, which is beneficial to the formation of stable heterogeneous nanocrystals. In the process of epitaxial growth, the mismatch of lattice constants will lead to lattice-mismatch strain effect. The introduction of mismatch strain has a significant effect on optimizing the material properties of heterostructures.

3.6.4 Crystal defects and atomic vacancies

In a narrow sense, crystal defects usually include point defects and line defects. Point defects include atom vacancy defects, interstitial atom defects, and impurity atom defects (also known as heteroatom doping defects), while line defects include step defects and dislocation defects (see Fig. 3.5M) [76]. In a broad sense, crystal defects usually include point defects (0 D), line defects (1 D), plane defects (2 D), and bulk defects (3 D). Plane defects include grain boundaries, phase boundaries, and stacking defects. Bulk defects are due to impurities, deposits, and voids being encased in the crystal (see Fig. 3.5N) [77]. On the other hand, defects can be divided into intrinsic defects and heteroatomic doping defects according to their different sources. Among them, intrinsic defects mainly include local point defects (such as vacancy defects), line defects (such as step and dislocation), and bulk defects (such as nanopore defects). There are also electronic defects including conduction band (CB) electrons and valence band (VB) holes in semiconductor nanocrystals.

In heterogeneous catalysts, defects can be classified into various types according to the type of catalytic materials. Taking point defects as an example, the defects in transition metal oxides include oxygen vacancies and metal vacancies, sulfur vacancies in sulfides, and some atomic doping belongs to doping defects. In addition, graphene contains a variety of topological defects (such as five-membered ring, seven-membered ring, 5-7-ring, etc.), and various defects such as atomic doping, surface steps, grain boundaries, twins, and holes can exist in the metal materials [77]. Several modes of action of defects affecting heterogeneous catalytic reactions are as follows: (1) adsorption molecules directly as active sites, (2) regulating the electronic structure of the catalyst and its adsorption energy for the reaction molecule, (3) reconfiguration and dynamic evolution of the defect structure regulate the activity. (4) interaction with the catalytic center regulates the activity and selectivity [77].

3.6.5 Crystal phase and phase transformation

The phase engineering of nanomaterials is a research hotspot in the field of materials at present. We all know that the atomic or molecular structure of matter has a decisive influence on its properties and properties that produce functions, coupled with function-oriented applications. The phase engineering of nanomaterials starts from the most basic aspect of chemistry, that is, the arrangement of atoms and molecules in materials, and synthesizes nanomaterials with new structures, properties, and functions by regulating the stacking of atoms and molecules. Generally, nanomaterials tend to exist in the most stable form in thermodynamics. For example, gold usually exists in the most stable FCC structure. However, at the nano or even sub—nanoscale, because the surface energy begins to dominate the system energy, we can adjust the arrangement of atoms and molecules of nanomaterials by adjusting the surface energy of materials. There are many kinds of metastable structures (including metastable crystalline structure and amorphous structure). The phase engineering research will greatly enrich the types of basic nanomaterials and broaden the breadth and depth of nanotechnology in synthesis, property, and application [70].

Nanomaterials usually present the same conventional phase as their bulk materials. However, some nanomaterials, such as metals, metal oxides, two-dimensional layered compounds, have been found to have unconventional phases that are usually unavailable in bulk materials. At present, the transformation between different conventional phases or the transformation between conventional phase and unconventional phase is a research hotspot in the field of nanomaterials. The unconventional phases nanomaterials can be obtained by phase-based epitaxial growth and the formation of alloys or intermetallics [70]. Our group (Changlin Yu) has published a typical research result in semiconductor heterojunction in-situ phase-transformation synthesis: Phase transformation synthesis of novel Ag_2O/Ag_2CO_3 heterostructures with high visible light efficiency in photocatalytic degradation of pollutants (Advanced materials, 26(6), 2014, 892—898) [83]. In 2019, Yu further published a review paper about the external-induced phase transformation of phase for preparing the heterojunction or homojunction, providing a new understanding of phase-transformation synthesis and photocatalysis application [84] (see Section 3.8.3 for details). Besides, in situ photocatalytic phase-transformation preparation of bismuth oxycarbonate ($Bi_2O_2CO_3$) nanosheets from bismuth-based oxide was also reported by our group (Zesheng Li) in 2021 [85]. In general, the phase transformation engineering is one effective method for the design and regulation of nanomaterials.

3.7 Confined effect

With the wide application of porous nanomaterials in various fields, some "unusual" physical and chemical phenomena are gradually revealed, which are as follows: When particles, molecules, or ions are confined in space less than a few nanometers, its way of action between individual (such as ligand, conformation), thermal motion, phase transition and its physical properties (such as viscosity, density), chemical properties (such as the catalytic behavior, photosensitivity) all show different from its bulk phase properties is different from its bulk phase properties (i.e., unconfined phase properties). This kind of special change caused by space limitation can be referred to as "nano confined effect" [86]. According to the scale of confined synthesis, the confined effects can be divided into self-confined effect of precursor, confined effect of nanospace, confined effect of chemical bond, and confined effect of multiscale integration (see Fig. 3.1C) [9]. High-efficiency electrocatalysts with definite nanostructures can be accurately prepared at macro, nano, and atomic levels by using the confined synthesis strategy. Here, we focus on the analysis and discussion of three effects: nanopore-confined effect, interlayer-confined effect, and atom-confined effect.

3.7.1 Nanopore-confined effect

Nano-confined catalysis and nano-confined adsorption are two typical applications in energy and environmental fields [87–93]. In recent years, the members of our research group have devoted to explore the nano-confined catalysis, including nanopore confined catalysis (see Fig. 3.6A–C) [87] and interlayer confined catalysis (see Fig. 3.6D and E) [88]. In 2013, Li, Pang, and Fang [87] jointly reported the synthesis of mesopore-functional carbon sphere nanochains (MCSNs) and their integration with PtRu alloy nanoparticles for enhanced electrochemical performance. The MCSNs were directly evolved from the colloidal carbon sphere nanochains (CCSNs) through a unique Li_2CO_3-molten salt pore-creating strategy (with a BET surface area of 543.4 m^2/g and a mean pore size of 14.7 nm) (see Fig. 3.6A). For the PtRu/MCSNs hybrid system, 2.5-nm-size small PtRu alloy nanoparticles were confined into the mesopores of MCSNs by a liquid-solid interface growth strategy (see Fig. 3.6B). Most nanoparticles are confined to the inner wall of the mesopore and a few to the surface of the carbon (see Fig. 3.6C). Due to the mesopore-confined effect, the PtRu/MCSN hybrid system exhibited superior catalytic properties toward methanol oxidation reaction (MOR) with greatly enhanced catalytic activity and desirable stability. This attractive efficiency can be ascribed to the functionalities of mesoporous carbon support, which affords more efficient electron transfer and better mass transport, maximizing the availability of nano PtRu catalysts [87].

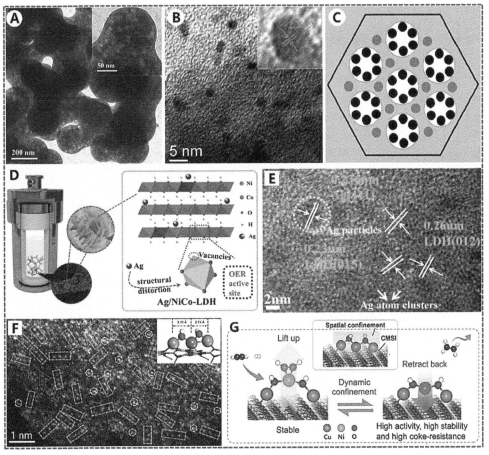

Figure 3.6 (A—C) Nanopore confined effect [87], (D and E) interlayer confined effect [88], (F and G) atomic-level chemical-bond confined effect [89,90].

3.7.2 Interlayer-confined effect

Layered double hydroxides (LDHs) are one of the most effective electrocatalysts. However, it is still necessary to improve the lower conductivity and limited active sites of LDHs to enhance their catalytic performance [91]. Recently (in 2021), Li and Pang designed and prepared novel 3D interlayer-confined hetero-electrocatalysts of NiCo-LDHs nanosheets incorporated with silver nanoclusters and nanoparticles (confined in interlayer of NiCo-LDHs) on a Ni foam (labeled as Ag@NiCo-LDH/NF) by a one-pot hydrothermal method (see Fig. 3.6D and E) [88]. The hetero-electrocatalysts of Ag/NiCo-LDH incorporated with in situ generation of Ag nanoclusters/nanoparticles have caused structural distortion and oxygen vacancy formation as a new active site (see Fig. 3.6D). The existence of Ag nanoclusters and nanoparticles on NiCo-LDHs was confirmed by high-resolution transmission electron microscopy (see Fig. 3.6E). Ag nanoclusters are incorporated into the LDH surface and interlaminar surface and replace nickel, which can result in interlaminar distance widening and oxygen vacancy generation. Altogether, the introduction of Ag species can alter the electronic structure of the catalyst and create new catalytically active sites for oxygen evolution reaction (OER) [88].

3.7.3 Atom-confined effect

Atomic-level chemical-bond confined effect is one latest and high-end tactical guideline for structuring sub−one-nano atomic structure materials. This chemical-bond confined effect has been widely used in the design of supported SACs [89,90]. The chemical bonding of coordination atoms (such as nitrogen, oxygen, carbon, etc.) on the support can make the single metal atoms exist independently and stably. Recently, Wei, Li, Lu, and group members, through the synergistic action (i.e., atomic-level chemical-bond confined effect) of "covalent metal-support interaction (CMSI)" and "atomic-space confinement effect (ASCE)," successfully prepared a linear tri-atomic catalyst ($Cu_1−Ni_1−Cu_1/g−C_3N_4$) with high-loading sites of atomic Ni (3.1 wt.%) and dense atomic Cu (8.1 wt.%) (with bridging O atoms (−OH) between Ni and Cu atoms) on the conjugated polymer support of graphitic carbon nitride ($g−C_3N_4$) (see Fig. 3.6F and G) [89]. In a recent review, we define this O-bridging SACs structure as a three-dimensional atomic foam catalyst (AFCs) [90]. The O atom (or −OH group) bridging belongs to the sophisticated 3-D atomic manipulation on the surface or defect edges of specific supports. Thanks to the atomic-level chemical-bond spatial confinement effect, the stereoscopic catalytic effect (i.e., dynamic confinement catalysis) of AFCs triggered by their 3-D atomic construction could be demonstrated incisively and vividly [90]. The most noteworthy feature is that the O bridging atoms have very high plasticity (the lift-up and retract-back effect of middle active M' atom) in the dynamic atomic confined catalytic process (see Fig. 3.6G), which may be an inherent property and attractiveness of 3-D atomic AFCs (influence on catalytic mechanism and stability by stereoscopic effect [90]).

Generally, the "nano confined effect" shows a special enhancement effect on multiple environmental pollution remediation technologies (including adsorption, catalytic oxidation, and membrane separation) [86]. For example, reductive adsorption removal of high-value heavy metals, selective transmission of ions in high-salt systems, and rapid and advanced oxidation degradation of organic wastewater. Porous material adsorption has attracted wide attention in water treatment because of its simple operation and low cost. Recently, Zhang and coworkers proved the selective sequestration of p-arsanilic acid (p-ASA) from water by using nano-hydrated zirconium oxide (HZO) confined inside the nanopores of hyper-cross-linked anion exchanger (HCA) (belongs to nanopore-confined adsorption) [92]. Compared with single HCA, HZO@HCA can remove p-ASA from solutions containing a large number of competitive anions (e.g., sulfate, chloride, and nitrate) due to HZO forming an inner ring complex with p-ASA and producing specific adsorption. Professor Kim's team also revealed that the special effect of manganese oxide on the spontaneous degradation of organic pollutants in water and its mechanism by controlling the "nanopore confinement" [93]. By preparing the membrane reactor with the function of "nanopore array," the spontaneous "slow reaction" environmental remediation process in nature can be greatly accelerated, thus providing a new theoretical and technical reserve for the application of environmental water treatment.

3.8 Interface effect

Heterogeneous interfacial catalysts constructed by optimized synthesis methods can achieve different interfacial effects and thus improve the selectivity of specific products. Professor Haobin Wu classifies interface effects into the following categories: spillover effect, charge transfer effect, synergistic effect, confined effect, stress effect, and microenvironmental effect (see Fig. 3.1E) [11]. The spillover effect involves the transfer of an active substance adsorbed or formed on one surface to another for further reduction. Charge transfer effect refers to the redistribution of electrons at heterogeneous interfaces driven by Fermi-level differences of different components to optimize the adsorption energy of intermediates. A synergistic effect is the combination of two or more substances so that an intermediate is more active or stable at a heterogeneous interface than either of the substances would appear to be by itself. The confined effect refers to limiting the diffusion of intermediates or the structural evolution of catalysts through interfacial interaction. The stress effect refers to the adjustment of the electronic structure of the heterogeneous interface due to the lattice distortion at the heterogeneous interface, so as to optimize the adsorption energy of the intermediate. Microenvironmental effects involve the regulation of the microenvironment near the active surface, thus affecting the selectivity of the product [11]. Professor Chunzhong Li recently described that the interface effects (via synergy of ensemble effect and electron effect) can break the activity limitation in atom heterogeneous interface engineering (see Fig. 3.1D) [10]. The ensemble effect helps to optimize the reaction pathway and enhance the reaction kinetics by creating favorable heterogeneous interfaces and electronic effects. The electron effect is to change the adsorption energy of the reaction intermediate by coupling the electrons at the interface. Then according to the composition and characteristics of the heterogeneous interface, the reasonable design of the target electrocatalyst is realized. Herein, we analyze and discuss the interface effects from three aspects: type of atom interface, metal-support interaction (MSI), and heterojunction effect.

3.8.1 Type of atom interface

Interfaces can be divided into planar interface, lateral interface, and hierarchical interface from two-phase contact mode. According to atom contact mode, interfaces can be divided into two categories: lattice mismatch interface and lattice match interface (see Fig. 3.1D) [10]. For nanoparticle materials, there are three types of atomic interfaces: alloy atomic interface, core-shell atomic interface, and double-particle heterojunction interface (see Fig. 3.7A) [94]. The synergistic interface effect between different metals can change the catalytic performance of catalysts. It is also very important to understand the interface effect between metals and supports for industrial production. The size-dependent corner, perimeter, and crystal plane numbers of metal nanoparticles on the supports directly affect the geometric and electronic structure of the catalyst, and ultimately affect the catalytic performance (see Fig. 3.7B) [95].

In addition to size-dependent effect (atoms, clusters, nanocrystals), the interface effect between metals and supports is closely related to the types and properties of metals and supports (see Fig. 3.7C) [17]. Changing the properties of supports, such as carbon, oxide, phosphide, nitride, sulfide, and metal, can modulate the geometric structure and chemical and electronic properties of metal species by differential MSI. In short, interface structures with different components, dimensions, and sizes can give different physico chemical properties.

3.8.2 Metal-support interaction

As the size of metal decreases (nanoparticles, nanoclusters, and single atoms), the catalytic behavior of supported metal species changes significantly for various chemical transformations. MSI is generally considered to play a key role in regulating the catalytic behavior of supported metal species. MSI is a very important research topic in the field of catalysis because of its significant influence on the geometrical structure and electronic properties of metal catalysts [17]. According to different modes of action and application conditions, Academician Zhang Tao and professor Qiao Botao divided MSI into four categories: CMSI (covalent MSI), OMSI (oxidative strong MSI), EMSI, and SMSI (strong metal-support interaction) (see Fig. 3.7D) [96]. Among them, SMSI is the earliest and most classical MSI, which is characterized by electronic structure changes and geometric interface movement (forming a new core-shell interface structure) between metal components and supports.

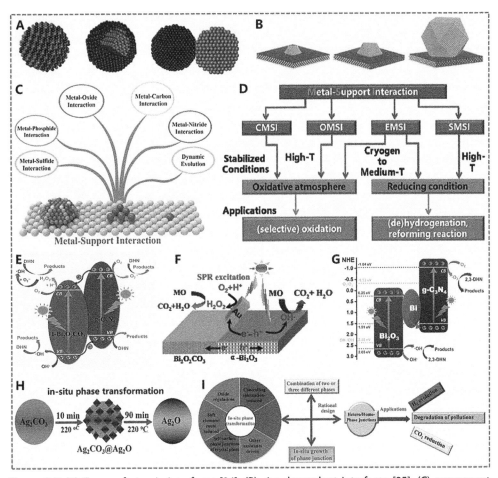

Figure 3.7 (A) Types of atomic interfaces [94], (B) size-dependent interfaces [95], (C) component-dependent interfaces [17], (D) metal-support interaction (MSI) [96], (E) I—Bi$_2$O$_2$CO$_3$—g—C$_3$N$_4$ heterojunction [97], (F) Au—Bi$_2$O$_2$CO$_3$—α—Bi$_2$O$_3$ heterojunction [71], (G) Bi—g—C$_3$N$_4$—Bi$_2$O$_3$ heterojunction [79], (H) Ag$_2$CO$_3$—Ag$_2$O heterojunction [83], (I) in situ phase-transformation synthesis of phase junctions [84].

The SMSI is first proposed by Tauster et al. in the late 1970s to explain the significant reduction of the chemisorption capacity of Pt/TiO$_2$ catalysts for H$_2$ and CO after high-temperature (high-T) H$_2$ treatment at reducing conditions [98]. Due to the strong interaction between the reducible support and the metal, the support transfers some electrons to the metal, thus reducing the chemisorption capacity of H_2. Philips Christopher reported a new method of regulating SMSI by adsorbents (HCO_x). The adsorbents (A) induce the formation of oxygen vacancies on the support, thus forming an A-SMSI overlay on Rh nanocrystals. The overlay core-shell interface is porous, facilitating the substrate to contact the active center Rh nanocrystals and increasing the stability of the catalyst. This study gives new impetus to the study of SMSI [99]. Metal-metal bonding, core—shell interface morphology, interfacial charge transfer, and mass transport are the most common explanations of the SMSI mechanism. In essence, the interaction is a kind of electron transfer effect. The popular explanation of metal-support strong interaction is that the number of "one-way" electron transfer between metal and support is more than the usual number of electron transfer, so the "interaction" is strong.

The EMSI is firstly proposed by Rodriguez and colleagues in 2012 as a new class of strong metal-carrier interactions for Pt clusters-CeO_2 support system (see Section 3.3.3 for details) [51]. When Pt clusters are dispersed on the CeO_2 support, the corresponding electronic perturbation at the interface between Pt clusters and substrates is denoted as EMSI, which greatly modulates the d-band center of the active site. Correspondingly, the EMSI effect was also observed on a variety of SACs by professor Xingfu Tang in 2014, regulating the charge state of the isolated metal centers [100]. Unlike SMSI (high temperature and reducing conditions), EMSI can be applied to a wide range of conditions (from cryogenic to moderate temperatures), and EMSI is applied to both reducing and oxidizing atmosphere (see Fig. 3.7D) [96]. It is worth mentioning that EMSI tends not to involve the formation of new geometric atomic interfaces, but rather focus more on interacting with electrons between metal and support.

The OMSI work (SMSI breakthrough work applicable to oxidizing atmosphere) came from Mou's research group in 2012 [101]. They found an oxygen-induced SMSI phenomenon in Au/ZnO catalyst. After oxidation at 300°C, Au nanoparticles will be wrapped by ZnO, accompanied by electron transfer from au to the carrier. This work extends the conditions for excitation of SMSI for the first time (from reducing conditions to oxidizing conditions). In 2016, Tang et al. found a similar oxidizing SMSI phenomenon in nonoxide (hydroxyapatite and phosphate) supported Au catalysts [102]. In addition, in 2018, Tang et al. confirmed that nonoxide and ZnO-loaded Pt group metals are also suitable for this oxidizing SMSI, and formally proposed the concept of "oxidizing strong metal-support interactions (OMSI)" to distinguish it from the classical SMSI triggered by reductive conditions [103]. Typically, the OMSI is applied to the medium-high temperature and oxidizing atmosphere conditions, which greatly expands the application of catalysts (e.g., oxidation or selective oxidation) (see Fig. 3.7D) [96].

Botao Qiao and Tao Zhang's team have been committed to the development of oxide-supported atomic catalysts and successively developed Pt, Au, Rh, and other atomic catalysts supported on iron oxide, titanium oxide, cerium oxide, and other oxides [96]. These research results not only contribute to the precise synthesis of atomic catalysts, but also provide new ideas for studying catalytic active centers and regulating catalytic properties. Based on the long-term exploration in this field, in 2015 Qiao and Zhang revealed for the first time that CMSI can occur in the Au_1/FeO_x single-atom catalytic system [104]. The studies revealed that the positively charged and surface-anchored Au_1 atoms with high valent states (high proportion of covalent bonds) formed by the CMSI, thus providing the ultra-stability and remarkable catalytic activity. The development of the CMSI in recent years not only promotes a new and deeper understanding of SMSI but also opens an alternative way to develop supported heterogeneous catalysts with better performance [105].

Influenced by various MSI, heterogeneous metal catalysts can be divided into two types: one is the hydrogenation and dehydrogenation of hydrocarbons, whose activity is greatly inhibited; The other is the reaction with CO participation, such as $CO + H_2$ reaction, $CO + NO$ reaction, its activity is greatly improved, selectivity is also enhanced. Generally, strengthening the MSI is very important for the internal stability (or activity) of active metal atoms. So far, various MSIs have been used to improve the stability (or activity) of supported metal catalysts. However, a thorough understanding and full utilization of these functions are far from being achieved (see Fig. 3.7D) [96]. In addition, strong interaction often leads to too strong binding support, possibly resulting in decreased activity. Therefore, how to solve this paradox, or how to better balance these two aspects, is still a matter of concern, which needs further research.

3.8.3 Heterojunction effect

In addition to electrocatalysis (see Fig. 3.7A—C) and thermocatalysis (see Fig. 3.7D), the composite interface nanomaterials (i.e., heterojunction) are also widely used in photocatalysis (see Fig. 3.7E—I). Semiconductor photocatalytic reactions involve at least five major steps: (i) light absorption by the semiconductor, (ii) formation of photogenerated electron-hole pairs, (iii) migration and recombination of the photogenerated electron-hole pairs, (iv) adsorption of reactants and desorption of products, (v) occurrence of redox reactions on the semiconductor surface. Strategies for effective separation of photoelectron-hole pairs in semiconductor photocatalysts involve nonmetal doping, metal loading, introducing heterojunctions. Several heterojunctions are as follows: conventional type II heterojunctions, p-n heterojunction, surface heterojunction, direct Z-type heterojunction, and semiconductor-graphene heterojunction [106]. The design of heterojunction mainly considers the matching of VB and CB of different components and interfacial charge transfer/separation.

Recently, Li and colleagues reported Iodine-doped $Bi_2O_2CO_3/g-C_3N_4$ heterojunctions consisting of graphitic carbon nitride ($g-C_3N_4$) and iodine-doped bismutite ($I-Bi_2O_2CO_3$) by a one-pot hydrothermal method for enhanced photodegradation activity under visible light (see Fig. 3.7E) [97]. Owing to the appropriate bandgaps, $g-C_3N_4$ and $I-Bi_2O_2CO_3$ were stimulated by visible light to generate charge carriers

(e^- and h^+). Photo-generated electrons on the CB of $g-C_3N_4$ reduced dissolved O_2 to $O_2\bullet^-$, due to the more negative potential than $E(O_2/O_2\bullet^-)$ (-0.33 eV vs. NHE). The h^+ on the VB oxidized OH^- to $\bullet OH$ ($E(\bullet OH/OH^-) = 1.99$ eV vs. NHE). The well-matched CB and VB positions of $g-C_3N_4$ and $I-Bi_2O_2CO_3$ promote the photogenerated electrons partially transferred from the CB of $g-C_3N_4$ to the CB of $I-Bi_2O_2CO_3$ rather than the opposite direction. The accumulated electrons on CB yielded oxidizing species and H_2O_2 ($O_2 + 2e^- + 2H^+ \rightarrow H_2O_2$, $E(O_2/H_2O_2) = 0.682$ eV vs. NHE) and $\bullet OH$ radicals ($H_2O_2 + O_2\bullet^- \rightarrow \bullet OH + OH^- + O^2$). Thus, the organic pollutant of 1,5-dihydroxynaphthalene (DHN) was eventually photodegraded by radicals ($O_2\bullet^-$ and $\bullet OH$) and oxidants (H_2O_2 and h^+). This study provides a rational approach for enhancing the visible-light catalytic activity of wide-bandgap $Bi_2O_2CO_3$, and reveals a new perspective on the removal mechanism of organic pollutants.

Previously, Yu and colleagues also reported an $Au@Bi_2O_2CO_3-\alpha-Bi_2O_3$ heterojunction via the phase-transformation method for superior visible-light-driven photocatalysis (see Fig. 3.7F) [71]. The potential of (CB: 0.11 eV) of $\alpha-Bi_2O_3$ is slightly negative than that of $Bi_2O_2CO_3$ (CB: 0.26 eV). Therefore, the photogenerated electrons in $\alpha-Bi_2O_3$ can be transferred to the CB of $Bi_2O_2CO_3$, leaving holes in the VB of $\alpha-Bi_2O_3$. The good interface charge transfer process promotes the effective separation of photoexcited electrons and holes, enhancing the photocatalytic activity of heterostructure. The integrated plasmonic Au on heterojunction may act as electron sinks to retard the recombination of the photogenerated electrons and holes so as to improve the charge separation. It is known that the Fermi level of gold is 0.5 V (vs. NHE), which is more positive than the CB edge of $\alpha-Bi_2O_3$ (0.11 eV). The SPR of Au could also enhance visible light absorption and photocatalytic efficiency.

More recently, Li and colleagues further reported a visible-light responsive Z-scheme $Bi@\beta-Bi_2O_3/g-C_3N_4$ heterojunction by in situ deposition-oxidation for efficient photocatalytic degradation (see Fig. 3.7G) [79]. The photogenerated electrons on the CB of $\beta-Bi_2O_3$ could transfer to the VB of $g-C_3N_4$ through the tightly coupled Bi-metal bridge (the electrons of $\beta-Bi_2O_3$ annihilated with the holes of $g-C_3N_4$). So, $Bi@\beta-Bi_2O_3/g-C_3N_4$ heterojunction exhibited extraordinary photodegradation capability compared with binary $\beta-Bi_2O_3/g-C_3N_4$ and single catalysts. Especially, Z-scheme heterojunction facilitated the spatial and temporal separation of respective electron-hole pairs of the two components and maintained the original oxidation and reduction center of correlative component. This study could inspire new ideas for building efficient metal-bridge Z-scheme heterojunctions, and provide novel insights into the elimination mechanism of polycyclic aromatic hydrocarbons and their derivatives in photocatalysis.

For the design of heterojunction interface photocatalytic materials, our research group has proposed a mature and universal design scheme, which is the in-situ phase transformation strategy (see Fig. 3.7H) [83]. This in situ topological phase transformation strategy has good controllability and reproducibility for the construction of two-component heterojunctions or homojunction phase junctions with controllable interfacial structure and electronic structure (see Fig. 3.7I) [84]. These in situ transformed phase junctions catalysts showed excellent performances in the field of photocatalytic hydrogen preparation, photocatalytic carbon dioxide reduction, and photocatalytic degradation (see Section 3.6.5 for details).

3.9 Synergistic effect

Compared with single-component pure-phase nanomaterials, multi-component composite nanomaterials have significant synergistic effects in electrochemical energy storage, which can effectively improve the electronic conductivity and ionic conductivity, electrochemical activity, and mechanical stability of the active materials. In addition, the composite nanomaterials can effectively fill in the performance differences between two active components with different energy storage mechanisms (synergistic complementary effect) [107]. Synergetic adsorption and synergetic catalysis are two important research topics in many catalytic fields, including electrocatalysis, photocatalysis, and thermocatalysis [108—110]. The excellent activity and selectivity of natural enzymes are derived from the synergistic interaction between multiple active sites, so it is particularly important to simulate natural enzymes to introduce multiple catalytic centers into nano-structured catalytic materials [111].

Generally, a "synergistic effect" can be loosely defined as the effect of "one plus one is greater than two." For catalysts, in a narrow sense, it can be understood that the effect of the integration of components A and B is greater than the sum of the effects of A and B alone or a new effect that neither A nor B has. In a broad sense, if the effect of the integration of major components A and B is greater than that of one of them (A or B), we can call it the "synergistic effect." The influence of MSI on catalysis is due to the interaction between metal nanoparticles and their support (see Fig. 3.8A) [112]. Typical MIS phenomena involve charge transfer, spillover effect, perimeter activation, NP-support interaction, and SMSI, NP structure effect, and synergistic interaction. These elements often interact with each other and play different roles in different catalytic reactions. It is worth mentioning that synergistic effect can unify the above aspects and then lead to the new subsynergistic effect: Synergistic electron effect, Synergistic adsorption effect, and Synergistic spillover effect; and a diatomic synergistic effect is also included for atomic structure catalysts (see Fig. 3.8 for details) [33,73,113—117].

3.9.1 Synergistic electron effect

Synergistic electronic effect refers to the interaction of different components to produce different electronic structures (such as electron state density, electronegativity, and binding

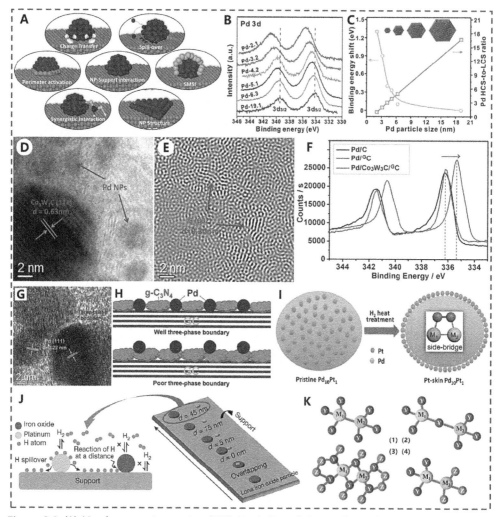

Figure 3.8 (A) Metal-support interaction (MSI) [112], (B and C) size-dependent electron effect [33], (D—F) two-phase synergistic electron effect [113], (G and H) three-phase synergistic electron effect [114], (I) synergistic adsorption effect [73,115], (J) synergistic spillover effect [116], and (K) diatomic synergistic effect [117].

energy) for a composite material than for a single material [118]. Previously, we described size-dependent electronic effects that lead to changes in catalytic properties of nanoparticles (see Section 3.2.3). That is, as the diameter of nanoparticles decreases, the ratio of low-coordination sites (LCSs) instead of high-coordination sites (HCSs) in the crystal changes, and the ratio of the former increases, resulting in a change in the electronic binding energy of nanoparticles (see Fig. 3.8B and C) [33]. The binding energy shift (~ 1 eV) of Pd nanoparticles is very obvious from 6.4 to 2.1 nm. Our previous research results show that the electronic structure of Pd can be changed (similar to the result of size-dependent electronic effect), through the interface interaction (interface synergistic electronic effect) of two different components (Pd and Co_3W_3C) (see Fig. 3.8D—F) [113]. With graphite carbon (GC) as a support (Pd/Co_3W_3C/GC), the Co_3W_3C can decrease the binding energy of Pd (in the same size of ~ 3.5 nm) by 1 eV, compared to that of Pd/GC and Pd/C. The electron transfer effect is synergistically occurred on the GC-supported Pd and Co_3W_3C components (i.e., synergistic electronic effect).

In many catalytic systems, the catalytic activity of the main catalyst can be effectively enhanced by adding a synergistic component (or called cocatalyst) due to the synergistic electronic effect caused by cocatalyst [118]. In general, cocatalysts can affect the electronic structures of noble metals and improve their catalytic activity, poisoning resistance, and stability. Recently, a series of transition metal oxides, phosphides, carbides, nitrides, and carbon nitride were widely used as cocatalysts for Pt and Pd catalysts. The transition metal element can provide an empty/half-full or full orbital, and the ligand provides a corresponding full/half-full or empty orbit for coordination to form a ligand compound [118]. We also report a novel graphitic carbon nitride/graphite carbon/palladium nanocomposite (Pd@g—C_3N_4/GC) as an efficient electrocatalyst for ethanol electro-oxidation. The ultra-thin g—C_3N_4 with "nano-islands"-like discrete distribution guarantees the formation of well three-phase solid boundary from the GC, g—C_3N_4, and Pd components (see Fig. 3.8G and H) [114]. It needs to be emphasized that the well three-phase solid boundary of support, main catalyst, and cocatalyst is the key condition to promote the synergistic electronic effect.

3.9.2 Synergistic adsorption effect

Synergistic adsorption effect can be divided into three categories: (1) selective adsorption and separation through the synergistic combination effect of different adsorbents; (2) specific adsorption of different molecules in series catalysis through the synergistic effect of two sites; (3) single molecule bridging adsorption in electrocatalysis through the synergistic effect of two sites. For example, a one-step separation of high-purity ethylene in a four-component mixed system (ethylene, acetylene, ethane, and carbon dioxide) can be achieved using synergistic adsorption effect between three different ultra-porous MOFs materials [119]. It was found that acetylene, ethane, and carbon dioxide were sequentially and efficiently removed by effectively connecting the three MOF materials in a single adsorption column, resulting in one-step separation and collection of high-purity ethylene (>99.9%) at the end of the adsorption column. Besides, the Pt–B two-site catalysts ($Pt_1/CoBO_x$) with a specific spatial configuration of single-atom Pt and Lewis acid B double site can achieve synergistic adsorption of different molecules and series catalytic reaction processes (such as selective hydrogenation of benzonitrile) [120]. Due to the spatial distance of 0.45 nm between Pt and B, the benzylamine molecule is easily condensed with the primary imine through the synergistic adsorption effect, thus the selective hydrogenation of benzonitrile to the secondary imine product is efficiently realized at the dual sites of Pt and B.

In the field of electrocatalysis, the catalytic reduction reactions of diatomic gases (e.g., O_2 and N_2) often require specific bridging side-type adsorption (diatomic gases molecule adsorbed on M_1 and M_2 dual sites) to improve the catalytic cracking of molecules and electrochemical conversion (see the inset in Fig. 3.8I) [115]. For example, the adsorption of O_2 on metal surfaces can generally be divided into three types: one end-to-end type (Pauling-type) and two side-type (Griffiths type and Yeager-type). The bridging side adsorption of O_2 is used to split the O–O bond, which may lead to a high selectivity of 4 e^- ORR, while the end adsorption of O_2 minimizes the O–O bond rupture, leading to inhibited 4 e^- ORR and promoting 2 e^- ORR (one of our recent review papers concludes that: the high metal site density catalysts are beneficial for the bridging side-type adsorption and 4 e^- ORR [121]). In particular, the $Pd_{10}Pt_1$ bimetallic alloys or Pd@Pt core-shell catalysts with Pt-rich skin have been designed by our research group to further enhance site interactions and promote the adsorption of O_2 molecules, thus improving the catalytic activity and stability of ORR (see Fig. 3.8I) [73].

3.9.3 Synergistic spillover effect

Spillover effect refers to the spillover phenomenon (such as hydrogen spillover) where the active center (original active center) on the surface of a solid catalyst is adsorbed to produce an ionic or free radical active species, which migrates to another active center (secondary active center). Hydrogen spillover can be seen as one of the forms of migration or movement of adsorbed species on the surface (or even in the shallow body phase), or as a special form of proton transfer [122]. The spillover phenomenon was discovered in the study of the dissociation adsorption of H_2 on Pt/Al_2O_3 in the early 1950s. Now it is found that the spillover phenomenon may occur when O_2 and other gas molecules are adsorbed. It can be seen from the spillover phenomenon that the active species of catalytic hydrogenation is not only H but should be a balanced composition of H^0, H^+, H_2, H^-, etc. The active species of catalytic oxidation is not only O, but should be a balanced composition of O^0, O^-, O_2^-, and O_2 [123]. In the thermocatalytic reaction, the hydrogen spillover or oxygen spillover effect can improve the catalytic activity of hydrogenation or oxidation reaction and reduce the reaction temperature. The spillover effect also has applications in electrocatalysis and photocatalysis.

Hydrogen spillover phenomenon is mainly manifested as the active hydrogen atom (H) formed by the dissociation and adsorption of hydrogen molecules on precious metal catalysts (such Pt). Then the H migrates easily on the catalyst surface and diffuses to the support, leading to the reduction or storage of H on the hydrogen acceptors (such as active metal oxides) adjacent to the catalyst in the controllable distance (0—45 nm) (see Fig. 3.8J for details) [116]. It has been found that hydrogen spillover can reduce iron oxide at a long distance (45 nm) on titanium oxide support, while it can only reduce iron oxide at a short distance (15 nm) on alumina support. Due to the simultaneous dissociation of H_2 and water molecules on the surface of platinum catalyst, the H^- and OH^- of competing adsorption sites of Al_{3c} are formed. As a result, the diffusion rate of H^- on the alumina is 10 orders of magnitude slower than that on the titanium oxide and can only reduce the metal oxides within a short distance. This discovery has greatly improved our understanding of the support-synergistic H migrating phenomenon of hydrogen spillover (i.e., the support-synergistic spillover effect) [116]. This type of synergistic spillover effect usually shows distance-dependent reactivity between metal and oxide components. The spatial separation of metal component and oxide components is helpful to elucidate their synergistic catalytic mechanism. For a separated two-component catalyst, varying their distance in the nanoscale may result in different spillover behavior. The controlled hydrogen behavior results in a lower oxidation state of the oxide component in the reactions [124].

In recent years, a new class of dual metals/support electrocatalysts has been derived based on the principle of hydrogen spillover for HER. In other words, hydrogen spillover can be used to connect the two metal components with strong and weak hydrogen adsorption capacity on the support surface as a whole. The proton in the electrolyte is highly adsorbed and activated on the strongly adsorbed metal component, and then the H_2 is released efficiently on the weakly adsorbed metal component through the support-synergistic spillover effect [125]. For example, by directly growing dual sulfide Ni_3S_2/Cr_2S_3 nanoparticles on the nickel foam (NF) support, Ni_3S_2/Cr_2S_3@NF synergistic catalyst can be obtained. This catalyst has an obvious synergistic effect, that is, the hydrogen spillover bridges Volmer/Tafel process at the Ni_3S_2/Cr_2S_3 (H_2O dissociation/H_2 formation) dual sites, thus greatly improving HER performances [126]. Based on the understanding of synergistic hydrogen spillover effect, researchers have designed bimetallic SACs, encapsulated metal catalysts, and spatially separated dual-component catalysts to effectively utilize the hydrogen spillover effect and improve the activity, selectivity, and stability of catalytic reactions.

3.9.4 Diatomic synergistic effect

While maintaining the advantages such as 100% atom utilization and excellent selectivity over single atom site catalysts (SACs), the diatomic catalysts (DACs) have emerged as a new frontier in the field of heterogeneous catalysis, because the synergistic effect between bimetallic atom sites (with or without metal bonds; symmetric or asymmetric ligand) can greatly enhance their catalytic activity (see Fig. 3.8K for details) [117]. Most of the symmetric DACs are supported by carbon-based materials, and their coordination structures can be abbreviated as $Y_3-M_1-M_2-Y_3$ (Fig 3.8K (1)) or $Y_3-M_1-Y-M_2-Y_3$ (Fig 3.8K (2)) or $M_1/M_2-Y_6-Z_x$ (Fig 3.8K (3)) (Y: coordination atoms, M_1/M_2: metal atoms ($M_1 = M_2$ or $M_1 \neq M_2$), and x: CN of the second coordination atoms). The asymmetric structure of DACs metal diatomic catalysts can be $Y_x-M_1-M_2-Z_y$ (Fig 3.8K (4)) (Y, Z: coordination atom, M_1/M_2: metal atom, x, y: CN of coordination atom). Based on different support, different coordination environments, and different dual metal atom interactions or MSIs, DACs show very different structural characteristics and catalytic properties [127].

The DACs have found extensive applications in most electrocatalysis and partial applications in thermocatalysis or photocatalysis. The principles of the synergistic effect mostly produce the hybridization coupling of electron orbitals to each other or the special spatial location between the two metal atom sites. The synergistic effect between adjacent diatomic sites has the following advantages: (1) the synergistic effect helps to tune the local electronic structure, thus improving the electrocatalytic performance [128]. (2) The synergistic effect can optimize the adsorption/desorption characteristics, reduce the overall reaction barrier, and finally promote reversible oxygen electrocatalysis [129]. (3) The synergistic effect resulting from the two-site synergistic adsorption could facilitate the transfer of electrons and thus optimize the hybridization and bond sum between the electron orbitals of metal atoms, reaching the role of optimal adsorption and cleavage of intermediates [130].

In a recent review [117], we have discussed the application progress and challenges of diatomic catalysts from three aspects: electrocatalysis thermocatalysis, and photocatalysis. For electrochemical applications, the DACs with synergistic effects can generally show good rechargeability and flexibility when used in batteries. The bimetallic synergistic effect may also enable the material to exhibit low overpotential, high electron transfer number, and good reversibility, thus facilitating the electrocatalytic OER/ORR reaction. In terms of thermochemistry part, the catalytic efficiency of DACs can immensely improve the catalyst activity due to the enhanced d electron density near the Fermi level and bifunctional synergistic adsorption-activation effect. In the selective hydrogenation of 4-nitrophenyl ethylene, the diatomic catalyst Ir_1Mo_1/TiO_2 shows excellent selectivity and activity. The theoretical calculation shows that Ir site promotes the activation of hydrogen and Mo site adsorbs nitrophenyl ethylene [131]. The DACs not only play a role in the conventional electrocatalysis and thermocatalysis but also play an important role in the field of photocatalysis by optimizing electronic structures. The Pt—Au DACs show better photocatalytic hydrogen production performance than the single atomic Pt and single atomic Au and exhibit the synergistic effect of the diatomic group [132]. It can be predicted that the diatomic catalysts with synergistic effects will definitely play a greater role in more catalytic fields in the near future, creating more conditions for realizing the possibility of diversified catalysis.

3.10 Summary

In this chapter, we comprehensively summarize the structure—performance relationship (namely various nano effects) of nanomaterials, based on their physical and chemical properties, toward the energy and environment applications. The structure—performance relationships of nanomaterials are systematically summarized from the following eight aspects: size effect, electronic effect, geometric effect, dimensional effect, crystal effect, confined effect, interface effect, and synergistic effect. For size effect, small size effect, quantum size effect, and size-dependent surface effect are included. We detailly summarized the key points of size-dependent surface CN, surface adsorption, and surface electron state. For electronic effect, charge transfer effect, d-band center theory, EMSI, and orbital potential theory are introduced. Geometric effect includes atomic-level, nano-level, and sub—micron-level geometric effect. Dimensional effect includes single, double, and multidimensional effect. Crystal effect includes four modules: atomic arrangement and amorphization, crystal plane and crystal boundary, lattice mismatch and lattice strain, crystal defects and atomic vacancies, and crystal phase and phase transformation. Nanopore-confined effect, interlayer-confined effect, atom-confined effect is summarized in detail. MSI and heterojunction effect are two key aspects of interface effects. For the so-called synergistic effect, the synergistic electron/adsorption/spillover effect as well as the diatomic synergistic effect are presented and analyzed systematically.

Acknowledgments

This book was supported by National Natural Science Foundation of China (22078071, 22272034), Natural Science Foundation of Guangdong Province (2021A1515010125, 2020A1515010344), Maoming Science and Technology Project (mmkj2020032), Guangdong Province Universities and Colleges Pearl River Scholar Funded Scheme (2019), Guangdong Basic and Applied Basic Research Foundation (2019A1515011249, 2021A1515010305), Key Research Project of Natural Science of Guangdong Provincial Department of Education (2019KZDXM010), Environment and Energy Green Catalysis Innovation Team of Colleges and Universities of Guangdong Province(2022KCXTD019), the program for Innovative Research Team of Guangdong University of Petrochemical Technology.

References

[1]   F.W. Halperin, Quantum size effects in metal particles, Reviews of Modern Physics 58 (3) (1986) 533.

[2]   P. Buffat, J.P. Borel, Size effect on the melting temperature of gold particles, Physical Review A 13 (6) (1976) 2287.

[3]   Y. Wang, N. Herron, Nanometer-sized semiconductor clusters: materials synthesis, quantum size effects, and photophysical properties, The Journal of Physical Chemistry 95 (2) (1991) 525−532.

[4]   G. Zhou, L. Xu, G. Hu, L. Mai, Y. Cui, Nanowires for electrochemical energy storage, Chemical Reviews 119 (20) (2019) 11042−11109.

[5]   J. Sato, H. Kobayashi, Y. Inoue, Photocatalytic activity for water decomposition of indates with octahedrally coordinated d10 configuration. II. Roles of geometric and electronic structures, The Journal of Physical Chemistry B 107 (31) (2003) 7970−7975.

[6]   G. Xiang, Y. Tang, Z. Liu, W. Zhu, H. Liu, J. Wang, X. Wang, Probing ligand-induced cooperative orbital redistribution that dominates nanoscale molecule−surface interactions with one-unit-thin TiO_2 nanosheets, Nano Letters 18 (12) (2018) 7809−7815.

[7]   https://mp.weixin.qq.com/s/0C07tj0V3V_pc2lMMS6q6g.

[8]   P.P. Edwards, R.L. Johnston, C.N.R. Rao, On the size-induced metal-insulator transition in clusters and small particles, Metal Clusters in Chemistry (1999) 1454−1481.

[9]   L.P. Yuan, T. Tang, J.S. Hu, L.J. Wan, Confinement strategies for precise synthesis of efficient electrocatalysts from the macroscopic to the atomic level, Accounts of Materials Research 2 (10) (2021) 907−919.

[10] Q. Xu, J. Zhang, H. Zhang, L. Zhang, L. Chen, Y. Hu, C. Li, Atomic heterointerface engineering breaks activity limitation of electrocatalysts and promises highly-efficient alkaline water splitting, Energy & Environmental Science 14 (2021) 5228−5259.

[11] X. Li, X. Wu, X. Lv, J. Wang, H.B. Wu, Recent advances in metal-based electrocatalysts with hetero-interfaces for CO_2 reduction reaction, Chem Catalysis 2 (2) (2022) 262−291.

[12] Amorphous metallic ultrathin nanostructures: a latent ultra-high-density atomic-level catalyst for electrochemical energy conversion to be published in, International Journal of Hydrogen Energy (2022). HE_HE-D-22-02246.

[13] https://mp.weixin.qq.com/s/dWZF8hRCsA5IdZFzQhlZzQ.

[14] https://mp.weixin.qq.com/s/7LCtj9ccGJksb9-deEnB9Q.

[15] https://www.zhihu.com/question/46430290.

[16] S. Monticone, R. Tufeu, A.V. Kanaev, E. Scolan, C. Sanchez, Quantum size effect in TiO_2 nanoparticles: does it exist? Applied Surface Science 162 (2000) 565−570.

[17] Y. Lou, J. Xu, Y. Zhang, C. Pan, Y. Dong, Y. Zhu, Metal-support interaction for heterogeneous catalysis: from nanoparticles to single atoms, Materials Today Nano 12 (2020) 100093.

[18] A.D. Yoffe, Low-dimensional systems: quantum size effects and electronic properties of semiconductor microcrystallites (zero-dimensional systems) and some quasi-two-dimensional systems, Advances in Physics 42 (2) (1993) 173−262.

[19] E. Roduner, Size matters: why nanomaterials are different, Chemical Society Reviews 35 (7) (2006) 583−592.

[20] H. Schmidt, F. Giustiniano, G. Eda, Electronic transport properties of transition metal dichalcogenide field-effect devices: surface and interface effects, Chemical Society Reviews 44 (21) (2015) 7715−7736.

[21] B. Hvolbæk, T.V. Janssens, B.S. Clausen, H. Falsig, C.H. Christensen, J.K. Nørskov, Catalytic activity of Au nanoparticles, Nano Today 2 (4) (2007) 14−18.

[22] Y. Yuan, N. Yan, P.J. Dyson, Advances in the rational design of rhodium nanoparticle catalysts: control via manipulation of the nanoparticle core and stabilizer, ACS Catalysis 2 (6) (2012) 1057−1069.

[23] F. Calle-Vallejo, J. Tymoczko, V. Colic, Q.H. Vu, M.D. Pohl, K. Morgenstern, A.S. Bandarenka, Finding optimal surface sites on heterogeneous catalysts by counting nearest neighbors, Science 350 (6257) (2015) 185−189.

[24] J. Kleis, J. Greeley, N.A. Romero, V.A. Morozov, H. Falsig, A.H. Larsen, K.W. Jacobsen, Finite size effects in chemical bonding: from small clusters to solids, Catalysis Letters 141 (8) (2011) 1067—1071.

[25] L. Li, A.H. Larsen, N.A. Romero, V.A. Morozov, C. Glinsvad, F. Abild-Pedersen, J.K. Nørskov, Investigation of catalytic finite-size-effects of platinum metal clusters, The Journal of Physical Chemistry Letters 4 (1) (2013) 222—226.

[26] S. Cao, F.F. Tao, Y. Tang, Y. Li, J. Yu, Size-and shape-dependent catalytic performances of oxidation and reduction reactions on nanocatalysts, Chemical Society Reviews 45 (17) (2016) 4747—4765.

[27] Z. Li, S. Ji, Y. Liu, X. Cao, S. Tian, Y. Chen, Y. Li, Well-defined materials for heterogeneous catalysis: from nanoparticles to isolated single-atom sites, Chemical Reviews 120 (2) (2020) 623—682.

[28] H. Wang, Y. Wang, Z. Zhu, A. Sapi, K. An, G. Kennedy, G.A. Somorjai, Influence of size-induced oxidation state of platinum nanoparticles on selectivity and activity in catalytic methanol oxidation in the gas phase, Nano Letters 13 (6) (2013) 2976—2979.

[29] Y. Zhou, A. Chen, J. Ning, W. Shen, Electronic and geometric structure of the copper-ceria interface on Cu/CeO_2 catalysts, Chinese Journal of Catalysis 41 (6) (2020) 928—937.

[30] F. Yang, D. Deng, X. Pan, Q. Fu, X. Bao, Understanding nano effects in catalysis, National Science Review 2 (2) (2015) 183—201.

[31] R. Xu, L. Du, D. Adekoya, G. Zhang, S. Zhang, S. Sun, Y. Lei, Well-defined nanostructures for electrochemical energy conversion and storage, Advanced Energy Materials 11 (15) (2021) 2001537.

[32] S. Sun, X. Zhou, B. Cong, W. Hong, G. Chen, Tailoring the d-band centers endows $(Ni_xFe_{1-x})_2P$ nanosheets with efficient oxygen evolution catalysis, ACS Catalysis 10 (16) (2020) 9086—9097.

[33] H. Wang, X.K. Gu, X. Zheng, H. Pan, J. Zhu, S. Chen, J. Lu, Disentangling the size-dependent geometric and electronic effects of palladium nanocatalysts beyond selectivity, Science Advances 5 (1) (2019) eaat6413.

[34] H. Wang, J. Lu, A review on particle size effect in metal-catalyzed heterogeneous reactions, Chinese Journal of Chemistry 38 (11) (2020) 1422—1444.

[35] G. Lin, Q. Ju, Y. Jin, X. Qi, W. Liu, F. Huang, J. Wang, Suppressing dissolution of Pt-based electrocatalysts through the electronic metal—support interaction, Advanced Energy Materials 11 (38) (2021) 2101050.

[36] J.K. Nørskov, F. Abild-Pedersen, F. Studt, T. Bligaard, Density functional theory in surface chemistry and catalysis, Proceedings of the National Academy of Sciences 108 (3) (2011) 937—943.

[37] B. Hammer, J.K. Nørskov, Theoretical surface science and catalysis-calculations and concepts, in: Advances in Catalysis vol 45, Academic Press, 2000, pp. 71—129.

[38] J. Yang, W.H. Li, S. Tan, K. Xu, Y. Wang, D. Wang, Y. Li, The electronic metal—support interaction directing the design of single atomic site catalysts: achieving high efficiency towards hydrogen evolution, Angewandte Chemie 133 (35) (2021) 19233—19239.

[39] Y. Shi, Z.R. Ma, Y.Y. Xiao, Y.C. Yin, W.M. Huang, Z.C. Huang, W. Chen, Electronic metal—support interaction modulates single-atom platinum catalysis for hydrogen evolution reaction, Nature Communications 12 (1) (2021) 1—11.

[40] G. Xiang, Y.G. Wang, Exploring electronic-level principles how size reduction enhances nanomaterial surface reactivity through experimental probing and mathematical modeling, Nano Research 15 (4) (2022) 3812—3817.

[41] Q. Liu, X. Wang, Sub-nanometric materials: electron transfer, delocalization, and beyond, Chem Catalysis 2 (6) (2022) 1257—1266.

[42] X. Sun, P. Han, B. Li, S. Mao, T. Liu, S. Ali, D. Su, Oxidative dehydrogenation reaction of short alkanes on nanostructured carbon catalysts: a computational account, Chemical Communications 54 (8) (2018) 864—875.

[43] S.F. Kurtoglu, A.S. Hoffman, D. Akgul, M. Babucci, V. Aviyente, B.C. Gates, A. Uzun, Electronic structure of atomically dispersed supported iridium catalyst controls iridium aggregation, ACS Catalysis 10 (21) (2020) 12354—12358.

[44] Z. Zhang, S.B. Peh, R. Krishna, C. Kang, K. Chai, Y. Wang, D. Zhao, Optimal pore chemistry in an ultramicroporous metal—organic framework for benchmark inverse CO_2/C_2H_2 separation, Angewandte Chemie International Edition 60 (31) (2021) 17198—17204.

[45] https://mp.weixin.qq.com/s/1K9ecYua0re9k6INRZOCmw.

[46] https://mp.weixin.qq.com/s/xaNgLkPEjxKbw10CkonntQ.

[47] B. Hammer, J.K. Norskov, Why gold is the noblest of all the metals, Nature 376 (6537) (1995) 238–240.

[48] J. Liang, F. Ma, S. Hwang, X. Wang, J. Sokolowski, Q. Li, D. Su, Atomic arrangement engineering of metallic nanocrystals for energy-conversion electrocatalysis, Joule 3 (4) (2019) 956–991.

[49] J. Shan, C. Ye, S. Chen, T. Sun, Y. Jiao, L. Liu, S.Z. Qiao, Short-range ordered iridium single atoms integrated into cobalt oxide spinel structure for highly efficient electrocatalytic water oxidation, Journal of the American Chemical Society 143 (13) (2021) 5201–5211.

[50] J. Zhou, Z. Han, X. Wang, H. Gai, Z. Chen, T. Guo, H. Jiang, Discovery of quantitative electronic structure-OER activity relationship in metal-organic framework electrocatalysts using an integrated theoretical-experimental approach, Advanced Functional Materials 31 (33) (2021) 2102066.

[51] A. Bruix, J.A. Rodriguez, P.J. Ramírez, S.D. Senanayake, J. Evans, J.B. Park, F. Illas, A new type of strong metal–support interaction and the production of H_2 through the transformation of water on Pt/CeO_2 (111) and $Pt/CeO_x/TiO_2$ (110) catalysts, Journal of the American Chemical Society 134 (21) (2012) 8968–8974.

[52] J. Li, Q. Guan, H. Wu, W. Liu, Y. Lin, Z. Sun, J. Lu, Highly active and stable metal single-atom catalysts achieved by strong electronic metal–support interactions, Journal of the American Chemical Society 141 (37) (2019) 14515–14519.

[53] Y. Hu, H. Li, Z.S. Li, B. Li, S. Wang, Y. Yao, Progress in batch preparation of single-atom catalysts and application in sustainable synthesis of fine chemicals, Green Chemistry 23 (2021) 8754–8794.

[54] M.S. Chen, D.W. Goodman, Structure–activity relationships in supported Au catalysts, Catalysis Today 111 (1–2) (2006) 22–33.

[55] B. Coq, F. Figueras, Structure–activity relationships in catalysis by metals: some aspects of particle size, bimetallic and supports effects, Coordination Chemistry Reviews 178 (1998) 1753–1783.

[56] V.R. Stamenkovic, B. Fowler, B.S. Mun, G. Wang, P.N. Ross, C.A. Lucas, N.M. Markovic, Improved oxygen reduction activity on Pt3Ni (111) via increased surface site availability, Science 315 (5811) (2007) 493–497.

[57] Y. Yu, Q. Zhang, B. Liu, J.Y. Lee, Synthesis of nanocrystals with variable high-index Pd facets through the controlled heteroepitaxial growth of trisoctahedral Au templates, Journal of the American Chemical Society 132 (51) (2010) 18258–18265.

[58] M. Tang, S. Luo, K. Wang, H. Du, R. Sriphathoorat, P. Shen, Simultaneous formation of trimetallic Pt-Ni-Cu excavated rhombic dodecahedrons with enhanced catalytic performance for the methanol oxidation reaction, Nano Research 11 (9) (2018) 4786–4795.

[59] B. Li, Z. Li, Q. Pang, Controllable preparation of N-doped Ni_3S_2 nanocubes@ N-doped graphene-like carbon layers for highly active electrocatalytic overall water splitting, Electrochimica Acta 399 (2021) 139408.

[60] S. Yang, B. Zhang, C. Ge, X. Dong, X. Liu, Y. Fang, Z. Li, Close-packed mesoporous carbon polyhedrons derived from colloidal carbon microspheres for electrochemical energy storage applications, RSC Advances 2 (27) (2012) 10310–10315.

[61] Y. Wang, Y. Liu, W. Liu, J. Wu, Q. Li, Q. Feng, Y. Lei, Regulating the coordination structure of metal single atoms for efficient electrocatalytic CO_2 reduction, Energy & Environmental Science 13 (12) (2020) 4609–4624.

[62] P. Wang, Z. Jin, P. Li, G. Yu, Design principles of hydrogen-evolution-suppressing single-atom catalysts for aqueous electrosynthesis, Chem Catalysis 2 (6) (2022) 1277–1287.

[63] Y. Shi, Z. Lyu, M. Zhao, R. Chen, Q.N. Nguyen, Y. Xia, Noble-metal nanocrystals with controlled shapes for catalytic and electrocatalytic applications, Chemical Reviews 121 (2) (2020) 649–735.

[64] S. Sun, X. Zhang, J. Cui, S. Liang, Identification of the Miller indices of a crystallographic plane: a tutorial and a comprehensive review on fundamental theory, universal methods based on different case studies and matters needing attention, Nanoscale 12 (32) (2020) 16657–16677.

[65] J. Nai, J. Zhang, X.W.D. Lou, Construction of single-crystalline Prussian blue analog hollow nanostructures with tailorable topologies, Chem 4 (8) (2018) 1967–1982.

[66] R. Jain, A.S. Lakhnot, K. Bhimani, S. Sharma, V. Mahajani, R.A. Panchal, N. Koratkar, Nanostructuring versus microstructuring in battery electrodes, Nature Reviews Materials (2022) 1–11.

[67] X. Zhang, Y. Wei, R. Yu, Multidimensional tungsten oxides for efficient solar energy conversion, Small Structures 3 (2) (2022) 2100130.

[68] Q. Zhu, D. Cai, X. Lan, G. Shi, K. Jin, J. Zhou, Y. Yu, Design of multidimensional nanocomposite material to realize the application both in energy storage and electrocatalysis, Science Bulletin 63 (2018) 152−154.

[69] S. Tan, Y. Jiang, Q. Wei, Q. Huang, Y. Dai, F. Xiong, L. Mai, Multidimensional synergistic nano-architecture exhibiting highly stable and ultrafast sodium-ion storage, Advanced Materials 30 (18) (2018) 1707122.

[70] Y. Chen, Z. Lai, Z. Fan, Q. He, C. Tan, H. Zhang, Phase engineering of nanomaterials, Nature Reviews Chemistry 4 (5) (2020) 243−256.

[71] C. Yu, W. Zhou, L. Zhu, G. Li, K. Yang, R. Jin, Integrating plasmonic Au nanorods with dendritic like α-Bi_2O_3/$Bi_2O_2CO_3$ heterostructures for superior visible-light-driven photocatalysis, Applied Catalysis B: Environmental 184 (2016) 1−11.

[72] C. Yu, H. He, Q. Fan, W. Xie, Z. Liu, H. Ji, Novel B-doped BiOCl nanosheets with exposed (001) facets and photocatalytic mechanism of enhanced degradation efficiency for organic pollutants, Science of the Total Environment 694 (2019) 133727.

[73] Z. Li, Y. Li, G. He, P.K. Shen, Novel graphene-like nanosheet supported highly active electrocatalysts with ultralow Pt loadings for oxygen reduction reaction, Journal of Materials Chemistry A 2 (40) (2014) 16898−16904.

[74] J. Liu, J. Zhang, Nanointerface chemistry: lattice-mismatch-directed synthesis and application of hybrid nanocrystals, Chemical Reviews 120 (4) (2020) 2123−2170.

[75] J. Zhao, B. Chen, F. Wang, Shedding light on the role of misfit strain in controlling core−shell nanocrystals, Advanced Materials 32 (46) (2020) 2004142.

[76] Z. Xiao, C. Xie, Y. Wang, R. Chen, S. Wang, Recent advances in defect electrocatalysts: preparation and characterization, Journal of Energy Chemistry 53 (2021) 208−225.

[77] C. Xie, D. Yan, H. Li, S. Du, W. Chen, Y. Wang, S. Wang, Defect chemistry in heterogeneous catalysis: recognition, understanding, and utilization, ACS Catalysis 10 (19) (2020) 11082−11098.

[78] N.D. Spencer, R.C. Schoonmaker, G.A. Somorjai, Structure sensitivity in the iron single-crystal catalysed synthesis of ammonia, Nature 294 (1981) 643−644.

[79] Y. Lan, Z. Li, D. Li, W. Xie, G. Yan, S. Guo, Visible-light responsive Z-scheme $Bi@$ β-Bi_2O_3/g-C_3N_4 heterojunction for efficient photocatalytic degradation of 2, 3-dihydroxynaphthalene, Chemical Engineering Journal 392 (2020) 123686.

[80] Z. Liu, Z. Zhao, B. Peng, X. Duan, Y. Huang, Beyond extended surfaces: understanding the oxygen reduction reaction on nanocatalysts, Journal of the American Chemical Society 142 (42) (2020) 17812−17827.

[81] Z. Chen, T. Wang, B. Liu, D. Cheng, C. Hu, G. Zhang, J. Gong, Grain-boundary-rich copper for efficient solar-driven electrochemical CO_2 reduction to ethylene and ethanol, Journal of the American Chemical Society 142 (15) (2020) 6878−6883.

[82] W. Huang, A.C. Johnston-Peck, T. Wolter, W.C.D. Yang, L. Xu, J. Oh, M. Cargnello, Steam-created grain boundaries for methane C−H activation in palladium catalysts, Science 373 (6562) (2021) 1518−1523.

[83] C. Yu, G. Li, S. Kumar, K. Yang, R. Jin, Phase transformation synthesis of novel Ag_2O/Ag_2CO_3 heterostructures with high visible light efficiency in photocatalytic degradation of pollutants, Advanced Materials 26 (6) (2014) 892−898.

[84] K. Yang, X. Li, C. Yu, D. Zeng, F. Chen, K. Zhang, H. Ji, Review on heterophase/homophase junctions for efficient photocatalysis: the case of phase transition construction, Chinese Journal of Catalysis 40 (6) (2019) 796−818.

[85] J. Zhou, M. Yu, J. Peng, R. Lin, Z. Li, C. Yu, Photocatalytic degradation characteristics of tetracycline and structural transformation on bismuth silver oxide perovskite nano-catalysts, Applied Nanoscience 10 (7) (2020) 2329−2338.

[86] S. Zhang, T. Hedtke, X. Zhou, M. Elimelech, J.H. Kim, Environmental applications of engineered materials with nanoconfinement, ACS ES&T Engineering 1 (4) (2021) 706−724.

[87] P. Qi, Y. Siyuan, G. Chunyu, L. Yingju, L. Xiaotang, F. Yueping, Z. Liya, Mesopore-functional carbon sphere nanochains and their integration with alloy nanoparticles for enhanced electrochemical performances, Electrochimica Acta 114 (2013) 334−340.

[88] B. Chu, Q. Ma, Z. Li, B. Li, F. Huang, Q. Pang, J.Z. Zhang, Design and preparation of three-dimensional hetero-electrocatalysts of NiCo-layered double hydroxide nanosheets incorporated with silver nanoclusters for enhanced oxygen evolution reactions, Nanoscale 13 (25) (2021) 11150−11160.

[89] J. Gu, M. Jian, L. Huang, Z. Sun, A. Li, Y. Pan, J. Lu, Synergizing metal−support interactions and spatial confinement boosts dynamics of atomic nickel for hydrogenations, Nature Nanotechnology 16 (10) (2021) 1141−1149.

[90] Z. Li, B. Li, Y. Hu, X. Liao, H. Yu, C. Yu, Emerging ultrahigh-density single-atom catalysts for versatile heterogeneous catalysis applications: redefinition, recent progress, and challenges, Small Structures (2022) 2200041.

[91] K. Fan, Z. Li, Y. Song, W. Xie, M. Shao, M. Wei, Confinement synthesis based on layered double hydroxides: a new strategy to construct single-atom-containing integrated electrodes, Advanced Functional Materials 31 (10) (2021) 2008064.

[92] Z. Zhao, P. Wu, Z. Fang, X. Zhang, Selective sequestration of p-arsanilic acid from water by using nano-hydrated zirconium oxide encapsulated inside hyper-cross-linked anion exchanger, Chemical Engineering Journal 391 (2020) 123624.

[93] S. Zhang, T. Hedtke, L. Wang, X. Wang, T. Cao, M. Elimelech, J.H. Kim, Engineered nanoconfinement accelerating spontaneous manganese-catalyzed degradation of organic contaminants, Environmental Science & Technology 55 (24) (2021) 16708−16715.

[94] S. Alayoglu, A.U. Nilekar, M. Mavrikakis, B. Eichhorn, Ru−Pt core−shell nanoparticles for preferential oxidation of carbon monoxide in hydrogen, Nature Materials 7 (4) (2008) 333−338.

[95] M. Cargnello, V.V. Doan-Nguyen, T.R. Gordon, R.E. Diaz, E.A. Stach, R.J. Gorte, C.B. Murray, Control of metal nanocrystal size reveals metal-support interface role for ceria catalysts, Science 341 (6147) (2013) 771−773.

[96] R. Lang, X. Du, Y. Huang, X. Jiang, Q. Zhang, Y. Guo, T. Zhang, Single-atom catalysts based on the metal−oxide interaction, Chemical Reviews 120 (21) (2020) 11986−12043.

[97] Y. Lan, Z. Li, W. Xie, D. Li, G. Yan, S. Guo, J. Wu, In situ fabrication of I-doped $Bi_2O_2CO_3$/g-C_3N_4 heterojunctions for enhanced photodegradation activity under visible light, Journal of Hazardous Materials 385 (2020) 121622.

[98] S.J. Tauster, S.C. Fung, R.L. Garten, Strong metal-support interactions. Group 8 noble metals supported on titanium dioxide, Journal of the American Chemical Society 100 (1) (1978) 170−175.

[99] J.C. Matsubu, S. Zhang, L. DeRita, N.S. Marinkovic, J.G. Chen, G.W. Graham, P. Christopher, Adsorbate-mediated strong metal−support interactions in oxide-supported Rh catalysts, Nature Chemistry 9 (2) (2017) 120−127.

[100] P. Hu, Z. Huang, Z. Amghouz, M. Makkee, F. Xu, F. Kapteijn, X. Tang, Electronic metal−support interactions in single-atom catalysts, Angewandte Chemie 126 (13) (2014) 3486−3489.

[101] X. Liu, M.H. Liu, Y.C. Luo, C.Y. Mou, S.D. Lin, H. Cheng, T.S. Lin, Strong metal−support interactions between gold nanoparticles and ZnO nanorods in CO oxidation, Journal of the American Chemical Society 134 (24) (2012) 10251−10258.

[102] H. Tang, J. Wei, F. Liu, B. Qiao, X. Pan, L. Li, T. Zhang, Strong metal−support interactions between gold nanoparticles and nonoxides, Journal of the American Chemical Society 138 (1) (2016) 56−59.

[103] H. Tang, Y. Su, Y. Guo, L. Zhang, T. Li, K. Zang, J. Wang, Oxidative strong metal−support interactions (OMSI) of supported platinum-group metal catalysts, Chemical Science 9 (32) (2018) 6679−6684.

[104] B. Qiao, J.X. Liang, A. Wang, C.Q. Xu, J. Li, T. Zhang, J.J. Liu, Ultrastable single-atom gold catalysts with strong covalent metal-support interaction (CMSI), Nano Research 8 (9) (2015) 2913−2924.

[105] K. Liu, X. Zhao, G. Ren, T. Yang, Y. Ren, A.F. Lee, T. Zhang, Strong metal-support interaction promoted scalable production of thermally stable single-atom catalysts, Nature Communications 11 (1) (2020) 1−9.

[106] J. Low, J. Yu, M. Jaroniec, S. Wageh, A.A. Al-Ghamdi, Heterojunction photocatalysts, Advanced Materials 29 (20) (2017) 1601694.

[107] L. Yu, H. Hu, H.B. Wu, X.W. Lou, Complex hollow nanostructures: synthesis and energy-related applications, Advanced Materials 29 (15) (2017) 1604563.

[108] C.S. Day, R.J. Somerville, R. Martin, Deciphering the dichotomy exerted by Zn (ii) in the catalytic sp^2 C−O bond functionalization of aryl esters at the molecular level, Nature Catalysis 4 (2) (2021) 124−133.

[109] X. Wu, S. Zhou, Z. Wang, J. Liu, W. Pei, P. Yang, J. Qiu, Engineering multifunctional collaborative catalytic interface enabling efficient hydrogen evolution in all pH range and seawater, Advanced Energy Materials 9 (34) (2019) 1901333.

[110] Q. Yang, T. Wang, Z. Zheng, B. Xing, C. Li, B. Li, Constructing interfacial active sites in Ru/g-C_3N_{4-x} photocatalyst for boosting H_2 evolution coupled with selective benzyl-alcohol oxidation, Applied Catalysis B: Environmental (2022) 121575.

[111] Z. Zhou, G. Roelfes, Synergistic catalysis in an artificial enzyme by simultaneous action of two abiological catalytic sites, Nature Catalysis 3 (3) (2020) 289−294.

[112] M. Ahmadi, H. Mistry, B. Roldan Cuenya, Tailoring the catalytic properties of metal nanoparticles via support interactions, The Journal of Physical Chemistry Letters 7 (17) (2016) 3519−3533.

[113] Z. Li, S. Ji, B.G. Pollet, P.K. Shen, A Co_3W_3C promoted Pd catalyst exhibiting competitive performance over Pt/C catalysts towards the oxygen reduction reaction, Chemical Communications 50 (5) (2014) 566−568.

[114] Z. Li, R. Lin, Z. Liu, D. Li, H. Wang, Q. Li, Novel graphitic carbon nitride/graphite carbon/palladium nanocomposite as a high-performance electrocatalyst for the ethanol oxidation reaction, Electrochimica Acta 191 (2016) 606−615.

[115] R. Li, D. Wang, Superiority of dual-atom catalysts in electrocatalysis: one step further than single-atom catalysts, Advanced Energy Materials 12 (9) (2022) 2103564.

[116] W. Karim, C. Spreafico, A. Kleibert, J. Gobrecht, J. VandeVondele, Y. Ekinci, J.A. van Bokhoven, Catalyst support effects on hydrogen spillover, Nature 541 (7635) (2017) 68−71.

[117] Y. Hu, Z. Li B. Li, C. Yu, Recent Progress of Diatomic Catalysts: General Design Fundamentals and Diversified Catalytic Applications.

[118] M. Yu, Z. Li, H. Shi, S. Lin, X. Zhang, F. Mo, D. Liang, Preparation of graphite carbon/Prussian blue analogue/palladium (GC/PBA/pd) synergistic-effect electrocatalyst with high activity for ethanol oxidation reaction, International Journal of Hydrogen Energy 47 (10) (2022) 6721−6733.

[119] K.J. Chen, D.G. Madden, S. Mukherjee, T. Pham, K.A. Forrest, A. Kumar, M.J. Zaworotko, Synergistic sorbent separation for one-step ethylene purification from a four-component mixture, Science 366 (6462) (2019) 241−246.

[120] S. Zhang, Z. Xia, Y. Zou, M. Zhang, Y. Qu, Spatial intimacy of binary active-sites for selective sequential hydrogenation-condensation of nitriles into secondary imines, Nature Communications 12 (1) (2021) 1−8.

[121] Z. Li, B. Li, Y. Hu, S. Wang, C. Yu, Highly-dispersed and high-metal-density electrocatalysts on carbon supports for the oxygen reduction reaction: from nanoparticles to atomic-level architectures, Materials Advances 3 (2) (2022) 779−809.

[122] G. Kyriakou, M.B. Boucher, A.D. Jewell, E.A. Lewis, T.J. Lawton, A.E. Baber, E.C.H. Sykes, Isolated metal atom geometries as a strategy for selective heterogeneous hydrogenations, Science 335 (6073) (2012) 1209−1212.

[123] https://mp.weixin.qq.com/s/R52HvBe22m4yRJlMjOUo5g.

[124] M. Xiong, Z. Gao, Y. Qin, Spillover in heterogeneous catalysis: new insights and opportunities, ACS Catalysis 11 (5) (2021) 3159−3172.

[125] J. Li, J. Hu, M. Zhang, W. Gou, S. Zhang, Z. Chen, Y. Ma, A fundamental viewpoint on the hydrogen spillover phenomenon of electrocatalytic hydrogen evolution, Nature Communications 12 (1) (2021) 1−12.

[126] H.Q. Fu, M. Zhou, P.F. Liu, P. Liu, H. Yin, K.Z. Sun, H. Zhao, Hydrogen spillover-bridged Volmer/Tafel processes enabling ampere-level current density alkaline hydrogen evolution reaction under low overpotential, Journal of the American Chemical Society 144 (13) (2022) 6028–6039.

[127] J. Zhang, Q.A. Huang, J. Wang, J. Wang, J. Zhang, Y. Zhao, Supported dual-atom catalysts: preparation, characterization, and potential applications, Chinese Journal of Catalysis 41 (5) (2020) 783–798.

[128] Y. Song, B. Xu, T. Liao, J. Guo, Y. Wu, Z. Sun, Electronic structure tuning of 2D metal (hydr) oxides nanosheets for electrocatalysis, Small 17 (9) (2021) 2002240.

[129] J. Su, S. Zhang, Q. Liu, G. Hu, L. Zhang, The Janus in monodispersed catalysts: synergetic interactions, Journal of Materials Chemistry A 9 (9) (2021) 5276–5295.

[130] Y. Lei, Y. Wang, Y. Liu, C. Song, Q. Li, D. Wang, Y. Li, Designing atomic active centers for hydrogen evolution electrocatalysts, Angewandte Chemie International Edition 59 (47) (2020) 20794–20812.

[131] J. Fu, J. Dong, R. Si, K. Sun, J. Zhang, M. Li, J. Huang, Synergistic effects for enhanced catalysis in a dual single-atom catalyst, Acs Catalysis 11 (4) (2021) 1952–1961.

[132] T. Wei, P. Ding, T. Wang, L.M. Liu, X. An, X. Yu, Facet-regulating local coordination of dual-atom cocatalyzed TiO_2 for photocatalytic water splitting, ACS Catalysis 11 (23) (2021) 14669–14676.

CHAPTER 4

Physicochemical basics and paradigms of nanomaterials

4.1 Introduction

The discipline of physical chemistry is developed on the basis of physics and chemistry. It takes a wealth of chemical phenomena and systems as its object, adopts a large number of theoretical achievements and experimental techniques of physics, explores, summarizes, and studies the basic laws and theories of chemistry, and forms the theoretical basis of chemical science. The research level of physical chemistry to a considerable extent reflects the depth of chemical development [1]. The discipline of physical chemistry can be traced back to 1887, more than 130 years from today, and was jointly started by Jacobus Henricus van't Hoff, Svante August Arrhenius, and Friedrich Wilhelm Ostwald. In early time, van't hoff, Ostwald, and Arrhenius have begun to work together to break through national boundaries and disciplinary boundaries and promote the establishment of this new discipline, Physical Chemistry. In 1887, an academic journal on Physical Chemistry founded by three originators, *Zeitschrift für Physikalische Chemie*), was published. Therefore, 1887 is regarded as the year when the discipline of Physical Chemistry was founded. The academic Journal of *Zeitschrift für Physikalische Chemie* (ZPC), covers the main developments in physical chemistry with emphasis on experimental and theoretical research (its influence factor (IF) is 4.315 in 2022) (see Fig. 4.1A for details) [2]. The ZPC represents a physicochemical combination of reaction kinetics and spectroscopy, quantum theory, surface research and electrochemistry, thermodynamics, and structure analysis of matter (including nanomaterials) in its various application conditions (including energy and environment applications). At present times, more academic journals related to physical chemistry have appeared, providing broad academic platforms for scientists to demonstrate the physicochemical properties of nanomaterials, as well as their energy and environment applications.

John B. Goodenough, the 2019 Nobel Prize winner in Chemistry, is one of the greatest scientists of our time (the intersection of physics and chemistry). Goodenough recognized the importance of interdisciplinarity in advancing science and engineering long before the advent of interdisciplinarity. Thus, in the early 1950s, he began his scientific research career, bridging the gap between chemistry and physics of solid–state materials in a unique way, thus achieving key technological advances in electrochemical storage and conversion (see Fig. 4.1B for details) [3]. As a physicist, Goodenough was able to bridge disciplinary gaps by working closely with chemists, an approach that allowed him to

Nanostructured Materials
ISBN 978-0-443-19256-2, https://doi.org/10.1016/B978-0-443-19256-2.00017-X

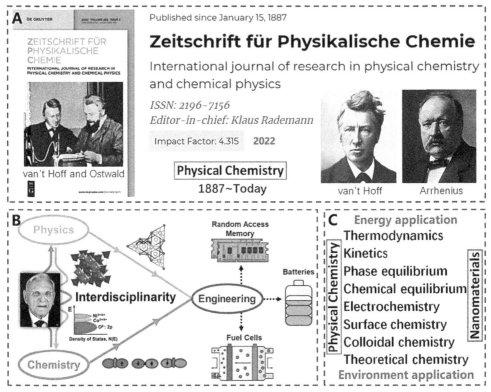

Figure 4.1 (A) Journal of physical chemistry (*Zeitschrift für Physikalische Chemie*) and its originators [2], (B) the interdisciplinarity of physics and chemistry by John B. Goodenough [3], (C) several important branches of physical chemistry related to nanomaterials for energy and environment applications.

delve deeply into problems between chemistry and physics, and to test his intuitions about physics, chemistry, or physical chemistry in a timely manner. The importance and richness of this physiochemically interdisciplinary research approach were vividly illustrated in his 1971 article on Metallic Oxides [4]. Goodenough's early knowledge and understanding of crystal chemistry, chemical bonding, redox reaction, and the interactions between electron and ion transport in solid-state materials, as well as the development of new nanomaterials or the exploration of new physicochemical properties, drove technological innovation in the field of modern energy [3,5].

Physical chemistry just is the long-term precipitated product of interdisciplinary scientific research by numerous scientists in physics, chemistry, and materials. At present, physical chemistry has been separated into more subdisciplines in scientific research, such as chemical thermodynamics, chemical dynamics, structural chemistry, surface chemistry, colloid chemistry, catalytic chemistry, quantum chemistry, solution chemistry, electrochemistry, and so on [6]. Thereinto, many subdisciplines are closely related to the preparation and characterization of nanomaterials, as well as energy and environmental applications. In this chapter, we will discuss the physicochemical basics and paradigms of nanomaterials from the following eight aspects: thermodynamics, kinetics, phase equilibrium, chemical equilibrium, electrochemistry, surface chemistry, colloidal chemistry, and theoretical chemistry (see Fig. 4.1C for details).

4.2 Thermodynamics of nanomaterials

Thermodynamics is a discipline that studies the properties and laws of thermal motion of matter from a macroscopic perspective. It is a branch of physical chemistry, which, together with statistical physics, constitutes the macroscopic and microscopic aspects of thermal theory in Chemistry [7]. Thermodynamics of nanomaterials (or called nano-thermodynamics) is earliest known as thermodynamics of small systems by Terrell L. Hill [8]. In 2000, Ralph V. Chamberlin published an article in Nature that treated a physical problem with Hill' theory and first used the term nano-thermodynamics [9]. In 2001, Hill officially endorsed the term nano-thermodynamics in nano-letters, introducing the discipline and the origin of this term [10]. The nano-thermodynamics is crucial for characterizing the thermal equilibrium distribution of independently relaxing regions inside bulk materials from a mesoscopic perspective, which extends the standard thermodynamics to facilitate finite-size effects on the scale of nanometers [11].

4.2.1 Basic functions of thermodynamics

Thermodynamics deals mainly with the thermal properties of matter from the point of view of energy transformation. It suggests the macroscopic laws that govern the transformation of energy from one form to another. The basic thermal laws include the zero law of thermodynamics, the first law of thermodynamics, the second law of thermodynamics, and the third law of thermodynamics. These laws are mostly described by different thermal functions (i.e., U, H, S, A, and G) and their equation relations.

4.2.1.1 Thermodynamic energy (U)

The first law of thermodynamics (namely, law of conservation and transformation of energy) refers to the law of conservation of different forms of energy (Q and W) in the process of transformation, expressed as (see Eq. 4.1):

$$\Delta U = Q + W \tag{4.1}$$

where ΔU is the change value of energy in system, Q is the heat exchange value between the system and environment, and W is the work exchange value between the system and the environment. The W done by the environment on the system, $W > 0$; The W done by the system on the environment, $W < 0$. The system absorbs heat from the environment, $Q > 0$, in reverse, $Q < 0$. The U of the system increases, $\Delta U > 0$, namely, ΔU is positive; The U of the system decreases, $\Delta U < 0$, that is, ΔU is negative. The first law of thermodynamics is the basis of thermodynamics and has a wide range of applications to energy, the material basis of human social activities.

4.2.1.2 Enthalpy (H)

Enthalpy (H) is an important state parameter describing the energy of a system in thermodynamics. H is equal to the sum of the products of internal energy (U), pressure (P), and volume (V). H is defined as follows (see Eq. 4.2):

$$H = U + PV \tag{4.2}$$

At some point, the H of a system has to be a certain value, but we can't measure the absolute value of H. What's important for thermodynamics is the change of H (ΔH), and that can be measured experimentally. The ΔH is important for chemical reactions because the heat absorbed (or given off) is equal to the change of internal energy (ΔU) plus the external volume W done during the change ($P\Delta V$) at a constant pressure (i.e., $\Delta H = \Delta U + P\Delta V$). In many biological or electrochemical systems, no volume W is done, so the ΔH is equal to the ΔU.

4.2.1.3 Entropy (S)

The concept of entropy (S) under constant pressure was put forward by the Clausius in 1865. It was proved that the essence of S is the "intrinsic disorder degree" of a system, and the more chaotic the system, the greater the S value. Clausius defined the change in S (ΔS) in a thermodynamic system as the rate of change of input heat (δQ) relative to temperature (T) during a reversible process (see Eq. 4.3):

$$dS = \left(\frac{\delta Q}{T}\right)_{reversible} \tag{4.3}$$

When a process is defined as "reversible," it means that the system maintains a state very close to equilibrium in every extremely short step of the change process, which is also known as "quasi-static process." The "reversibility" of the process here involves a physical principle closely related to "S," called the "principle of entropy increase," also known as the "second law of thermodynamics": in an isolated system, the actual process always tends to increase the S of the whole system.

4.2.1.4 Helmholtz free energy (A)

Helmholtz function is an important thermodynamic parameter, also known as Helmholtz free energy (work), work function, commonly represented by A (see Eq. 4.4).

$$A = U - TS \qquad (4.4)$$

In thermodynamics, the Helmholtz free energy is a thermodynamic potential, the maximum "useful" work that can be obtained from a closed thermodynamic system at constant temperature and volume. For such a system, the negative value of the helmholtz energy difference(ΔA) is equal to the maximum work (W_{max}) output of a reversible process at constant temperature and volume.

4.2.1.5 Gibbs free energy (G)

Gibbs free energy (G), also known as Gibbs function, is an important parameter in thermodynamics, often represented by G, which is defined as (see Eq. 4.5):

$$G = H - TS(\text{or } G = U - TS + PV \text{ or } G = A + PV) \qquad (4.5)$$

where U is the internal energy of the system, T is temperature (absolute temperature, K), S is entropy, P is pressure, V is volume, and H is enthalpy. ΔG is negative for spontaneous processes, positive for nonspontaneous processes, and zero for processes in equilibrium, that is, sufficient free energy is required for reactants to change state. Gibbs free energy (G) is the ability of a system to do reversible work, or maximum work, at constant pressure and temperature.

4.2.1.6 The size-dependent Gibbs free energy (G)

The actual influencing factor of the change of Gibbs free energy (G) of metal nanomaterials is the increase of surface free energy. Under constant temperature and pressure in reversible conditions, the surface area of the system is increased by moving the atoms inside the metal material to the crystal surface. At the same time, the increased effective surface area (ΔA) by this process is proportional to the increase in Gibbs free energy (ΔG) of the system (see Eq. 4.6):

$$\Delta G^{nano} = G^{nano} - G^{bulk} = \gamma \cdot \Delta A \qquad (4.6)$$

where ΔG^{nano} is equal to the free energy of the nanomaterial (G^{nano}) minus the free energy of the bulk material (G^{bulk}), γ is the specific surface energy, and ΔA is the effective surface area change. In an ideal nanocrystal, all metal atoms (radius r_0) are located in the equilibrium lattice position. If the metal nanocrystal is a perfect spherical crystal (radius R), the ΔA and G^{nano} are as follows (see Eqs. 4.7 and 4.8):

$$\Delta A = 4\pi R^2 \qquad (4.7)$$

$$G^{nano} = \gamma \cdot 4\pi R^2 \qquad (4.8)$$

When all atoms are completely on the metal surface, the total surface free energy (G_O) of these atoms (with number of N) can be expressed as (see Eq. 4.9):

$$G_o = N \cdot 4\pi r_o^2 \cdot \gamma \tag{4.9}$$

To sum up, the ΔG^{nano} of metal nanomaterials can be expressed as (see Eq. 4.10):

$$\Delta G^{nano} = G_o - G^{nano} = \gamma \cdot 4\pi \cdot r^2 \cdot N \cdot \left(1 - \frac{r}{R} \cdot \frac{1}{\xi}\right) \tag{4.10}$$

The above equation is the relationship between Gibbs free energy of metal nanomaterial and nanometer size. For the change of Gibbs free energy at different temperatures, it can be further extended as (see Eq. 4.11):

$$\Delta G^{nano} = G_o - G^{nano} = \left(r_o + \frac{d\gamma}{dT}(T - T_{mo})\right) \cdot 4\pi \cdot r^2 \cdot N \cdot \left(1 - \frac{r}{R} \cdot \frac{1}{\xi}\right) \tag{4.11}$$

Since the enthalpy change (ΔH^{nano}) of metal nanomaterials is equal to the diffusion activation energy, and the entropy change (ΔS^{nano}) is also very small (close to zero), the following relationship can be obtained (see Eq. 4.12):

$$\Delta G^{nano} = \Delta H^{nano} - T\Delta S^{nano} = \Delta Q_r - T\Delta S^{nano} \tag{4.12}$$

If ΔS^{nano} is zero, the Gibbs free energy of metal nanomaterials is approximately equal to the ΔH^{nano} or diffusion activation energy. In other words, the size effect of the Gibbs free energy function can be verified by using the change of the diffusion activation energy. By parity of reasoning, other surface thermodynamic functions of nanomaterials can be measured by sophisticated calorimeters [12,13].

4.2.2 Standard thermodynamic functions for nanomaterials

When the size of matter enters the nanometer scale, the traditional thermodynamic theory faces severe challenges, and some thermodynamic quantities such as entropy, enthalpy, free energy, melting temperature, ordering temperature, Debye temperature, specific heat, and so on, change with the change of the dimension, size, and morphology of nanomaterials [14]. Using modern microcalorimetric technology with high precision and sensitivity to monitor the in-situ synthesis of nano-materials online, people can obtain the characteristic parameters of non-equilibrium growth of nanomaterials, and correlate the growth process of nanomaterials with the size, morphology, and structure of nano materials, which is conducive to the study of the growth mechanism of nano-crystals and provides theoretical guidance for the controlled synthesis of nanomaterials [15]. The standard thermodynamic functions of nanomaterials are the key intrinsic properties of nanomaterials, determining the efficiency of the nano-reaction system. Taking the block materials as the reference standard, according to the thermos kinetic equation and the transition state theory of chemical dynamics, scientists have successfully obtained the standard molar entropy, standard molar formation enthalpy, and standard molar formation Gibbs free energy of nanomaterials [16–18]. Huang et al. innovatively designed three schemes, integrating the chemical thermodynamic potential function method, the electrochemical principle of reversible batteries, the transition state theory of chemical kinetics, and the modern thermodynamic principle and reported the accurate determination of standard molar entropy, standard molar formation enthalpy, and standard molar formation Gibbs free energy of nanomaterials. Three bottleneck problems in the determination of standard molar thermodynamic functions of nanomaterials are solved [19,20]. These thermodynamic properties of nanomaterials (entropy, enthalpy, and Gibbs free energy) determine the applications of nanomaterials in catalysis, energy storage, sensing, and adsorption.

4.2.3 Dissolution thermodynamics of nanomaterials

The physical and chemical stability of nanomaterials is critical in energy and environmental applications. The solubility of nanomaterials in aqueous/nonaqueous solution determines their service life, and the study of the dissolution thermodynamics of nanomaterials is helpful to explore the stability mechanism. At present, many studies have shown that the dissolution thermodynamic properties of nanomaterials are related to the properties of the materials themselves (crystal structure, nano scale, etc.) and are also related to the properties of the solution (concentration, components, etc.). Recently, Nakamura et al. have confirmed that, by embedding Mn into the lattice of Co_3O_4 spinel, the dissolution thermodynamics of Co_2MnO_4 is inhibited, which can extend the lifetime of the catalyst from several hours to hundreds or even thousands of hours in acidic system, while maintaining the activity of the catalyst [21]. Using Ag_3PO_4 microcrystals with different crystal planes as models, Huang et al. studied the crystal plane effect of the thermodynamic function of dissolution of nanomaterials [22]. The results show that the standard molar dissolution Gibbs free energy, standard molar dissolution enthalpy and standard molar dissolution entropy of rhombic dodecahedron Ag_3PO_4 with {110} crystal faces are the highest, the cube Ag_3PO_4 with {100} crystal faces is the second and the tetrahedron Ag_3PO_4 with {111} crystal faces is the smallest. In battery applications, the high concentration of solvent-in-salt and water-in-salt electrolyte can not only broaden the electrochemical window, but also greatly reduce the thermodynamically controlled dissolution of electrode materials (such as transition metal manganese oxide and sulfur electrode) and provide outstanding electrode cycle stability [23].

Sodium–ion battery (SIB) is considered to be the most promising battery technology in the postlithium era due to the abundance of sodium. For sodium-ion battery, the dissolution process of sodium salts is very important which can be divided into two separate processes, including lattice dissociation (splitting) determined by lattice energy (U) and physical dissolution with solvent determined by dissolution energy (ΔH_h). The simplified Born-Haber cycle of dissolution process is shown in Fig. 4.2, where

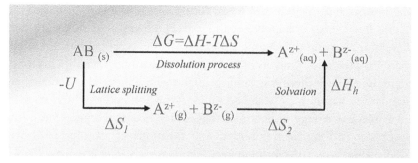

Figure 4.2 Energy parameters for dissolution of salts: Lattice energy (U) and dissolution energy (ΔH_h) [24].

$\Delta H = -U + \Delta H_h$, $\Delta S = \Delta S_1 + \Delta S_2$ [24]. According to this cycle, a smaller Gibbs free energy (ΔG) represents that the dissolution process is easier to proceed. Higher lattice energy will decrease the solubility of salt, and higher solubility energy will increase it. Due to the univalent nature of Na^+ ions, the valence or oxidation state of cations/anions is not important. Therefore, emphasis is placed on the solubility of salts.

Two thermodynamic variables can also be used to describe the dissolution behavior of sodium salts: binding energy (ΔE_b) and dissolution-free energy (ΔG_{sol}) [24]. The ΔE_b reflects the strength of interaction between cations and solvent molecules, which can be calculated from the difference in energy between the solvated complex and the components that make up the complex (solvent molecules and Na^+ ions) (see Eq. 4.13). The ΔG_{sol} refers to the part of a thermodynamic process in which the reduced internal energy can be converted into external work. When $\Delta G_{sol} < 0$, solvation is more likely to occur. For the solvation process, ΔG_{sol} can be calculated as follows (see Eq. 4.13).

$$\Delta E_b = E_{(complex)} - \left(n^* E_{(SM)} + E_{(Na+ion)}\right) \tag{4.13}$$

$$\Delta G_{(sol)} = \Delta G_{(complex)} - \left(n^* G_{(SM)} + E_{(Na+ion)}\right) \tag{4.14}$$

4.2.4 Nucleation thermodynamics of nanomaterials

In general, the bottom-up synthesis of nanomaterials must go through the nucleation stage. Nucleation is divided into homogeneous nucleation and heterogeneous nucleation [25]. For homogeneous nucleation, the essential point is supersaturation: solid precipitation and nucleation occur only when the monomers (atoms and molecules) of nanocrystals reach supersaturation concentration in solution. The change of Gibbs free energy (ΔG_{homo}) of nanocrystals during homogeneous nucleation is composed of two opposite parts, namely, the change of bulk free energy (decrease) and the change of surface free energy (increase). It is assumed that the crystal nucleus has smooth and continuous surface and the value of surface energy is $\gamma_{\alpha m}$ (see Fig. 4.3A) [26]. Thus, the ΔG_{homo} during nucleation can be calculated by Eq. (4.15). Where, r is the nucleus radius, ΔG_v is the change of free energy corresponding to the change of unit volume of crystal nucleus. $\gamma_{\alpha m}$ is the change of free energy corresponding to unit surface area of crystal nucleus. ΔG_v is determined by supersaturation S, molar volume of crystal nucleus v, and system temperature T, as shown in Eq. (4.16).

$$\Delta G_{homo} = \frac{4}{3}\pi r^3 \Delta G_V + 4\pi r^2 \gamma_{\alpha m} \tag{4.15}$$

$$\Delta G_V = \frac{-K_B T \ln(S)}{v} \tag{4.16}$$

On the other hand, the heterogeneous nucleation allows us to circumvent the uncertainty of homogeneous nucleation and achieve controlled growth of nanomaterials in a two-step process [25]. Heterogeneous nucleation can add monomers (precursors) to preformed nanocrystals (so-called the seed crystals) at their concentrations less than supersaturated one. In this process, the monomer directly transforms on the seed surface to obtain a new nanocrystalline phase [27]. Modeling this process requires two additional surface energy contributions: basal-dielectric surface energy ($\gamma_{\beta m}$) and core-substrate surface

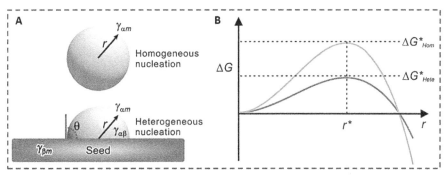

Figure 4.3 Homogeneous nucleation and heterogeneous nucleation: (A) Schematic diagram, (B) ΔG variation with nucleus radius r [26].

energy ($\gamma_{\alpha\beta}$) (see Fig. 4.3A) [26]. According to Young's equation, the contact Angle between crystal nucleus and substrate in equilibrium state is shown as Eq. (4.17). We can further calculate the energy barrier for heterogeneous nucleation, as shown in Eq. (4.18). Based on this, the energy barrier for heterogeneous nucleation is smaller than that for homogeneous nucleation [25]. In particular, when the nucleus morphology is hemispheric and $\theta = 90$, the energy barrier for heterogeneous nucleation is just half of the barrier for homogeneous nucleation (see Fig. 4.3B) [26].

$$\cos\theta = \left(\frac{\gamma_{\beta m} - \gamma_{\alpha\beta}}{\gamma_{\alpha m}}\right) \tag{4.17}$$

$$\Delta G^*_{\text{hetero}} = \left(\frac{2 - 3\cos\theta + \cos^3\theta}{4}\right)\Delta G^*_{\text{homo}} \tag{4.18}$$

4.2.5 Phase-transition thermodynamics of nanomaterials

Due to the large surface/volume ratio of nanomaterials, the surface and interface properties obviously affect the overall properties and surface state of nanomaterials. In order to manufacture nano devices with definite physical, chemical, and mechanical properties, it is necessary to determine the phase-transition thermodynamic parameters such as melting temperature, melting entropy, interfacial energy, interfacial stress, and their dependence on the material size [27]. Jiang et al. confirmed that the determination of melt thermodynamic quantity mentioned above not only proposed a new dimension variable in the aspect of thermodynamics theory, but also provided potential application prospects for nanomaterials in various industrial fields. The size-dependence models of melting temperature and melting entropy of nanoparticles, nanowire, and nanofilm crystals without free parameters were established. Their universal thermodynamic model without free parameters provides a convenient thermodynamic tool for understanding the thermal stability and surface state of nanomaterials [28–30].

In addition to the conventional phase transition (solid–liquid–gas two-phase transition), the crystalline transition (amorphous and ordered phases) thermodynamics of nanomaterials is also a hot topic recently, such as the thermodynamic stability of atomic-arrangement engineering and plane-stacking engineering [31]. In principle, the stability of a nanoparticle is determined by its thermodynamic state, and the size, shape, composition, crystal structure, and external environment are important factors affecting the thermodynamic state. The most stable structural state has the lowest Gibbs free energy (G), which in turn depends on enthalpy (H), entropy (S), and temperature (T), ($G = H - TS$). Therefore, in atomic-arrangement engineering, the difference of Gibbs free energy between the disordered phase and the ordered phase ($\Delta G_{d \to o}$) can be determined by the formula ($\Delta G_{d \to o} = \Delta H_{d \to o} - T\Delta S_{d \to o}$). Where the d and o represent the disordered phase and the ordered phase, respectively. Free energy diagram can be used to determine thermodynamically stable states from metastable phase of nanoparticles. The metal species and composition of binary alloys play an important role in the order-disorder transition [31]. In atomic arrangement engineering, we mainly focus on binary systems where entropy plays an important role. In plane-stacking engineering, however, entropy is not so important, single metal environment and stress thermodynamics are the main research object. For phase transition, the stress thermodynamics can also be adjusted by external pressure. So, the preparation of a new crystalline phase is achieved by precisely adjusting the pressure during wet chemical synthesis [31].

4.2.6 Reaction thermodynamics of nanomaterials

In chemical reactions, the surface energy of solid reactants also participates in chemical reactions, so the particle size of nanomaterials in the reaction system will definitely affect the thermodynamic properties of chemical reactions. In the previous section (4.2.2), we have emphasized the importance of the standard thermodynamic functions of nanomaterials in surface reactivity. Compared with the bulk materials, the particle size of the nanomaterials with small particle size has a significant effect on the standard thermodynamic functions of the multi-phase reaction. With the decrease of the particle size, $\Delta_r H^\theta_m$, $\Delta_r S^\theta_m$ and $\Delta_r G^\theta_m$ decrease, while K^θ increases. It can be seen that the thermodynamic properties of nanomaterials are different from those of bulk materials in all aspects, so it is of great scientific significance and application value to study the thermodynamic properties of nanomaterials [32].

Compared with conventional chemical reaction methods, the cation exchange method is an effective method to prepare nanomaterials with stable structure and controllable morphology [33]. Cation exchange reactions based on templates provided by specific nanomaterials (such as metal sulfides and oxides) can result in targeted nanocrystalline products with controllable morphology and composition. In this case, the target nanocrystalline preserves the size and shape of the parent material. The total cation exchange reaction can be expressed as (see Eq. 4.19):

$$M^{n+} + CA \Leftrightarrow MA + C^{n+} \tag{4.19}$$

where M is the substituted metal cation, C and A are the cation and anion in the parent material, respectively. The total cation exchange reaction can be divided into four basic reactions (see Eqs. 4.20—4.23):

$$CA \Leftrightarrow C^0 + A^0 - \left(\Delta G^0_f\right)_{CA} \tag{4.20}$$

$$A^0 \Leftrightarrow A^{n+} + ne^- - \left(E^0\right)_{A^{n+}} \tag{4.21}$$

$$M^0 + A^0 \Leftrightarrow MA \left(\Delta G^0_f\right)_{MA} \tag{4.22}$$

$$M^{n+} + ne^- \Leftrightarrow M^0 \left(E^0 \right)_{M^{n+}} \tag{4.23}$$

The thermodynamic regulation of cation exchange is the primary task of this method. In the above formula, ΔG_f^0 is the standard free energy of the formation of metal cation, and E^0 is the standard reduction potential of metal cation. The thermodynamic driving force for calculating the total cation exchange reaction is (see Eq. 4.24):

$$\Delta G_{reaction} = \left(\Delta G_f^0 \right)_{MA} - \left(\Delta G_f^0 \right)_{CA} - nF\left[\left(E^0 \right)_{M^{n+}} - \left(E^0 \right)_{A^{n+}} \right] \tag{4.24}$$

Here, F is Faraday's constant. By calculating the driving force of the total reaction, the possibility of cation exchange reaction can be predicted. However, in actual reactions, cation exchange reactions may behave quite differently from thermodynamic predictions. This is because kinetic factors (such as activation energy) determine the feasibility of the reaction under practical conditions [33].

4.2.7 Adsorption thermodynamics of nanomaterials

Adsorption equilibrium is one of the most important physicochemical aspects in evaluating the adsorption process of nano-porous materials, and its equilibrium constant is very important to determine the thermodynamic parameters of adsorption. Gibbs free energy change (ΔG), enthalpy change (ΔH), and entropy change (ΔS) are three important thermodynamic parameters usually studied in adsorption process. The negative or positive sign of ΔG indicates spontaneous or other modes of adsorption process. ΔH is positive for endothermic adsorption process, negative for exothermic process, and its value indicates the mechanism involved: physical adsorption is less than 20 kJ/mol^{-1}, and chemical adsorption is between 80 and 400 kJ/mol^{-1}. Positive ΔS indicates an increase in adsorbent affinity that may accompany some structural modifications, which also implies an increase in the degree of freedom of adsorbent molecules [34].

The electro-adsorption process of nano-porous materials can realize fast electron transfer by exchanging electrons through electric double layers (EDLs), which can be used for high-power energy storage. Under thermodynamic conditions, the charging process of EDLs will follow the principle of minimum free energy increase (ΔG_{min}). The adsorption of different ions is energy unfavorable because the ions entering the pores of nanomaterials will reduce the entropy of the system ($\Delta S < 0$). When ions of the same charge accumulate in the carbon channel, the enthalpy change (ΔH) is also unfavorable. The process of energy storage is dominated by ion exchange mechanism. The total ion concentration in the channel remains constant, reducing the enthalpy change (ΔH) and entropy change (ΔS) caused by dense ion accumulation, which is favorable in terms of energy. The same ion desorption reduces the enthalpy change (ΔH) due to the charge interaction. It also increases the entropy change (ΔS), so it increases the capacitance [35].

For the electrocatalytic application of nanomaterials, the adsorption mechanism of reaction molecules or intermediates at the catalyst site is the focus of current research.

Hydrogen evolution reaction (HER) is one of the two half-reactions of electrolytic decomposing water. An important parameter to be considered in this reaction is the adsorption-free energy of hydrogen (ΔG_{H*}) (see Eq. 4.25):

$$\Delta G_{H*} = \Delta E_H + \Delta E_{ZPE} + T\Delta S_H \qquad (4.25)$$

where ΔE_H represents the calculated hydrogen adsorption energy, ΔE_{zpe} is the difference of zero energy between adsorbed state and gaseous state, ΔS_H represents the adsorption entropy of $1/2$ H_2. For her reaction catalyst, the adsorption of adsorbed hydrogen atoms on the catalyst surface cannot be too strong or too weak [36]. For other multielectron and multistep catalytic reactions, such as oxygen evolution reaction (OER) and oxygen reduction reaction (ORR), the adsorption process of intermediates on the catalytic surface is more complex. Often, we can clarify the adsorption-free energy (ΔG) relationship between each step through theoretical calculation, and then determine the adsorption mechanism and catalytic mechanism [37].

4.3 Kinetics of nanomaterials

Designing and synthesizing nanomaterials with customized properties is a complex task. In the synthesis of nanomaterials, reactions often produce nonequilibrium kinetic by-products, rather than thermodynamic equilibrium phases. Hance, understanding the competitive relationship between thermodynamics and kinetics is the basic step to realize the directional synthesis of target materials, which is of great significance. In the catalytic reaction of nano materials, kinetics is a more important research direction, and the diameter determines the reaction rate and effect.

4.3.1 Basic equations of kinetics

4.3.1.1 Kinetic equation of first-order reaction

The formula of the first-order reaction rate equation is $v = -dc_A/dt = k_Ac$ (c_A is the concentration of reactant A, k_A is the rate constant of the reaction, t is the reaction time). First-order reaction refers to the reaction whose reaction speed is only proportional to the first power of reactant concentration. First-order reactions exist widely in nature: the transformation of most radioactive atoms and molecular rearrangement. There are also some hydrolysis reactions, such as the hydrolysis of sucrose. The definite integral form of the first-order reaction rate equation is as follows (see Eq. 4.26):

$$1n\frac{c_{A,0}}{c_A} = k_At \qquad (4.26)$$

After deformation, the above formula can express the following linear equation (see Eq. 4.27), that is, the graph of $\ln\{c_A\} \sim \{t\}$ is a straight line, and k_A can be obtained from the slope of the straight line (the slope $= -k_A$).

$$\ln\{c_A\} = -k_At + \ln\{c_{A,0}\} \qquad (4.27)$$

Learn to master the mechanism of the first-order reaction, promote industrial production or catalytic reaction, and find the best reaction time and way. For most experiments of photocatalytic degradation of organic compounds, it can be treated as first-order or pseudo-first-order reaction. Put the sample into a constant temperature water bath at different temperatures, take samples regularly to measure its concentration and calculate the concentration change at different times at different temperatures. Plot the time with concentration or other functions of concentration to judge the reaction order. If ln C plots a straight line against t, it is a first-order reaction. From the slope of the straight line, the rate constant k at each temperature can be calculated, and the activation energy of the reaction can be further calculated.

4.3.1.2 Kinetic equation of second-order reaction

The formula of the first-order reaction rate equation is $v = -dc_A/dt = k_A c^2$ (c_A is the concentration of reactant A, k_A is the rate constant of the reaction, t is the reaction time).

First-order reaction refers to the reaction whose reaction speed is only proportional to the second power of reactant concentration. The definite integral form of the second-order reaction rate equation is as follows (see Eq. 4.28):

$$\frac{1}{c_A} - \frac{1}{c_{A,0}} = k_A t \tag{4.28}$$

After deformation, the above formula can express the following linear equation (see Eq. 4.29), that is, the graph of $\ln\{1/c_A\} \sim \{t\}$ is a straight line, and k_A can be obtained from the slope of the straight line (the slope $= k_A$).

$$\frac{1}{c_A} = k_A t + \frac{1}{c_{A,0}} \tag{4.29}$$

4.3.1.3 Arrhenius equation

Arrhenius equation is an empirical formula of the relationship between chemical reaction rate constant and temperature founded by Arrhenius in Sweden. In 1889, when studying the effect of acidity on the conversion rate of sucrose at different temperatures, Arrhenius proposed an empirical formula of two parameter rate constant (see Eq. 4.30):

$$k = A e^{\frac{-E_a}{RT}} \tag{4.30}$$

where R is the gas constant, T is the thermodynamic temperature, and A and E_a are the empirical constants obtained in the experiment, which are called preexponential factor and apparent activation energy, respectively.

The differential form of Arrhenius equation is as follows (see Eq. 4.31):

$$\frac{d\ln k}{dT} = \frac{E_a}{RT^2} \tag{4.31}$$

The indefinite integral form of Arrhenius equation is as follows (see Eq. 4.32):

$$\ln k = \frac{-E_a}{RT} + \ln A \qquad (4.32)$$

The definite integral form of Arrhenius equation is as follows (see Eq. 4.33):

$$ln\frac{k_2}{k_1} = \frac{-E_a}{R}\left(\frac{1}{T_2} - \frac{1}{T_1}\right) \qquad (4.33)$$

Arrhenius equation is based on the assumption that E_a is constant. E_a can be determined by measuring the rate constants at different reaction temperatures. The equation is applicable to elementary reactions, nonelementary reactions, and even some heterogeneous reactions (such as photocatalytic degradation reaction).

4.3.2 Growth kinetics of nanomaterials

In the past, thermodynamics and dynamics were often regarded as independent concepts in the Growth of nanomaterials. The latest research results show that they are closely coupled in the early stage of material formation. The fast reaction kinetics in the multistage crystallization process is the result of a large thermodynamic driving force, while a small driving force will lead to slow kinetics. At this time, the completion of the reaction requires a higher reaction temperature. The authors [38] believe that the high reaction energy obtained from the precursor controls the composition and structure of the first formed phase by thermodynamics, and the subsequent transformation can usually be dynamically selected through simple composition changes or topological variable layer shifts. Through a better understanding of the complex relationship between thermodynamics and dynamics in the formation of materials, the conclusion of this paper provides convenience for the design of more complex strategies to achieve the target synthesis of inorganic nanomaterials [38].

Crystallization is a key step in the manufacture of various types of nanomaterials. However, the dynamics of this first-order phase transition are often complex, and there is still a lack of theory at the basic level. The embryo develops from the liquid phase through the nucleation process. Small nuclei grow only when they exceed the critical size, which corresponds to the free energy barrier. The formation of critical nuclei in the initial stage is crucial, but it is difficult to measure because of the extremely small space and time scales. Recently, Professor Yilong Han of Hong Kong University of science and technology commented on the article "Kinetic pathways of crystalization at the nanoscale" recently published in nature materials (see Fig. 4.4 for details) [39]. The authors combined the particle tracking of low-dose liquid phase transmission electron microscopy (TEM) with Monte Carlo simulation to obtain a high spatial-temporal resolution description of colloidal crystallization [40]. The authors also found that the crystallization of colloidal nanoparticles followed a two-step nucleation kinetic pathway (including

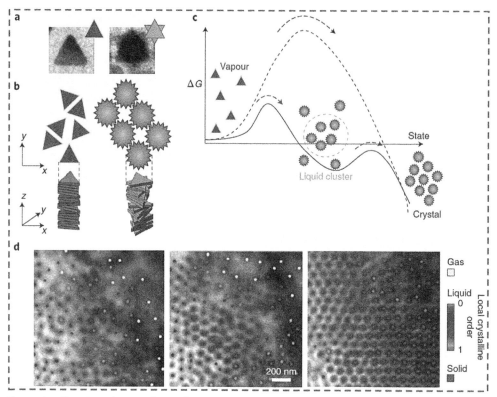

Figure 4.4 Kinetic pathways of crystalization at the nanoscale: (A) TEM images of a single and a double misaligned particle imaged from the top, (B) schematic diagram of nano stacking, (C) the sum of the free-energy, (D) TEM images showing the crystallization process [39,40].

dense and amorphous intermediates in nanoscale). Due to the van der Waals force, the nanosheets are stacked in columns along the z direction (Fig. 4.4A and B). Each column can be considered as "nanoparticles" spreading on the xy plane, and the author uses particle algorithm to track these particles. Research shows that the "particles" (gas phase) with good initial dispersion will condense into metastable liquid clusters with long life and then nucleate into nanocrystals (Fig. 4.4C) [39].

Because the interface energy is dominant when the atomic nucleus is small, the liquid—gas interface energy is lower than the crystal gas interface energy, making the initial atomic nucleus tend to be liquid. Other types of two-step pathways were observed in colloidal microspheres, that is, liquid from higher-density liquid clusters to crystals, and liquid from ordered low-density clusters to crystals. In fact, it is not always possible to directly transform the system into an ideal final state, especially when the energy barrier between the two states is very high. In these cases, the indirect route through the intermediate metastable state (separated by multiple lower barriers) may be the most advantageous option (see Fig. 4.4D for details) [39,40].

Controlling the shape and size of metal nanoparticles is very important for achieving excellent electronic, optical, and catalytic properties. The nucleation of nanocrystals is the first step in the growth process of materials. The reduction kinetics of the nucleation process is closely related to the morphology of the final nanoparticles. Professor Pan and Wu reported a study on the characterization of platinum precursors at the atomic scale and the formation kinetics of platinum nanoparticles from K_2PtCl_4 precursors [41]. The reaction kinetics of different stages including decomposition, reduction, and nucleation were captured and revealed in situ by double spherical aberration-corrected TEM. Through in situ experiments, three stages of the nucleation process were captured: decomposition into K^+ and $[PtCl_4]^{2-}$, conversion from $[PtCl_4]^{2-}$ to $PtCl_2$, and reduction of divalent Pt^{2+} to Pt. These processes followed the order of chemical energy and bond energy. This study clearly reveals the dynamic process and reaction kinetics of platinum from its precursor to nanocrystals at the atomic scale. This work provides a deeper understanding of how to regulate the path of solid-state reaction, so as to realize the control of the size and shape of nanomaterials and promote the application of nanomaterials in energy and environmental fields [41].

4.3.3 Catalytic reaction kinetics of nanomaterials

Heterogeneous catalysis is not only the central discipline in the current chemical and energy industry but also will play a vital role in the future development of these industries. The key scientific problem of heterogeneous catalysis is the mechanism of interfacial reaction and the structure-activity relationship of catalyst. The structure-activity relationship and the structure of active sites of catalyst can be clarified through kinetic research. For example, Xu et al. determined the reaction order of CO catalytic oxidation through kinetic research and measured the adsorption isotherm of CO on the catalyst surface in situ, so as to obtain the reaction order of adsorbed CO [42]. Our research group is committed to the study of kinetic parameters (first-order reaction kinetic constants) of photocatalytic degradation of organic compounds in a variety of nano catalyst systems (such as graphite phase carbon nitride [43], bismuth phosphate [44], silver vanadate [45], bismuth tungstate [46], bismuth oxycarbonate [47], etc.). The first-order reaction kinetics measurement method of photocatalytic reaction is often based on the absorbance method and the standard curve to determine the relationship between the concentration of reactants at different times and further calculate the kinetic constant (see 4.3.1.1 "Kinetic equation of first order reaction" for details).

The measurement of catalytic reaction apparent activation energy (E_a) is also an important part of kinetic research, whether in photocatalysis, electrocatalysis, or thermal catalysis. The energy required for a molecule to change from a normal state to an active state prone to chemical reactions is called molecule activation energy. The activation energy in Arrhenius formula derived from dynamics is also called Arrhenius activation energy or empirical activation energy. In a kinetic-limited chemical reaction, the activation energy E_a is the difference between the average molar energy of activation collisions and the average molar energy of all collisions. The energy barrier E is the difference between the zero energy of the activated complex and the reactant. According to Arrhenius indefinite integral equation, draw 1/T with Ln k, and calculate A and E_a according to slope and intercept (see 4.3.1.3 "Arrhenius equation" for details).

For example, through apparent activation energy E_a by Arrhenius equation, Qian et al. investigated intrinsic activity of the interface site in Co@CoO catalyst. The results showed that Co@CoO there is a negative linear correlation between TOF (turnover frequency) and E_a. In addition, the two catalytic descriptors (E_a and hydrogen production rate k) are also linearly correlated with the material descriptors (oxygen vacancy (O_V) concentration and lattice strain), which proves that the lattice strain induced by O_V plays a key role in the catalytic hydrogen production of formaldehyde at the Co@CoO interface site [48]. Yu and co-worker also investigated that adding tungsten carbide to platinum carbon catalyst can effectively reduce the activation energy and accelerate the kinetic process of electrocatalytic methanol oxidation [49]. Li and his colleagues have been exploring the mechanism and differences of various metal catalysts (Pt, Pd, Ru, Ni) in reducing the activation energy of different electrocatalytic reactions (oxygen reduction, alcohol oxidation, and water decomposition) [50−55].

In addition, the microdynamics is a powerful tool to deal with surface catalytic reactions, which is of great significance for improving the level of surface computational catalysis and in-depth analysis of the catalytic process. At the same time, it is also a bridge between theoretical calculation and experiment [36,37]. The reaction rate under actual conditions can be obtained by calculating the free energy change and free energy barrier of each elementary reaction through microdynamics. In fact, all the basic principles of microdynamics are introduced in detail in "Physical Chemistry" textbook (refer to the chapter on statistical thermodynamics in physical chemistry by Fu Xiancai [1]). For example, based on the reaction rate constant, the microkinetic model can be used to carry out theoretical research on electrocatalytic CO_2 reduction reaction. By comparing the kinetic behavior of corr on the surface of different Cu single crystals, it is proved that the first step of CO proton-coupled electron transfer reaction to generate CHO* or COH* is the decisive step of the whole reaction [34]. By jointly exploring the electronic effects of metal nano catalysts, a reaction kinetic model containing mechanism information such as surface adsorption, activation energy, and key reaction steps can be established, which can be used to guide the design of catalysts, as a "bridge" between the electronic structure and macro catalytic behavior [56].

4.3.4 Energy storage kinetics of nanomaterials

For electrochemical energy storage (such as supercapacitors and lithium-ion batteries), kinetic studies mainly focus on ion diffusion kinetics and redox reaction kinetics. The main electrochemical methods include cyclic voltammetry (investigating the reaction kinetic parameters at different scanning rates) and electrochemical impedance (investigating ion diffusion kinetics at different potential) [57,58]. Our research group has long been committed to the research on the rate performance and energy storage dynamics of supercapacitors and lithium-ion batteries, involving nano-materials including three-dimensional graphene [59—63], high specific surface area activated carbon [64—66], manganese dioxide [67,68], tin oxide [69,70], nickel sulfide, etc [71]. In short, the porous structure, nanostructure, and composition of electrode materials collectively determine the electrochemical energy storage dynamics and rate performance of these nanomaterials. For multi-electron reaction high energy density batteries, the feasible ways of kinetic optimization mainly include composite material construction, electrode structure design, electrode morphology regulation, electrolyte optimization, storage mechanism improvement, etc [72].

It is worth mentioning that the molecular dynamics simulation based on classical Newtonian mechanics is considered to be one of the most beneficial tools to explore the energy storage behavior of supercapacitors. With the help of classical potential function, molecular dynamics simulation can reveal the micromechanism and dynamic process of energy storage at the atomic level, such as the law of ion adsorption and desorption in nanopores and the transmission mechanism driven by field, providing theoretical guidance for the optimal design of supercapacitors. The research group of Professor Zheng Bo of Zhejiang University systematically discussed the progress of molecular dynamics simulation from traditional porous carbon to new nanomaterials, focusing on the internal relationship between energy storage performance and pore size distribution, geometric morphology, and surface modification of electrode materials [73]. In addition, Chen and Zhang discussed that the molecular dynamics simulation method also has potential advantages in exploring the physical and chemical properties such as electrolyte structure, ionic conductivity, and interface reaction mechanism for rechargeable batteries and is playing an increasingly important role in electrolyte research [74].

4.3.5 Adsorption reaction kinetics of nanomaterials

Here, the adsorption reaction kinetics of nano materials includes three levels: the physicochemical adsorption kinetics of nano-porous materials on metal ideal or organic molecules, the adsorption and dissociation kinetics of molecules in heterogeneous catalysis, and the ion adsorption kinetics of electrochemical energy storage system. For porous material adsorption, the nano pore geometry of adsorbent can change the mass transfer mechanism in particles and the efficiency of guest molecules, thus affecting the adsorption rate. Clarifying the role and contribution of nano-pore geometry in adsorption kinetics can guide the optimization of porous material structure and further improve the adsorption efficiency in practical applications. The interconnection of macropores and mesopores is conducive to the rapid transfer of molecules and the accessibility of adsorption sites. Micropores connected with mesopores not only provide adsorption sites but also promote the concentration distribution of guest molecules in the pores of porous materials [75]. Previously, our research group confirmed that the surface modification of porous materials (including oxygen functional groups [76] and molecular grafting [77]) can greatly improve the adsorption kinetics and change the adsorption mechanism. For example, the dynamic adsorption processes of coconut-based activated carbon fibers to methylene blue, Congo red, and neutral red were all in accordance with the second-order kinetic model [76]. The modified sugarcane bagasse (MSB) with acrylonitrile (AN) also showed the pseudo-second-order model and chemical adsorption as the rate-controlling step. The calculated activation energy (E_a) was 254.5 kJ/mol^{-1}, which indicates that the adsorption of Cd (II) onto MSB was under chemical control [77].

The kinetic study of molecular dissociation and adsorption on metal surface plays an important role in industrial processes such as heterogeneous catalysis. In the past 20 years, scientists have made great efforts to develop reliable theories to accurately describe the dissociation and adsorption kinetics of molecules on solid surfaces. Due to the possible quantum effects in the reaction, such as quantum tunneling, zero-point energy, reaction resonance, etc., the study of quantum dynamics is the most reliable, especially the full dimensional quantum dynamics calculation based on the reaction of polyatomic molecules on the metal surface is commendable. The research method of full-dimensional quantum dynamics can be widely used in the study of the dissociation and adsorption dynamics of polyatomic molecules on metal surfaces, which provides an important theoretical method for accurately simulating polyatomic molecule surface reactions. Recently, Zhang's research team successfully calculated the dissociation and adsorption probability of H_2O on the Cu (111) surface at the full dimensional (9-dimensional) level on its fitted full domain potential energy surface, thus realizing the full dimensional quantum dynamics study of the reaction of a three-atom molecule on the metal surface for the first time, which was praised by the reviewer as "an important milestone in understanding the surface reaction dynamics" [78].

The large radius of potassium ion causes the extremely slow ion storage dynamics of the positive pole, which further aggravates the dynamic mismatch between the positive and negative poles and the poor stability of the potassium ion hybrid capacitor. Wang et al. realized a potassium ion hybrid capacitor with excellent cycle stability by synchronously regulating the adsorption kinetics of cation and anion in carbon materials, and explored the dynamic mechanism of energy storage of this carbon material through the combination of theory and experiment [79]. With the help of first-principle calculation and other analysis methods, Ma et al. proved that the promotion of active nitrogen functional groups on potassium ion batteries is not only reflected in the enhanced adsorption reaction activity (enhanced partial space ion adsorption) but also in that it greatly improves the diffusion kinetics of potassium ions in carbon materials and realizes the efficient storage of potassium ions [80].

4.4 Phase equilibrium of nanomaterials

The part with completely uniform physical and chemical properties inside the system is called the phase. There is an obvious interface between phases under specified conditions, and the change of macroscopic properties on the interface is a leap. The total number of phases in the system is called the phase number, which is expressed by Φ. The judgment criteria of phase number are as follows: (1) no matter how many kinds of gases are mixed, there is only one gas phase. (2) Liquids can form one phase, two phases, or three phases according to their mutual solubility. (3) Generally, a solid has a phase. No matter how evenly mixed the two solid powders are, they are still two phases (except the solid solution). (4) Solid solution: in solid alloys, alloys containing other elements in the lattice structure of one element are called solid solutions [1].

4.4.1 Definition of phase equilibrium

Phase equilibrium refers to the limit state of each phase change in a multiphase system. At this time, no matter is transferred between phases macroscopically, but substances with opposite directions are still transferred between phases microscopically, and the speed is equal, so the net speed of transfer is zero. Phase equilibrium is one of the important applications of thermodynamics in the field of physical chemistry. The thermodynamic condition of phase equilibrium is that the temperature and pressure of each phase are equal, and the chemical potential of any component in each phase is equal. Therefore, phase equilibrium is characterized by a physical and chemical equilibrium between phases at the same time. The equilibrium of two-phase system in the thermodynamics of nanomaterials includes gas-liquid equilibrium, gas-solid equilibrium, liquid-liquid equilibrium, liquid-solid equilibrium, and solid-solid equilibrium. Systems with more than two phases include gas-liquid-solid equilibrium, gas-liquid-liquid equilibrium, gas-solid-solid equilibrium, etc.

4.4.2 Gibbs phase rule

Phase rule is the law of interdependence and change between the number of phases (Φ), component number (C) and temperature (T), pressure (P), composition, and other factors in a multiphase system. It is a basic law generally observed by thermodynamic equilibrium system. The mathematical expression of the phase rule is as follows (see Eq. 4.34):

$$F = C - \Phi + 2 \tag{4.34}$$

where F is the degree of freedom, 2 usually refers to two variables, T and P [1]. If the electric field, magnetic field, or gravity field has an effect on the equilibrium state, the two in the phase ratio should be 3, 4 and 5. If the system studied is a solid substance, the influence of pressure can be ignored, and 2 in the phase law should be 1.

4.4.3 Lever rule in two-phase equilibrium

The lever rule is widely used in phase equilibrium, which can be briefly described as the quantity of one phase multiplied by the length of the line segment on this side is equal to the quantity of the other phase multiplied by the length of the line segment on the other side. In the phase diagram of a multicomponent system, the system point falls in the two-phase coexistence area of the temperature-composition diagram (or pressure-composition diagram), and the system is in two-phase equilibrium. The intersection of the horizontal line of the system point and the two-phase lines is two-phase points, and the connection line of the two-phase points is called the connection line. The system point divides the connection line into two segments, and the length of the segment and the quantity of each phase can prove the lever rule [1].

4.4.4 Phase diagram for the synthesis of nanomaterials

Phase diagram, also known as phase equilibrium diagram, is a diagram used to show the relationship between the composition of phase equilibrium system and some parameters (such as temperature and pressure) [1]. The phase diagram is a collective expression of the trajectories of thermodynamic variables and intensity variables after the equilibrium between the phases in the system under given conditions. It plays an important role in physical chemistry, mineralogy, and material science. For a multiphase system, the intertransformation of phases, the formation of new phases, and the disappearance of old phases are related to temperature, pressure, and composition. From the phase diagram, one can intuitively see the various states of aggregation and their conditions (temperature, pressure, composition) in the multiphase system. Based on this, some phase diagrams in textbooks (such as the two-component solid-liquid equilibrium phase diagram [1]) can be used to guide the controlled synthesis of various nanomaterials (including gas-phase, liquid-phase, or solid-phase synthesis of 2D nanosheets, 1D nanowires, 1D nanotubes, or 0D nanoparticles) (Fig. 4.5 for details) [81–84].

The construction of one-dimensional (1D) nanostructures is mainly based on gas-liquid-solid (VLS) [81] and liquid-solid-solution (SLS) [82] growth mechanisms, which can all be analyzed by phase diagrams and related phase equilibrium rules. The VLS growth mechanism was proposed by Wagner et al. in the 1960s to analyze the growth process of silicon whisker by chemical vapor deposition (CVD) method [85]. In 2001, Yang Peidong's group observed the generation process of 1D Ge nanowires in situ for the first time by using TEM, providing direct and effective evidence for VLS growth

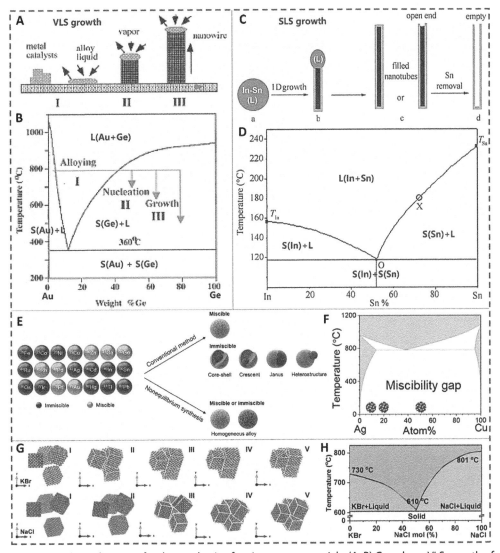

Figure 4.5 Phase diagrams for the synthesis of various nanomaterials: (A, B) Gas-phase VLS growth of 1D nanowires [81], (C, D) liquid-phase SLS growth of 1D nanotubes [82], (E, F) nonequilibrium synthesis of bimetallic 0D nanoparticles [83], (G, H) solid-phase synthesis of 2D nanosheets [84].

(see Fig. 4.5A and B) [81]. In general, the growth mechanism of VLS consists of three steps: Alloying, nucleation, and growth. The reactant Ge gas molecule is dissolved in Au metal catalyst (droplet) through carrier gas transport to form alloy liquid (see Fig. 4.5A). From the phase diagram, it means that the composition of the alloy liquid moves to the right continuously. When it reaches the saturation state of nucleation, solid Ge crystal is precipitated out of the alloy liquid (see Fig. 4.5B). The above "dissolution-saturation-precipitation" process is repeated in VLS growth process, which provides continuous power for the growth of 1D Ge nanowires. The growth temperature of Ge nanowires is determined by the alloying phase diagram of Au and Ge, and the diameter of nanowires is determined by the diameter of catalyst particles.

The growth mechanism of SLS is similar to VLS and developed on the basis of VLS in 1995, when 1D nanostructures of III-V compound semiconductors were prepared at relatively low temperatures by Buhro [86]. The main difference between VLS and SLS is that the reactants required for transport in SLS are supplied by solution, while VLS is supplied by the gas phase. The synthesis process of SLS takes low melting point metals (such as Bi, In, Sn, etc.) as droplet catalysts, metal-organic compounds as precursors, and aromatic compounds as solvents to complete the synthesis of target products in the liquid phase environment. Fang et al. reported the synthesis of Sn-filled $In(OH)_3$ nanotubes using liquid droplets of an In—Sn mixture, which serves as both catalyst and reagents for the 1D nanotube growth, from an ethanol-containing aqueous solution under an oxidative atmosphere (see Fig. 4.5C and D) [82]. The binary phase diagram of In and Sn showed that the melting points of In and Sn are 156.6 and 231.8°C, respectively, so Sn is expected to dissolve slowly in the molten In to form In—Sn liquid droplets at 180°C with less than 65% Sn (point X), above which solid Sn starts to precipitate (see Fig. 4.5D). In is preferentially oxidized to $In(OH)_3$ in the form of Sn-filled nanotubes by the oxygen in the solution. This work suggests a general mechanism for the growth of core-shell 1D nanostructure by a simple solution procedure.

Many bimetal systems show a very wide miscible gap on the phase diagram. Bimetal nanomaterials obtained by some traditional preparation methods, such as coreduction, thermal decomposition, crystal seed-induced growth, and electrochemical replacement methods, mostly present core-shell or some other heterostructures (see Fig. 4.5E) [83]. According to the binary phase diagram, Cu is immiscible with many elements, such as Ag, Ni, Sn, In, etc (see Fig. 4.5F) [83]. When using the traditional binary metal preparation method, Cu and many metals will not form a uniform alloy, but will form some phase separation structures. Recently, Yang et al. [83] developed a nonequilibrium synthesis strategy to overcome the immiscibility problem between many bimetallic components. By using this method, they prepared a series of Cu-based bimetallic homogeneous alloy nanoparticles and proved that this nonequilibrium synthesis strategy is applicable to Cu and almost all metals [83].

A team led by Wei Liu of the Shanghai University of Science and Technology has successfully achieved air carbonization without inert gases through a new binary dynamic salt (NaCl and KBr) coating method, reducing the preparation cost of 2D carbon nanosheet materials (see Fig. 4.5G and H) [84]. The carbon sources used in this method range from small molecules (glucose), large molecules (polyvinylidene fluoride, PVDF), biomass (camphor leaf) to metal–organic skeleton materials (zeolite imidazole-67, ZIF-67). In a typical process, the core is a mixture of carbon precursor/NaCl particles, and KBr is then coated as a shell to form a carbon precursor/NaCl@KBr. Carbon nanosheet materials can be obtained by carbonizing carbon precursors in the carbon precursor/NaCl@KBr [84]. Reasonable solid phase reaction temperature and component ratio can be obtained according to the binary phase diagram of NaCl and KBr (see Fig. 4.5H). The yield of carbon nanosheet materials prepared by this dynamic salt coating method is close to that in inert atmosphere. This cost-effective method can be used to prepare materials for other similar reaction processes.

4.5 Chemical equilibrium of nanomaterials

From a kinetic point of view, the reaction starts with a higher concentration of reactants and a lower concentration of products, so the forward rate is higher than the reverse rate. As the reaction progresses, the concentration of reactants decreases, and the concentration of products increases, so the forward reaction rate decreases and the reverse reaction rate increases. When the forward and reverse reaction rates are equal, the concentration of each substance in the system does not change, and the reaction reaches dynamic chemical equilibrium. Or from a thermodynamic point of view, when a reversible reaction goes its change in Gibbs free energy (ΔG) is equal to zero, that is chemical equilibrium at constant temperature and pressure [1].

4.5.1 Standard equilibrium constant in chemical equilibrium

Standard equilibrium constant is an equilibrium constant calculated from a standard thermodynamic function of chemical matters. It is expressed as an K^θ and is a function of temperature. The standard equilibrium constant is expressed as follows [1]:

For a gas reaction system, when the gas phase system reaches chemical equilibrium at a certain temperature, the ratio of the partial pressure of the gases involved in the reaction to the thermodynamic standard pressure is a constant product of the power of the measurement coefficients in the equation (see Eqs. 4.35 and 4.36).

$$H_2(g) + I_2(g) \rightleftharpoons 2HI(g) \tag{4.35}$$

$$K^\theta = \frac{\left[p(HI)/p^\theta\right]^2}{\left[p(H_2)/p^\theta\right]\left[p(I_2)/p^\theta\right]} = \left[p(HI)/p^\theta\right]^2 \cdot \left[p(H_2)/p^\theta\right]^{-1}\left[p(I_2)/p^\theta\right]^{-1} \tag{4.36}$$

For a solution reaction system, the relationship is expressed in terms of ionic concentrations and standard concentrations (see Eqs. 4.37 and 4.38).

$$Sn^{2+}(aq) + 2Fe^{3+}(aq) \rightleftharpoons Sn^{4+}(aq) + 2Fe^{2+}(aq) \tag{4.37}$$

$$K^\theta = \frac{[c(Sn^{4+})/c^\theta][c(Fe^{2+})/c^\theta]^2}{[c(Sn^{2+})/c^\theta][c(Fe^{3+})/c^\theta]^2} \tag{4.38}$$

For the general chemical reaction, when the reactants or products simultaneously exist in the solution state, gas state, solid state, the reaction equilibrium constant expression of the gas is represented by partial pressure, solution is represented by ionic concentration, solid matter does not participate in the calculation (see Eqs. 4.39 and 4.40).

$$dS = \left(\frac{\delta Q}{T}\right)_{reversible} \tag{4.39}$$

$$K^\theta = \frac{[p(X)/p^\theta]^x[C(Y)/C^\theta]^y}{[p(A)/p^\theta]^a[C(B)/C^\theta]^b} \tag{4.40}$$

Generally, the larger the K^θ was, the more complete the reaction was. The smaller the K^θ was, the less complete the reaction was. The K^θ were not too big or too small (as in $10^{-3} < K^\theta < 10^3$) and the reactants were partially converted to the products.

4.5.2 Nanomaterials for changing chemical equilibrium

Since most chemical reactions are reversible, they follow the law of chemical equilibrium: under certain circumstances, a chemical reaction can reach equilibrium. Le Chatelier's principle states that increasing the reactant concentration or removing the reaction product increases the equilibrium conversion rate of chemical a reaction. Industrial production of esters, for example, is governed by the law of chemical equilibrium. In order to increase the yield of esterification, excess reactants and dehydrants are usually used to drive the reaction. However, these methods not only consume a lot of energy but also create additional difficulties in separating the final product. Recently, Jia Zhu and Bin Zhu of Nanjing University reported a photothermal catalytic esterification system based on graphene oxide aerogel (SGA) at nanoscale interface, which broke through the chemical equilibrium limit of esterification reaction [87]. Due to local photothermal heating and different molecular bond affinity, the resulting products evaporate from the reaction site, resulting in a local excess of reactants, which thermodynamically drives the reaction in favor of ester formation (the process requires no excess reactants or dehydrants). Catalysis is an important phenomenon in nature that can change the rate of chemical reactions without affecting chemical equilibrium. This interfacial photothermal catalytic design not only provides a new way for ester synthesis in chemical production but also facilitates the development of various reversible chemical reactions toward sustainable development [87].

Nanomaterials changing chemical equilibrium also is reflected in series reactions. In thermodynamics, series catalysis actively promotes a shift in chemical equilibrium, since subsequent reactions consume the products of the previous reaction as reactants, i.e., by altering the thermodynamic diagram to increase yield. Therefore, it is possible for series catalysis to improve the efficiency of the whole reaction by coupling the multistep reaction. At present, series catalysis has been widely used in nature to produce biological macromolecules with multiple enzymes through coupling reaction steps, which is also a strategy that can effectively improve the performance of carbon dioxide reduction reaction (CO_2RR) with the help of nanomaterials [88]. In series reactions, nanomaterial-based series catalysts offer the possibility of decoupling the adsorption energy of intermediates at different active sites, which is beneficial to the control of chemical equilibrium because the reaction requires multiple steps and intermediates.

4.5.3 Thermodynamic equilibrium constant in reaction system of nanomaterials

Chemical equilibrium plays an important role in nano-catalytic reaction system. Taking the association mechanism of ORR under alkaline conditions as an example, the reaction process goes through the formation of *OOH, *O, and *OH intermediates, and finally generates OH^- (OER is the reverse process of ORR) (see Eqs. 4.41−4.45).

$$* + O_2(g) + H_2O(1) + e^{-\circ} \leftrightarrow HOO^* + OH^{-\circ} \tag{4.41}$$

$$HOO^* + e^{-\circ} \leftrightarrow O^* + OH^{-\circ} \tag{4.42}$$

$$O^* + H_2O(1) + e^{-\circ} \leftrightarrow HO^* + OH^{-\circ} \tag{4.43}$$

$$OH^* + e^{-\circ} \leftrightarrow OH^{-\circ} + * \tag{4.44}$$

$$\text{Overall:} \quad \cdot O_2^\circ + 4e^{-\circ} + 2H_2O \leftrightarrow 4OH^{-\circ} \tag{4.45}$$

The adsorption energy and reaction rate of reaction intermediates follow linear free energy relationships, which can be expressed as $\ln k = a \ln K + b$, where k is the reaction rate, K is the thermodynamic equilibrium constant, and a and b are coefficients. The catalyst makes the reaction easier by reducing the activation energy of the reaction. Based on the above formula, the thermodynamic equilibrium constant K is a very critical parameter, which has an effect on determining the thermodynamics or kinetics of ORR catalysis reactions of nanomaterials [89].

Chemical equilibrium is a theoretical system of equilibrium including dissolution equilibrium, ionization equilibrium, hydrolysis equilibrium, etc. Chemical equilibrium is the core of this system and the basis of analyzing other equilibrium systems. Chemical equilibrium also plays an important role in the synthesis of nanomaterials. Due to the different equilibrium constants of Co^{2+} and Mn^{2+} ions in liquid environment, the local separation of cobalt and manganese oxides is often observed during the synthesis by coprecipitation method. Therefore, it is very important to develop an effective method for the synthesis of $Co_xMn_{1-x}O_y$ nanostructured catalyst. Recently, Zhang's research group confirmed that $Co_xMn_{1-x}O_y$ can be synthesized efficiently through mechanochemical redox process [90]. The motion energy and heat energy released in the mechanical ball milling process in a short time are used to drive the redox reaction of potassium permanganate and cobalt chloride in alkaline environment (controllable chemical equilibrium process), so as to generate cobalt manganese bimetallic oxides.

4.6 Electrochemistry of nanomaterials

Electrochemistry is an important branch part of physical chemistry. It is not only related to inorganic chemistry, organic chemistry, analytical chemistry, and chemical engineering, but also permeates into the fields of environmental science, energy science, biology, and metal industry. Electrochemistry is a science that investigates the changes in charge and electron transfer that occur at the interface formed by two types of conductors (electronic conductors, such as metals or graphite, and ionic conductors, such as electrolyte solutions) [1]. In the past, electrochemistry was considered mainly to study the conversion between electrical energy and chemical energy, such as galvanic cells and electrolytic cells, but now electrochemistry has been expanded to the study of electrodes, ions, electrochemical corrosion of metals, etc., and involves the content of kinetics and thermodynamics in various electrochemical systems.

4.6.1 Important equations in electrochemistry

4.6.1.1 Faraday's law and its application

Faraday summarized a basic law in 1833 on the basis of a large number of electrolysis experiment results, that is, after electrification of electrolyte solution, the amount of substance with chemical changes on the electrode (that is, the interface between two phases) is proportional to the amount of charge through the electrode, known as Faraday's law. The mathematical expression of Faraday's law is $Q = z\xi F$. In the above formula: z is charge number of electrode reaction, ξ is progress of reaction, F is Faraday's constant. Faraday's law describes the relationship between the amount of charge passing through an electrode and the amount of the electrode reactants, also known as the law of electrolysis. Faraday's law is the earliest quantitative basic law in electrochemistry, which reveals the quantitative relationship between the incoming charge and the precipitated matter. This law can be applied at any temperature and pressure and there is no limit to how this law can be used [1].

Faraday's law plays an important role in electrochemical energy storage and conversion as well as the preparation of nanomaterials by electrodeposition. Several processes of electrochemical energy storage occur at solid-state electrodes: (1) through the formation of EDL, (2) through surface redox reactions, (3) through the insertion of ions in electrochemical intercalation, and (4) through alloying, decomposition, or conversion reactions [91]. The last three processes obey Faraday's law and take place charge transfer reactions on the electrochemical surface, where surface redox reactions and some ion insertion reactions are called pseudo-capacitance reactions. One strategy for achieving efficient electrochemical storage is to use reversible surface or near-surface Faraday reactions to store charge by pseudo-capacitive materials. This allows them to exceed the capacity limits of electric double-layer capacitors and the mass transfer limits of batteries [91]. Faraday's law is a very important guiding principle in electrochemical deposition synthesis of nanomaterials [92] and electrocatalytic conversion on nano-catalyst [93]. The charge transfer and charge conservation determine the transformation efficiency of matter and energy in electrode and electrolyte interface.

4.6.1.2 Nernst equation and its application

The Nernst equation is an equation used to quantitatively describe the diffusion potential of a certain ion between A and B systems. The equation shows the quantitative relationship between the electromotive force (E) of a reversible battery and the concentration of each component participating in the battery reaction at a certain temperature. The Nernst equation, derived by the German chemist and physicist W.H. Nernst in 1889, relies on thermodynamics (see Eqs. 4.46 and 4.47):

$$aA + bB = cC + dD \tag{4.46}$$

$$E = E^{\ominus} - \frac{RT}{nf} \ln \frac{[C]^c [D]^d}{[A]^a [B]^b} \tag{4.47}$$

In the formula, E is the electrode potential of the electric pair at a certain concentration, E^{θ} is the standard electrode potential of the electric pair, n is the number of electron transfer in the electrode reaction, and R is the molar gas constant, T is thermodynamic temperature, and F is Faraday constant.

In electrochemistry, the Nernst equation is used to calculate the equilibrium voltage of a specified redox pair at an electrode relative to the standard potential. The Nernst equation only makes sense if there are two substances in a redox pair. This equation connects chemical energy with galvanic electrode potential and makes a significant contribution to electrochemistry.

Lewis proposed and developed the concept of activity and activity coefficient to deal with nonideal solutions. After replacing concentration with activity, the Nernst equation becomes the following form (see Eqs. 4.48 and 4.49):

$$E = -\frac{\Delta G}{nF} = E^{\theta} - \frac{RT}{nF} \ln J \tag{4.48}$$

where E^{θ} and E are standard and actual battery emf, respectively, F is Faraday constant, R is gas constant, T is absolute temperature, n is the charge number of battery reaction, J is the activity product of each component in battery reaction.

$$J = \prod_{B} a_B^{\nu_B} \qquad (4.49)$$

where a_B is the concentration of the component and ν_B is the reaction number of the component.

The Nernst equation is the basis of battery thermodynamics, which can be used to describe the electromotive force of battery in equilibrium state and establish the relationship between chemical thermodynamics and battery thermodynamics. When a current flows through the battery, the electrode usually deviates from its reversible electrode potential, exhibiting an overpotential due to the activation energy barrier required for charge transfer at the metal-solution surface.

Recently, Professor Liping Wang of The University of Electronic Science and Technology of China and his collaborators successfully explained the influence of electrolyte components such as lithium-ion concentration and solvent type on the working voltage and energy density of Li/CF$_x$ batteries by using the Nernst equation (see Eqs. 4.50–4.53). It is suggested that the working voltage of Li/CF$_x$ battery can be increased by decreasing the concentration of lithium and increasing the coordination number of solvent and Li$^+$.

$$E(-) = E_{Li}^{\circ} + 2.303 \frac{RT}{F} \lg \frac{c_{Li^+} \cdot s_n}{c_{sfree}^n} \qquad (4.50)$$

$$E(+) = E_{CF}^{\circ} - 2.303 \frac{RT}{F} \lg \frac{c_{sfree}^{n-z}}{c_{Li^+} \cdot s_n} \qquad (4.51)$$

$$E = E(+) - E(-) \; E_{CF}^{\circ} - E_{Li}^{\circ} + 2.303 \frac{RT}{F} \lg c_{sfree}^z \qquad (4.52)$$

$$\Delta E = 2.303 \frac{RT}{F} \lg c_{sfree}^z \qquad (4.53)$$

When z is 3, the actual discharge voltage displacement curves of CF$_{1.12}$ and CF$_{0.88}$ are in good agreement with the theoretical voltage displacement curves. Therefore, in LiTFSI/DMSO electrolyte, solvated Li$^+$ is coembedded in the positive fluorinated carbon material in the form of Li$^+$(DMSO)$_3$ [94].

4.6.1.3 Tafel equation and its application

According to the electrochemical theory, when a current passes through the irreversible electrode, the potential value of the irreversible electrode will deviate from the equilibrium value when no current passes through. This phenomenon is called electrode polarization, and the potential difference of deviation is called overpotential. In 1905, Tafel proposed an empirical formula to express the quantitative relationship between hydrogen overpotential and current density, called Tafel formula, which is an important formula in electrode reaction kinetics, and its specific form is as follows: $\eta = a + b\log j$, where η is the overpotential, j is the current density, a and b are constants, respectively [95]. Where, a is the overpotential (the intercept between Tafel line and potential axis) at current density $= 1$ A/cm^{-1}, and b is the slope of the line in the η-log$j$ image, called the Tafel slope. The smaller a value is, the stronger the antipolarization ability of the electrode is. The value of a is related to the electrode material, electrode surface state, solution concentration, and temperature. The b value represents the influence degree of polarization current density change on electrode overpotential. The smaller b value is, the rapider catalytic reaction kinetics of the electrode is.

Around 1930, Bulter and Volmer assumed that the steps of gaining or losing electrons were elementary steps, and applied the transition state theory and Nernst equation in chemical dynamics to derive the basic equation of the kinetics of the electrode process—Butler—Volmer equation (B—V equation) (see Eq. 4.54) [96].

$$i = i_{fd} - i_{rev} = i_0 \exp\left(\frac{\alpha\eta F}{RT}\right) - i_0 \exp\left(\frac{-1(1-\alpha)\eta F}{RT}\right) \tag{4.54}$$

Where i_{fd} is forward current density, i_{rev} is reverse current density , i_0 is exchange current density. The B—V equation consists of two parts: anode current and cathode current. The net current of the electrochemical reaction is equal to the sum of the anode and cathode currents during the electrode process. When the cathode overpotential is large, the reduction current density increases, while the oxidation current density decreases, so that the reduction current density is rapidly much larger than the oxidation current density, so the oxidation current density can be ignored, and vice versa. The simplified equation is as follows (see Eq. 4.55):

$$\eta = -\left(\frac{2.303RT}{\alpha F}\right)\log i_0 + \left(\frac{2.303RT}{\alpha F}\right)\log i \tag{4.55}$$

The empirical constants $a = (2.303RT\log i_0)/(\alpha F)$ and $b = (2.303RT)/(\alpha F)$ when compared with The Tafel formula. Some important parameters of the electrode process, such as exchange current density and charge transfer coefficient, can be calculated by using Tafel formula and current logarithm and overpotential diagram.

The Tafel equation is derived from experiments in which the measured Tafel slope b is the apparent value of the multistep electrochemical reaction, which corresponds to the apparent electron transfer number. Most electrochemical reactions involve multiple electron transfers (ORR and OER), so the apparent electron transfer numbers (n) include α^* of rate-determining step (RDS) and n of those steps that precede RDS. Therefore, the

Tafel slope of overall reaction should be b = $(2.303RT)/((\alpha^*+n)F)$. If RDS involves an electron transfer step, i.e. $\alpha^* = 0.5$, then b = $(2.303RT)/((0.5 + n)F)$: (1) n = 0, then b = 118 mV, and the steps before RDS do not involve electron transfer, (2) n = 1, then b = 40 mV, and the number of electron transfer before RDS is 1. If RDS involves zero electron transfer steps, i.e. $\alpha^* = 0$, then b = $(2.303RT)/(nF)$: (1) n = 1, then b = 60 mV, the steps before RDS do not involve electron transfer, (2) n = 2, then b = 30 mV, and the number of electron transfer before RDS is 1 [97].

4.6.2 Three electrode systems in electrochemistry

Electrolysis or battery system are two electrode system, only positive and negative electrode, but in electrochemical testing process, we often choose three-electrode system. The reason is that in the process of electrochemical testing, we need to study a single electrode (i.e., the working electrode). If we choose a two-electrode system, we will default to the opposite electrode (also known as the auxiliary electrode) as a reference. In fact, as soon as an electric current passes through the system, the opposite electrode polarizes, causing a potential change, and the working electrode is measuring an incorrect potential. Generally, a reversible reference electrode is added on the basis of two electrodes to construct a three-electrode system to solve the above problems, and the two-electrode system also has the problem of solution voltage drop when the current flows, so the three-electrode system is obviously the first choice. The working electrode and the opposite electrode form a loop, the opposite electrode only plays the role of current conduction, and the reference electrode is used as a reference to measure or apply the potential of the working electrode, so the potential of the working electrode is the potential relative to the reference electrode [98]. Common reversible reference electrodes include saturated calomel electrode (SCE), silver-silver chloride electrode, mercury-mercury oxide electrode, and reversible hydrogen electrode (RHE).

4.6.3 Electrolytic cells in electrochemistry

Electrolytic cell (or electrolyzer) is the key factor of electrochemical measurement system, the cell structure is different for different reactions. Recently, Shen developed an integrated electrolytic cell for ORR electrocatalytic reactions involving reversible reference electrodes (see Fig. 4.6A) [99]. The RHE can be prepared in situ to ensure the purity and freshness of the hydrogen. In Fig. 4.6A, one and two are Pt wire electrodes in RHE, three is a piston, 4 is a socket for the working electrode five is a fixed (oxygen) inlet, six is opened for insertion into the counterelectrode, seven is the main body of the electrolytic cell and eight is a Luggin capillary. At first, the piston three is first opened during use, and the same solution as the electrolyte solution in the electrolytic cell is filled with the RHE glass tubes one and two to communicate with the solution in the electrolytic cell, and then the piston three is closed in time. The two Pt wire electrodes of A and B are

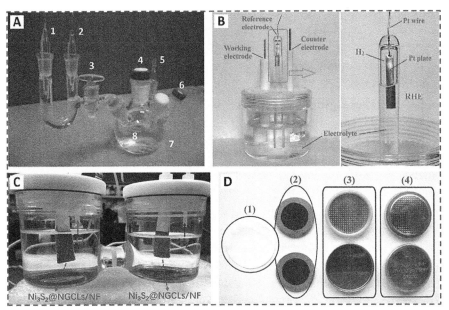

Figure 4.6 Three electrode cells in electrochemistry: (A) Electrolyzer and reference electrode for rotating the ring electrode of ORR [99], (B) electrolyzer and simple RHE reference electrode [100]; two electrode cells in electrochemistry: (C) Electrolyzer for water-splitting reaction [36], (G, H) button-like capacitor or battery reactors [68].

respectively connected to a potentiostat or a regulated power supply, the positive electrode is connected to the electrode 1, and the negative electrode is connected to the electrode 2. Then, the electrolysis of H_2O is started. At this time, the piston of the one electrode can be pulled apart to make the O_2 generated to maintain the internal pressure balance. According to the electrochemical reaction, the electrode one generates O_2 and the electrode two generates H_2. When the position of the hydrogen-discharging solution produced by electrolysis is about half of the Pt wire electrode exposed, the electrolysis can be stopped to prevent the H_2 from discharging the solution below the Pt wire electrode. Close the piston of electrode one to keep the hydrogen in a stable position. Finally, the piston three is opened, and the electrolyte in the U-tube is electrically connected to the electrolytic cell through the Luggin capillary 8.

Recently, our research group (Zesheng Li) also designed a simple three-electrode electrolyzer system (including RHE) for performance testing of supercapacitors (see

Fig. 4.6B) [100]. This three-electrode system consists of a working electrode, a counter-electrode, and a reference electrode. The work electrode was prepared by coating the active material on a glassy carbon electrode. A Pt plate (1 cm^2) was used as the counter electrode. 1 mol L^{-1} KOH aqueous solution was used as electrolyte. The RHE was used as the reference electrode. The RHE is made up of sealed H$_2$, Pt wire-plate, and electrolyte (see Fig. 4.6B **right**). The sealed H$_2$ in RHE is prepared via electrolysis of water (at 3 V DC) in the same 1 mol L^{-1} KOH electrolyte. In principle, the three-electrode cell is similar to Shen's design, but our system is much simpler and easier to use and shows a wider range of applications.

For two-electrode test systems, two devices are most commonly used: (1) the two-chamber cell (see Fig. 4.6C) [36] and (2) the button-like cell (see Fig. 4.6D) [68]. Recently, we designed a fully decomposed water two-electrode electrolytic cell, consisting of two electrode chambers and a connected glass tube. A porous plug is fixed in the middle of the glass tube to prevent interference from different gases from the two electrodes on two sides (see Fig. 4.6C). Previously, we also designed a universal button-like supercapacitor cell consisting of a porous membrane (1), electrodes (2), a negative cell case (3), and a positive cell case (4) (see Fig. 4.6D) [68]. Two-electrode system is relatively simple in cell structure, a common characteristic is that the two electrodes need to be separated by porous plug or porous membrane, to ensure that the system is relatively independent and prevent internal short circuit.

4.7 Interface chemistry of nanomaterials

Surface chemistry (or interface chemistry) is one important branch of physical chemistry, mainly covering surface chemistry and surface physics. Surface chemistry explores the basic principles of physical and chemical processes on solid surfaces, and has extensive applications in the fields of multiphase catalysis, electrochemistry, energy chemistry, and nanotechnology. Professor Gerhard Ertl, winner of the 2007 Nobel Prize in chemistry, has pointed out that "the whole field of nanotechnology is, in effect, controlled by surface reactions" [101]. With the rapid development of modern surface science and technology and the progress of theoretical chemistry, it is now possible to reveal surface physicochemical processes (physical and electronic structures) at atomic and molecular levels. Despite the rapid development of surface chemistry, some classical surface-chemistry principles and equations are still shining in nanomaterials and their energy and environmental applications.

4.7.1 Classical equations in surface chemistry
4.7.1.1 Young's equation and its application
In 1805, British scientist Thomas Young described the quantitative relationship between interfacial tension and contact Angle in his study about the wetting and

capillarity. For more than 200 years, Young's equation has become one of the most basic theories in the field of wetting. It is the relationship between the interfacial tension γ_{s-g}, γ_{s-l}, γ_{l-g}, and the contact Angle θ, also known as the wetting equation, the expression is: $\gamma_{s-g} - \gamma_{s-l} = \gamma_{l-g} \cos \theta$, suitable for uniform surface and the equilibrium state between solid and liquid without special interaction (see Fig. 4.7A) [1]. Although this equation can be derived from thermodynamic energy minimization, researchers have been trying to explain Young's equation from a mechanical perspective and verify its validity at the nanoscale. At present, nanomaterial-based energy electrocatalytic reactions (such as water decomposition, carbon dioxide reduction, fuel cells, etc.) still have many problems that need to be solved (such as poor selectivity, high overpotential, low efficiency, and slow electrocatalytic reaction kinetics, etc.). The core problem is closely related to the solid—liquid—gas three-phase interface (SLG-TPI) of nanomaterials (see Fig. 4.7B) [102]. It is gradually recognized that the SLG-TPI involving catalyst, electrolyte, and active gas plays an important role in controlling the electrochemical performance of different electrocatalytic systems. In addition to extensive research on catalyst development, there is increasing attention to regulating gas transport/diffusion behavior in photocatalytic reactions involving gases, with a view to creating industrially viable catalytic systems with high reaction rates and excellent long-term stability. Bionic surfaces and systems with special wetting capabilities and structural advantages could provide ideas for future design of electrodes and solve long-standing challenges (see Fig. 4.7C) [103].

Researchers from Lanzhou Institute of Chemical Physics, Chinese Academy of Sciences also carried out systematic research work on optimization design of micro—nano-structures on the surface of biomimetic materials [107—110]. Starting from the parameters of size, geometry, and intrinsic contact Angle of micro-/nanostructures, they studied the theoretical criteria of surface wetting state transition of different micro-/nanostructures by using classical theory and thermodynamics. The direct relation between geometrical surface, intrinsic contact angle, and surface wettability of micro-/nanostructure is also systematically analyzed [107—110]. Surface roughness is very important in the preparation of practical bionic superhydrophobic surfaces. Chemical intrinsic contact Angle, droplet size, environmental vibration energy, and other factors also affect the anisotropic wetting behavior of the surface of micro-/nanostructures. All the same, there are still many key scientific problems to be solved in this field: on the one hand, as a key factor controlling droplet dynamics, the capillary force acting on the three-phase contact line of solid, liquid, and gas is not clearly reflected in Young's equation and is easy to be confused with the concept of interfacial tension. On the other hand, the verification of Young's equation has always been controversial because it is difficult to accurately measure the interfacial tension in experiments [111].

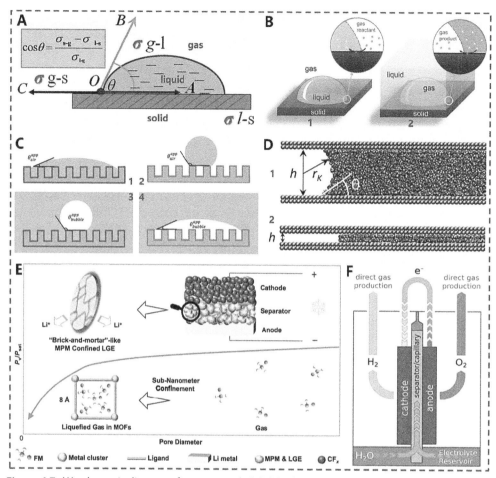

Figure 4.7 (A) schematic diagram of contact angle [1], (B) schematic diagram of three phase interface structure [102], (C) schematic diagram of bionic surfaces and contact angle [103], (D) schematic diagram of capillary condensation [104], (D) sub—nanoconfined capillary condensation of MOFs [105], (D) schematic diagram of capillary electrolyzer [106].

4.7.1.2 Kelvin equation and its application

The Kelvin equation is considered as one of the three classical theories in the field of solid-liquid interface wetting, which describes the vapor pressure change caused by the curved liquid-gas interface in capillary theoretically. The Kelvin equation can be written as follows (see Eq. 4.56):

$$\ln\frac{p}{p_0} = \frac{2\gamma V_m}{rRT} \tag{4.56}$$

where P is the actual vapor pressure of curved liquid surface, P_0 is the saturated vapor pressure, γ is the surface tension, V_m is the molar volume of the liquid, R is the universal gas constant, r is the radius of curvature, and T is the temperature. The equilibrium vapor pressure depends on the radius of curvature. For convex surface, r is positive, then, $P > P_0$; For a concave liquid surface, r is negative, then, $P < P_0$ [1].

A typical application of the Kelvin Equation is to analyze capillary condensation. Capillary condensation refers to the phenomenon that gas in capillary channel space can condense and turn into liquid without reaching supersaturated state due to $P < P_0$ for concave liquid surface (see Fig. 4.7D) [104]. Capillary condensation is a key scientific issue in nanoconfined mechanics and a hot topic in mesoscale science, which is related to macroscopic solid-liquid interface wetting and microscopic intermolecular mechanical interaction. However, when the channel diameter is reduced to nanometer or subnanometer scale, only a few atoms, the channel may allow only one or two layers of water molecules, bending liquid surface curvature, contact Angle and other concepts are difficult to define accurately, the Kelvin equation is not applicable. Recently, Fengchao Wang and his collaborators revealed the size effect of solid—liquid interface energy, modified the classical Kelvin equation, and established a new theory of nanoconfined capillary condensation. The latest experimental results and mechanical mechanism of this limit scale (within 10 nm) are explained reasonably, and the important role of solid-liquid interface mechanics in the capillary condensation of nanometer/subnanometer scale is expounded [104].

Metal-organic frameworks (MOFs) are a class of porous crystalline solids composed of organic connectors and metal ions/nodes that are ideal candidates for capturing frequency-modulated molecules by capillary condensation to reduce internal pressure in cells using liquefied gas electrolytes (LGE). Guorui Cai et al. demonstrated capillary condensation of fluoromethane (FM) gaseous electrolytes by designing a class of flexible MOF-polymer membranes (MPMs) that provide dense and continuous microporous (0.8 nm) networks (see Fig. 4.7E) [105]. The effect of MPMs on the concentration of FM molecules was studied by experiments and computer simulation. Using the significant capillary condensation of sub—nanopores in MPMs, the authors show that LGE can operate below its vapor pressure. This research not only provides insights into the behavior of molecules in a nano-enclosed environment ("brick-and-mortar"-like

MPMs-confined LGE), but also opens up a potential avenue for the safer operation of gaseous electrolytes by this sub—nanoconfinement strategy.

Recently, Gerhard F. Swiegers et al. from the University of Wollongong reported the development of a very unique concept of electrocatalytic water decomposition, which enables the transport of water-based electrolyte to hydrogen and oxygen electrodes via capillary and capillary interactions along porous interelectrode partitions, thus achieving a bubble-free electrode electrocatalytic hydrogen production (see Fig. 4.7F) [106]. Electrocatalytic decomposition of water via capillary transport has higher energy efficiency than commercial electrolytic cells. Working at the current density of 0.5 A/cm^{-1} and 85°C, the voltage of the electrolytic cell is only 1.51 V, the energy efficiency of the electrolytic cell reaches 98%, and the energy consumption of hydrogen production reaches 40.4 kWh/kg^{-1} H$_2$. At the same time, the structure of capillary-based electrolytic cell is very simple, so it provides a new opportunity to realize affordable renewable hydrogen energy closer to commercialization.

4.7.1.3 Langmuir equation and its application

Langmuir equation, one of the commonly used adsorption isotherm equations, was put forward by physical chemist Langmuir Itying in 1916 on the basis of molecular motion theory and some assumptions. Now it is widely used in adsorption. Langmuir's work suggested that atoms or molecules on solid surfaces had an outward residual valence force that could trap gas molecules. The range of action of this residual valence force is similar to the molecular diameter, so only monolayer adsorption can occur on the surface of the adsorbent. Langmuir equation is presented as $\theta = \Gamma/\Gamma_m = kp/(1 + kp)$, where θ is the adsorbent surface coverage rate, Γ and Γ_m is the actual and saturated adsorption capacity, P is pressure of gas, k is the Langmuir equilibrium constant, $k = k_a/k_d$, k_a and k_d are the rate constant of adsorption and desorption, respectively [1].

Langmuir adsorption isotherm equation can be used to describe the adsorption isotherms in low or medium pressure range. When the pressure of adsorbent in gas is high and close to the saturated vapor pressure, the deviation of this equation occurs. This is because adsorbents can be condensed in fine capillaries, and the assumption of monolayer adsorption is not valid. Langmuir adsorption isotherm equation can be also used to calculate the monolayer adsorption capacity. Because the Langmuir equation is based on the assumption of uniform surface, while real surface is not uniform, it is often necessary to correct the heterogeneity of surface in practice.

4.7.2 Surface catalysis in physical chemistry

Surface catalysis is one of the important research directions in surface physical chemistry. The core mission of catalysis is to transform raw materials into high value-added chemicals and fuels in a more economical, efficient, and environmentally friendly way, involving major pillar industries such as chemistry, food, medicine, automobile, and petrochemical industry, which plays a pivotal role in the progress of human civilization and economic development. More than 90% of the processes in large-scale chemical industries such as energy and chemicals involve heterogeneous catalysis [1].

Catalysis is generally divided into heterogeneous and homogeneous catalysis. Based on the way of energy supply, catalysis can be divided into thermal catalysis, electrocatalysis, and photocatalysis. The heterogeneous catalytic process mainly occurs on the solid surface or interface of the catalyst. The research is usually divided into two parts: (1) From the perspective of solid surface, including the interface composition, structure, electronic properties, and energy of the solid surface; (2) From the perspective of reactive molecules, including molecular structural changes and chemical bond breaking and formation. The study of surface physical chemistry of heterogeneous catalysis covers the design and preparation of catalysts, catalytic reaction performance, surface active sites, reaction mechanism, and energy change, etc. In particular, it is expected that the physical and chemical processes on the surface of practical and model catalysts can be studied in detail at the atomic and molecular levels by combining ultra-high spatial and time-resolved surface technologies and methods, providing a scientific basis for the development of novel catalytic systems [112].

Our research groups (Zesheng Li and Changlin Yu) have been developing methods and theories for the control of well-defined micro-/nanostructures and mesoscopic system surface interface and studying the internal relationship between the surface structures of nanomaterials and related surface catalysis properties in complex systems from the level of atomic and molecular structures [43–47,50–55,113–116]. The structure–effect relationship, that is, the relationship between the structure and properties of the catalytic system, was revealed. It provides theoretical guidance for the design and application of related materials in electrocatalysis, photocatalysis, and other complex systems. More research on basic principles and laws is needed in the research and development of energy and environmental nanomaterials and their applications. Guided by controllable preparation of nanomaterials, the research on new nanomaterials and energy environment is carried out from the perspective of physical chemistry and the structure–activity relationship between nanomaterials and their surfaces/interfaces.

4.8 Colloidal chemistry of nanomaterials

Colloidal chemistry is a branch of physical chemistry that studies the properties and laws of colloid, macromolecular solutions and emulsions, and systems associated with interfacial phenomena. Its connotation is broad, not only involves the most basic theory of chemistry, but also has a very wide range of practicability, and intersects with many disciplines. Energy and environmental sciences are also extensively concerned with some basic principles and methods of colloid chemistry. An important feature of colloidal systems is that they have a large surface area and small colloidal nucleus in nanostructure

(1.100 nm). Complex physical or chemical phenomena can occur at any two-phase interface of colloidal nucleus and environment mediums.

4.8.1 Electric double-layer theory of colloid

EDL refers to the charged characteristics of colloidal nanoparticles: colloidal nanoparticles surface first adsorbed a layer of potential ions (positive or negative charge), and this layer of potential ions can attract ions (negative or positive) of opposite charge in solution around to the first layer of potential ions by electrostatic action. In this way, positive-negative or negative-positive EDLs are formed in the interface region of the medium around the nanomaterial.

The concept of flat plate EDL was first proposed by Helmholtz in 1853 (the inner and outer Helmholtz planes OHP) were proposed by Grahame in 1947). Later (1909−1913), Gouy and Chapman put forward the idea of diffusion layer of counterions on the basis of compact layer of Helmholtz. Considering the volume effect and solvation effect, Stern further proposed the Stern EDL model in 1924. Rice proposed the theory of electronic model of EDL in 1928 (see Fig. 4.8A) [117]. The models of flat-plate EDL (1), diffusion-layer EDL (2), and Stern EDL (3) are vividly described in Fig. 4.8A [118]. Helmholtz's flat-plate model consists of two planes with equal numbers but opposite charges, where the spacing between two parallel planes (i.e., EDL) is equivalent to the counterion radius (<1 nm), and the resulting capacitance is usually many orders of magnitude higher than the value of dielectric capacitor (see Fig. 4.8B (1)). Gouy and Chapman's diffusion-layer model emphasizes that the thermodynamic potential (Φ_e) decreases exponentially from the electrode surface to the solution bulk (Φ_s) (see Fig. 4.8B (2)). Stern EDL model emphasizes hydrodynamic motion of the ionic species in the diffuse layer and the accumulation of ions close to the electrode surface (see Fig. 4.8B (3)). Stern plane marks the distance of the closest approach of the ions to the charged surface and the absence of charges/ions in the Stern layer. The diffuse layer starts in the range of 10−100 nm from the electrode surface [118].

Our research group (Zesheng Li) is also devoted to the exploration of EDL structure model and its electrochemical energy storage mechanism [58−61,121]. Recently, we have demonstrated the schematic diagram for the Stern-model of electrical double layer and the ideal desolvation model of KOH aqueous solution in 0.8 nm cylindrical micropores (see Fig. 4.8C and D) [100]. In this model, the potential difference between the solid surface and the bulk solution is called the thermodynamic potential (Φ_0). The potential difference between the Stern interface and the bulk solution is called the Stern potential (Φ_δ), and that between the sliding interface and the bulk solution is called the Zeta potential (ζ) (see Fig. 4.8C). The key theories of Stern model include: ions are of a certain size and ions exist solvation effect. Because of the existence of van der Waals force in the ions and solvent molecules, the surface of the ions is surrounded by solvent molecules to

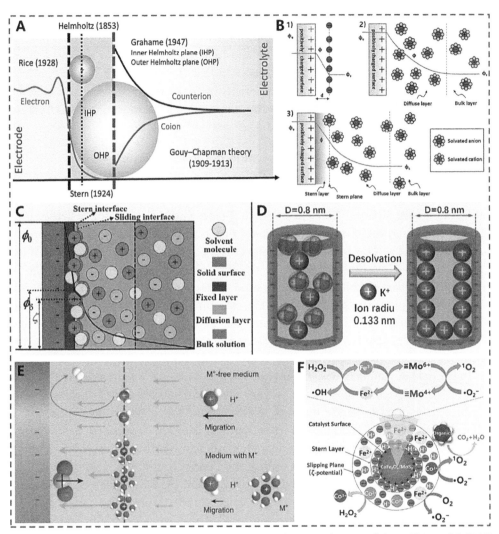

Figure 4.8 (A) Historical course of EDL theory [117], (B) schematic diagram of three EDL models [118], (C) schematic diagram for the Stern-model and (D) ideal desolvation model of KOH aqueous solution in 0.8 nm cylindrical micropores [100], (E) the hydrated alkali metal ions adsorbed on the cathode change the distribution of the double-layer electric field in electrocatalytic application [119], (F) micelle structure and ζ potential regulation for Fenton reaction system in environmental remediation application [120].

form the so-called "solvated ions," which is the real carrier of the charges in EDL capacitors (EDLCs). In this case, 0.8 nm cylindrical micropores in porous carbon is chose for constructing desolvation model. The bare and hydrated ion radius of K^+ is 0.133 and 0.331 nm, respectively. Thus, it can be deduced that the hydrated K^+ with 0.662 nm diameter can grudgingly diffuse into cylindrical micropores with 0.8 nm diameter, and then the compact EDL structure can be developed due to the de-solvation effect (see Fig. 4.8D).

4.8.2 Application of zeta potential in nanomaterials

When electro-kinetic phenomenon occurs, Stern layer moves with solid particles and slips relative to diffusion layer. The interface between Stern layer and diffusion layer is called the sliding surface. The Zeta potential (ζ) is the potential difference between the sliding surface and the solution body. The ζ potential reflects the degree of charge of solid nanoparticles. The higher the ζ potential, the more charged the particle. When $\zeta = 0$, the particles are not charged, so no electrokinetic phenomena occur. At the same time, uncharged colloidal particles tend to agglomerate and sink, so ζ potential can be used to judge the stability of micelle structure. The Stern model gives the definite physical meaning of ζ potential, reasonably explains the electrokinetic phenomenon and makes people have a deeper understanding of the structure of double electric layers.

In the field of nanomaterials, the importance of ζ potential is mainly reflected in two aspects: (1) To determine the positive and negative charge on the surface of nanoparticles, which can be used to guide the next modification, modification, or application of different systems. (2) To evaluate whether nanoparticles can disperse stably in the medium and guide the improvement of the stability of nanoparticles in the solution system [122]. Recently, Professor Xile Hu's team at the Federal Institute of technology in Lausanne showed that by using alkali metal ions to inhibit HER, effective electrocatalytic CO_2 reduction can be carried out in acidic media, thus overcoming the carbonate problem [119]. Among three typical catalysts (SnO_2/C, Au/C, and Cu/C), this cationic effect has been proved to be universal, resulting in Faraday efficiency of formic acid and CO formation as high as 90%. The results showed that the hydrated alkali metal ions (M^+) physically adsorbed on the cathode can change the distribution of the double-layer electric field (see Fig. 4.8D), thus inhibiting the migration of hydrated hydrogen ions (H^+), hindering the precipitation of hydrogen, and promoting the reduction of CO_2 by stabilizing key intermediates [119]. Essentially, the change of double-layer electric field can be attributed to the change in ζ potential in EDL structure. In the medium containing M^+ (such as K^+), chemically inert hydrated K^+ layer is formed on OHP due to the competitive adsorption of hydrated K^+ ion and hydronium ion on OHP, and the electric field on the cathode is shielded in a wide potential window. Thus, the migration of hydronium ions is greatly inhibited [119].

Recently, Prof. Mingyang Xing and his team from East China University of Science and Technology prepared $CoFe_2O_4/MoS_2$ heterogeneous Fenton catalyst for efficient pollutant control in environmental application [120]. Compared with blank $CoFe_2O_4$, MoS_2 can construct an "acidic microenvironment" through chemical bonding on the "Slipping plane" of $CoFe_2O_4$ particles, which significantly improved the activity of decomposition of H_2O_2 and phenol degradation in the macroscopic pH range of 3.0–9.0. Moreover, it can still degrade phenol efficiently in neutral buffer solution. The ζ potential is known to be the potential of particles on the "Slipping plane" into the bulk phase solution (see Fig. 4.8F) [120]. The ions at the "Slipping plane" do not move with the movement of particles, which means that there are a large number of positively charged cations at the "Slipping plane" of $CoFe_2O_4/MoS_2$. It was found that the activity of heterogeneous Fenton was mainly related to the "acidic microenvironment" of the catalyst surface and was not affected by the pH of the macroenvironment. It promotes iron ion cycling ($\equiv Fe^{3+}/\equiv Fe^{2+}$) on the "Slipping plane" of the catalyst, exposing the "fresh" Fenton reaction "active site" on the catalyst surface all the time. By using the ζ potential theory in colloid chemistry, the authors confirmed the existence of "acidic microenvironment" on the surface of nanostructured catalysts, which made Fenton technology really get rid of the limitation of pH of macroscopic environment and was expected to expand the application range of Fenton technology [120].

4.8.3 Basic concepts and application of Sol and Gel

Colloid is a dispersed system with a small particle size. The mass of particles in the dispersed phase is negligible, and the interaction between particles is mainly short-range force. Sol is generally a colloidal system with liquid characteristics. The dispersed particles are solid or macromolecular nanoparticles with sizes ranging from 1 to 100 nm. Gel is generally a colloidal system with solid characteristics. The dispersed nanoparticles form a continuous network skeleton, and the void of the skeleton is filled with liquid (i.e., hydrogel) or gas (i.e., aerogel). The content of the dispersed phase in the Gel is very low, generally between 1 wt.% and 3 wt.% [1].

Sol-gel method is a common method for preparation of nanomaterials, which has been highly concerned by science and technology. It has the advantages of simple process, low cost of equipment, energy saving, wide doping range of materials, easy to control the reaction process, and so on. By using compounds containing high chemical active components as precursors, the liquid-phase water or organic solvent is mixed evenly with these raw materials, after hydrolysis and chemical reaction, the solution can form a stable transparent Sol system. The Gel with three-dimensional space network structure is formed by the slow polymerization of aged colloidal particles, and the gel network is filled with liquid solvents. The gel becomes a kind of dry gel with porous space structure after drying and removing the solvent. Finally, the materials with nano substructure are prepared by sintering and curing. More importantly, the sol–gel method can achieve uniform mixing at molecular levels, which has special advantages for the preparation of uniform materials and uniform doping, making it widely used in the field of material preparation more than 100 years after its invention [123].

4.9 Theoretical chemistry of nanomaterials

Theoretical chemistry is the application of pure theoretical calculation rather than experimental methods to study the essence of chemical reactions, theoretical chemistry research fields mainly include five aspects: quantum chemistry, statistical mechanics, chemical thermodynamics, nonequilibrium thermodynamics, and molecular reaction dynamics. These aspects may be involved in different degrees in studying the structure of substances, predicting the reactivity of compounds, and studying the microscopic nature of reactions. There are two sections in the physical chemistry textbook, quantum mechanics and statistical thermodynamics, which are closely related to the theoretical (computational) chemistry [124].

A large part of theoretical chemistry can be classified as computational chemistry, although computational chemistry usually refers to the specific application of theoretical chemistry and the design of some approximations, such as some post-Hartree-Foker-type methods, density functional theory (DFT), semiempirical methods (such as PM3) or various force field methods. Some chemical theorists use statistical mechanics to provide a bridge between the microscopic phenomena of the quantum world and the macroscopic properties of the bulk matter of the system. According to the principle of interaction between nucleus and electron and its basic law of motion, the algorithm of solving Schrödinger equation directly after some approximate processing according to specific requirements by using the principle of quantum mechanics is commonly called the first principle. The generalized first principles include two major categories, ab Initio based on Hartree-Fock self-consistent field calculations, and DFT calculations. DFT is a quantum mechanical method to study the electronic structure of multielectron systems, which is widely used in physics and chemistry, especially in studying the properties of molecules and condensed matter. It is one of the most commonly used methods in computational physics and computational chemistry. Many of the mechanisms of electrochemical conversion and environmental catalysis of nanomaterials in this book can be calculated using DFT method [36,37].

In different types of catalytic applications (electrocatalysis, photocatalysis, and thermocatalysis), the DFT calculations can be used to study the electronic structure and catalytic reaction mechanism of nanomaterials (including reaction thermodynamics and kinetic mechanism). Through the study of the path, intermediate state and transition state of catalytic reaction, and the discussion of the basic concepts of photogenerated carrier and band edge, a new dimension is opened for the study of chemical reaction. According to the recent literature works, several hot directions of theoretical calculation of nanostructured catalysis are summarized as follows: (1) The theoretical calculation of thermodynamic free energy step curve of electrocatalytic reaction (the difference between free energy of intermediates and thermodynamic overpotential electrochemical potential can forcibly break the thermodynamic equilibrium between reactants and products); (2) The theoretical calculation of relationship between catalytic activity and adsorption energy, namely volcanic curve (volcanic curve can clearly show the linear proportional relationship of catalyst surface activity, and provide the design standard for the best catalyst); (3) The theoretical calculation of molecular orbital (bonding and antibonding orbital) and d-band center (electronic structure of metal surface) (the binding strength of adsorbent and surface metal has a significant impact on catalytic properties); (4) The theoretical calculation of semiconductor photocatalysis band gap engineering (providing a theoretical basis for the effective separation of photogenerated carriers and the regulation of photocatalytic activity such as heterojunction photocatalysis); (5) The theoretical calculation of semiconductor photocatalysis energy band potential matching (surface work function and energy band matching are closely related to the photocatalytic activity of heterojunction); (6) The theoretical calculation of ion diffusion properties of electrochemical energy storage (ion diffusion is a control step in the kinetic process of nanomaterials in energy storage) [125,126].

4.10 Summary

In this chapter, we comprehensively discuss the physicochemical principles and case analysis of nanomaterials from the following eight branch aspects of physical chemistry: thermodynamics, kinetics, phase equilibrium, chemical equilibrium, electrochemistry, surface chemistry, colloidal chemistry, and theoretical chemistry. For thermodynamics, the core contents include basic functions of thermodynamics (thermodynamic energy (U), enthalpy (H), entropy (S), Helmholtz free energy (A), Gibbs free energy (G)), size-dependent Gibbs free energy, standard thermodynamic functions, dissolution thermodynamics, nucleation thermodynamics, phase-transition thermodynamics, reaction thermodynamics, and adsorption thermodynamics of nanomaterials. For kinetics, the core contents include kinetic equation of first/second order reaction, Arrhenius equation, growth kinetics, catalytic reaction kinetics, energy storage kinetics, and adsorption reaction kinetics of nanomaterials. Gibbs phase rule, lever rule, phase diagram, and standard equilibrium constant are introduced in phase or chemical equilibrium. Faraday's Law, Nernst equation, Tafel equation, and their applications are introduced in electrochemistry. Young's equation, Kelvin equation, Langmuir equation, and surface catalysis are introduced in surface chemistry. Basic concepts and application of sol and gel, zeta potential, EDL theory are introduced in colloidal chemistry. Theoretical chemistry including quantum mechanics and statistical thermodynamics is also included in the last part.

Acknowledgments

This book was supported by National Natural Science Foundation of China (22078071, 22272034), Natural Science Foundation of Guangdong Province (2021A1515010125, 2020A1515010344), Maoming Science and Technology Project (mmkj2020032), Guangdong Province Universities and Colleges Pearl River Scholar Funded Scheme (2019), Guangdong Basic and Applied Basic Research Foundation (2019A1515011249, 2021A1515010305), Key Research Project of Natural Science of Guangdong Provincial Department of Education (2019KZDXM010), Environment and Energy Green Catalysis Innovation Team of Colleges and Universities of Guangdong Province (2022KCXTD019), the program for Innovative Research Team of Guangdong University of Petrochemical Technology.

References

[1]   X.C. Fu, W.X. Shen, T.Y. Yao, W.H. Hou, Physical Chemistry, Higher Education, Beijing, 2005.
[2]   https://www.degruyter.com/journal/key/zpch/html.
[3]   A. Manthiram, John Goodenough's 100th Birthday Celebration: His Impact on Science and Humanity, 2022, https://doi.org/10.1021/acsenergylett.2c01343.
[4]   J.B. Goodenough, Metallic oxides, Progress in Solid State Chemistry 5 (1971) 145−399.
[5]   J.B. Goodenough, How we made the Li-ion rechargeable battery, Nature Electronics 1 (3) (2018) 204.
[6]   R.J. Silbey, R.A. Alberty, M.G. Bawendi, Physical Chemistry, Wiley, 2005.
[7]   D.R. Gaskell, D.E. Laughlin, Introduction to the Thermodynamics of Materials, CRC press, 2017.
[8]   T.L. Hill, Thermodynamics of small systems, The Journal of Chemical Physics 36 (12) (1962) 3182−3197.
[9]   R.V. Chamberlin, Mean-field cluster model for the critical behaviour of ferromagnets, Nature 408 (6810) (2000) 337−339.
[10] T.L. Hill, Perspective: Nanothermodynamics 1 (3) (2001) 111−112.
[11] R.V. Chamberlin, The big world of nanothermodynamics, Entropy 17 (1) (2014) 52−73.
[12] X. YU, Study on the Effect of Nano-Size on Mechanical and Thermodynamic Properties of Materials [D], Kunming University of Science and Technology, 2014.
[13] Z.H. Li, D.G. Truhlar, Nanothermodynamics of metal nanoparticles, Chemical Science 5 (7) (2014) 2605−2624.
[14] W. Qi, Nanoscopic thermodynamics, Accounts of Chemical Research 49 (9) (2016) 1587−1595.
[15] http://www.tiaozhanbei.net/project/16933/.
[16] G. Fan, J. Jiang, Y. Li, Z. Huang, Thermodynamic functions of the ZnO nanoweeds, Materials Chemistry and Physics 130 (3) (2011) 839−842.
[17] G. Fan, L. Sun, Z. Huang, J. Jiang, Y. Li, Thermodynamic functions of the grain-like ZnO nanostructures, Materials Letters 65 (17−18) (2011) 2783−2785.
[18] X. Li, G. Fan, Z. Huang, Synthesis and surface thermodynamic functions of CaMoO4 nanocakes, Entropy 17 (5) (2015) 2741−2748.
[19] Z. Huang, C. Fan, J. Chen, Y. Ma, L. Wang, Y. Guo, Study on in situ growth and prescribed thermodynamic function of nanomaterials, in: Abstracts of the 4th Session of the 28th Annual Conference of The Chinese Chemical Society, 2012.
[20] Huang Z., Li X., Nanomaterials and Photocatalysis Physical Chemistry, Chemical Industry Press.
[21] A. Li, S. Kong, C. Guo, H. Ooka, K. Adachi, D. Hashizume, …R. Nakamura, Enhancing the stability of cobalt spinel oxide towards sustainable oxygen evolution in acid, Nature Catalysis 5 (2) (2022) 109−118.
[22] H. Zijun, X. Ming, M. Xiangying, Q. Jiangyuan, X. Biyuan, Q. Fanghong, H. Zaiyin, Facet and temperature effects on dissolution thermodynamic functions of Ag_3PO_4 microcrystals, Chemical Journal of Chinese Universities 40 (5) (2019) 959−964.

[23] J. Yue, L. Lin, L. Jiang, Q. Zhang, Y. Tong, L. Suo, …L. Chen, Interface Concentrated-Confinement Suppressing Cathode Dissolution in Water-in-Salt Electrolyte, Advanced Energy Materials 10 (36) (2020) 2000665.

[24] Z. Tian, Y. Zou, G. Liu, Y. Wang, J. Yin, J. Ming, H.N. Alshareef, Electrolyte solvation structure design for sodium ion batteries, Advanced Science 9 (22) (2022) 2201207.

[25] https://mp.weixin.qq.com/s/Rtm0Bkk-n_SxAT-BjB6Tlw.

[26] Y. Xia, K.D. Gilroy, H.C. Peng, X. Xia, Seed-mediated growth of colloidal metal nanocrystals, Angewandte Chemie International Edition 56 (1) (2017) 60−95.

[27] N.T.K. Thanh, N. Maclean, S. Mahiddine, Chemical Reviews 114 (2014) 7610.

[28] Q. Jiang, H.X. Shi, M. Zhao, Melting thermodynamics of organic nanocrystals, The Journal of Chemical Physics 111 (5) (1999) 2176−2180.

[29] Q. Jiang, H.X. Shi, M. Zhao, Free energy of crystal−liquid interface, Acta Materialia 47 (7) (1999) 2109−2112.

[30] Q. Jiang, Z. Zhang, J.C. Li, Melting thermodynamics of nanocrystals embedded in a matrix, Acta Materialia 48 (20) (2000) 4791−4795.

[31] J. Liang, F. Ma, S. Hwang, X. Wang, J. Sokolowski, Q. Li, …D. Su, Atomic arrangement engineering of metallic nanocrystals for energy-conversion electrocatalysis, Joule 3 (4) (2019) 956−991.

[32] J. Jiang, Z. Huang, M. Yan, Y. Li, A. Yuan, Research status and prospect of thermodynamics of nanomaterials, Progress in Chemistry 22 (06) (2010) 1058.

[33] T. Ling, M. Jaroniec, S.Z. Qiao, Recent progress in engineering the atomic and electronic structure of electrocatalysts via cation exchange reactions, Advanced Materials 32 (46) (2020) 2001866.

[34] Z.N. Garba, I. Lawan, W. Zhou, M. Zhang, L. Wang, Z. Yuan, Microcrystalline cellulose (MCC) based materials as emerging adsorbents for the removal of dyes and heavy metals−a review, Science of the Total Environment 717 (2020) 135070.

[35] https://mp.weixin.qq.com/s/FyuBwpvv2GBh3FpU6sxkBA.

[36] B. Li, Z. Li, Q. Pang, J.Z. Zhang, Core/shell cable-like Ni_3S_2 nanowires/N-doped graphene-like carbon layers as composite electrocatalyst for overall electrocatalytic water splitting, Chemical Engineering Journal 401 (2020) 126045.

[37] D. Lyu. S. Yao, A. Ali, Z.Q. Tian, P. Tsiakaras, P.K. Shen, N, S codoped carbon matrix-encapsulated Co_9S_8 nanoparticles as a highly efficient and durable bifunctional oxygen redox electrocatalyst for rechargeable Zn−air batteries, Advanced Energy Materials 11 (28) (2021) 2101249.

[38] M. Bianchini, J. Wang, R.J. Clément, B. Ouyang, P. Xiao, D. Kitchaev, G. Ceder, The interplay between thermodynamics and kinetics in the solid-state synthesis of layered oxides, Nature Materials 19 (10) (2020) 1088−1095.

[39] Y. Han, Seeing crystal formation one particle at a time, Nature Materials 19 (4) (2020) 377−378.

[40] Z. Ou, Z. Wang, B. Luo, E. Luijten, Q. Chen, Kinetic pathways of crystallization at the nanoscale, Nature Materials 19 (4) (2020) 450−455.

[41] W. Gao, P. Tieu, C. Addiego, Y. Ma, J. Wu, X. Pan, Probing the dynamics of nanoparticle formation from a precursor at atomic resolution, Science Advances 5 (1) (2019) eaau9590.

[42] https://mp.weixin.qq.com/s/iKY8JR45IEAd-xwqvy83uA.

[43] Z. Li, Q. Chen, Q. Lin, Y. Chen, X. Liao, H. Yu, C. Yu, Three-dimensional P-doped porous g-C3N4 nanosheets as an efficient metal-free photocatalyst for visible-light photocatalytic degradation of Rhodamine B model pollutant, Journal of the Taiwan Institute of Chemical Engineers 114 (2020) 249−262.

[44] Z. Li, S. Yang, J. Zhou, D. Li, X. Zhou, C. Ge, Y. Fang, Novel mesoporous g-C3N4 and BiPO4 nanorods hybrid architectures and their enhanced visible-light-driven photocatalytic performances, Chemical Engineering Journal 241 (2014) 344−351.

[45] D. Chen, B. Li, Q. Pu, X. Chen, G. Wen, Z. Li, Preparation of Ag-AgVO3/g-C3N4 composite photo-catalyst and degradation characteristics of antibiotics, Journal of Hazardous Materials 373 (2019) 303−312.

[46] Z. Li, M. Luo, B. Li, Q. Lin, X. Liao, H. Yu, C. Yu, 3-D hierarchical micro/nano-structures of porous Bi_2WO_6: controlled hydrothermal synthesis and enhanced photocatalytic performances, Microporous and Mesoporous Materials 313 (2021) 110830.

[47] Y. Lan, Z. Li, W. Xie, D. Li, G. Yan, S. Guo, J. Wu, In situ fabrication of I-doped $Bi_2O_2CO_3$/g-C_3N_4 heterojunctions for enhanced photodegradation activity under visible light, Journal of Hazardous Materials 385 (2020) 121622.

[48] K. Qian, Y. Yan, S. Xi, T. Wei, Y. Dai, X. Yan, R. Li, Elucidating the strain—vacancy—activity relationship on structurally deformed Co@CoO nanosheets for aqueous phase reforming of formaldehyde, Small 17 (51) (2021) 2102970.

[49] Y. Zhou, X. Li, C. Yu, X. Hu, Y. Yin, S. Guo, S. Zhong, Synergistic and durable Pt-WC catalyst for methanol electro-oxidation in ionic liquid aqueous solution, ACS Applied Energy Materials 2 (12) (2019) 8459—8463.

[50] Z. Li, B. Li, Y. Hu, X. Liao, H. Yu, C. Yu, Emerging ultrahigh-density single-atom catalysts for versatile heterogeneous catalysis applications: redefinition, recent progress, and challenges, Small Structures (2022) 2200041.

[51] Z. Li, B. Li, Y. Hu, S. Wang, C. Yu, Highly-dispersed and high-metal-density electrocatalysts on carbon supports for the oxygen reduction reaction: from nanoparticles to atomic-level architectures, Materials Advances 3 (2) (2022) 779—809.

[52] Z. Li, Y. Li, G. He, P.K. Shen, Novel graphene-like nanosheet supported highly active electrocatalysts with ultralow Pt loadings for oxygen reduction reaction, Journal of Materials Chemistry A 2 (40) (2014) 16898—16904.

[53] Z. Li, S. Ji, B.G. Pollet, P.K. Shen, A Co 3 W 3 C promoted Pd catalyst exhibiting competitive performance over Pt/C catalysts towards the oxygen reduction reaction, Chemical Communications 50 (5) (2014) 566—568.

[54] S. Yang, C. Zhao, C. Ge, X. Dong, X. Liu, Y. Liu, Z. Li, Ternary Pt—Ru—SnO_2 hybrid architectures: unique carbon-mediated 1-D configuration and their electrocatalytic activity to methanol oxidation, Journal of Materials Chemistry 22 (15) (2012) 7104—7107.

[55] B. Li, Z. Li, Q. Pang, Controllable preparation of N-doped Ni_3S_2 nanocubes@ N-doped graphene-like carbon layers for highly active electrocatalytic overall water splitting, Electrochimica Acta 399 (2021) 139408.

[56] W. Chen, J. Cao, J. Yang, Y. Cao, H. Zhang, Z. Jiang, ...X. Duan, Molecular-level insights into the electronic effects in platinum-catalyzed carbon monoxide oxidation, Nature Communications 12 (1) (2021) 6888.

[57] A.C. Michael, L. Borland, Electrochemical Methods for Neuroscience, CRC press, 2006.

[58] Z. Li, J. Lin, B. Li, C. Yu, H. Wang, Q. Li, Construction of heteroatom-doped and three-dimensional graphene materials for the applications in supercapacitors: a review, Journal of Energy Storage 44 (2021) 103437.

[59] B. Li, M. Yu, Z. Li, C. Yu, Q. Li, H. Wang, Three-dimensional activated carbon nanosheets modified by graphitized carbon dots: one-step alkali pyrolysis preparation and supercapacitor applications, Journal of Energy Storage 51 (2022) 104515.

[60] Z. Li, B. Li, Z. Liu, D. Li, H. Wang, Q. Li, One-pot construction of 3-D nitrogen-doped activated graphene-like nanosheets for high-performance supercapacitors, Electrochimica Acta 190 (2016) 378—387.

[61] Y. Li, Z. Li, P.K. Shen, Simultaneous formation of ultrahigh surface area and three-dimensional hierarchical porous graphene-like networks for fast and highly stable supercapacitors, Advanced Materials 25 (17) (2013) 2474—2480.

[62] Z. Li, K. Xiao, C. Yu, H. Wang, Q. Li, Three-dimensional graphene-like carbon nanosheets coupled with MnCo-layered double hydroxides nanoflowers as efficient bifunctional oxygen electrocatalyst, International Journal of Hydrogen Energy 46 (69) (2021) 34239—34251.

[63] Z. Li, L. Zhang, B. Li, Z. Liu, Z. Liu, H. Wang, Q. Li, Convenient and large-scale synthesis of hollow graphene-like nanocages for electrochemical supercapacitor application, Chemical Engineering Journal 313 (2017) 1242—1250.

[64] Z. Li, X. Hu, D. Xiong, B. Li, H. Wang, Q. Li, Facile synthesis of bicontinuous microporous/mesoporous carbon foam with ultrahigh specific surface area for supercapacitor application, Electrochimica Acta 219 (2016) 339—349.

[65] H. Wang, Z. Li, J. Yang, Q. Li, X. Zhong, A novel activated mesocarbon microbead (aMCMB)/ Mn_3O_4 composite for electrochemical capacitors in organic electrolyte, Journal of Power Sources 194 (2) (2009) 1218–1221.

[66] Q.Y. Li, Z.S. Li, L. Lin, X.Y. Wang, Y.F. Wang, C.H. Zhang, H.Q. Wang, Facile synthesis of activated carbon/carbon nanotubes compound for supercapacitor application, Chemical Engineering Journal 156 (2) (2010) 500–504.

[67] H.Q. Wang, G.F. Yang, Q.Y. Li, X.X. Zhong, F.P. Wang, Z.S. Li, Y.H. Li, Porous nano-MnO_2: large scale synthesis via a facile quick-redox procedure and application in a supercapacitor, New Journal of Chemistry 35 (2) (2011) 469–475.

[68] H.Q. Wang, Z.S. Li, Y.G. Huang, Q.Y. Li, X.Y. Wang, A novel hybrid supercapacitor based on spherical activated carbon and spherical MnO_2 in a non-aqueous electrolyte, Journal of Materials Chemistry 20 (19) (2010) 3883–3889.

[69] B. Zhang, X. Yu, C. Ge, X. Dong, Y. Fang, Z. Li, H. Wang, Novel 3-D superstructures made up of SnO_2@C core-shell nanochains for energy storage applications, Chemical Communications 46 (48) (2010) 9188–9190.

[70] X. Yu, S. Yang, B. Zhang, D. Shao, X. Dong, Y. Fang, H. Wang, Controlled synthesis of SnO_2@ carbon core-shell nanochains as high-performance anodes for lithium-ion batteries, Journal of Materials Chemistry 21 (33) (2011) 12295–12302.

[71] Z. Li, B. Li, C. Liao, Z. Liu, D. Li, H. Wang, Q. Li, One-pot construction of 3-D graphene nanosheets/Ni_3S_2 nanoparticles composite for high-performance supercapacitors, Electrochimica Acta 253 (2017) 344–356.

[72] Y.X. Huang, F. Wu, R.J. Chen, Thermodynamic analysis and kinetic optimization of high-energy batteries based on multi-electron reactions, National Science Review 7 (8) (2020) 1367–1386.

[73] Z. Bo, C. Li, H. Yang, K. Ostrikov, J. Yan, K. Cen, Design of supercapacitor electrodes using molecular dynamics simulations, Nano-Micro Letters 10 (2) (2018) 1–23.

[74] N. Yao, X. Chen, Z.H. Fu, Q. Zhang, Applying classical, ab Initio, and machine-learning molecular dynamics simulations to the liquid electrolyte for rechargeable batteries, Chemical Reviews 122 (2022).

[75] L. Xu, M. Zhang, Y. Wang, F. Wei, Highly effective adsorption of antibiotics from water by hierarchically porous carbon: effect of nanoporous geometry, Environmental Pollution 274 (2021) 116591.

[76] L. Zhang, L.Y. Tu, Y. Liang, Q. Chen, Z.S. Li, C.H. Li, W. Li, Coconut-based activated carbon fibers for efficient adsorption of various organic dyes, RSC Advances 8 (74) (2018) 42280–42291.

[77] X. Niu, L. Zheng, J. Zhou, Z. Dang, Z. Li, Synthesis of an adsorbent from sugarcane bagass by graft copolymerization and its utilization to remove Cd (II) ions from aqueous solution, Journal of the Taiwan Institute of Chemical Engineers 45 (5) (2014) 2557–2564.

[78] Z. Zhang, T. Liu, B. Fu, X. Yang, D.H. Zhang, First-principles quantum dynamical theory for the dissociative chemisorption of H2O on rigid Cu (111), Nature Communications 7 (1) (2016) 1–7.

[79] G. Wang, W. Wang, X. He, J. Li, L. Yu, B. Peng, G. Zhang, Concurrent manipulation of anion and cation adsorption kinetics in pancake-like carbon achieves ultrastable potassium ion hybrid capacitors, Energy Storage Materials 46 (2022) 10–19.

[80] L. Ma, Z. Li, J. Li, Y. Dai, C. Qian, Y. Zhu, W. Mai, Phytic acid-induced nitrogen configuration adjustment of active nitrogen-rich carbon nanosheets for high-performance potassium-ion storage, Journal of Materials Chemistry A 9 (45) (2021) 25445–25452.

[81] Y. Wu, P. Yang, Direct observation of vapor–liquid–solid nanowire growth, Journal of the American Chemical Society 123 (13) (2001) 3165–3166.

[82] Y. Fang, X. Wen, S. Yang, Hollow and tin-filled nanotubes of single-crystalline in $(OH)_3$ grown by a solution–liquid–solid–solid route, Angewandte Chemie International Edition 45 (28) (2006) 4655–4658.

[83] C. Yang, B.H. Ko, S. Hwang, Z. Liu, Y. Yao, W. Luc, L. Hu, Overcoming immiscibility toward bimetallic catalyst library, Science Advances 6 (17) (2020) eaaz6844.

[84] N. Zheng, X. Zhang, C. Zhang, X. Hu, J. Pan, C. Wu, W. Liu, Dynamic salt capsulated synthesis of carbon materials in air, Matter 5 (5) (2022) 1603–1615.

[85]   R.S. Wagner, The vapor-liquid-solid mechanism of crystal growth and its application to silicon, Trans. Metallur. Soc. AIME 233 (1965) 1053−1064.

[86]   T.J. Trentler, K.M. Hickman, S.C. Goel, A.M. Viano, P.C. Gibbons, W.E. Buhro, Solution-liquid-solid growth of crystalline III-V semiconductors: an analogy to vapor-liquid-solid growth, Science 270 (5243) (1995) 1791−1794.

[87]   P. Yao, H. Gong, Z.Y. Wu, H. Fu, B. Li, B. Zhu, J. Zhu, Greener and higher conversion of ester-ification via interfacial photothermal catalysis, Nature Sustainability 5 (4) (2022) 348−356.

[88]   Y. Zhu, X. Cui, H. Liu, Z. Guo, Y. Dang, Z. Fan, W. Hu, Tandem catalysis in electrochemical CO_2 reduction reaction, Nano Research 14 (12) (2021) 4471−4486.

[89]   X.M. Liu, X. Cui, K. Dastafkan, H.F. Wang, C. Tang, C. Zhao, …Q. Zhang, Recent advances in spinel-type electrocatalysts for bifunctional oxygen reduction and oxygen evolution reactions, Journal of Energy Chemistry 53 (2021) 290−302.

[90]   J. Bao, H. Chen, S. Yang, P. Zhang, Mechanochemical redox-based synthesis of highly porous CoxMn1-xOy catalysts for total oxidation, Chinese Journal of Catalysis 41 (12) (2020) 1846−1854.

[91]   S. Fleischmann, J.B. Mitchell, R. Wang, C. Zhan, D.E. Jiang, V. Presser, V. Augustyn, Pseudocapa-citance: from fundamental understanding to high power energy storage materials, Chemical Reviews 120 (14) (2020) 6738−6782.

[92]   M.T. Molares, V. Buschmann, D. Dobrev, R. Neumann, R. Scholz, I.U. Schuchert, J. Vetter, Sin-gle-crystalline copper nanowires produced by electrochemical deposition in polymeric ion track membranes, Advanced Materials 13 (1) (2001) 62−65.

[93]   F. Zhou, A. Izgorodin, R.K. Hocking, L. Spiccia, D.R. MacFarlane, Electrodeposited MnO_x films from ionic liquid for electrocatalytic water oxidation, Advanced Energy Materials 2 (8) (2012) 1013−1021.

[94]   J. Jiang, H. Ji, P. Chen, C. Ouyang, X. Niu, H. Li, L. Wang, The influence of electrolyte concen-tration and solvent on operational voltage of Li/CF_x primary batteries elucidated by Nernst Equation, Journal of Power Sources 527 (2022) 231193.

[95]   J. Tafel, Über die Polarisation bei kathodischer Wasserstoffentwicklung[J], Zeitschrift für physikali-sche Chemie 50 (1) (1905) 641−712.

[96]   E.J. Dickinson, A.J. Wain, The Butler-Volmer equation in electrochemical theory: origins, value, and practical application, Journal of Electroanalytical Chemistry 872 (2020) 114145.

[97]   Y.H. Fang, Z.P. Liu, Tafel kinetics of electrocatalytic reactions: from experiment to first-principles, ACS Catalysis 4 (12) (2014) 4364−4376.

[98]   https://mp.weixin.qq.com/s/6Wy7GVD1BaMNVw3fnFIwBw.

[99]   J. Cheng, X. Lin, P.K. Shen, The measurements of the oxygen reduction reaction, in: Electrochem-ical Oxygen Reduction, Springer, Singapore, 2021, pp. 29−83.

[100]   Z. Li, L. Zhang, X. Chen, B. Li, H. Wang, Q. Li, Three-dimensional graphene-like porous carbon nanosheets derived from molecular precursor for high-performance supercapacitor application, Elec-trochimica Acta 296 (2019) 8−17.

[101]   G. Ertl, Reactions at surfaces: from atoms to complexity (Nobel lecture), Angewandte Chemie In-ternational Edition 47 (19) (2008) 3524−3535.

[102]   H. Jiang, R. Luo, Y. Li, W. Chen, Recent advances in solid−liquid−gas three-phase interfaces in electrocatalysis for energy conversion and storage, EcoMat (2022) e12199.

[103]   G. Liu, W.S. Wong, M. Kraft, J.W. Ager, D. Vollmer, R. Xu, Wetting-regulated gas-involving (photo) electrocatalysis: biomimetics in energy conversion, Chemical Society Reviews 50 (18) (2021) 10674−10699.

[104]   Q. Yang, P.Z. Sun, L. Fumagalli, Y.V. Stebunov, S.J. Haigh, Z.W. Zhou, A.K. Geim, Capillary condensation under atomic-scale confinement, Nature 588 (7837) (2020) 250−253.

[105]   G. Cai, Y. Yin, D. Xia, A.A. Chen, J. Holoubek, J. Scharf, Z. Chen, Sub-nanometer confinement enables facile condensation of gas electrolyte for low-temperature batteries, Nature Communications 12 (1) (2021) 1−11.

[106]   A. Hodges, A.L. Hoang, G. Tsekouras, K. Wagner, C.Y. Lee, G.F. Swiegers, G.G. Wallace, A high-performance capillary-fed electrolysis cell promises more cost-competitive renewable hydrogen, Na-ture Communications 13 (1) (2022) 1−11.

[107] L. Tie, Z. Guo, W. Li, Optimal design of superhydrophobic surfaces using a paraboloid microtexture, Journal of Colloid and Interface Science 436 (2014) 19—28.

[108] L. Tie, Z. Guo, W. Liu, Anisotropic wetting properties on various shape of parallel grooved microstructure, Journal of Colloid and Interface Science 453 (2015) 142—150.

[109] L. Tie, Z. Guo, W. Liu, PH-manipulated underwater—oil adhesion wettability behavior on the micro/nanoscale semicircular structure and related thermodynamic analysis, ACS Applied Materials and Interfaces 7 (19) (2015) 10641—10649.

[110] Z. Ji, C. Yan, S. Ma, X. Zhang, X. Jia, X. Wang, F. Zhou, Biomimetic surface with tunable frictional anisotropy enabled by photothermogenesis-induced supporting layer rigidity variation, Advanced Materials Interfaces 6 (2) (2019) 1801460.

[111] J. Fan, J. De Coninck, H. Wu, F. Wang, Microscopic origin of capillary force balance at contact line, Physical Review Letters 124 (12) (2020) 125502.

[112] https://mp.weixin.qq.com/s/m7imGAp3BF9yGkhQSPPTwA.

[113] K. Yang, X. Li, C. Yu, D. Zeng, F. Chen, K. Zhang, H. Ji, Review on heterophase/homophase junctions for efficient photocatalysis: the case of phase transition construction, Chinese Journal of Catalysis 40 (6) (2019) 796—818.

[114] C. Yu, G. Li, S. Kumar, K. Yang, R. Jin, Phase transformation synthesis of novel Ag_2O/Ag_2CO_3 heterostructures with high visible light efficiency in photocatalytic degradation of pollutants, Advanced Materials 26 (6) (2014) 892—898.

[115] C. Yu, Z. Wu, R. Liu, D.D. Dionysiou, K. Yang, C. Wang, H. Liu, Novel fluorinated Bi_2MoO_6 nanocrystals for efficient photocatalytic removal of water organic pollutants under different light source illumination, Applied Catalysis B: Environmental 209 (2017) 1—11.

[116] C. Yu, W. Zhou, H. Liu, Y. Liu, D.D. Dionysiou, Design and fabrication of microsphere photocatalysts for environmental purification and energy conversion, Chemical Engineering Journal 287 (2016) 117—129.

[117] J. Wu, Understanding the electric double-layer structure, capacitance, and charging dynamics, Chemical Reviews 122 (12) (2022) 10821—10859.

[118] F. Béguin, V. Presser, A. Balducci, E. Frackowiak, Carbons and electrolytes for advanced supercapacitors, Advanced Materials 26 (14) (2014) 2219—2251.

[119] J. Gu, S. Liu, W. Ni, W. Ren, S. Haussener, X. Hu, Modulating electric field distribution by alkali cations for CO_2 electroreduction in strongly acidic medium, Nature Catalysis 5 (4) (2022) 268—276.

[120] Q. Yan, C. Lian, K. Huang, L. Liang, H. Yu, P. Yin, M. Xing, Constructing an acidic microenvironment by MoS_2 in heterogeneous Fenton reaction for pollutant control, Angewandte Chemie International Edition 60 (31) (2021) 17155—17163.

[121] B. Li, M. Yu, Z. Li, C. Yu, H. Wang, Q. Li, Constructing Flexible All-Solid-State Supercapacitors from 3D Nanosheets Active Bricks via 3D Manufacturing Technology: A Perspective Review, Advanced Functional Materials, 2022, p. 2201166.

[122] P. Liu, Y. Zhao, R. Qin, S. Mo, G. Chen, L. Gu, N. Zheng, Photochemical route for synthesizing atomically dispersed palladium catalysts, Science 352 (6287) (2016) 797—800.

[123] X.P. Wang, W.K. Wang, X.Z. Wang, Physical Chemistry, Higher Education, Beijing, 2017.

[124] S.L. Li, X. Fang, J.J. Liu, Y.P. Zhou, Physical Chemistry, Higher Education, Beijing, 2017.

[125] https://mp.weixin.qq.com/s/wLfIOr17P6yR3XijaL-Lhw.

[126] https://mp.weixin.qq.com/s/hY14q1tYO4fXIR9OKqbc3Q.

CHAPTER 5

Synthesis methods and paradigms of nanomaterials

5.1 Introduction

The rational design, controllable synthesis, and macropreparation of nanomaterials are the prerequisite of their technical applications in energy and environment fields. Efficient and clean preparation methods can promote the sustainable development of nanotechnology [1−3]. There are many different kinds of preparation methods for nanometer materials, in general these methods can be divided into two categories: (1) "Top-down" approach (mainly is a physical method, such as planet ball-milling, machinery crushing, laser ablation, and ultrasonic grinding, and other high energy physics methods) and (2) "Bottom-up" approach (mainly chemical method, such as hydrothermal/solvothermal method, coprecipitation, sol-gel method, chemical vapor deposition (CVD), and electrodeposition method, etc.) (see Fig. 5.1A for details) [4,5]. Among them, the "top-down" approach usually produces nanomaterials by physical dimension descending and refinement of large materials (such as micron materials or bulk materials larger than 1 mm), which is a dispersion process of dimensionality reduction and size reduction. The "bottom-up" approach is based on the connection and accumulation of atom, ion, or molecular basic units (less than 1 nm) to build low-dimensional (L-D) nanomaterials, which is a process of dimension and size control, mostly by chemical methods. Stacking arrangement with atoms as basic units can form sub-nanometer scale clusters, which do not form regular crystal nanostructures. When the size of materials goes beyond the scope of clusters, that is, nano-scale materials that can be regulated and constructed in different dimensions (0D, 1D, 2D, and 3D), which is the fascinating L-D nanostructured materials (see Fig. 5.1A) [4,5]. Through different preparation methods (including gas–phase, solution-phase, and solid-phase methods), most nanomaterials are expected to achieve their structure regulation and macropreparation, which lays the foundation for their practical application in energy and environment sciences.

In our world the states of matter are chiefly gas, liquid and solid. The preparation methods of nanomaterials can be simply divided into "gas-phase synthesis method", "liquid (solution)-phase synthesis method" and "solid-phase synthesis method" according to the states of reactants (see Fig. 5.1B) [6]. The gas-phase synthesis method mainly includes physical vapor deposition (PVD) (such as gas condensation and sputtering method) and CVD (such as super vacuum CVD and simple quasi-CVD method). The solution-phase synthesis method mainly includes hydrothermal/solvothermal method,

Nanostructured Materials
ISBN 978-0-443-19256-2, https://doi.org/10.1016/B978-0-443-19256-2.00030-2

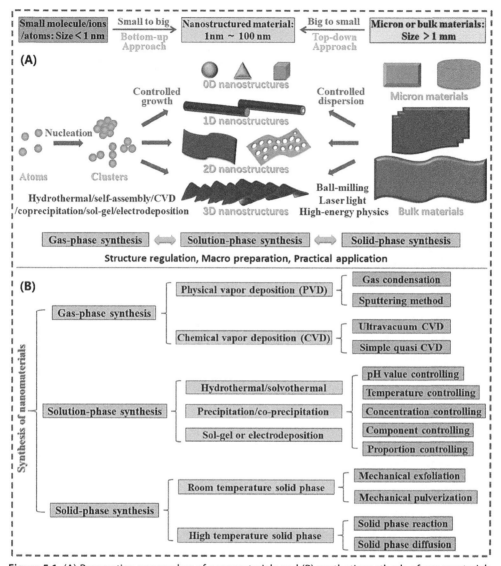

Figure 5.1 (A) Preparation approaches of nanomaterials and (B) synthetic methods of nanomaterials.

precipitation/coprecipitation, sol–gel method, and electrodeposition method. The pH and temperature of the reaction solution and the composition, concentration, and proportion of the reactants are the key control parameters for the solution–phase synthesis. The solid–phase synthesis can be roughly divided into room-temperature solid–phase synthesis and high-temperature solid–phase synthesis. The former is mostly used for mechanical exfoliation of layered materials and mechanical pulverization of bulk materials, while the latter is mostly used for solid–phase (solid–solid or solid–gas) chemical reactions and solid–phase atomic diffusion (such as thermal migration of metal atoms). By these methods, the morphology, size, crystal phase, and composition of nanomaterials can be controlled, and even the distribution of elements and single atoms in nanomaterials can be precisely controlled by atomic diffusion strategy [7]. For ease of reading and understanding, in this chapter micron will introduce the preparation of nanomaterials according to different synthesis techniques, including hydrothermal/solvothermal method, chemical coprecipitation method, sol-gel synthesis method, electrodeposition method, CVD method, high temperature solid phase method, mechanochemistry method, and other high energy physics methods. In summarizing these preparation methods of nanomaterials, we pay special attention to the description of the physicochemical principles of different synthesis methods and the paradigm summary of our or other group's work in recent years.

5.2 Hydrothermal/solvothermal method

5.2.1 Definitions and history of hydrothermal/solvothermal method

Hydrothermal/solvothermal method is an important controllable low-temperature liquid-phase synthesis method of nanomaterials. Hydrothermal/solvothermal method is to use aqueous solvent (or organic solvent) as the reaction medium in a special closed reaction vessel (generally with polytetrafluoroethylene as the liner and stainless steel as the protective shell), and create a reaction environment with moderate temperature (100−300°C) and high pressure (1−50 MPa) by heating the reaction vessel, so that the usually insoluble or inert substances are dissolved and further participate in the liquid phase reaction, and crystallize and grow corresponding products. In the hydrothermal/solvothermal reaction process, the solvent plays versatile roles: (1) participating in the chemical reaction as an effective component, (2) acting as a solvent and expansion promoter, (3) acting as a pressure transfer medium. By controlling the temperature and time of the reaction, the physical and chemical factors in the reaction system can be adjusted to realize the controllable growth of inorganic nanostructures. Hydrothermal/solvothermal reaction has been widely used in the preparation of various inorganic nanomaterials, and inorganic nanomaterials have become a very active research field [8].

Hydrothermal method was first developed by French scholars Daubree and Xenalmon. The main purpose was to synthesize hydrothermal minerals and explore their formation conditions in nature, laying a foundation for the hydrothermal synthesis of industrial minerals and crystals. Academician Yitai Qian of China developed solvothermal synthesis technology into an important solid synthesis method, creatively developed inorganic synthesis chemistry in organic phase, realized a series of new inorganic reactions in organic phase, and made great contributions in the field of nanomaterials [9]. In 1996, Qian published a paper in *Science*, in which nanocrystalline GaN was prepared by benzene thermal synthesis technology at 280°C, which contains ultrahigh pressure phase rock salt Gan phase [10]. This work established the important position of solvothermal synthesis technology in nano synthesis. Under the guidance of keeping the chemical bond geometry of reactants in the product, using Wurtz reaction, carbon tetrachloride and hexachlorobenzene were reduced with metal sodium at relatively low-temperature condition to prepare diamond powder and multi walled carbon nanotubes [11]. The article was published in *J Am Chem Soc*, which was rated as "straw turns gold" by "American Chemical and Engineering News" and was also selected as one of the top 10 Science and Technology news in 1998 by the Ministry of education of China [12].

5.2.2 Physicochemical principles of hydrothermal/solvothermal method

Under subcritical and supercritical hydrothermal/solvothermal conditions, the reaction is at the molecular level, the reaction activity is improved, so hydrothermal reaction can replace some high-temperature solid-state reactions. Because the homogeneous and heterogeneous nucleation mechanism of hydrothermal/solvothermal reaction is different from the diffusion mechanism of solid-phase reaction, new compounds and materials that cannot be prepared by other methods can be created in this method. These advantages can be attributed to the special physical and chemical factors of hydrothermal/solvothermal synthesis. The physicochemical principles of hydrothermal/solvothermal method include chemical equilibrium principle, phase equilibrium principle, reaction kinetics principle, etc. The principle of chemical equilibrium is as follows: in a constant-volume and closed system, the ions in the solution can easily react according to stoichiometry, and it is easy to reach the chemical equilibrium state conducive to the product. Phase equilibrium principle: nanograins can grow according to their crystallization habits. During the crystallization process, harmful impurities can be discharged into the solution by themselves to produce crystalline powder with high purity. The principle of reaction kinetics is as follows: with the increase of temperature and autogenous pressure, the solvent becomes a gaseous mineralizer with great depolymerization ability, the chemical reaction speed is fast, and can prepare multi-component or single-component ultra-fine nanopowders.

5.2.3 Paradigms and analysis of hydrothermal/solvothermal method

The controllable conditions of hydrothermal/solvothermal synthesis often include reaction temperature, reactant ratio, reactant concentration, pH of reaction solution, additives, etc. The change of these conditions can affect the crystallinity, apparent morphology, pore structure, and even crystalline phase of nanomaterials. Our research group has been devoted to the regulation of hydrothermal or solvothermal reaction conditions and the controllable preparation of various nanomaterials for many years. Recently, we prepared a series of porous Bi_2WO_6 photocatalysts with 3-D hierarchical micro/nano-structures (HMNSs) by hydrothermal method via adjusting the concentration of reactants (see Fig. 5.2A) [13]. In this work, the hydrothermal synthesis without any additives is proposed, i.e., the Bi_2WO_6 3-D HMNSs photocatalysts with adjustable nanostructures are successfully prepared by just controlling the concentration of reactants. Generally, in hydrothermal synthesis, the concentration of the reactants can affect the type, distribution, and amount of charge on the crystal nucleus, thus the crystal

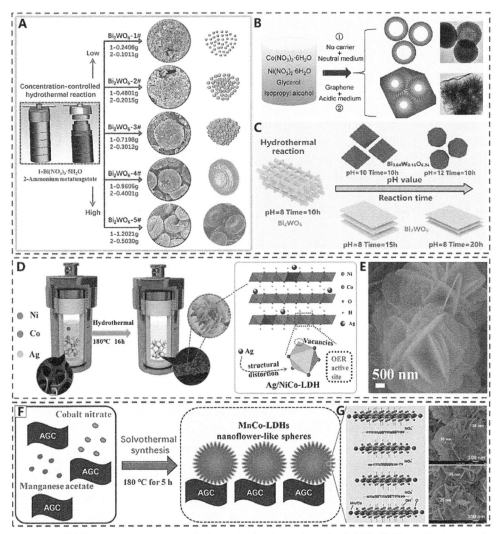

Figure 5.2 (A) The concentration regulation in hydrothermal synthesis [13], (B) The pH value regulation in solvothermal synthesis [14], (C) The pH value regulation in hydrothermal synthesis [15], (D) The heterogeneous doping regulation in hydrothermal synthesis [16], (E) The composite structure regulation in hydrothermal synthesis [17].

orientation and growth rates are affected. The reactant concentration will affect the crystalline structure of the catalyst, including the degree of crystallinity, crystal size, and the pore structure, so lead to the different structures and morphology of the products. These Bi_2WO_6 products show the different crystalline size and different morphology, mainly due to the different reaction kinetics and assembly degree of nanocrystals under the different reactant concentrations. In the hydrothermal process, the reactant components are anisotropic, when the reactant concentration is low, it is difficult for the self-assemble of low-crystallinity nanoparticles. With the concentration increasing, these nanoparticles automatically cluster to form self-assembled 3-D HMNSs microspheres, which further form particular forms, namely, erythrocyte-like superstructures (see Fig. 5.2A) [13].

We also carried out research on pH controlling for hydrothermal/solvothermal synthesis, where different morphology [14] and crystal phase structure [15] can be obtained with different pH conditions. In 2017, we reported hollow and mesoporous flower-like $NiCo_2O_4$ construction with 3D hierarchical nano-sheets, by means of the controllable solvothermal synthesis strategy with appropriate amount of graphene oxide aqueous solution (see Fig. 5.2B) [14]. It is generally known that the pH value of precursor solution is a pivotal factor affecting the morphology of nanomaterials during hydrothermal synthesis process. It is also established that the hierarchical nanostructures of metal oxides can be readily produced in acidic reaction conditions, due to the distinguished "dissolution-precipitation" mechanism [18]. In the present case, the graphene oxide solution used in the experiment is a typical acidic aqueous solution (pH value is about 3.0) that is prepared by sulfuric acid oxidation system. The sphere-like structures were gradually evolved into the flower-like structures with the increase of the amount of graphene oxide solution (with the increase of pH value). The result suggested that the increase in acidity of reaction solution can accelerate the disintegration of sphere-like structures and the generation flower-like structures based on the "dissolution-precipitation" mechanism [14].

In 2021, we further prove that pH regulation can achieve different nano-morphologies and crystal phase structures of hydrothermal products (see Fig. 5.2C) [15]. With the increase of pH (pH = 8, 10, 12), the products gradually changed from orthogonal phase Bi_2WO_6 to cubic $Bi_{3.84}W_{0.16}O_{6.24}$ and the morphology changed from lamellas made of nanorods to octahedral or spherical particles. The Bi_2WO_6-8 (pH = 8) is a lamellar structure formed by directional growth of regular nanorods, $Bi_{3.84}W_{0.16}O_{6.24}$-10 (pH = 10) is a double cone octahedral structure with a regular square on the bottom. The edges and corners of $Bi_{3.84}W_{0.16}O_{6.24}$-12 (pH = 12) gradually become smooth and have the tendency to develop into spherical particles. In addition, the Bi_2WO_6-8 (pH = 8) becomes thin or ultra-thin nanosheets with the prolongation of hydrothermal reaction time from 10 to 15h or 20h. Generally, this study showed the transformation of morphology and phase structure of hydrothermal products with different pH and reaction time [15]. In acidic aqueous solutions of different dosages, we also prepared metal oxides of different crystal types by hydrothermal method: in low-dosage acidic aqueous solution (5 mL HNO_3), hydrothermal preparation of α-MnO_2 nanosilks is realized [19], while in high-dosage acidic aqueous solution (15 mL HNO_3) hydrothermal preparation of β-MnO_2 nanorods is realized [20]. In general, the pH (acidic and basic capacity) regulation is an efficient strategy for hydrothermal synthesis of nanomaterials with specific phase, structure, and morphology.

Hydrothermal synthesis is an effective method to realize hetero-element doping of nanomaterials. The hetero-doping structure has abundant hetero-interfaces that can modulate the intrinsic properties of active sites, resulting in a greatly improved catalytic activity. Recently, Li and Pang designed and prepared novel 3D hetero-electrocatalysts of NiCo-layered double hydroxide (LDH) nanosheets incorporated with silver nanoclusters (atomic-level metal doping) on a Ni foam (labeled as Ag@NiCo-LDH/NF) by a one-pot hydrothermal method (see Fig. 5.2D) [16]. The macroporous structure of Ni foam ensured that silver nanoclusters were uniformly deposited on NiCo-LDH-nanosheets during the hydrothermal process. In particular, the hydrothermal synthesis of Ag doping causes the surface of the NiCo-LDH catalyst to be rich in anionic defects (i.e., oxygen vacancy). This work provides a facile hydrothermal strategy for designing efficient Ni and Co-based LDH electrocatalysts by creating a high density of oxygen vacancies and new active sites on the LDH catalyst surface.

Hydrothermal synthesis is also an effective method to obtain the composite interface structure of nanomaterials. More recently, Li and coworkers further designed and prepared MnCo-layered double hydroxides nanoflowers (MnCo-LDHs) supported on the active graphene-like carbon (AGC) nanosheets by a convenient solvothermal method (see Fig. 5.2E) [17]. This 3-D nanocomposite (AGC/MnCo-LDHs) showed a thinner nanosheet structure of MnCo-LDHs due to the composite structure regulation by AGC nanosheets. The hydrothermal reaction process (at 180°C for 5 h) leads to the close contact (formation of chemical bonds) between AGC nanosheets and MnCo-LDHs nanoflowers, which promotes the interfacial electron transfer and interfacial catalytic properties. The expansion of the interlayer region is occurred due to the intercalation of anions, such as NO_3^{-1} derived from one (cobalt nitrate) of the reactants in solvothermal synthesis. This study proves that the hydrothermal/solvothermal method is an efficient method for the design of composite nanomaterials.

5.3 Chemical coprecipitation method

5.3.1 Definitions and history of chemical coprecipitation method

Chemical coprecipitation method usually mixes substances with different chemical components in the state of solution, adds appropriate precipitant to the mixed solution to prepare precursor precipitate, and then dries or calcines the precipitate to prepare corresponding powder particles. Strictly speaking, coprecipitation method refers to the method that contains two or more cations in the solution, which exist in the solution in homogeneous phase. After adding precipitant, uniform precipitation of various components can be obtained after the precipitation reaction. It is an important method to prepare multi-metal oxide or multi-metal alloy or multi-metal heterojunction ultra-fine powder containing two or more metal elements [21]. More broadly, some redox reactions in solution (such as comproportionation between different metal valence states) can also be understood as chemical coprecipitation (or precipitation) reactions. The advantages of the coprecipitation method are as follows: firstly, nano-powder materials with uniform chemical composition can be obtained directly through various chemical reactions in solution; secondly, nano-powder materials with small particle size and uniform distribution can be easily prepared by regulating precipitation reaction kinetics. Coprecipitation method has also the advantages of simple preparation, easy control of conditions, and low synthesis cost.

Coprecipitation from solution is one of the oldest techniques for the preparation of mixed oxides before 1990s [21], such as the transparent conductive mixed oxide of stannic antimony oxide (ATO) in 1979 [22]. In recent decades, this technique has been extended to liquid-phase synthesis for many multicomponent nanomaterials, including single-phase coprecipitation (such as bimetallic oxide and alloy) and mixture coprecipitation (such as mixed oxides and interfacial heterojunctions) [23]. So far, coprecipitation method has been a mature and widely used method for the preparation of nanoscale metal catalysts. The guiding concern is that coprecipitation is one of the first means to synthesize single-atom catalysts (SACs). On the basis of long-term research on high-dispersion catalysts, academician Zhang Tao's research group first prepared Pt_1/FeO_x SACs by coprecipitation method in 2011 [24]. The specific steps are as follows: firstly, the aqueous solution of precious metal precursor (chloroplatinic acid) and ferric nitrate solution are mixed and titrated in an appropriate proportion under the condition of stirring in an alkaline environment. The obtained coprecipitate is filtered, washed, and calcined, and finally, Pt_1/FeO_x SACs is obtained. In the report, Tao Zhang proposed the concept of "single atom catalysis" for the first time, and this achievement was selected as one of the "top 10 scientific research achievements" in the field of chemistry and chemical engineering in 2016 by the chemical and Engineering News of the American Chemical Society [25].

5.3.2 Physicochemical principles of chemical coprecipitation method

The physicochemical principles of chemical coprecipitation method include chemical equilibrium principle, phase equilibrium principle, reaction kinetics principle, etc. Coprecipitation is seen as a multicomponent reverse of dissolved substances (multicomponent solid-liquid phase diagram), in the precipitation process, it is only when the concentration of dissolved substances in the solution more than the critical saturation, precipitation will occur spontaneously (supersaturated solution is the prerequisite for precipitation). Coprecipitation existed dissolution-precipitation dynamic balance in the reaction solution. For example, complexation (NH$_3$) and precipitation (OH$^-$) are inter-dependent and competitive in the preparation of polymetallic hydroxide by coprecipita-tion method: as the total ammonia concentration increases, higher pH values are required to precipitate the transition metal ions completely [26]. Chemical coprecipitation also in-volves chemical reactions and equilibria between precursors, so the reaction temperature and concentration can affect the chemical equilibrium shift. For the reaction kinetics of coprecipitation, it is necessary to strictly control the parameters, such as the adding speed of precursor, droplet size, mixing rates, solution shear rate, pH value, and so on. The composition control, purity, and morphology of the resulting product are good by coprecipitation. However, different rates of precipitation of each individual compound may lead to microscopic inhomogeneity or even sectional aggregates [21]. According to the relative strength of complexation and precipitation ($R_{c/p}$), the hydroxide coprecipi-tation reaction can be divided into three parts: (1) Incomplete precipitation region ($R_{c/p} > 10.1$); (2) Time correlation region ($R_{c/p} = 0.1-10.1$); (3) Reaction difficult control area ($R_{c/p} < 0.1$). The precipitation and complexation rates in the time-controlled region are the precondition for uniform growth of nanoparticles by copreci-pitation method [27,28].

5.3.3 Paradigms and analysis of chemical coprecipitation method

In terms of chemical coprecipitation or chemical precipitation, our group has made a number of typical achievements in the last 10 years, including single metal oxides, mixed metal oxides, phosphate-carbon nitride composites, and bimetallic alloys [29−33]. In 2010, we proposed a coprecipitation strategy based on comproportionation redox reaction to achieve the chemical deposition of small size MnO$_2$ nanosheets on the surface of activated mesocarbon microbeads (AMCMB) (see Fig. 5.3A−C) [29]. Firstly, after the activation treatment, the MCMB becomes a–MCMB with a high adsorption capacity. Secondly, the a–MCMB were added into the KMnO$_4$ (Mn^{7+}) solution, where the Mn^{7+} are adsorbed on the surface of a–MCMB and formed mixture (a–MCMB + KMnO$_4$). Finally, Mn(Ac)$_2 \cdot$4H$_2$O (Mn^{2+}) are added into the solution drop by drop during stirring, the Mn^{2+} sis in situ oxidized to the Mn^{4+} on the surface a–MCMB, the resulting Mn^{4+} interacted with water to produce MnO$_2$ (see Eqs. 5.1 and 5.2):

$$3Mn^{2+} + 5Mn^{7+} \rightarrow 5Mn^{4+} \tag{5.1}$$

$$Mn^{4+} + 2H_2O \rightarrow MnO_2 + 4H^+ \tag{5.2}$$

Comproportionation reaction refers to the redox reaction of different substances composed of the same element, and the two valences (one high and one low) of the element is close to the middle (the comproportionation reaction is opposite to dispropor-tionation reaction). Since the metal element of the product come from the two reactants,

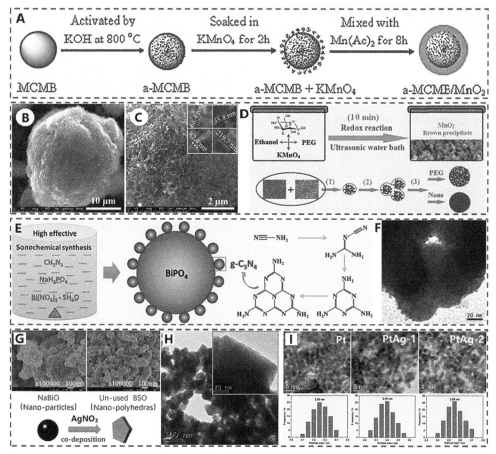

Figure 5.3 (A–C) The comproportionation reaction in coprecipitation synthesis [29], (D) The quick-redox reaction in precipitation synthesis [30], (E and F) The interfacial assemble of phosphate-carbon nitride composites by precipitation synthesis [31], (D) The coprecipitation synthesis of BSO mixed oxides [32], (E) The coprecipitation synthesis of PtAg bimetallic alloys [33].

the comproportionation reaction can be regarded as a special homogeneous coprecipitation reaction [29].

Whether chemical coprecipitation or precipitation, the reaction rate of redox determines the nanostructure and crystal structure of precipitation products. In 2010, we also reported a new type of porous nano-MnO_2 synthesized by a sonochemistry-assisted quick-redox reaction between $KMnO_4$ and D-glucose (i.e., quick chemical precipitation) (see Fig. 5.3D) [30]. The redox precipitation reaction can be completed within 10 min in a high–intensity ultrasonic source (so-called quick-redox precipitation reaction). The results show that the porous MnO_2 nanoparticles in the range 20–50 nm are interestingly composed of nanorods with diameters of about 2 nm and lengths of 4–8 nm (no obvious particle agglomeration with the help surfactant PEG). Most importantly, the rapid redox reaction ensures the occurrence of large-area homogeneous nucleation, and the growth kinetic process is inhibited. Therefore, amorphous nanostructures with low crystallinity and small size can be harvested through this reaction.

Chemical coprecipitation or precipitation methods can also be used to design composite interface nanomaterials. In 2014, we reported a novel 0D-on-0D composite architecture made of graphitic carbon nitride (g-C_3N_4) quantum dots and bismuth phosphate (BiPO$_4$) nanocrystals by chemical precipitation method (see Fig. 5.3E and F) [31]. For the synthesis of composite architectures, a sonochemical precipitation and heat-treating synthesis were introduced, by using CH_2N_2, NaH_2PO_4 and $Bi(NO_3)_3 \cdot 5H_2O$ as precursors. During chemical precipitation, CH_2N_2 is evenly adsorbed on the surface of $BiPO_4$ nanocrystals under ultrasonic dispersion. Then, g-C_3N_4 quantum dots are formed and assembled on the surface of $BiPO_4$ at heat-treating procedure. It can be seen that the combination of chemical precipitation and in situ interface growth can construct unique heterojunction interface nanomaterials.

More recently (in 2020), our groups (Zesheng Li and Changlin Yu) synthesized a new-fashioned bismuth silver oxide (BSO) nanocrystal by a simple coprecipitation method, from the silver nitrate ($AgNO_3$) and bismuth acid sodium ($NaBiO_3$) raw materials (see Fig. 5.3G and H) [32]. After the coprecipitation reaction, the solid $NaBiO_3$ nanoparticles were transformed into BSO nanocrystals with polyhedral structures. Because $NaBiO_3$ is difficult to dissolve in water, this coprecipitation reaction belongs to solid–liquid interface reaction or in-situ phase transformation reaction. The BSO nanocrystals prepared by coprecipitation of Ag ion and $NaBiO_3$ have a stable polyhedral structure and chemical property. This study provides a unique in situ phase transformation coprecipitation strategy for nanostructured material design.

Previously (in 2017), Zesheng Li et al. developed a coprecipitation strategy (via glycerine co-reduction of Pt and Ag ionic precursors) to structure bimetallic PtAg alloyed nanoparticles (NPs) with high metal density and ultrafine particle size ($\sim$2.5 nm) (see Fig. 5.3I) [33]. This coprecipitation reduction method can be used to uniformly deposit ultrafine PtAg NPs onto 3-D conductive networks of mesoporous graphene (3DMGS). The combination of ultrafine PtAg NPs and 3DMGS conductive networks provides a relatively stable macroporous composite architecture, which offers convenient binary channels for both electron transport and ion diffusion. This study demonstrated that the PtAg/3DMGS composite material fabricated by coprecipitation strategy (coreduction method) is a promising electrocatalyst with high catalytic activity and high stability for the oxygen reduction reaction.

5.4 Sol-gel synthesis method

5.4.1 Definitions and history of sol-gel synthesis method

Sol–Gel method is a common method for preparation of nanomaterials, which has attracted much attention in academia and industry. By using compounds containing high chemical active components as precursors, water or organic solvent is used as a medium to disperse these raw materials, after hydrolysis and chemical reaction, the solution can form a stable transparent Sol system. Sol is a colloidal system with liquid characteristics, where solid nanoparticles or macromolecular with sizes ranging from 1 to 100 nm are uniformly dispersed in liquid-phase medium. Gel with a network structure is formed by slow polymerization of aged colloidal particles, and the gel network is filled with liquid solvents. Gel is a colloidal system with solid characteristics, where the dispersed nanoparticles or macromolecular become a continuous network skeleton. The Gel can become a kind of dry gel with porous structures after removing the solvent by freeze-drying and long-term air drying. Finally, the powder or aerogel nanomaterials with porous structures can be prepared by curing and sintering at elevated temperatures.

In 1846, the French chemist J. J. Ebelmen found that the hydrolysis of Tetrasilicate in the air would form a gel, thus ushering in a new era of Sol-Gel chemistry. Taking metal alkoxide as precursor, sol is formed through hydrolysis and alcoholization of the precursor, and finally, gel products are formed through polycondensation. The sol-gel method is a unique wet chemical method for preparing ultra-fine nanomaterials, and a commercial sol-gel coating applied to glass plates appeared in the early 1960s. However, the real development of Sol-Gel science began with the "First International Symposium on the preparation of glass and ceramics by gel method" held in Padua in 1981. Since then, the research on sol-gel method has experienced significant growth, and a large number of the literature on the basic research and applied research of sol-gel technology have appeared. At present, the sol-gel method has been widely used in the preparation of multifunctional nanomaterials in energy and environment applications [34].

5.4.2 Physicochemical principles of sol-gel synthesis method

From the birth of sol-gel technology to now, the research of sol-gel synthesis has made great progress, and the corresponding basic theories have been established from polymer science, physical chemistry, coordination chemistry, metal organic chemistry, and other related disciplines. The physicochemical principles of sol-gel synthesis method include colloidal chemistry principle, surface chemistry principle, phase equilibrium principle, reaction kinetics principle, etc. The preparation process of aerogel gel is divided into two steps: preparing wet gel (involving reaction kinetics principle in hydrolysis and condensation reaction) and drying the wet gel by special means (involving solid-gas phase equilibrium principle in freeze drying). Due to the effect of surface tension, under normal conditions, the volatilization of liquid in gel will cause the fragile skeleton of the gel to collapse. This problem can be solved by freeze-drying technology in sublimation principle. In addition, the electric double layer principle of colloid and the precipitation principle of colloid should also be considered in the study of sol-gel synthesis method. It is believed that the sol-gel technology will be more widely used with the deepening of basic research work on the physicochemical mechanism of sol and the nanostructures of gel, as well as their crystalline transition process [35].

5.4.3 Paradigms and analysis of sol-gel synthesis method

In recent years, our research groups (Zesheng Li and Changlin Yu) have focused on the optimization of sol-gel synthesis method and its application in the synthesis of nanomaterials for electrochemistry and photochemistry. Through research and summary, we confirm that the preparation process of nanomaterials by sol-gel method includes three aspects: (I) sol preparation, (II) gel formation, and (III) subsequent heat treatment.

(I) The sol preparation includes three steps: (1) Selecting a specific chemical reagent to configure it as a precursor of metal inorganic salt (or metal organic alkoxide); (2) The precursor is dissolved in liquid solvent (water or organic solvent) to form a uniform solution; (3) Adding an appropriate amount of additives to the solution to hydrolyze, alcoholize or polymerize the precursor salt to form a uniform and stable sol system (other active components can be added if necessary).

(II) The gel formation also includes three steps: (1) A hydrogel (or organic gel) system in which the sol is concentrated or polymerized into a network structure after a long time of placement (so-called aging) or partial evaporation; (2) After further freeze-drying, the hydrogel (or organic gel) is transformed into aerogel; (3) Or the Sol can be directly (or coated on substrate) applied to low-temperature drying under vacuum to obtain colloidal powder (or dry gel film).

(III) Subsequent heat treatment: The uniform functional nanomaterials of powder (or aerogel) can be obtained by oxidation, high-temperature solid reaction or removal of organic components in air atmosphere or protective atmosphere. It was found that the conditions of subsequent heat treatment process (such as sintering, carbonization, or high-temperature reaction) affected the structure and morphology of nanomaterials.

Through the reasonable design and optimization of the above three aspects, we have prepared a series of functional nanomaterials by sol-gel method. They mainly include nanoporous materials (nanoparticles in sol as sacrificial template for porous structure) [36], mixed oxide nanomaterials (sol component + foreign active component) [37,38], elemental metal nanomaterials (entire organic Sol + single metal precursor) [39], quantum dots-on-particles nanostructures (entire organic Sol + double metal precursors) [40]. Detailed research results are shown as follows (see Fig. 5.4 for details).

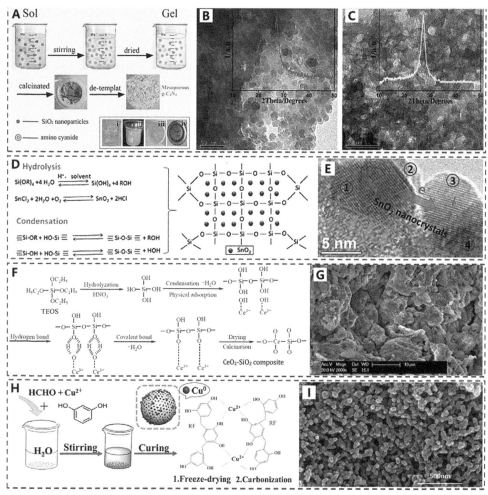

Figure 5.4 (A–C) Synthesis of nanoporous g-C$_3$N$_4$ materials by sol-gel method [36], (D and E) Synthesis of mixed oxide (SiO$_2$–SnO$_2$) nanomaterials by sol-gel method [37], (F and G) Synthesis of mixed oxide (SiO$_2$–CeO$_2$) nanomaterials by sol-gel method [38], (H) Synthesis of elemental metal (Cu^0) nanoparticles by sol-gel method [39], (I) Synthesis of CdS quantum dots on TiO$_2$ nanoparticles by sol-gel method [40].

In 2013, Zesheng Li and coworkers proposed a high-efficiency solution-based sol-gel synthesis for large-scale production of mesoporous g-C_3N_4, by using amino cyanide solution and the silica colloidal dispersion liquid as the reaction precursors (see Fig. 5.4A—C) [36]. Firstly, 50 mL amino cyanide solution was mixed in 50 mL of silica colloidal dispersion liquid, after the mixed solution was magnetic stirring at room temperature for 5 h, the homogeneous and viscous solution (Sol) was then dried at 343 K for 1 h to get a transparent Gel. Secondly, the gel was transferred into a porcelain boat and calcinated at 823 K for 4 h under N_2 protection. Finally, the resulting dark yellow sample was treated with a 4 M NH_4HF_2 solution to remove the silica template. This study indicated that the Sol-gel synthetic method is a simple, efficient, and viable technique for the large-scale production of mesoporous polymeric materials.

In 2012, Zesheng Li and coworkers also proposed a convenient Sol-gel synthesis route to synchronously synthesize ultra-high-density SnO_2 small nanocrystals (6—8 nm) anchored on amorphous silica matrix, by using tetraethoxysilane (TEOS) and $SnCl_2$ as the reaction precursors (see Fig. 5.4D and E) [37]. Firstly, SnO_2/silica hybrid gels were prepared by hydrolysis and condensation of the ethanol-diluted TEOS in the presence of acetic acid catalysts, coupled with a synchronous hydrolysis of $SnCl_2$. The amorphous SnO_2 is formed by the hydrolysis of $SnCl_2$ and supported onto the silica during the formation of the gel, and crystal SnO_2 is formed during the process of sintering. The close-packed SnO_2 nanocrystals on silica matrix could offer excellent electronic transfer capability and good stability for electrochemical energy storage applications.

In 2014, Changlin Yu and coworkers reported that the mixed oxide (SiO_2—SnO_2) nanomaterials with large surface areas can be synthesized by using a Sol-gel process under acidic conditions (TEOS and $Ce(NO_3)_3$ as the reaction precursors) (see Fig. 5.4F and G) [38]. The formation process could include several steps such as hydrolysis of TEOS, condensation, dehydration, and calcination. Firstly, under acidic conditions, the hydrolysis of TEOS takes place, producing orthosilicic acid. The orthosilicic acid is transformed into a silicate polymer by condensation and dehydration. Ce^{3+} could be adsorbed by the hydroxy (—OH) groups in the silicate polymer. Drying and calcination produce a SiO_2—SnO_2 mixed oxide with good dispersion and a large surface area. The active component, such as Ni, can be loaded onto the as-synthesized mixed oxides, producing supported Ni catalysts for catalytic partial oxidation of methane to syngas.

In 2019, Changlin Yu and coworkers reported that Cu^{2+} can be embedded into a polycondensation structure (entire organic Sol) of resorcinol (R) and formaldehyde (F) via sol-gel reaction, and the complex was then calcined at high temperature to obtain copper (Cu^0) nanoparticles dispersed on carbon aerogels (Cu/CA) (see Fig. 5.4H) [39]. The Cu^{2+} can be fixed into the 3D framework formed by the polycondensation of RF. The hydrogen bond in the solution also contributes a strong connection between RF and Cu^{2+}. After curing step, a certain amount stable Cu^{2+} embedded into xerogel structure can be obtained. Then, the sample was then freeze-dried, further carbonization, and further activated sequentially under CO^2 and N^2 to obtain 3D carbon aerogel with uniformly distributed Cu nanoparticles. The entire organic Sol strategy can be endowed with high purity of carbon material compared to other metal-organic Sol. In 2017, Yu and coworkers also reported an entire organic Sol strategy (with triblock copolymer Pluronic P123 as precursor) to prepare CdS quantum dots distributed on TiO_2 nanoparticles by the sol-gel method (see Fig. 5.4I) [40]. Uniform TiO_2 and CdS/TiO_2 with different ratios of CdS were successfully obtained via this sol-gel method under mild conditions.

5.5 Electrodeposition method

5.5.1 Definitions and history of electrodeposition method

Electrodeposition is an electrochemical process, and its research focus is "cathode deposition." Electrodeposition is to apply an electric current in a solution containing plated metal ions to discharge positively charged cations on the cathode, so as to obtain a metal film. Electrodeposition is usually carried out in aqueous solution, but it can also be carried out in nonaqueous solution, such as polar organic compounds. The methods of electrodeposition include direct current electrodeposition, alternating current electrodeposition, pulse electrodeposition, composite electrodeposition, and so on. In the electrodeposition solution, it is usually necessary to add a suitable crystallization refining surfactant, which is conducive to obtaining the nanocrystalline structure with grain refinement. The morphology of deposits is related to the properties of metal ions (such as valence state and redox potential) and also depends on the composition of electrolyte, pH value, temperature, current density, and other factors.

Electrodeposition was first called electroplating, which began with the discovery of electricity, from 1792 when Galvani discovered animal electric currents to 1800 when Volt invented the battery pack, and to 1805 when Brugatelly successfully plated gold to silver with the battery pack. The electroplating alloys began with copper zinc alloys (brass) and precious gold alloys in the 1840s. In basic research areas such as energy materials or more broadly nanomaterials, scientists prefer to use "electrodeposition" to describe this electrosynthesis technique. Since 1991, when El-Sherikt reported the preparation of ultrafine nickel nanocrystals ($\sim$20 nm) by DC electroplating technology, there has been increasing interest in electrodeposition of nanomaterials [41]. At present, electrodeposition has proved to be a promising method for the preparation of different nanomaterials, which has the following advantages: (1) The structure of nanomaterials can be easily controlled by changing electroplating parameters (deposition time, voltage and electrolyte concentration, etc.); (2) The uniformly dispersed nanomaterials can be controlled quickly and easily without the need for additional capping agents or reducing agents; (3) This method is simple and highly scalable at ambient condition [42].

5.5.2 Physicochemical principles of electrodeposition method

The physicochemical principles of electrodeposition method include electrochemical principle, surface chemistry principle, reaction kinetics principle, etc. Electrodeposition usually takes place in a two or three-electrode system with a reactant electrolyte solution (including the compact layer, diffusion layer, and bulk solution) between the electrodes (see Fig. 5.5A and B) [43]. During electrodeposition, by controlling the applied potential or deposition current, the reactants in the solution are oxidized/reduced and continuously deposited on the working electrode. Therefore, by changing the electrodeposition

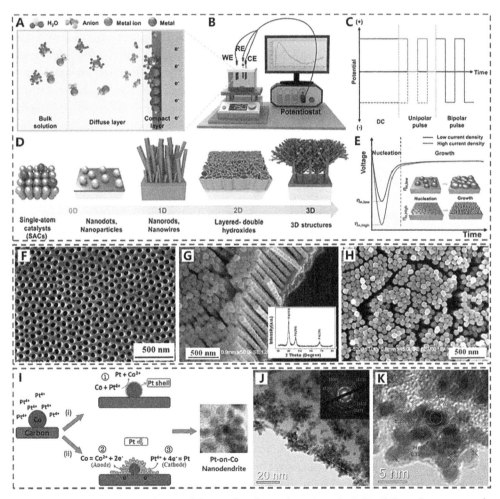

Figure 5.5 (A–E) Systems and control factors for electrodeposition [43], (F–H) Template strategy for electrodeposition [44], (I–K) Oxygen regulation for underpotential deposition method [45].

mode (DC/pulse) (see Fig. 5.5C), overpotential, solution concentration, solution viscosity, stirring speed additive, and deposition parameters, deposition products ranging from a single atom (0D) to complex three-dimensional (3D) nanostructures can be obtained (see Fig. 5.5D). Meanwhile, nucleation and growth rates of crystals can be controlled by different current densities to obtain different film morphology and deposition sizes (see Fig. 5.5E). For example, 3D hierarchical structures can be formed by electrodeposition with limited growth under nonequilibrium conditions, and atomic-level structures can be achieved by surface confinement of underpotential deposition (UPD) [43].

In the process of electrodeposition, when metal ions are transferred to the cathode, adsorption atoms are formed due to charge transfer reaction, and finally, the lattice is formed. The key step in the electrodeposition process is the generation of new crystal nucleus and the growth of crystal (following reaction kinetics principle). The competition between these two steps directly affects the size of the generated crystal grain in the deposit coating, which is determined by the inconsistency between the diffusion rate of the adsorption surface and the charge transfer reaction rate. Among them, the dialectical relationship is as follows: if there is a high surface diffusion rate on the electrode surface, the small number of adsorbed atoms due to the slow charge transfer reaction and the low overcharge potential will be beneficial to the crystal growth. On the contrary, the low surface diffusion rate and the large number of adsorbed atoms as well as the high overpotential will increase the nucleation rate. It is shown that high electrode overpotential, high total number of adsorbed atoms, and low surface mobility of adsorbed atoms are necessary conditions for mass nucleation and reduced grain growth.

Nucleation rate is denoted by J, then:

$$J = K_1 \exp \left[\frac{-bs\varepsilon^2}{zekT\eta} \right] \tag{5.3}$$

where K_1 is the rate constant, b is the geometric exponent, s is the area of an atom in the lattice, ε is the boundary energy, k is Boltzmann constant, z is the ionic charge, e is electron charge; T is the absolute temperature, η is the overpotential.

Tafel formula is as follows:

$$\eta = \alpha + \beta \log i \tag{5.4}$$

where α and β are constants, i is the current density.

According to Eqs. (5.3) and (5.4), the main electrochemical factor affecting nucleation rate is overpotential, and the main factor affecting overpotential is current density. Therefore, when the current density during electrodeposition is increased, the overpotential and nucleation rate will be increased. Therefore, the important electrochemical factor of nanocrystalline generation is to effectively improve the current density (namely improve overpotential) during electrodeposition. In conclusion, the average grain size of electrodeposited crystal metals depends on the overpotential. At a high overpotential, that is, at a high current density, crystal or nanocrystalline coatings with smaller average grain size can be obtained [46].

5.5.3 Paradigms and analysis of electrodeposition method

Electrochemical deposition method opens up a new field for controllable preparation of multifarious nanomaterials. Compared with other methods, electrochemical method has many advantages such as simple equipment, convenient operation, and low energy consumption. In particular, the electrodeposition method can prepare the 1D nanowire array materials with the assistance of the porous membrane template, and the diameter and length of the nanowires can be controlled by the pore and thickness of the template. In template electrodeposition, porous membrane electrode material is selected as cathode, and the electrochemical reduction reaction in the cathode makes the metal component enter the nanometer pore channel directionally. The hole wall of the template will limit the shape and size of metal nanomaterial, so as to obtain 1D nanomaterial. In 1987, Martin et al. prepared metal (Pt) nanowire arrays for the first time through a combination of electrodeposition and template method, that is, electrodeposition assisted by porous polycarbonate membrane template [47]. The shape and size of nanowires are limited by the pore structure of porous membrane template, where the uniformity of nanopores affects the uniformity of nanowires.

Up to now, many porous membrane materials have been developed for template electrodeposition of different 1D nanomaterials (including metal and metal compound nanowires). The preparation of nanostructured materials with porous anodic aluminum oxide (AAO) as template has attracted much attention due to its unique advantages and has been studied deeply in recent years. It has been widely reported that various ordered nanowire arrays were prepared by electrochemical deposition using porous AAO as template. For example, Xu and coworkers reported highly ordered Pd nanowire arrays by template-electrodeposition method with porous AAO template (see Fig. 5.5F—H) [44]. The Pd nanowire arrays showed high active surface and excellent catalytic properties for ethanol electrooxidation in alkaline media. The micrometer-sized pores and channels in nanowire arrays act as structure units. They make liquid fuel diffuse into and products diffuse out of the catalysts layer much easier; therefore, the utilization efficiency of catalysts gets higher. In a word, this study opens a new opportunity for the application of 1D noble metal nanomaterials in electrocatalysis.

UPD, as a special in situ electrodeposition, refers to the phenomenon that a metal can be deposited on another substrate at a positive potential than its thermodynamically reversible potential, which is an important electrochemical phenomenon closely related to the electrode/solution structure. So far, a large number of UPD experiments have been reported. It is considered that the UPD phenomenon occurs when the interaction energy between the deposited atom M and the external matrix atom S (ψ M-S) is greater than that between the deposited atoms (ψ M-M) [48]. In other words, the UPD phenomenon occurs only when the metal with smaller energy functions is deposited to the metal with larger energy functions. For example, because the work function of Cu is smaller than that of Au, Cu can form a UPD monolayer on the surface of Au electrode, while the UPD does not occur during the deposition of Au on Cu electrode. It is believed that the UPD monolayer is formed because the interaction between the deposited metal atoms and the base metal atoms is larger than that between the deposited metal atoms. The combination of sustained UPD, galvanic replacement reaction, and control of nanocrystalline growth, is a versatile strategy for engineering the architectural diversity of complex heterogeneous metallic nanocrystals [49]. Particularly, the UPD-monolayer-induced galvanic replacement reaction can be used to design high-performance catalysts with single or multilayer atomic structure (namely core-shell or core-shell-like nanostructured atomic-level catalyst) [50].

Recently, our research group (Zesheng Li) proposed a new microscopic electrodeposition strategy, a carbon-regulated galvanic replacement reaction (galvanic cell reaction), to construct 3D Pt nanoflower structures (Pt-on-Co nanodendrites) (see Fig. 5.5I−K) [45]. We propose a "two-path" growth mechanism to analyze the formation process of the novel 3D nanostructures: (1) in situ chemical replacement reactions, in which positive tetravalent platinum Pt^{4+} ($PtClO_4^-$) is reduced to metallic platinum (Pt^0) ($Co + Pt^{4+} = Co^{2+} + Pt$) and (2) spontaneous galvanic cell reactions (Anode: $Co = Co^{2+} + 2e^-$; Cathode: $Pt^{4+} + 4e^- + Pt$). The carbon-supported Co nano-particles might initiate innumerable microzone galvanic battery reactions over the surface of carbon support. Spatially separated Pt particles can be readily produced apart from the Co particles because of the electron shuttling effect of carbon matrix. Subjected to an epitaxial growth mechanism, these spatially separated Pt particles can serve as catalytic sites for further galvanic reduction of the Pt precursor and thus desirable tridimensional dendritic nanostructures would be developed on carbon matrix in this system. It is confirmable that the carbon-supported Co particles could react partially or completely with various amounts of $PtClO_4^-$ and thus result in the 3-D Pt-on-Co nanodendrites or Pt nanodendrites with tunable Pt content [45].

5.6 Chemical vapor deposition method

5.6.1 Definitions and history of chemical vapor deposition method

CVD is a technology to form solid deposits by chemical reactions of gaseous or vaporous chemical substances on the gas phase or gas-solid interface in a reactor by means of chemical reactions using various energy sources such as heating, plasma excitation, or light radiation. Briefly, the CVD is when two or more gaseous raw materials are introduced into a reaction chamber, where they react with each other to form a new material that is deposited on the substrate surface. The CVD is a new technique for preparing inorganic materials developed in recent decades. These inorganic materials include oxides, sulfides, nitrides, carbides, as well as binary or ternary interelemental compounds in III–V, II–IV, IV–VI groups. CVD has become a new field of inorganic synthetic chemistry. The CVD synthetic technology is a process that uses gaseous substances to produce chemical reactions and transport reactions on solids to produce solid sediments. It roughly consists of three steps: (1) forming volatile substances, (2) transfer of the substances to the sedimentary area, (3) produce chemical reactions on solids and produce solid substances [51]. The most basic CVD synthesis includes thermal decomposition reaction, chemical synthesis reaction, and chemical transport reaction. In brief, the CVD synthesis of new inorganic materials has become the main subject of modern materials science.

The use of CVD technology can be traced back to ancient times, when dark carbon layers are left on cave walls or rocks due to heating and barbecuing. Modern CVD technology began in the 1950s, when it was mainly used to make coatings on knives. Since 1960s and 1970s, with the development of semiconductor and integrated circuit technology, CVD technology has made great progress. The CVD technology can be classified by reaction type or pressure, including low-pressure CVD (LPCVD), atmospheric pressure CVD (APCVD), subatmospheric CVD (SACVD), ultra-high vacuum CVD (UHVCVD), plasma enhanced CVD (PECVD), high-density plasma CVD (HDPCVD), rapid thermal CVD (RTCVD) and metal-organic CVD (MOCVD). The CVD technology became a breakthrough in the production of precious metal coatings in 1988, when NASA successfully tried to produce composite nozzles using rhenium iridium as a coating in MOCVD process [52]. The UHVCVD is especially useful to study the initial stages of the CVD processes in 1991, to prepare ultrathin films, and to investigate the composition of deposited films without interference from ambient impurities [53]. According to the nature of the precursors, the CVD technology also includes a simple quasi-CVD (QCVD) method proposed by An in 2016 [54], where the precursors are in a liquid state or solid state and must be gasified or pyrolyzed before being introduced into the container [55]. The QCVD technology does not need super vacuum condition and the precursors are easily available, so it has wide application prospects and technical significance.

5.6.2 Physicochemical principles of chemical vapor deposition method

In the CVD process, the forms of solids precipitated from the gas phase are mainly as follows: thin films, whiskers, and grains are formed on the solid surface, and nanoparticles are formed in the gas. Therefore, the main physicochemical principles of CVD synthetic design include surface/interface chemistry principle, chemical equilibrium principle, and growth kinetics principle. By using a substrate material (a material with particular surface tension), the sediments can be easily separated from the substrate after reaching a certain thickness, so that free sediments of various shapes can be obtained. In CVD technology, the deposition reaction can only take place in the gas phase through the control of growth dynamics, and the inorganic substance obtained in this way is very fine powder, or even nano-scale particles called nano ultrafine powder. Chemical reactions in CVD include pyrolysis (thermal decomposition), photolysis (photodecomposition), reduction (or hydrogenation reactions), oxidation, and redox reactions. Therefore, the chemical equilibrium control and kinetic control are slightly different for different reaction types. Chemical equilibrium thermodynamic calculation can be used to estimate the partial pressure of the gas species in equilibrium with the solid phase of a particular component in the CVD deposition system, which can be used to predict the degree of deposition and the influence of various reaction parameters on the deposition process [56].

5.6.3 Paradigms and analysis of chemical vapor deposition method

CVD is widely used in the preparation of low-dimensional nanomaterials (such as two-dimensional (2D) or 2D-built 3D nanomaterials). Recently, using 2D transition metal choriocarbides (TMDCs) as an example, Huiming Cheng and coauthors reviewed the progress of 2D materials grown by CVD method, summarized the promising growth strategies established by researchers in recent years, and focused on the key scientific and technical problems involved in 2D materials grown by CVD method (see Fig. 5.6A) [57]. Control strategies and methods include nonmetallic precursors, metal precursors, substrate engineering, temperature, airflow, etc. Article points out the CVD growth of 2D future research direction in the field of materials, including the preparation of new 2D materials (such as stable p-type semiconductor material, high mobility of 2D material, broadband gap 2D material, narrow band gap 2D material), the CVD growth combined with postprocessing to obtain a new 2D material and heterostructure, novel physical properties and application of exploration. This paper is of guiding significance to the design of CVD growth system, the improvement of growth controllability, the preparation of high-quality 2D materials, and the understanding of the preparation mechanism of relevant materials [57].

The CVD is an effective method to prepare high-quality 3D graphene nanomaterials in large scale. From the point of view of chemical thermodynamics, the growth process of 3D graphene on surfaces of metal substrates (also the 3D templates) can be divided into three steps: catalytic decomposition of carbon-containing precursors on the surface of substrate, nucleation and growth of graphene (sp^2 carbon deposited on the substrate), the removal of templates and purification of 3D graphene materials (see Fig. 5.6B) [58]. Peculiarly, the doping-type 3D graphene can be prepared on the substrates in one-step synthesis, by using the mixed precursor of carbon source and doped source gasses. This method can realize the controllable doping of large area 3D graphene, and facilitate subsequent device preparation and application. The typical example is the preparation of N-doped 3D graphene by CVD method: methane (CH_4) and ammonia (NH_3) are used to provide carbon and nitrogen sources and the simultaneous nucleation and doping reactions take place in a high-temperature reactor.

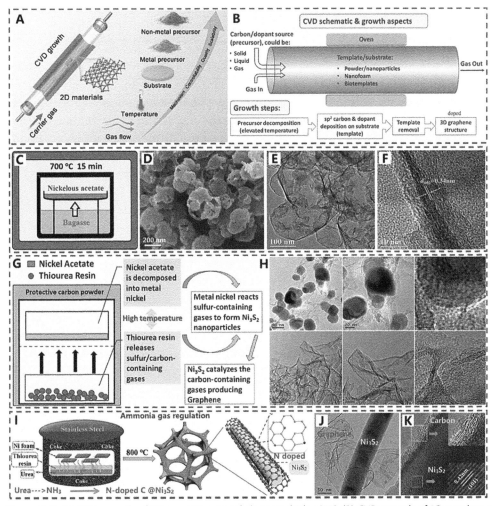

Figure 5.6 (A) CVD growth of 2D transition metal choriocarbides [57], (B) CVD growth of 3D graphene structures [58], (C–F) QCVD growth of 3D graphene nanocages [59], (G–H) QCVD growth of 3D graphene nanosheets [60], (I–K) QCVD growth of Ni_3S_2@graphene core-shell nanowires [61].

The N atoms in NH_3 will precipitate together with the C atoms on the substrate, and the final material on the substrate is the mixed film of carbon atoms and nitrogen atoms (namely N-doped 3D graphene) [62].

Quasi-chemical vapor deposition (QCVD) is a low-cost and widely applicable synthesis technology for 3-D graphene materials. The basic feature of QCVD technology is that the solid precursor is used as the carbon source, the carbon-containing gas is released through pyrolysis of solid precursor, and then the graphene layer is deposited on the surface of transition metal template. The choice of solid carbon sources is extensive including various biomass and polymers. Different carbon sources can produce 3D graphene products with different morphologies. Moreover, the ways of heat treatment can also be diversified, which can be carried out either under traditional tubular furnace or under muffle furnace [62]. Li's research group early reported a novel 3-D graphene powders, hollow graphene nanocages (HGNCs), by QCVD method using biomass bagasse as carbon source and nickel acetate as catalyst precursor (see Fig. 5.6C−F) [59]. Typically, the solid carbon source (bagasse) is placed in the lower layer of the crucible, the catalyst precursor (nickel acetate) is placed in the upper layer of the crucible, the cover heat treatment is carried out in muffle furnace (700°C for 15 min), the HGNCs in upper layer can be obtained after nickel template is removed by acid treatment. The HGNCs have a typical hollow structure with ultra-thin nanowalls ($\sim$10 nm), a unique hierarchical porous structure with multiple mesopores (2.5, 9.2, and 45 nm), and a wide range of macropores (50−200 nm) [59]. In order to prepare 3-D graphene powders with network structure, Li et al. further proposed thiourea resin as carbon source, by a similar QCVD method in muffle furnace using nickel acetate as catalyst precursor (see Fig. 5.6G−H) [60]. Firstly, 3-D graphene network@nickel sulfur nanoparticles (Ni_3S_2@3-D GE) were prepared by synchronous thermal decomposition of thiourea resin and nickel acetate, where the Ni_3S_2 nanoparticles serve as 3-D template and catalyst. Afterward, the template was removed by pickling and 3-D graphene powders with cross-linked mesoporous network structure were easily obtained [60]. The QCVD technology also shows a high degree of universality in the preparation of other nanostructured materials (including carbon materials, metal-based materials, or their composites) [55,61].

Recently, our research group further designed and synthesized core/shell cable-like Ni_3S_2 nanowires@N-doped graphene free-standing nanomaterials by one-pot QCVD technology, by using macro-porous nickel foam as catalyst and template, thiourea resin as carbon source, and urea as a nitrogen source (see Fig. 5.6I−K) [61]. The Ni_3S_2@graphene core-shell nanowires exhibited a unique architecture with a well-defined core-shell cable-like 1D nanostructure in which graphene acts as conductive shell and Ni_3S_2 nanowire as active core. The composite has a nitrogen content of 6.39% in atomic ratio. Using nickel foam as a template, the binder-free bulk electrode materials can be obtained, which is beneficial to further electrochemical applications. Ammonia decomposed by urea can not only realize nitrogen doping, but also play a role in gas regulation for the formation of one-dimensional Ni_3S_2 nanostructures.

5.7 High-temperature solid phase method

5.7.1 Definitions and history of high-temperature solid phase method

High-temperature solid-state synthesis refers to the formation of solid products, such as carbon-based materials, metal-based materials, composite oxide materials, etc., between solid-state reactants through four stages: interface contact, molecular diffusion, chemical reaction, crystal nucleation, and crystal growth at high temperature ($600-1500°C$). In a narrow sense, solid-state reaction often refers to the process of chemical reaction between solids to produce new solid products. Broadly speaking, any chemical reaction involving solid phase can be called solid phase reaction. For example, the thermal decomposition and oxidation of solids, as well as the chemical reactions between solids and liquids, and between solids and gases, all belong to the category of solid-state reactions. According to different reaction properties, the high-temperature solid-state reaction can be divided into high-temperature oxidation reaction, reduction reaction, addition reaction, substitution reaction, and decomposition reaction. According to different reaction mechanism, the high-temperature solid-state reaction can be also divided into diffusion control reaction, chemical reaction speed control reaction, nucleation rate control reaction, and sublimation control reaction.

High-temperature solid phase method is a traditional powder-making process, which was first used in the preparation of ceramic materials and cement materials over 100 years ago. Although it has its inherent shortcomings, such as large energy consumption, low efficiency, powder is not fine enough, easy to mix with impurities, etc., because the powder particles prepared by this method have no agglomeration, good filling, low cost, large yield, simple preparation process, and other advantages, so far high-temperature solid phase method is still a commonly used method in the preparation of energy materials and environmental materials. For example, high-performance lithium iron phosphate battery materials can be prepared by high-temperature solid-phase method in 1997 [63]. According to the properties of each raw material, nano-sized crushing, mixing, granulation, and prefiring are carried out to obtain the precursor of lithium iron phosphate. After nano crushing, mixing with carbon source and granulation of precursor, secondary high-temperature sintering was carried out to obtain high-quality nano-sized lithium iron phosphate cathode material in 2008 [64]. At present, various nanometer powder materials with uniform particle size and excellent properties can be prepared by the combination of mechanical ball milling and high-temperature solid phase reaction.

5.7.2 Physicochemical principles of high-temperature solid phase method

The physicochemical principles of high-temperature solid phase synthetic method include surface/interface chemistry principle, chemical equilibrium principle, reaction thermodynamics, and growth kinetics principle. High-temperature solid-state reaction method is to mix the reactants evenly to generate a precursor or amorphous product, and then calcination at high temperature to make the reaction complete and crystallization of the product. For the solid phase reaction, the atoms and ions of each component in the reaction are limited by the cohesion of the crystal, and cannot migrate freely as in the liquid phase or gas phase reaction. The fineness and uniformity of the powder are very important for the solid phase reaction. Solid phase reaction at high temperature is a universal physical and chemical phenomenon. High-temperature solid-state reaction is limited to the preparation of thermodynamically stable compounds, while low-temperature metastable compounds or kinetically stable compounds are not suitable for high-temperature synthesis. In fact, the solid reaction is the reactant through the particle contact surface diffusion in the lattice, the diffusion rate is usually the determining factor of the speed and degree of the solid phase reaction. In order to increase the reaction rate, it needs to be heated to higher temperature. Therefore, both thermodynamics and kinetics are of great significance in the high-temperature solid phase reaction. On the other hand, high-temperature solid phase reaction is completed by diffusion and transport of solid atoms or ions. First, the reaction occurs at the contact point between the reactant components, and then gradually diffuses into the interior of the phase for reaction, so the reactants must be in full contact with each other during the reaction process. Therefore, grinding the reactants and mixing them thoroughly can increase the contact interface area between reactants and make the diffusion transport of atoms or ions easier to carry out, so as to increase the reaction rate. In a word, the smaller the particle size of the reactant, the larger the specific surface area, the larger the contact area between the components, and the larger the particle-free energy on the surface, so that the reaction and diffusion ability is enhanced, so the faster the reaction speed [65].

5.7.3 Paradigms and analysis of high-temperature solid phase method

In recent years, our group has proposed several strategies in the high-temperature solid-state synthesis of nanomaterials: (1) Template-assisted high-temperature solid-state method: using specific templates to mix with reactants, then high-temperature solid-state reaction and removing templates to obtain nanomaterials with specific structures. (2) Ion-localization high-temperature solid-state method: using ion exchange resin to enrich reactant metal ions, and then obtain carbon-supported nanomaterials by high-temperature carbonization and high-temperature solid state reaction. (3) Oxidation-driven high-temperature solid-state method: specific reaction precursors are treated at high temperature in an aerobic environment, and specific nanomaterials can be obtained through oxidation-driven action (see Fig. 5.7 for details) [66–70].

Li's research group has synthesized hollow hemispherical macroporous graphene-tungsten carbide-platinum (HMG-WC-Pt) 3-D nanocomposites by template-assisted

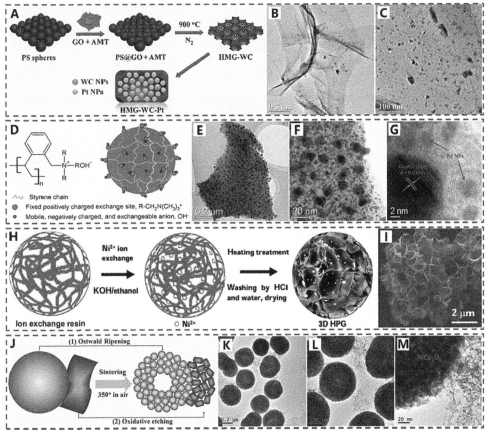

Figure 5.7 (A–C) Template-assisted high-temperature solid-state method [66], (D) Ion exchange resin with ion exchange function [67], (E–G) Ion-localization high-temperature solid-state method [68], (H–I) Ion-localization catalytic graphitization [69], (J–M) Oxidation-driven high-temperature solid-state method [70].

high–temperature solid-state method with polystyrene (PS) spheres preprepared template from graphene oxide (GO) (see Fig. 5.7A–C) [66]. Firstly, PS spheres, GO and ammonium metatungstate (AMT) were uniformly mixed with distilled water to form mixed precursors (PS@GO) before subsequent freeze drying. In the high-temperature treatment, PS spheres are decomposed into atmosphere containing carbon, and AMT reacts with carbon atom in GO to form tungsten carbide (WC) nanoparticles to produce

HMG-WC nanocomposites. Finally, the HMG-WC-Pt nanostructures were formed on HMG-WC after loading of Pt. It is obvious that the PS sphere is the key spherical template to form 3-D hollow hemispherical macroporous graphene structure in the high-temperature solid-state synthesis process.

Ion exchange resin is a special polymer material with ion exchange function. Its own unfixed ions can be exchanged with similarly charged ions in the surrounding environment (ion-localization function). Ion exchange is a reversible chemical reaction process, which generally refers to the process of equal exchange between the same charged ions in solution and the ions of the exchanger (see Fig. 5.7D) [67]. Recently, our research group realized the design and synthesis of Co_3W_3C/GC (GC is graphite carbon) catalyst through a new type of ion exchange assisted (i.e., ion-localization) high-temperature solid-state synthesis process (see Fig. 5.7E—G) [68]. The typical process is as follows: 50 g of macroporous acrylic-type anion-exchange resin (D314) was firstly exchanged with 1000 mL of 0.1 M ammonium metatungstate hydrate $((NH_4)_6H_2W_{12}O_{40})$ and sodium hexanitrocobaltate $(Na_3Co(NO_2)_6)$ solution. The resulting resin complex (Co and W contained anions) was then sintered at 1400°C for 2 h under a pure Ar flow. After cooling to room temperature, the resulting Co_3W_3C/GC product was shattered into fine powder by mechanical milling. The $Co_3W_3C/GC/Pd$ catalyst can be further prepared by loading Pd nanoparticles on Co_3W_3C/GC obtained by high-temperature solid-state synthesis.

Previously, Li and coworkers have developed a novel KOH activation and Ni catalytic graphitization-associated technology to synchronously synthesize 3-D hierarchical porous graphene (3-D HPG) network powders from a cheap solid precursor of ion exchange resin (see Fig. 5.7H—I) [69]. In this synthesis strategy, cation exchange resin was used to adsorb nickel ions (Ni^{2+}), followed by heat treatment and Ni catalytic growth of graphene by the ion-localization high-temperature solid-state method. The obtained 3-D HPG products show a good 3-D porous network with interconnected graphene nanosheets. Meanwhile, during the Ni catalytic graphitization, KOH is synchronously introduced as a pore-forming agent for the activation etching of carbon. Therefore, the multiple design concepts of high graphitization, high specific surface area, and hierarchical porous structure are realized at the same time.

More recently, we further reported a newly $g-C_3N_4$ quantum dots/$NiCo_2O_4$ hollow spheres (i.e., $g-C_3N_4$ QDs/$NiCo_2O_4$ HSs) hybrid architecture prepared by a convenient synchronous heat treatment technology under air environment (i.e., oxidation-driven high-temperature solid-state method) (see Fig. 5.7J—M) [70]. During heat treatment, the spherical NiCo-precursors are driven by oxidation and become $NiCo_2O_4$ hollow nanospheres by Ostwald ripening, while $g-C_3N_4$ nanosheets are oxidized and etched into $g-C_3N_4$ quantum dots synchronously. And the electrochemical performances of the $g-C_3N_4$ QDs/$NiCo_2O_4$ HSs have been investigated as a promising nonnoble metal catalyst for methanol electrooxidation. In a word, the oxidation-driven high-temperature solid-state method is a highly efficient synthesis strategy for the preparation of nanostructured metallic oxides and ultrafine quantum dots.

5.8 Mechanochemistry method

5.8.1 Definitions and history of mechanochemistry method

Mechanochemistry is a new subject that studies the chemical reactions, physical and chemical properties, or internal microstructural changes of materials induced and acted by mechanical forces. Mechanochemistry is the product of the combination of mechanical processing and chemical reaction at the molecular level, including mechanical crushing, chemical reaction under mechanical pressure, mechanical degradation of polymers, ultrasonic physical and chemistry reactions, etc. Mechanochemical reaction mainly refers to the application of mechanical force to condensed substances such as solid and liquid by means of shear, friction, impact, extrusion, etc., to induce changes in their structure and physicochemical properties, as well as induce chemical reaction transformations. Unlike ordinary thermochemical reactions, the driving force of mechanochemical reactions is mechanical energy rather than heat energy, so the reaction can be completed without high temperature, high pressure, and other harsh conditions. With the development of the mechanical industry, the continuous emergence of various high-energy grinding equipment (such as planetary ball milling) has made mechanochemistry applied in many chemical fields. In addition, because almost no solvent is used, the reaction is relatively safe, clean, and efficient. Mechanochemical synthesis method can also be said to be a synthesis method that conforms to the principle of "green chemistry."

In ancient times, people drilling wood for fire is a kind of mechanochemical phenomenon. In 1988, Shingu et al. first reported the preparation of aluminum-iron nanocrystalline materials by high-energy ball milling. Since then, the simple and convenient way to prepare nanomaterials by ball milling has attracted people's attention. In the early 1990s, Rowlands et al. [71] used the mechanochemical method in the treatment of halogenated organic compounds and found that all organochlorides were converted into calcium chloride and graphite after 12 h of ball milling. This amazing effect attracted wide attention, and thus opened the prelude to the study of mechanochemical treatment. The symbol of modern mechanochemistry is that the grinding method is used to replace conventional experimental devices, such as ball milling instead of heating and stirring, ball milling tank instead of flask and beaker, and ball milling medium instead of solvent. In industrial-grade equipment, the centrifugal force produced by the motion of this "planetary ball milling" mimics the effect of gravity, and provides a direct link between mechanochemistry and large-scale industrial production. The material of the grinding ball and grinding tank is stainless steel, zirconia, tungsten carbide, polytetrafluoron, and so on. The transparent polymethyl methacrylate (PMMA) which is easy to observe is often used in the production of ball grinding tank. Stainless steel, with a density of about 7.5 g mL^{-1}, is the most commonly used material, but may bring metallic contamination. Zirconia (a density of about 5.6 g mL^{-1}) does not have this problem [72].

5.8.2 Physicochemical principles of mechanochemistry method

The basic principle of mechanochemistry is to use mechanical energy to induce chemical reactions and to induce changes in the structure and properties of materials, so as to prepare new materials or modify materials. The physicochemical principles of mechanochemistry method include surface/interface chemistry principle, phase equilibrium principle, reaction thermodynamics, and kinetics principle. Solid phase synthesis based on mechanochemistry usually has the following physical and chemical characteristics: (1) mechanical solid phase reaction generally includes two processes: the reaction of substances at the phase interface and the migration of substances. (2) Generally, it needs to be carried out at a certain temperature (ball milling self-heating effect) and in a specific atmosphere (inert gas or other reaction atmosphere). (3) The whole mechanical solid-state reaction speed is controlled by the slowest speed (such as interfacial material migration). (4) The products of mechanical solid-state reaction have several phase stages: raw materials → initial products → intermediate products → final products. The principle of mechanochemistry is quite complex. Under the action of strong mechanical force, solid is subjected to violent impact, while the crystal structure is destroyed, local plasma process will also occur, accompanied by excited electron radiation and other phenomena, which can induce chemical reactions between substances and reduce the temperature and activation energy of chemical reactions [73].

5.8.3 Paradigms and analysis of mechanochemistry method

In the preparation of energy and environmental-related nanomaterials, mechanochemistry method mainly includes the following three forms: (1) Mechanical dispersion of micron materials: transforming micron materials into nanomaterials through mechanical force (such as mechanical stripping and mechanical crushing). (2) Preparation of nanomaterials by mechanochemical reaction: nanomaterials are obtained by promoting chemical reaction under environmental conditions through high-energy mechanical milling. (3) Mechanochemical-assisted preparation of nanomaterials: the preproducts are first obtained by mechanical ball milling, and then the nanomaterials are obtained by high-temperature reaction. In particular, the mechanochemical or mechanical-assisted chemical synthesis for the repreparation of atomic-structured materials also shows exciting potential and prospect (see Fig. 5.8 for details) [66,74—79].

Recently, our research group prepared porous graphite foam material with micron structure by ion-localization high-temperature solid state method, and then successfully obtained graphite sheet material with nanostructure by mechanical ball milling (see Fig. 5.8A—B) [66]. After ball milling, the micron graphite is transformed into graphene-like nanocrystals (200 nm in width and 10 nm in thickness). The shear force and impact force of ball milling can realize the separation of layered graphite microcrystal layers and obtain graphene-like nanosheets with few-layer structure. The mechanical

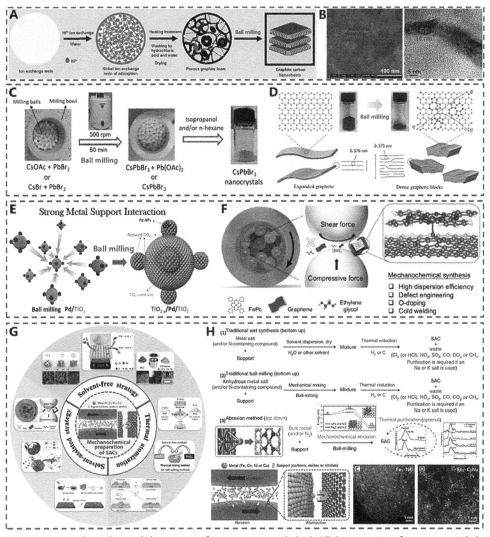

Figure 5.8 (A—B) Mechanical dispersion of micron materials [66], (C) Preparation of nanomaterials by mechanochemical reaction [74], (D) Crystal defect construction by mechanical ball milling [75], (E) SMSI construction by mechanical ball milling [76], (F) Covalent bond construction by mechanical ball milling [77], (G) Preparation of SACs by mechanochemical reaction [78], (H) Preparation of SACs by mechanochemical abrasion [79].

dispersion (such as mechanical stripping and mechanical crushing) of micron materials into nanomaterials is an important method for mass preparation of nanomaterials. For macroscopic materials, they first need to be processed by mechanical pulverizer to obtain micron-structured particles and then are ground by ball milling to obtain nanostructured materials. The revolving speed and milling time of ball milling are the basic factors that determine the size of nanomaterials.

The preparation of nanomaterials by mechanochemical reaction can be implemented under normal temperature and pressure conditions by high-energy ball milling. Recently, the team of Professor Salvador Eslava successfully synthesized a gram $CsPbBr_3$ nanomaterial by using a mechanochemical process (solvent-free ball milling with zirconia balls) (see Fig. 5.8C) [74]. The pathway used to prepare $CsPbBr_3$ nanocrystals was a surfactant-free mechanochemical synthesis. During milling, the kinetic energy of the balls was transferred to both Cs and Pb precursors, allowing their collision and chemical reaction to form CsPbBr3 nanocrystals, as shown in the following equation for the use of CsOAc as a reactant: $2CsOAc + 3PbBr_2 \rightarrow 2CsPbBr_3 + Pb(OAc)_2$. Pure $CsPbBr_3$ nanocrystals were obtained for a minimum of 1 h ball-milling time at 500 rpm and after workup to remove $Pb(OAc)_2$ byproduct. The as-prepared $CsPbBr_3$ nanocrystals have excellent crystallinity and adjustable morphology, which can be comparable with the products obtained by conventional solution synthesis.

Mechanical ball milling is also an efficient strategy for the construction of vacancy defects of nanomaterials. Recently, Song and his collaborators reported a strategy for the design and regulation of defective structures in graphene using a simple ball milling process (see Fig. 5.8D) [75]. The authors prepared expanded graphene (EG) from natural graphite by Hummers oxidation and thermal reduction, and then prepared defective graphene blocks (DGB) by mechanical ball milling under argon atmosphere. Various active sites (including heteroatoms, functional groups, defective structures, etc.) were designed to improve the sodium storage capacity of carbon materials. The resulting DGB with defective structures exhibits extremely high mass and volume-specific capacity as a sodium storage material and excellent rate performance. The defect structure could be used as the active site to significantly improve the sodium storage capacity of graphene materials. Meanwhile, the densification effect brought by ball milling also significantly improved the volume properties of graphene materials.

Mechanical ball milling strategies also play a key role in facilitating interactions between nanomaterials and support materials, such as strong metal support interactions (SMSI). Precious metals are very important in electrochemical catalytic reactions. However, excessive overpotential and poor long-term stability still hinder its application in many reactions such as oxygen evolution/reduction. It is urgent to improve its overall electrocatalytic performance (activity, selectivity, and stability). Based on this, Liu and Zhang regulated the SMSI over an oxidized TiC electrocatalyst loaded with Pd by an unprecedented time-dependent machining (ball milling) method (see Fig. 5.8E) [76].

The ball milling-induced SMSI greatly improved the activity, selectivity, and stability of electrosynthesis of H_2O_2.

The mechanochemical (such as ball milling) strategies can be used to construct covalent bonds between different nanomaterials and form new composite nanomaterials. Adjusting the electronic and geometric structure of $Fe-N_4$ active center of SACs with axial coordination has been proven to be an effective mean to improve the electrocatalytic performance. Recently, Li and coworkers reported the fixation of molecular-dispersed FePc onto graphene with in-situ oxygen-carbon defects (via $Fe-O$ covalent bond axial coordination) using mechanochemical wet ball milling (see Fig. 5.8F) [77]. In ethylene glycol liquid medium of wet ball milling, the local shear and compression force can scatter FePc aggregates into a single molecule and knockout carbon atoms on graphene (oxygen impurity atoms introduced from ethylene glycol), ultimately successfully build the molecular dispersion FePc from reactive oxygen species of graphene by the $Fe-O$ covalent bond axial coordination.

A high-energy ball milling process will spontaneously generate strong shear force and a high local temperature, which will reconstruct the chemical bonds of materials and renovate the surface chemistry characteristics. The ball milling method is a simple and robust strategy to synthesize nanomaterials, and it can also be used to synthesize SACs. Recently, we systematically summarized the strategy and principle of ball milling strategy to for the preparation of SACs: Solvent-assisted ball-milling strategy, solvent-free ball-milling strategy, and mechanochemistry-thermal atomization joint strategy (see Fig. 5.8G) [78]. Particularly, Li, Jeong, and Baek jointly proposed a top-down ball milling method (mechanical abrading method) for the preparation of SACs (including iron, cobalt, nickel, and copper), in which the metals are directly atomized onto different supports, such as carbon skeleton, oxides, and nitride (see Fig. 5.8H) [79]. The mechanical abrading mechanism is to generate defects in situ on the carrier through mechanical forces and then capture and stably isolate the atomized metal by abrading effect of various metallic balls. The experimental results showed that the proposed abrading strategy can be used as a general green strategy for SACs preparation.

5.9 High energy physics method

5.9.1 High-energy physical vapor deposition

PVD technology refers to the gasification of solid or liquid surfaces of source materials into gaseous atoms and molecules or partial ionization into ions under vacuum conditions by high-energy physical methods (such as thermal evaporation or particle beam bombardment). And through low-pressure gas (or plasma) process, deposition on the surface of the substrate has a special function of the film technology (a controllable atomic transfer technology from the source material to the film). The vacuum evaporation, magnetron sputtering, and arc ion deposition are the three typical PVD technology for the preparation of nanomaterials. In recent years, the development of thin film technology and thin film materials has made remarkable progress. On the original basis of PVD technology, there have been ion beam enhanced deposition technology, electric spark deposition technology, electron beam PVD technology, and multilayer jet deposition technology. The PVD techniques can be utilized to expand the fundamental understanding of battery materials (such as the influence of crystalline structure, crystal orientation, and defects on electronic and ionic conductivity, electrochemical performance, and underlying material transformations) [80].

5.9.2 High-energy laser liquid phase synthesis

Since the feasibility of laser liquid phase synthesis of nanomaterials was first reported in 1993, after nearly 30 years of development, this process has been proven to have the advantages of simple process, high flexibility, and wide applicability. A variety of simple metal targets can be selectively converted into high-activity, multiscale, multicomponent (metal, alloy, nitride, carbide, oxide, hydroxide, etc.) functional nanomaterials, and has shown many advantages and great application potential in the fields of energy and environment. In the liquid synthesis of nanomaterials, pulsed laser technology generated by chemical and optical control can produce high-precision nanomaterials with uniform, multicomponent, nonequilibrium control at the nanometer and atomic scales. Laser liquid phase synthesis includes pulsed laser ablation in liquid, pulsed laser fragmentation in liquid, pulsed laser melting in liquid. At present, the pulsed laser liquid synthesis has become a viable technology for manufacturing innovative nanomaterials due to its many advantages in the obtained materials and its applicability for remote control operation. These nanomaterials have independent and precisely controlled properties such as the size, composition, morphology, defect density, and atomic structure of the nanoparticles inside and on the surface [81].

5.10 Summary

In this chapter, we comprehensively discuss the preparation methods (definitions and history), physicochemical principles, and case analysis for synthesizing nanomaterials from the following methods: hydrothermal/solvothermal method, chemical coprecipitation method, sol-gel synthesis method, electrodeposition method, CVD method, high-temperature solid phase method, mechanochemistry method, and other high energy physics methods. In general, these preparation methods can be divided into two categories: (1) "top-down" approach (mainly a physical method) and (2) "bottom-up" approach (mainly a chemical method). These preparation methods of nanomaterials can also be simply divided into "gas-phase synthesis method," "liquid (solution)-phase synthesis method," and "solid-phase synthesis method" according to the states of reactants. Through different preparation methods (including gas-phase, solution-phase, and solid-phase methods), most nanomaterials are expected to achieve their structure regulation and macroscopic preparation, which lays the foundation for their practical application in energy and environment sciences.

Acknowledgments

This book was supported by National Natural Science Foundation of China (22078071, 22272034), Natural Science Foundation of Guangdong Province (2021A1515010125, 2020A1515010344), Maoming Science and Technology Project (mmkj2020032), Guangdong Province Universities and Colleges Pearl River Scholar Funded Scheme (2019), Guangdong Basic and Applied Basic Research Foundation (2019A1515011249, 2021A1515010305), Key Research Project of Natural Science of Guangdong Provincial Department of Education (2019KZDXM010), Environment and Energy Green Catalysis Innovation Team of Colleges and Universities of Guangdong Province (2022KCXTD019), the program for Innovative Research Team of Guangdong University of Petrochemical Technology.

References

[1] H.W. Liang, J.W. Liu, H.S. Qian, S.H. Yu, Multiplex templating process in one-dimensional nanoscale: controllable synthesis, macroscopic assemblies, and applications, Accounts of Chemical Research 46 (7) (2013) 1450−1461.

[2] Z. Li, B. Li, Y. Hu, X. Liao, H. Yu, C. Yu, Emerging ultrahigh-density single-atom catalysts for versatile heterogeneous catalysis applications: redefinition, recent progress, and challenges, Small Structures 3 (6) (2022) 2200041.

[3] B. Li, M. Yu, Z. Li, C. Yu, H. Wang, Q. Li, Constructing flexible all-solid-state supercapacitors from 3D nanosheets active bricks via 3D manufacturing technology: a perspective review, Advanced Functional Materials 32 (29) (2022) 2201166.

[4] S. Yu, Preparation Methodology of Low Dimensional Nano Materials, Science Press, 2019.

[5] M.R. Gao, Y.F. Xu, J. Jiang, S.H. Yu, Nanostructured metal chalcogenides: synthesis, modification, and applications in energy conversion and storage devices, Chemical Society Reviews 42 (7) (2013) 2986−3017.

[6] G.A. Ozin, A. Arsenault, Nanochemistry: A Chemical Approach to Nanomaterials, Royal Society of Chemistry, 2015.

[7] L. Lin, Z. Chen, W. Chen, Single atom catalysts by atomic diffusion strategy, Nano Research 14 (12) (2021) 4398−4416.

[8] J. Li, Q. Wu, J. Wu, Synthesis of nanoparticles via solvothermal and hydrothermal methods, in: Handbook of Nanoparticles, Springer, Cham, 2016, pp. 295−328.

[9] Y. Xie, W. Wang, Y. Qian, X. Liu, Preparation of nano indium phosphide by hydrothermal method in non-aqueous system, Chinese Science Bulletin (11) (1996) 997−1000.

[10] Y. Xie, Y. Qian, W. Wang, S. Zhang, Y. Zhang, A benzene-thermal synthetic route to nanocrystalline GaN, Science 272 (5270) (1996) 1926−1927.

[11] Y. Jiang, Y. Wu, S. Zhang, C. Xu, W. Yu, Y. Xie, et al., A catalytic-assembly solvothermal route to multiwall carbon nanotubes at a moderate temperature, Journal of the American Chemical Society 122 (49) (2000) 12383−12384.

[12] http://www.hfnl.ustc.edu.cn/detail?id=9091.

[13] Z. Li, M. Luo, B. Li, Q. Lin, X. Liao, H. Yu, et al., 3-D hierarchical micro/nano-structures of porous Bi_2WO_6: controlled hydrothermal synthesis and enhanced photocatalytic performances, Microporous and Mesoporous Materials 313 (2021) 110830.

[14] Z. Li, R. Yang, B. Li, M. Yu, D. Li, H. Wang, et al., Controllable synthesis of graphene/$NiCo_2O_4$ three-dimensional mesoporous electrocatalysts for efficient methanol oxidation reaction, Electrochimica Acta 252 (2017) 180−191.

[15] M. Yu, Q. Pu, X. Liao, H. Yu, S. Lin, Z. Li, et al., Controllable synthesis of bismuth tungstate photo-catalysts with different morphologies for degradation of antibiotics under visible-light irradiation, Journal of Materials Science: Materials in Electronics 32 (13) (2021) 17848–17864.

[16] B. Chu, Q. Ma, Z. Li, B. Li, F. Huang, Q. Pang, et al., Design and preparation of three-dimensional hetero-electrocatalysts of NiCo-layered double hydroxide nanosheets incorporated with silver nano-clusters for enhanced oxygen evolution reactions, Nanoscale 13 (25) (2021) 11150–11160.

[17] Z. Li, K. Xiao, C. Yu, H. Wang, Q. Li, Three-dimensional graphene-like carbon nanosheets coupled with MnCo-layered double hydroxides nanoflowers as efficient bifunctional oxygen electrocatalyst, International Journal of Hydrogen Energy 46 (69) (2021) 34239–34251.

[18] H.Q. Wang, Z.S. Li, Y.G. Huang, Q.Y. Li, X.Y. Wang, A novel hybrid supercapacitor based on spherical activated carbon and spherical MnO_2 in a non-aqueous electrolyte, Journal of Materials Chemistry 20 (19) (2010) 3883–3889.

[19] Z. Li, Z. Liu, B. Li, D. Li, Q. Li, H. Wang, MnO_2 nanosilks self-assembled micropowders: facile one-step hydrothermal synthesis and their application as supercapacitor electrodes, Journal of the Taiwan Institute of Chemical Engineers 45 (6) (2014) 2995–2999.

[20] Z. Li, Z. Liu, B. Li, D. Li, Z. Liu, H. Wang, et al., Large area synthesis of well-dispersed β-MnO_2 nanorods and their electrochemical supercapacitive performances, Journal of the Taiwan Institute of Chemical Engineers 65 (2016) 544–551.

[21] P. Cousin, R.A. Ross, Preparation of mixed oxides: a review, Materials Science and Engineering: A 130 (1) (1990) 119–125.

[22] G. Frank, H. Köstlin, A. Rabenau, X-ray and optical measurements in the In_2O_3-SnO_2 system, Physica Status Solidi (A) 52 (1) (1979) 231–238.

[23] M. Behrens, Coprecipitation: an excellent tool for the synthesis of supported metal catalysts—From the understanding of the well known recipes to new materials, Catalysis Today 246 (2015) 46–54.

[24] B. Qiao, A. Wang, X. Yang, L.F. Allard, Z. Jiang, Y. Cui, et al., Single-atom catalysis of CO oxidation using Pt1/FeOx, Nature Chemistry 3 (8) (2011) 634–641.

[25] https://mp.weixin.qq.com/s/_DLVoTM1_H2F2BLEhuLjNA.

[26] Y. Shen, H. Xue, S. Wang, D. Zhang, D. Yin, L. Wang, et al., Ammonia-low coprecipitation synthesis of lithium layered oxide cathode material for high-performance battery, Chemical Engineering Journal 411 (2021) 128487.

[27] Z. Wang, H. Zhu, H. Yu, H. Jiang, C. Li, Research progress on preparation of high Ni oxide cathode precursors by coprecipitation method, Chemical Industry and Engineering Progress 40 (9) (2021) 5097–5106.

[28] Y. Shen, Y. Wu, H. Xue, S. Wang, D. Yin, L. Wang, et al., Insight into the coprecipitation-controlled crystallization reaction for preparing lithium-layered oxide cathodes, ACS Applied Materials and Interfaces 13 (1) (2021) 717–726.

[29] Z.S. Li, H.Q. Wang, Y.G. Huang, Q.Y. Li, X.Y. Wang, Manganese dioxide-coated activated mesocarbon microbeads for supercapacitors in organic electrolyte, Colloids and Surfaces A: Physicochemical and Engineering Aspects 366 (1–3) (2010) 104–109.

[30] H.Q. Wang, G.F. Yang, Q.Y. Li, X.X. Zhong, F.P. Wang, Z.S. Li, et al., Porous nano-MnO_2: large scale synthesis via a facile quick-redox procedure and application in a supercapacitor, New Journal of Chemistry 35 (2) (2011) 469–475.

[31] Z. Li, B. Li, S. Peng, D. Li, S. Yang, Y. Fang, Novel visible light-induced g-C_3N_4 quantum dot/ $BiPO_4$ nanocrystal composite photocatalysts for efficient degradation of methyl orange, RSC Advances 4 (66) (2014) 35144–35148.

[32] J. Zhou, M. Yu, J. Peng, R. Lin, Z. Li, C. Yu, Photocatalytic degradation characteristics of tetracycline and structural transformation on bismuth silver oxide perovskite nano-catalysts, Applied Nanoscience 10 (7) (2020) 2329–2338.

[33] Z. Li, Y. Li, C. He, P.K. Shen, Bimetallic PtAg alloyed nanoparticles and 3-D mesoporous graphene nanosheet hybrid architectures for advanced oxygen reduction reaction electrocatalysts, Journal of Materials Chemistry A 5 (44) (2017) 23158–23169.

[34] R. Ciriminna, A. Fidalgo, V. Pandarus, F. Beland, L.M. Ilharco, M. Pagliaro, The sol–gel route to advanced silica-based materials and recent applications, Chemical Reviews 113 (8) (2013) 6592–6620.

[35] K. Baskaran, M. Ali, K. Gingrich, D.L. Porter, S. Chong, B.J. Riley, et al., Sol-gel derived silica: a review of polymer-tailored properties for energy and environmental applications, Microporous and Mesoporous Materials (2022) 111874.

[36] S. Yang, W. Zhou, C. Ge, X. Liu, Y. Fang, Z. Li, Mesoporous polymeric semiconductor materials of graphitic-C_3N_4: general and efficient synthesis and their integration with synergistic AgBr NPs for enhanced photocatalytic performances, RSC Advances 3 (16) (2013) 5631−5638.

[37] J. Cai, Z. Li, S. Yao, H. Meng, P.K. Shen, Z. Wei, Close-packed SnO_2 nanocrystals anchored on amorphous silica as a stable anode material for lithium-ion battery, Electrochimica Acta 74 (2012) 182−188.

[38] J. Hu, C. Yu, Y. Bi, L. Wei, J. Chen, X. Chen, Preparation and characterization of Ni/CeO_2-SiO_2 catalysts and their performance in catalytic partial oxidation of methane to syngas, Chinese Journal of Catalysis 35 (1) (2014) 8−20.

[39] X. Xiao, Y. Xu, X. Lv, J. Xie, J. Liu, C. Yu, Electrochemical CO_2 reduction on copper nanoparticles-dispersed carbon aerogels, Journal of Colloid and Interface Science 545 (2019) 1−7.

[40] P. Zhou, Y. Xie, J. Fang, Y. Ling, C. Yu, X. Liu, et al., CdS quantum dots confined in mesoporous TiO_2 with exceptional photocatalytic performance for degradation of organic polutants, Chemosphere 178 (2017) 1−10.

[41] G. Palumbo, D.M. Doyle, A.M. El-Sherik, U. Erb, K.T. Aust, Intercrystalline hydrogen transport in nanocrystalline nickel, Scripta metallurgica et materialia 25 (3) (1991) 679−684.

[42] M.B. Kale, R.A. Borse, A. Gomaa Abdelkader Mohamed, Y. Wang, Electrocatalysts by electrodeposition: recent advances, synthesis methods, and applications in energy conversion, Advanced Functional Materials 31 (25) (2021) 2101313.

[43] S.A. Lee, J.W. Yang, S. Choi, H.W. Jang, Nanoscale electrodeposition: dimension control and 3D conformality, Exploration 1 (3) (2021) 20210012.

[44] H. Wang, C. Xu, F. Cheng, S. Jiang, Pd nanowire arrays as electrocatalysts for ethanol electrooxidation, Electrochemistry Communications 9 (5) (2007) 1212−1216.

[45] Z. Li, C. He, M. Cai, S. Kang, P.K. Shen, A strategy for easy synthesis of carbon supported Co@Pt core−shell configuration as highly active catalyst for oxygen reduction reaction, International Journal of Hydrogen Energy 37 (19) (2012) 14152−14160.

[46] L. Guo, P.C. Searson, On the influence of the nucleation overpotential on island growth in electrodeposition, Electrochimica Acta 55 (13) (2010) 4086−4091.

[47] R.M. Penner, C.R. Martin, Preparation and electrochemical characterization of ultramicroelectrode ensembles, Analytical Chemistry 59 (21) (1987) 2625−2630.

[48] E. Herrero, L.J. Buller, H.D. Abruña, Underpotential deposition at single crystal surfaces of Au, Pt, Ag and other materials, Chemical Reviews 101 (7) (2001) 1897−1930.

[49] Y. Yu, Q. Zhang, Q. Yao, J. Xie, J.Y. Lee, Guiding principles in the galvanic replacement reaction of an underpotentially deposited metal layer for site-selective deposition and shape and size control of satellite nanocrystals, Chemistry of Materials 25 (23) (2013) 4746−4756.

[50] H. Yang, Platinum-based electrocatalysts with core−shell nanostructures, Angewandte Chemie International Edition 50 (12) (2011) 2674−2676.

[51] S. Hofmann, P. Braeuninger-Weimer, R.S. Weatherup, CVD-enabled graphene manufacture and technology, The Journal of Physical Chemistry Letters 6 (14) (2015) 2714−2721.

[52] J.T. Harding, J.M. Kazaroff, M.A. Appel, Iridium-Coated Rhenium Thrusters by CVD (No. E-4304), 1988.

[53] J.P. Lu, R. Raj, Ultra-high vacuum chemical vapor deposition and in situ characterization of titanium oxide thin films, Journal of Materials Research 6 (9) (1991) 1913−1918.

[54] T. An, J. Tang, Y. Zhang, Y. Quan, X. Gong, A.M. Al-Enizi, et al., Photoelectrochemical conversion from graphitic C_3N_4 quantum dot decorated semiconductor nanowires, ACS Applied Materials and Interfaces 8 (20) (2016) 12772−12779.

[55] J. Zhu, Q. Wu, J. Key, M. Wu, P.K. Shen, Self-assembled superstructure of carbon-wrapped, single-crystalline Cu_3P porous nanosheets: one-step synthesis and enhanced Li-ion battery anode performance, Energy Storage Materials 15 (2018) 75−81.

[56] H.P. Tang, L. Vescan, H. Lüth, Equilibrium thermodynamic analysis of the Si-Ge-Cl-H system for atmospheric and low pressure CVD of Si1-xGex, Journal of Crystal Growth 116 (1−2) (1992) 1−14.

[57]   L. Tang, J. Tan, H. Nong, B. Liu, H.M. Cheng, Chemical vapor deposition growth of two-dimensional compound materials: controllability, material quality, and growth mechanism, Accounts of Materials Research 2 (1) (2020) 36–47.

[58]   S. Ullah, M. Hasan, H.Q. Ta, L. Zhao, Q. Shi, L. Fu, et al., Synthesis of doped porous 3D graphene structures by chemical vapor deposition and its applications, Advanced Functional Materials 29 (48) (2019) 1904457.

[59]   Z. Li, L. Zhang, B. Li, Z. Liu, Z. Liu, H. Wang, et al., Convenient and large-scale synthesis of hollow graphene-like nanocages for electrochemical supercapacitor application, Chemical Engineering Journal 313 (2017) 1242–1250.

[60]   Z. Li, B. Li, C. Liao, Z. Liu, D. Li, H. Wang, et al., One-pot construction of 3-D graphene nanosheets/Ni$_3$S$_2$ nanoparticles composite for high-performance supercapacitors, Electrochimica Acta 253 (2017) 344–356.

[61]   B. Li, Z. Li, Q. Pang, J.Z. Zhang, Core/shell cable-like Ni$_3$S$_2$ nanowires/N-doped graphene-like carbon layers as composite electrocatalyst for overall electrocatalytic water splitting, Chemical Engineering Journal 401 (2020) 126045.

[62]   Z. Li, J. Lin, B. Li, C. Yu, H. Wang, Q. Li, Construction of heteroatom-doped and three-dimensional graphene materials for the applications in supercapacitors: a review, Journal of Energy Storage 44 (2021) 103437.

[63]   A.K. Padhi, K.S. Nanjundaswamy, J.B. Goodenough, Phospho-olivines as positive-electrode materials for rechargeable lithium batteries, Journal of the Electrochemical Society 144 (4) (1997) 1188.

[64]   Y. Wang, Y. Wang, E. Hosono, K. Wang, H. Zhou, The design of a LiFePO$_4$/carbon nanocomposite with a core–shell structure and its synthesis by an in situ polymerization restriction method, Angewandte Chemie International Edition 47 (39) (2008) 7461–7465.

[65]   E.R. Kupp, S. Kochawattana, S.H. Lee, S. Misture, G.L. Messing, Particle size effects on yttrium aluminum garnet (YAG) phase formation by solid-state reaction, Journal of Materials Research 29 (19) (2014) 2303–2311.

[66]   Z. Li, R. Lin, Z. Liu, D. Li, H. Wang, Q. Li, Novel graphitic carbon nitride/graphite carbon/palladium nanocomposite as a high-performance electrocatalyst for the ethanol oxidation reaction, Electrochimica Acta 191 (2016) 606–615.

[67]   G. He, Z. Yan, M. Cai, P.K. Shen, M.R. Gao, H.B. Yao, et al., Ion-exchange-assisted synthesis of Pt-VC nanoparticles loaded on graphitized carbon: a high-performance nanocomposite electrocatalyst for oxygen-reduction reactions, Chemistry–A European Journal 18 (27) (2012) 8490–8497.

[68]   Z. Li, S. Ji, B.G. Pollet, P.K. Shen, A Co$_3$W$_3$C promoted Pd catalyst exhibiting competitive performance over Pt/C catalysts towards the oxygen reduction reaction, Chemical Communications 50 (5) (2014) 566–568.

[69]   Y. Li, Z. Li, P.K. Shen, Simultaneous formation of ultrahigh surface area and three-dimensional hierarchical porous graphene-like networks for fast and highly stable supercapacitors, Advanced Materials 25 (17) (2013) 2474–2480.

[70]   Facile Construction of G-C$_3$n$_4$ Quantum dots/NiCo$_2$O$_4$ Hollow Spheres Hybrid Architecture as Bifunctional Electrocatalyst for OER and HER, International Journal of Hydrogen Energy submitting.

[71]   S.A. Rowlands, A.K. Hall, P.G. McCormick, R. Street, R.J. Hart, G.F. Ebell, et al., Destruction of toxic materials, Nature 367 (6460) (1994) 223.

[72]   J.L. Do, T. Friščić, Mechanochemistry: a force of synthesis, ACS Central Science 3 (1) (2017) 13–19.

[73]   F. Fischer, K.J. Wenzel, K. Rademann, F. Emmerling, Quantitative determination of activation energies in mechanochemical reactions, Physical Chemistry Chemical Physics 18 (33) (2016) 23320–23325.

[74]   S. Kumar, M. Regue, M.A. Isaacs, E. Freeman, S. Eslava, All-inorganic CsPbBr$_3$ nanocrystals: gram-scale mechanochemical synthesis and selective photocatalytic CO$_2$ reduction to methane, ACS Applied Energy Materials 3 (5) (2020) 4509–4522.

[75]   Y. Dong, X. Lin, D. Wang, R. Yuan, S. Zhang, X. Chen, et al., Modulating the defects of graphene blocks by ball-milling for ultrahigh gravimetric and volumetric performance and fast sodium storage, Energy Storage Materials 30 (2020) 287–295.

[76] J. Zhang, J. Ma, T.S. Choksi, D. Zhou, S. Han, Y.F. Liao, et al., Strong metal—support interaction boosts activity, selectivity, and stability in electrosynthesis of H_2O_2, Journal of the American Chemical Society 144 (5) (2022) 2255—2263.

[77] X. Tan, H. Li, W. Zhang, K. Jiang, S. Zhai, W. Zhang, et al., Square-pyramidal Fe-N_4 with defect-modulated O-coordination: two-tier electronic structure fine-tuning for enhanced oxygen reduction, Chem Catalysis 2 (4) (2022) 816—835.

[78] Mechanochemical Preparation of Single Atom Catalysts: A Perspective Review, Material Today Accept (n.d.).

[79] G.F. Han, F. Li, A.I. Rykov, Y.K. Im, S.Y. Yu, J.P. Jeon, et al., Abrading bulk metal into single atoms, Nature Nanotechnology 17 (4) (2022) 403—407.

[80] S. Lobe, A. Bauer, S. Uhlenbruck, D. Fattakhova-Rohlfing, Physical vapor deposition in solid-state battery development: from materials to devices, Advanced Science 8 (11) (2021) 2002044.

[81] R.C. Forsythe, C.P. Cox, M.K. Wilsey, A.M. Muller, Pulsed laser in liquids made nanomaterials for catalysis, Chemical Reviews 121 (13) (2021) 7568—7637.

CHAPTER 6

Characterization techniques and paradigms of nanomaterials

6.1 Introduction

Nanotechnology has become an important foundation for the development of energy and environmental science in the last 2 decades. The chemical composition, crystal structure, and microstructure of nanomaterials are the key factors that determine their properties and applications. Advanced characterization technology is very important for the structural modification and performance optimization of nanomaterials. Powerful and comprehensive characterization technology is essential for analyzing much information about nanomaterials, such as phase state, chemical composition, element composition, morphological characteristics, micro or surface structure, electronic properties, and so on. At present, the common instrumental analysis methods used for the characterization of nanomaterials include the following: X-ray technology, electron spectroscopy technology, electron microscopy technology, spectroscopy technology, thermal analysis technology, selected area electron diffraction (SAED) technology, and inductively coupled plasma (ICP) technology (see Fig. 6.1 for details) [1–5].

The commonly used X-ray technologies include X-ray diffraction (XRD), small angle X-ray diffraction (SAXRD), X-ray absorption near edge spectroscopy (XANES), etc. The main electron spectroscopy technologies are X-ray photoelectron spectroscopy (XPS), energy dispersive spectroscopy (EDS), and electron energy loss spectroscopy (EELS). The electron microscopy techniques used in nano-characterization include scanning electron microscope (SEM), transmission electron microscope (TEM), scanning transmission electron microscope (STEM), atomic force microscopy (AFM), etc. The spectroscopy technology mainly includes ultraviolet-visible (UV-Vis) spectrum, Fourier transform infrared spectroscopy (FTIR), Raman spectrum, and so on. Thermal analysis techniques (determination of thermal stability or property of nanomaterials or carbon content) include differential thermal analysis, differential scanning calorimetry, thermogravimetric analysis, etc. According to different detection methods, the ICP (determination of metal content) can be divided into ICP-atomic emission spectrometry (ICP-AES) and ICP-mass spectrometry (ICP-MS) [1–5].

From the perspective of characterization technology, the main characterization methods of nanomaterials are shown in Fig. 6.1. However, in order to better understand the role of these characterization technologies, we introduce the characterization

Nanostructured Materials
ISBN 978-0-443-19256-2, https://doi.org/10.1016/B978-0-443-19256-2.00033-8

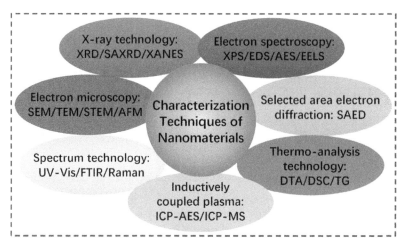

Figure 6.1 Common characterization techniques of nanomaterials [1–5].

methods from the perspective of nanomaterials, mainly from the eight aspects: crystal phase, morphology, crystal structure, electronic structure, atomic structure, element composition, porous structure, and theoretical calculation of nanomaterials. We also pay special attention to the description of the definition and physicochemical principles of different characterization methods, as well as the paradigm summary of our or other group's work in recent years.

6.2 Crystal phase characterization

6.2.1 Definition and principle of XRD

X-ray diffraction, also known as XRD, is a research method to obtain phase information such as the composition of materials and the structure of atoms or molecules inside materials by analyzing their diffraction patterns through X-ray diffraction of materials. XRD is not only used for phase analysis of solid samples but also used to determine cell parameters of crystal structure, lattice patterns, and atomic coordinates of simple structures. The principle of X-ray diffraction analysis for phase analysis is that the crystal plane spacing determined by the angular position of each diffraction peak and their relative intensity is inherent characteristics of the material. Each substance has a specific cell size and crystal structure, which correspond to diffraction intensity and diffraction Angle. Therefore, the crystal phase and crystal structures of nanomaterials can be identified according to diffraction data.

When the diffraction conditions are satisfied, Bragg formula can be applied: $2d\sin\theta = \lambda$. X-ray of known wavelength can be used to measure θ Angle, so as to calculate the crystal plane spacing d, which is used for X-ray structure analysis. Another method is to measure θ Angle with crystal with known d, so that the wavelength of characteristic X-ray can be calculated, and the elements contained in the sample can be determined from available data. In addition, according to XRD diffraction pattern, Schererr formula can be used to determine the grain size of nanoparticle: $D = K\gamma/B\cos\theta$ (D is the average thickness of the grain perpendicular to the crystal plane, K is Scherrer's constant, B is the half-height width of the diffraction peak or the integral height width of the diffraction peak of the measured sample, θ is the diffraction Angle, γ is the X-ray wavelength, 0.154056 nm). If B is the half-width of the diffraction peak, then $K = 0.89$; if B is the integral height and width of the diffraction peak, then $K = 1$. In the calculation process, the diffraction Angle θ needs to be replaced by radians (rad) [2].

6.2.2 Paradigm and summary of XRD

The XRD paradigm summary of our group's work in recent years is summarized in Fig. 6.2 [6–11]. Generally, in XRD characterization, the following information can be obtained from the XRD diffraction peaks: (1) the substance composition and crystal phase of the material can be determined by the diffraction peak at a specific position (2θ peak position of substance); (2) the crystallinity of the crystal (or the relative proportion of each component in the composite) can be preliminarily judged by the height and width of the diffraction peak; (3) the variation of crystal lattice parameters (such as crystal plane spacing and alloying degree) can be determined by the position shifting of diffraction peak; (4) the average size of crystal size of nanomaterials was calculated by Schererr formula ($D = K\gamma/B\cos\theta$) [6–11].

In 2012, Li and Shen reported a carbon-supported 3D Pt-on-Co nanodendrites as high-performance electrocatalysts. Fig. 6.2A and B presents the X-ray diffraction (XRD) patterns of the as-synthesized (A) carbon-supported Co nanoparticles (NPs) and (B) carbon-supported 3-D Pt-on-Co nanodendrites [6]. The XRD pattern of the Co NPs shows three peaks at 44.2° (111), 51.5° (200), and 75.8° (220), indicating the Co NPs are polycrystalline (JCPDS, 15–0806). The calculated average size according to the diffraction peak of Co (111) was 4.1 nm. The XRD patterns of 3-D Pt-on-Co nanodendrites can be indexed as the face-centered cubic (fcc) phase (JCPDS, 65–2868) with clear Pt (111), (200), (220), (311), and (222) facets. For the carbon-supported 3-D Pt-on-Co nanodendrites, two reflection peaks of Co NPs can be observed, indicating that Co component was preserved in the sample after Pt loading. The calculated average particle from the diffraction peak of Pt (111) was 3.8 nm, while that calculated from the diffraction peak of Pt (220) was 2.9 nm according to Schererr formula [6].

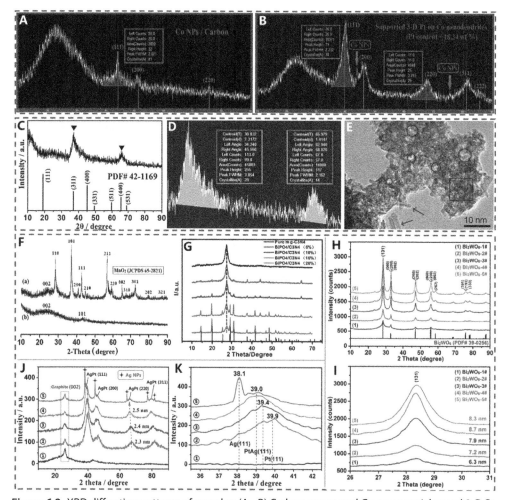

Figure 6.2 XRD diffraction patterns of samples: (A—B) Carbon-supported Co nanoparticles and 3-D Pt-on-Co nanodendrites [6], (C—E) MnO₂ nanocrystalline short-rods [7], (F) Carbon and carbon-supported MnO₂ nanowires [8], (G) BiPO₄/g-C₃N₄ composite nanomaterial [9], (H—I) Bi₂WO₆ nanocrystals with different crystal size [10], and (J—K) Graphite carbon-supported AgPt alloy nanoparticles [11].

In 2010, Li and Wang reported an ultrafine low–crystallinity MnO₂ nanocrystalline short-rods (see Fig. 6.2C—E) [7]. The XRD pattern showed that only two characteristic peaks of (311) and (400) are very obvious for this MnO₂ (PDF# 42-1169), while other peaks are almost nonexistent. The calculated mean sizes according to the diffraction peaks of (311) and (400) were found to be 2.8 and 4.4 nm, respectively. The weak peak signals observed in the XRD pattern suggest the sample is in a poorly crystalline state with only a short-range crystal form (nanocrystalline short-rods). In 2011, Li and Wang further reported a carbon-supported MnO_2 nanowires with high-crystallinity structure (see Fig. 6.2F) [8]. The sharp and clear diffraction peaks clearly indicate a good crystallinity of MnO_2 component. All the reflections of the MnO_2 can be indexed to a pure tetragonal phase of MnO_2 (JCPDS 65-2821). For the carbon support, the (002) and (101) two diffraction peaks of carbon, are very broad and weak, which suggests that the carbon has a typical amorphous structure of porous carbonaceous materials.

In 2014, Li and Fang reported a mesoporous g-C_3N_4 and $BiPO_4$ nanorods composite architectures with different $BiPO_4$ contents (see Fig. 6.2G) [9]. The XRD peaks of the pure g-C_3N_4 have a strongest peak at $2h = 27.5°$, corresponding to the interplanar distance of $d = 0.324$ nm, which can be indexed as the (002) peak of the stacking of the conjugated aromatic system, the other weak peak at $13.1°$ can be indexed as (100) diffraction planes. For the $BiPO_4$/g-C_3N_4 composites, as compared to the pure g-C_3N_4, diffraction peaks of the $BiPO_4$ (JCPDS 15−0766) had been detected. With the increasing of $BiPO_4$ content, the intensity of diffraction peaks of $BiPO_4$ increased, while the intensity of diffraction peaks of g-C_3N_4 decreased in composites. The above result revealed the relative proportion of $BiPO_4$ and g-C_3N_4 components in the $BiPO_4$/g-C_3N_4 composites can be demonstrated by XRD.

In 2021, Li and Yu reported a series of porous Bi_2WO_6 photocatalysts with different crystal sizes synthesized by hydrothermal method via adjusting the concentration of reactants (see Fig. 6.2H−I) [10]. Sample numbers one to five are in reaction concentrations from low to high. It can be seen that the five samples show very similar diffraction patterns, and the positions of all diffraction peaks of these samples are consistent with those of the standard Bi_2WO_6 (JCPDS card No. 39-0256). The approximate values of (131) crystalline sizes for Bi_2WO_6-1# ~ 5# samples are 6.3, 7.2, 7.9, 8.7, and 8.3 nm, respectively. The results show that the higher reactant concentrations can generate the larger crystal size of Bi_2WO_6 to a certain extent. On the other hand, some crystal parameters (such as lattice spacing) can be reflected by XRD peak position. The lattice spacing of Bi_2WO_6-1# ~ 5# samples are 0.3181, 0.3180, 0.3179, 0.3177, and 0.3182, respectively. As reactant concentration increases, the (131) diffraction peaks of samples move gradually to the left, which results in decreasing lattice spacing of (131) plane.

In 2017, Li and Shen also reported a graphite carbon-supported bimetallic PtAg alloyed nanoparticles (NPs) with different alloying degree and proportion (see Fig. 6.2J and K) [11]. For the PtAg/graphite carbon samples, all diffraction peaks of PtAg alloy are shied gradually to lower 2θ values with the increasing proportion of the Ag component (from sample 1−5); this reflects the increase of lattice distances via the replacement of Pt with Ag and further manifests the increase in the alloying degree of these PtAg alloy NPs. Since the XRD is mass sensitive, a small fraction of larger particles in the samples will lead to narrower diffraction peaks (e.g., the Ag NPs in sample 5). On the contrary, the diffraction peaks with broad shoulders suggest that the as-prepared PtAg alloy NPs exist in small particle sizes with a narrow size distribution. Using Scherrer's equation, the average sizes of the Pt or PtAg nanoparticles based on (220) planes are estimated to be 2.3, 2.4, and 2.5 nm for samples 1−5, respectively.

6.3 Morphology characterization

6.3.1 Definition and principle of SEM and TEM

Scanning electron microscope (SEM): SEM is a more modern cell biology research tool invented in 1965. It mainly uses secondary electron signal imaging to observe the surface morphology of samples, that is, scanning samples with an extremely narrow electron beam, and producing various effects through the interaction between electron beam and samples, mainly the secondary electron emission of samples. The secondary electron can produce an enlarged morphological image of the sample surface, which is established according to the time sequence when the sample is scanned, that is, the amplified image is obtained by using the point-by-point imaging method. The SEM is a multifunctional and widely used instrument with many superior properties. The uses of SEM include (1) observation and analysis of three-dimensional morphology of nanomaterials; (2) when observing the surface morphology, the composition analysis of the microarea can be carried out by energy spectrum (such as EDS) [2].

Transmission electron microscope (TEM): TEM projects the accelerated and aggregated electron beam onto a very thin (less than 100 nm) sample, and the electrons collide with the atoms in the sample to change the direction, resulting in solid angle scattering. The size of the scattering angle is related to the density and thickness of the sample, so different light and dark images can be formed. The images will be displayed on imaging devices (such as fluorescent screen, film, and photosensitive coupling components) after amplification and focusing. Because the de Broglie wavelength of the electron is very short, the resolution of the TEM is very high, which can reach 0.1−0.2 nm, and the magnification is tens of thousands to millions of times. Therefore, the TEM can be used to observe the fine structure of the sample, and even the structure of only one column of atoms (by the high-resolution (HR) TEM) [2].

6.3.2 Paradigm and summary of SEM and TEM

The SEM and TEM paradigm summary of our group's work in recent years are summarized in Fig. 6.3 [12−15]. Generally, in SEM and TEM characterization, the following information can be obtained from the SEM and TEM images: (1) The overall morphology of the sample can be observed by low-magnification SEM, and the surface nano-structures of the sample can be observed by high-magnification SEM; (2) The internal structure (such as hollow structures) of the sample can be observed

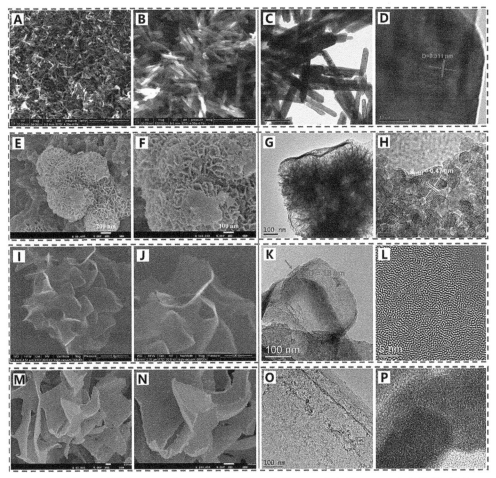

Figure 6.3 SEM and TEM images of samples: (A—D) well-dispersed MnO$_2$ nanorods [12], (E—H) three-dimensional graphene/NiCo$_2$O$_4$ composite [13], (I—L) three-dimensional active graphene nanosheets [14], (M—P) three-dimensional active carbon nanosheets [15].

by low-magnification TEM, and the nanocrystal structure (such as crystal plane spacing) of the sample can be observed by high-magnification TEM; (3) The surface and internal structure of nanomaterials can be fully and scientifically demonstrated through comparative analysis of SEM and TEM images [12—15].

In 2016, Li and coworkers reported the large area synthesis of well-dispersed MnO_2 nanorods (see Fig. 6.3A—D) [12]. The diameter and length distribution of these MnO_2 nanorods have been achieved by the SEM measurement (see Fig. 6.3A and B). The diameter of nanorods ranges from 48 to 66 nm, and the dominant diameter would be about 56 nm. And the length of nanorods ranges from 460 to 550 nm, and the dominant diameter would be about 510 nm. The results suggest a desirable structural uniformity and dimensional controllability of these MnO_2 nanorods. On the other hand, Fig. 6.3C and D shows the typical TEM images of the MnO_2 nanorods sample at different magnifications. It is in agreement with the SEM findings that a great number of the well-defined nanorods can be seen from the lower-magnification image. The higher-magnification image further reveals that these nanorods have relatively uniform diameters throughout their overall lengths. The HR-TEM image shows the lattice fringes with spacings of 0.311 nm, which correspond to the (110) plane of MnO_2.

In 2017, Li and coworkers reported the controllable synthesis of graphene/$NiCo_2O_4$ three-dimensional mesoporous composite nanomaterials (see Fig. 6.3E—H) [13]. The SEM images show that graphene/$NiCo_2O_4$ composite manifests an interesting three-dimensional flower-like construction (with a poriferous sheet-like surface) (Fig. 6.3E and F). The flat nanosheet on the nanoflower is graphene. These poriferous three-dimensional constructions of nanomaterials can provide a larger specific surface area and improve the electrochemical performances. In order to investigate the internal microstructure of the samples, the TEM images are further shown in Fig. 6.3G and H. The sample has three-dimensional flower-like construction of $NiCo_2O_4$ which is firmly supported on the surface graphene nanosheets. The flower-like $NiCo_2O_4$ possesses a hollow nanostructure with the pore diameter of 20—30 nm. The average particle size of $NiCo_2O_4$ nanoparticles on graphene is about 4.5 nm. In addition, a lattice space in 0.47 nm for (111) crystal plane of $NiCo_2O_4$ can be identified from high-resolution TEM images.

In 2016, Li and coworkers reported the synthesis of three-dimensional nitrogen-doped activated graphene-like nanosheets (3-D NAGNs) (see Fig. 6.3I—L) [14]. The microstructure and morphology of the 3-D NAGNs sample were examined by SEM and TEM. The SEM images (Fig. 6.3I and J) exhibit that the sample possesses an outstanding 3-D architecture assembled by interconnected camber-like carbon nanosheets with ultrathin 2-D structures. The TEM image (Fig. 6.3K and L) further confirms the interconnected structures of these nanosheets, and the thickness of one typical nanosheet is measured to be 18 nm. Interestingly, the high-magnification TEM image taken on the edge of this nanosheet reveals a highly poriferous network structure formed by numerous intertwined nanocrystals.

In 2022, Li and coworkers further reported the synthesis of three-dimensional activated carbon nanosheets modified by graphitized carbon dots (3-D ACNs/GCDs) (see Fig. 6.3M—P) [15]. The surface morphology and structure of the material were characterized by SEM (Fig. 6.3M and N), showing that the 3-D ACNs/GCDs sample has an obvious three-dimensional porous network structure and interrelated nanosheet morphology. These 3-D carbon nanosheets have leaf-like branching structure and cuspate morphology. The thickness of these nanosheets is about 20 nm. In particular, there are some GCDs nanoparticles (~ 20 nm) on the surface of the nanosheet. The TEM images (Fig. 6.3O and P) of 3-D ACNs/GCDs sample further indicate that the surface of the nanosheet is rough and has many GCDs nanoparticle (5—20 nm). The GCDs nanoparticle has clear graphited lattice fringes (0.34 nm in D (002) spacing), indicating that these carbon nanoparticles are typical graphitized carbon dots (GCDs).

6.4 Crystal structure characterization

6.4.1 Definition and principle of HRTEM and STEM

HRTEM (namely high-resolution transmission electron microscope) has a relatively high resolution, so it can do what the general transmission electron microscope can do. However, the pole shoe spacing of the objective lens of the HRTEM is relatively small, so the rotation angle of the double tilt table is smaller than that of the analytical electron microscope. HRTEM is a kind of transmission electron microscope, which shows the crystal plane spacing through the image of light and dark stripes. By measuring the spacing of light and dark stripes, and then comparing it with the standard crystal plane spacing d of the crystal, determine which crystal plane it belongs to. In this way, it is very convenient to calibrate the crystal plane orientation or the growth direction of the material. The structure and composition information of nanoparticles can be obtained by combining the results of HRTEM image and EDS analysis.

Scanning transmission electron microscope (STEM) has both features of TEM and SEM. STEM scans the surface of the sample with an electron beam, and images the sample through electron penetration. STEM technology requires high vacuum, and the electronic system is more complex than TEM and SEM. The STEM is a new development of transmission electron microscope. The scanning coil forces the electron probe to scan on the thin-film sample. The difference from the STEM is that the detector is placed under the sample, and the detector receives the transmission electron beam or elastic scattering electron beam. After amplification, the bright field image and dark field image of the STEM corresponding to the conventional TEM are displayed on the fluorescent screen. As one of the most important STEM imaging methods, high-angle dark-field (HAADF) is a popular characterization method in various scientific research fields in recent years. The image strength of HAADF-STEM is proportional to the density of the material, mapping the material to sub-nanometer resolution.

6.4.2 Paradigm and summary of HR-TEM and STEM

The HR-TEM and STEM paradigm summary of our and other cooperative group's work in recent years are summarized in Fig. 6.4 [16–20]. Generally, in HR-TEM and STEM characterization, the following information can be obtained from the HR-TEM and STEM images: (1) the distance of light–dark fringe on different crystal planes

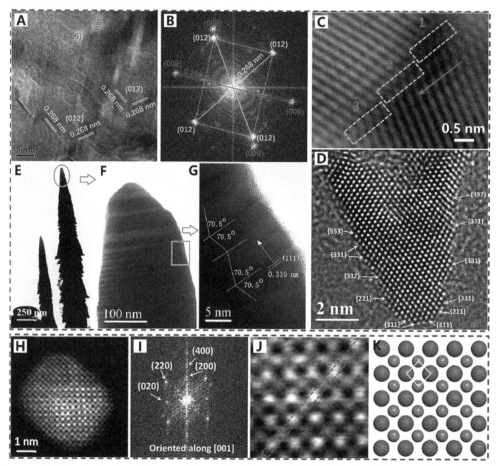

Figure 6.4 HR-TEM or STEM images of samples: (A and B) MnCo-LDHs [16], (C) Crystal boundary of PdPt alloy nanoparticles [17], (D) PtCu nanoframes with high-index facets [18], (E–G) Periodically twinned HgSe nanotowers [19], (H–K) Atomic-resolution HAADF-STEM image, FFT pattern, atomic columns, atomic structure of the PtCo nanoparticle (blue and red spheres is Pt and Co atoms) [20].

can be accurately measured by HR–TEM images and their fast Fourier transform (FFT) images; (2) the high index facet, twined crystal, and crystal boundary of nanomaterials can be also measured by HR–TEM images; (3) the atomic arrangement construction (atomic columns and atomic structures) of nanocrystals can be clearly characterized by HAADF-STEM images [16−20].

In 2021, Li and coworkers reported MnCo-layered double hydroxides (LDHs) with good nanocrystal structures (see Fig. 6.4A and B) [16]. Fig. 6.4A and B shows the enlarged high-resolution HR–TEM image and Fourier transform image, respectively. It can be clearly seen that the MnCo-LDHs nanocrystal is of obvious lattice stripes, and the lattice stripe shows the plane spacing values of 0.260 and 0.268 nm, corresponding to the (009) and (012) crystal planes of MnCo-LDHs, respectively. In 2014, Li and coworkers constructed ultra-low Pt loading $Pd_{10}Pt_1$ bimetallic catalyst with the structure of nanoparticles in close contact (see Fig. 6.4C) [17]. The two nanocrystals have the same lattice spacing between (111) planes of 0.225 nm, which shows an evident crystal dislocation. As a result, a distinct three-step twin boundary is readily observed for the two nanocrystals. This step boundary structure of the crystallographic plane is predicted to be of affinity with the superior catalytic properties of catalysts.

Metal nanocrystals (NCs) coated by high-index-facet (HIF) have attracted many attentions because of their excellent properties and potential advantages. The HIF is defined by a set of Miller index {HKL} with at least one of the indices greater than 1. The most prominent feature of the high HIF is the high density of step atoms and kink atoms, and the low coordination number (CN) [21]. The surface energy of HIF nanocrystals is usually higher than low-index-facet ones due to the presence of high-density low-coordination surface atoms. In 2017, Shen and coworkers reported an atomic-scale PtCu nanoframes with high-index facets (see Fig. 6.4D) [18]. The atomic-resolution HRTEM image of the foot oriented along the [011] zone axis showed that the nano frame possesses abundant stepped atoms and various HIFs, such as {553}, {332}, {331}, {311}, {221}, and {211} in the outer layer atoms order surface. The low coordination surface atoms of HIF are rich in suspended bonds, which can easily interact with reactants and become reactive centers, enhancing catalytic activity.

Recently, periodic twinned nanostructures of semiconductor materials, such as ZnSe, ZnS, GaP, and InP nanowires, have been demonstrated, which showed excellent physical and chemical properties. With a hydrothermal method, Fang and coworkers have fabricated the periodically twinned nanotowers of HgSe crystals simply by judiciously choosing participating reactants and their molar ratios and concentrations (see Fig. 6.4E−G) [19]. The HRTEM image taken from the square of the nanotower reveals the alternating twins along the [111] axis of the nanotowers. We also notice a lattice spacing of (3.39 ± 0.05) Å along the nanotower direction, which matches up well with the distance between the adjacent (111) crystal planes of HgSe and thus confirms the preferential growth of the HgSe nanotower along [111] as well as the relationship between the twins. The twin relationship is manifested by a zigzag angle of $141°$ ($70.5° + 70.5°$), in accordance with the relative rotational angle of (111) twin crystals in face-centered cubic (fcc) structures. It is thus obvious that the alternate twinning takes place along the [111] axis, which evolves continuously toward the HgSe nanotower direction.

More recently, Shen and coworkers reported the one-step solid-state synthesis of PtCo nanocubes and their characterization by the atomic-resolution HAADFSTEM (see Fig. 6.4H−K) [20]. A 5 nm PtCo nanocube viewed along the [001] zone axis, an ordered alloy single phase is clearly and directly identified by HAADFSTEM image. The corresponding FFT pattern of the PtCo nanocube shows a characteristic fcc structure viewed along the [001] zone axis. The brightness of each dot in the HAADF-STEM image represents scattering intensity of the element associated with the number of electrons per atom (Z) and the number of atoms in the column. Since Z_{Pt} (78) is significantly higher than Z_{Co} (27), the Pt columns (indicated by blue arrows) will have higher intensity than that of the Co columns (indicated by red arrowhs), shown in the intensity profile obtained from projecting the atomic columns along the red line shows the schematic diagram of the atomic structure of the PtCo nanocube.

6.5 Electronic structure characterization

6.5.1 Definition and principle of XPS and EELS

X-ray photoelectron spectroscopy, abbreviated as XPS or ESCA, is to irradiate the surface of a sample with X-rays, so that the electrons of its atoms or molecules are excited and emitted, and measure the energy distribution of these photoelectrons, so as to obtain the required information. XPS has developed into a powerful surface analysis instrument with the functions of surface element analysis, chemical state and energy band structure analysis, and microchemical state imaging analysis. According to Einstein's energy relation formula: $by = E_b + E_k$, the incident photon energy by is known. With the help of photoelectron spectrometer, the photoelectron energy E_k excited by the incident photon in the photoelectric process can be measured, so the orbital binding energy E_b of the inner electron can be calculated. Because all kinds of atoms have certain structures, the sample can be analyzed and identified after knowing the E_b value. The XPS is one of the most important means to study the electronic and atomic structure of the surface and interface of materials. In principle, XPS can determine most elements except hydrogen and helium in the periodic table of elements [2].

EELS has the following characteristics: (1) EELS can realize the regional component analysis with horizontal resolution of 10 nm and depth of 0.5−2 nm; (2) EELS has the ability to microanalysis that X-ray photo spectroscopy (XPS) does not have; (3) EELS has more surface and sensitive characteristics than Auger electron spectroscopy (AES); (4) EELS can distinguish the structure and chemical properties of atoms and molecules adsorbed on the surface; (5) EELS is better than X-ray energy spectrometry (EDS) in detecting ultra-light elements. Importantly, the EELS can study the following problems: (1) Electronic transition of adsorbed molecules; (2) Through the study of the surface state, the optical properties, interface state, and bonding of the film coating are studied; (3) By studying the vibration of adsorbed substances, one can understand the structural symmetry, bond length and order of adsorbed molecules, as well as the identification of surface compounds; (4) Surface bonding and relaxation are studied by surface phonons; (5) By studying the optical properties of metals and semiconductors, one can understand the carrier concentration distribution and relaxation process in the space charge region [22].

6.5.2 Paradigm and summary of XPS and EELS

The XPS and EELS paradigm summary of our and other group's work in recent years are summarized in Fig. 6.5 [11,23–25]. Generally, the main functions of XPS testing include: (1) Firstly, it can test element types and percentage content of samples (including mass percentage and atomic percentage); (2) The band and electronic structure of semiconductor materials can be determined by the binding energy position of characteristic peaks; (3) The different valence states of elements (by using Gaussian peak-splitting model) and their relative contents (based on peak area ratio) were analyzed according to the high-resolution spectrogram; (4) The electron orientation transfer and electron state density can be demonstrated according to the shift direction (red shift or blue shift) of binding energy of different samples [11,23–25].

In 2020, Li and coworkers reported the synthesis of Bi@β-Bi$_2$O$_3$/g-C$_3$N$_4$ heterojunction at different temperatures with different electronic properties (see Fig. 6.5A–C) [23]. The XPS analysis was performed to analyze elemental compositions: evident peaks of C, N, O and Bi in FU200, FU230, FU260, and FU290, and revealed the presence of C and N in g-C$_3$N$_4$. The low-intensity O peak in CN corresponded to adsorbed H$_2$O or O$_2$. The binding energy of sp^2 C in the composites was shifted to a lower value compared with the sp^2 C of g-C$_3$N$_4$ at 288.1 eV, implying the increased electron density of C atoms for g-C$_3$N$_4$ component. Further comparison in the Bi 4f and O 1s spectra indicated that the Bi and O binding energies of β-Bi$_2$O$_3$ in FU230 were reduced compared with FU260 and FU290, revealing the increased electron density of β-Bi$_2$O$_3$ in FU230. And the binding energies of Bi-metal in FU230 were shifted to higher values relative to FU200 that consisted mainly of Bi/g-C$_3$N$_4$, confirming bismuth acted as an electron donor in the composite and electrons migrated from Bi-metal to β-Bi$_2$O$_3$.

In 2017, Li and coworkers synthesized hybrid architectures of bimetallic PtAg alloyed nanoparticles and 3-D mesoporous graphene sheets (PtAg/3DMGS) with different electronic properties (see Fig. 6.5D–G) [11]. The XPS was used to elucidate the surface

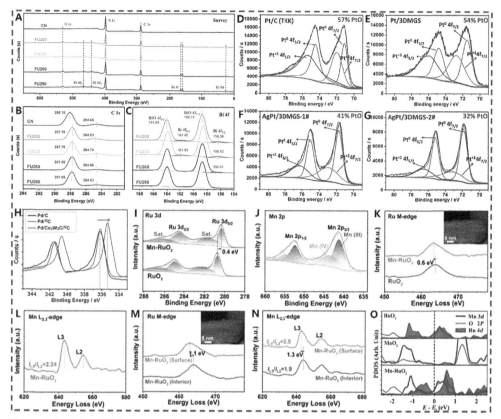

Figure 6.5 XPS or EELS images of samples: (A—C) Bi@β-Bi$_2$O$_3$/g-C$_3$N$_4$ heterojunction with different electronic properties [23], (D—G) PtAg/3DMGS with different electronic properties [11], (H) Pd/Co$_3$W$_3$C/GC [24], (I—O) Mn-Ruo$_2$ double site catalyst [25].

oxidation states of platinum in commercial Pt/C, Pt/3DMGS, PtAg/3DMGS-1#, and PtAg/3DMGS-2# catalysts. All these Pt 4f spectra are composed of the 4f$_{5/2}$ and 4f$_{7/2}$ characteristic peaks of Pt^{2+} (PtO) and Pt^0 (Pt). It can be seen that the atomic ratios of PtO to Pt in these samples are in the increasing order of 32% (PtAg/3DMGS-2#) < 41% (PtAg/3DMGS-1#) < 54% (Pt/3DMGS) < 57% (Pt/C), which suggest that the alloyed PtAg catalysts have higher oxidation resistance than the single Pt catalysts. Therefore, the alloy-induced oxidation resistance of the PtAg/3DMGS catalyst should be one of the basic factors accounting for its advanced catalytic performance. Furthermore, the poisoning resistance (better CO resistance) of the Pt-based alloyed catalysts is another key parameter for practical applications.

Charge transfer effect, also known as synergistic electron effect (see Sections 3.3.1 and 3.9.1), is based on the interface charge transfer between different components to achieve directional regulation of charge density of nanomaterials. One of our previous research results showed that the electronic structure of Pd can be changed, through the interface charge transfer effect (or interface synergistic electronic effect) of two different components (Pd and Co_3W_3C) (see Fig. 6.5H) [24]. With graphite carbon (GC) as a support (Pd/Co_3W_3C/GC), the Co_3W_3C can decrease binding energy of Pd (in the same size of ~ 3.5 nm) by 1 eV, compared to that of Pd/GC and Pd/C. The electron transfer effect is synergistically occurred on the GC-supported Pd and Co_3W_3C components (i.e., synergistic electronic effect). In addition, Zhou et al. also investigated the electronic structure of Mn–RuO_2 catalyst by XPS, the results showed that the incorporation of Mn causes the negative shift of Ru binding energy and proved that Ru has a low oxidation state in Mn–RuO_2, and the 2p peak of Mn shows the coexistence of Mn^{3+} and Mn^{4+} (see Fig. 6.5I and J) [25]. In short, the XPS is an effective way to prove electron transfer effect on catalyst surface, where the binding energy position shift proves interfacial charge transfer (the lower binding energy means the higher electron density).

The low oxidation state of Ru in Mn–RuO_2 catalyst can also be proved by EELS, while Mn^{3+} and Mn^{4+} coexist (see Fig. 6.5K−O) [25]. The EELS analysis on the surface and interior of a single Mn–RuO_2 catalyst shows that the valence states of Ru and Mn on the surface are lower than those in the interior of the catalyst. The density functional theory (DFT) theoretical calculation can also prove that the valence state on the surface of Mn–RuO_2 two-site catalyst is lower than that of pure RuO_2 and MnO_2, and the Mn-O bond length is larger than that of MnO_2. Such tensile strain makes the D-band center move up, enhances its adsorption on oxygen intermediate species, and thus improves its oxygen reduction reaction (ORR) electrocatalytic activity. In short, the EELS can effectively characterize the internal and surface oxidation states and electronic structures of nanomaterials, providing direct evidence for the improvement of intrinsic catalytic activity when designing high-performance catalyst.

6.6 Atomic structure characterization

6.6.1 Definition and principle of XAS and AC-TEM

With the development of technology and research progress, we can easily use electron microscopy technology to see the surface structure and element distribution of materials, ICP, XPS to get the type of elements, XRD crystal structure, and so on. However, the research on nanomaterials is no longer satisfied with these but pursues more accurate atomic structure identification. The synchrotron X-ray absorption spectroscopy (XAS) can provide valuable information about the coordination environment and the chemical state of the detected atom, and hard X-ray has the ability to study the dynamic process of in situ electrochemical reaction, which is conducive to the establishment of more accurate structure—activity relationship. The XAS spectrum consists of absorption edge and a series of oscillating structures, which can be divided into two regions: Extended X-ray absorption fine structure (EXAFS) is located at the absorption edge of 40—1500 eV region, providing local structure information; X-ray absorption near edge structure (XANES) is located in the ± 50 eV region of absorption edge and can provide a lot of chemical information (identifying the electron and coordination structures) [26].

Spherical aberration-corrected transmission electron microscopy (AC-TEM) is a state-of-the-art analytical instrument (acceleration voltage: 0—200 KV; maximum resolution: 0.08 nm) used in the fields of nanomaterials science, physics, and chemical engineering. With the emergence of atomic-structure nanomaterials, the AC-TEM has entered the field of common researchers in the last decade. The AC-TEM can work in two modes, namely, "TEM mode" and "STEM mode." In TEM mode, the morphology is can be observed, and in STEM mode, EDS and EELS component line scanning and mapping can be done. In STEM mode, HADDF images can be collected using bright and dark field probes, and its advantage is that clear images of atomic structure can be obtained. Particularly, during AC-TEM testing, the accurate chemical information of nanomaterials (even those with atomic structures) can be obtained by using EELS and X-ray energy dispersive spectroscopy (EDS) under the sub-nanometer atomic-level microdomain [27].

6.6.2 Paradigm and summary of XAS and AC-TEM

The XAS and AC-TEM (including EELS and EDS) paradigm summary of work on single atomic materials in recent years are summarized in Fig. 6.6 [28—34]. Generally, the structure characterization of single atomic materials includes several aspects: (1) Analyzing the single dispersed atomic structure of metal (proving that there is no metal bond) and the coordination structure of metal atoms (metal and nonmetal coordination) by XAS (EXAFS and XANES); (2) The atomic phase structure of metal atoms was directly observed by AC-TEM to confirm the atomic-scale dispersed structure; (3) The EELS and EDS were used to prove the distribution characteristics of metal elements and nonmetals in the sub-nanometer region [28—34]. Recently, our research group has published three review papers on single-atomic materials: (1) emerging ultra-high-density single-atom catalysts for versatile heterogeneous catalysis applications: redefinition, recent progress, and challenges [35]; (3) progress in batch preparation of single-atom catalysts and application in green synthesis of fine chemicals [36];

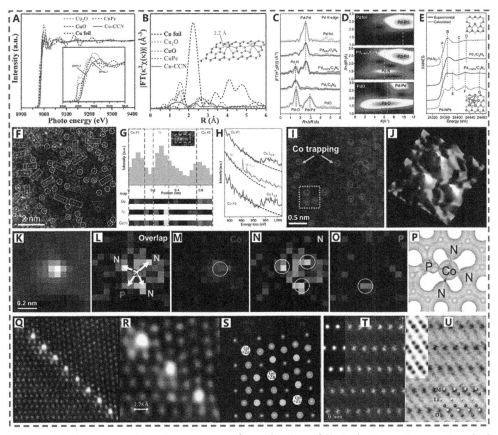

Figure 6.6 XAS and AC-TEM (or EELS) images of samples: (A and B) single atomic Cu on g-C₃N₄ [28], (C—E) single atomic Pd on g-C₃N₄ [29], (F—H) single atomic Cu—Ni—Cu on g-C₃N₄ [30], (I and J) single atomic Co on SiO₂ [31], (K—P) Co-N₃P₁ coordination of single atomic Co on carbon [32], (Q—S) HAADF-STEM images of Mg-Gd-Zn ternary alloy [33], (T and U) HAADF (or ABF)-STEM images of LiTMO₂ [34].

(2) recent progress of diatomic catalysts: general design fundamentals and diversified catalytic applications [37]. Some structure characterizations of single atomic materials are included in these review papers.

In 2020, Li and coworkers synthesized crystalline carbon nitride supported copper single atoms (single atomic Cu on g-C₃N₄ or Cu-CNN) and XAS (XANES and EXAFS) analysis (see Fig. 6.6A and B) [28]. The XANES (Fig. 6.6A) of Cu–CCN sample showed a curve similar to that of CuPc, suggesting that the coordination conditions of Cu atoms in Cu-CCN samples and the CuPc are also similar. The spectrum of Cu-CCN samples is shifted relative to the CuPc samples, indicating that the coordination of Cu atoms in Cu-CCN sample may be only N without C. The EXAFS (Fig. 6.6B) of Cu-CCN sample showed a distinct peak at 1.5 Å, which is close to that of Cu_2O, CuO, and CuPc references. The reason for this phenomenon may be that it is difficult to distinguish the coordination bond between the C, N, and O elements and Cu atoms. Particularly, the Cu-Cu coordination bond does not exist in Cu-CCN sample. The EXAFS curve-fitting plot revealed the coordination numbers of Cu-N in Cu-CCN sample is around 6, which indicates that the Cu atom was introduced into a six-fold cavity of g-C_3N_4.

In 2022, Liu et al. proposed the synergistic effect of single palladium atom (Pd_1) and palladium nanoparticles (Pd NP) supported on g-C_3N_4 in photocatalysis (see Fig. 6.6C–E) [29]. In order to determine the chemical state and coordination structure of Pd atom in the sample, XANES and EXAFS were used for measurement. In XANES curve (Fig. 6.6E), the absorption edge position of Pd_1/C_3N_4 is close to that of PdO, which indicates that Pd species in Pd_1/C_3N_4 are in an almost +2 oxidation state. At the same time, the absorption edge of Pd NP/C_3N_4 is very close to that of Pd foil, so the valence state of Pd is close to 0. The Pd_{1+NP}/C_3N_4 is located between Pd_1/C_3N_4 and Pd NP/C_3N_4, showing a medium average oxidation state of Pd. In EXAFS curve (Fig. 6.6C), Pd_{1+NP}/C_3N_4 has two peaks at 1.5 and 2.5 Å, which are attributed to Pd-C/N and Pd-Pd bonds, respectively. The wavelet transform analysis (Fig. 6.6D) of Pd further confirms this point: Pd_{1+NP}/C_3N_4 shows two maximum intensity values at the wave vector of 6.0 and 9.7 Å^{-1}, which are designated as Pd-C/N and Pd-Pd scattering, respectively.

In 2021, Lu and his collaborators designed and synthesized a Ni_1Cu_2 dynamic triatomic catalyst with high loading and high stability on g-C_3N_4 support (see Fig. 6.6F–H) [30]. A large number of linear three-atom structures with significant catalytic activity were observed by atomic resolution spherical aberration correction electron microscopy (i.e., HADDF-TEM), while the other single-atom and triangular three-atom structures showed no catalytic activity. Using atomic-resolved AR-EELS experiments, they found that these linear three-atom structures, with Ni atoms in the middle and two Cu atoms on both sides, directly demonstrated the existence of linear Cu-Ni-Cu structures. Based on the strong metal-support interaction between metal (Cu and Ni) and abundant nitrogen on g-C_3N_4 support and the limitation of predeposited Cu atoms on Ni atoms, the Cu-Ni-Cu triatomic catalysts with high loading were prepared on g-C_3N_4 support (3.1 wt.% Ni and 8.1 wt.% Cu).

In 2022, Wu et al. constructed a SiO_2 with ultra-short 3D channels for effective trapping of Co single atoms (see Fig. 6.6I and J) [31]. The self-assembled SiO_2@ polymer composite was used to vaporize carbon in an air atmosphere, forming an ultra-short 3D channel. A large number of oxygen (O*) defects are generated in the channel during the decarbonization process, which can anchor the free Co_1 species to form a sintering-resistant Co_1/SiO_2 catalyst (with unsaturated $Co-O_3$ sites). The HADDF-TEM image (Fig. 6.6I) and the selected-area structural model (Fig. 6.6J) demonstrate the well atomic structure of isolated metal Co species. Using the AR-EELS mapping, the atomic and coordination structures of single-atom catalysts (SACs) can be clearly demonstrated. The AR-EELS mapping at a relatively low beam current to minimize electron-beam perturbations to provide strong evidence of $Co_1-N_3P_1$ structure (see Fig. 6.6K—P) [32]. The Co L-edge EELS spectrum presents a clear Co signal, providing direct evidence for the presence of atomically dispersed Co species. The existence of N, P coordination with Co site is revealed by identifying the surrounding heteroatoms. Electron-density surface of Co atoms (blue color is positive charge and red color is negative charge) manifests asymmetric electron structure in $Co_1-N_3P_1$ by introducing heteroatom P.

In 2013, Nie et al. used high-resolution HAADF-STEM to characterize the twinning boundary of Mg-Gd-Zn ternary alloy at atomic scale and found periodic segregation of Gd and Zn atoms at the twinning boundary (see Fig. 6.6Q—S) [33]. Since the brightness of the atomic columns in HAADF-STEM is proportional to the atomic number, the atomic columns of Gd and Zn can be clearly observed at the twin boundary. The periodic segregation of Gd and Zn on the twin interface can effectively reduce the elastic strain energy of the twin and pin the movement of the twin, thus producing a certain strengthening effect. In 2013, Zhou et al. also used high-resolution HAADF-STEM and annular bright-field STEM (ABF-STEM) to reveal the atomic scale structure of LLOs ($LiTMO_2$) material (see Fig. 6.6T and U) [34]. The Li atom cannot be observed in HAADF image (Fig. 6.6T) due to its very low scattering electron intensity, while it can be clearly observed in ABF image (Fig. 6.6U). The lithium manganese oxide layer (LLOs) is the most attractive cathode material in lithium-ion batteries. The clear observation of Li atom is very important to the electrochemical mechanism.

6.7 Elemental composition characterization

6.7.1 Definition and principle of EDS

SEM is often used as an accessory to SEM, TEM, or AC-TEM. Each element has its own X-ray characteristic wavelength, and the characteristic wavelength depends on the characteristic energy $\triangle E$ released in the energy level transition process. Energy spectrometer uses the characteristic of the different X-ray photon energy of different elements to analyze the composition. EDS can analyze the elements in samples qualitatively and quantitatively. Although organic elements such as C, N, and O can also be analyzed, the analysis of inorganic elements with larger Ordinal Numbers is more accurate. EDS can be used for phase analysis, component analysis, and inclusion morphological composition identification of metal materials. Using qualitative and quantitative analysis of the microarea components on the surface of materials, the surface, line, and point distribution of elements on the material surface can be analyzed by EDS technique.

6.7.2 Paradigm and summary of EDS

The SEM-based EDS and TEM-based EDS (or AC-TEM-based EDS) paradigm summary of our and other group's work in recent years are summarized in Fig. 6.7 [8,16,38−43]. Generally, the main functions of EDS testing include (1) the SEM-based EDS can be used to analyze the element composition and distribution of materials with micron structure (or micron region of materials); (2) the TEM-based EDS can be used to analyze the elemental composition and distribution of nanostructured materials (or nano regions of materials); (3) the AC-TEM-based EDS can be used to analyze the element composition and distribution of atomic-structure materials (or atomic regions of materials) [8,16,38−43].

Previously, our research group used SEM-based EDS to study the element distribution of activated mesophase carbon microspheres (AMCMB) supported nanostructured manganese oxides and self-supporting $ZnGa_2O_4$ nanorods. Fig. 6.7A shows the SEM and EDS images of the AMCMB and AMCMB/Mn_3O_4 nanoparticles composite [38]. There are numberless Mn_3O_4 about 200 nm dispersed uniformly onto the surface of AMCMB, and the C, Mn, and O element distributions were further illustrated by EDS pattern (element mapping). Fig. 6.7B shows the SEM and EDS images of the AMCMB/MnO_2 nanowires composite [8]. The vertical MnO_2 nanowires are well dispersed onto the surface of AMCMB, and the element distribution can be further illustrated by EDS mapping. Fig. 6.7C shows the SEM and EDS images of the self-supporting $ZnGa_2O_4$ nanorods [39], which also demonstrate the uniform distribution of Ga, Zn, and O elements. Nonetheless, the SEM-based EDS mapping cannot reveal the one-dimensional element distribution of nanowire or nanorods due to its low resolution.

Recently, our research group used TEM-based EDS to study the element distribution of Ag@NiCo-LDH/NF [40], Ag-$AgVO_3$/g-C_3N_4 [41], MnCo-LDH nanospheres [16], and Ni_3S_2 nanocubes [42]. The TEM-based EDS elemental mapping of Ag@NiCo-LDH/NF (Fig. 6.7D) shows homogeneous distribution of Ni, Co, Ag, and O, which indicates that Ag nanomaterials and NiCo-LDH nanosheets have formed hybrid structures. The HAADF-STEM and element mapping of the Ag-$AgVO_3$/g-C_3N_4 (Fig. 6.7E) shows that the C, N, O, V, Ag elements have been dispersed and distributed evenly. The STEM-HAADF and element mapping demonstrates the ideal distribution uniformity of Mn, Co, and O in the MnCo-LDH nanospheres (Fig. 6.7F). The HAADF-STEM and EDS elements mapping reveal that the N-Ni_3S_2@NG nanocubes (Fig. 6.7G) are mainly composed of Ni, S, C, and N elements, which homogenously

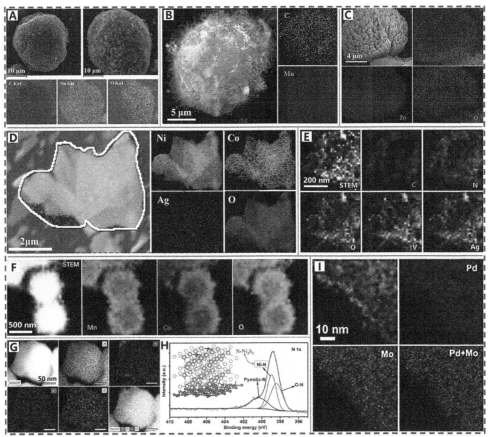

Figure 6.7 SEM-based EDS images of samples: (A) AMCMB/Mn₃O₄ nanoparticles [38], (B) AMCMB/MnO₂ nanowires [8], (C) self-supporting ZnGa₂O₄ nanorods [39]; TEM-based EDS images of samples: (D) Ag@NiCo-LDH/NF [40], (E) Ag–AgVO₃/g-C₃N₄ [41], (F) MnCo-LDH nanospheres [16], (G and H) Ni₃S₂ nanocubes [42]; AC-TEM-based EDS images of samples: (I) Pd₁/α-MoC atomic-structured material [43].

distribute to form an entire cube-like nanostructure. The AC-TEM-based EDS mapping can be used to prove the single-atom-dispersed structure of Pd₁/α-MoC high-density atomic material (Fig. 6.7I) [43]. The AC-TEM (HAADF-STEM) has ultra-high resolution EDS mapping, which can obtain the clear elements mapping of 10 nm nanostructured images. In general, the TEM-EDS mapping can obtain nano-structure and even atomic-structure element images, providing useful chemical information on multielement nanomaterials and single-atomic materials.

6.8 Porous structure characterization

6.8.1 Definition and principle of N_2 adsorption isotherm (BET model)

BET is the acronym of three scientists (Brunauer, Emmett, and Teller). The multimolecular layer adsorption formula derived by the three scientists from the classical statistical theory, namely, the famous BET equation, has become the theoretical basis of particle surface adsorption science and has been widely used in the study of particle surface adsorption performance and the data processing of related detection instruments (see Fig. 6.8A) [2]. The basic assumptions of the model used in the derivation of BET multilayer adsorption theoretical equation are (1) the solid surface is uniform, and multilayer adsorption occurs; (2) Except for the adsorption heat of the first layer, the adsorption heat of other layers is equal to the liquefaction heat of adsorbate. BET multilayer adsorption is different from Langmuir single-layer adsorption. The former is physical adsorption, and

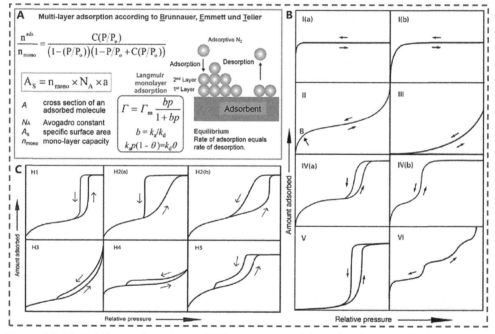

Figure 6.8 (A) Multi-layer adsorption and BET equation [2]; (B) Six classifications of adsorption isotherms, (C) Five classifications of hysteresis loops [44].

the latter is chemical adsorption. The nitrogen (N_2) adsorption equilibrium isotherm is a curve with the adsorption capacity of adsorbent on adsorbent as ordinate and pressure as abscissa under constant temperature. Pressure is usually expressed as relative pressure. The BET-specific surface area and pore size distribution can be obtained N_2 adsorption and desorption isotherm.

The shape of equilibrium isotherm is closely related to the pore structure of materials. We usually use six classifications of adsorption isotherms of IUPAC (see Fig. 6.8B) [44]: Type I indicates the adsorption on microporous adsorbent (I(a) is ~1 nm narrow microporous material, I(b) is ~2 nm wide microporous material); type II indicates the adsorption on the macroporous adsorbent, where there is a strong interaction between the adsorbate and the adsorbent; type III refers to the adsorption on the macroporous adsorbent, but there is a weak interaction between the adsorbate molecules and the adsorbent surface, and the interaction between the adsorbate molecules has a great impact on the adsorption isotherm; type IV is monolayer adsorption with capillary condensation on the mesoporous adsorbent (IV(a) has hysteresis loop, IV(b) has no hysteresis loop); type V demonstrates the multilayer adsorption with capillary condensation on the mesoporous and macroporous adsorbent; type VI refers to the multilayer adsorption on nonporous adsorbents with uniform surface.

Capillary condensation phenomenon is also known as hysteresis loop of adsorption. The noncoincidence of adsorption isotherm and desorption isotherm constitutes a hysteresis loop. This phenomenon often occurs in adsorbents with mesoporous or macroporous structures. IUPAC divides the phenomenon of adsorption isotherm retention loop into five classifications (see Fig. 6.8C) [44]: (1) Type I loop is found in materials that exhibit a narrow range of uniform mesopores; (2) Type II loop is found in materials with complex mesoporous structures in which network effects are important (II(a) is narrow mesoporous material, II (b) is wide mesoporous material); (3) Type III loop is found in layered structure materials and slitting mesoporous and macroporous materials; (4) Type IV loop is found in plate-like particles with nonrigid aggregates; (5) Type VI loop is found in materials with both open and partially blocked mesopores.

6.8.2 Paradigm and summary of N_2 adsorption isotherm (BET model)

The N_2 adsorption-desorption isotherm paradigm summary of our group's work in recent years is summarized in Fig. 6.9 [13,16,45−47]. Fig. 6.9A and B shows the N_2 adsorption-desorption isotherm and pore size distribution of 3D graphene-like carbon nanosheet hierarchical porous structure [45]. The BET-specific surface area of the sample is calculated to be 2017.3 $m^2 \ g^{-1}$, in which the micropore area is 1836.1 $m^2 \ g^{-1}$ and the external surface area is 181.2 $m^2 \ g^{-1}$. For a porous material with micropores, mesopores, and macropores (namely hierarchical porous structures), its adsorption isotherm usually contains the following five stages (see the rectangles in Fig. 6.9A): (1) Microporous filling

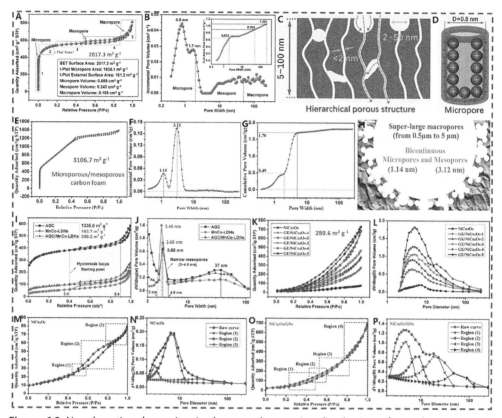

Figure 6.9 N$_2$ adsorption-desorption isotherm and pore size distribution of samples: (A–D) 3-D graphene-like carbon nanosheet [45], (E–H) microporous/mesoporous carbon foam [46], (I and J) AGC/MnCo-LDHs composite [16], (K and L) GE/NiCo$_2$O$_4$ composite [13], (M–P) NiCo$_2$O$_4$ and NiCo$_2$O$_4$/GNs composite [47].

stage: at very low relative pressure (P/P$_0$ less than 0.01), the initial segment of the adsorption isotherm increases sharply, because the interaction between adsorbent and adsorbate is extremely strong in the narrow micropores, resulting in microporous filling at very low pressure. (2) Monolayer adsorption stage: as the adsorption goes on micropores are fully filled, the adsorbate molecules will form a single molecule layer on the surface of the whole adsorbent (including mesopores and macropores), and the adsorption isotherm presents a unique "knee" shape (P/P$_0$ = 0.01–0.2). (3) Multilayer adsorption stage:

the surface of adsorbent occurs the multimolecular layer adsorption, and the adsorption curve enters the platform area ($P/P_0 = 0.2-0.4$). (4) Mesoporous capillary condensation stage: when P/P_0 is in range of $0.4-0.8$, the surface of adsorbent continues to the multi-layer adsorption, and the adsorption curve begins to rise slowly that is accompanied by mesoporous capillary condensation (the obvious hysteresis loop in this stage is the basic characteristic of mesoporous materials). (5) Macroporous capillary condensation stage: when the P/P_0 is greater than 0.8, the adsorption curve shows a rapidly upward trend without any platform until P/P_0 reaches up to 1.0, which can be attributed to the unsaturated macroporous capillary condensation (the macropores usually cannot be filled completely by the capillary condensates due to their large pore diameter and high permeability) [45].

The pore size distribution (incremental pore volume mode) further confirms that the 3D graphene-like carbon nanosheet has a unique hierarchical porous structure, with microporous range of $0.4-2.0$ nm (two peak values of 0.8 and 1.7 nm), mesoporous range of $2.0-3.0$ nm and $5.5-50$ nm, and macroporous range of $50-220$ nm (see Fig. 6.9B) [45]. The inset shows the pore width distribution in form of cumulative pore volume. The cumulative pore volumes until 2, 50 and 220 nm are 0.659, 0.902 and 1.061 $cm^3 \, g^{-1}$, respectively. The mesoporous structure is an important bridge for the formation of 3-D ion transport channels in hierarchical porous carbon (see Fig. 6.9C and D). The micropores can endow with the abundant locations for the charge accommodation, and the mesopores provide 3-D channels for the rapid transport of ions, while the additional macropores in the material act as efficient ion-buffering reservoirs for electrochemical energy storages (such as supercapacitor) [45].

Fig. 6.9E—H shows the N_2 adsorption-desorption isotherm, pore size distribution, and pore structure model of bi-continuous microporous/mesoporous carbon foam [46]. This carbon foam possesses an ultrahigh specific surface area (up to 3106.7 $m^2 \, g^{-1}$) and unique hierarchical porous structure composed of superlarge macropores ($0.5-5$ mm), bicontinuous large micropores (~ 1.14 nm) and small mesopores (~ 3.12 nm). The incremental pore volume of the sample displays that the total pore volume is 1.82 $cm^3 \, g^{-1}$, the micropore ($0.4-2$ nm) volume is 0.49 $cm^3 \, g^{-1}$, the mesopore ($2-5$ nm) volume is 1.21 $cm^3 \, g^{-1}$. Such interconnected and continuous hierarchical microporous—mesoporous—macroporous structures can guarantee a low-resistance path for electrolyte ion transport and provide a high electrode/electrolyte contact area for the designing of high-performance supercapacitors [46].

Fig. 6.9I and J shows the N_2 adsorption-desorption isotherm and pore size distribution of AGC/MnCo-LDHs composite [16]. The adsorption-desorption isotherms of the samples show that they have the comprehensive characteristics of type-II and type-IV isotherms (knee-like and inverted-L-like curves) and belong to the typical hierarchical porous materials. The H_3 and H_4 hybrid hysteresis curves of mesoporous—macroporous materials were shown in the isotherms, and the starting points of the hysteresis curves were all around 0.4, and they were upwarped after 0.9 in relative pressure. These samples have mesoporous (2–50 nm) and macroporous (> 50 nm) structures and have narrow mesopores between three and 4.6 nm. Fig. 6.9K and L shows the N_2 adsorption-desorption isotherm and pore size distribution of $GE/NiCo_2O_4$ composite [13]. The absorption/desorption curves of $GE/NiCo_2O_4$ samples exhibit gradually increasing adsorption quantity and spindly hysteresis loops at $P/P_0 = 0.0$–1.0, indicating that the adsorption/desorption curves of these materials are III-type isotherms with H_3 hysteresis loops. The pore size distribution of all these $GE/NiCo_2O_4$ samples is from 2 to 100 nm, showing the characteristic of hierarchical mesoporous and macroporous structures.

Fig. 6.9M–P shows the N_2 adsorption-desorption isotherm and pore size distribution of $NiCo_2O_4$ and $NiCo_2O_4/GNs$ composite [47]. It is worth mentioning that, for the first time, our research group used the gaussian peak splitting method to split the continuous distribution curve into several small peaks. The pore size distribution indicates that the $NiCo_2O_4$ has a satisfactory small mesopores (2–4 nm in region (1)) and abundant medial mesopores (4–10 nm in region (2)), while a little large mesopores and macropores (10–100 nm in region (3)). It is worth noting that the region (1)–(3) in pore size distribution can be corresponding with region (1)–(3) in isotherms. The pore size distribution reveals that the $NiCo_2O_4/GNs$ composite has a continuous hierarchical porous structure from 2 to 200 nm, the four peak values of pores (region (1)–(4)) are 4.5 nm, 8.5 nm, 20 nm, and 70 nm, respectively. Likewise, the region (1)–(4) in pore size distribution can be matched by region (1)–(4) in isotherms.

6.9 Theoretical calculation characterization

6.9.1 Density of electronic states

6.9.1.1 Definition and principle of DOS

Density of electronic states or density of states (DOS) is the number of electronic states per unit energy interval in the case of quasi-continuous distribution of electronic energy levels. The electronic structure is a macroscopic quantity, while the DOS is a microscopic quantity, so the electronic structure is not suitable to explain the properties caused by the size change of nanoparticles but should be explained by the DOS. The DOS can be used as a visual result of the band structure. Many analyses correspond to the results of band analysis, and many terms are related to band analysis. But because the DOS is more visualized, it is used more broadly in the discussion of electronic properties of materials than band analysis of valence state. Analysis of electronic properties plays an important role in first-principles calculation; hence the DOS is indispensable in the fields of light, electricity, and catalysis.

For example, the conductivity of materials can be judged by the size of the band gap to distinguish direct and indirect band gap semiconductors. If Fermi level is in the range of DOS value zero, it indicates that the system is a semiconductor or an insulator. The system is metal if there is a shingle DOS crossing the Fermi level. In addition, the density of partial DOS (PDOS) and local DOS (LDOS) can be drawn to study the bonding at each point in more detail. The concept of pseudo-gap can also be introduced from DOS diagram. There are two peaks on either side of the Fermi level (the DOS between the two spikes is not zero). The pseudo-gap from DOS directly reflects the strength of the bonding covalence of the system: the wider the gap, the stronger the covalence. The DOS with even distribution and no local spike in whole energy interval corresponds to the sp band, indicating that the electron has strong nonlocal property. In contrast, for general transition metals, the DOS of d orbitals is generally a large spike, indicating that the d electrons are relatively localized and the band is relatively narrow [48].

6.9.1.2 Paradigm and summary of DOS

Recently, our research group reported a P-doped porous g-C_3N_4 nanosheets for visible-light photocatalytic degradation (see Fig. 6.10A and B) [49]. In order to understand the acceleration of photocatalysis by P doping, theoretical calculations were carried out based on the DFT. The as-obtained structural models and its partial density of states (PDOS) of g-C_3N_4 and P-doped g-C_3N_4 are shown in Fig. 6.10A and B, respectively. From the PDOS, it is obvious that the characteristics of PDOS change significantly because of the P doping. For g-C_3N_4 (Fig. 6.10A), the electronic state density of the valence band top near Fermi level is mainly composed of 2p orbital of N, showing semiconductor characteristics and poor electronic conductivity of g-C_3N_4. For P-doped g-C_3N_4 (Fig. 6.10B), Fermi level moves up and impurity level appears in the forbidden band, which is the typical characteristic of N-type semiconductor. It is worth noting that, the band gap of P-doped g-C_3N_4 is greatly reduced and the electrical conductivity is greatly increased due to the P doping. The latent carbon vacancies in g-C_3N_4 can suppress the charge recombination, and the increased electrical conductivity by P doping can accelerate the mobility of photogenerated charge carriers.

Recently, our research group also reported theoretical and experimental research of novel F-doped hierarchical Sn_3O_4 with excellent photocatalytic performance (see Fig. 6.10C and D) [50]. Total density of states (TDOS) of Sn_3O_4 was mainly composed of PDOS of Sn^{4+} s orbit, Sn^{2+} porbit, O^{2-} s orbit and O^{2-} p orbit. TDOS of F doping Sn_3O_4 was mainly contributed by the PDOS of Sn^{4+} p orbit, Sn^{2+} p orbit, O^{2-} s orbit, O^{2-} p orbit, F-s orbit, and F-p orbit. On the basis of the fact that DOS crossed the Fermi levels, Sn_3O_4 and Sn_3O_4-Rx possessed half-metallic characteristic, in which Sn_3O_4-Rx showed strong half-metallic characteristic. DOS of Sn_3O_4-Rx were remarkably strengthened and changed from discontinuity to continuity (from VB edge to CB edge) compared with Sn_3O_4, which could imply that Sn_3O_4-Rx would possess improved light harvesting and photo-response.

In 2020, our research group also reported PDOS research of novel F-doped hierarchical Sn_3O_4 with excellent photocatalytic performance (see Fig. 6.10E—H) [51]. The

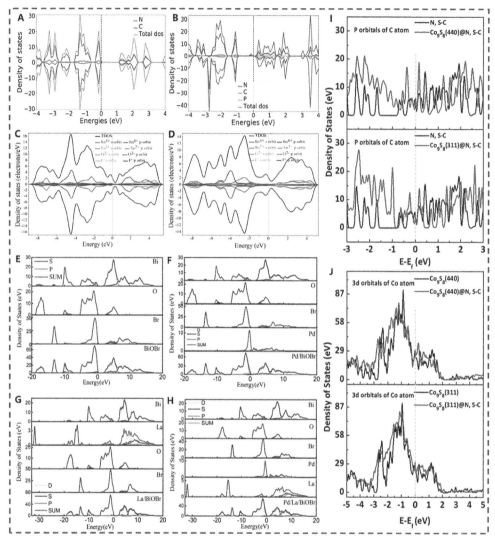

Figure 6.10 Density of states (DOS) of samples: (A and B) g-C$_3$N$_4$ and P-doped g-C$_3$N$_4$ [49], (C and D) F-doped Sn$_3$O$_4$ [50], (E−H) Pd/La/BiOBr [51], (I and J) Co$_9$S$_8$@N,S-C [52].

deeper valence bands and conduction bands are mainly contributed from the Bi 6p, O 2p, and Br 3p orbitals, and the band gap structure of BiOBr-(102) is greatly affected by both La and Pd. The La-doped BiOBr-(102) sample reveals the narrowed band gap with the presence of Pd 5s and La 5d energy states from the bottle of conductive band, the band gaps are decreased to 1.933 and 1.469 eV for La/BiOBr-(102) and Pd/La/BiOBr-(102), respectively. The degenerate levels of doping and the conductive band below the Fermi level are called as Moss-Brustein shift (ΔE), an electron from the top of the valence band can only be excited into conduction band above the Fermi level, since all the states below the Fermi level occupy the states.

In 2021, Shen and coworkers investigate DOS and the interaction of N, S codoped carbon-encapsulated Co_9S_8 (Co_9S_8@N,S-C) (see Fig. 6.10I and J) [52]. From p orbital of the C atoms in Fig. 6.10I, two effects can be identified: (1) the states associated with C atoms close to Co_9S_8 are significantly modified in energy below the Fermi level ($-3-0$ eV), exhibiting a higher-DOS feature than N, S-C and charge transfer from Co_9S_8 to N, S-C layer; (2) when Co_9S_8 encapsulates in N, S-C, the center of p orbital (denoted as E_p) of C is positively shifted relatively to Fermi level (E_f). The encapsulation of Co_9S_8 improves the p orbitals energy of C in N, S-C layer, which moves the antibonding state upward above the Fermi level, reduces the filling of electrons in the antibonding state, and enhances adsorption. From 3d orbital of the Co atoms in Fig. 6.10J, the D-band center of Co is negatively shifted when N, S-C is covered on Co_9S_8. At E_f, it is obvious that the empty orbit of Co_9S_8@N, S-C is larger than Co_9S_8, indicating the charge transfer from Co atom to C atom. The changes in the DOS of the p orbital of C and the d orbital of Co explain the synergistic effect of Co_9S_8 and N, S-C layer.

6.9.2 Adsorption Gibbs free energy

6.9.2.1 Definition and principle of adsorption ΔG

Gibbs free energy (G) is a thermodynamic function introduced in chemical thermodynamics to determine the direction in which a process proceeds. Also known as free enthalpy or free energy. Free energy refers to the part of the system's reduced internal energy that can be converted to work during a thermodynamic process. Free energy is usually expressed as G, which is defined as $G = U - TS + pV = H - TS$, where U is the internal energy of the system, T is temperature, S is entropy, P is pressure, V is volume, and H is enthalpy ($\Delta G = \Delta H - T\Delta S$ for thermostatic process). The differential form of the Gibbs free energy is $dG = -SdT + Vdp + \mu dN$, where μ is the chemical potential, that is, the average Gibbs free energy per particle is equal to the chemical potential (see Section 4.2.1.5 for details).

Calculation of HER adsorption ΔG: The reactivity of hydrogen evolution reaction (HER) is closely related to the adsorption energy of a single H atom. Calculating the free energy of H* ($\Delta G(H^*)$) is an effective way to evaluate HER activity. The lower the

$\Delta G(H^*)$ value is, the better the HER activity is. The free energy of H^* can be calculated by the following formula:

$$\Delta G(H^*) = \Delta E(H^*) + \Delta ZPE - T\Delta S \tag{6.1}$$

ΔE (H^*): hydrogen binding energy; ΔZPE: zero point energy difference between adsorbed hydrogen and gaseous hydrogen; ΔS: H^* entropy change of adsorption. $\Delta E(H^*) = E\text{slab} - H^* - E\text{slab} - 1/2\ E_{H_2}$, $E\text{slab} - H^*$ is the total energy of the slab model adsorbed H^*, $E\text{slab}$ is the total energy of the original slab, and E_{H_2} is the total energy of a single hydrogen molecule. ΔS can be obtained by calculation formula for the following: $\Delta S = S(H^*) - 1/2\ S(H_2)$, due to the vibration of the entropy H^* ($S(H^*)$) can be ignored, so $\Delta S \approx -1/2\ S(H_2)$. At 298K, 1 ATM, $TS(H_2) = 0.40$ eV, so $T\Delta S = -0.20$ eV, and $\Delta ZPE = ZPE(H^*) - 1/2\ ZPE(H_2)$.

Calculation of OER adsorption ΔG: Oxygen evolution reaction (OER) involves four electron transfer processes, consisting of four basic steps:

$$H_2O + * \rightarrow HO^* + H^+ + e^- \tag{6.2}$$

$$HO^* \rightarrow O^* + H^+ + e^- \tag{6.3}$$

$$O^* + H_2O \rightarrow HOO^* + H^+ + e^- \tag{6.4}$$

$$HOO^* \rightarrow * + O_2 + H^+ + e^- \tag{6.5}$$

Each step contains electron transfer and proton output, where * and M* represent the adsorption site and the M intermediate adsorbed on the surface, where the only energy of $H^+ + e^-$ can be regarded as half of H_2 formation at 288 K and 1 ATM. The free energy of OER can be calculated by the following formula: $\Delta G = \Delta E + \Delta ZPE - T\Delta S$. ΔE can be calculated by crystal geometry, while ΔZPE and ΔS are determined by the calculated vibration frequencies and standard tables of gas phase reactants and products. Assuming that the entropy of the adsorbed atom/molecule at the surface active site is zero, the dependence of enthalpy on temperature is ignored in the calculation. In addition, an external bias U is applied to each step by adding the $-eU$ term when calculating the free energy of the reaction. Therefore, the free energy (ΔG) of the reaction at each step can be expressed as the following formulas:

$$\Delta G_1 = E(HO^*) - E(*) - E_{H_2O} + 1/2E_{H_2} + (\Delta ZPE - T\Delta S)_a - eU \tag{6.6}$$

$$\Delta G_2 = E(O^*) - E(HO^*) + 1/2E_{H_2} + (\Delta ZPE - T\Delta S)_b - eU \tag{6.7}$$

$$\Delta G_3 = E(HOO^*) - E(O^*) - E_{H_2O} + 1/2E_{H_2} + (\Delta ZPE - T\Delta S)_c - eU \tag{6.8}$$

$$\Delta G_4 = E(*) - E(HOO^*) + E_{O_2} + 1/2E_{H_2} + (\Delta ZPE - T\Delta S)_d - eU \tag{6.9}$$

E (*), E (HO*), E* (O), E (HOO*) is calculated DFT energy of pure surface and adsorption surface of HO*, O* and HOO*. The E_{H_2O}, E_{H_2} and E_{O_2} are the calculated energies of separate H_2O, H_2 and O_2 molecules, respectively. From the equation: $H_2O \rightarrow 1/2O_2 + H_2$, the change in free energy is fixed at the experimental value of 2.46 eV per water molecule. When to form a molecule of O_2, reaction steps and reaction-free energy can be expressed as: $\Delta G_{(2H_2O \rightarrow O_2+2H_2} = 4.92\,\text{eV} = E_{O_2} + 2E_{H_2} - 2E_{H_2O} + (\Delta ZPE - T\Delta S)_{(2H_2O \rightarrow O_2+2H_2}$. The overpotential can be obtained by calculating the difference between minimum voltage required for OER and the corresponding voltage required to turn all free energy steps downhill.

Calculation of ORR adsorption ΔG: It is well accepted that the ORR and OER happen by following four-electron ($4e^-$) steps as the following formulas:

$$O_2* + H_2O(l) + e^- \rightarrow OOH* + OH^- \tag{6.10}$$

$$OOH* + e^- \rightarrow O* + OH^- \tag{6.11}$$

$$O* + H_2O(l) + e^- \rightarrow OH* + OH^- \tag{6.12}$$

$$OH* + e^- \rightarrow OH^- \tag{6.13}$$

The relevant OER mechanism is recognized as the reverse process of ORR. The adsorption energies (ΔE_{ads}) of OOH*, OH*, and O* are calculated by referring their DFT total energy to that of NSP, and H_2O and H_2 in the gas phase. The adsorption free energy (ΔG_{ads}) is obtained by: $\Delta G_{ads} = \Delta E_{ads} + \Delta ZPE - T\Delta S + GPH$, where ΔZPE and ΔS are the contributions to the free energy from the zero-point vibration energy and entropy, respectively. For each reaction step in ORR/OER, the Gibbs free energy of formation is given by: $\Delta G = \Delta E + \Delta ZPE - T\Delta S - eU + \Delta GPH$, GPH is the correction of the H^+ free energy by the concentration dependence of the entropy: $\Delta GPH = -kBT \ln [H^+]$. The overpotentials of ORR can be determined by the standard hydrogen electrode (SHE) method developed by Norskov et al. The ORR overpotentials can be computed by the equations as follows ($\Delta G_1 + \Delta G_2 + \Delta G_3 + \Delta G_4 = 4.92$ eE):

$$G^{ORR} = \min \{\Delta G_1, \Delta G_2, \Delta G_3, \Delta G_4\} \tag{6.14}$$

$$\eta^{ORR} = 1.23\,\text{V} - \mid G^{ORR} \mid / e \tag{6.15}$$

where ΔG_1, ΔG_2, ΔG_3, and ΔG_4 are the free energy of reaction, respectively [52].

6.9.2.2 Paradigm and summary of adsorption ΔG

The adsorption ΔG (such as basic step's adsorption ΔG of ORR, OER, and HER) paradigm summary of our and cooperative group's work in recent years are summarized in Fig. 6.11 [40,52,53]. By calculating the free energy of the intermediate (including total

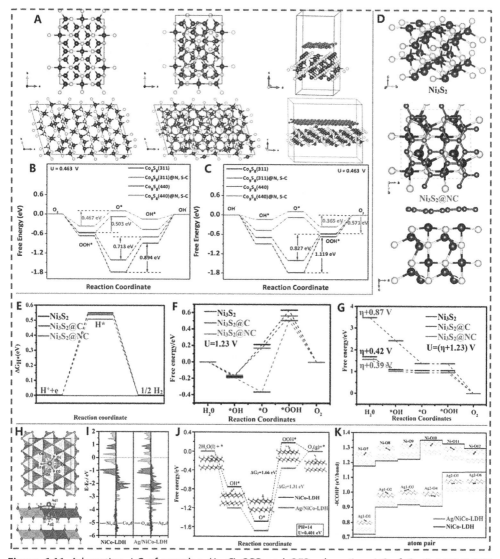

Figure 6.11 Adsorption ΔG of samples: (A–C) ORR and OER adsorption ΔG of Co$_9$S$_8$@N,S-C [52], (D–G) HER and OER adsorption ΔG of Ni$_3$S$_2$@NC [53], (H–K) OER adsorption ΔG of Ag@NiCo-LDH [40].

energy, zero vibration energy, and entropy), the reaction kinetic process of each step, the influence of voltage on the free energy, the step diagram of HER/OER/ORR can be drawn. The adsorption energy of intermediate species on the surface of electrocatalyst has a great influence on the performance of electrocatalyst (affecting thermodynamics, catalytic kinetics, and catalytic efficiency).

The key factor for the high electrocatalytic activity of the bifunctional ORR/OER is the favorable strength of the adsorption interaction (adsorption ΔG) between the catalyst and the reaction intermediate species (including the OOH*, O*, and OH*). To better understand the electrocatalytic activity of the Co_9S_8@N, S-C, Shen and coworkers investigated the detailed adsorption mechanism by using DFT calculations: Models containing crystal plane of Co_9S_8 (311)/(440) nanoparticle and an N, S codoped carbon layer covered on it are used in calculations (see Fig. 6.11A−C) [52]. When an electrode potential (U) is added, which is equal to the equilibrium potential of 0.463 V (in 0.1 m KOH (pH ≈ 13), URHE = 1.23 V), the adsorption ΔG of ORR and OER process is shown in Fig. 6.11B and C. For ORR, under $U = 0.463$ V, the rate-determining step (RDS) of the overall ORR reaction is the O* transformation to OH*, for energy barrier of 0.894 and 0.713 eV for Co_9S_8 (311) and Co_9S_8 (440), respectively. The RDS of the overall ORR reaction is the OOH* → O* stage overpotential values are 0.894 and 0.713 V. For OER, under $U = 0.463$ V, the RDS on the Co_9S_8 (311) and Co_9S_8 (440) is the O* transformation to OOH*, where the energy barriers are 1.119 and 0.827 eV, respectively. Overall analysis, for Co_9S_8 (311) and Co_9S_8 (440), the adsorption free energy of O intermediate is too big, by contrast, after it being encapsulated with N, S codoped carbon layer, the free energy of O intermediate becomes smaller. This proves that by encapsulating N, S-C, the resulted Co_9S_8@N, S-C has a favorable adsorption energy for O intermediates and the as-prepared catalyst material has higher catalytic activity than the Co_9S_8 alone [52].

In order to study the electrocatalytic performances of Ni_3S_2@NC, Li and Pang calculated the Gibbs free energy (ΔG) for HER and OER by using DFT calculations (see Fig. 6.11D−G) [53]. Free-energy diagram of HER is calculated at equilibrium potential (E). Free-energy diagram for the four steps of the OER is calculated at applied potentials of (F) $U = 1.23$ V and (G) $U = \eta + 1.23$ V. The ΔG (H*) value (0.51 eV) of Ni_3S_2@NC is much lower than that of Ni_3S_2 and Ni_3S_2@C: C and NC are not exactly matched to the lattice of Ni_3S_2, which will cause the compression of Ni_3S_2 lattice, while NC changes Ni_3S_2 lattice, thus causing a significant increase in hydrogen evolution activity for Ni_3S_2@NC. The PDS step for OER is *OOH generation step. The PDS values were calculated by the difference value of free energy of *OOH and *O, which are 0.42, 0.87, and 0.39 eV, for Ni_3S_2, Ni_3S_2@C and Ni_3S_2@NC, respectively. With applied potential $U = 1.23$ V, some steps are downhill and others are uphill. Therefore, the potential must be applied to make every step of the energy diagram downhill for all these samples. The required overpotential values for Ni3S2, Ni3S2@C and Ni3S2@NC are 0.42, 0.87, and 0.39 V, respectively. The computational studies indicate that the Ni_3S_2@NC possesses better catalytic activity for the OER than Ni3S2 and Ni3S2@C [53].

In order to clarify the electrocatalytic mechanism of Ag@NiCo-LDH, Li and Pang further calculated the Gibbs free energy (ΔG) of OER by using DFT calculations (see Fig. 6.11H−K) [40]. The calculated results show that O*→OOH* is the rate-determining step. Therefore, ΔG_3 is the overpotential for the samples in $U = 0.401$ eV, pH = 14. The more positive the valence state of adsorbed O atoms is, the easier it is to be attacked by H_2O to form OOH*, and therefore, ΔG_3 on Ag@NiCo-LDH is lower ($\Delta G_3 = 1.31$ eV) than that of NiCo-LDH ($\Delta G_3 = 1.66$ eV). These results show that depositing Ag onto NiCo-LDH can change the electronic structure of NiCo-LDH and increase the number of active sites on the surface, thus improving the catalytic performance of NiCo-LDH, which is consistent with our experimental results. The Ag doped in Ag@NiCo-LDH coordinates with three O atoms, and the total –ICOHP of O and Ag ranges from 0.718 to 1.136 eV. The lower total ICOHP indicates that Ag@NiCo-LDH is not as stable as Ni in NiCo-LDH. The Ag-O bond is easy to break, resulting in the formation of Ag atom clusters, and O is easy to leave and form oxygen vacancies [40].

6.9.3 Combination of D-band central theory and adsorption Gibbs free energy

Based on PDOS analysis, the central position of D-band (relative to Fermi level) is closely related to the adsorption properties of the catalyst intermediates or products (adsorption-free energy and desorption capacity). The DFT calculation shows that the moderate D-band center location can obtain the optimal adsorption capacity of intermediates and desorption capacity of products, which is helpful to realize the efficient electrocatalytic process [54]. The reduction of D-band energy, that is, the reduction of D center also reduces the antibond band generated by coupling, and more parts of the antibond band are lower than the Fermi level, thus being filled by electrons, which reduces the stability of bond and leads to the reduction of adsorption energy. On the contrary, the increased metal D-band center can enhance the adsorption energy of the catalytic site to the substrate (see Section 3.3.2 for details).

Recently, Professor Yin constructed PtCo-PtSn/C heterojunction catalyst and reduced the D-band center of Pt by using the well-structured interfacial effect and charge redistribution, so as to improve the activity and stability of the catalyst (see Fig. 6.12A−C) [55]. The XPS and Bader results show that there is a strong charge transfer between PtCo and PtSn, and the electron redistribution adjusts the electronic structure of Pt. The D-band center of PtCo−PtSn/C heterojunction decreases to −2.45 eV. The downward

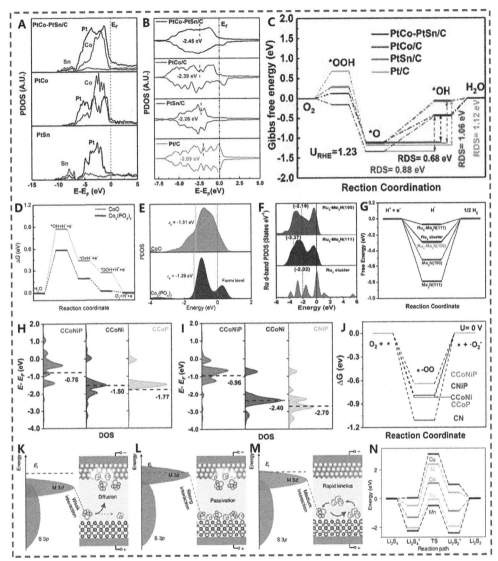

Figure 6.12 The combination of D-band central and adsorption ΔG of samples: (A—C) PtCo-PtSn/C heterojunction [55], (D and E) $Co_3(PO_4)_2$ nanosheets [56], (F and G) $Ru-Mo_2N$ nanorods [57], (H—J) $Co/Ni-N_3P_1$ SACs [58], (K—N) cation-doped ZnS catalysts [59].

shift of D–band center optimizes the adsorption energy of O-containing intermediates, thus enhancing the intrinsic activity of ORR. At the same time, the strong electronic interaction between PtCo and PtSn interface can effectively prevent the separation of the two phases, limit the leaching of nonnoble metals, reduce Ostwald maturation and Pt migration, and improve the durability of the catalyst. These results indicate that the heterostructure formed between PtCo and PtSn can effectively regulate the electronic structure of Pt and the balance between adsorption and desorption of O reaction intermediates, which can effectively enhance the activity and stability of ORR [55].

According to DFT calculation, the center of D-band of $Co_3(PO_4)_2$ nanosheets is far away from Fermi level and binds with *OH to occupy the antibonding orbital, which is beneficial to optimize the adsorption free energy and reduce the overpotential of OER (see Fig. 6.12D and E) [56]. The energy difference between the D-band center of Co and the P-band center of O in $Co_3(PO_4)_2$ is 3.22 eV, which is less than the 3.38 eV in CoO, which will form a larger Co-O covalence, which is more conducive to the transfer of reaction intermediates between the two, thus increasing the OER kinetics. Moreover, the P-band center of O in $Co_3(PO_4)_2$ is more negative than that of CoO, indicating that lattice oxygen in $Co_3(PO_4)_2$ is more conducive to OER stability. The interfacial electron interaction between Ru and Mo_2N results in charge redistribution in the interfacial region of Ru−Mo_2N nanorods, which makes Ru in a slightly positive oxidation state (see Fig. 6.12F and G) [57]. The energy reduction of the D-band center of the Ru nanocluster not only reduces the binding strength of the reaction intermediates but also improves the thermodynamics of HER on the Ruthenium surface.

Synergistic effects on D-band center via coordination sites of $M-N_3P_1$ (M = Co and Ni) in metal dual single atoms (DSAs) also proved to enhance photocatalytic performances (see Fig. 6.12H−J) [58]. The atomically dispersed Co and Ni atoms anchored on the carbon nitride substrate with Co/Ni-N_3P_1 coordination sites were synthesized by PH_3-assisted pyrolysis. Combined with DFT calculation (Fig. 6.12H and I shows the D-band centers of Co and Ni, respectively), it is confirmed that multiple coordination of Co/Ni-N and Co/Ni-P can adjust the D-band center position, thus regulating Gibbs free energy diagram for $\bullet O_2^-$ and improving the catalytic activity of Co/Ni-N_3P_1 DSAs (see Fig. 6.12J). The formed multiple midgap levels can extend optical absorption ranges. The P-introduction can change the coordination, suppress the conversion trend of SAs to high valence state, and improve electron separation. The above characteristics can provide the effective degradation of tetrachlorobisphenol under visible light irradiation, the removal rate reaches 100%, and the dechlorination rate reaches 44.1%.

Recently, Huigang Zhang and Jun Lu reported a fundamental study on how polysulfide adsorption determines catalytic activity by conjoint analysis of D-band central and adsorption ΔG (see Fig. 6.12K−N) [59]. By examining the activity of a series of transition metal dopants (Mn^{2+}, Fe^{2+}, Co^{2+}, Ni^{2+}, or Cu^{2+}) in the ZnS lattice, it is found that enhanced adsorption does not necessarily lead to increased catalytic activity, especially when the desorption of the dissolved polysulfide (Li_2S_2/Li_2S) is rate limited. The strong adsorption of Li_2S_2/Li_2S may lead to the passivation of the ZnS catalyst. Only moderate D-band central location and moderate adsorption of polysulfide (namely, the medium interactions of polysulfides with catalysts and medium) can improve the conversion of Li_2S_4 and promote the desorption of Li_2S_2/Li_2S, thus showing the highest catalytic activity, where the activity and adsorption strength has a volcanic trend. The activity regulation strategy between adsorption and catalysis provides a reasonable perspective for analyzing polysulfide conversion and designing efficient $Co_{0.125}Zn_{0.875}S$ catalysts.

6.10 Summary

In this chapter, we have discussed the characterization technologies and characterization methods of nanomaterials from the following eight aspects: phase characterization, morphology characterization, crystal structure characterization, electronic structure characterization, atomic structure characterization, element composition characterization, porous structure characterization, and theoretical calculation characterization. The common instrumental analysis methods for the characterization of nanomaterials include X-ray technology, electron spectroscopy technology, electron microscopy technology, spectroscopy technology, thermal analysis technology, selected area electron diffraction (SAED) technology, and ICP technology. We also discussed the definition and principle of several typical characterization methods (XRD, SEM, TEM, HR-TEM, STEM, AC-TEM, XPS, EELS, XAS, EDS, BET, DOS, D-band center, adsorption ΔG) and the paradigm summary of our or other group's work in recent years.

Acknowledgments

This book was supported by National Natural Science Foundation of China (22078071, 22272034), Natural Science Foundation of Guangdong Province (2021A1515010125, 2020A1515010344), Maoming Science and Technology Project (mmkj2020032), Guangdong Province Universities and Colleges Pearl River Scholar Funded Scheme (2019), Guangdong Basic and Applied Basic Research Foundation (2019A1515011249, 2021A1515010305), Key Research Project of Natural Science of Guangdong Provincial Department of Education (2019KZDXM010), Environment and Energy Green Catalysis Innovation Team of Colleges and Universities of Guangdong Province (2022KCXTD019), the program for Innovative Research Team of Guangdong University of Petrochemical Technology.

References

[1]   https://mp.weixin.qq.com/s/-NT-qyzY3uqAs_vLP6sawA.
[2]   https://mp.weixin.qq.com/s/fQflUWyliQLDpoSn3P6u1w.
[3]   https://mp.weixin.qq.com/s/2i9Qjojytqlu8RNDn8dJXw.

[4] https://mp.weixin.qq.com/s/SFnpO95oQ7KzMHqX4xBaSA.

[5] https://mp.weixin.qq.com/s/En2HYwdtf9A8wDZEr86GOQ.

[6] Z. Li, C. He, M. Cai, S. Kang, P.K. Shen, A strategy for easy synthesis of carbon supported Co@Pt core—shell configuration as highly active catalyst for oxygen reduction reaction, International Journal of Hydrogen Energy 37 (19) (2012) 14152—14160.

[7] H.Q. Wang, G.F. Yang, Q.Y. Li, X.X. Zhong, F.P. Wang, Z.S. Li, et al., Porous nano-MnO_2: large scale synthesis via a facile quick-redox procedure and application in a supercapacitor, New Journal of Chemistry 35 (2) (2011) 469—475.

[8] Z. Li, Q. Li, Y. Fang, H. Wang, Y. Li, X. Wang, Unique mesoporous carbon microsphere/1-D MnO_2-built composite architecture and their enhanced electrochemical capacitance performance, Journal of Materials Chemistry 21 (43) (2011) 17185—17192.

[9] Z. Li, S. Yang, J. Zhou, D. Li, X. Zhou, C. Ge, et al., Novel mesoporous g-C_3N_4 and $BiPO_4$ nanorods hybrid architectures and their enhanced visible-light-driven photocatalytic performances, Chemical Engineering Journal 241 (2014) 344—351.

[10] Z. Li, M. Luo, B. Li, Q. Lin, X. Liao, H. Yu, et al., 3-D hierarchical micro/nano-structures of porous Bi_2WO_6:controlled hydrothermal synthesis and enhanced photocatalytic performances, Microporous and Mesoporous Materials 313 (2021) 110830.

[11] Z. Li, Y. Li, C. He, P.K. Shen, Bimetallic PtAg alloyed nanoparticles and 3-D mesoporous graphene nanosheet hybrid architectures for advanced oxygen reduction reaction electrocatalysts, Journal of Materials Chemistry A 5 (44) (2017) 23158—23169.

[12] Z. Li, Z. Liu, B. Li, D. Li, Z. Liu, H. Wang, et al., Large area synthesis of well-dispersed β-MnO_2 nanorods and their electrochemical supercapacitive performances, Journal of the Taiwan Institute of Chemical Engineers 65 (2016) 544—551.

[13] Z. Li, R. Yang, B. Li, M. Yu, D. Li, H. Wang, et al., Controllable synthesis of graphene/$NiCo_2O_4$ three-dimensional mesoporous electrocatalysts for efficient methanol oxidation reaction, Electrochimica Acta 252 (2017) 180—191.

[14] Z. Li, B. Li, Z. Liu, D. Li, H. Wang, Q. Li, One-pot construction of 3-D nitrogen-doped activated graphene-like nanosheets for high-performance supercapacitors, Electrochimica Acta 190 (2016) 378—387.

[15] B. Li, M. Yu, Z. Li, C. Yu, Q. Li, H. Wang, Three-dimensional activated carbon nanosheets modified by graphitized carbon dots: one-step alkali pyrolysis preparation and supercapacitor applications, Journal of Energy Storage 51 (2022) 104515.

[16] Z. Li, K. Xiao, C. Yu, H. Wang, Q. Li, Three-dimensional graphene-like carbon nanosheets coupled with MnCo-layered double hydroxides nanoflowers as efficient bifunctional oxygen electrocatalyst, International Journal of Hydrogen Energy 46 (69) (2021) 34239—34251.

[17] S. Luo, M. Tang, P.K. Shen, S. Ye, Atomic-scale preparation of octopod nanoframes with high-index facets as highly active and stable catalysts, Advanced Materials 29 (8) (2017) 1601687—1601692.

[18] A.M. Qin, X.S. Zhou, Y.F. Qiu, Y.P. Fang, C.Y. Su, S.H. Yang, Periodically twinned nanotowers and nanodendrites of mercury selenide synthesized via a solution—liquid—solid route, Advanced Materials 20 (4) (2008) 768—773.

[19] Z. Li, Y. Li, G. He, P.K. Shen, Novel graphene-like nanosheet supported highly active electrocatalysts with ultralow Pt loadings for oxygen reduction reaction, Journal of Materials Chemistry A 2 (40) (2014) 16898—16904.

[20] C. He, S. Zhang, J. Tao, P.K. Shen, One-step solid state synthesis of PtCo nanocubes/graphene nanocomposites as advanced oxygen reduction reaction electrocatalysts, Journal of Catalysis 362 (2018) 85—93.

[21] C. Xiao, B.A. Lu, P. Xue, N. Tian, Z.Y. Zhou, X. Lin, et al., High-index-facet-and high-surface-energy nanocrystals of metals and metal oxides as highly efficient catalysts, Joule 4 (12) (2020) 2562—2598.

[22] https://mp.weixin.qq.com/s/qf4ICLi8AY-jlRHboFcKwQ.

[23] Y. Lan, Z. Li, D. Li, W. Xie, G. Yan, S. Guo, Visible-light responsive Z-scheme Bi@ β-Bi_2O_3/g-C_3N_4 heterojunction for efficient photocatalytic degradation of 2, 3-dihydroxynaphthalene, Chemical Engineering Journal 392 (2020) 123686.

[24] Z. Li, S. Ji, B.G. Pollet, P.K. Shen, A Co_3W_3C promoted Pd catalyst exhibiting competitive performance over Pt/C catalysts towards the oxygen reduction reaction, Chemical Communications 50 (5) (2014) 566—568.

[25] C. Zhou, X. Chen, S. Liu, Y. Han, H. Meng, Q. Jiang, et al., Superdurable bifunctional oxygen electrocatalyst for high-performance zinc−air batteries, Journal of the American Chemical Society 144 (6) (2022) 2694−2704.

[26] H. Fei, J. Dong, D. Chen, T. Hu, X. Duan, I. Shakir, et al., Single atom electrocatalysts supported on graphene or graphene-like carbons, Chemical Society Reviews 48 (20) (2019) 5207−5241.

[27] https://mp.weixin.qq.com/s/kcn5K06Ax3CGoMyUDIqfQw.

[28] Y. Li, B. Li, D. Zhang, L. Cheng, Q. Xiang, Crystalline carbon nitride supported copper single atoms for photocatalytic CO_2 reduction with nearly 100% CO selectivity, ACS Nano 14 (8) (2020) 10552−10561.

[29] P. Liu, Z. Huang, X. Gao, X. Hong, J. Zhu, G. Wang, et al., Synergy between palladium single atoms and nanoparticles via hydrogen spillover for enhancing CO_2 photoreduction to CH_4, Advanced Materials 34 (16) (2022) 2200057.

[30] J. Gu, M. Jian, L. Huang, Z. Sun, A. Li, Y. Pan, et al., Synergizing metal−support interactions and spatial confinement boosts dynamics of atomic nickel for hydrogenations, Nature Nanotechnology 16 (10) (2021) 1141−1149.

[31] W. Wang, Y. Wu, T. Liu, Y. Zhao, Y. Qu, R. Yang, et al., Single Co sites in ordered SiO_2 channels for boosting nonoxidative propane dehydrogenation, ACS Catalysis 12 (4) (2022) 2632−2638.

[32] H. Jin, P. Li, P. Cui, J. Shi, W. Zhou, X. Yu, et al., Unprecedentedly high activity and selectivity for hydrogenation of nitroarenes with single atomic Co_1-N_3P_1 sites, Nature Communications 13 (1) (2022) 1−9.

[33] J.F. Nie, Y.M. Zhu, J.Z. Liu, X.Y. Fang, Boundaries periodic segregation of solute atoms in fully coherent twin, Science 340 (2013) 957−960.

[34] H. Yu, R. Ishikawa, Y.G. So, N. Shibata, T. Kudo, H. Zhou, et al., Direct atomic-resolution observation of two phases in the $Li_{1.2}Mn_{0.567}Ni_{0.166}Co_{0.067}O_2$ cathode material for lithium-ion batteries, Angewandte Chemie International Edition 52 (23) (2013) 5969−5973.

[35] Z. Li, B. Li, Y. Hu, X. Liao, H. Yu, C. Yu, Emerging ultrahigh-density single-atom catalysts for versatile heterogeneous catalysis applications: redefinition, recent progress, and challenges, Small Structures 3 (6) (2022) 2200041.

[36] Y. Hu, H. Li, Z.S. Li, B. Li, S. Wang, Y. Yao, Progress in batch preparation of single-atom catalysts and application in sustainable synthesis of fine chemicals, Green Chemistry 23 (2021) 8754−8794.

[37] Y. Hu, Z.S. Li, B. Li, C. Yu, Recent progress of diatomic catalysts: general design fundamentals and diversified catalytic applications, Small 18 (46) (2022) e2203589.

[38] H. Wang, Z. Li, J. Yang, Q. Li, X. Zhong, A novel activated mesocarbon microbead (aMCMB)/Mn_3O_4 composite for electrochemical capacitors in organic electrolyte, Journal of Power Sources 194 (2) (2009) 1218−1221.

[39] Z. Li, B. Li, Z. Liu, D. Li, C. Ge, Y. Fang, Controlled synthesis of $ZnGa_2O_4$ nanorod arrays from hexagonal ZnO microdishes and their photocatalytic activity on the degradation of RhB, RSC Advances 4 (89) (2014) 48590−48595.

[40] B. Chu, Q. Ma, Z. Li, B. Li, F. Huang, Q. Pang, et al., Design and preparation of three-dimensional hetero-electrocatalysts of NiCo-layered double hydroxide nanosheets incorporated with silver nanoclusters for enhanced oxygen evolution reactions, Nanoscale 13 (25) (2021) 11150−11160.

[41] D. Chen, B. Li, Q. Pu, X. Chen, G. Wen, Z. Li, Preparation of Ag-$AgVO_3$/g-C_3N_4 composite photo-catalyst and degradation characteristics of antibiotics, Journal of Hazardous Materials 373 (2019) 303−312.

[42] B. Li, Z. Li, Q. Pang, Controllable preparation of N-doped Ni_3S_2 nanocubes@N-doped graphene-like carbon layers for highly active electrocatalytic overall water splitting, Electrochimica Acta 399 (2021) 139408.

[43] Y. Ma, Y. Ren, Y. Zhou, W. Liu, W. Baaziz, O. Ersen, et al., High-density and thermally stable palladium single-atom catalysts for chemoselective hydrogenations, Angewandte Chemie International Edition 59 (48) (2020) 21613−21619.

[44] M. Thommes, K. Kaneko, A.V. Neimark, J.P. Olivier, F. Rodriguez-Reinoso, J. Rouquerol, et al., Physisorption of gases, with special reference to the evaluation of surface area and pore size distribution (IUPAC technical report), Pure and Applied Chemistry 87 (9−10) (2015) 1051−1069.

[45] Z. Li, L. Zhang, X. Chen, B. Li, H. Wang, Q. Li, Three-dimensional graphene-like porous carbon nanosheets derived from molecular precursor for high-performance supercapacitor application, Electrochimica Acta 296 (2019) 8–17.

[46] Z. Li, X. Hu, D. Xiong, B. Li, H. Wang, Q. Li, Facile synthesis of bicontinuous microporous/mesoporous carbon foam with ultrahigh specific surface area for supercapacitor application, Electrochimica Acta 219 (2016) 339–349.

[47] Z. Li, B. Li, J. Chen, Q. Pang, P. Shen, Spinel $NiCo_2O_4$ 3-D nanoflowers supported on graphene nanosheets as efficient electrocatalyst for oxygen evolution reaction, International Journal of Hydrogen Energy 44 (31) (2019) 16120–16131.

[48] R.E. Belardinelli, V.D. Pereyra, Fast algorithm to calculate density of states, Physical Review E 75 (4) (2007) 046701.

[49] Z. Li, Q. Chen, Q. Lin, Y. Chen, X. Liao, H. Yu, et al., Three-dimensional P-doped porous g-C_3N_4 nanosheets as an efficient metal-free photocatalyst for visible-light photocatalytic degradation of Rhodamine B model pollutant, Journal of the Taiwan Institute of Chemical Engineers 114 (2020) 249–262.

[50] D. Zeng, C. Yu, Q. Fan, J. Zeng, L. Wei, Z. Li, et al., Theoretical and experimental research of novel fluorine doped hierarchical Sn_3O_4 microspheres with excellent photocatalytic performance for removal of Cr (VI) and organic pollutants, Chemical Engineering Journal 391 (2020) 123607.

[51] X. Chen, K. Zhang, Y. Yang, K. Yang, Q. Fan, C. Yu, et al., Pd/BiOBr tetragonal platelets with controllable facets by the decoration of La dopant enabling highly efficient photocatalytic activity, CrystEngComm 22 (40) (2020) 6699–6712.

[52] D. Lyu, S. Yao, A. Ali, Z.Q. Tian, P. Tsiakaras, P.K. Shen, N, S codoped carbon matrix-encapsulated Co_9S_8 nanoparticles as a highly efficient and durable bifunctional oxygen redox electrocatalyst for rechargeable Zn–air batteries, Advanced Energy Materials 11 (28) (2021) 2101249.

[53] B. Li, Z. Li, Q. Pang, J.Z. Zhang, Core/shell cable-like Ni_3S_2 nanowires/N-doped graphene-like carbon layers as composite electrocatalyst for overall electrocatalytic water splitting, Chemical Engineering Journal 401 (2020) 126045.

[54] F. Du, J. Li, C. Wang, J. Yao, Z. Tan, Z. Yao, et al., Active sites-rich layered double hydroxide for nitrate-to-ammonia production with high selectivity and stability, Chemical Engineering Journal 434 (2022) 134641.

[55] J. Chen, G. Qian, B. Chu, Z. Jiang, K. Tan, L. Luo, et al., Tuning d-band center of Pt by PtCo-PtSn heterostructure for enhanced oxygen reduction reaction performance, Small 18 (12) (2022) 2106773.

[56] Y. Shao, X. Xiao, Y.P. Zhu, T.Y. Ma, Single-crystal cobalt phosphate nanosheets for biomimetic oxygen evolution in neutral electrolytes, Angewandte Chemie International Edition 58 (41) (2019) 14599–14604.

[57] X. Zhang, R. Sa, S. Yang, F. Zhou, Z. Jiang, R. Wang, A non-carbon catalyst support upgrades the intrinsic activity of ruthenium for hydrogen evolution electrocatalysis via strong interfacial electronic effects, Nano Energy 75 (2020) 104981.

[58] Y. Zhou, W. Qin, X. Sun, Y. Zhu, J. Niu, Synergistic effects on d-band center via coordination sites of M-N_3P_1 (M = Co and Ni) in dual single atoms that enhances photocatalytic dechlorination from tetrachlorobisphenol A, Journal of Hazardous Materials 430 (2022) 128419.

[59] Z. Shen, X. Jin, J. Tian, M. Li, Y. Yuan, S. Zhang, et al., Cation-doped ZnS catalysts for polysulfide conversion in lithium–sulfur batteries, Nature Catalysis 5 (6) (2022) 1–9.

PART 2

Application types of nanomaterials in energy and environment fields

CHAPTER 7

Supercapacitor: basic principles, electrode materials, and applications

7.1 Introduction

As a new type of electrochemical energy storage device, supercapacitor has been widely concerned by the scientific and industrial circles due to its advantages such as long cycle life, high power density, wide range of temperature, and wide application fields. The power density of supercapacitors is much higher than that of secondary batteries such as lithium-ion batteries, and their energy density is much higher than that of conventional capacitors. Supercapacitors can be classified according to the following criteria. The first category is based on the energy storage mechanism, which can be divided into three categories: hybrid supercapacitor (HSC), Faraday pseudocapacitor (PC), and electric double-layer supercapacitor (EDLC). The second category is according to the different electrolytes, which can also be divided into two categories: water-based supercapacitors and organic system (including ionic liquid) supercapacitors. Among them, the water-electrolyte voltage is 1.23 V, but the decomposition voltage of organic solutes can reach $3 \sim 4$ V. Energy storage technology has become an important part of the sustainable development of new energy. It is particularly important to research and develop new energy storage devices with environmental protection, high energy, high power, and high adaptability. Therefore, the supercapacitor has become a green energy storage technology [1−3].

7.2 Basic principles

7.2.1 Principle of electric double layer capacitor (EDLC)

Electric double-layer capacitors (EDLC): The storage and release of charge only occur on the interface of the "electric double layer" structure (see Section 4.8.1), and the whole process is a physical process (no chemical reaction occurs). Therefore, the EDLC has high stability and relatively ideal service life. In the charging process of EDLC, the anion and cation in electrolyte will transfer to the positive and negative direction of the capacitor, so it will form an electric double layer attached to the surface of the porous electrode. After charging, the electrolyte ions on electrode cannot migrate to the electrolyte due to the attraction between the positive and negative charges in electric double layer. Hence, the stable potential difference between the positive and negative electrodes can be maintained so as to achieve the storage of electric energy.

Nanostructured Materials
ISBN 978-0-443-19256-2, https://doi.org/10.1016/B978-0-443-19256-2.00001-6

When the EDLC is discharged, the electrons collected on the negative electrode are transferred to the positive electrode by the loading, and the electric double-layer balance between the electrode and the electrolyte is broken, and the electrolyte ions will return to the electrolyte. This is a similar mechanism to conventional capacitors, but the distance between the double layer and the electrode is only ionic radius; therefore, EDLC capacitors have a much larger capacitance than conventional capacitors (see Fig. 7.1A for details) [4].

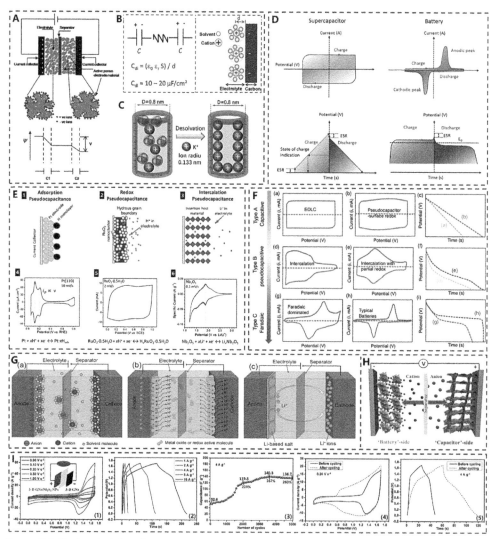

Figure 7.1 Basic principles of various supercapacitor: (A) EDLC mechanism on porous electrode [4], (B) Charge distribution on electrode [5], (C) Desolvation in micropore <1 nm [6], (D) Capacitor and battery performance curves [7], (E) PC mechanism and (F) PC performance curves [8], (G) supercapacitor schematic diagram [9], (H) HSC schematic diagram [10], (I) HSC performance curves [11].

In principle, when an external voltage is applied between EDLC electrodes, the electron charge accumulated on the electrode surface is balanced by absorbing the opposite ionic charge in the electrolyte. The capacitance (C_{dl}) of EDLC created by this charge separation at electrode and electrolyte interface resulting from electrostatic charge separation can be given by:

$$C_{dl}=(\varepsilon_0 \varepsilon_r S)/d \tag{7.1}$$

where ε_0 is the permittivity of the vacuum ($\varepsilon_0 = 8.85 \times 10^{-12}$ F m^{-1}), ε_r is the relative dielectric constant of the electrolyte (dimensionless), d is the average approaching distance of ions to the electrode surface (m), and S is the accessible surface area of porous electrode (m^2). Considering conventional values for the ε_r of electrolyte (less than 100) and the approaching distance d (a few 10^{-10} m), the C_{dl} values span the range of 10–20 μF cm^{-2} (see Fig. 7.1B for details) [5]. In general, the distribution of charged ions on the electrode surface is accompanied by a solvation phenomenon. Therefore, the value of approaching distance d is larger than the radius of the individual metal ions (depending on the size of the solvent molecules). For porous electrodes, the accessible surface area S is the sum area of all available surface of the pore (including micropore, mesopore, and macropore). The desolvation in tiny micropore (<1 nm) can provide a huge EDLC capacitance for microporous electrode with high specific surface area (see Fig. 7.1C for details) [6]. Even so, in actual porous electrode, the capacitance formation and evaluation of EDLC capacitance are more complex, due to the complex pore structure of the electrode.

In a three-electrode system, the capacitance (C) of porous electrodes can be evaluated with $C = Q/U=It/U$. For the two-electrode supercapacitor cell, it contains two parallel electrodes, in which the positive and negative electrodes are equivalent to two capacitors assembled in series. Therefore, the cell capacitance (C_{cell}) of the device is calculated by the following formula:

$$C_{cell} = \frac{C_+ C_-}{C_+ + C_-} \tag{7.2}$$

where the C_+ and C_- are the capacitances of the positive and negative electrode, respectively. Energy density and power density are the two main performance indicators of EDLC cell. The energy density E (Wh) is calculated by the following formula:

$$E = \frac{1}{2}C_{cell}\Delta U^2 \frac{1}{3600} \tag{7.3}$$

where U is the operating voltage window (V). The maximum power P_{max} (W) supply of the supercapacitors is given by the following formula:

$$P_{max} = \frac{U_{max}^2}{4R_s} \qquad (7.4)$$

where R_s is the series resistance (Ohm). And the average power P_a (W) is associated with the energy delivered per unit time (s) and can be expressed by the following formula:

$$P_a = \frac{E}{t_D} \qquad (7.5)$$

where t_D is the discharge time during the testing of two-electrode supercapacitor cell.

Cyclic voltammetry (CV) and constant-current charge and discharge (CD) are common evaluation methods for the electrochemical performance of supercapacitors. The CV curve of EDLC is often rectangular, while the CDC curve is often an isosceles triangle. This is quite different from the curve of the battery. The CV curve of the battery has an obvious anode peak and cathode peak, while the CDC curve of the battery has an obvious CD platform (see Fig. 7.1D for details) [7]. These differences are mainly attributed to the different energy storage mechanisms of supercapacitors and batteries.

7.2.2 Principle of pseudocapacitor (PC)

PC: underpotential deposition of active substances and highly reversible chemical adsorption/desorption or redox reactions on the electrode surface and in the two-dimensional or quasi-two-dimensional space of bulk phase under appropriate applied voltage to achieve electrochemical energy storage. Pseudocapacitance can be generated not only on the surface of the electrode, but also in the whole electrode, so that higher capacitance and energy density can be obtained than EDLC. For the same electrode area, the pseudocapacitance can be $10-100$ times ($1-2$ orders of magnitude) the capacitance of the EDLC. Although Ps follow Faraday's CD principle, they will not produce continuous Faraday current, but they still have the basic characteristics of EDLC capacitors, such as linear relationship between potential and time, similar rectangular relation in CV curve (may there are localized redox current peaks), and measuring the electric energy storage by the specific capacitance (F g^{-1}).

Pseudocapacitance (PC) can be divided into three types from electrochemical mechanism: (1) underpotential deposition, (2) redox pseudocapacitance, and (3) intercalated pseudocapacitance. Underpotential deposition is a process in which metal ions in solution adsorb on the surface of another metal to form a single metal layer under its redox potential. This process occurs between two different metals and is typically exemplified by the deposition of lead on the surface of a gold electrode by underpotential deposition. The redox pseudocapacitance refers to the process in which ions in solution are electrochemically adsorbed to the surface or near the surface of active substances, and then undergo redox reactions with transferred electrons to convert electrons/ions into charges and store them. Although redox pseudocapacitance follows Faraday's principle, it generates rapid Faraday current. Intercalated pseudocapacitance is a new type of pseudocapacitance for tunneling or layered materials. Ions in the solution intercalate into pores or layers of the materials, where they undergo redox reactions with surrounding atoms and electrons. Unlike the intercalation of lithium-ion batteries, this intercalated pseudocapacitance does not undergo a material phase transition.

Recently (in 2021), V. Augustyn and coworker summarized the basic classification of pseudocapacitance: (I) adsorption pseudocapacitance, (II) redox pseudocapacitance, and (III) intercalation pseudocapacitance (see Fig. 7.1E (1) $\sim$ (3) for details) [8]. In each of these, the extent of reaction (ξ) (based on the surface coverage, surface redox, or intercalation) depends linearly or almost linearly on the potential (V), leading to the thermodynamic definition of pseudocapacitance as simply $\Delta\xi/\Delta V$. Fig. 7.1E (4) shows the case study of adsorption pseudocapacitance: Cyclic voltammogram of a Pt (110) surface in aqueous 0.1 MHClO$_4$ solution cycled at 50 mV s^{-1}. The adsorption-desorption Faradaic peak current (i_p) is inversely proportional to the scan rate (ν) (Pt + xH$^+$ + xe$^-$ $\leftrightarrow$ Pt·xH$_{ads}$). The dotted lines indicate the high reversibility of the Faradaic adsorption processes. Fig. 7.1E (5) shows the case study of redox pseudocapacitance: Cyclic voltammogram of a RuO$_2$·0.5H$_2$O electrode in aqueous 0.5M H$_2$SO$_4$ solution cycled at 2 mV s^{-1}. It should be noted that the hydrous RuO$_2$ lacks obvious features of surface Faradaic reactions in the electrochemical response (RuO$_2$·0.5H$_2$O + xH$^+$ + xe$^-$ $\leftrightarrow$ H$_x$RuO$_2$·0.5H$_2$O). Fig. 7.1E (6) shows the case study of intercalation pseudocapacitance: cyclic voltammogram of Nb$_2$O$_5$ nanocrystalline film in a nonaqueous Li$^+$ electrolyte cycled at 0.1 mV s^{-1}. The dashed line indicates the high reversibility of the Faradaic intercalation process (Nb$_2$O$_5$ + xLi$^+$ + xe$^-$ $\leftrightarrow$ Li$_x$Nb$_2$O$_5$). The electrochemical response of certain pseudocapacitive materials lacks obvious Faradaic peaks, due to the combination of dominant double-layer and partial Faradaic processes. It should be highlighted that the formalism can lead to a potential-dependent pseudocapacitance, even when accounting for the presence of successive Faradaic reactions and the interactions between species [8].

The electrochemical characteristics of PC materials are usually tested by cyclic voltammetry and constant current charge discharge test. Fig. 7.1 F further shows the cyclic voltammograms and constant current discharge curves of various representative PC materials [8]. In this classification, type A is a typical capacitive process (including EDLC of carbon materials and surface redox pseudocapacitance of nitrogen-doped carbon); type B is a typical pseudocapacitance of Faraday in nature (including intercalation pseudocapacitance and intercalation-redox pseudocapacitance); type C is a typical Faraday mechanism and is not capacitance in nature (Faraday dominated battery reaction). Cyclic voltammetry is a common characterization technique for studying PC materials, because it is easy to identify the "mirror image" criterion and the relationship between current and scanning rate. The pseudo-linearity and hysteresis platform of the constant current discharge curve can also be used to evaluate the pseudo-capacitance [8]. The "mirror image" criterion can be used to identify pseudocapacitive materials from battery materials: in cyclic voltammetry, pseudocapacitive materials are characterized by very wide charge transfer peaks. During cathode and anode scanning, they are mirror images of each other, and quickly convert from cathode current to anode current. The relationship between peak potential and scanning rate can also identify pseudocapacitive materials: the peak position of pseudocapacitive materials hardly changes with the change of scanning rate, and the energy storage efficiency of pseudocapacitive material will be very high even in rapid CD process [8].

7.2.3 Principle of hybrid supercapacitor (HSC)

Two-electrode symmetrical EDLC supercapacitors usually include two carbon electrodes, which are separated from each other by a separator. When a voltage is applied to the two electrodes, the solvated charges in the electrolyte are arranged on the surface of the oppositely charged electrodes to form an electric double layer. In this case, no redox reactions are involved, so EDLC supercapacitors can theoretically be charged as many times as they want and thus have a very high service life. The power density of the EDLC supercapacitor is also high; however, the energy density is much lower than a lithium-ion battery. HSC: one electrode is an EDLC material and the other electrode is a pseudocapacitive material (or Faraday battery material). Combining the advantages of the two electrode materials, the two capacitors with different storage mechanisms can be complementary, and the hybrid capacitor with energy density, storage capacity, and cycle life in line with expectations can be prepared (see Fig. 7.1G for details) [9]. Two-electrode asymmetrical HSC based on EDLC material and Faraday battery material tends to exhibit higher energy density and storage capacity (see Fig. 7.1H for details) [10]. In particular, the high voltage ($3 \sim 4$ V) and high capacitance ($200-1000$ F g^{-1}) of HSC based on the organic electrolyte give the device an extremely high energy density ($100-150$ Wh kg^{-1}) [12].

Recently, our research group reported three-dimensional graphene nanosheets/transition metal sulfide nanoparticles (i.e., 3-D GNs/Ni$_3$S$_2$ NPs) composite by efficient quasi-chemical vapor deposition (Q-CVD) technique for high-performance supercapacitors (see Fig. 7.1I for details) [11]. To investigate the practical applications of the samples, a HSC was assembled by using 3-D GNs/Ni$_3$S$_2$ NPs as the cathode and 3-D GNs as the anode, separated by a porous separator in 1 mol L^{-1} KOH aqueous electrolyte. The theoretical charge balance of the cathode and anode corresponds to a ratio $R = m_+/m_- = C_-/C_+$, where m_+ and m_- are the active material masses of cathode and anode, and C_+ and C_- are the capacitance of cathode and anode, respectively. An optimized specific capacitance of 140.3 F g^{-1} at 1 A g^{-1} and an ultrahigh stability of 97.4% from

3600th to 5000th cycle was demonstrated for the HSC assembled with 3-D GNs/Ni_3S_2 NPs cathode and 3-D GNs anode. Within the potential window from 0.0 to 1.7 V, the CV curves of supercapacitor exhibited both the properties of EDLCs and PCs, where the rectangular section is contributed by the electric double-layer capacitance of 3-D GNs while the redox peak sections are contributed by the pseudo-capacitance of Ni_3S_2 NPs. The contrastive CV curves before and after 5000 cycles showed that the CV curve after 5000 cycles has an extra increased area in the potential range of 0.6—1.3 V after 5000 cycles, when compared to the CV curve before 5000 cycles. These results suggest that the increment in capacitance after cycling test mainly attributed to the contribution from the pseudocapacitive component (i.e., Ni_3S_2) in cathode by electrochemical activation [11].

7.3 Electrode materials

7.3.1 Carbon-based materials

Carbon-based materials include activated carbon, glass carbon, carbon fiber, carbon aerogel, expanded graphite, carbon foam, carbon nanotubes, graphene, and so on. For carbon materials, a large capacitance can be obtained by using a high specific surface area. According to the electric double layer theory, the double electric layer capacitance on the electrode surface is can be 20 $\mu F\ cm^{-2}$. If the specific surface area is 1000 $m^2\ g^{-1}$, the specific capacitance of the capacitor is 200 $F\ g^{-1}$. At present, the specific surface area of activated carbon can reach more than 2000 $m^2\ g^{-1}$. However, due to the different sizes of pores in porous carbon materials, it can be divided into micropores (<2 nm), mesoles (2—50 nm) and macropores (>50 nm). For electrode materials of supercapacitors, only pores larger than 1 nm (aqueous solution system) or 3 nm (organic solution system) are conducive to the formation of double-layer capacitance. Therefore, the carbon electrode materials used in supercapacitors not only require large specific surface area but also have appropriate pore size distribution. At present, the actual electrode capacitance of commercial carbon materials is only 80—120 $F\ g^{-1}$, which needs to be further improved by effective strategies (such as introducing pseudocapacitance materials) [13].

7.3.2 Metal-based materials

The metal oxide supercapacitors in the initial study mainly use RuO_2 as the electrode material, which has better performance because its conductivity is two orders of magnitude greater than that of carbon and it is stable in sulfuric acid solution. The reported redox pseudocapacitance of RuO_2 electrode is 1000 $F\ g^{-1}$ [14], but the high price of RuO_2 has hindered its commercial application. Therefore, researches on other cheaper metal oxide substitutes have been carried out. Anderson et al. prepared ultrathin MnO_2 by sol-gel method has a specific capacity of up to 698 $F\ g^{-1}$, and the specific capacity remains above 90% after 1500 cycles [15]. Although this type of supercapacitor has a specific electrode capacity of up to 500 $F\ g^{-1}$ or even higher, the metal-based materials cannot meet the requirements of commercialization because nanoparticles are easy to agglomerate, the structure is easy to be damaged, and there are a series of shortcomings such as poor reversibility in CD, poor power characteristics, and serious self-discharge. Since the Faradaic capacitance of metal material is much larger than that of carbon material, and carbon material itself has good conductivity and stability, metal material-carbon material composite has attracted extensive attention [16].

7.3.3 Conductive polymer materials

Compared with the previous two kinds of electrode materials, conductive polymer is a relatively new electrode material, with short charging and discharging time and low cost, and its capacitance is usually 3—5 times higher than that of activated carbon. Conductive polymers generate large Faradaic capacitance by generating fast N-type or P-type doping/dedoping redox reactions on the polymer film in the charging and discharging process. The commonly used conductive polymer materials include polyaniline, polythiophene, polypyrrole, and their derivatives, which belong to redox PC materials. Although the conductivity of most conductive polymers is not strong, when the material is doped by proton, its conductivity is significantly improved, and its electrical activity is significantly increased. Due to the large number of microporous structures and 3D structures in conductive polymer material, the transfer of electrons and ions in the electrode material can be completed through the exchange of ions in the electrolyte and then obtain excellent electrochemical performances [17].

7.4 Applications

Compared with traditional capacitors, supercapacitors have larger specific capacitance, faster CD rate, wider operating temperature range and longer service life, environmental protection, and so on. Therefore, supercapacitors are widely used in industrial power, consumer electronics, energy management, memory backup systems, uninterruptible power supply, electric hybrid electric vehicle, and storage of energy produced by wind or solar cells (i.e., energy storage in distributed grids). Especially, the capacitor combined with batteries, it can apply to the higher performance of hybrid-power electric vehicle, including accelerating the faster, the recovery of braking energy, and increase the service life of batteries. Therefore, in the field of energy conversion and storage, some shortages of batteries can be compensated by supercapacitors. With the exhaustion of fossil energy and the advent of the era of electrification, the research and development of energy storage components with practical application value has become an obligatory topic for many scientists and engineers, and the high-performance supercapacitors undoubtedly give people great hope and a bright outlook [18].

7.5 Summary

In this chapter, we have discussed the basic classification and energy storage mechanism of supercapacitors, including the electric double-layer supercapacitor (EDLC), Faraday PC, and HSC. Electrode materials of supercapacitors, including the carbon-based materials, metal-based materials, and conductive polymer materials, are also summarized. Supercapacitor is a new type of energy storage device between the traditional capacitor and battery. Its mechanism is physical energy storage, the device does not heat, has the advantages of large power, long life, and good safety, and it is irreplaceable in many application fields.

Acknowledgments

This book was supported by National Natural Science Foundation of China (22078071, 22272034), Natural Science Foundation of Guangdong Province (2021A1515010125, 2020A1515010344), Maoming Science and Technology Project (mmkj2020032), Guangdong Province Universities and Colleges Pearl River Scholar Funded Scheme (2019), Guangdong Basic and Applied Basic Research Foundation (2019A1515011249, 2021A1515010305), Key Research Project of Natural Science of Guangdong Provincial Department of Education (2019KZDXM010), Environment and Energy Green Catalysis Innovation Team of Colleges and Universities of Guangdong Province (2022KCXTD019), the program for Innovative Research Team of Guangdong University of Petrochemical Technology.

References

[1] Y. Li, Z. Li, P.K. Shen, Simultaneous formation of ultrahigh surface area and three-dimensional hierarchical porous graphene-like networks for fast and highly stable supercapacitors, Advanced Materials 25 (17) (2013) 2474−2480.

[2] Z. Li, J. Lin, B. Li, C. Yu, H. Wang, Q. Li, Construction of heteroatom-doped and three-dimensional graphene materials for the applications in supercapacitors: a review, Journal of Energy Storage 44 (2021) 103437.

[3] B. Li, M. Yu, Z. Li, C. Yu, H. Wang, Q. Li, Constructing flexible all-solid-state supercapacitors from 3D nanosheets active bricks via 3D manufacturing technology: a perspective review, Advanced Functional Materials 32 (2022) 2201166.

[4] L.L. Zhang, X.S. Zhao, Carbon-based materials as supercapacitor electrodes, Chemical Society Reviews 38 (9) (2009) 2520−2531.

[5] H. Shao, Y.C. Wu, Z. Lin, P.L. Taberna, P. Simon, Nanoporous carbon for electrochemical capacitive energy storage, Chemical Society Reviews 49 (10) (2020) 3005−3039.

[6] Z. Li, L. Zhang, X. Chen, B. Li, H. Wang, Q. Li, Three-dimensional graphene-like porous carbon nanosheets derived from molecular precursor for high-performance supercapacitor application, Electrochimica Acta 296 (2019) 8−17.

[7] Y. Shao, M.F. El-Kady, J. Sun, Y. Li, Q. Zhang, M. Zhu, et al., Design and mechanisms of asymmetric supercapacitors, Chemical Reviews 118 (18) (2018) 9233−9280.

[8] S. Fleischmann, J.B. Mitchell, R. Wang, C. Zhan, D.E. Jiang, V. Presser, et al., Pseudocapacitance: from fundamental understanding to high power energy storage materials, Chemical Reviews 120 (14) (2020) 6738−6782.

[9] X. Chen, R. Paul, L. Dai, Carbon-based supercapacitors for efficient energy storage, National Science Review 4 (3) (2017) 453−489.

[10] J. Ding, W. Hu, E. Paek, D. Mitlin, Review of hybrid ion capacitors: from aqueous to lithium to sodium, Chemical Reviews 118 (14) (2018) 6457–6498.

[11] Z. Li, B. Li, C. Liao, Z. Liu, D. Li, H. Wang, et al., One-pot construction of 3-D graphene nanosheets/Ni_3S_2 nanoparticles composite for high-performance supercapacitors, Electrochimica Acta 253 (2017) 344–356.

[12] H.Q. Wang, Z.S. Li, Y.G. Huang, Q.Y. Li, X.Y. Wang, A novel hybrid supercapacitor based on spherical activated carbon and spherical MnO_2 in a non-aqueous electrolyte, Journal of Materials Chemistry 20 (19) (2010) 3883–3889.

[13] E. Frackowiak, Carbon materials for supercapacitor application, Physical Chemistry Chemical Physics 9 (15) (2007) 1774–1785.

[14] F. Pico, E. Morales, J.A. Fernandez, T.A. Centeno, J. Ibáñez, R.M. Rojas, et al., Ruthenium oxide/carbon composites with microporous or mesoporous carbon as support and prepared by two procedures. A comparative study as supercapacitor electrodes, Electrochimica Acta 54 (8) (2009) 2239–2245.

[15] S.C. Pang, M.A. Anderson, T.W. Chapman, Novel electrode materials for thin-film ultracapacitors: comparison of electrochemical properties of sol-gel-derived and electrodeposited manganese dioxide, Journal of the Electrochemical Society 147 (2) (2000) 444.

[16] M. Kandasamy, S. Sahoo, S.K. Nayak, B. Chakraborty, C.S. Rout, Recent advances in engineered metal oxide nanostructures for supercapacitor applications: experimental and theoretical aspects, Journal of Materials Chemistry A 9 (33) (2021) 17643–17700.

[17] Q. Meng, K. Cai, Y. Chen, L. Chen, Research progress on conducting polymer based supercapacitor electrode materials, Nano Energy 36 (2017) 268–285.

[18] M.A. Scibioh, B. Viswanathan, Materials for Supercapacitor Applications, Elsevier, 2020.

CHAPTER 8

Metal-ion battery: basic principles, electrode materials, and applications

8.1 Introduction

Lithium–ion batteries (LIBs) are a kind of secondary battery (rechargeable battery), which mainly depends on the movement of lithium ions (Li^+) between the positive and negative electrodes. During charging and discharging, Li^+ is inserted and deinserted back and forth between the two electrodes: during charging, Li^+ is deinserted from the positive electrode and embedded into the negative electrode through electrolyte, and the negative electrode is in a lithium-rich state. The opposite is true when discharging (so-called the "rocking-chair battery"). The commercial LIBs were first developed by Sony Corporation in 1991. In 2019, the Royal Swedish Academy of Sciences announced that the Nobel Prize in chemistry is awarded to John Goodenough, Stanley Whittingham, and Akira Yoshino in recognition of their contributions to the field of LIBs research and development [1]. Currently, LIBs have a low energy density, which cannot meet the long endurance and high safety requirements of electric vehicles. In addition, LIBs are becoming more expensive to manufacture as the price of lithium continues to rise. Therefore, it is necessary to develop high-performance electrode materials and suitable electrolytes to build high specific energy LIBs. On the other hand, low cost or high safety metal-ion batteries (MIBs) such as sodium (Na), potassium (K), and zinc (Zn) ion batteries need to be developed to replace LIB. As an important part of batteries, the electrode material is the key to build high-performance MIBs [2].

8.2 Basic principles
8.2.1 Development history of LIBs

Recently, Zhang and coworkers summarized the background of "rocking-chair electrodes concept" and the development of LIBs (see Fig. 8.1A for details) [3]. In the earliest, Rüdorff and Rouxel proved the chemical intercalation of alkali metals from their liquid ammonia solutions was very fast between the S-Ti-S slabs in 1965 and 1971. The first lithium battery, made by Wintingham, used TiS_2 as anode and lithium as cathode, in 1976. The birth of the "rocking-chair battery" concept dated from the late 1970s. Scrosati reported Li_xWO_2 | $LiClO_4$/propylene carbonate (PC) | TiS_2 the first "rocking-chair" LIBs resulted in a voltage of ~ 2 V and good reversibility. The first working

Nanostructured Materials
ISBN 978-0-443-19256-2, https://doi.org/10.1016/B978-0-443-19256-2.00020-X

lithium-ion graphite electrode came from Bell LABS, and SONY of Japan released the first commercial LIB in 1991. The identification of suitable electrode materials ($LiCoO_2$, $LiMn_2O_4$ and $LiFePO_4$) follows in the 1980s by Goodenough and the commercialization of LIBs in the 1990s and key improvements of LIBs achieved from the 1990s to 2000s (see Fig. 8.1A) [3].

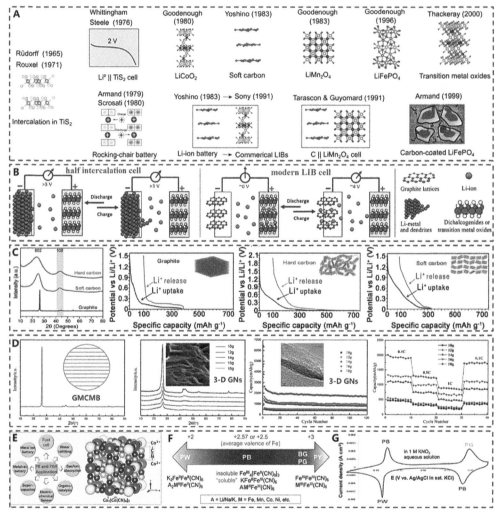

Figure 8.1 (A) Development history of LIBs [3], (B) "rocking-chair mechanism" of LIBs [4], (C) various carbon electrodes of LIBs [5], (D) 3D graphene nanosheets for LIBs [6], (E) application and structure of Prussian blue [7], (F) Prussian blue for Li/Na/K MIBs [8], and (G) CV curve of Prussian blue [9].

8.2.2 Basic principles of LIBs

The cathode material of lithium battery is manganese dioxide or thionyl chloride, and the cathode is lithium. After the battery is assembled, the battery has voltage (>3 V) and does not need to be charged. This kind of battery may avalso be charged, but the cycle performance is not good. During the charge and discharge cycle, lithium dendrites are easy to form, causing internal short circuit of the battery, so generally, this kind of battery is prohibited from charging (see Fig. 8.1B for details) [4]. Sony Corporation of Japan invented the carbon material as the negative electrode and the lithium-containing compound as the positive electrode. In the process of charging and discharging, there is no metal lithium, only lithium ion, which is the modern LIBs ($\sim$4 V). When the battery is charged, lithium ions are generated on the positive pole of the battery, and the generated lithium ions move to the negative pole through the electrolyte. The carbon as the negative electrode has a layered structure, which has many micropores. Lithium ions reaching the negative electrode are embedded into the micropores of the carbon layer. Similarly, when the battery is discharged, the lithium-ion embedded in the carbon layer of the negative pole will come out and move back to the positive pole. In the process of charging and discharging, Li-ion moves as follows: positive electrode $\rightarrow$ negative electrode $\rightarrow$ positive electrode. The Li-ion diffusion is like a rocking chair in charging and discharging, so LIBs are also called rocking-chair Batteries (see Fig. 8.1B) [4].

8.3 Electrode materials

8.3.1 Cathode materials of LIBs

Goodenough's group began working on oxide cathode materials (through the band principle) at Oxford in the 1980s, in order to increase battery voltages and develop cathode materials that already contained lithium [10]. In the sulfide positive electrode, the top of the S^{2-}: 3p band at higher energies limits the cell voltage to <2.5 V. In contrast, the top of the lower energy O^{2-}: 2p band can enter the lower band with the higher oxidation state and basically raise the cell voltage to $\sim$4 V. This basic idea led Goodenough's team, together with visiting scientists from three different parts of the world, to discover three classes of oxide positives in the 1980s: Layered oxide positive electrode studied by Mizushima, spinel oxide positive electrode studied by Thackeray, and polyanionic oxide positive electrode studied by Manthiram. The layered $LiCoO_2$ containing octahedral lithium ions increases the cell voltage from <2.5 V in TiS_2 to $\sim$4 V. Spinel $LiMn_2O_4$ containing tetrahedral lithium ions increases the battery voltage from 3 to $\sim$4 V, while reducing the cost. The polyanionic oxide $Li_xFe_2(SO_4)_3$ provides an alternative method to increase the cell voltage to 3.6 V by induction effects of <2.5 V in a simple oxide like Fe_2O_3, further reducing cost and improving thermal stability and safety [11]. In 1996, Goodenough et al. proposed a phospho-olivine material, lithium iron phosphate ($LiFePO_4$), as a promising positive electrode material [12]. However, the poor electronic conductivity of LiFePO$_4$ impeded its practical application in LIBs. A breakthrough toward implementation of this material was made by Armand et al. who proposed the carbon-coated LiFePO$_4$ particles and today this active positive electrode material is produced in thousands of tons per year [13]. Surface carbon coating requirements for the positive electrode include: (1) thin and uniform, (2) ionic and electronic conductivity, (3) high mechanical properties and highly stable after the charge/discharge cycle; (4) the coating process is simple and extensible.

8.3.2 Anode materials of LIBs

The anode material of commercial LIBs is mainly graphite material. According to the lithium storage mechanism of LiC$_6$ between graphite layers, its theoretical specific capacity is only 372 mAh g^{-1}, which means that the space for improvement is very limited, and the lithium diffusion between graphite layers also limits its rate performance. As a new type of anode material, hard carbon has similar lithium potential and higher specific capacity as graphite. Even at 3000°C, hard carbon will not form graphite, can only form short-range ordered, long-range disordered graphite microcrystal structures in lowest graphitization degree compared with graphite and soft carbon. This unique structure can not only provide more lithium storage sites but also facilitate the removal of lithium ions between graphite layers (>600 mAh g^{-1}) (see Fig. 8.1C for details) [5]. Recently, we demonstrated a 3D interconnected graphene-like nanosheet (3DGNs) developed from graphite microspheres. When used as an anode in LIBs, the 3DGN is capable of reaching an extremely high reversible discharge capacity of 2795 mA h g^{-1} while maintaining a good electrochemical stability (see Fig. 8.1D for details) [6]. More Recently, alloy lithium storage anode materials (including silicon, germanium, and tin-based materials) with higher lithium storage capacity have become the most potential replacement materials for graphite anode materials in the future [14]. At the nanoscale, the volume change effect can be buffered and protected, and the electrochemical cycle and rate performance can be effectively improved, which fully shows a good application prospect in high-performance LIBs.

8.3.3 Electrode materials of other MIBs

LIBs are one of the best high-energy density devices and have been commercially available for decades. However, the scarcity of lithium resources limits the application on a large scale. In this regard, Na-ion batteries (NIBs) and K-ion batteries (KIBs) have an advantage due to the much greater abundance of sodium and potassium. Compared with LIBs, NIBs and KIBs are ideal for next-generation electrical energy storage due to their low cost and high energy/power density. However, the intercalation kinetics of larger Na$^+$ ($r = 1.02$ Å) and K$^+$ ($r = 1.38$ Å) in tightly packed materials is much slower than that of Li$^+$ with an ionic radius (r) of 0.76 Å, and usually causes more significant structural changes, resulting in poor electrochemical stability of the active materials. Therefore, efforts have been made to develop new structures that allow faster and more reversible intercalation of Na^+ and K^+. Prussian blue (PB) and Prussian blue analogs (PBAs) are of a wide range of applications in the energy field because of their unique crystal structures (see Fig. 8.1E for details) [7]. In the search for viable electrode materials for NIBs and KIBs, Prussian blue analogs (PBAs), with their inherently rigid and open frames and large intergap holes, have shown the ability to accommodate large alkali metal ions without structural collapse (see Fig. 8.1F for details) [8]. In particular, iron hexacyanoferric (HCF) PBA, which uses abundant iron $(CN)_6$ resources, is one of the most interesting subgroups in PBA, capable of providing specific capacities of $70-170$ mAh g^{-1} and voltages of $2.5-3.8$ V in NIBs/KIBs (see Fig. 8.1G for details) [9]. Prussian blue analogs are one of the most studied cathode materials and one of the most potential low-cost cathode materials for high-performance MIBs in the future.

8.4 Applications

LIBs are widely used in energy storage power systems (such as water power, firepower, wind power, and solar power stations), uninterruptible power supply for post and telecommunications, personal electric tools (mobile phones, computers, tablets, digital cameras and so on), electric bicycles, electric motorcycles, electric vehicles, military equipment, aerospace, and other fields. With the development of microelectronic technology in the 20th century, the number of miniaturized equipment is increasing, which puts forward high requirements for power supply. Micro-LIBs then entered the stage of large-scale utility (for example, used in pacemakers and micromonitor) [15].

8.5 Summary

In this chapter, we have discussed the brief history and energy storage mechanism of LIBs. Cathode and anode materials of LIBs, and electrode materials of other MIBs are also introduced. LIBs are "rocking-chair battery." Metal compound containing Li ($LiCoO_2$, $LiMn_2O_4$, and $LiFePO_4$) are the most widely used cathode materials. And graphite is the most widely used anode material. The LIBs are the most common energy storage technology in the market at present, which is widely used in various personal electronic products, mobile devices, and even the onboard battery of electric vehicles.

Acknowledgments

This book was supported by National Natural Science Foundation of China (22078071, 22272034), Natural Science Foundation of Guangdong Province (2021A1515010125, 2020A1515010344), Maoming Science and Technology Project (mmkj2020032), Guangdong Province Universities and Colleges Pearl River Scholar Funded Scheme (2019), Guangdong Basic and Applied Basic Research Foundation (2019A1515011249, 2021A1515010305), Key Research Project of Natural Science of Guangdong Provincial Department of Education (2019KZDXM010), Environment and Energy Green Catalysis Innovation Team of Colleges and Universities of Guangdong Province(2022KCXTD019), the program for Innovative Research Team of Guangdong University of Petrochemical Technology.

References

[1]   https://mp.weixin.qq.com/s/Ghllegd01tdVFBkQZ6aTZA.

[2]   Y. Dong, H. Shi, Z.S. Wu, Recent advances and promise of MXene-based nanostructures for high-performance metal ion batteries, Advanced Functional Materials 30 (47) (2020) 2000706.

[3]   H. Zhang, C. Li, G.G. Eshetu, S. Laruelle, S. Grugeon, K. Zaghib, et al., From solid-solution electrodes and the rocking-chair concept to today's batteries, Angewandte Chemie 132 (2) (2020) 542–546.

[4]   M. Winter, B. Barnett, K. Xu, Before Li ion batteries, Chemical Reviews 118 (23) (2018) 11433–11456.

[5]   L. Xie, C. Tang, Z. Bi, M. Song, Y. Fan, C. Yan, et al., Hard carbon anodes for next-generation Li-ion batteries: review and perspective, Advanced Energy Materials 11 (38) (2021) 2101650.

[6]   H.Q. Wang, G.H. Yang, L.S. Cui, Z.S. Li, Z.X. Yan, X.H. Zhang, et al., Controlled synthesis of three-dimensional interconnected graphene-like nanosheets from graphite microspheres as high-performance anodes for lithium-ion batteries, Journal of Materials Chemistry A 3 (42) (2015) 21298–21307.

[7]   M. Yu, Z. Li, H. Shi, S. Lin, X. Zhang, F. Mo, et al., Preparation of graphite carbon/Prussian blue analogue/palladium (GC/PBA/pd) synergistic-effect electrocatalyst with high activity for ethanol oxidation reaction, International Journal of Hydrogen Energy 47 (10) (2022) 6721–6733.

[8]   A. Zhou, W. Cheng, W. Wang, Q. Zhao, J. Xie, W. Zhang, et al., Hexacyanoferrate-type Prussian blue analogs: principles and advances toward high-performance sodium and potassium ion batteries, Advanced Energy Materials 11 (2) (2021) 2000943.

[9]   P. Padigi, J. Thiebes, M. Swan, G. Goncher, D. Evans, R. Solanki, Prussian green: a high rate capacity cathode for potassium ion batteries, Electrochimica Acta 166 (2015) 32–39.

[10] A. Manthiram, John Goodenough's 100th Birthday Celebration: His Impact on Science and Humanity, 2022, https://doi.org/10.1021/acsenergylett.2c01343.

[11] A. Manthiram, A reflection on lithium-ion battery cathode chemistry, Nature Communications 11 (1) (2020) 1–9.

[12] A.K. Padhi, K.S. Nanjundaswamy, J.B. Goodenough, Phospho-olivines as positive-electrode materials for rechargeable lithium batteries, Journal of the Electrochemical Society 144 (4) (1997) 1188.

[13] N. Ravet, S. Besner, M. Simoneau, A. Vallee, M. Armand, CA2270771A1, 1999.

[14] W. Li, X. Sun, Y. Yu, Si-, Ge-, Sn-based anode materials for lithium-ion batteries: from structure design to electrochemical performance, Small Methods 1 (3) (2017) 1600037.

[15] M. Li, J. Lu, Z. Chen, K. Amine, 30 years of lithium-ion batteries, Advanced Materials 30 (33) (2018) 1800561.

CHAPTER 9

Metal-sulfur battery: basic principles, electrode materials, and applications

9.1 Introduction

With the rapid development of lithium-ion batteries, their energy density has approached the theoretical limit. The most promising strategy for further breakthroughs is to replace the traditional intercalation materials with conversion materials with higher capacity. Lithium-sulfur (Li-S) batteries based on conversion reactions have high theoretical specific energy (2600 Wh kg^{-1}), which is considered as the development direction of a new generation of secondary batteries. However, there are still some problems that limit the technological development of Li-S batteries, such as the insulation of active sulfur and discharge product Li-sulfide; the shuttle effect caused by soluble intermediate lithium polysulfides (LiPSs) is produced in the process of charging and discharging. Low utilization rate of active substances and rapid decline of battery capacity are caused by the slow kinetics of LiPSs conversion. In order to solve the above problems, it is necessary to provide the conductivity of sulfur electrode, inhibit the shuttle effect of LiPSs, and improve the kinetics of LiPSs conversion reaction fundamentally. Anchoring of porous carbon materials and adsorption of defective supports are preferential strategies to enhance the conductivity and stability of sulfur electrodes. On the other hand, nanostructured or atomic-structured electrocatalysts are widely used to accelerate cathodic sulfur conversion kinetics. Among them, the interaction between electrocatalyst, solvent, and lithium salt greatly determines the actual performances of Li-S batteries [1–3].

9.2 Basic principles

In the 1960s, scientists (Herbert and Ulam) proposed the concept of a lithium-sulfur (Li-S) battery system consisting of a metal lithium anode and an elemental sulfur anode. The Li-S battery is a kind of lithium-based rechargeable battery with sulfur element as the positive electrode ($S_8 + 16Li^+ + 16e^- \leftrightarrow 8Li_2S$) and lithium metal as the negative electrode (Li $\leftrightarrow$ Li$^+$ + e$^-$) (see Fig. 9.1A for details) [4]. In theory, the complete reaction of lithium and elemental sulfur can achieve electronic reaction. The theoretical specific capacity of sulfur electrode is as high as 1675 mAh g^{-1}, and the theoretical capacity of lithium metal negative electrode is as high as 3860 mAh g^{-1}. Therefore, the theoretical energy density of Li-S secondary battery system based on elemental sulfur and lithium metal reaches 2600 Wh kg^{-1}. If the energy density of the actual battery system can

Nanostructured Materials
ISBN 978-0-443-19256-2, https://doi.org/10.1016/B978-0-443-19256-2.00028-4

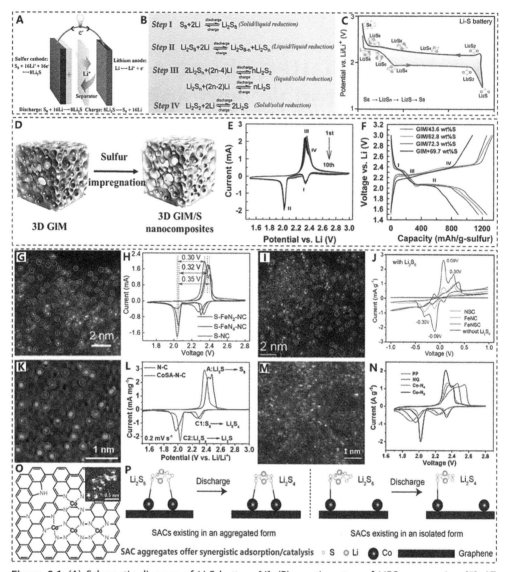

Figure 9.1 (A) Schematic diagram of Li-S battery [4], (B) reaction step of LiPSs conversion [5], (C) charge-discharge curve of Li-S battery [6], (D—F) 3-D graphene anchored S for Li-S battery [7], (G—P) single atomic catalysts (Fe SACs and Co SACs) for Li-S batteries [3,8—12].

achieve 20% of the theoretical energy density, the energy density of the lithium/sulfur battery can reach 500 Wh kg^{-1}. Therefore, Li-S battery system has great development potential and has become one of the research hotspots and focuses in the field of high energy density secondary batteries in recent years [4].

The discharge/charging process of Li-S battery is achieved by electrochemical cleavage and recombination of sulfur-sulfur bonds and is associated with a four-step redox reaction and complex phase transfer of various LiPSs (see Fig. 9.1B and C for details) [5,6]. Step 1 (solid/liquid reaction): During the discharge process, elemental sulfur (S$_8$) first combines with Li ions through solid/liquid reduction to form soluble Li$_2$S$_8$. Step 2 (liquid/liquid reaction): The Li$_2$S$_8$ reacts with Li ions to generate a LiPSs chain intermediate (Li$_2$S$_n$, $4 \leq n \leq 8$) through liquid/liquid reduction. These two steps lead to a theoretical capacity of 419 mAh g^{-1}. The sequential reduction of S$_8$ to S$_6^{2-}$ and S$_4^{2-}$ results in a reduction in the length of sulfur chain (the discharge potential plateau is between 2.2 and 2.3 V). The long-chain Li$_2$S$_n$ can be soluble and diffused into organic electrolyte from cathode. Step 3 (liquid/solid reaction): long-chain Li$_2$S$_n$ is further reduced to short-chain Li$_2$S$_2$ or low-solubility Li$_2$S in the electrolyte by a continuous discharge process (the discharge potential plateau is between 1.9 and 2.1 V). This step led to a theoretical capacity of 1256 mAh g^{-1}. Step 4 (solid/solid reaction): the insulation and insolubility of Li$_2$S$_2$ and Li$_2$S lead to large polarization and slow reaction kinetics at the last solid/solid reduction. During the charging process, Li$_2$S$_2$ and Li$_2$S are gradually oxidized to LiPSs intermediates and finally converted to elemental sulfur [5,6]. At present, the bottleneck of lithium-sulfur batteries (that is most difficult problem) is the cathodic reaction intermediates easily dissolved in the organic electrolyte and degradation, leading to the negatively charged polysulfide through the electrolyte from cathode to anode (so called "shuttle effect"), and Li metal anode surface precipitation, resulting in loss of active substances and lithium metal anode corrosion (damaging the efficiency and cycle life of the battery) [13]. The chemical reaction between dissolved sulfur and negative lithium is directly generated in the negative electrode Li$_2$S, because Li$_2$S in the negative electrode, recharging also cannot make it back to S$_8$, the legendary polysulfide "shuttle effect," in fact, is a "loss effect" that never comes back, resulting in performance attenuation and cycle life reduction of Li-S batteries [14].

9.3 Electrode materials

The main drawback hindering the success of Li-S batteries is the severe leakage and migration of soluble LiPSs intermediates during cycling. The loss of active sulfur results in a significant decrease in battery capacity and battery life. Therefore, many efforts have been made to develop various host materials that can effectively anchor sulfur and polysulfide. The main host materials include (1) porous carbon-based materials, (2) porous inorganic compounds, and (2) two-dimensional layered nanomaterials. A rational design and synthesis of sulfur-carbon nanocomposites by infiltrating into 3-D graphene-like material (GlM) with hierarchical pores has been achieved by our group, and the resulting 3D GlM/S nanocomposite shows a highly stable capacity and reversible high charge/discharge rate performance (see Fig. 9.1D–F for details) [7]. The ideal porous carbon matrix of sulfur-carbon composites should include (1) high conductivity to improve the utilization of sulfur, (2) high electrochemical affinity for sulfur to achieve high capacity, (3) small pores without large outlet to stabilize polysulfides, (4) large specific surface area to load enough sulfur, (5) suitable structure of active materials to sulfur infiltration to receive liquid electrolytes, (6) stable framework to maintain the strain caused by the volume change of the active material during the cycle [7].

The key to achieve high theoretical energy of Li–S batteries is to stabilize polythioides while ensuring high sulfur content. In 2015, Al-Salem et al. proposed an electrocatalytic approach to demonstrate preferential adsorption of soluble polysulfide species formed during discharge at the anchor site of graphene/Pt catalyst and accelerated conversion reactions to long-chain polysulfides during redox processes (with a capacity increase of 40%) [15]. The metal catalyst accelerates the reduction process of polysulfide in Li-sulfur batteries: $Li_2S_8 \rightarrow Li_2S_6 \rightarrow Li_2S_4 \rightarrow Li_2S_2/Li_2S$, thus accelerating the reaction kinetics and improving the capacity and rate performance of the batteries [16]. For adsorption, limitation, and catalysis strategies, heterojunction engineering has received much attention in recent years. Taking the porous carbon/metal nanocatalysts as an example, porous carbon is responsible for absorbing polysulfide and reducing the loss of active substances, while metal nanocatalysts catalyze the conversion of polysulfide, so as to inhibit the shuttle effect of sulfide. More importantly, the enhanced chemical coupling between metal components and carbon materials enhances the interelectrode charge transfer and redox kinetics [17].

At present, one of the most effective strategies to solve shuttle effect is to introduce metal single-atom catalysts (SACs) to improve the electrochemical performance of sulfur cathode, so as to produce excellent adsorption and catalysis for polysulfide Li_2S_n. The introduction of SACs can accelerate the conversion of Li_2S_n, inhibit the shuttle effect from the source and improve the cycle performance of Li–S batteries. More recently, we summarize the recent advances in the application of high-density SACs (Fe SACs and Co SACs) for Li–S batteries with an emphasis on the synergistic catalysis of adjacent active sites (see Fig. 9.1G–P for details) [3]. From the coordination structure (Fig. 9.1G and H) [8] and chemical environment (Fig. 9.1I and J) [9] aspects, the two works have successfully optimized the catalytic efficiency of polysulfide conversion by the Fe-based SACs, showing the great feasibility and validity in practical application of Li–S batteries. On the other hand, N-doped carbon supported Co-based SACs also showed excellent catalytic properties for polysulfide conversion in Li–S batteries (Fig. 9.1K–P) [10–12]. Electrochemical evaluation confirmed that these high-density metal SACs with unique coordination achieved strong sulfur fixation and catalysis conversion (in small potential spacing of redox current peaks from their CV curves) for Li–S batteries.

9.4 Applications

The research of Li-S battery started in 1970s, which is an energy storage system composed of sulfur (S) composite positive electrode, lithium metal (Li) negative electrode, and electrolyte between them. It is considered as a promising new secondary battery system due to its high energy density (2600 Wh kg^{-1}), wide operating temperature (-30 to $60°C$) and low electrode material cost. Currently, it is reported that Japan has used Li-S batteries as energy propulsion devices in its nuclear submarines. British companies OXIS and CODEMGE have teamed up with Brazilian blue-chip companies to electrify regional jets, buses, and trucks using Li-S batteries and are working with Brazilian aircraft manufacturers to build electric planes in Brazil. Throughout the development history of Li-S battery, it has been intermittent for more than 50 years since its birth. The scientists believe that its development history can be divided into three stages: (1) How to cycle the Li-S battery in 1970−2002; (2) How to improve the Li-S battery cathode in 2002−2014; (3) How to protect the Li-S battery anode in 2014~present. Since then, how to protect the anode of Li metal in Li-S batteries has become the key factor for Li-S batteries to go to the market. The complexity of Li protection lies in the consideration of the characteristics of Li metal itself, the characteristics of electrolyte, and the thermodynamic and electrochemical corrosion of Li metal by polysulfides [18].

9.5 Summary

In this chapter, we have discussed the brief history and energy storage mechanism of Lithium-sulfur (Li-S) batteries. The reaction mechanism of lithium polysulfides (LiPSs) and the "shuttle effect" mechanism of dissolved sulfur species is also introduced in detail. The sulfur-carbon composites and metal catalyst can be used to effectively adsorb polysulfide and promote reduction conversion. The SACs not only promoted the uniform deposition of lithium at the negative electrode but also effectively absorbed soluble LiPSs and promoted the catalytic conversion at cathode. The Li-S batteries have high energy density and long cycle life, which provides a broad prospect for large-scale energy storage.

Acknowledgments

This book was supported by National Natural Science Foundation of China (22078071, 22272034), Natural Science Foundation of Guangdong Province (2021A1515010125, 2020A1515010344), Maoming Science and Technology Project (mmkj2020032), Guangdong Province Universities and Colleges Pearl River Scholar Funded Scheme (2019), Guangdong Basic and Applied Basic Research Foundation (2019A1515011249, 2021A1515010305), Key Research Project of Natural Science of Guangdong Provincial Department of Education (2019KZDXM010), Environment and Energy Green Catalysis Innovation Team of Colleges and Universities of Guangdong Province (2022KCXTD019), the program for Innovative Research Team of Guangdong University of Petrochemical Technology.

References

[1] W. Hou, Y. Yang, L. Fang, Y. Mao, W. Sun, Y. Bai, et al., Perovskite with in situ exsolved cobalt nanometal heterostructures for high rate and stable lithium-sulfur batteries, Chemical Engineering Journal 409 (2021) 128079.

[2] X.Y. Li, S. Feng, C.X. Zhao, Q. Cheng, Z.X. Chen, S.Y. Sun, et al., Regulating lithium salt to inhibit surface gelation on an electrocatalyst for high-energy-density lithium—sulfur batteries, Journal of the American Chemical Society 144 (32) (2022) 14638—14646.

[3] Z. Li, B. Li, Y. Hu, X. Liao, H. Yu, C. Yu, Emerging ultrahigh-density single-atom catalysts for versatile heterogeneous catalysis applications: redefinition, recent progress, and challenges, Small Structures 3 (2022) 2200041.

[4] Z.W. Seh, Y. Sun, Q. Zhang, Y. Cui, Designing high-energy lithium—sulfur batteries, Chemical Society Reviews 45 (20) (2016) 5605—5634.

[5] Q. Zhang, Q. Huang, S.M. Hao, S. Deng, Q. He, Z. Lin, et al., Polymers in lithium—sulfur batteries, Advanced Science 9 (2) (2022) 2103798.

[6] X. Zhao, C. Wang, Z. Li, X. Hu, A.A. Razzaq, Z. Deng, Sulfurized polyacrylonitrile for high-performance lithium sulfur batteries: advances and prospects, Journal of Materials Chemistry A 9 (35) (2021) 19282—19297.

[7] Y. Li, Z. Li, Q. Zhang, P.K. Shen, Sulfur-infiltrated three-dimensional graphene-like material with hierarchical pores for highly stable lithium—sulfur batteries, Journal of Materials Chemistry A 2 (13) (2014) 4528—4533.

[8] J. Wang, W. Qiu, G. Li, J. Liu, D. Luo, Y. Zhang, et al., Coordinatively deficient single-atom Fe-nc electrocatalyst with optimized electronic structure for high-performance lithium-sulfur batteries, Energy Storage Materials 46 (2022) 269—277.

[9] H. Zhao, B. Tian, C. Su, Y. Li, Single-atom iron and doped sulfur improve the catalysis of polysulfide conversion for obtaining high-performance lithium—sulfur batteries, ACS Applied Materials & Interfaces 13 (6) (2021) 7171—7177.

[10] Y. Li, J. Wu, B. Zhang, W. Wang, G. Zhang, Z.W. Seh, et al., Fast conversion and controlled deposition of lithium (poly) sulfides in lithium-sulfur batteries using high-loading cobalt single atoms, Energy Storage Materials 30 (2020) 250—259.

[11] D. Fang, P. Sun, S. Huang, Y. Shang, X. Li, D. Yan, et al., An exfoliation—evaporation strategy to regulate N coordination number of Co single-atom catalysts for high-performance lithium—sulfur batteries, ACS Materials Letters 4 (1) (2021) 1—10.

[12] X. Meng, X. Liu, X. Fan, X. Chen, S. Chen, Y. Meng, et al., Single-atom catalyst aggregates: size-matching is critical to electrocatalytic performance in sulfur cathodes, Advanced Science 9 (2021) e2103773.

[13] S. Ohno, W.G. Zeier, Toward practical solid-state lithium—sulfur batteries: challenges and perspectives, Accounts of Materials Research 2 (10) (2021) 869—880.

[14] R. Xu, H.A. Tang, Y. Zhou, F. Wang, H. Wang, M. Shao, et al., Enhanced catalysis of LiS_3·radical-to-polysulfide interconversion via increased sulfur vacancies in lithium—sulfur batteries, Chemical Science 13 (2022) 6224—6232.

[15] H. Al Salem, G. Babu, C.V. Rao, L.M.R. Arava, Electrocatalytic polysulfide traps for controlling redox shuttle process of Li—S batteries, Journal of the American Chemical Society 137 (36) (2015) 11542—11545.

[16] M. Cheng, R. Yan, Z. Yang, X. Tao, T. Ma, S. Cao, et al., Polysulfide catalytic materials for fast-kinetic metal—sulfur batteries: principles and active centers, Advanced Science 9 (2) (2022) 2102217.

[17] C. Ye, L. Zhang, C. Guo, D. Li, A. Vasileff, H. Wang, et al., A 3D hybrid of chemically coupled nickel sulfide and hollow carbon spheres for high performance lithium—sulfur batteries, Advanced Functional Materials 27 (33) (2017) 1702524.

[18] https://mp.weixin.qq.com/s/v3qkWHJHkyRorik-Fq20YA.

CHAPTER 10

Metal-air battery: basic principles, electrode materials and applications

10.1 Introduction

Metal air battery is a kind of special fuel cell which takes metal as fuel and produces electric energy by a redox reaction with oxygen in the air. The metal-air battery has the advantages of safety and high energy density with active metal as an anode. It has a good development and application prospect and is even expected to replace the current lithium-ion power battery for vehicles. Metal-air battery mainly includes aluminum-air battery, magnesium-air battery, zinc-air battery, lithium-air battery, and so on. Lithium-air battery (Li-air battery) is a very potential high-specific capacity battery technology. It uses the reversible reaction between lithium metal and oxygen to achieve the upper limit of the theoretical energy density of 11,000 Wh kg^{-1} (excluding oxygen mass), far exceeding the actual energy density of lithium-ion batteries of 250 Wh kg^{-1} at present [1]. The Li-air battery has a higher energy density than lithium-ion batteries because their cathodes (mostly porous carbon) are light and oxygen is taken from the environment rather than stored in the battery. Zinc-air battery (Zn-air battery) relies on the chemical reaction between zinc metal and air in the aqueous electrolyte to obtain electrical energy. The positive active material is oxygen in the air, and the negative active material is zinc. The Zn-air battery has great appeal in portable electronics, electric vehicles, and other fields due to its high energy density, abundant raw material reserves, and higher safety [2].

10.2 Basic principles

10.2.1 Basic principles for Li-air batteries

Because of the consumption and pollution of fossil fuels such as gasoline, new alternative energy sources are needed. But the current Li-ion battery ($LiCoO_2$ material) 250 Wh kg^{-1} energy density and gasoline 1750 Wh kg^{-1} index is too big to meet the vehicle demand. Fig. 10.1A shows the actual energy density, estimated driving distance, and packaging price of typical rechargeable batteries [3]. The actual energy density of Li-air batteries is estimated to be in the range of 500−900 Wh kg^{-1}, which is at least 2−3 times that of Li-ion batteries. The Li-air batteries are sufficient to provide a driving distance of

Nanostructured Materials
ISBN 978-0-443-19256-2, https://doi.org/10.1016/B978-0-443-19256-2.00019-3

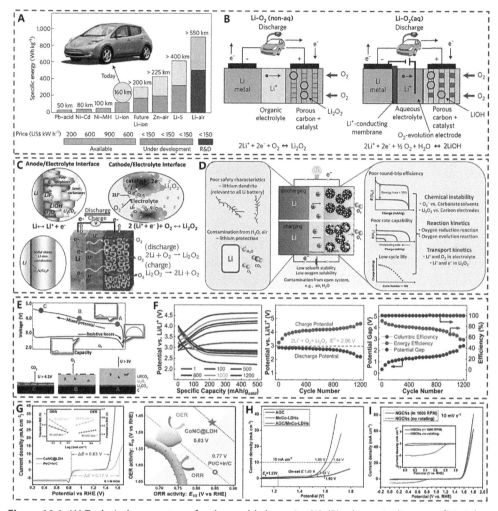

Figure 10.1 (A) Technical parameters of rechargeable batteries [3], (B) schematic diagram of Li-air battery [3], (C) by-products of Li-air battery [4], (D) property regulation of Li-air battery [5], (E) cyclic voltammetry and impedance of Li-air battery [6], (F) charge and discharge of Li-air battery [7], (G) ORR and OER of CoNC@LDH [8], (H) OER of AGC/MnCo-LDH [9], (I) ORR and OER of NGCNs [10].

more than 550 km and a packaging price of less than US\$150 kWh^{-1}. If Li-S battery is the next generation of Li–ion battery, then Li-air battery will be the final form of Li–ion battery. The strict definition of Li-air battery is Li-oxygen battery (Li-O$_2$). In fact, the most important problem to be solved for Li-air batteries is to suppress the complex reaction between lithium metal and other components in the air environment.

The Li–air batteries use oxygen in the air as a reactant at the cathode and lithium as the anode. In the discharge process, lithium at the anode releases electrons and becomes a lithium cation (Li^+). The Li^+ passes through the electrolyte and battery membrane, combines with oxygen at the cathode, and electrons flow through the external circuit to form lithium oxide (Li_2O) or lithium peroxide (Li_2O_2), and stays at the cathode. When charged, the Li_2O or Li_2O_2 is broken down into lithium and oxygen, which involves an oxygen reduction reaction (ORR) and oxygen evolution reaction (OER) (see Fig. 10.1B for details) [3]. The Li–air batteries have different reaction equations depending on the electrolyte:

$$2Li^+ + 2e^- + O_2 \leftrightarrow Li_2O_2 \text{ (Nonaqueous electrolyte)}$$

$$2Li^+ + 2e^- + {}^1\!/_2\ O_2 + H_2O \leftrightarrow 2LiOH \text{ (Aqueous electrolyte)}$$

Compared with $LiCoO_2$ and Li-S electrode, the reaction equation of Li–air batteries is simpler, but there are also a series of side reactions in the reaction process, LiOH, and $Li_2(CO_3)$ is the main side reaction products. In order to reduce by–products and improve cycle efficiency, researchers mostly react with pure oxygen O_2 environment, so Li–air battery is also called Li-O_2 battery (see Fig. 10.1C for details) [4]. The fundamental battery chemistry during discharge in Li–air batteries is thought to be the electrochemical oxidation of lithium metal at the anode and the reduction of oxygen from the air at the cathode. The most important challenge is to understand the chemical reactions occurring in Li–air batteries and improve the selectivity and kinetics of the main reaction by developing new catalyst materials.

In the application of Li–air batteries, the safety caused by lithium metal dendrites, the side reaction of air and water impurity (carbon dioxide), low oxygen solubility, and other problems cannot be ignored. Chemical stability, reaction kinetics, and lithium-ion migration kinetics are the key factors for regulating the performance (round-trip efficiency, ratio performance, and cycle performance) of Li–air batteries (see Fig. 10.1D for details) [5]. For studying the kinetic properties, it is very important to measure the electrochemical impedance of Li_2O_2 formation and decomposition at different charge stages during charging and discharging (see Fig. 10.1E for details) [6]. A substantial increase in polarization resistance occurs toward the end of the discharge, whereas at the beginning of the charging, this polarization resistance decreases compared to that at the end of the prior discharge. The layers of Li_2CO_3 (and other insulating byproducts) accumulate at the Li_2O_2-cathode and Li_2O_2-electrolyte interfaces with deeper states of charging and over repeated cycles, where the interfacial Li_2CO_3 likely plays a decisive role in determining the sluggish oxidation kinetics of Li–air batteries [6].

Currently, the main drawbacks of the most advanced Li–air batteries are low energy efficiency and limited cycle life due to the lack of efficient cathodic catalysts that can drive oxygen reduction and evolution reactions (ORR and OER) at high speed at the thermodynamic potential. Recently, Asadi reported that the inexpensive tri molybdenum phosphate (Mo_3P) nanoparticles have exceptional catalytic activity for Li-air batteries: at 2.0 and 4.2 V (relative to Li/Li^+), the ORR and OER current densities are as high as 7.21 and 6.85 mA cm^{-2} (in oxygen-saturated nonaqueous electrolyte), respectively (see Fig. 10.1F for details) [7]. The charge and discharge performance of this Li-air battery can be 1200 cycles, which should be a breakthrough in history (after 100 cycles the charging potential rises significantly).

10.2.2 Basic principles for Zn-air batteries

Zinc-air battery (Zn-air battery) is also known as zinc-oxygen battery. The cathode active material is oxygen in the air, the anode active material is active metal zinc, and the electrolyte is potassium hydroxide aqueous solution containing saturated zinc oxide. The working principle of Zn-air battery is found by Leclanch in 1868, he noticed that when the volume of electrolyte only accounts for half of the holding cell volume, the upper of cathode manganese dioxide/carbon composites are not soaked in the electrolyte. The oxygen reduction reaction (ORR) in the air of the wet part occurred, and the performance of zinc-manganese dioxide/carbon battery was improved. The Zn-air battery in KOH electrolyte can be expressed as:

$$(-) \text{ Zn} \mid \text{KOH} \mid O_2 \text{ } (+)$$

The electrochemical reaction between the anode and cathode during the discharge of zinc-air battery is as follows:

$$\text{Zn} + 4OH^- \rightarrow Zn(OH)_4{}^{2-} + 2e^- \text{ (Anode reaction 1)}$$

$$Zn(OH)_4{}^{2-} \rightarrow ZnO + 2OH^- + H_2O \text{ (Anode reaction 2)}$$

$$O_2 + 2H_2O + 4e^- \rightarrow 4OH^- \text{ (Cathode reaction)}$$

The total battery reaction is:

$$2Zn + O_2 \rightarrow 2ZnO$$

Normally, this reaction produces a voltage of 1.4 V, but the current and discharge depth can cause the voltage to vary. Air must flow continuously to the cathode, and holes must be cut in the positive shell to allow a steady flow of oxygen in order for the battery to react chemically.

The Zn-air battery has attracted more and more attention due to its advantages of high energy density and low cost. High-performance ORR and OER bifunctional catalytic materials play a key role in the advancement of Zn-air battery technology. Based on rational nano design, Li et al. recently reported a composite bifunctional catalyst CoNC@LDH with extremely high catalytic activity (see Fig. 10.1G for details) [8]. The ORR and OER bifunctional performance of CoNC@LDH are $E_{1/2} = 0.84$ V and $E_{10} = 1.47$ V, respectively, thus achieving the ultra-high bifunctional catalytic performance of $\triangle E = 0.63$ V, much better than the noble metal based catalyst ($\triangle E = 0.77$ V). The Co species on NC is the active catalytic component of ORR, while NiFe-LDH is the active catalytic component of OER. Through in-depth mechanism analysis, this work reveals the internal synergism between the components of composite catalysts, which provides strategic guidance for the rational design of ORR-OER bifunctional catalysts.

Recently, our research group also reported two ORR and OER bifunctional catalysts: (1) AGC/MnCo-LDH (see Fig. 10.1H) [9] and NGCNs (containing Ni species) (see Fig. 10.1I) [10]. The favorable 3-D porous architecture (fast ion diffusion) of MnCo-LDHs and the carrier effect of AGC (high electron conductivity) were the key contributing factors for their excellent ORR-OER electro-catalytic performances of nanocomposites [9]. The 3D NGCNs-supported atomic Ni species catalyst was also assembled into ORR and OER electrodes for electro-catalytic evaluation, and the possible synergistic effect between Ni single atom and Ni cluster or N-doped carbon and Ni in NGCNs was also suggested [10]. Electrochemical oxygen reduction reaction (ORR) and oxygen evolution reaction (OER) play an important role in the process of discharge and charging energy conversion for Li or Zn-air batteries.

10.3 Electrode materials

10.3.1 Cathode materials of metal-air battery

In the air cathode, the reported ORR and OER dual-functional electrocatalytic materials can be divided into two main categories: carbon-based material (nitrogen-doped carbon material) and transition metal-based material (Ru, Rh, Pt, and Fe, Co, Ni, and other transition metals and their compounds). Through nano-design and surface chemistry, these catalytic materials can achieve high intrinsic activity regulation. For electrocatalysts with high intrinsic activity, rapid gas, electrolyte, and electron transport are also required to obtain high apparent activity. By combining high intrinsic activity and good microstructure, the electrocatalyst of metal-air batteries can reduce the charge and discharge overpotential of the cells, so as to obtain high power density and high round-trip efficiency. Carbon materials have been widely studied as air electrode electrocatalysts and carriers of metal-air batteries due to their high conductivity, large specific surface area, and porous structure, which is beneficial to achieve high discharge capacity and rate capability. Noncarbon air electrode materials for metal-air batteries have attracted much attention in recent years: many materials, such as noble metals and transition metal oxides, are active for aprotic oxygen reduction and evolution reactions [11].

10.3.2 Anode materials of metal-air battery

In the metal anode, the nanostructures, interfacial effects, and phase balance of metal's deposition are crucial to the performance of metal-air batteries, including electrical conductivity, electrochemical activity, stability, and safety. For example, the deposition of insulated ZnO on zinc electrodes leads to the passivation of zinc, which is a key factor limiting the discharge capacity of Zn-air batteries. The optimized structure of the Zn electrode by regulating the deposition of ZnO can control the dissolution/precipitation process of Zn and ZnO, and minimize the shape change of the Zn electrode under a long time cycle. In addition, the chemical properties, interfacial structure, and stability of zinc electrodes can be adjusted by adding additives or surface coatings. Similar to the Zn dendrites, Li dendrites have clearly unfavorable degradation effects for Li-air batteries. More seriously, since Li is more active than Zn, perforation of the diaphragm and short circuits can cause serious safety problems. The performance of Li metal electrodes can be improved by using 3D Li electrodes, adjusting electrode composition, and surface coating. By controlling the current distribution and ion flow, the nucleation and deposition behavior of Li can be realized to inhibit the growth of Li dendrites. The solid electrolyte interface (SEI) formed on the surface of the Li electrode as a protective layer is beneficial to the recycling ability of Li-air batteries. Therefore, much work has been done to improve the stability and homogeneity of SEI or to build an artificial SEI to stabilize the Li electrode for Li-air batteries [11].

10.4 Applications

Li-air batteries can exhibit superior theoretical energy density (11,429 Wh kg^{-1}, based on the mass of Li metal), high specific capacity (3860 mAh g^{-1}, based on the mass of Li metal), and up to 2.96 V battery voltage. For Zn-air batteries, the theoretical energy density is 1350 Wh kg^{-1} (based on the mass of Zn metal), which is five times higher than Li-ion batteries. In addition, Zn-air batteries cost (\$10 kW^{-1} h^{-1}) s much less than Li-ion batteries (\$400 $\sim$ \$800 kW^{-1} h^{-1}). Therefore, the metal-air battery family has great potential as a next-generation electrochemical energy storage device [11]. At present, Li-air batteries can only be charged and discharged in laboratory conditions, and are still not directly applicable to phones or cars. The application of Li-air battery in segmental energy storage of the power grid is possible: using Li-air battery to store energy in the power grid during the low period, discharge in the peak period, relieve the power supply pressure of the power grid, reduce the waste of energy. The Zn-air batteries have been widely used in audiphone or hearing AID, but there are still many problems to be faced in large-scale industrial applications, such as hydrogen evolution and dendrite. Recently, a big step has been made in the large-scale application of Zn-air batteries, and the Ah-class battery soft pack design has been realized. The battery has an energy density of 460 Wh kg^{-1} or

$1389\ \text{Wh L}^{-1}$, a battery life of 6000 cycles at 25 mA cm^{-2} current density, and is flexible enough to achieve good battery performance over a wide temperature range of -20 to 80°C [12].

10.5 Summary

In this chapter, we have discussed the general features, energy storage mechanisms, and cathode and anode design principles of metal-air batteries (such as Li-air batteries and Zn-air batteries). As a promising energy device in the new generation of electronic products, electric transportation, and electric energy storage, the most outstanding advantage of metal-air battery is that they can combine high energy density metal anode with active air anode material with an open structure. The occurrence of side reactions of the metal anode and air cathode, the growth of metal dendrites, the pollution of electrolytes, and the instability of the air cathode structure are the problems that need to be solved in the application of metal-air battery.

Acknowledgments

This book was supported by the National Natural Science Foundation of China (22078071, 22272034), Natural Science Foundation of Guangdong Province (2021A1515010125, 2020A1515010344), Maoming Science and Technology Project (mmkj2020032), Guangdong Province Universities and Colleges Pearl River Scholar Funded Scheme (2019), Guangdong Basic and Applied Basic Research Foundation (2019A1515011249, 2021A1515010305), Key Research Project of Natural Science of Guangdong Provincial Department of Education (2019KZDXM010), Environment and Energy Green Catalysis Innovation Team of Colleges and Universities of Guangdong Province(2022KCXTD019), the program for Innovative Research Team of Guangdong University of Petrochemical Technology.

References

[1] J. Dahn, Electrically Rechargeable Metal-Air Batteries Compared to Advanced Lithium-Ion Batteries. Scalable Energy Storage: Beyond Lithium Ion, San Jose, CA, USA, 2009.

[2] C. Wang, J. Li, Z. Zhou, Y. Pan, Z. Yu, Z. Pei, et al., Rechargeable zinc-air batteries with neutral electrolytes: recent advances, challenges, and prospects, EnergyChem 3 (4) (2021) 100055.

[3] P.G. Bruce, S.A. Freunberger, L.J. Hardwick, J.M. Tarascon, Li$-$O$_2$ and Li$-$S batteries with high energy storage, Nature Materials 11 (1) (2012) 19$-$29.

[4] G. Girishkumar, B. McCloskey, A.C. Luntz, S. Swanson, W. Wilcke, Lithium$-$air battery: promise and challenges, The Journal of Physical Chemistry Letters 1 (14) (2010) 2193$-$2203.

[5] Y.C. Lu, B.M. Gallant, D.G. Kwabi, J.R. Harding, R.R. Mitchell, M.S. Whittingham, et al., Lithium$-$oxygen batteries: bridging mechanistic understanding and battery performance, Energy & Environmental Science 6 (3) (2013) 750$-$768.

[6] T. E Liu, J.P. Vivek, E.W. Zhao, J. Lei, N. Garcia-Araez, C.P. Grey, Current challenges and routes forward for nonaqueous lithium$-$air batteries, Chemical Reviews 120 (14) (2020) 6558$-$6625.

[7] A. Kondori, Z. Jiang, M. Esmaeilirad, M. Tamadoni Saray, A. Kakekhani, K. Kucuk, et al., Kinetically stable oxide overlayers on Mo$_3$P nanoparticles enabling lithium$-$air batteries with low overpotentials and long cycle life, Advanced Materials 32 (50) (2020) 2004028.

[8]   C.X. Zhao, J.N. Liu, J. Wang, D. Ren, J. Yu, X. Chen, et al., A $\Delta E=$ 0.63 V bifunctional oxygen electrocatalyst enables high-rate and long-cycling zinc—air batteries, Advanced Materials 33 (15) (2021) 2008606.

[9]   Z. Li, K. Xiao, C. Yu, H. Wang, Q. Li, Three-dimensional graphene-like carbon nanosheets coupled with MnCo-layered double hydroxides nanoflowers as efficient bifunctional oxygen electrocatalyst, International Journal of Hydrogen Energy 46 (69) (2021) 34239—34251.

[10] M. Yu, Z. Li, X. Liang, B. Li, C. Yu, P. Shen, N-Doped Graphene-like Carbon Nanocages Modified by Trace Nickel Species for Efficient ORR and OER Bifunctional Electrocatalyst, International Journal of Hydrogen Energy (2023).

[11] H.F. Wang, Q. Xu, Materials design for rechargeable metal-air batteries, Matter 1 (3) (2019) 565—595.

[12] S.S. Shinde, J.Y. Jung, N.K. Wagh, C.H. Lee, D. Kim, S.H. Kim, et al., Ampere-hour-scale zinc—air pouch cells, Nature Energy 6 (6) (2021) 1—13.

CHAPTER 11

Fuel cells: basic principle, electrode material, and applications

11.1 Introduction

At present, there are several fuel cell technologies: proton exchange membrane fuel cell (PEMF), phosphate fuel cell, alkaline fuel cell, molten carbonate fuel cell, and solid oxide fuel cell. PEMFCs are the most important development direction in the market due to their significant advantages in operating temperature and start-up time. Driven by policy and performance advantages, the downstream applications of PEMFC are mainly focused on transportation. The PEMFCs, as a green power plant that can replace internal combustion engine, do not depend on carbon-containing fossil energy in theory. Therefore, the development and application of PEMFCs are of great significance to achieve the national strategic goal of "peak carbon dioxide emission" and "carbon neutrality." Platinum group metals (PGMs) are irreplaceable catalyst materials for current commercial PEMFCs. Because the global reserves and production of PGM are extremely limited, PGM will be the main cost (about 40% of the total cost) when fuel cells are scaled up. Therefore, it is critical to reduce platinum loading in commercial fuel cells without compromising performance, such as the development of high-performance alloy or core-shell nanocatalysts with ultra-low platinum loading, as well as single atomic platinum electrocatalysts with 100% utilization rate of metal platinum [1]. In order to replace PGM catalysts, people have done a lot of research on non-noble metal catalysts, and the research on M-N-C (M = Fe and Co) catalysts has made a series of landmark breakthroughs, which has become the focus of attention [2].

11.2 Basic principles

Fuel cell is a chemical device that directly converts the chemical energy of fuel into electric energy, also known as electrochemical generator. Fuel cells are highly efficient because they convert the chemical energy of fuel into electricity through electrochemical reactions, which are not limited by Carnot cycle effects. When the fuel cell works, the fuel (hydrogen, methanol, ethanol, formic acid, etc.) and oxidant (oxygen) are supplied externally to react. In principle, fuel cells can generate electricity continuously under efficient cathodic and anodic catalysts as long as reactants are fed in and reaction products are removed (see Fig. 11.1A for details) [3]. Herein, hydrogen-oxygen (H_2 and O_2) PEMFCs are taken as an example to illustrate the basic structure and reaction principle of fuel cells.

Nanostructured Materials
ISBN 978-0-443-19256-2, https://doi.org/10.1016/B978-0-443-19256-2.00023-5

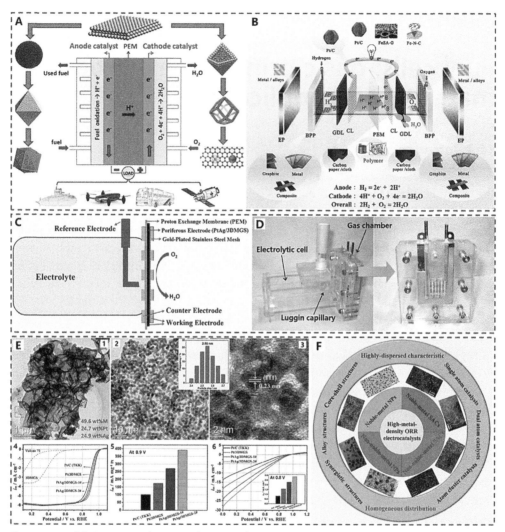

Figure 11.1 (A) Reaction schematic diagram of PEMFCs [3], (B) structural schematic diagram of PEMFCs [4], (C–E) three-electrode test system based on membrane electrode assembly (MEA) for PEMFCs [5], (F) High-metal-density oxygen reduction reaction (ORR) electrocatalysts for PEMFCs [6].

The electrode reactions (anodic H_2 oxidation and cathodic O_2 reduction reactions) are shown as follows:

$$Anodic\ reaction:\ H_2 \rightarrow 2H^+ + 2e^-$$

$$Cathodic\ reaction:\ 2H^+ + 1/2O_2 + 2e^- \rightarrow H_2O$$

$$Total\ reaction:\ H_2 + 1/2O_2 = H_2O$$

PEMFCs is a power generation device that uses hydrogen as fuel and proton exchange membrane (PEM) as electrolyte to convert chemical energy into electric energy through electrochemical reaction. The electrochemical reaction is characterized by the oxidation reaction of hydrogen input at the anode and the reduction reaction of oxygen or air input at the cathode, and the formation of water under the action of catalysts. The PEMFC has seven layers of structures, the middle is PEM, on both sides of the catalyst layer, and then outward is the gas diffusion layer (GDL), the five layers become membrane electrode (MEA), on both sides of the membrane electrode for bipolar plate, this seven-layer structure combined with the outer end plate constitutes a whole assembly, multiple battery components by stacking the fuel cell stack (see Fig. 11.1B for details) [4]. Compared with the rapid oxidation of hydrogen at anode, the high platinum loading, slow oxygen reduction kinetics, and the difficulty of oxygen mass transfer at cathode have become the key limiting factors for the cost, performance, and lifetime of membrane electrodes.

The electrocatalytic activity of cathodic oxygen reduction catalysts can be evaluated by the membrane electrode half-cells (MEHC) in a three-electrode test system (see Fig. 11.1C—E for details) [5]. Fig. 11.1C and D illustrate the schematic structure and picture of an MEHC: A poriferous electrode (carbon paper sprayed with cathodic catalysts) was bonded onto one side of a piece of PEM, and the resulting assembly was linked to an electrolytic cell in which the membrane faced the electrolyte solution. Oxygen is supplied by the gas chamber on the side of the poriferous electrode instead of the O_2-saturated electrolyte solution. Since the membrane is selective, it allows only cations, such as H^+, to pass through, and anions, such as ClO_4^-, are forbidden. Therefore, this structure of MEHC mimics the situation in a real PEMFC to a large extent, which can provide accurate and valuable parameters for the performance evaluation of cathodic oxygen reduction catalysts (Fig. 11.1E) [5].

11.3 Electrode materials

11.3.1 Cathode catalyst materials

In PEMFCs, the design of cathode "oxygen reduction" electrocatalyst is more important and complex than anode "hydrogen oxidation." The main reasons include the following two aspects: (1) The kinetics of oxygen reduction is very slow, and its exchange current density is only 1/100 of that of anodic hydrogen oxidation, which has become the restrictive step of electrocatalytic reaction of PEMFCs; (2) The process of oxygen reduction is relatively complex, involving multistep elementary steps and a variety of intermediates, which often leads to the decrease of energy conversion efficiency and the increase of oxygen reduction over-potential. Therefore, the design and development of high-performance oxygen reduction electrocatalyst are of great significance in promoting the development of PEMFCs. Electrocatalysts for cathode oxygen reduction reaction (ORR) mainly include platinum-based alloy/core-shell catalysts, synergistic-enhanced low-platinum catalysts, M-N-C transition metal catalysts, and carbon-based non-metallic catalysts. The synthesis of highly-dispersed and high-metal-density ORR electrocatalysts (e.g., nanoscale and atom-level structures) on carbon supports with strong durability is extremely desirable but remains challenging. In a recent review, we summarized the advancements in carbon-supported nanoscale and atom-level ORR electrocatalysts with high metal density (namely high loading) for PEMFCs (see Fig. 11.1F for details) [6].

Carbon-supported high-loading noble metal catalysts with nanoscale structures (e.g., Pt-based nanoparticles) are the most widely used catalysts with the best catalytic performances. Single-atom catalysts that integrate the merits of homogeneous and heterogeneous catalysts have been attracting considerable attention in recent years. The development of ORR electrocatalyst with high performance and low cost is of great strategic significance in the development of advanced energy conversion devices. In essence, Pt is still the most effective ORR electrocatalyst. However, its high price has restricted the development of PEMFCs. At present, effective measures include (1) reducing the use of Pt by optimizing the utilization of Pt catalyst, (2) reducing the use of Pt by improving the performance of Pt catalyst, and (3) developing other catalysts that can replace Pt metal. Therefore, the design direction of ORR electrocatalyst mainly includes "low-Pt electrocatalyst", "Pt-free electrocatalyst" and "non-noble-metal electrocatalyst." The low-Pt electrocatalyst can be divided into three types: (1) core-shell-structure low-Pt electrocatalyst, (2) alloy-structure low-Pt electrocatalyst, and (3) synergistic-effect low-Pt electrocatalyst (synergistic co-catalyst). The Pt-free electrocatalyst refers to other lower-price noble-metal electrocatalysts such as palladium (Pd), iridium (Ir), and silver (Ag). Non-noble-metal electrocatalyst refers to the transition metal catalyst represented by iron (Fe) and cobalt (Co), which is an alternative electrocatalyst with rich resources and low prices. These ORR electrocatalysts have their own advantages, and they are related to each other, and even complement each other in specific dimension and environment [6].

11.3.2 Anode catalyst materials

The anodic oxidation reaction of fuel cell (acidic PEMFCs and alkaline fuel cells) mainly includes hydrogen oxidation reaction (HOR), methanol oxidation reaction (MOR), ethanol oxidation reaction (EOR), and formic acid oxidation reaction (FAOR).

Platinum carbon (Pt/C) catalysts are commonly used in commercial fuel cell anodes, but they are prone to severe carbon monoxide (CO) poisoning. This makes the cheap hydrogen produced by reforming methane-containing CO molecules cannot be directly used as fuel for PEMFCs, and the CO impurity gas needs to be further purified to reach the use standard stipulated by the International Organization for Standardization (< 0.2 PPM). But the process carries a significant increase in hydrogen fuel costs for PEMFCs [7]. High-index-facet nanocrystals (such as tetrahexahedral Pt nanocrystals), alloy nanoparticles (such as PtRu alloy), and their support effects (N-doped carbon support) of anodic catalysts can improve the catalytic activity and stability of HOR and MOR (including high resistance to CO poisoning) [3]. It was found that the introduction of F atom into Pd/N-carbon catalyst could improve the environment around Pd and improve the activity and durability of the EOR reaction. The experimental results show that the introduction of F atoms builds a more N-rich Pd surface, which is conducive to EOR catalysis. In addition, the durability of the catalyst was significantly improved by inhibiting Pd migration and reducing carbon corrosion [8]. The mass activity of the atomically dispersed Rh (SA-Rh/CN) synthesized on N-doped carbon for FAOR is 28 and 67 times higher than Pd/C and Pt/C, respectively. Moreover, the SA-Rh/CN has good sintering resistance, catalytic stability, and resistance to CO toxicity [9]. Nanostructured catalysts and atomic-structured catalysts are key catalytic materials for anodic oxidation (they have their own advantages and complement each other).

11.4 Applications

Fuel cells have a history of nearly 200 years. It is estimated that by 2035, the whole hydrogen energy industry chain will bring a market capacity of five trillion yuan. The industrial chain includes manufacturing, transportation, and storage in the upstream, fuel cell reactors and systems in the midstream, and transportation and power supply in the downstream. Key applications of fuel cells include (1) portable power supply: the year-over-year growth in the portable power supply market has attracted many power supply technologies, including laptops, mobile phones, radios, and other mobile devices that require a power supply. At present, direct methanol fuel cells and PEMFC have been applied to the military individual power supply and mobile charging devices. (2) Fixed power supply: Fixed power supply includes emergency standby power supply, uninterrupted electrotherapy, independent power station in remote areas, etc. Fuel cells have played an important role in disaster relief by being used as independent power stations in many terrestrial disasters. (3) Transportation power supply: transportation power supply has always been a major inducer for clean energy technology research and development. In 2015, Toyota Motor Corporation began to sell the world's first Mirai with PEMFC as the main power supply, marking a new era in the application of fuel cell technology in automotive power [10].

11.5 Summary

In this chapter, we have discussed the general features, energy storage mechanisms, and cathode and anode electrocatalysts of PEMFCs. Fuel cell technology is considered as one of the new environmentally efficient power generation technologies in the 21st century. Particularly, the PEMFCs have shown wide application prospects due to their advantages of fast start-up speed and high energy conversion efficiency. With continuous breakthroughs in research, the PEMFCs have been used in power plants, micro-power sources. and other applications. Catalyst is the core component of fuel cell, which is mainly composed of carbon support and platinum or platinum alloy and other low platinum or non–platinum catalysts, and plays the role of catalyzing chemical reactions in the PEMFCs.

Acknowledgments

This book was supported by National Natural Science Foundation of China (22078071, 22272034), Natural Science Foundation of Guangdong Province (2021A1515010125, 2020A1515010344), Maoming Science and Technology Project (mmkj2020032), Guangdong Province Universities and Colleges Pearl River Scholar Funded Scheme (2019), Guangdong Basic and Applied Basic Research Foundation (2019A1515011249, 2021A1515010305), Key Research Project of Natural Science of Guangdong Provincial Department of Education (2019KZDXM010), Environment and Energy Green Catalysis Innovation Team of Colleges and Universities of Guangdong Province (2022KCXTD019), the program for Innovative Research Team of Guangdong University of Petrochemical Technology.

References

[1]   Z. Zhao, Z. Liu, A. Zhang, X. Yan, W. Xue, B. Peng, Y. Huang, Graphene-nanopocket-encaged PtCo nanocatalysts for highly durable fuel cell operation under demanding ultralow-Pt-loading conditions, Nature Nanotechnology (2022) 1—8.

[2]   L. Ding, T. Tang, J.S. Hu, Recent progress in proton-exchange membrane fuel cells based on metal-nitrogen-carbon catalysts, Acta Physico-Chimica Sinica 37 (2020) 2010048.

[3]   N. Tian, B.A. Lu, X.D. Yang, R. Huang, Y.X. Jiang, Z.Y. Zhou, S.G. Sun, Rational design and synthesis of low-temperature fuel cell electrocatalysts, Electrochemical Energy Reviews 1 (1) (2018) 54—83.

[4]   R. Haider, Y. Wen, Z.F. Ma, D.P. Wilkinson, L. Zhang, X. Yuan, J. Zhang, High temperature proton exchange membrane fuel cells: progress in advanced materials and key technologies, Chemical Society Reviews 50 (2) (2021) 1138—1187.

[5]   Z. Li, Y. Li, C. He, P.K. Shen, Bimetallic PtAg alloyed nanoparticles and 3-D mesoporous graphene nanosheet hybrid architectures for advanced oxygen reduction reaction electrocatalysts, Journal of Materials Chemistry A 5 (44) (2017) 23158—23169.

[6]   Z. Li, B. Li, Y. Hu, S. Wang, C. Yu, Highly-dispersed and high-metal-density electrocatalysts on carbon supports for the oxygen reduction reaction: from nanoparticles to atomic-level architectures, Materials Advances 3 (2) (2022) 779—809.

[7]   Y. Yang, F.Y. Gao, X.L. Zhang, S. Qin, L.R. Zheng, Y.H. Wang, M.R. Gao, Suppressing electron back-donation for a highly CO-tolerant fuel cell anode catalyst via cobalt modulation, Angewandte Chemie 61 (42) (2022) e202208040.

[8]   J. Chang, G. Wang, M. Wang, Q. Wang, B. Li, H. Zhou, Y. Yang, Improving Pd—N—C fuel cell electrocatalysts through fluorination-driven rearrangements of local coordination environment, Nature Energy 6 (12) (2021) 1144—1153.

[9]   Y. Xiong, J. Dong, Z.Q. Huang, P. Xin, W. Chen, Y. Wang, Y. Li, Single-atom Rh/N-doped carbon electrocatalyst for formic acid oxidation, Nature Nanotechnology 15 (5) (2020) 390—397.

[10] https://mp.weixin.qq.com/s/R1Nd6HkK-_kYuYL3NAlvNw.

CHAPTER 12

Solar cells: basic principles, electrode materials, and applications

12.1 Introduction

Under the condition of decreasing fossil fuels, facing the huge demand for energy and the increasingly serious environmental pollution problem, solar energy is an inexhaustible energy treasure house endowed by nature to human beings. A solar cell (or photovoltaic cell) is a device that directly converts light energy into electricity through a photoelectric or photochemical effect [1]. In order to develop high-efficiency and low–cost solar cells and promote the utilization of solar energy, the photovoltaic technology is constantly updated and developed, and the types of solar cell materials are also increasing. According to its material structure, solar cell materials can be divided into the following three categories: (1) silicon–based photovoltaic cells: monocrystalline silicon, polycrystalline silicon photovoltaic cells, etc; (2) thin–film photovoltaic cell: gallium arsenide, cadmium telluride, copper indium gallium selenium thin–film photovoltaic cell, etc; (3) new photovoltaic cells: new concept cells with high theoretical conversion efficiency and low-cost advantages, mainly dye-sensitized photovoltaic cells, perovskite photovoltaic cells, organic solar cells, and quantum dot solar cells [2]. The analysis and summary of the basic principle, the latest electrode materials, and the current application prospect of solar cells are of great significance to deepen readers' understanding and promote the application of solar energy conversion and utilization.

12.2 Basic principles

The basic principle of solar cells is to convert light energy directly into electricity through photoelectric or photochemical effects. Crystalline silicon solar cells based on photovoltaic effect are the mainstream, while thin-film cells based on photochemical effect are still in their infancy. Photovoltaic solar cell chips are semiconductor materials (made of P-type and N-type semiconductors) with photoelectric effect. Semiconductors tend not to conduct electricity, but if different impurities are added to them, P-type and N-type semiconductors can be made [3]. When the sunlight shines, the light energy excites the electrons in the silicon atom, and the convection of electrons (e^-) and holes (h^+) is generated, which will be attracted by N-type and P-type semiconductors, respectively, and gather at both ends affected under the built-in potential. At this time, if the external electrodes are connected, a loop is formed to generate current, which is the principle of

Nanostructured Materials
ISBN 978-0-443-19256-2, https://doi.org/10.1016/B978-0-443-19256-2.00015-6

solar cells to generate electricity (see Fig. 12.1A for details) [4]. It shows the layout of the Schottky barrier α-Si solar cell in a classic model of metal electrode and transparent conductive oxide (TCO) layer. The illustration of a Schottky barrier amorphous silicon (α-Si) solar cell demonstrates a highly doped p-type region adjacent to the Schottky

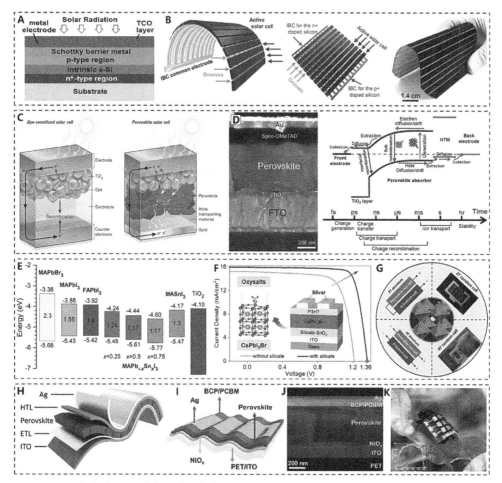

Figure 12.1 (A) The layout of the Schottky barrier α-Si solar cell [4], (B) corrugated flexible wafer-scale monocrystalline Si solar cell [5], (C) dye-sensitized solar cells and perovskite solar cells [6], (D) charge carrier dynamics of perovskite solar cells [7], (E) band gap width and position of perovskite solar cells [8], (F) oxysalts passivation effect of perovskite solar cells [9], (G) 2 and 4T perovskite/crystalline silicon stacked cells [10], (H) flexible perovskite solar cells [11], (I—K) flexible perovskite solar cells [12].

barrier high work function metal. The Schottky barrier α-Si solar cell is constructed with a metal-to-N junction rather than a P—N semiconductor junction.

In addition to the traditional electrode (metal electrode + TCO layer), the interdigitated back contact (IBC) is an efficient electrode model for solar cells. The biggest feature of IBC electrode is that the P—N junction and metal contact are on the back side of solar cells, and the front side is free from the influence of metal electrode occlusion, which has higher solar conversion efficiency. Hussain and coworkers proposed an IBC solar cell (corrugated and flexible wafer-scale crystalline-Si solar cell) with an area of 127×127 mm^2 (see Fig. 12.1B for details) [5]. In order to achieve extreme flexibility, corrugation architecture was utilized on the IBC wafers with an alternating region of thinned and rigid Si discontinuities. Each Si wafer comprises an interdigitated P and N regions on a bulk silicon wafer with $\approx 260\ \mu$m thickness. The optical image in Fig. 12.1B **(right)** of the corrugated crystalline-Si solar cell demonstrates extreme mechanical bending flexibility.

In addition to crystalline Si solar cells, dye-sensitized solar cells and perovskite solar cells (PSCs) are two hot research directions at present (see Fig. 12.1C for details) [6]. In 1991, O'Regan and Grätzel reported in Nature a dye-sensitized solar cell with a simple design, relatively low cost, and conversion efficiency of 7%. For more than 30 years, scientists have continued to develop low-cost solar cells with higher efficiency. Especially in the past 10 years, the continuous development of PSCs has achieved the conversion efficiency of more than 22%. A conventional consists of a film of titanium dioxide (TiO$_2$) nanoparticles, on which dye molecules are deposited. When sunlight hits the dye, a negatively charged electron (e$^-$) and a positively charged hole (h$^+$) are produced. The electron diffuses through the TiO$_2$ film to an electrode and is subsequently transferred to a counter-electrode. Finally, the electron enters a liquid electrolyte before recombining with the hole and being reabsorbed by the dye (see Fig. 12.1C **left** for details) [6]. In a modern solid-state PSCs, the liquid electrolyte is replaced with a hole-transporting material, and chemical compounds called perovskites act as the light harvesters. In PSCs, gold is commonly used as the counter-electrode material to further enhance the efficiency (see Fig. 12.1C **right** for details) [6]. The charge carrier dynamics play an important role in photoelectric conversion of PSCs. In view of this, the charge carrier dynamics of PSCs in the time range from ultra-fast sub-picosecond to ultra-slow second are summarized by Shi and Meng, and the physical model and mechanism are discussed in detail (see Fig. 12.1D for details) [7].

12.3 Electrode materials

After more than half a century of development, solar cells have experienced the first generation of crystal silicon solar cells, the second generation of thin film solar cells, the third generation of efficient solar cells. At present, the market is a large number of monocrystalline silicon and polycrystalline silicon solar cells. With the increasing maturity of industrial production technology, the high-efficiency cell of the laboratory is also gradually used in industrial production. In recent years, perovskite thin film solar cells have made great progress in the photoelectric conversion performance, and their photoelectric conversion efficiency exceeds that of already commercial polycrystalline silicon, cadmium telluride, and copper indium gallium selenium cells. The rapid development of perovskite cells is mainly due to their excellent semiconductor photoelectric properties, controllable crystal growth, and adjustable electronic structure (width and position of the band gap) (see Fig. 12.1E for details) [8]. SCs use organic-inorganic crystalline materials (organometallic trihalides such as $CH_3NH_3PbX_3$, usually abbreviated as $MAPbX_3$, X = I, Br, Cl) as optical absorption materials, have suitable band structures and band gap widths (corresponding to the absorption cut-off wavelength and showing good optical absorption performance).

The design of composite materials, such as oxysalt-perovskite [9] and perovskite/silicon [10] composites, can effectively improve cell performance. Yang et al. designed a strategy to passivate the interface defects of perovskite ($CsPbI_2Br$). Through theoretical calculation and experimental characterization, the interaction between a series of oxysalts (NO_3^-, SO_4^{2-}, CO_3^{2-}, PO_4^{3-} and SiO_3^{2-}) and the surface of perovskite was investigated. The mechanism of the passivation effect of different oxysalts on the surface of perovskite is revealed: the adsorption follows the principle of bond order conservation, that is, when the inner central ion of oxysalts has a weak interaction with oxygen ion, the interaction strength between oxygen ion and metal site on the surface of perovskite can be promoted (see Fig. 12.1F for details) [9]. Cheng and He reviewed and summarized the research progress of perovskite/crystalline silicon stacked solar cells. This paper describes the working principle and development history of perovskite/crystalline silicon stacked solar cells and summarizes the design of the middle connecting layer of the stacked solar cells, the device structure regulation of perovskite top cells, the optimization of perovskite film, and the way to reduce optical loss (see Fig. 12.1G for details) [10]. After several years of development, the certification efficiency of 2 and 4T perovskite/crystalline silicon stacked cells has reached 29.5% and 28.2%, respectively, which is higher than that of perovskite and crystalline silicon single junction solar cells.

Flexible energy storage and conversion devices are ideal for meeting the growing demand for wearable electronics. Flexible PSCs have attracted much attention due to their broad commercial prospects. Huang et al. found that by precisely controlling the thickness and morphology of tin dioxide (SnO_2) in the electron transport layer (ETL), flexible PSCs achieved a power conversion efficiency (PCE) of up to 19.51%, and also showed good bending resistance (about 95% of the initial PCE was retained after 6000 bends) (see Fig. 12.1H for details) [11]. Li et al. also reported an optically rechargeable lithium-ion capacitor (LIC) powered by a flexible PSC that mixes energy harvesting and storage for self-powered wearable strain sensors, thus enabling synergy of energy harvesting, storage, and utilization within a smart system, that is expected to provide significant benefits for practical self-powered wearable electronics (see Fig. 12.1I—K for details) [12]. These flexible solar cells can simultaneously achieve higher PCE, excellent mechanical properties, and robust stability, providing a wide range of opportunities for wearable, implantable electronic devices.

12.4 Applications

Solar energy is the best energy choice known to be available, clean and safe, and able to meet the future needs of mankind. In the field of batteries, solar cells also have a broad market space (for spacecraft, artificial satellites, lighthouse power supply, and civil power supply). As a potential renewable energy, solar cells have been gradually promoted on the ground, and photovoltaic power generation is an ideal way to solve the problem of electricity consumption for dispersed peasants and citizens (solar street lamp, yard lighting, water heater), with huge market potential. At present, the most widely used solar cells in the world are monocrystalline silicon solar cells, polycrystalline silicon solar cells, and amorphous silicon solar cells, which each account for about 1/3 of the market. Flexible solar cell is a kind of thin film solar cell, mainly including amorphous silicon flexible cell, copper indium gallium selenium thin film cell, organic solar cell, dye-sensitized solar cell, and so on. In recent years, with the progress and application of solar cell technology, the solar energy industry has developed rapidly. Renewables are expected to account for more than 50% of the world's total energy mix by 2040. As the main source of renewable energy, solar photovoltaic generation accounts for 20% of the world's total electricity supply. It can be seen that photovoltaic power generation will occupy an important strategic position in the future energy field, and solar cells are worthy of the name of "energy star of tomorrow" [13].

12.5 Summary

In this chapter, we have discussed the general features, energy storage mechanisms, and electrode materials of solar cells (photovoltaic cells). The solar cell is a device that converts light energy into electricity by photovoltaic effect or photochemical effect. Solar photovoltaic power generation is considered as an important way to solve the space energy supply and civil energy supply due to its advantages such as convenient utilization, environmental friendliness, simple maintenance, and long life. There are three generations of solar cell materials in the world: the first generation is crystalline silicon solar cell materials, the second generation is inorganic thin film solar cell materials, and the third generation is organic thin film solar cell materials. Solar cells on the market are generally still silicon cells, divided into monocrystalline silicon solar cells, polycrystalline silicon solar cells, and amorphous silicon solar cells. Compared with traditional silicon solar cells, film shape flexible solar cells have the advantages of light weight, softness, and low cost, which can be widely used in wearable electronic devices and integrated photovoltaic power generation. However, wearable flexible solar cells are still at the laboratory stage and are not ready for large-scale commercial use.

Acknowledgments

This book was supported by National Natural Science Foundation of China (22078071, 22272034), Natural Science Foundation of Guangdong Province (2021A1515010125, 2020A1515010344), Maoming Science and Technology Project (mmkj2020032), Guangdong Province Universities and Colleges Pearl River Scholar Funded Scheme (2019), Guangdong Basic and Applied Basic Research Foundation (2019A1515011249, 2021A1515010305), Key Research Project of Natural Science of Guangdong Provincial Department of Education (2019KZDXM010), Environment and Energy Green Catalysis Innovation Team of Colleges and Universities of Guangdong Province(2022KCXTD019), the program for Innovative Research Team of Guangdong University of Petrochemical Technology.

References

[1]   https://mp.weixin.qq.com/s/2PmrBYkkOfIXlPi6BraX5Q.
[2]   https://mp.weixin.qq.com/s/aQ33WB4pR4mHma5jo5CSoQ.
[3]   https://mp.weixin.qq.com/s/zw-t98NQN0Hl3LQonswicg.
[4]   T.D. Lee, A.U. Ebong, A review of thin film solar cell technologies and challenges, Renewable and Sustainable Energy Reviews 70 (2017) 1286−1297.
[5]   R.R. Bahabry, A.T. Kutbee, S.M. Khan, A.C. Sepulveda, I. Wicaksono, M. Nour, M.M. Hussain, Corrugation architecture enabled ultraflexible wafer-scale high-efficiency monocrystalline silicon solar cell, Advanced Energy Materials 8 (12) (2018) 1702221.
[6]   M.K. Nazeeruddin, Twenty-five years of low-cost solar cells, Nature 538 (7626) (2016) 463−464.
[7]   J. Shi, Y. Li, Y. Li, D. Li, Y. Luo, H. Wu, Q. Meng, From ultrafast to ultraslow: charge-carrier dynamics of perovskite solar cells, Joule 2 (5) (2018) 879−901.
[8]   H.S. Jung, N.G. Park, Perovskite solar cells: from materials to devices, Small 11 (1) (2015) 10−25.
[9]   Z.Q. Lin, H.J. Lian, B. Ge, Z. Zhou, H. Yuan, Y. Hou, H.G. Yang, Mediating the local oxygen-bridge interactions of oxysalt/perovskite interface for defect passivation of perovskite photovoltaics, Nano-micro Letters 13 (1) (2021) 1−14.
[10]   Y. Cheng, L. Ding, Perovskite/Si tandem solar cells: fundamentals, advances, challenges, and novel applications, SusMat 1 (3) (2021) 324−344.
[11]   K. Huang, Y. Peng, Y. Gao, J. Shi, H. Li, X. Mo, J. Yang, High-performance flexible perovskite solar cells via precise control of electron transport layer, Advanced Energy Materials 9 (44) (2019) 1901419.
[12]   C. Li, S. Cong, Z. Tian, Y. Song, L. Yu, C. Lu, Z. Liu, Flexible perovskite solar cell-driven photo-rechargeable lithium-ion capacitor for self-powered wearable strain sensors, Nano Energy 60 (2019) 247−256.
[13]   https://mp.weixin.qq.com/s/o_lNe4k6hVyfPWpWOQIGSA.

CHAPTER 13

Electrocatalysis for energy conversion and environmental protection: fundamentals

13.1 Introduction

The searching for sustainable and low-cost energy has become a key area of global in-depth research, which is crucial to the sustainable development of modern society. New energy industry technologies such as fuel cells and water electrolysis are highly anticipated, and their performance depends heavily on electrochemical conversion processes: electrochemical catalytic reactions that create and store chemical energy by breaking or forming chemical bonds [1]. In recent years, electrocatalytic water desorption of hydrogen and oxygen evolution (HER, OER) and reduction of oxygen and carbon dioxide (ORR, CO_2RR) have attracted researchers' attention as important means to solve global energy and environmental problems. However, these energy conversion processes are limited by the low efficiency and low durability of electrocatalysis. The lack of understanding of the catalytic active site and reaction mechanism also restricts the development of efficient electrocatalysts [2]. Therefore, the design of high-performance electrocatalyst and the exploration of catalytic reaction mechanism have important guiding significance for the further optimization of electrocatalytic reaction performances.

The environment treatment technology based on electrocatalysis reaction has the following advantages: (1) Without additional reagent, can avoid secondary pollution; (2) Reaction conditions are mild, and reactions can occur at room temperature and pressure; (3) It can simultaneously realize the purpose of water purification and wastewater resource utilization. Electrocatalysis includes electrocatalytic oxidation and electrocatalytic reduction: (1) Electrocatalytic oxidation: substances (such as organic molecules) lose electrons on the surface of the anode and are oxidized or active substances such as $\cdot OH$, Cl_2 produced by electrolysis are oxidized; (2) Electrocatalytic reduction: direct or indirect reduction of substances (such as heavy metal ions) on the cathode surface. In the electrocatalytic reaction system, electrocatalytic oxidation and electrocatalytic reduction exist simultaneously [3].

Nanostructured Materials
ISBN 978-0-443-19256-2, https://doi.org/10.1016/B978-0-443-19256-2.00011-9

13.2 Basic principles

13.2.1 Basic principles of electrocatalysis for energy conversion

13.2.1.1 OER and HER electrocatalytic mechanism

As a high-energy and zero-carbon energy carrier, hydrogen is considered as a promising green energy source. Electrocatalytic hydrolysis is an efficient technology for hydrogen production. Oxygen evolution reaction (OER) is the key factor (multielectron transfer process and kinetic reaction) that restricts the efficiency of the whole hydroelectricity electrolysis device. The mechanism of OER adsorption evolution involves the process of adsorption and desorption of intermediates, namely, $OH_{ads} \rightarrow O_{ads} \rightarrow OOH_{ads} \rightarrow O_{2ads}$ process. In both alkaline and acidic media, the OER mechanism consists of four steps (Eqs. 13.1–13.12) (each step is coupled to an electron) and involves multiple intermediates (OH_{ads}, O_{ads}, OOH_{ads}, and O_{2ads}). In both alkaline and acidic media, the Gibbs free energy required for the OER reaction is 4.92 eV (Eq. 13.6 or Eq. 13.12), and the Gibbs free energy required for the two intermediate steps is 3.2 eV (Eqs. 13.2 and 13.3 or Eqs. 13.9 and 13.10). The steps with high Gibbs free energies are the OER rate-determining steps (RDS).

The steps of OER primitives under alkaline conditions are as follows:

$$OH^- + * \rightarrow OH_{ads} + e^- \tag{13.1}$$

$$OH_{ads} + OH^- \rightarrow O_{ads} + H_2O + e^- \tag{13.2}$$

$$O_{ads} + OH^- \rightarrow OOH_{ads} + e^- \tag{13.3}$$

$$OOH_{ads} + OH^- \rightarrow O_{2ads} + H_2O + e^- \tag{13.4}$$

$$O_{2ads} \rightarrow O_2 + * \tag{13.5}$$

$$\text{Overall: } 4OH^- \rightarrow 2H_2O + O_2 + 4e^- \tag{13.6}$$

The steps of OER primitives under acidic conditions are as follows:

$$H_2O + * \rightarrow OH_{ads} + H^+ + e^- \tag{13.7}$$

$$OH_{ads} \rightarrow O_{ads} + H^+ + e^- \tag{13.8}$$

$$O_{ads} + H_2O \rightarrow OOH_{ads} + H^+ + e^- \tag{13.9}$$

$$OOH_{ads} \rightarrow O_{2ads} + H^+ + e^- \tag{13.10}$$

$$O_{2ads} \rightarrow O_2 + * \tag{13.11}$$

$$\text{Overall: } 2H_2O \rightarrow 4H^+ + O_2 + 4e^- \tag{13.12}$$

where the * represents the active sites on the catalyst surface, and the "ads" represents adsorbed state of intermediates (OH_{ads}, O_{ads}, OOH_{ads}, and O_{2ads}).

Under standard conditions, the thermodynamic equilibrium potential of OER is 1.23 V, but in the actual reaction process, there are unfavorable kinetic factors to hinder the reaction, and an additional potential is needed, namely, the overpotential. Usually, in the process of OER catalyzed by a metallic (M) catalyst (including noble metals and transition metals), the M-O bonding interaction has a significant role in stabilizing intermediates on the catalyst surface, which has a pronounced impact on the overall electrocatalytic efficiency. In both alkaline and acidic media, the OER reaction mechanism can be written as follows (the green arrow in the middle shows the possibility of forming oxygen, not M-OOH intermediates) (see Fig. 13.1A for details) [4].

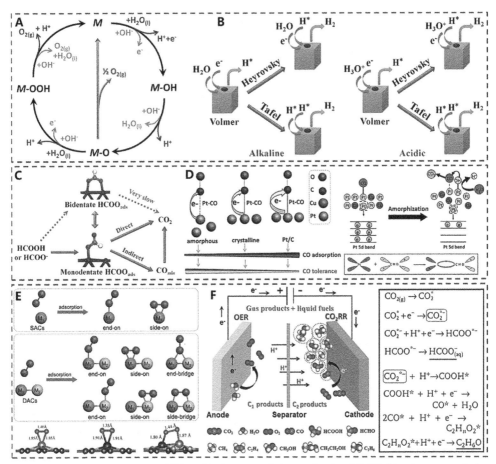

Figure 13.1 (A) OER, (B) HER, and (C) FAOR electrocatalytic mechanism [4], (D) CO tolerance and electronic effect for precious metal electrocatalysts for FAOR, EOR, and MOR [5], (E) Adsorption model of O_2 or N_2 on metal atomic site for ORR or NRR [6], (F) Schematic diagram and mechanism of CO_2RR [7].

Hydrogen evolution reaction (HER) catalytic activity is related to the adsorption-free energy of hydrogen (ΔG_{H*}). HER can occur based on Volmer-Heyrovsky mechanism or Volmer–Tafel mechanism (see Fig. 13.1B for details) [4]. In alkaline (left) or acidic (right) media, the evolution steps of HER are similar. The first step of HER is to generate H* by Volmer reaction with H_3O^+ in acidic medium and H* by reaction with H_2O in alkaline medium (see Eqs. 13.13 and 13.16). The second step is the RDS, which depends on the activity of these catalysts (see Eqs. 13.14, 13.15, 13.17, and 13.18). For example, Pt-based catalysts, Tafel reaction adsorbs H* and H* to generate H_2, while transition metal catalysts usually react with H_2O (alkaline) or H_3O^+ (acid) and H* to generate H_2. The reason for different reaction paths is that the ΔG_{H*} on Pt metal is close to zero, while the ΔG_{H*} on transition metal is very high.

The steps of HER primitives under alkaline conditions are as follows:

$$H_2O + e^- \rightarrow OH^- + H_{ads} \text{ (Volmer)} \tag{13.13}$$

$$H_{ads} + H_2O + e^- \rightarrow OH^- + H_2 \text{ (Heyrovsky)} \tag{13.14}$$

$$\text{or } 2H_{ads} \rightarrow H_2 \text{ (Tafel)} \tag{13.15}$$

The steps of HER primitives under acidic conditions are as follows:

$$H^+ + e^- + * \rightarrow H_{ads} \text{ (Volmer)} \tag{13.16}$$

$$H_{ads} + H^+ + e^- \rightarrow H_2 \text{ (Heyrovsky)} \tag{13.17}$$

$$\text{or } 2H_{ads} \rightarrow H_2 \text{ (Tafel)} \tag{13.18}$$

where the * represents the active sites on the catalyst surface, and the "ads" represents adsorbed state of intermediates (H_{ads}).

13.2.1.2 FAOR, EOR, and MOR electrocatalytic mechanism

The exploitation of formic-acid oxidation reaction (FAOR) catalysts is the key to the preparation of direct formic acid fuel cells. Currently, the widely accepted formic-acid oxidation mechanism is the so-called "dual pathway mechanism" (including direct pathway and indirect pathway) based on metal single-atom-site adsorption model (see Fig. 13.1C for details) [4]. Rather than bidentate-adsorbed formate, monodentate-adsorbed formate is the intermediate for the production of both CO_2 and adsorbed CO. The dual-atom-site bridged formate acts as a site-blocking role rather than an active intermediate. Generally, the noble metal Pd-catalyzed formic-acid oxidation favors the direct pathway (see Eqs. 13.19 and 13.20), where the rate-determining step is the dissociation of HCOOH. While a very high overpotential is required to remove CO_{ads} toxic species (that is easily adsorbed on crystal surface of noble metal Pt) for the indirect pathway formic-acid oxidation (see Eqs. 13.21 and 13.22).

$$HCOOH + * \rightarrow HCOO_{ads} + H^+ + e^- \tag{13.19}$$

$$HCOO_{ads} \rightarrow CO_2 + H^+ + e^- \tag{13.20}$$

$$HCOOH + * \rightarrow CO_{ads} + H_2O \tag{13.21}$$

$$CO_{ads} + HO_{ads} \rightarrow CO_2 + H^+ + 2e^- \tag{13.22}$$

where the * represents the active sites on the catalyst surface, the "ads" represents adsorbed state of intermediates (CO_{ads} and HO_{ads}).

Ethanol oxidation reaction (EOR) and methanol oxidation reaction (MOR) are important anodic reactions for direct ethanol fuel cells (DEFCs) and direct methanol fuel cells (DMFCs), respectively. Palladium (Pd)-based nanostructures have attracted much attention as electrocatalysts for EOR in DEFCs due to their inherent high catalytic activity in alkaline solutions and lower cost relative to the Pt. The widely accepted catalytic mechanism for EOR in alkaline medium are as follows (see Eqs. 13.23−13.26):

$$M + OH^- \rightarrow M\text{-}OH_{ads} + e^- \tag{13.23}$$

$$M + C_2H_5OH \rightarrow M\text{-}(C_2H_5OH)_{ads} \tag{13.24}$$

$$M\text{-}(C_2H_5OH)_{ads} + 3OH^- \rightarrow M\text{-}(CH_3CO)_{ads} + 3H_2O + 3e^- \tag{13.25}$$

$$M\text{-}(CH_3CO)_{ads} + M\text{-}OH_{ads} \rightarrow M\text{-}CH_3COOH + M \tag{13.26}$$

where the M represents the active Pd metal sites on the catalyst surface, the "ads" represents adsorbed state of intermediates ($C_2H_5OH_{ads}$, CH_3CO_{ads}, and OH_{ads}).

Platinum (Pt)-based alloy nanostructures are efficient electrocatalysts for the MOR in DMFCs. The CO stripping test showed that the amorphous CuPt alloy catalyst has the weakest CO adsorption and strongest CO tolerance, and the highest MOR activity and stability among the three catalysts (see Fig. 13.1D left for details) [5]. It is revealed that the successful avoidance of CO poisoning is mainly responsible for the excellent MOR performances of the Pt-based alloy catalysts. If the CO tolerance ability of the alloy is further improved by adjusting the amorphous level and atomic ratio of M atoms, the MOR activity of the Pt-M alloyed catalyst would be further improved. It is noteworthy that the decrease of d electron density of Pt atom may have high activity for the oxidation of adsorbed water (see Eq. 13.27). In addition, based on the so-called "bifunctional mechanism," Pt-OH formed by water oxidation contributes to the removal of CO intermediates (see Eq. 13.28). Based on the above reasons, it can be concluded that the unique interaction between Pt and Cu atoms in the amorphous CuPt alloy greatly reduces the d electron density of Pt atom, enhances the oxidation ability of adsorbed water and the removal ability of CO, and thus improving the activity and stability of MOR (see Fig. 13.1D right for details) [5].

$$M\text{-}OH_2 \rightarrow M\text{-}OH_{ads} + H^+ + e^- \tag{13.27}$$

$$M\text{-}CO_{ads} + M\text{-}OH_{ads} \rightarrow 2M + CO_2 + H^+ + e^- \tag{13.28}$$

where the M represents the active Pt metal sites on the catalyst surface, the "ads" represents adsorbed state of intermediates (OH_{ads}, and CO_{ads}).

13.2.1.3 ORR, NRR, and CO₂RR electrocatalytic mechanism

Oxygen reduction reaction (ORR) electrocatalysts are essential for a variety of efficient energy conversion applications, such as fuel cells and metal-air batteries. In order to accelerate the ORR kinetics, a catalyst with high activity and stability at the cathode is required. The ORR follows a multielectron reaction mechanism in which oxygen molecules are reduced to H_2O by either a direct four-electron or two-electron pathway. In the two-electron pathway, oxygen molecules are first reduced to peroxide (H_2O_2) and then further reduced to H_2O. Oxygen molecules can be reduced to form water through direct "four-electron mechanism" (taking metal Pt as an example) (see Eqs. 13.29–13.32):

$$2\,Pt + O_2 \rightarrow 2\,Pt\text{-}O \tag{13.29}$$

$$2\,Pt\text{-}O + 2H^+ + 2e^- \rightarrow 2\,Pt\text{-}OH \tag{13.30}$$

$$2\,Pt\text{-}OH + 2H^+ + 2e^- \rightarrow Pt + 2H_2O \tag{13.31}$$

The total reaction is

$$O_2 + 4H^+ + 4e^- \rightarrow 2H_2O \quad E = 1.23 \text{ V vs. SHE } (25°C) \tag{13.32}$$

(ii) Oxygen molecule can also be reduced by "two-electron mechanism," that is, two electrons can be obtained to be reduced to hydrogen peroxide (see Eqs. 13.33 and 13.34):

$$O_2 + 2H^+ + 2e^- \rightarrow H_2O_2 \quad E = 0.68 \text{ V vs. SHE } (25°C) \tag{13.33}$$

The intermediate product H_2O_2 can be further reduced to water:

$$H_2O_2 + 2H^+ + 2e^- \rightarrow 2H_2O \quad E = 1.77 \text{ V vs. SHE } (25°C) \tag{13.34}$$

From the above reaction process, it can be seen that the theoretical potential of four electron process is 1.23 V (Eq. 13.32), while that of two-electron process is only 0.68 V (Eq. 13.33). The electron transfer number of the four-electron process is twice that of the two-electron process, that is, the energy is converted twice. Therefore, in the design of electrocatalyst for cathode ORR, we should strive to be conducive to the four-electron process, so as to improve the catalytic efficiency of oxygen reduction process and the whole cell system [8].

Electrochemical nitrogen reduction reaction (NRR) is considered an ideal alternative to the Haber-Bosch process, which can produce ammonia from nitrogen and water under ambient conditions using the catalysis of electrocatalysts. However, due to the strong nonpolar bond of N_2 and the competitive HER, the yield and Faradaic efficiency of electrochemical ammonia synthesis are seriously reduced. In order to solve these problems, it is urgent to develop efficient catalysts to reduce the N_2 activation barrier and limit the occurrence of side reactions of hydrogen evolution [9]. For the ORR or NRR electrocatalytic mechanism, O_2 or N_2 molecules have different adsorption modes at metal sites (top and bridge sites), which can change the adsorption condition of molecules on the metal atoms, promote the activation of inert species, and thus affect the catalytic reaction (see Fig. 13.1E for details) [6]. Green and orange balls represent two metal atoms, and blue balls represent the adsorbed molecules, such as O_2 or N_2. The reactant molecule can only bond to the only metal atom at single-atom sites. However, at dual-atom sites, one atom of the reactant molecule can bond to two metal atoms, or two of them can bond to two metal atoms separately. Thus, moderate adsorption is more likely by increasing the way reactant molecules bond to the catalyst.

Electrochemical energy conversion (such as CO_2 reduction reaction (CO_2RR)) powered by renewable energy is a cost-effective, environmentally friendly way to convert unwanted substances into valuable chemicals and fuels. For the electrocatalytic reduction of CO_2 into formic acid (HCOOH) and/or ethanol (CH_3CH_2OH) liquid fuels, their selectivity (often accompanied by CO, CH_4, and C_2H_4 gas products), and Faraday efficiency (accompanied by severe hydrogen evolution competition reaction) are still difficult to meet the actual production requirements (see Fig. 13.1F left for details) [7]. Compared with crystalline materials, amorphous materials usually have a large number of low coordination atoms, so there are a lot of defects and then produce more catalytic active sites to improve the electrochemical performances. For example, amorphous Cu catalyst (a-Cu) has a large electrochemical active area and strong CO_2 adsorption capacity, and amorphous atomic structure can be used to promote CO_2RR to produce C_1 and C_2 liquid fuels with high utilization value (see Fig. 13.1F right for details) [7]. The preparation of multicarbon (C_{2+}) liquid fuel by electro-catalytic CO_2RR is challenging, which is mainly limited by the stability of reaction intermediates and their subsequent C-C coupling.

13.2.2 Basic principles of electrocatalysis for environmental protection

Electrochemical water treatment technology is a kind of green water treatment technology, its main principle is to use the potential difference to regulate the electron flow direction, so that the pollution substances in the electrode interface or solution complete the degradation or transformation process, in order to achieve water purification. Electrochemical water treatment technology has unique advantages over traditional water treatment technology: clean, flexible, simple, and controllable. In recent years, electrochemical water treatment technology has gradually become a research hotspot in the field of water pollution treatment. Electrocatalytic oxidation treatment of organic pollutant is a special advanced oxidation technology (the power supply includes Dc constant current or constant voltage and pulse constant current or constant voltage). The critical principle of this technology is to make the strong oxidizing substances (represented by hydroxyl ·OH radical) produced on the surface of the anode (see Fig. 13.2A for details) [10]. The ·OH radical is fully contacted and reacted with the organic molecules in the solution, so that the organic molecules are gradually oxidized and decomposed into carbon dioxide and water. It is worth noting that the contact of this strong oxidizing material

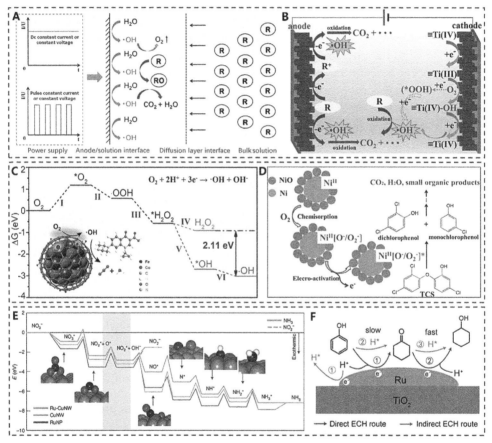

Figure 13.2 (A) Electrocatalytic oxidation treatment of organic pollutant [10], (B) combination of anodic oxidation and electric Fenton [11], (C) Reaction paths and Gibbs free energies for electrocatalytic reduction of molecular oxygen [12], (D) Electrically assisted Catalytic wet air oxidation (CWAO) [13], (E) electro-catalytic conversion of NO_3^- into NH_3 [14], (F) Electrocatalytic hydrogenation (ECH) of phenol [15].

with organic molecules is crucial. This contact can only be achieved by the migration of organic molecules to the electrode/solution interface, thus making the mass transfer process the most limiting step in electrocatalytic oxidation.

Electrochemical anodic oxidation (AO) technology has been recognized as a promising wastewater treatment technology due to its strong oxidation performance and environmental compatibility. However, due to side reactions such as hydrogen evolution on the cathode and oxygen evolution on the anode, the energy consumption of pollutant removal by this technology is high. Electric Fenton (EF) technology combined with AO can not only produce •OH for pollutant degradation, but also improve the current efficiency. Wang et al. successfully fabricated a Ti^{3+} self-doped TiO_2 nanotube array (Ti^{3+}/TNTAs) electrode and used it as both cathode and anode for wastewater treatment, and systematically investigated the cooperative electrocatalytic process between EF and AO (see Fig. 13.2B for details) [11]. Recently, Zhao et al. proposed using molecular oxygen as the green oxidant and 3-electron selective electrocatalytic reduction to generate hydroxyl radicals in situ, which can be used for rapid and efficient removal of environmental pollutants. The Gibbs free energies corresponding to the reaction steps I, II, and III are 1.18, 0.57, and −0.58 eV, respectively, indicating that the adsorption of molecular oxygen on the electrode surface is the most rapid step in the whole electrocatalytic process (see Fig. 13.2C for details) [12]. This study breaks through the classical concept of using hydrogen peroxide as oxidant in the traditional Fenton method, without adding hydrogen peroxide and ferric salt reagent, and provides a new method for green and efficient water treatment technology.

Catalytic wet air oxidation (CWAO) uses a catalyst to promote oxygen oxidation under mild conditions and can save energy better than traditional wet air oxidation. The NiO is a promising oxygen carrier that adsorbs O_2 from the air and provides reactive oxygen species for oxidizing organic molecules. Although the high-efficiency catalyst greatly reduces the operating temperature of CWAO, its practical application at room temperature is still a great challenge. To this end, the anodic electric field provides a possible method to assist the CWAO process at room temperature. Recently, Sun et al. reported an electrically assisted (ECWAO) process using partially oxidized nickel (Ni@NiO)-loaded graphite felt (GF) as a catalytic anode (see Fig. 13.2D for details) [13]. In ECWAO, oxygen is transferred from O_2 molecules to triclosan (TCS) molecules by chemisorption of oxygen on NiO. Chemisorbed oxygen species are activated by electrooxidation reactions in an electric field, allowing them to oxidize TCS at room temperature. NiO in the Ni@NiO/GF electrode provides the active site to accommodate chemisorbed oxygen species, and Ni ensures the conductivity of the catalyst during the electroactivation reaction. This method has shown broad effectiveness and good stability at room temperature for the deep oxidation of various organic pollutants.

As a rich source of nitrogen, nitrate ions (NO_3^-) are widely present in industrial wastewater and groundwater, which is one of the causes of global nitrogen cycle imbalance.

The electro-catalytic conversion of high-concentration NO_3^- ion into NH_3 in waste-water is expected to alleviate the industrial demand for traditional ammonia production, which not only helps to solve environmental problems but also may reduce energy consumption. Wang and colleagues reported a high-performance Ru-dispersed Cu nano-wire electrocatalyst, which was able to provide an industrial-grade NO_3^- reduction current density of 1 A cm^{-2} while maintaining a high NH_3 Faraday production efficiency of up to 93% (see Fig. 13.2E for details) [14]. The DFT calculations showed that the highly dispersed Ru atoms could be used as active nitrate reduction sites, while the surrounding Cu atoms could inhibit the main side reaction, hydrogen evolution.

Electrocatalytic hydrogenation (ECH), as a kind of organic substances conversion technology with low energy consumption and mild conditions, has attracted more and more attention in the field of energy and environmental catalysis. Recently, Gu et al. constructed an efficient ECH system by preparing nano-Ru/TiO$_2$ catalytic electrodes to convert and remove high-concentration phenol (1–10 mM) in wastewater (see Fig. 13.2F for details) [15]. It was confirmed that cyclohexanol was the final product of the reaction, which could achieve rapid recovery and greatly reduce the toxicity of the product. This study is expected to provide technical support for the treatment and resource utilization of highly concentrated phenol-containing wastewater and provide theoretical guidance for the construction of a new energy-saving, low-carbon, and resource-reuse wastewater treatment model.

13.3 Catalysis materials

Faced with the energy crisis and environmental pollution caused by the depletion of nonrenewable fossil fuels, there is an urgent need to develop efficient technologies for chemical and energy conversion. However, most of these technologies rely on various electrocatalysis processes. Therefore, it is very important to design efficient electrocatalysts with high selectivity and rapid reaction rate. At present, noble metal-based catalysts (Pt, Pd, Au, Ag, Ru, Fh, Ir, etc.) are considered as the most advanced type of catalysts due to their unique intrinsic characteristics and irreplaceable catalytic activity. However, the serious scarcity and high cost of precious metals seriously hinder their large-scale production. The design of unique nanostructures (such as alloys and core-shell structures) and monoatomic noble metal catalysts can effectively improve the catalytic activity and metal utilization, thereby reducing the material cost [16].

Due to the high cost and scarcity of noble metal catalysts, nonnoble metal catalysts have become the focus and hotspot in the field of electrocatalysis. Electrocatalysts based on inexpensive transition metal group elements such as Fe, Co, Ni, and Cu (including metal elements, oxides, nitrides, sulfides, and phosphates) have potential advantages in terms of cost and performance and are expected to be alternative electrocatalysts for various electrocatalysis applications (including energy and the environment fields) [17]. Electrocatalytic nanocarbons (EN), defined as any form of chemically modified graphite carbon nanocarbon, are a class of metal-free electrocatalysts for energy conversion and environmental remediation. Although graphite nanocarbon is chemically inert, the catalytic activity of EN is introduced through defects and heteroatom doping, both metallic and nonmetallic doping. In general, defects are induced by heat or radiation treatment of the existing graphitic carbon, while doping atoms are introduced by the reaction of carbon precursors containing heteroatoms at high temperatures [18].

13.4 Applications

Energy and environment are the basis of the development of modern society and the frontier of technological change. By the traction of great target of "emission peak, carbon neutralization," the safe access to clean energy and improvement of ecological environment management is an important issue of scientific development in China. Electrocatalysis can not only produce clean energy efficiently but also realize the recycling of wastewater and exhaust gas, which is the key to solve the existing energy and environmental problems [19]. In recent years, the electrocatalytic technology for energy and environment has made great progress. In particular, the green hydrogen production by electrolytic water, fuel cells, electrocatalytic conversion and utilization of greenhouse gases, and AO degradation of pollutants has ushered in significant development opportunities, and some important original breakthroughs have been made. The clean and efficient energy storage and conversion (or environmental treatment and purification) can be realized through these sustainable electrocatalytic reactions, which have attracted great attention to address the energy and environmental problems caused by the overuse of fossil fuels [20].

13.5 Summary

In this chapter, we have discussed the fundamentals, electrocatalytic mechanisms, and electrode materials of different electrocatalytic reactions in the fields of energy conversion and environmental protection. For the electrochemical energy conversion, electrocatalytic mechanisms of OER, HER, FAOR, EOR, MOR, ORR, NRR, and CO_2 reduction reaction (CO_2RR) are introduced and summarized in detail. The basic principles and case studies of several environmental electrocatalysis applications are also discussed: Electrocatalytic oxidation treatment of organic pollutant, combination of AO and EF, electrically assisted CWAO, electro-catalytic conversion of NO_3^- into NH_3, and ECH of phenol. In general, the function of electrocatalysts is dominated by surface properties.

We should pay more attention to the chemistry and structure of the electrode surface, which can essentially improve the research quality in the field of electrocatalysis (including energy and environmental applications).

Acknowledgments

This book was supported by National Natural Science Foundation of China (22078071, 22272034), Natural Science Foundation of Guangdong Province (2021A1515010125, 2020A1515010344), Maoming Science and Technology Project (mmkj2020032), Guangdong Province Universities and Colleges Pearl River Scholar Funded Scheme (2019), Guangdong Basic and Applied Basic Research Foundation (2019A1515011249, 2021A1515010305), Key Research Project of Natural Science of Guangdong Provincial Department of Education (2019KZDXM010), Environment and Energy Green Catalysis Innovation Team of Colleges and Universities of Guangdong Province(2022KCXTD019), the program for Innovative Research Team of Guangdong University of Petrochemical Technology.

References

[1] Z. Fang, P. Li, G. Yu, Gel electrocatalysts: an emerging material platform for electrochemical energy conversion, Advanced Materials 32 (39) (2020) 2003191.

[2] X. Li, H.Y. Wang, H. Yang, W. Cai, S. Liu, B. Liu, In situ/operando characterization techniques to probe the electrochemical reactions for energy conversion, Small Methods 2 (6) (2018) 1700395.

[3] Y. Xiao, Y. Chen, G. Wang, W. Shi, L. Sun, Y. Chen, et al., Advances in electrocatalytic treatment of refractory wastewater, Industrial Water Treatment 40 (6) (2020) 1−6.

[4] Z. Li, B. Li, M. Yu, C. Yu, P. Shen, Amorphous metallic ultrathin nanostructures: a latent ultra-high-density atomic-level catalyst for electrochemical energy conversion, International Journal of Hydrogen Energy 47 (63) (2022) 26956−26977.

[5] Y. Zhao, J. Liu, C. Liu, F. Wang, Y. Song, Amorphous CuPt alloy nanotubes induced by $Na_2S_2O_3$ as efficient catalysts for the methanol oxidation reaction, ACS Catalysis 6 (7) (2016) 4127−4134.

[6] R. Li, D. Wang, Superiority of dual-atom catalysts in electrocatalysis: one step further than single-atom catalysts, Advanced Energy Materials 12 (9) (2022) 2103564.

[7] W. Zhang, Y. Hu, L. Ma, G. Zhu, Y. Wang, X. Xue, et al., Progress and perspective of electrocatalytic CO2 reduction for renewable carbonaceous fuels and chemicals, Advanced Science 5 (1) (2018) 1700275.

[8] Z. Li, B. Li, Y. Hu, S. Wang, C. Yu, Highly-dispersed and high-metal-density electrocatalysts on carbon supports for the oxygen reduction reaction: from nanoparticles to atomic-level architectures, Materials Advances 3 (2) (2022) 779−809.

[9] K. Chu, Y. Luo, P. Shen, X. Li, Q. Li, Y. Guo, Unveiling the synergy of O-vacancy and heterostructure over MoO_3-x/MXene for N_2 electroreduction to NH_3, Advanced Energy Materials 12 (3) (2022) 2103022.

[10] H. Xu, J. Jordan, Z. Xu, H. Guo, S. Chen, X. Xu, et al., Application of electrocatalytic oxidation technology in organic wastewater treatment, Industrial Water Treatment 41 (3) (2021) 1−9.

[11] K. Wang, K. Zhao, X. Qin, S. Chen, H. Yu, X. Quan, Treatment of organic wastewater by a synergic electrocatalysis process with Ti^{3+} self-doped TiO_2 nanotube arrays electrode as both cathode and anode, Journal of Hazardous Materials 424 (2022) 127747.

[12] F. Xiao, Z. Wang, J. Fan, T. Majima, H. Zhao, G. Zhao, Selective electrocatalytic reduction of oxygen to hydroxyl radicals via 3-electron pathway with FeCo alloy encapsulated carbon aerogel for fast and complete removing pollutants, Angewandte Chemie International Edition 60 (18) (2021) 10375−10383.

[13] M. Sun, Y. Zhang, S.Y. Kong, L.F. Zhai, S. Wang, Excellent performance of electro-assisted catalytic wet air oxidation of refractory organic pollutants, Water Research 158 (2019) 313−321.

[14] F.Y. Chen, Z.Y. Wu, S. Gupta, D.J. Rivera, S.V. Lambeets, S. Pecaut, et al., Efficient conversion of low-concentration nitrate sources into ammonia on a Ru-dispersed Cu nanowire electrocatalyst, Nature Nanotechnology 17 (2022) 1—9.

[15] Z. Gu, Z. Zhang, N. Ni, C. Hu, J. Qu, Simultaneous phenol removal and resource recovery from phenolic wastewater by electrocatalytic hydrogenation, Environmental Science & Technology 56 (7) (2022) 4356—4366.

[16] F. Zhang, Y. Zhu, Q. Lin, L. Zhang, X. Zhang, H. Wang, Noble-metal single-atoms in thermocatalysis, electrocatalysis, and photocatalysis, Energy & Environmental Science 14 (5) (2021) 2954—3009.

[17] B. Ma, H. Zhao, T. Li, Q. Liu, Y. Luo, C. Li, et al., Iron-group electrocatalysts for ambient nitrogen reduction reaction in aqueous media, Nano Research 14 (3) (2021) 555—569.

[18] E.J. Askins, M.R. Zoric, M. Li, Z. Luo, K. Amine, K.D. Glusac, Toward a mechanistic understanding of electrocatalytic nanocarbon, Nature Communications 12 (1) (2021) 1—15.

[19] https://mp.weixin.qq.com/s/3VNxIdO5O3a9g4TgI4yCmA.

[20] Y. Li, H. Wang, C. Priest, S. Li, P. Xu, G. Wu, Advanced electrocatalysis for energy and environmental sustainability via water and nitrogen reactions, Advanced Materials 33 (6) (2021) 2000381.

CHAPTER 14

Photocatalysis energy conversion and environmental protection: fundamentals

14.1 Introduction

Solar energy is a kind of clean and pollution-free renewable energy, most of the energy on earth comes from solar energy. Photocatalysis is an efficient way to use light energy to transform substances, which is a chemical reaction of substances under the action of light and catalyst. Photocatalyst is a chemical contact agent that can play a catalytic role under the excitation of photons. Photocatalysis is a new interdisciplinary research field, such as catalytic chemistry, photochemistry, semiconductor physics, materials science, energy science, and environmental science. Photocatalysis was discovered by professor Akira Fujima in 1967 when he irradiated a single crystal of titanium oxide (TiO_2) into water with ultraviolet light and found that water was decomposed into oxygen and hydrogen. In 1972, Fujima published this phenomenon in Nature (Electrochemical photolysis of water at a semiconductor electrode, Nature 1972, 238, 37−38, has been cited more than 30,000 times), ushering in a new era of multiphase photocatalysis [1]. In 1976, Carey et al. found that TiO_2 could effectively decompose polychlorinated biphenyls under ultraviolet light irradiation, which was considered as the creative work of photocatalysis technology in the elimination of environmental pollutants, and further promoted the research boom of photocatalysis [2]. Photocatalytic technology draws on the photosynthesis of green plants and simulates this process artificially, to achieve efficient utilization and conversion of solar energy, to convert light energy into clean fuels or chemicals, and to achieve environmental purification. After decades of development, photocatalysis has been widely used in hydrogen production from water decomposition, pollutant degradation, heavy metal ion reduction, air purification, CO_2 reduction, antibacterial, self-cleaning, and other aspects, which is one of the hot research fields in the field of heterogeneous catalysis [3].

14.2 Basic principles of photocatalysis for energy conversion

Using solar photocatalysis to decompose water to produce hydrogen and storing solar energy in the form of hydrogen energy is one of the ideal ways to solve the energy problem. The hydrogen production system by photocatalytic decomposition of water

Nanostructured Materials
ISBN 978-0-443-19256-2, https://doi.org/10.1016/B978-0-443-19256-2.00008-9

is usually composed of semiconductor photocatalysts (such as CdS, TiO_2, and $g-C_3N_4$), electron transport agent or medium that absorbs light energy, and cocatalyst that catalyzes chemical reaction (carried on semiconductor surface or dispersed in reaction medium). Among them, the use of co-catalyst can effectively reduce the activation energy of the reaction and accelerate the rate of chemical reaction. At present, most co-catalysts for hydrogen production are precious metals (such as Pt, Ru, Rh, and Pd), which have high hydrogen production activity. However, their high price and low abundance limit the large-scale application of these materials in photocatalytic hydrogen production. Therefore, the development of efficient, stable, and inexpensive co-catalysts for hydrogen production, from nonprecious metals (such as MoC_x, NiS, and CoP), is a key scientific issue to realize the practical application of photocatalytic decomposition technology in hydrogen production from water [4]. As the hydrogen production active sites, these co-catalysts can not only effectively capture and activate H^+ ions on the surface of the semiconductor photocatalysts, but also greatly reduce the hydrogen evolution barrier. For an excellent hydrogen evolution co-catalyst, the electron configuration of the active site must match that of the adsorbed H atoms (H_{ads}). In this case, according to Sabatier's principle, the binding strength of the active site-HADs should be neither too strong nor too weak [5].

In general, the semiconductor-based photocatalytic reactions rely heavily on three reaction processes: light harvesting, charge transport and separation, and surface catalytic reactions. For photocatalytic H_2 production on semiconductors using cocatalysts, there are four processes in the photocatalytic process: (1) light harvesting, (2) separation of photogenerated carriers, (3) transfer of charge carriers between the bulk and the interface (or between the semiconductor and the cocatalyst), and (4) charge carriers capturing by cocatalyst and surface electrocatalytic reactions (see Fig. 14.1A for details) [6]. Improving the separation of photogenerated carriers (that is, preventing recombination of electrons and holes) and accelerating the surface reaction kinetics are more critical to improving the overall efficiency of photocatalytic hydrogen production than increasing light harvesting by narrowing the bandgap of semiconductors.

Compared with single co-catalyst, the introduction of dual co-catalysts (oxidation/reduction co-catalyst) can not only achieve electron and hole extraction from the surface of photocatalyst but also promote the synergistic effect between dual co-catalysts to promote more charge carriers to the corresponding co-catalyst sites (raise the utilization ratio of solar energy). The surface of the dual co-catalysts has more catalytic sites, lower reaction over-potential and reactant adsorption energy, and higher product selectivity. According to the latest reports, the configurations of oxidation/reduction co-catalysts are mainly divided into randomly supported and spatially separated supported types (see Fig. 14.1B for details) [7]. The spatial separation supported type can be subdivided into inner and outer loading types based on core-shell structure, hetero plane loading types based on single crystal, tip and side wall loading types based on one-dimensional structure,

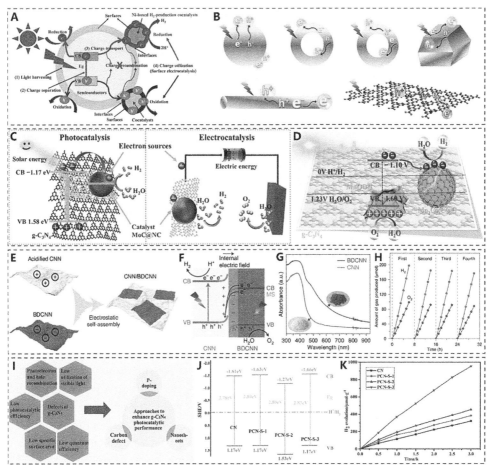

Figure 14.1 (A) Photocatalytic H_2 production process [6], (B) oxidation/reduction dual cocatalysts [7], (C) the relationship between photocatalysis and electrocatalysis [8], (D) mechanism of photocatalytic whole hydrogen and oxygen production [9], (E−H) Z-type g-C_3N_4 for photocatalytic whole hydrogen and oxygen production [10], (I−K) P-dopped g-C_3N_4 for efficient photocatalytic hydrogen production [11].

and center and edge loading types based on two-dimensional material. The integration of oxidation/reduction dual co-catalysts is mainly used in several important photocatalytic reactions such as total water decomposition hydrogen production, hydrogen production coupled with organic conversion, CO_2 reduction, oxygen reduction, etc.

In fact, the photocatalyst of whole hydrogen and oxygen production can be regarded as a microelectrode with redox capacity, where the conduction band with photoelectrons (e^-) is equivalent to the electrocatalytic cathode (the electrode where the reduction reaction occurs, $H_2O \rightarrow H_2$), and the valence band with photoholes (h^+) is equivalent to the electrocatalytic anode (the electrode where the oxidation reaction occurs, $H_2O \rightarrow O_2$) (see Fig. 14.1C for details) [8]. The potential difference between valence band and conduction band can be considered as the voltage difference between two electrodes (including theoretical potential and over-potential). In other words, the photogenerated electrons are equivalent to electrons in electrocatalysis (participating in cathodic reduction reactions), and photogenerated holes are equivalent to electrically catalyzed electron-deficient media (participating in anodic oxidation reactions). Therefore, in the photocatalytic process, the role of hydrogen evolution reaction (HER) cocatalyst is similar to that in the electrocatalytic process (reducing the cathodic activation energy and over-potential). Similarly, the oxygen evolution reaction (OER) cocatalyst plays a similar role as it does in electrocatalysis (reducing the anodic activation energy and over-potential).

Fig. 14.1D shows the charge transfer mode of g-C_3N_4 supported with Mn_2Co_2C@C (HER cocatalyst) and MnOOH (OER cocatalyst) and the mechanism of photocatalytic total water decomposition by Fang and coworkers [9]. Under light irradiation, electrons in the valence band of g-C_3N_4 are excited to the conduction band of g-C_3N_4. The photoelectrons excited to the conduction band of g-C_3N_4 are subsequently transferred to Mn_2Co_2C@C to participate in the HER. At the same time, the photogenerated holes in the valence band of g-C_3N_4 are transferred to MnOOH to participate in the OER, because MnOOH can improve the activity of oxygen evolution. In addition, the spatial separation loading of HER cocatalyst and OER cocatalyst ensures the separation of incompatible photocatalytic oxidation and reduction active sites, promotes the separation of photogenerated electrons and holes and promotes the redox reaction of water molecules. Therefore, the g-C_3N_4 modified with Mn_2Co_2C@C and MnOOH dual cocatalyst has an excellent photocatalytic activity of hydrogen production by whole water decomposition.

Fig. 14.1E−H shows the charge transfer mode and photocatalytic performance of B-doped N-deficient g-C_3N_4 nanosheets (BDCNN) and acidified CNN (Z-scheme heterostructures) for photocatalytic overall water splitting by Shen and coworkers [10]. In order to develop a Z-type water decomposition system, two core requirements must be met: One is to determine the photocatalyst with suitable energy band structure for H_2 and O_2 production, and the other is to realize effective charge transfer between the two photocatalysts through the formed Z-type heterostructure interface. The ultrathin BDCNN and acidified CNN were designed and synthesized as photocatalysts for HER and OER, respectively. Then, through strong intermolecular interaction, 2D/2D polymer Z-type heterostructures were formed by electrostatic self-assembly for photocatalytic total water decomposition. Considering that the relatively large energy gap

(~ 2.72 eV) of acidified CNN limits the absorption of visible light, BDCNN with narrow band gap is therefore used as HER catalyst to combine with another BDCNN as OER catalyst, which further improves the performance of photocatalytic total water hydrolysis. The photocatalytic activity of the synthesized 2D/2D Z-type g-C_3N_4 nanosheets heterostructure to hydrolysate was greatly improved.

Fig. 14.1I—K shows the band structure diagram and photocatalytic performance of P-doped C-deficient g-C_3N_4 nanosheets for efficient photocatalytic hydrogen production by Li and coworkers [11]. The CB potential of P-doped samples is all negative the reduction potential of proton (0 eV), demonstrating that this condition is favorable to promote the process of hydrogen colliding and producing hydrogen molecules. At the same time, the band gap of the catalysts synthesized with a different quality ratio of P was apparently broader than that without doping, and the band gap of PCN—S-3 was broadest hence has a better photocatalytic performance. Highly efficient P-doped g-C_3N4 nanosheets with the high photocatalytic activity of 318 μmol/h/g, 2.9 times higher than that of pure g-C_3N_4, were prepared by a facile, eco-friendly, and scalable thermal treatment strategy (calcinating the mixture of g-C_3N_4 and NaH_2PO_2). This study paves a new avenue, which is simple, environment-friendly, and sustainable, to synthesize highly efficient P doping g-C_3N_4 nanosheets for solar energy conversion.

14.3 Basic principles of photocatalysis for environmental protection

Because the photocatalyst is mostly semiconductor material, so the default photocatalysis is semiconductor photocatalysis. Different from conductors or insulators, the band structure of semiconductors is discontinuous. The region between the valence band filled with electrons and the empty conduction band is called the band gap. The energy difference between the highest valence band and the lowest conduction band is the band gap width, which is generally represented by E_g. The photocatalytic process can be simplified into the following steps: (1) When the incident light energy hv is not less than the band gap width E_g, the electron (e^-) of valence band (VB) absorbs light energy and jumped to the conduction band (CB), and the VB produces hole (h^+) at the same time. (2) The generated e^- and h^+ migrate to the semiconductor surface respectively under the action of electric field or diffusion. (3) The e^- with reducing ability and h^+ with oxidizing ability induce the redox reactions for the substances adsorbed on the semiconductor surface, such as pollutant degradation, water decomposition to produce hydrogen, and so on [12]. Because there are some crystal defects and surface dangling bonds on nanomaterials, which play the role of capturing e^- and h^+ and preventing them from recombining, which is beneficial to generate effective redox potential. Through electron acceptor A and electron donor B, strong oxidizing species are generated, such as superoxide radical ($O_2^-\cdot$) and hydroxyl radical ($OH\cdot$). $OH\cdot$ and O_2^- which can oxidize organic pollutants into CO_2, H_2O, and other inorganic small molecules (see Fig. 14.2A for details) [13].

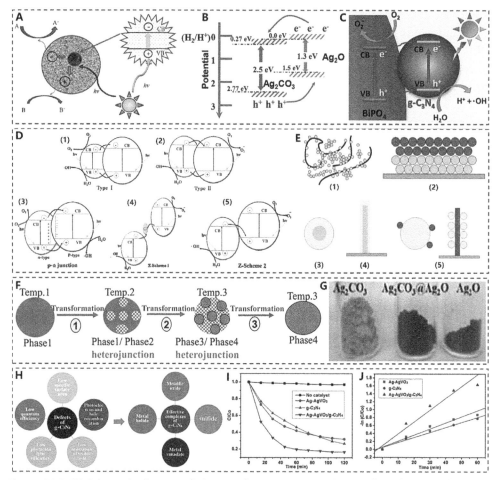

Figure 14.2 (A) Schematic diagram of photocatalysis process [13], (B) Interface diagram of Ag₂CO₃/Ag₂O heterojunction [14], (C) Interface diagram of g-C₃N₄/BiPO₄ heterojunction [15], (D) Schematic diagram of five types of heterojunction systems [16], (E) Schematics of heterojunction dimension structure [17], (F) Schematic diagram of semiconductor phase transition in the construction of heterojunctions [16], (G) Picture of Ag₂CO₃/Ag₂O heterojunction [18], (H−J) Performance of Ag−AgVO₃/g-C₃N₄ heterojunction [19].

The formation of heterojunction could largely promote the electron/hole pair separation, resulting in highly photocatalytic activity and stability. The Ag-based semiconductors as promising visible light-driven photocatalysts have aroused much interesting due to their strong visible light responsibility. The band gap energies of Ag_2CO_3 and Ag_2O were 2.5 and 1.3 eV, respectively; the potentials of Ag_2CO_3 valence band (VB) and conduction band (CB) were 2.77 and 0.27 eV, respectively; the potentials of Ag_2O VB and CB were 1.5 and 0.2 eV (see Fig. 14.2B for details) [14]. In this Ag_2O/Ag_2CO_3 heterojunction, Ag_2O has more negative CB and VB than Ag_2CO_3. Under visible light irradiation, the photoproduced electrons on Ag_2O can quickly move to Ag_2CO_3 surface. At the same time, the photoproduced holes on Ag_2CO_3 surface can transfer to Ag_2O surface, thus increasing the separation efficiency of electrons and holes for each other. The photocatalytic activity of Ag_2O/Ag_2CO_3 for the degradation of methyl orange was 67 and 31 times than that of Ag_2CO_3 and Ag_2O, respectively. Novel heterojunction architectures made up of $g-C_3N_4$ quantum dots/$BiPO_4$ nanocrystals were also synthesized as a visible light-induced photocatalyst for efficient degradation of methyl orange (see Fig. 14.2C for details) [15]. The efficient separation and transport of photogenerated electron-hole pairs at the $g-C_3N_4/BiPO_4$ results in greatly enhanced photocatalytic activity and stabilization.

The construction of heterojunction can effectively enhance the photocatalytic activity and improve the stability of the material. These heterojunction materials can be classified into two types (I and II) junctions (1—2) based on the relative positions of the two semiconductor bands, and into P—N junction (3) and Z-types (I and II) junctions based on different electron transfer paths (see Fig. 14.2D for details) [16]. When different semiconductors, such as P-type (holes as majority carriers) or N-type (electrons as majority carriers), form hetero-phase junctions by close contact, a potential difference will be established between the two sides of the junctions due to differences in their energy bands and other properties. The existence of spatial potential difference enables photogenerated carriers to inject charged particles from one semiconductor energy level to another, thus promoting the separation of electrons and holes and enhancing the efficiency of photocatalysis. The in situ growth of heterojunction can be controlled by the nanostructures or surface morphologies. Nanoscale heterogeneity includes (1) mixed type, (2) laminated type, (3) core-shell type, (4) coaxial type, (5) surface dispersion type (see Fig. 14.2E for details) [17]. The motion patterns of the electrons and holes generated by photoexcitation are dependent on the crystallization and surface state of the materials.

The phase transition of semiconductor is an efficient strategy for design of heterojunction photocatalysts. Semiconductor phase transitions usually occur in a stepwise manner due to the control of thermodynamics and phase transition dynamics. When the temperature of the system rises to temperature 1, the first phase transition occurs in the semiconductor. By controlling the phase transition rate, a two-phase coexistence system can be obtained. Since the phase transition occurs inside the catalyst, the heterogeneous structures of phases 1 and 2 can be formed in close contact, and the heterogeneous structures of crystalline phases 2 and 3 or crystalline phases 3 and 4 can also be formed (see Fig. 14.2F for details) [17]. Once the heterogeneous structure is formed, the potential difference between the two semiconductor crystal phases with energy level matching will be generated, which will establish the internal electric field, accelerate the separation of photogenerated electrons and holes, and enhance the activity and stability of the photocatalytic reaction. The $Ag_2CO_3@Ag_2O$ heterostructure obtained by the Ag_2CO_3 phase transition shows obvious color changes of different samples, which proved that the constructed $Ag_2CO_3@Ag_2O$ had a matching energy level structure (see Fig. 14.2G for details) [18].

At present, graphitic carbon nitride (g-C_3N_4) is considered as a kind of potential photocatalyst, which stands out in many photocatalysts. A new type of Ag−$AgVO_3$/ g-C_3N_4 surface plasmon heterostructure photocatalyst has been synthesized by hydrothermal method for the catalytic degradation of antibiotics under visible light (see Fig. 14.2H−J for details) [19]. The catalytic effect and degradation rate of Ag−$AgVO_3$/g-C_3N_4 heterostructure are obviously better than that of g-C_3N_4 and Ag−$AgVO_3$. The degradation reaction rate constants of Ag−$AgVO_3$/g-C_3N_4 heterostructure were 0.0298 min, 2.4 and 2.0 times that of g-C_3N_4 (0.0125 min) and Ag−$AgVO_3$ (0.0152 min), respectively. At 120 min, the degradation rate of heterostructure reached 83.6%. The excellent photocatalytic performance is mainly due to the enhancement of optical absorption and effective separation efficiency of photo-generated carriers.

14.4 Catalytic materials

The semiconductor photocatalytic materials include metal oxides, metal sulfides, other metal compounds, organic substances, and elemental semiconductors. The metal oxides include TiO_2, Fe_2O_3, WO_3, ZnO, Bi_2O_3, In_2O_3, SnO_2, Cu_2O,and so on. The CdS and MoS_2 are two representative materials in the application of sulfides in the field of photocatalysis. They have two-dimensional layered structure and adjustable energy band. When they change from multilayer to single-layer, the band gap widens, and the optical and electrical properties will also change. Bismuth halooxide BiOX (X = Cl, Br, I) material has a unique layered structure. The built-in electric field formed between $[Bi_2O_2]_2^+$ layer and X-layer contribute to the effective separation of electron-hole pairs, prolongs the life of photogenerated carriers, and improves its photocatalytic activity. $BiVO_4$, Bi_2WO_6, Bi_2MoO_6, Ag_3PO_4 and Ag_2CrO_4 have also been widely studied for their visible light catalytic properties. The g-C_3N_4, as a nonmetallic semiconductor photocatalyst, has a suitable band gap width, can respond to visible light, its chemical stability, thermal stability are good. In addition, metal-organic frame materials (MOFs), conjugated microporous polymers (CMPs) and covalent organic frame materials (COFs) have also been used in the field of photocatalysis. Red P has the properties of P-type semiconductor. Under the Pt as co-catalyst and visible light, red P can decompose H_2O into H_2. The α-S(S8) is a visible light-responsive element semiconductor photocatalytic material, which can degrade organic molecules and decompose water under ultraviolet light or visible light [20].

14.5 Applications

The photocatalytic applications and directions include water pollution treatment, water decomposition for hydrogen production, the CO_2 reduction, air purification, antibacterial, and organic synthesis. Compared with traditional water pollution treatment methods, photocatalytic method is green and environmentally friendly, without secondary pollution. In addition to common dyes, such as methylene blue (MB), Rhodamine B (RhB), methyl orange (MO), other colorless pollutants, such as phenol, bisphenol A(BPA), antibiotics, and pesticides can be degraded. In addition, photocatalysis can also reduce toxic heavy metal ions in water, such as Cr^{6+}, Pt^{4+}, Au^{3+}, to low-price ions, and reduce their toxicity. Photocatalysis can be used to decompose water into H_2 and O_2, and hydrogen energy is used to replace fossil energy, which is environmentally friendly and low cost. However, the efficiency of hydrogen production is still relatively low, and there is still a long way to go before the actual industrial application. With the increasing concentration of CO_2 in the atmosphere, the greenhouse effect becomes more and more obvious. Photocatalytic technology is also used to reduce CO_2 to methane, methanol, formic acid, and other organic compounds, which have high application value. Pollutants contained in the air mainly include nitrogen oxides (NO_2, NO, etc.), sulfur oxides (SO_2, SO_3, etc.), various volatile organic compounds (toluene, benzene, xylene, acetaldehyde, formaldehyde, etc.). Photocatalysis as a new green technology, low cost, wide application, further shows a broad application prospect in air purification [20].

14.6 Summary

In this chapter, we have discussed the fundamentals, photocatalytic mechanisms, and photocatalytic materials of different photocatalytic reactions in the fields of energy conversion and environmental protection. Usually, in the visible light photocatalytic reaction, photocatalyst is a semiconductor that can capture light energy and convert visible light into chemical energy. Using this technology has promoted the development of many important researches, such as photocatalytic water decomposition, organic matter oxidation, CO_2 reduction, and solar energy harvesting. Cocatalyst can effectively improve the activity and stability of semiconductor catalysts: improve the efficiency of semiconductor charge separation, reduce the activation energy of H_2 and O_2 generation to inhibit photocorrosion, and inhibit the reverse reaction. We emphasize the importance of establishing structure—activity relationship between nanomaterials and photocatalytic activity, providing guidance for achieving high performance photocatalytic reactions in the energy and environmental fields.

Acknowledgments

This book was supported by National Natural Science Foundation of China (22078071, 22272034), Natural Science Foundation of Guangdong Province (2021A1515010125, 2020A1515010344), Maoming Science and Technology Project (mmkj2020032), Guangdong Province Universities and Colleges Pearl River Scholar Funded Scheme (2019), Guangdong Basic and Applied Basic Research Foundation (2019A1515011249, 2021A1515010305), Key Research Project of Natural Science of Guangdong Provincial Department of Education (2019KZDXM010), Environment and Energy Green Catalysis Innovation Team of Colleges and Universities of Guangdong Province (2022KCXTD019) the program for Innovative Research Team of Guangdong University of Petrochemical Technology.

References

[1] A. Fujishima, K. Honda, Electrochemical photolysis of water at a semiconductor electrode, Nature 238 (5358) (1972) 37—38.

[2] J.H. Carey, J. Lawrence, H.M. Tosine, Photodechlorination of PCB's in the presence of titanium dioxide in aqueous suspensions, Bulletin of Environmental Contamination and Toxicology 16 (6) (1976) 697—701.

[3] H. Kisch, Semiconductor Photocatalysis: Principles and Applications, John Wiley and Sons, 2015.

[4] L. Tian, S. Min, Y. Lei, S. Chen, F. Wang, Vanadium carbide: an efficient, robust, and versatile cocatalyst for photocatalytic hydrogen evolution under visible light, Chemical Communications 55 (48) (2019) 6870—6873.

[5] D. Gao, J. Xu, L. Wang, B. Zhu, H. Yu, J. Yu, Optimizing atomic hydrogen desorption of sulfur-rich NiS1+x cocatalyst for boosting photocatalytic H2 evolution, Advanced Materials 34 (6) (2022) 2108475.

[6] R. Shen, J. Xie, Q. Xiang, X. Chen, J. Jiang, X. Li, Ni-based photocatalytic H2-production cocatalysts2, Chinese Journal of Catalysis 40 (3) (2019) 240—288.

[7] B. Qiu, M. Du, Y. Ma, Q. Zhu, M. Xing, J. Zhang, Integration of redox cocatalysts for artificial photosynthesis, Energy and Environmental Science 14 (2021) 5260—5288.

[8] X. Zhou, Y. Tian, J. Luo, B. Jin, Z. Wu, X. Ning, X. Zhou, MoC quantum dots@N-Doped-Carbon for low-cost and efficient hydrogen evolution reaction: from electrocatalysis to photocatalysis, Advanced Functional Materials (2022) 2201518.

[9] X. Zhou, J. Li, X. Cai, Q. Gao, S. Zhang, S. Yang, Y. Fang, In situ photo-derived MnOOH collaborating with Mn2Co2C@ C dual co-catalysts boost photocatalytic overall water splitting, Journal of Materials Chemistry A 8 (33) (2020) 17120—17127.

[10] D. Zhao, Y. Wang, C.L. Dong, Y.C. Huang, J. Chen, F. Xue, L. Guo, Boron-doped nitrogen-deficient carbon nitride-based Z-scheme heterostructures for photocatalytic overall water splitting, Nature Energy 6 (4) (2021) 388—397.

[11] Q. Lin, Z. Li, T. Lin, B. Li, X. Liao, H. Yu, C. Yu, Controlled preparation of P-doped g-C3N4 nanosheets for efficient photocatalytic hydrogen production, Chinese Journal of Chemical Engineering 28 (10) (2020) 2677—2688.

[12] B. Jing, C.W. Chow, C. Saint, Recent developments in photocatalytic water treatment technology, Water Research 44 (10) (2010) 2997—3027.

[13] Li Z., He W., Wu Z., Huang Z., Cheng H., & Zhou J. Preparation and photocatalytic performance test of bismuth molybdate nanosheets. Chemistry Education, 42(4), 69-72.

[14] J. Li, W. Fang, C. Yu, W. Zhou, Y. Xie, Ag-based semiconductor photocatalysts in environmental purification, Applied Surface Science 358 (2015) 46—56.

[15] Z. Li, B. Li, S. Peng, D. Li, S. Yang, Y. Fang, Novel visible light-induced g-C3N4 quantum dot/ BiPO4 nanocrystal composite photocatalysts for efficient degradation of methyl orange, RSC Advances 4 (66) (2014) 35144—35148.

[16] K. Yang, X. Li, C. Yu, D. Zeng, F. Chen, K. Zhang, H. Ji, Review on heterophase/homophase junctions for efficient photocatalysis: the case of phase transition construction, Chinese Journal of Catalysis 40 (6) (2019) 796—818.

[17] H.S. YU, X. QUAN, Nano-heterojunction photocatalytic materials in environmental pollution controlling, Progress in Chemistry 21 (0203) (2009) 406—418.

[18] C. Yu, G. Li, S. Kumar, K. Yang, R. Jin, Phase transformation synthesis of novel Ag2O/Ag2CO3 heterostructures with high visible light efficiency in photocatalytic degradation of pollutants, Advanced Materials 26 (6) (2014) 892—898.

[19] D. Chen, B. Li, Q. Pu, X. Chen, G. Wen, Z. Li, Preparation of Ag-AgVO3/g-C3N4 composite photo-catalyst and degradation characteristics of antibiotics, Journal of Hazardous Materials 373 (2019) 303—312.

[20] https://mp.weixin.qq.com/s/55ToMvcs5vWC51l4p23Ang.

CHAPTER 15

Thermocatalysis for energy conversion and environmental protection: fundamentals

15.1 Introduction

Catalysis is the soul of chemistry, and catalysis is the engine of the chemical industry. Catalyzed technological innovation underpins the basic needs of modern humans for food, clothing, shelter, and transportation. Chemical industry catalysis plays a key role in solving the problems of food, energy, and the environment. Industrial catalysis based on thermocatalysis is the science and technology of utilizing the principle of catalysis and the chemical industry to achieve large-scale production of chemicals [1]. There are many kinds of catalysts and various classification methods, which can be classified according to the state, purpose, and also according to the use industry. According to the field of use of catalysts, industrial catalysts are divided into four categories: chemical fertilizer catalysts, oil refining catalysts, petrochemical catalysts, and environmental catalysts. In the new energy system, the green and efficient preparation of hydrogen has attracted extensive attention in both industry and academia [2]. The vast majority of industrial hydrogen is currently produced through coal gasification and steam methane reforming, both of which require significant amounts of energy and result in significant carbon dioxide emissions. Methanol steam reforming is considered an alternative to conventional hydrogen production from coal and methane due to its mild conditions and low carbon footprint [3]. On the other hand, catalytic oxidation technology based on thermocatalysis is less affected by changes in environmental conditions and has a high oxidation capacity, which can deal with most refractory organic pollutants, so it has attracted more and more attention in pollutant treatment [4]. In general, thermocatalysis shows broad prospects in the production of traditional energy and green hydrogen energy. At the same time, thermocatalysis also has important value in environmental protection and treatment.

15.2 Basic principles
15.2.1 Basic principles of thermocatalysis for energy conversion
15.2.1.1 Water gas shift (WGS) reaction
Water gas conversion (WGS) reaction ($CO + H_2O \rightarrow CO_2 + H_2$) provides an important way to simultaneously extract hydrogen from water and purify CO. Its combination with steam reforming reaction is the main industrial technology for cheap hydrogen

Nanostructured Materials
ISBN 978-0-443-19256-2, https://doi.org/10.1016/B978-0-443-19256-2.00026-0

production at present. At the same time, with the development of the hydrogen economy, the hydrogen fuel cell has become an important new energy application platform. In order to prevent the toxicity of a small amount of carbon monoxide (CO) in hydrogen fuel to fuel cell catalyst, a water gas conversion reaction can be used to purify hydrogen fuel [5]. The H_2 production efficiency of the traditional WGS catalyst is low, which cannot meet the needs of the effective integration of the low-temperature hydrogen fuel cell system. It is of great scientific significance and practical value to develop a new generation of low-temperature WGS catalysts. Recently, Shi and coworkers constructed a bifunctional carbide-supported gold (Au) catalyst Au/α-MoC$_{1-x}$: cubic phase α-MoC$_{1-x}$ active dissociation of H_2O at low temperature by taking advantage of the good thermal stability of transition metal carbide and strong interaction with the dispersed Au metal. The dispersed Au metal promoted the adsorption and activation of low-temperature CO, completed the renormalization reaction at the interface, and generated H_2. The catalyst can greatly reduce the temperature of the water-gas conversion reaction to 120°C, and the CO conversion rate is more than 95%, which effectively solves the problem that a high conversion rate and high reaction rate cannot be achieved at low temperature (see Fig. 15.1A for details) [5].

At present, the WGS reaction is the main method used to produce H_2 on a large scale in the industry. However, the WGS process usually needs to be carried out under the conditions of high temperature (180—250°C) and high pressure (1.0—6.0 MPa). In addition to harsh reaction conditions, H_2 produced by WGS reaction often contains about 1%—10% CO residue and reaction products such as CO_2 and CH_4, so further separation and purification are required for downstream application. In view of this, Deng et al. combined the traditional WGS reaction with an electrochemical method and proposed a new concept of low-energy electrochemical WGS (EWGS) reaction at room temperature to produce high-purity hydrogen: 99.99% high-purity H_2 can be prepared under mild conditions (25°C and 0.1 MPa) and the Faradaic efficiency of H_2 production is close to 100% (see Fig. 15.1B for details) [6]. Through the design of the catalyst and the optimization of the electrode structure, the initial potential of the EWGS reaction was reduced to 0 V, which was significantly lower than the theoretical anode potential of water electrolysis (1.23 V). Compared with traditional WGS reactions and water electrolysis reactions, EWGS has the advantages of low energy consumption and high energy efficiency. Therefore, the EWGS process provides a new idea with an attractive prospect for the production of high-purity H_2.

15.2.1.2 Methanol steam reforming
The on-site H_2 production by methanol reforming provides a scheme for H_2 energy storage and transportation and hydrogen supply to hydrogen fuel cells. Among many catalytic materials, Cu-based catalysts are widely used because of their low price, high activity, and low carbon monoxide selectivity. There have been many studies on the mechanism of methanol steam-reforming reactions catalyzed by Cu-based catalysts. In

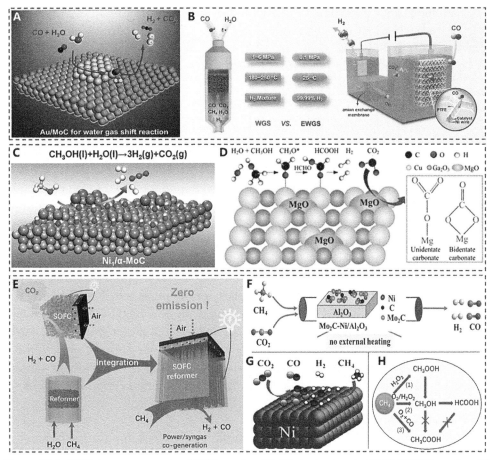

Figure 15.1 (A) Water gas conversion (WGS) reaction [5], (B) electrochemical WGS (EWGS) reaction [6], (C) methanol steam reforming [7], (D) sorption-enhanced steam reforming of methanol [8], (E) integrated SOFC methane reforming reactor [9], (F) methane dry reforming on MO_2C-Ni/Al_2O_3 [10], (G) methane dry reforming on Ni [11], (H) reaction pathways of direct methane oxidation into chemicals [12].

the early stage, it was believed that methanol first decomposed to produce CO and then produced CO_2 through the WGS reaction. The specific reaction mechanism is shown in Eqs. (15.1) and (15.2).

$$CH_3OH \rightarrow 2H_2 + CO \tag{15.1}$$

$$CO + H_2O \rightarrow CO_2 + H_2 \tag{15.2}$$

With the gradual deepening of research on the reaction mechanism of Ni_1/α-MoC catalyst, researchers put forward another mechanism, that is, methanol and steam first generate CO_2 and H_2, and then part of CO_2 and H_2 generates CO through inverse WGS reaction, as shown in Eqs. (15.3) and (15.4) (see Fig. 15.1C for details) [7]:

$$CH_3OH + H_2O \rightarrow 3H_2 + CO_2 \tag{15.3}$$

$$CO_2 + H_2 \rightarrow CO + H_2O \tag{15.4}$$

The sorption-enhanced steam reforming of methanol (SE-SRM) is a promising method for producing high-purity H_2. Adding CO_2 adsorbent in the reaction chamber, the adsorption reaction of CO_2 and SRM is coupled to promote the forward H_2 production reaction and the WGS reaction (Le Charlier principle). A recent study confirmed that the methanol conversion (99.70%) could be achieved at 200°C, and the H_2 selectivity was 100% for Ga doping of Cu–MgO. The density functional theory (DFT) calculation based on $Cu(111)Ga_2O_3(202)MgO(200)$ model shows that the Ga doping increases the adsorption energy of methanol and carbon dioxide, promotes the activation of methanol, and increases the absorption capacity of carbon dioxide (see Fig. 15.1D for details) [8]. On the one hand, Ga doping can promote the dispersion of active component Cu and strengthen the interaction between Cu and support, and improve the catalytic activity and stability. On the other hand, Ga and Mg have similar ionic radii, which is expected to build more defect sites on the surface of MgO crystals through ion substitution between Ga and Mg ions, and improve the CO_2 adsorption performance of MgO.

15.2.1.3 Methane steam reforming

Methane steam reforming is a relatively mature technology for the preparation of hydrogen for industrial applications. It has been in industrial application for more than 90 years since 1926 and has been continuously developed and perfected. The chemical reactions of methane steam reforming are shown in Eqs. (15.5) and (15.6):

$$CH_4 + H_2O \rightarrow CO + 3H_2 \ (\Delta H = +206 \text{ kJ mol}^{-1}) \tag{15.5}$$

$$CO + H_2O \rightarrow CO_2 + H_2 \ (\Delta H = -41 \text{ kJ mol}^{-1}) \tag{15.6}$$

The above reaction is carried out by a catalyst at high temperature (750–920°C) and high pressure (2–3 MPa). There are two main types of catalysts used in the methane steam reforming process: nonnoble metal catalysts (mainly Ni) and noble metal catalysts (such as Pt), usually with MgO, Al_2O_3 as the supports.

Solid oxide fuel cells (SOFC) can generate electricity directly from hydrocarbon fuels, such as natural gas (CH_4). Recent studies have shown that the traditional catalyst bed reactor integrated into the anode support body can achieve the material and thermal coupling between methane reforming reaction and fuel electrochemical oxidation reaction, which can achieve efficient and stable electrical symbiosis (see Fig. 15.1E for details) [9]. The methane reforming reactor and SOFC integrate to realize the double coupling of material and heat between the methane reforming reaction and fuel electro-chemical oxidation reaction, carry out efficient electrical symbiosis, and achieve zero-emission natural gas power generation.

15.2.1.4 Methane dry reforming

Hydrogen production by methane dry reforming is the reaction between methane (CH_4) and carbon dioxide (CO_2) reforming, as shown in Eq. (15.7):

$$CH_4 + CO_2 \rightarrow 2CO + 2H_2 \ (\Delta H = +247 \text{ kJ mol}^{-1}) \tag{15.7}$$

CH_4 and CO_2 are typical greenhouse gases, and the process of reforming CH_4 and CO_2 to syngas (CO)/hydrogen (H_2) is a technological route of large-scale comprehensive utilization of carbon and hydrogen sources and transformation of greenhouse gases. Hydrogen production from natural gas by CO_2 reforming has the following advantages: CH_4 and CO_2 are used at the same time, and the carbon emission reduction benefit is significant.

At present, nickel-based catalysts are mainly used for methane dry reforming reactions, but they are prone to carbon deposition and sintering at high temperatures (>700°C), leading to catalyst deactivation. Recently, Shi and coworkers prepared MO_2C-Ni/Al_2O_3 composite bifunctional catalyst by mechanical mixing method, and used plasma coupled with MO_2C-Ni/Al_2O_3 catalyst for methane dry reforming reaction (see Fig. 15.1F for details) [10]. Through a series of characterizations, the role of β-MO_2C promoter in the structure, discharge properties, and reaction performance of the catalyst was revealed. Lunkenbein observed the dynamic evolution of the surface structure of the catalyst at temperatures up to 900°C by using a temperature-controlled reaction cell with an implanted environmental scanning electron microscope cavity, which was correlated with the product characteristics analysis results of the online mass spectrometry detector (see Fig. 15.1G for details) [11]. The active phase characteristics of methane dry reforming reaction catalyzed by Ni catalyst and its dynamic evolution with temperature and reaction atmosphere were revealed for the first time.

15.2.1.5 Methane partial oxidation

The mechanism of partial catalytic oxidation of methane is relatively complex, and two mechanisms are widely accepted at present. One is an indirect synthesis of syngas, as shown in Eqs. (15.8) and (15.9), and the other is directly made into syngas, as shown in Eq. (15.10) [13]:

$$0.5CH_4 + O_2 \rightarrow 0.5CO_2 + H_2O \ (\Delta H = -445.15 \text{ kJ mol}^{-1}) \tag{15.8}$$

$$CH_4 + CO_2 \rightarrow 2CO + 2H_2 \ (\Delta H = +247 \ kJ \ mol^{-1}) \tag{15.9}$$

$$CH_4 + 0.5O_2 \rightarrow CO + 2H_2 \ (\Delta H = -36 \ kJ \ mol^{-1}) \tag{15.10}$$

In recent years, the direct oxidation of methane to produce high value-added chemicals (such as methanol and other C_1 (formic acid) or even C_2 (acetic acid) oxygenates) in the presence of hydrogen peroxide (H_2O_2), oxygen (O_2), and other oxidants have attracted extensive attention due to its mild reaction conditions and environmental friendliness (see Fig. 15.1H for details) [12]. However, the direct conversion of methane to fine chemicals is a major challenge in catalysis, which usually requires high-energy input to overcome the reaction energy barrier, compared to the partial oxidation of methane to produce syngas.

15.2.2 Basic principles of thermocatalysis for environmental protection

15.2.2.1 Environmental catalysis and nanomaterials

Environmental catalysis based on thermocatalysis includes the catalytic science and technology used in the following processes: (1) elimination of pollutants already produced (narrow definition of environmental catalysis); (2) reduce the production of harmful substances in the process of energy conversion (such as natural gas catalytic combustion, diesel catalytic desulfurization, etc.); (3) Conversion of waste into useful things (such as recycling of methane and carbon dioxide). In a broad sense, any green catalytic process involving the reduction of pollutant emissions can belong to the category of environmental catalysis [14]. Noble metal nanomaterials are not only important chemical catalysts in the field of thermal catalysis because of their unique physicochemical properties, but are also widely used in the field of environmental catalysis (catalytic oxidation of organic pollutants or VOCs and catalytic reduction of nitrogen oxides) (see Fig. 15.2A for details) [15]. Different pollutants and catalytic methods have different requirements for noble metal nanocatalysts. The properties of noble metal nanocatalysts mainly depend on their size, composition, and support parameters. Based on this, many researchers are committed to improving the catalytic degradation effect of pollutants by regulating the size, composition, and carrier of noble metal nanomaterials.

15.2.2.2 Thermocatalysis degradation of organic pollutant

In recent years, great progress has been made in the degradation of organic pollutants by thermocatalysis in a dark atmosphere without adding other chemicals and energy. Compared with other advanced oxidation technologies, this method has the advantages of simple operation and cost-saving in the treatment of organic wastewater. Chen et al. systematically summarized the mechanisms of various thermocatalysis treatments of organic wastewater under a dark atmosphere, including the following four aspects (see Fig. 15.2B for details) [16].

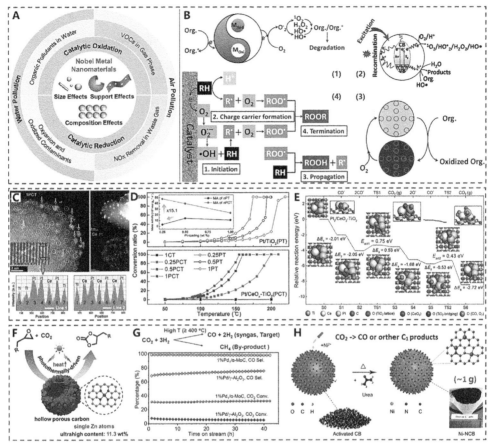

Figure 15.2 (A) Thermocatalysis of noble metal nanomaterials [15], (B) thermocatalysis treatment of organic wastewater [16], (C—E) thermocatalysis PROX of CO [17,18], (F) cycloaddition reaction of CO_2 on epoxide [19], (G) RWGS reactions for CO_2 conversion [20], (H) chemical reduction of CO_2 [21].

(1) Diagram of surface electron transport mechanism of organic pollutant degradation: adsorbed organic pollutants inject their electrons into the catalyst through the catalyst conduction band or redox pair, thereby obtaining the captured electrons and partially oxidized organic pollutant cations. The trapped electrons then react with adsorbed oxygen to generate reactive oxygen species, which lead to the degradation of organic pollutants.

(2) Diagram of jump mechanism of degradation of organic pollutants: When the catalyst is subjected to an energy equal to or higher than the band gap width, its valence band electrons are excited to the conduction band, leaving holes in the valence band. Holes can directly oxidize water to form hydroxyl radicals. Conduction band electrons can react with adsorbed oxygen to generate reactive oxygen species, achieving thermal catalytic degradation of organic molecules.

(3) Diagram of Mars-Van Krevelen mechanism of organic pollutant degradation: The mechanism includes oxidation of organic pollutants by catalyst lattice oxygen and regeneration of oxygen in the catalyst. For this process, catalysis is similar to an oxygen conduction medium.

(4) Diagram of free radical chain autoxidation for degradation of organic pollutants: organic matter interacts with a catalyst to generate R•, H^+, and reduced state catalysts. The reduced state catalyst can be regenerated by reacting with adsorbed oxygen to generate HO•, and HO• can react with organic matter to obtain R• and water. R• can react with oxygen to form ROO•, which initiates the radical chain autoxidation reaction.

Due to the complex and changeable characteristics of the reaction system, it is necessary to systematically study the thermal catalytic reaction in a dark atmosphere to clarify the intrinsic catalytic sites. Investigating the generation and extinction of reactive oxygen species, electron transport, and the interaction between target pollutants/intermediates and catalysts, can accurately understand the reaction process, explain the reaction mechanism, and promote the application prospect of thermal catalysts in wastewater treatment [16].

15.2.2.3 Thermocatalysis oxidation of CO

Thermal catalytic oxidation of carbon monoxide (CO) can be used in the neutralization of vehicle exhaust or the removal of the trace amount of CO in hydrogen feedstock (via the reaction of $CO+1/2O_2 \rightarrow CO_2$). Due to the easy CO poisoning of Pt metal, the removal of CO from hydrogen is important when Pt metal is used as a catalyst in fuel cells, where hydrogen purification by preferential oxidation (PROX) of CO becomes crucial. By uniformly loading Pt single atom catalysts (SACs) on the surface of metal oxides, each Pt atom can be used as the active site of reaction, which is conducive to giving full play to its performance. However, it is difficult to obtain good catalytic performance when Pt SACs are used in the CO oxidation reaction because the single-atom structure is usually unstable and prone to CO poisoning [17]. Recently, Kim and coworkers used CeO_x/TiO_2 bicomponent oxides to support CO-tolerant dense Pt single (or dual) atom catalyst, and obtained excellent performances of PROX of CO by adjusting the chemical properties of the interface between two oxides (see Fig. 15.2C—E for details) [18]. The CeO_x/TiO_2 mixed oxide interface was formed by adding 1 wt.% Ce onto TiO_2 nanoparticles, which could stabilize high-density Pt single (or dual) atoms (in rich Pt_1-O_x entities) through the strong electronic metal-support interactions (the electron donation from Pt to oxides) (see Fig. 15.2C). Different amounts of Pt were deposited on the CeO_x-TiO_2 (1 wt.% Ce) hybrid support (i.e., Pt/CeO_x-TiO_2) (denote as nPCT, where the n = 0.25, 0.5, and 1.0 wt.% Pt), where the 1PCT showed the optimal catalytic characteristics due to the high-density catalyst has synergistic properties. Particularly, the nPCT catalysts PROX of CO more actively than the nPT catalysts (i.e., Pt/TiO_2) with the same Pt loading, where the 1PCT reached 100% CO conversion at 160 °C (while the 1 PT reached 100% at 175°C) (see Fig. 15.2D). Compared with the conventional $Pt-TiO_2$ (0.25 wt.% Pt) catalyst, the mass activity of the Pt/CeO_x-TiO_2 (0.25 wt.% Pt) catalyst was 15.1 times that of the former toward CO oxidation at 140°C, showing the highest mass activity (47.5×10^{-5} mol $CO/g_{Pt}/s$) among similar systems reported previously (see the inset in Fig. 15.2D). The interface of CeO_x-TiO_2 mixed oxides can provide strong binding sites and rich coordinated oxygen for Pt single (or dual) atoms and activate the Mars-van Krevelen (MvK) CO-oxidation mechanism (protecting Pt single-atoms from CO poisoning) (see Fig. 15.2E). The interfacial oxygen ion bridging the Ce and the Ti ions and binding the Pt_2 cluster (namely the lattice oxygen at the triphase interface of $Pt-CeO_x-TiO_2$) can oxidize a Pt-bound CO molecule ($Pt-CO^*$) through the interface-mediated MvK mechanism. The formation of an $O-C-O$ intermediate requires an activation energy barrier (E_{act1}) of 0.75 eV (TS1), and an E_{act2} of 0.43 eV is required for dissociation of the Ce-bound O_2 (TS2) (see Fig. 15.2E). The relatively higher E_{act1} indicates that activation of the lattice oxygen at the $Pt_2-CeO_x-TiO_2$ interface is the rate-determining step. This study provides a novel design strategy for building high-density Pt SACs by atomic interface engineering toward efficient catalytic oxidation reaction (the above content is from one of our review papers [17]).

15.2.2.4 Thermocatalysis conversion of CO$_2$

With the increase of CO_2 emissions, environmental problems such as global warming and ocean acidification have emerged. The fixation and conversion of CO_2 have become an important topic for scientists. The preparation of high-added cyclic carbonate by cycloaddition reaction of CO_2 on epoxide is an effective method in CO_2 transformation, where the cyclic carbonate is an organic solvent with excellent performance and is a multifunctional organic intermediate as well [12]. Recently, Jiang and coworkers synthesized hollow porous carbon spheres with high-content Zn single atoms (11.3 wt.%) by pyrolysis hollow ZIF-8 microspheres at high temperature, and the dispersed Zn/N sites can be used as Lewis acid/base sites to activate epoxy compounds and CO_2 molecules respectively (see Fig. 15.2F for details) [19]. The hollow cavity structure can cause the incident light to reflect many times, thus increasing the efficiency of light utilization and improving the catalytic effect in photothermal catalyzed reactions. The reverse water-gas shift (RWGS) reaction can convert greenhouse gas of CO_2 into more valuable CO, where this reverse process is currently recognized as the most promising approach for green CO_2 conversion [17]. At present, the development of low-temperature, high-efficiency, and highly-stable Pd-based catalysts of RWGS reactions for CO_2 conversion is of great significance to the sustainable development of "carbon neutrality" (see Fig. 15.2G for details) [20]. The chemical reduction of CO_2 to produce high-value-added products (fuels and fine chemicals) has attracted more and more attention all over the world. Chemical reduction of CO_2 involves electrocatalytic reduction, thermal catalytic reduction, photocatalytic reduction, as well as joint reduction (see Fig. 15.2H for details) [21]. In a word, the green conversion of CO_2 into high-value-added chemicals by thermocatalysis is an efficient "carbon neutrality" strategy in the field of environmental catalysis.

15.3 Catalysis materials

The precious metals Pt, Pd, Ru, and Rh catalysts are widely used in thermal catalytic reactions, and the transition metals Fe, Co, Ni, and Cu catalysts are the cheapest and more efficient thermal catalysts. α-MoC is recently used as a "star" catalyst carrier to achieve ultraefficient hydrogen energy production. Compared with β-MoC, α-MoC interacts more strongly with metals (Au, Pt, Ni, etc.), which can achieve atomic-level dispersion of metals. At the same time, α-MoC shows extremely high hydrolytic dissociation activity. The abundant surface hydroxyl group is produced in the reaction process, which accelerates the hydrogen production reaction (WGS reaction, methanol steam reforming reaction, etc.). Because of its high low-temperature catalytic activity, the α-MoC support has great application potential in the field of WGS hydrogen production. Martin et al. from Peking University conducted in-depth research on α-MoC, and published three articles on α-MoC in Nature and Science [22].

Ternary catalyst (such as $Cu/ZnO/Al_2O_3$, Pt/Rh/Pd) is one of the most important industrial catalysts, catalytic low-temperature water-gas transformation, methanol synthesis, methanol steam reforming reaction, and exhaust (CO, hydrocarbons, and NO_x) removal. Compared with traditional catalysis, SACs can achieve 100% atomic utilization in theory, which is the key to the upgrading of modern thermal chemical catalytic technology. The thermal catalytic reaction is often accompanied by a series of side reactions, the surface of the catalyst is easy to form carbon deposition, which will lead to catalyst poisoning, in addition, high temperature is easy to cause the catalyst sintering and make the catalyst fail. In order to reduce the formation of carbon, avoid the poisoning of the catalyst and reduce the activity of the catalyst, the addition of Mg, La, Ce, and other elements in the catalyst can effectively inhibit the formation of carbon deposition and improve the activity of catalyst [23].

15.4 Applications

Chemistry changes life and catalysis changes chemistry. According to statistics, more than 90% of chemical products need to be synthesized under the action of catalysts, and 50% of the catalysts need to use precious metals. Noble metal nanostructure and atomic structure catalysts can produce target products more efficiently, improve energy utilization and reduce carbon emissions, helping to achieve the "double carbon" goal. Precious metal thermal catalysts are widely used in environmental governance, the chemical industry, energy, and other fields, which are closely related to the national economy and people's livelihoods and the sustainable and healthy development of economic society. 70% of the world's rhodium, 40% of platinum, and 50% of palladium are used in the preparation of thermal catalysts [24]. Thermal catalysis (thermocatalysis), as one of the most widely known catalytic categories, is commonly used in conventional industrial processes (water-gas conversion reactions, selective hydrogenation or oxidation, and various reforming reactions, and others) and environmental catalytic processes due to its high efficiency and applicability to large-scale production.

15.5 Summary

In this chapter, we have discussed the fundamentals, thermocatalytic mechanisms, and thermocatalytic materials of different thermocatalytic reactions in the fields of energy conversion and environmental protection. In a thermocatalytic reaction, the catalyst interacts with the reactant, changing the reaction path and thereby reducing the activation energy of the reaction. For nearly a century, chemical catalysis has been an important part of industrial production. At present, more than 85% of chemical products cannot be separated from catalytic reactions. Thermal catalysis plays a crucial role in energy conversion and environmental protection. The energy conversion typically includes water gas conversion, methanol steam reforming, methane steam reforming, methane dry reforming, and methane partial oxidation. Compared with other advanced oxidation environmental technologies, the thermocatalytic method has the advantages of simple operation and cost-saving in the treatment of organic wastewater.

Acknowledgments

This book was supported by National Natural Science Foundation of China (22078071, 22272034), Natural Science Foundation of Guangdong Province (2021A1515010125, 2020A1515010344), Maoming Science and Technology Project (mmkj2020032), Guangdong Province Universities and Colleges Pearl River Scholar Funded Scheme (2019), Guangdong Basic and Applied Basic Research Foundation (2019A1515011249, 2021A1515010305), Key Research Project of Natural Science of Guangdong Provincial Department of Education (2019KZDXM010), Environment and Energy Green Catalysis Innovation Team of Colleges and Universities of Guangdong Province(2022KCXTD019), the program for Innovative Research Team of Guangdong University of Petrochemical Technology.

References

[1] https://mp.weixin.qq.com/s/zrZKWCLI38H2QFZ7zFOKqg.
[2] R.A. Sheldon, I. Arends, U. Hanefeld, Green Chemistry and Catalysis, John Wiley and Sons, 2007.
[3] D.R. Palo, R.A. Dagle, J.D. Holladay, Methanol steam reforming for hydrogen production, Chemical Reviews 107 (10) (2007) 3992—4021.
[4] Y. Huang, Y. Lu, Y. Lin, Y. Mao, G. Ouyang, H. Liu, Y. Tong, Cerium-based hybrid nanorods for synergetic photo-thermocatalytic degradation of organic pollutants, Journal of Materials Chemistry A 6 (48) (2018) 24740—24747.
[5] S. Yao, X. Zhang, W. Zhou, R. Gao, W. Xu, Y. Ye, D. Ma, Atomic-layered Au clusters on α-MoC as catalysts for the low-temperature water-gas shift reaction, Science 357 (6349) (2017) 389—393.
[6] X. Cui, H.Y. Su, R. Chen, L. Yu, J. Dong, C. Ma, X. Bao, Room-temperature electrochemical water—gas shift reaction for high purity hydrogen production, Nature Communications 10 (1) (2019) 1—8.
[7] L. Lin, Q. Yu, M. Peng, A. Li, S. Yao, S. Tian, D. Ma, Atomically dispersed Ni/α-MoC catalyst for hydrogen production from methanol/water, Journal of the American Chemical Society 143 (1) (2020) 309—317.
[8] Z. Sun, J. Liu, R. Zhang, Y. Wu, H. Li, S. Toan, Z. Sun, Fabricating Ga doped and MgO embedded nanomaterials for sorption-enhanced steam reforming of methanol, Journal of Materials Chemistry A 10 (13) (2022) 7300—7313.
[9] D. Fan, F. Liu, J. Li, T. Wei, Z. Ye, Z. Wang, Z. Shao, A microchannel reactor-integrated ceramic fuel cell with dual-coupling effect for efficient power and syngas co-generation from methane, Applied Catalysis B: Environmental 297 (2021) 120443.
[10] Y. Diao, X. Zhang, Y. Liu, B. Chen, G. Wu, C. Shi, Plasma-assisted dry reforming of methane over Mo2C-Ni/Al2O3 catalysts: effects of β-Mo2C promoter, Applied Catalysis B: Environmental 301 (2022) 120779.
[11] L. Sandoval-Diaz, M. Plodinec, D. Ivanov, S. Poitel, A. Hammud, H.C. Nerl, T. Lunkenbein, Visualizing the importance of oxide-metal phase transitions in the production of synthesis gas over Ni catalysts, Journal of Energy Chemistry 50 (2020) 178—186.
[12] Y. Hu, H. Li, Z.S. Li, B. Li, S. Wang, Y. Yao, Progress in batch preparation of single-atom catalysts and application in sustainable synthesis of fine chemicals, Green Chemistry 23 (2021) 8754—8794.
[13] J. Wang, Q. Wang, T. Zhu, X. Zhu, B. Sun, Analysis of research status of hydrogen production by methane reforming, Modern Chemical Industry 40 (7) (2020) 15—20.
[14] https://mp.weixin.qq.com/s/mnqriOH_1qUC2EMRPKjtFA.
[15] Y. Lin, Y. Cao, Q. Yao, O.J.H. Chai, J. Xie, Engineering noble metal nanomaterials for pollutant decomposition, Industrial and Engineering Chemistry Research 59 (47) (2020) 20561—20581.
[16] H. Chen, J. Ku, L. Wang, Thermal catalysis under dark ambient conditions in environmental remediation: fundamental principles, development, and challenges, Chinese Journal of Catalysis 40 (8) (2019) 1117—1134.
[17] Z. Li, B. Li, Y. Hu, X. Liao, H. Yu, C. Yu, Emerging Ultrahigh-Density Single-Atom Catalysts for Versatile Heterogeneous Catalysis Applications: Redefinition, Recent Progress, and Challenges, Small Structures, 2022, p. 2200041.
[18] M. Yoo, Y.S. Yu, H. Ha, S. Lee, J.S. Choi, S. Oh, H.Y. Kim, A tailored oxide interface creates dense Pt single-atom catalysts with high catalytic activity, Energy and Environmental Science 13 (4) (2020) 1231—1239.
[19] Q. Yang, C.C. Yang, C.H. Lin, H.L. Jiang, Metal—organic-framework-derived hollow N-doped porous carbon with ultrahigh concentrations of single Zn atoms for efficient carbon dioxide conversion, Angewandte Chemie 131 (11) (2019) 3549—3553.
[20] Y. Ma, Y. Ren, Y. Zhou, W. Liu, W. Baaziz, O. Ersen, Y. Liu, High-density and thermally stable palladium single-atom catalysts for chemoselective hydrogenations, Angewandte Chemie International Edition 59 (48) (2020) 21613—21619.

[21] H. Yang, L. Shang, Q. Zhang, R. Shi, G.I. Waterhouse, L. Gu, T. Zhang, A universal ligand mediated method for large scale synthesis of transition metal single atom catalysts, Nature Communications 10 (1) (2019) 1—9.

[22] https://mp.weixin.qq.com/s/Yayc4v6YtwUIKrvRYA8y7A.

[23] W.X. Fu, X. Liu, Hydrogen production from natural gas reforming and its application in fuel cells, Gas and Heat 33 (6) (2013) 16—21.

[24] https://mp.weixin.qq.com/s/B0lrYhdh0XirQrW7fezJ8Q.

CHAPTER 16

Selective separation and storage of energy gases: fundamentals

16.1 Introduction

Gas separation is the process of separation of each component in the mixed gas by cryogenic method (distillation principle), adsorption method (molecular polarity), membrane method (membrane filtration), and other methods. Cryogenic method: commonly used concepts such as air separation, air components are separated, commonly used methods for cryogenic method, cryogenic air separation equipment is commonly known as the air separation equipment, also called oxygen machine. Adsorption separation: Adsorption operation has a wide range of applications in the chemical industry, light industry, oil refining, metallurgy, and environmental protection. Such as the removal of water in the gas, solvent recovery, aqueous solution or organic solution decolorization, deodorization, organic alkane separation, refining of aromatic hydrocarbons, etc. [1]. According to the difference in adsorption capacity between adsorbent and adsorbent, adsorption operations can be divided into two categories: physical adsorption and chemical adsorption. Membrane separation is a general term for the selective transmission of certain components in a liquid using a special film. For the separation of impurity gas in energy gas (such as hydrogen, carbon monoxide, methane, acetylene, etc.), the adsorption method is often used for selective separation. The commonly used adsorbent is metal organic frameworks (MOFs), covalent organic frameworks (COFs), porous organic polymers, and porous carbon with microporous structures or special functional groups [2].

16.2 Basic principles
16.2.1 Basic principles of selective separation of energy gases
16.2.1.1 Selective separation of C_2H_2 and CO_2

Acetylene (C_2H_2) is a hydrocarbon with the highest degree of unsaturation. This unique carbon-carbon triple bond can participate in a variety of addition reactions to convert it into a variety of high-value-added chemical products, such as polyvinyl chloride, neoprene rubber, and acrylic acid. In industrial production, C_2H_2 usually contains some impurities, such as CO_2, H_2, CO, and so on. The boiling point of CO_2 is close to that of C_2H_2 (CO_2:194.7K; C_2H_2:189.3k) and similar molecular size (CO_2: $3.18 \times 3.33 \times 5.36$ Å^3; C_2H_2: $3.32 \times 3.34 \times 5.7$ Å^3), and the molecular morphology is linear, and the kinetic diameter is almost the same, 3.3 Å (see Fig. 16.1A for details) [3].

Nanostructured Materials
ISBN 978-0-443-19256-2, https://doi.org/10.1016/B978-0-443-19256-2.00031-4

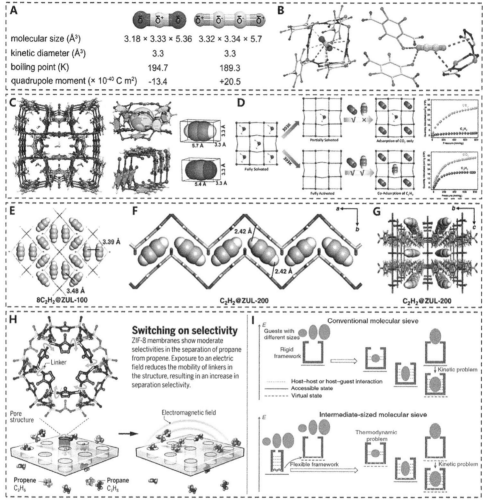

Figure 16.1 (A and B) CO_2/C_2H_2 separation by Cl atom-inserting MOFs [3], (C and D) CO_2/C_2H_2 separation by Cu−F-pymo MOFs [4], (E−G) C_2H_2/C_2H_4 separation by 2-D fluorinated MOFs [5], (H) C_3H_6/C_3H_8 separation by electric-field lattice-fixing MOFs [6], (I) Selective separation of styrene in mixture by intermediate-sized molecular sieve (iSMS) [7].

Therefore, the selective separation of CO_2 from C_2H_2 is a particularly important but extremely difficult task. Metal organic frameworks (MOFs) have various structures and functions and have been widely studied for the separation of different gases. By introducing a highly chlorinated organic aromatic linker tetrachloroterephthalic acid (BDC-Cl$_4$), the ultramicroporous MOFs of the pillar layer, [Zn(atz) (BDC-Cl4)$_{0.5}$]$_n$(1) (Hatz = 3-amino-1,2,4-triazole), containing electronegative Cl atoms and one-dimensional rhomboid channels, was successfully constructed. These ultramicroporous MOFs can selectively adsorb CO_2 in C_2H_2 after activation, showing a CO_2/C_2H_2 (V:V = 1:1) adsorption selectivity of 2.4 at 285 K and 100 kPa (see Fig. 16.1B for details) [3]. In addition, efficient selective separation of CO_2/C_2H_2 was also achieved in the ultramicroporous MOFs (Cu−F−pymo). At 303K, partially activated Cu−F−pymo can preferentially adsorb CO_2, while the preferred binding site of C_2H_2 is occupied by H_2O molecules, thus inhibiting the adsorption of C_2H_2. The adsorption experiments showed that the high-efficiency screening effect avoided the coadsorption of C_2H_2 and CO_2 gases, and high selectivity was obtained (10^5). In this way, CO_2 can be removed in one step without an additional desorption process, resulting in high-purity C_2H_2 (> 99.9%) (see Fig. 16.1C and D for details) [4]. This report highlights the importance of modifying the pore channels by occupying the adsorption sites of the guest in MOFs, which will have implications for the future development of energy gas-separating porous materials.

16.2.1.2 Selective separation of C_2H_2 and C_2H_4

The huge demand for high-purity gas in the industry has greatly promoted the development of gas separation and adsorption technology. In terms of economy and product quality, gas adsorption technology has advantages over traditional solvent absorption and catalytic hydrogenation technology, when it is necessary to separate trace amounts of impurity gases (e.g., acetylene (C_2H_2)) from gas streams (e.g., ethylene (C_2H_4)). The ideal adsorbent should have both selectivity and high adsorption capacity for trace gases. However, conventional adsorption materials such as zeolite, activated carbon and resin do not have these characteristics. Yang et al. from Zhejiang University reported a strategy to improve the efficiency of adsorption separation using two-dimensional (2-D) fluorinated MOFs with adjustable interlayer and intra-layer space (see Fig. 16.1E−G for details) [5]. This strategy can achieve record low-pressure C_2H_2 capacity and record high purity (99.9999%) C_2H_4 production and excellent stability. Acetylene in C_2H_2/ C_2H_4 (1/99, V/V) mixture can be quickly absorbed by ZUL-100, its adsorption rate can reach 2200 min/g, and the adsorption rate of acetylene by ZUL-200 was 1958 min/g. In addition to setting a benchmark for C_2H_2/C_2H_4 separation, the strategy described in this study demonstrates a novel crystal engineering approach for the synthesis of new porous materials that can enable the capture and separation of other trace gases.

16.2.1.3 Selective separation of C₃H₆ and C₃H₈

The MOFs is a porous crystalline substance composed of organic ligands and metal nodes. However, due to the dynamic changes of ligands and structures, many MOFs have large structural flexibility, so the separation of molecules with similar dynamic sizes is not satisfactory for many MOFs. In light of this, Knebel and Caro reported A strategy to enhance the precise separation of gaseous mixtures such as propane (C_3H_8) and propylene (C_3H_6) by fixing the lattice and pore dimensions of MOFs (ZIF-8) via an electric field (see Fig. 16.1H for details) [6]. The ZIF-8 films were treated with an electric field of 500 V/mm, resulting in lattice polarization, the transition of crystal structure from cubic phase to monoclinic and triclinic polytype structures, and crystal pore size from 0.34 to 0.36 nm. The electric field limits the mobility of the organic ligand, and the lattice flexibility is correspondingly reduced to become stiffer and the pore size dynamics change less. This study experimentally demonstrated that electric fields can control the crystal structure of MOFs, thus opening new windows in a range of application areas such as membrane separation and molecular switching.

16.2.1.4 Selective separation of CO₂ and H₂

The chemical process that captures carbon involves the reaction of syngas (a mixture of H_2 and CO) with water vapor (to produce H_2 and CO_2). For example, the water gas conversion (WGS) reaction ($CO + H_2O \rightarrow CO_2 + H_2$) provides an important way to simultaneously extract hydrogen from water and purify CO. Therefore, porous materials with high selectivity for CO_2 and H_2 separation can be used for CO_2 capture and H_2 purification. Recently, Fu and coworkers demonstrated that MOFs can be grown on the covalent organic frameworks (COFs) membrane to fabricate COFs-MOFs composite membranes [8]. The COFs-MOFs composite membranes showed higher separation selectivity of H_2/CO_2 gas mixtures than the individual COFs and MOFs membranes. Yang et al. also designed a simple in situ growth combined with a novel preparation strategy of domain-limited interface polymerization, a new concept of metal-organic frameworks soft-solid composite membrane (MOFs SSCM) (soft polyamide-solid $Zn_2(Bim)_4$ connected modular network structure) was proposed [9]. A high precision separation of H_2/CO_2 gas mixtures with minimal size difference is realized. For the Mg/Cu-BTC(MOFs)@MWCNT composite adsorbent, the adsorption strength of the adsorbent to each gas in the syngas can be ranked as $CO_2 > CO > CH_4 > H_2$ [10]. This study confirmed that the doping of Mg metal and hydrophobic MWCNT materials is an efficient way to improve the CO_2 adsorption performance (The CO_2/H_2 selectivity is as high as 14.28).

16.2.1.5 Selective separation of styrene in the mixture

Recently, professor Jiepeng Zhang proposed a new adsorption separation principle, called intermediate-sized molecular sieve (iSMS), which can adsorb only intermediate-size target components in a complex mixture to solve major needs such as styrene separation and purification (see Fig. 16.1I for details) [7]. To achieve this particular adsorption behavior, the porous material must be suitably flexible, thereby excluding non-target components by combining thermodynamic principles (molecules too small to open the flexible frame) and kinetic principles (molecules too large to open the pore window). They designed and synthesized a coordination polymer porous material (MAF-41), a coordination polymer with restricted flexibility, to achieve ultra-efficient (selectivity of 3300) purification of styrene from a mixture of ethylbenzene, styrene, toluene, and benzene, with a single adsorption-desorption cycle to obtain > 99.9% pure styrene. The MAF-41 also has ultra-high thermal stability (500°C), water stability (boiling water, pH 3−14), and superhydrophobic properties, which are beneficial for practical applications in the selective separation of styrene in the mixture.

16.2.2 Basic principles of storage of energy gases

As promising energy gases, methane (CH_4) and hydrogen (H_4) are both alternatives to gasoline and could potentially be used as fuels in the transportation industry. Methane is considered a bridge fuel because its combustion still emits CO_2, but less than gasoline. In contrast, hydrogen is envisioned as the "real green fuel of the future" because hydrogen fuel cell vehicles are zero-emission vehicles. However, the transport, storage, and operation of hydrogen- and methane-powered vehicles currently require high-pressure compression (i.e., 700 bar for H_2 and 250 bar for CH_4), which is both expensive and unsafe. To encourage research in this important area, the US Department of Energy (DOE) has established metrics for onboard storage and transport systems for the development of alternative fuels in the transportation sector. The development of novel and high-capacity adsorbent materials is one of the strategies to achieve the goal of safe and cost-effective storage of methane and hydrogen [11].

Porous materials with high surface area (generally have a surface area of 2000 m^2/g or greater) have been investigated for their wide range of potential adsorbents for vehicular clean energy gas storage (e.g., metal-organic frameworks (MOFs), porous carbon, covalent organic skeletons, and porous organic polymers adsorbents). The properties of these adsorbents allow gas loads to power methane- and hydrogen-powered vehicles at low load pressures. After years of research, there is no shortage of ultra-high porosity MOFs materials for clean energy gas storage. However, it is difficult for these MOFs materials to achieve both weight adsorption and volume adsorption of methane and hydrogen. Recently, Farha and his group took a unique approach and developed a super MOFs material based on the metal tri-core cluster (NU-1501-M (M = Al or Fe)) with ultra-high porosity and ultra-high surface area, achieving a balance between the weight and volume storage properties of clean hydrogen and methane. The NU-1501-Al has an extremely high BET area for gravimetric analysis (7310 m^2/g) and BET area for volumetric analysis (2060 m^2/cm^3), which are the highest data values ever reported [11].

16.3 Adsorption materials

Metal–organic frameworks (MOFs) and covalent organic frameworks (COFs) provide irreplaceable molecular platforms for designing frameworks and pores for structurally specific functions such as semiconductors, adsorption and separation, and catalysts. Recently, Chemical Society Reviews has published two review articles on MOFs and COFs, focusing on their applications in selective gas separation and clean energy gas storage. Fluorinated metal–organic skeletons (F-MOFs), a rapidly growing group of porous materials, have revolutionized the field of gas separation due to their adjustable pore size, attractive chemical properties, and excellent stability [12]. A thorough understanding of their structure-performance relationship is essential for the synthesis and development of new F-MOFs. The COFs are an emerging class of crystalline porous polymers with highly tunable structures and functionalities. The COFs have been proposed as ideal materials for applications in the energy-intensive field of molecular separation due to their notable intrinsic features such as low density, exceptional stability, high surface area, and readily adjustable pore size and chemical environment [13]. Mixed matrix membranes (MMMs), which are organic-inorganic hybrid membranes, have been proposed as the alternative approach to intensify the comprehensive gas separation performance of polymeric membranes [14]. Gas separation processes are the most important operations in refineries and gas-related industries. Recently, many efforts are being dedicated to modifying the gas separation properties of existing organic or inorganic membranes to further expand their use for extensive industrial gas separation applications.

16.4 Applications

Gas separation technology has been developed since the beginning of the 20th century and has been widely used. Gas separation is when the gas is a mixture, the composition of the adsorbed phase is different from that of the gas phase due to the difference of attraction on the solid surface to different gas molecules. This difference in density and composition between the gas phase and the adsorbed phase constitutes the basis of the gas adsorption separation technology. Gas separation is the use of the porous material adsorption method, this way can use adsorbent (MOFs, COFs, activated carbon, etc.) porous structure of various hydrocarbons' adsorption capacity is different, so some useful components in the gas mixture can be separated. There are two advantages in the process of gas separation using porous adsorbents: one is the "type-selection ability", the topological structure of adsorbents determines the pore size, which means that it has a special screening effect on the target gas; The second is the "selective separation ability", due to the difference of polarity and saturation among the target gases, the difference of diffusion rate and the difference of interaction intensity between the target gases and the adsorbent. In conclusion, the selective adsorption (physical or chemical adsorption) of microporous materials provides a good molecular platform for the separation, purification, and storage of different energy gases (methane, acetylene, hydrogen, etc) [15].

16.5 Summary

In this chapter, we have discussed the basic principles, adsorption mechanisms, and adsorption materials for selective separation and storage of all kinds of energy gases (methane, acetylene, hydrogen, etc). Among these energy gases, acetylene is a wide range of energy chemical raw materials, which can be prepared into high-value-added chemicals. Methane and hydrogen can be directly used as fuel gas to replace gasoline used in a vehicle, which is green and continuous energy gases in modern society. The metal-organic frameworks (MOFs) and covalent organic frameworks (COFs) can provide well molecular platforms for designing frameworks and pores for selective separation and storage of different energy gases. These microporous polymer materials provide a structural basis for the preparation, storage, and utilization of green energy gases.

Acknowledgments

This book was supported by National Natural Science Foundation of China (22078071, 22272034), Natural Science Foundation of Guangdong Province (2021A1515010125, 2020A1515010344), Maoming Science and Technology Project (mmkj2020032), Guangdong Province Universities and Colleges Pearl River Scholar Funded Scheme (2019), Guangdong Basic and Applied Basic Research Foundation (2019A1515011249, 2021A1515010305), Key Research Project of Natural Science of Guangdong Provincial Department of Education (2019KZDXM010), Environment and Energy Green Catalysis Innovation Team of Colleges and Universities of Guangdong Province(2022KCXTD019), the program for Innovative Research Team of Guangdong University of Petrochemical Technology.

References

[1] R.B. Lin, S. Xiang, W. Zhou, B. Chen, Microporous metal-organic framework materials for gas separation, Chem 6 (2) (2020) 337−363.

[2] L. Dai, K. Huang, Y. Xia, Z. Xu, Two-dimensional material separation membranes for renewable energy purification, storage, and conversion, Green Energy and Environment 6 (2) (2021) 193−211.

[3] X.Y. Li, Y. Song, C.X. Zhang, C.X. Zhao, C. He, Inverse CO2/C2H2 separation in a pillared-layer framework featuring a chlorine-modified channel by quadrupole-moment sieving, Separation and Purification Technology 279 (2021) 119608.

[4] Y. Shi, Y. Xie, H. Cui, Y. Ye, H. Wu, W. Zhou, B. Chen, Highly selective adsorption of carbon dioxide over acetylene in an ultramicroporous metal−organic framework, Advanced Materials 33 (45) (2021) 2105880.

[5] J. Shen, X. He, T. Ke, R. Krishna, J.M. van Baten, R. Chen, Q. Ren, Simultaneous interlayer and intralayer space control in two-dimensional metal− organic frameworks for acetylene/ethylene separation, Nature Communications 11 (1) (2020) 1−10.

[6]   A. Knebel, B. Geppert, K. Volgmann, D.I. Kolokolov, A.G. Stepanov, J. Twiefel, J. Caro, Defibrillation of soft porous metal-organic frameworks with electric fields, Science 358 (6361) (2017) 347–351.

[7]   D.D. Zhou, P. Chen, C. Wang, S.S. Wang, Y. Du, H. Yan, J.P. Zhang, Intermediate-sized molecular sieving of styrene from larger and smaller analogues, Nature Materials 18 (9) (2019) 994–998.

[8]   J. Fu, S. Das, G. Xing, T. Ben, V. Valtchev, S. Qiu, Fabrication of COF-MOF composite membranes and their highly selective separation of H2/CO2, Journal of the American Chemical Society 138 (24) (2016) 7673–7680.

[9]   L. Shu, Y. Peng, R. Yao, H. Song, C. Zhu, W. Yang, Flexible soft-solid metal−organic framework composite membranes for H2/CO2 separation, Angewandte Chemie International Edition 61 (14) (2022) e202117577.

[10] Y. Zhang, H. Wibowo, L. Zhong, M. Horttanainen, Z. Wang, C. Yu, M. Yan, Cu-BTC-based composite adsorbents for selective adsorption of CO2 from syngas, Separation and Purification Technology 279 (2021) 119644.

[11] Z. Chen, P. Li, R. Anderson, X. Wang, X. Zhang, L. Robison, O.K. Farha, Balancing volumetric and gravimetric uptake in highly porous materials for clean energy, Science 368 (6488) (2020) 297–303.

[12] A.E. Amooghin, H. Sanaeepur, R. Luque, H. Garcia, B. Chen, Fluorinated metal−organic frameworks for gas separation, Chemical Society Reviews 51 (2022) 7427–7508.

[13] Z. Wang, S. Zhang, Y. Chen, Z. Zhang, S. Ma, Covalent organic frameworks for separation applications, Chemical Society Reviews 49 (3) (2020) 708–735.

[14] A.R. Kamble, C.M. Patel, Z.V.P. Murthy, A review on the recent advances in mixed matrix membranes for gas separation processes, Renewable and Sustainable Energy Reviews 145 (2021) 111062.

[15] J.R. Li, R.J. Kuppler, H.C. Zhou, Selective gas adsorption and separation in metal−organic frameworks, Chemical Society Reviews 38 (5) (2009) 1477–1504.

CHAPTER 17

Adsorption in the treatment of three wastes: fundamentals

17.1 Introduction

Adsorption refers to the process that when fluid (gas or liquid) contacts with solid porous material, one or more components in the fluid are transferred to the outer surface of porous material and the inner surface of micropores to enrich and form monolayer or multimolecular layer on these surfaces. The adsorbed fluid is called adsorbate, and the porous solid particle itself is called adsorbent. Adsorption method refers to the use of porous solid adsorption of some or several pollutants in the environment, in order to recover or remove pollutants, so as to purify the environment [1]. Nanoadsorption technology based on porous materials provides an effective treatment scheme for the treatment and recycling of "three wastes" (waste gas, waste water and waste residue). When achieving the standard discharge of "three wastes," the useful organic matter, volatile solvents, salts and water resources are recovered by adsorption method, and the pollutants lacking recovery value are thoroughly oxidized and decomposed, so as to realize the "recycling, reduction, and harmless" treatment of pollutants [2]. Adsorbents generally have a large specific surface, suitable pore structure and surface structure (such as porous carbon, zeolite, molecular sieve, metal-organic frameworks (MOFs), and so on). These porous materials (adsorbents) have strong adsorption capacity for various adsorbates, such as waste gas (volatile organic compounds (VOCs)), waste water (organic molecules and heavy metal ions (HMIs)), and waste residue (water-soluble leaching solution from residue) [3].

17.2 Basic principles

17.2.1 Adsorption mechanism and isotherm

According to the different forces between porous materials (adsorbents) and pollutant molecules or ions (adsorbates) in the adsorption process, adsorption can be divided into two categories: physical adsorption and chemical adsorption (see Fig. 17.1A for details) [4]. In the adsorption process, when the force between porous materials and the pollutant molecules is van der Waals force (or electrostatic attraction) called physical adsorption; When the force between porous materials and pollutant molecules is a chemical bond, it is called chemical adsorption. The adsorption heat, adsorption rate, adsorption activation energy, adsorption temperature, selectivity, adsorption layer number, and

Nanostructured Materials
ISBN 978-0-443-19256-2, https://doi.org/10.1016/B978-0-443-19256-2.00013-2

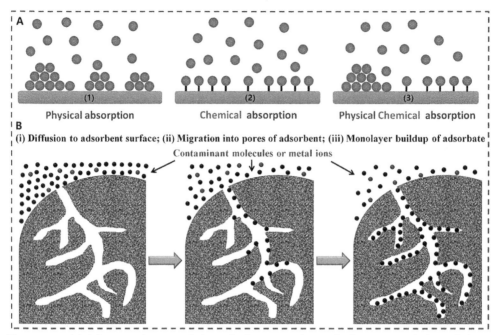

Figure 17.1 (A) Schematic diagram of physical adsorption, chemical adsorption and physical chemical adsorption [4]; (B) adsorption process diagram of porous materials: (i) Surface contact (external diffusion), (ii) adsorption (internal diffusion), (iii) monolayer adsorption equilibrium [5].

adsorption spectrum of physical adsorption and chemical adsorption are different due to their different bond forces. Usually, in practice, the porous structure and functional groups of porous materials give the adsorbent a dual adsorption mechanism (that is, the association mechanism of physical and chemical adsorption).

The adsorption removal of pollutant molecules or ions (adsorbates) by the porous materials (adsorbents) should take place by a three-stage adsorption mechanism as follows: (i) diffusion of adsorbate to adsorbent surface, (ii) migration of adsorbate into pores of adsorbent, and (iii) monolayer buildup of adsorbate on the adsorbent (see Fig. 17.1B for details) [5]. However, for the removal of HMIs, the core mechanism may be ion exchange: due to the presence of different functional groups (such as hydroxyl, carbonyl, carboxyl, etc.) on the surface of porous carbon adsorbents, these functional groups can become active ion exchange sites for effectively trapping HMIs. The physical adsorption of gas molecules on porous materials has the following principles: (1) The diameter of the molecule is larger than the diameter of the pore, because of steric hindrance, the molecule cannot enter the pore, so it is not adsorbed; (2) The molecular diameter is equal to the diameter of the pore, and the adsorbent has a strong capturing force, which is very suitable for low-concentration adsorption; (3) The molecular diameter is less than the diameter of the pore, capillary condensation occurs in the pore, and the adsorption capacity is large; (4) Molecular diameter is much smaller than the diameter of the pore, adsorbed molecules are easy to desorption (namely the desorption rate is higher than adsorption rate), low concentration of adsorption is small [6].

The rational perception of adsorbent processes on surface, type of adsorbate monolayer or multilayer and adsorbent capacity can be simplified by the adsorption isotherms. The adsorption isotherm is an equation relating the amount of solute adsorbed onto the solid and the equilibrium concentration of the solute in a solution at a given temperature. The most often used isotherms for "three wastes" treatment (Langmuir, Langmuir–Frendlich, Toth, Sips, etc.) are presented in Table 17.1 [7]. The adsorption capacity of adsorbent is determined by adsorption isotherm. The choice of a particular equation depends on many factors: composition of the system (one or multicomponent), properties of the adsorbent (single or multilayer adsorption), and the type of adsorption (physical, chemical, or ionexchange adsorption). The integral adsorption equation gives an opportunity to determine the mutual inter-dependence between the shape of the overall adsorption isotherm and the energy distribution function (see Table 17.1 for details).

17.2.2 Adsorption of volatile organic compounds (VOCs)

VOCs are mostly toxic, mutagenic, and carcinogenic, which seriously threaten human health and ecological environment. The continuous increase in VOCs and strict regulations makes it more urgent to reduce VOC emissions. At present, a variety of VOC treatment technologies such as incineration, condensation, biodegradation, adsorption and catalytic oxidation have emerged. Among them, adsorption technology is recognized as an efficient and economical control strategy due to its great potential of adsorbent and adsorbent recycling. Carbon-based adsorbents are widely used in gas purification, especially for VOC treatment and recovery, because of their large specific surface area, rich porous structure and large adsorption capacity. The key factors affecting VOC adsorption mainly include three aspects: (1) physicochemical properties of adsorbates (molecular structure, molecular polarity, and boiling point), (2) structural properties of adsorbents (specific surface area, pore structure, and functional groups), and (3) adsorption conditions (temperature, humidity, and fluid viscosity) (see Fig. 17.2A for details) [8]. Porous carbon-based adsorption technology is considered to be one of the most promising and economical strategies for VOCs emission control and resource recovery in industrial processes due to its high efficiency and low cost. The core problems of porous carbon adsorption usually involve high adsorption capacity, stable physical and chemical properties, and high desorption. Therefore, many porous carbon adsorbents, such as activated carbon, activated carbon fiber, biochar, graphene, carbon nanotubes and ordered mesoporous carbon, have been studied and developed, and are used to remove or recover VOCs. Most of the current studies improve the selectivity of porous carbon adsorbents by regulating the structure of porous carbon adsorbents, such as pore

Table 17.1 Adsorption isotherm for one- and poly-component systems [7].

Name of isotherm	Equation	References
Henry's law	$q_e = K q_m C$	Dąbrowski (2001)
Langmuir	$q_e = \dfrac{K q_m C}{1+KC}$	Dąbrowski (2001)
Freundlich	$q_e = A C^B$	Appel (1973), Liu (2005)
Brunauer–Emmett–Teller (BET theory)	$q_e = \dfrac{K q_e C_r}{[1+(K-1)C_r][1-C_r]}$	Maciej (2009), Caurie (2006)
Brunauer–Deming–Deming–Tellet (BDDT theory)	$q_e = \dfrac{K q_m C_r \left[1+m(g-1)C_r^{m-1}+g C_r^{m-1}(2g-1)C_r^m\right]}{(1-C_r)\left(1+[K-1]C_r+K(g-1)C_r^{\,}+C_r^m -g C_r^{m-1}\right)}$	Caurie (2006)
Redlich–Peterson	$q_e = \dfrac{K q_m C}{(1+KC^B)}$	Wu et al. (2010)
Langmuir–Freundlich	$q_e = \dfrac{A q_m C^B}{1+AC^B}$	Azizian et al. (2007)
Sips	$q_e = q_m \left[\dfrac{AC}{1+AC}\right]^B$	Ahmed (2012)
Toth	$q_e = \dfrac{KC}{\left(\dfrac{c^B}{1+\dfrac{c^B}{A}}\right)+\left(1+\dfrac{c^B}{A}\right)}$, where $n_M = KA^{\frac{1}{B}}$	Terzyk et al. (2003)
Yoon–Nelson	$\dfrac{C_c}{C_o} = \dfrac{1}{1+\exp[k_{YN}(\tau-(V/Q))]}$	Yazici et al. (2009)
Dubinin–Radushkevich	$q_e = q_m \exp^*\left\{2\left[\left(\dfrac{k_s e}{b_o}\right)^2\right]\right\}$	Misra (1969), Condon (2000)
Dubinin–Astakhov	$q_e = q_m \exp^*\left\{-\left[\left(\dfrac{k_s e}{b_o}\right)^2\right]\right\}$	Jaroniec and Marczewski (1984), Stoeckli (1981), Condon (2000)
Temkin	$q_c = \dfrac{R_s T}{b_T}\ln(A_T C_e)$	Khan (2012)
Fritz–Schlunder	$q_c = \dfrac{q_{m1}K_{FS}C_e^n FS}{1+K_{FS}C_e^m FS}$	Jossens et al. (1978)
Bi Langmuir	$q_c = \dfrac{q_{m1}K_{Bil,1}C_e}{1+K_{Bil,1}C_e} + \dfrac{q_{m2}K_{Bil,2}C_e}{1+K_{Bil,2}C_e}$	Yamamoto et al. (1993)

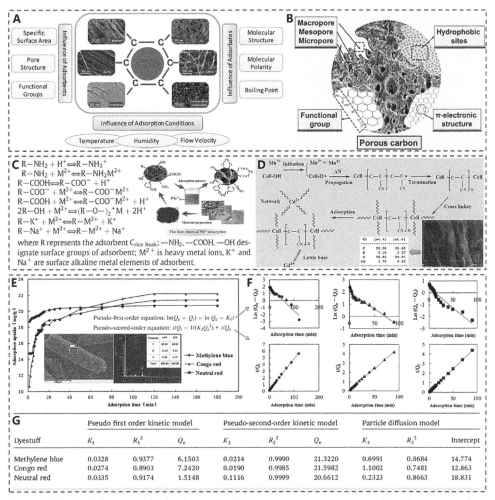

Figure 17.2 (A) Carbon-based adsorbents for VOCs treatment and recovery [8]; (B) porous carbon-based adsorption of VOCs [9]; (C) ion exchange combined with physical adsorption of heavy metal ion Pb^{2+} [10]; (D) modified sugarcane bagasse adsorption of heavy metal ion Cd^{2+} [11]; (E–G) activated carbon fibers adsorption of various organic dyes [12].

structure, hydrophobic point, π-electronic structure, and functional groups and are used for the recovery of high-value VOCs and purification and elimination of low-value VOCs (see Fig. 17.2B for details) [9].

17.2.3 Adsorption of heavy metal ions (HMIs)

At present, there are many methods to treat heavy metal pollution (such as Cu(II), Cd(II), and Pb(II) ions) in water, among which porous material adsorption method is considered as the most promising treatment method due to its advantages of simplicity, high efficiency and low pollution. A series of carbon materials are prepared by combination of the KOH activation method and steam activation method and their Pb^{2+} adsorption performances are evaluated (Ion exchange is the main process for Pb^{2+} adsorption) (see Fig. 17.2C for details) [10]. The results illustrated that the surface oxygen-containing functional groups such as carboxyl, lactone group, phenolic hydroxyl, and other alkaline metal ions like Na^+ and K^+ have significant effect on the adsorption process. And a reasonable mechanism of Pb^{2+} adsorption is proposed that the ion exchange combining with physical adsorption play key roles on the adsorption process. The detailed adsorption mechanism proposed by this study is as follows:

$$R-NH_2 + H^+ \Leftrightarrow R-NH^{3+}$$

$$R-NH_2 + M^{2+} \Leftrightarrow R-NH_2M^{2+}$$

$$R-COOH \Leftrightarrow R-COO^- + H^+$$

$$R-COO^- + M^{2+} \Leftrightarrow R-COO^-M^{2+}$$

$$R-COOH + M^{2+} \Leftrightarrow R-COO^-M^{2+} + H^+$$

$$2R-OH + M^{2+} \Leftrightarrow (R-O-)^{2+}M + 2H^+$$

$$R-K^+ + M^{2+} \Leftrightarrow R-M^{2+} + K^+$$

$$R-Na^+ + M^{2+} \Leftrightarrow R-M^{2+} + Na^+$$

Where the R represents the adsorbent; $-NH_2$, $-COOH$, $-OH$ designate surface groups of adsorbents; M^{2+} is HMIs, K^+ and Na^+ are surface alkaline metal elements of adsorbent. In addition, the effects of Cu^{2+}, Zn^{2+} on the Pb^{2+} adsorption capacity with the carbon adsorbents are also studied and the results demonstrate that other heavy metals play positive effects on the adsorption of Pb^{2+} [10].

Recently, our research group presented a novel adsorbent, modified sugarcane bagasse (MSB) developed by graft copolymerization, which can be used to remove cadmium ions (Cd (II)) from aqueous solution (see Fig. 17.2D for details) [11]. During the modification process, the cellulose in sugarcane bagasse first reacts with the initiator and the free radical sites formed in the cellulose structure, which leads to the changes of the valences of Mn ions (Mn^{7+} became Mn^{3+} and Mn^{2+}). This in turn continues to initiate the graft copolymerization reaction until the termination. As a result, the functional groups ($-CN$) from AN could be introduced into cellulose by the monomer and a three-dimensional cross-linked structure formed by a cross-linker reaction. In the adsorption process, the nitrogen of the $-CN$ group was a strong Lewis base due to its vacant double electrons, which could provide a complex for coordination with chemical entities low in electrons such as Cd (II) ions. Meanwhile, the three-dimensional cross-linked structure in cellulose affix Cd (II) ions to the network structures. The calculated activation energy (E_a) of 254.5 kJ mol^{-1} indicated that the adsorption of Cd (II) onto MSB is chemical control. The adsorption kinetics were best described by the pseudo-second-order kinetic model, which confirms that chemical adsorption is the rate-controlling step.

17.2.4 Adsorption of organic pollutant molecules (OPMs)

With the acceleration of human industrialization, water pollution is becoming more and more serious worldwide. Organic wastewater is of concern because they contain refractory or persistent organic pollutants (dyes, antibiotics, phenols, etc.). At present, in the treatment of organic wastewater, the photocatalytic method has some shortcomings, such as low utilization rate of light energy and difficult recovery, while the adsorption method has some problems, such as incomplete adsorption. Due to their high specific surface area, developed pore structure, the advantages of easy to surface modification, porous carbon materials in heterogeneous elements doping, can make its double function mechanism (direct adsorption and assisted catalytic oxidation) for organic wastewater treatment. Recently, we summarized the research progress of preparation methods and adsorption applications of heterogeneous element doped hierarchical porous carbon materials. It is hoped that by summarizing the basic theoretical knowledge of doped porous carbon materials, the application research of porous carbon materials in organic wastewater treatment can be promoted, so as to provide theoretical basis for the large-scale preparation and practical application of porous carbon materials with high surface area, developed pore structure and high adsorption performances [13].

More recently, by using coconut fibers as raw material, activated carbon fibers were prepared via carbonization and KOH activation processes by our research group for efficient adsorption of various organic dyes (see Fig. 17.2E—G for details) [12]. The specific surface area and the pore volume of the activated carbon fibers reach 1556 m^2 g^{-1} and 0.72 cm^3 g^{-1}, respectively. The adsorption capacities of the activated carbon fibers in methylene blue, Congo red, and neutral red systems reached equilibrium at 150, 120, and 120 min, and the maximum adsorption capacities were 21.3, 22.1, and 20.7 mg g^{-1}, respectively. The adsorption of three kinds of dye solutions, namely, methylene blue, Congo red, and neutral red dye was investigated. The adsorption capacity (Q_e) was calculated as follows:

$$Q_e = (C_0 - C_e) \times V/m$$

where C_0 (mg L^{-1}) is the initial concentration of dye solution, C_e (mg L^{-1}) is the residual concentration of dye solution, V (L) is the volume of dye solution, and m (g) is the mass of activated carbon fibers. The adsorption rate (D) was determined as follows:

$$D = (C_0 - C_e)/C0 \times 100\%$$

In order to analyze the adsorption kinetics, three kinds of adsorption kinetics models including pseudo-first-order equation, pseudo-second-order equation, and intraparticle diffusion equation were applied as follows:

$$\text{Pseudo-first-order equation: } \ln(Q_e - Q_t) = \ln Q_e - K_1 t$$

where Q_t is the adsorption capacity at time t (min), Q_e (mg g^{-1}) is the equilibrium adsorption capacity, and K_1 is the constant of quasi-first-order equation.

$$\text{Pseudo-second-order equation: } t/Q_t = 1/(K_2 Q_e^2) + t/Q_e$$

where K_2 is the constant of quasi-second-order equation.

$$\text{Intraparticle diffusion equation: } Q_t = K_p t^{1/2} + C$$

where K_p is the constant of particle diffusion constant and C is the experimental constant.

The results indicated that the dynamic adsorption processes of coconut-based activated carbon fibers to methylene blue, Congo red, and neutral red were all in accordance with the second-order kinetic model, and the equations are as follows: $t/Q_t = 0.1028 + t/21.3220$, $t/Q_t = 0.1128 + t/21.5982$ and $t/Q_t = 0.0210 + t/20.6612$. The optimal pH values of methylene blue, Congo red, and neutral red were 9, 3, and 9, respectively [12].

17.3 Functional materials

Common adsorbent materials mainly include molecular sieve, activated carbon, silica gel, activated alumina four categories. Molecular sieve has regular micropore structure, specific surface area of about 500–1500 m^2 g^{-1}, mainly micropores, pore size distribution between 0.4 and 1 nm. The adsorption characteristics of molecular sieve can be changed by adjusting the structure, composition and balance of cation types. Active carbon has abundant microporous and mesoporous structure, and the specific surface area is about 800–3000 m^2 g^{-1}, and the pore size distribution is mainly in 2–50 nm. Activated carbon mainly depends on the van der Waals force produced by adsorption and adsorbent, mainly used in adsorption of organic compounds, heavy hydrocarbon organic matter adsorption removal, deodorant, etc. Silica gel has a specific surface area of about $300-500 \, m^2 \, g^{-1}$, mainly mesoporous, pore size distribution in 2—50 nm, the internal surface of the pore has rich surface hydroxyl, mainly used for adsorption drying and pressure swing adsorption CO_2 production, etc. Activated alumina has a specific surface area of $200-500 \, m^2 \, g^{-1}$, mainly mesoporous, pore size distribution in 2—50 nm, mainly used in drying dehydration, acid waste gas purification, and so on [1]. Novel nanostructured or ultraporous adsorption materials (e.g., metal-organic frameworks) are being developed and hold fascinating prospects for future adsorption (especially gas adsorption) applications.

17.4 Applications

Adsorption as a phenomenon exists everywhere. At present, solid adsorbents have been widely used in environmental purification and waste treatment. The gas and liquid on the solid surface have the tendency to accumulate automatically on the solid surface in order to reduce the surface energy. The phenomenon that the concentration of gas or liquid on solid surface is higher than its bulk concentration is called solid surface adsorption. With environmental adsorption materials as the core, the key applications of various adsorption materials in future environmental research include: heavy metal adsorption in sewage, arsenic, and fluorine adsorption in drinking water, perfluorinated compounds adsorption of emerging pollutants in water and CO_2 adsorption of greenhouse gas in gas phase. For promoting the application of nanoporous materials in environmental remediation and governance, we should systematically study the preparation method (mass technology), performance characterization (adsorption capacity, adsorption rate, selectivity and regeneration) of efficient adsorption materials, and explore the adsorption characteristics and adsorption mechanism of different pollutants.

17.5 Summary

In this chapter, we have discussed the basic principles, adsorption mechanisms, and adsorption materials for the treatment and recycling of "three wastes" (waste gas, waste water, and waste residue). The porous materials (adsorbents), such as molecular sieve and activated carbon, have strong adsorption capacity for various adsorbates, including the waste gas (VOCs), waste water (organic molecules and HMIs), and waste residue (water-soluble leaching solution from residue). The adsorption mechanism and Isotherm, adsorption of VOCs, adsorption of HMIs, and adsorption of organic pollutant molecules (OPMs) are analyzed and summarized in detail. Nanoadsorption technology based on porous materials provides an effective treatment scheme for the treatment and recycling of "three wastes."

Acknowledgments

This book was supported by National Natural Science Foundation of China (22078071, 22272034), Natural Science Foundation of Guangdong Province (2021A1515010125, 2020A1515010344), Maoming Science and Technology Project (mmkj2020032), Guangdong Province Universities and Colleges Pearl River Scholar Funded Scheme (2019), Guangdong Basic and Applied Basic Research Foundation (2019A1515011249, 2021A1515010305), Key Research Project of Natural Science of Guangdong Provincial Department of Education (2019KZDXM010), Environment and Energy Green Catalysis Innovation Team of Colleges and Universities of Guangdong Province (2022KCXTD019), the program for Innovative Research Team of Guangdong University of Petrochemical Technology.

References

[1] https://mp.weixin.qq.com/s/xmCm_UzRqqsjPayGMk0SjA.
[2] https://mp.weixin.qq.com/s/bf076PynUG8_ERUaQsHHMQ.
[3] X. Li, L. Zhang, Z. Yang, P. Wang, Y. Yan, J. Ran, Adsorption materials for volatile organic compounds (VOCs) and the key factors for VOCs adsorption process: a review, Separation and Purification Technology 235 (2020) 116213.
[4] X.C. Fu, W.X. Shen, T.Y. Yao, W.H. Hou, Physical Chemistry, Higher Education, Beijing, 2005.
[5] R. Blaszczak, Choosing an Adsorption System for VOC: Carbon, Zeolite, or Polymers, EPA-456/F-99-004, North Carolina, 1999.
[6] https://mp.weixin.qq.com/s/eoGJ7azBjrHoq5rRA9n7kw.
[7] E. Iakovleva, M. Sillanpää, The use of low-cost adsorbents for wastewater purification in mining industries, Environmental Science and Pollution Research 20 (11) (2013) 7878−7899.
[8] X. Zhang, B. Gao, A.E. Creamer, C. Cao, Y. Li, Adsorption of VOCs onto engineered carbon materials: a review, Journal of Hazardous Materials 338 (2017) 102−123.
[9] W. Zhang, G. Li, H. Yin, K. Zhao, H. Zhao, T. An, Adsorption and desorption mechanism of aromatic VOCs onto porous carbon adsorbents for emission control and resource recovery: recent progress and challenges, Environmental Science: Nano 9 (2022) 81−104.
[10] M. Song, Y. Wei, S. Cai, L. Yu, Z. Zhong, B. Jin, Study on adsorption properties and mechanism of Pb^{2+} with different carbon based adsorbents, Science of the Total Environment 618 (2018) 1416−1422.
[11] X. Niu, L. Zheng, J. Zhou, Z. Dang, Z. Li, Synthesis of an adsorbent from sugarcane bagass by graft copolymerization and its utilization to remove Cd (II) ions from aqueous solution, Journal of the Taiwan Institute of Chemical Engineers 45 (5) (2014) 2557−2564.
[12] L. Zhang, L.Y. Tu, Y. Liang, Q. Chen, Z.S. Li, C.H. Li, W. Li, Coconut-based activated carbon fibers for efficient adsorption of various organic dyes, RSC Advances 8 (74) (2018) 42280−42291.
[13] S. Zhai, Z. Liu, Z. Li, Q. Chen, H. Liao, Research Progress on Preparation of Doped Graded Porous Carbon Materials and Adsorption of Organic Pollutants, Guangdong Chemical Industry, 2020.

CHAPTER 18

Advanced oxidation in the treatment of three wastes: fundamentals

18.1 Introduction

The advanced oxidation process (AOP) refers to the technology of using strong oxidizing free radicals to degrade organic pollutants, and generally refers to the chemical oxidation technology in which a large number of hydroxyl radicals ($\cdot$OH) participate in the reaction process [1]. By using a catalyst, radiation, or a variety of chemical reagents, the reaction system produces highly reactive free radicals. The addition, substitution, and electron transfer reaction between free radicals and pollutants can make the refractory organic macromolecular oxidized and degraded into low toxic or nontoxic small molecular, or even directly degraded into CO_2 and H_2O by complete mineralization [2]. It can be said that the production of $\cdot$OH radical is the fundamental mark and characteristic of the AOP. Advanced oxidation technology has become an important means of controlling refractory organic toxic pollutants, and has been applied in the wastewater treatment of printing and dyeing, the chemical industry, pesticide, papermaking, electroplating and printed board, pharmaceutical, hospital, mine, landfill leachate and so on [3]. At present, advanced oxidation technologies mainly include chemical oxidation (Fenton reagent oxidation and ozone oxidation), persulfate oxidation, electrochemical oxidation, wet oxidation, photocatalytic oxidation, supercritical water oxidation, and ultrasonic oxidation methods [4]. These advanced oxidation technologies show application prospects in "three wastes" treatment: waste gas (volatile organic compounds (VOCs)), wastewater (organic molecules and heavy metal ions), and waste residue (water-soluble leaching solution from residue). In this chapter, we mainly focus on the presentation of basic principles, catalytic materials, and application prospects of Fenton reagent oxidation and persulfate activation oxidation methods.

18.2 Basic principles

18.2.1 Basic principles for fenton reaction

Fenton reagent oxidation technology originated in the mid-1890s, put forward by the French scientist H. J. Furenton, under acidic conditions, H_2O_2 under the catalytic action of Fe^{2+} ions can effectively oxidize tartaric acid, and applied to the oxidation of malic acid. For a long time, the main principle of Fenton oxidation by default is to use ferrous ions as the catalyst for hydrogen peroxide, and the hydroxyl radical generated under

Nanostructured Materials
ISBN 978-0-443-19256-2, https://doi.org/10.1016/B978-0-443-19256-2.00018-1

acidic conditions. Fenton reaction uses ferrous ion (Fe^{2+}) as a catalyst to catalyze hydrogen peroxide (H_2O_2), making it produce hydroxyl radical ($\cdot OH$) to oxidize organic matter. Hydroxyl radical has a strong oxidation ability. It can react with most refractory organic matter (such as phenol and aniline), thereby destroying organic matter molecules and making them mineralized until transformed into inorganic matter such as CO_2 and H_2O. At the same time, Fe^{2+} can be oxidized into iron ion (Fe^{3+}), and the reaction between Fe^{3+} and H_2O_2 can produce Fe^{2+} and trigger a chain reaction (including chain initiation, development, and termination) to produce more other free radicals ($\cdot OH$, $\cdot HO_2$ and $\cdot R$) [5].

Chain initiation reactions:

$$Fe^{2+} + H_2O_2 \rightarrow \cdot OH + OH^- + Fe^{3+}$$

$$Fe^{3+} + H_2O_2 \rightarrow Fe^{2+} + \cdot HO_2 + H^+$$

$$\cdot HO_2 + H_2O_2 \rightarrow \cdot OH + O_2 + H_2O$$

Chain development reactions:

$$RH \text{ (organic substance)} + \cdot OH \rightarrow \cdot R + H_2O$$

$$\cdot R + Fe^{3+} \rightarrow R^+ + Fe^{2+}$$

The chain reaction results:

$$R^+ + O_2 \rightarrow ROO^+ \rightarrow CO_2 + H_2O$$

Termination of chain reactions:

$$\cdot OH + \cdot OH \rightarrow H_2O_2$$

$$\cdot OH + \cdot R \rightarrow ROH$$

With the in-depth study of the Fenton method, in recent years, ultraviolet light (UV), oxalate, and complexing agent are introduced into the Fenton method or developing photo-Fenton reagent, electro-Fenton reagent, and ligand-Fenton reagents can greatly enhance the oxidation capacity of Fenton method. Fe (III) salt solution, soluble iron, and iron oxide minerals (such as hematite, goethite, etc.) can also catalyze the decomposition of H_2O_2 to produce $\cdot OH$, so as to achieve the purpose of degrading organic pollutants. A Fenton reagent composed of such catalysts is called a Fenton-like reagent (the source of iron is relatively wide for the Fenton-like method). The main parameters affecting the reaction of the Fenton reagent include the solution pH, residence time, temperature, hydrogen peroxide, and Fe^{2+} concentration [6].

Fenton oxidation, as one of the commonly used advanced oxidation technologies, plays an irreplaceable role in water environmental remediation. However, because

Fenton oxidation contains many complex reaction processes, it has the disadvantages of low iron cycling efficiency, easy-to-produce iron mud, poor stability, and high operation cost, which limits its practical application. The conversion of Fe^{3+} to Fe^{2+} can be effectively promoted by adding a certain amount of cocatalysts in the Fenton system, so as to improve the reaction efficiency. The common cocatalysts include organic acid, zero-valent metal, single-atom metal, and metal sulfide. Organic acids can be used as excellent ligands for chelating Fe^{3+}. The conversion rate of Fe^{3+} to Fe^{2+} can be increased by charge transfer, and the pH range of the Fenton reaction can be expanded. Zero-valent metal is not only the catalyst of the Fenton reaction but also the reducing agent of the reduction reaction, which plays an important role in performance improvement. The metal reduction sites in metal sulfide can significantly accelerate the conversion of Fe^{3+}/Fe^{2+} and reduce the amount of Fenton reagent, indicating a new method for improving the efficiency of the Fenton reaction. Single-atom metal can maximize atomic efficiency and single-atom Fenton technology has achieved remarkable results in environmental remediation, enriching the modification strategies available for Fenton reactions (see Fig. 18.1A for details) [7].

Singlet oxygen ($^1O_2$) is a kind of reactive oxygen species with selective oxidation ability, which has a wide application prospect in the field of environmental pollution control. However, the formation mechanism of $^1O_2$ in the Fenton reaction system is still unclear, especially the transformation mechanism from superoxide radical ($\cdot O^-$) to $^1O_2$ is controversial. The activation of H_2O_2 in the Fenton reaction will produce a large number of hydroxyl radicals ($\cdot OH$), and $\cdot OH$ can through its own disproportionation reaction generate $^1O_2$. This interferes with the study of the conversion mechanism of $\cdot O^-$ to $^1O_2$ in Fenton reaction, and also makes it difficult to realize the regulation of reactive oxygen species (ROS) of Fenton oxidation. In order to solve this problem, Professor Xing used molybdenum (Mo) powder as a cocatalyst and made use of the highly reductive active site Mo^0 on the surface of Mo powder to realize the quenching of $\cdot OH$ in the Fenton reaction process, eliminating its interference on the formation mechanism of $^1O_2$. At the same time, the exposed oxidation active site Mo^{6+} on the surface of Mo powder makes $\cdot O^-$ overcome the thermodynamic reaction energy barrier and realize its directional transformation to $^1O_2$. Compared with $\cdot OH$ and other ROS, $^1O_2$ has a relatively long life and migration distance, which can achieve the removal of Rhodamine B, phenol, norfloxacin, sulfadiazine, and other aromatic organic pollutants in water (see Fig. 18.1B for details) [8].

Many studies have shown that porous catalysts can achieve high efficiency of advanced oxidation degradation and mineralization of pollutants. However, most studies only stay at the phenomenon level, and there is no clear definition of the "confinement effect" (see Section 3.7.1). Recently, Professor Kim reported a research paper on the mechanism of heterogeneous Fenton reaction kinetics enhancement under nanoscale spatial confinement. The nanoreactor can rapidly degrade the pollutants within only a

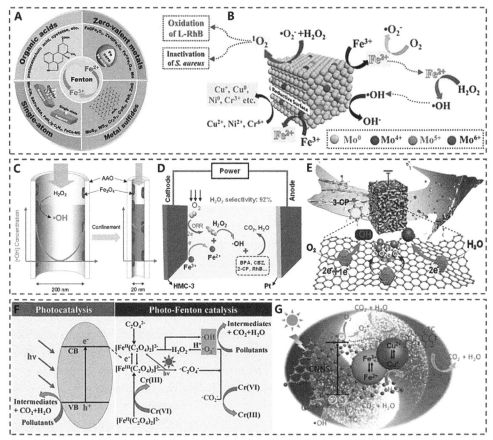

Figure 18.1 (A) Fenton oxidation cocatalysts for conversion of Fe^{3+} to Fe^{2+} [7]; (B) Mo cocatalysts for Fenton oxidation [8]; (C) Nano confinement effect for Fenton oxidation [9]; (D) Electro Fenton process of two-electron O_2 reduction [10]; (E) Electro Fenton process on PdFe alloy/CA cathode [11]; (F) Photo Fenton on Fe (III)/oxalate ($C_2O_4^{2-}$) system [12]; (G) Photo Fenton on 0D Cu-Fe QDs/2D g-C_3N_4 system [13].

few tens of seconds, and the degradation efficiency is greatly improved with the decrease of the reactor pore size (from 200 to 20 nm). Under confinement conditions, the exposure intensity of ·OH per unit catalytic area was increased by up to 23 times, and the half-reaction period was shortened to 14 s, which was much smaller than the catalytic reaction without confinement (at least 3 h). This study reveals the phenomenon and mechanism of $\cdot OH$ oxidation kinetics enhancement due to the confinement effect of nanoreactor, which is of guiding significance for the research and design of new reactors for advanced oxidized water treatment (see Fig. 18.1C for details) [9].

Electro Fenton process is considered a promising advanced oxidation technology for the degradation and removal of persistent organic pollutants in wastewater. In the electro-Fenton reaction, oxygen generates H_2O_2 in situ at the cathode through a two-electron reduction process, which reacts with Fe^{2+} to generate a strong oxidizing hydroxyl radical ($\cdot OH$), which rapidly oxidizes organic pollutants. Recently, Luo et al. prepared a porous biocarbon catalyst doped with O and N using a peanut shell as the precursor. The catalyst has a specific surface area of 1875 $cm^2\ g^{-1}$, good electronic conductivity, and abundant active defect site. The presence of the O and N functional group make the catalyst has excellent two-electron selectivity for the electric generation of H_2O_2. Meanwhile, the coordination of the N functional group and Fe accelerates the regeneration of Fe^{2+}, thus achieving the stable accumulation of $\cdot OH$ and improving the electro-Fenton efficiency. The HMC-3 electro-Fenton system can efficiently degrade and mineralize a variety of persistent organic pollutants, and the system shows good cycle stability and strong adaptability to different surface water bodies (see Fig. 18.1D for details) [10].

Carbon aerogel (CA) is a new type of carbon-based electrode material with a high specific surface area, rich porosity, high conductivity, and adjustable pore size. Recently, Zhao and collaborators reported that "In situ Formed PdFe Nanoalloy and Carbon Defects In Synergic reduced-oxidation of Chlorinated materials Unsustainable in Electro-Fenton Process". In this study, an integrated PdFe alloy/CA cathode was constructed, a new heterogeneous electro-Fenton method for the codegradation of pollutants by electrochemical reduction-oxidation. On the same cathode material, the electrocatalytic reduction of molecular O_2 can produce $\cdot OH$ and electrocatalytic hydrogen evolution of H_2O can produce $[H]_{ads}$, which can be used for the advanced treatment of halogenated pollutants in water and typical disinfection by-products (halogenated acetamide) in drinking water. It has a 100% mineralization rate and dechlorination rate, low electrochemical energy consumption, high electrode stability, and mechanical strength, and has a good application prospect (see Fig. 18.1E for details) [11].

In recent years, as a typical advanced oxidation process (AOP), the photo Fenton strategy has been widely used to remove organic pollutants and heavy metal ions in water. Persistent organic pollutants (POPs) in wastewater, such as industrial dyes, antibiotics, and hexavalent chromium (VI), have attracted great attention due to their difficult degradation and persistent environmental pollution. Different from the traditional Fenton reaction, the Fe (III)/oxalate ($C_2O_4^{2-}$) system, under visible light, can achieve rapid iron cycling without additional addition of H_2O_2, and produce a large number of strong redox reactive oxygen radicals ($\cdot O^{2-}$ and $\cdot OH$). The $FeWO_4$ exposed to {001} crystal surface enhanced the ability of activated oxalic acid to produce H_2O_2, $\cdot O^{2-}$ and $\cdot OH$.

The main oxidizing radicals of the FeWO$_4$/Fe (III)/oxalate system are $\cdot O^{2-}$ and $\cdot OH$, while the main reducing radical is $\cdot CO^{2-}$, which shows greatly enhanced activities for the mineralization of organic pollutants and reduction of Cr (VI). This study provides the theoretical reference for understanding the mechanism of surface photo-Fenton reaction dependent on crystal surface (see Fig. 18.1F for details) [12].

It is very important to develop multi-component catalysts with multiple active centers to improve the oxidation performances for the photo Fenton process. Liu et al. successfully prepared a 0D Cu-Fe bimetallic oxide QDs/2D g-C$_3$N$_4$ composite through a gentle one-step synthesis strategy, which has incomparable advantages over single metal 0D/2D quantum dots in photo Fenton catalysis. Thanks to the synergistic effect of g-C$_3$N$_4$ and Cu-Fe site, the composite can efficiently remove tetracycline in a wide pH range. Experiments and DFT calculations show that in addition to rapid charge separation and transport, the above synergistic effects can also achieve the optimal H$_2$O$_2$ adsorption and activation tradeoff at the Cu–Fe site, and can also change the adsorption of tetracycline, resulting in multiple synergistic effects of adsorption-catalytic degradation and photo Fenton oxidation (see Fig. 18.1G for details) [13].

18.2.2 Basic principles for persulfate activation

Sulfate radical (SO$_4^-\cdot$) is a radical with high redox potential ($E_0 = 2.5-3.1$ V), so sulfate radical is considered to be able to oxidize the vast majority of organic matter under ideal conditions. The general action mode of sulfate and organic matter: hydrogen capture, electron transfer, addition, oxidation. Fenton and Fenton-like reactions can produce highly reactive oxygen species from peroxygens (such as peroxydualsulfate (PDS), peroxymonosulfate (PMS), hydrogen peroxide (H$_2$O$_2$), etc.) and have developed into powerful technologies for chemical synthesis, bacterial sterilization, environmental remediation, especially for the degradation of emerging refractory organic pollutants. The persulfates can be excited by light, heat, catalysis, and other ways, the dioxygen bond is broken, and the highly reactive sulfate radical (SO$_4^-\cdot$) is produced. The activation principle is shown as follows [6]:

$$SO_5^{2-} + heat/UV/else \rightarrow SO_4^- \cdot + [O]$$

The toxicological effects, pollution risk, and control of polycyclic aromatic hydrocarbons (PAHs) derivatives have attracted extensive attention. Advanced oxidation technology is often used for the oxidative degradation of toxic organic compounds in the environment. However, how to choose catalysts and oxidants to degrade PAHs derivatives is a difficult problem in the treatment of such pollutants. Recently, Professor Gao from the Nanjing Agricultural University of China used advanced oxidation technology combined with computational chemistry to construct an oxidative degradation system with nano-MoO$_2$ as a catalyst and peroxymono-sulfate (PMS) as an oxidant (see Fig. 18.2A for details) [14]. Mo (IV) can be regenerated from the reduction of Mo

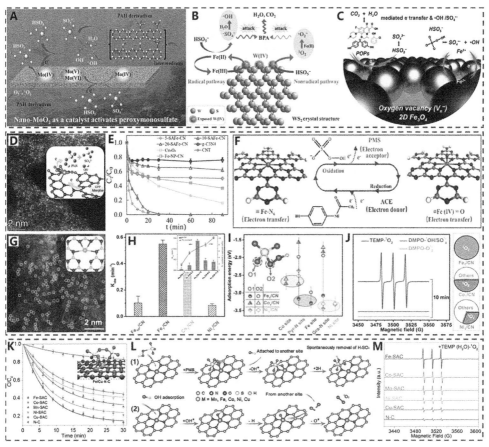

Figure 18.2 (A) PMS activation and degradation of PAHs by nano-MoO$_2$ [14]; (B) WS$_2$ cocatalyzes the degradation of BPA by Fe(II)/PMS [15]; (C) Fe$_3$O$_4$ cocatalyzes the degradation of POPs by Fe(II)/PMS [16]; PMS activation by SACs [17]: (D and E) SAFe-CN [18], (F) Fe-SA/PHCNS [19], (G—J) Fe$_1$/CN [20], (K—M) M-SACs (M = Fe, Co, Mn, Ni and Cu) [21]; the inset in (K) is FeCu bimetallic SACs [22]).

(VI) on the nano-MoO$_2$ surface. It was found that the system could effectively degrade naphthalene and its derivatives, such as 1-methylnaphthalene, 1-nitronaphthalene, 1-chlornaphthalene, 1-naphthalamine, and 1-naphthol. By electron paramagnetic resonance spectroscopy and X-ray photoelectron spectroscopy, it was found that nano

MoO_2 cleaved the O-O bond of PMS to produce $SO_4^-\cdot$ through electron transfer from nano-MoO_2 to PMS, and part of $SO_4^-\cdot$ could be further converted to $\cdot OH$, which promoted the degradation of naphthalene and its derivatives in water (the nano-MoO_2 is a novel activator with high activity on PMS). The results showed that the substituents on the PAHs derivatives caused the uneven distribution of electron cloud density on the whole molecular surface, which affected the electron transfer and electrophilic reaction between $SO_4^-\cdot$ and OH and pollutants, resulting in the difference of degradation efficiency between the different PAHs derivatives and the parent PAHs [14].

Sulfate-based AOPs are often inhibited by the slow Fe(III) to Fe(II) transformation cycle. Therefore, it is necessary to seek an effective strategy to enhance the activation of PMS to achieve the desired degradation effect of organic pollutants. Recently, Chen et al. demonstrated that transition metal sulfide (WS_2) can significantly enhance PMS activation and organic pollutant degradation through enhanced Fe(III)/Fe(II) cycling (see Fig. 18.2B for details) [15]. In this system, 99.4% of BPA can be degraded within 20 min, which can be extended to degrade other refractory organic pollutants and treat real leachate. Quenching test and ESR analysis showed that sulfate ($SO_4^-\cdot$) and hydroxyl ($\cdot OH$) contributed to the ideal degradation of BPA. The singlet oxygen ($^1O_2$) generated by WS_2-induced PMS activation reacts with Fe(II) to form $\cdot O_2^-$, which also leads to BPA degradation.

In the Fenton-like reaction of permono-sulfate (PMS) activation, iron-based catalysts are considered the most promising transition metal catalysts due to their wide source of raw materials, non-toxicity, and low processing cost. Recently, Wang et al. constructed an ultra-thin two-dimensional (2D) Fe_3O_4 for Fenton-like PMS activation (see Fig. 18.2C for details) [16]. By introducing oxygen vacancies into the interface of the 2D Fe_3O_4 catalyst, the surface electronic states of the transition metal oxides were skillfully regulated to improve their catalytic performance. The existence of oxygen vacancies on Fe_3O_4 can promote the Fe^{3+}/Fe^{2+} cycle, and effectively enhance the reactivity of traditional iron-based catalysts. The rapid oxidation of POP pollutants involves a degradation process accompanied by nonradical mechanisms (mediated electron transfer) and radical oxidation mechanisms ($SO_4^-\cdot$ and $\cdot OH$).

The N-coordinated metal (M-N_x) single atom catalysts (SACs) (such as g-C_3N_4 and N-doped carbon-supported Fe SACs) have atomically-dispersed metal active sites with tunable coordination structures and easily increased atom density, which can efficiently catalyze the activation of persulfates (PDS or PMS) [17]. By adjusting coordination structures and active site densities of SACs, it is expected to realize the nonfree radical persulfate activation, which lays a structural foundation for studying the intrinsic activity and simplifying descriptors of catalysts (see Fig. 18.2D–M for details) [18–22]. Among nonfree radical mechanisms, singlet oxygenation ($^1O_2$), high valence Fe species (HV-Fe), and mediated electron transfer are the three most prominent mechanisms [17]. Recently, Duan et al. designed an atomically dispersed Fe catalyst (SAFe-CN) with high atomic density ($\sim$8 atoms nm^{-2}) supported on g-C$_3$N$_4$ (in Fe-N$_2$O$_2$ moiety) and used it to PMS activation for efficient removal of o-phenylphenol (OPP) (removal rate reached 99% in 20 min) where the mediated electron transfer is the dominant mechanism (Fig. 18.2D and E) [18]. More recently, Wang et al. synthesized a single-atom Fe catalyst (Fe-SA/PHCNS) immobilized on graphitic carbon nitride in the form of $\equiv$Fe-N$_6$ with modest atomic density ($\sim$2 atoms nm^{-2}), which can achieve efficient PMS activation and oxidation removal of organic medicine of acetaminophen (ACE) (Fig. 18.2D and F) [19]. This study clarified the mechanism and advantages of "HV-Fe-oxo" single-atom species-mediated oxidation pathway, promoting the popularization of this new pathway in AOP.

Singlet oxygen (^{1}O$_2$) is known as a highly active species that can selectively degrade diversified organic pollutants, while it is still a great challenge to realize high yield and high selectivity in the production of ^{1}O$_2$. Recently, Zou and coworkers reported the preparation of high-density Fe SACs (Fe$_1$/CN) loaded with up to 11.2 wt.% Fe by a supramolecular method, which could activate PMS effectively to produce ^{1}O$_2$ with an amazing selectivity of 100% (Fig. 18.2G–J) [20]. The PMS activated by Fe$_1$/CN can degrade p-chlorophenol (4-CP) efficiently and selectively. The Fe$_1$/CNs in different Fe loading (1.7–11.2 wt.%) exhibited normal distribution of the degradation rates of 4-CP. Compared with Co and Ni sites, Fe sites in Fe$_1$/CN are more likely to adsorb the terminal O of PMS, thus promoting the oxidation of PMS to SO$_5^-\cdot$, and effectively generating ^{1}O$_2$ with 100% selectivity. The high-density Fe SACs realize the highly efficient activation of PMS and open up a new way for the highly selective production of ^{1}O$_2$, showing a wide application prospect in the degradation of organic pollutants.

Recently, Cheng and coworkers synthesized a series of N-doped carbon (NC) supported single-atom metal catalysts (M-SACS, M = Mn, Fe, Co, Ni, Cu) by a universal metallic molecule pyrolysis method for the comparative analysis of PMS activation with different metal centers (Fig. 18.2K–M) [21]. The structure-property relationship for these M-SACs has been analyzed, and their activity trend and reaction mechanism in the activation of PMS to ^{1}O$_2$ have been revealed systematically. The degradation of bisphenol A (BPA) by M-SACs/PMS system showed the following active order: Fe-SAC > Co-SAC > Mn-SAC > Ni-SAC > Cu-SAC. Combined with the experimental results, theoretical calculation proved that PMS $\rightarrow$ OH* $\rightarrow$ O* $\rightarrow$ ^{1}O$_2$ is the most reasonable reaction pathway for these M-SACs. The ^{1}O$_2$ was proved to be the main active oxygen species in the system with the same active order in BPA degradation. In particular, adjacent metal atoms (or bimetallic atoms) can lead to changes in electronic structure that favor molecular adsorption and chemical bond activation (see the inset in Fig. 18.2K) [22]. Because the distance of the atomic pair is often less than 0.3 nm, bimetallic SACs can provide an opportunity to adsorb two O atoms of PDS molecules by the bimetallic atom pair.

18.3 Functional materials

Nanotechnology has played an increasing role in facilitating iron cycling in the Fenton system. For example, zero-valent iron and single–atom cocatalytic Fentons are both dependent on nanotechnology. For example, FeS_2/C nanocomposites can be used as efficient and stable cocatalysts in the Fenton treatment of organic water pollutants. Nano-zero-valent iron is widely used in the Fenton system and persulfate oxidants to generate free radicals for rapid and thorough degradation and removal of organic matter due to its large specific surface area and strong reducing ability. The nano-structured CuO is confirmed to be oxidized by PMS to form Cu(III). The electrophilicity of Cu(III) makes it more inclined to directly oxidize phenolic organic compounds, thus inhibiting the reaction of Cu(III) with PMS to form singlet oxygen. Layered double hydroxides (e.g., CoFe-LDHs) can also be used to activate peroxymono-sulfate (PMS) to degrade quinolone antibiotics. The promoting mechanism of electric field on the activation of persulfates by new growing amorphous nanostructured MnO_2 provides a new idea for the efficient utilization of transition metal oxide in the water oxidation treatment process. N- and O-codoped carbon materials with porous structures (NOPC-X) have been used to activate PMS to degrade bisphenol. In general, nanostructured zero-valent metals (including single atom metals), metal oxides, metal sulfides, metal hydroxides, and even porous carbon materials are widely used as active materials or carrier materials in advanced oxidation technology.

18.4 Applications

The essence of the Fenton method is that the chain reaction between divalent iron ion (Fe^{2+}) and hydrogen peroxide (H_2O_2) catalyzes the generation of hydroxyl radical ($\cdot OH$), which has strong oxidation ability, and its oxidation potential is second only to fluorine, up to 2.80 V. In addition, the OH has a high electronegativity, or electrical, the electron affinity is as high as 569.3 kJ, and have very strong addition reaction characteristics. Fenton reagent (use of ferrous sulfate and hydrogen peroxide) can be no selective oxidation of most of the organic matter in water, especially suitable for oxidation treatment of biological refractory wastewaters or those general chemical oxidations difficult to work. Persulfates include permonosulfate (PMS, HSO_5^-) and perdisulfide (PDS, $S_2O_8^{2-}$). Both PMS and PDS have O-O bonds in their structures, which are stable at room temperature with a low reaction rate and general degradation effect on organic pollutants. Once PS is activated, O-O bond breakage will produce $SO_4^-\cdot$ and OH with higher redox potential in the system, which greatly enhances the oxidative degradation ability of organic matter. With the development and progress of science and technology, the methods of activated persulfates will be more abundant, the degradation mechanism in the oxidation process will be further studied, and the application scope will be gradually extended to the advanced treatment of soil, waste gas, refractory organic wastewater and drinking water, etc.

18.5 Summary

In this chapter, we have discussed the basic principles, oxidation mechanisms, and functional materials for the advanced oxidation process (AOP). The oxidation capacity of AOP exceeds all common oxidants or the oxidation potential is close to or reaches the level of hydroxyl radical $HO\cdot$, which can carry out a series of free radical chain reactions with harmful organic pollutants in the water, thereby destroying their structure and gradually degrading them into harmless low molecular weight organic matter. The final degradation to harmless CO_2, H_2O, and other minerals (N_2, O_2, SO_4^{2-}, PO_3^{4-}). Fenton reaction (traditional Fenton, photo Fenton, and electro Fenton) and persulfate activation have short reaction time, fast reaction speed, controlled process, no selectivity, and can degrade a variety of organic pollutants in the water. The nanostructured and atomic-structured materials are widely used in advanced oxidation technology.

Acknowledgments

This book was supported by National Natural Science Foundation of China (22078071, 22272034), Natural Science Foundation of Guangdong Province (2021A1515010125, 2020A1515010344), Maoming Science and Technology Project (mmkj2020032), Guangdong Province Universities and Colleges Pearl River Scholar Funded Scheme (2019), Guangdong Basic and Applied Basic Research Foundation (2019A1515011249, 2021A1515010305), Key Research Project of Natural Science of Guangdong Provincial Department of Education (2019KZDXM010), Environment and Energy Green Catalysis Innovation Team of Colleges and Universities of Guangdong Province (2022KCXTD019), the program for Innovative Research Team of Guangdong University of Petrochemical Technology.

References

[1] R. Andreozzi, V. Caprio, A. Insola, R. Marotta, Advanced oxidation processes (AOP) for water purification and recovery, Catalysis Today 53 (1) (1999) 51−59.

[2] M.E. Sillanpää, T.A. Kurniawan, W.H. Lo, Degradation of chelating agents in aqueous solution using advanced oxidation process (AOP), Chemosphere 83 (11) (2011) 1443−1460.

[3] Y. Deng, R. Zhao, Advanced oxidation processes (AOPs) in wastewater treatment, Current Pollution Reports 1 (3) (2015) 167−176.

[4] R. Guan, X. Yuan, Z. Wu, L. Jiang, Y. Li, G. Zeng, Principle and application of hydrogen peroxide based advanced oxidation processes in activated sludge treatment: a review, Chemical Engineering Journal 339 (2018) 519−530.

[5] https://mp.weixin.qq.com/s/eNnlv0SyKF3JBhwpNXml8Q.

[6] https://mp.weixin.qq.com/s/oZ0SiovSyepNtPNSNgSfqA.

[7] Q. Yan, J. Zhang, M. Xing, Cocatalytic fenton reaction for pollutant control, Cell Reports Physical Science 1 (8) (2020) 100149.

[8] Q. Yi, J. Ji, B. Shen, C. Dong, J. Liu, J. Zhang, et al., Singlet oxygen triggered by superoxide radicals in a molybdenum cocatalytic Fenton reaction with enhanced REDOX activity in the environment, Environmental Science & Technology 53 (16) (2019) 9725−9733.

[9] S. Zhang, M. Sun, T. Hedtke, A. Deshmukh, X. Zhou, S. Weon, et al., Mechanism of heterogeneous Fenton reaction kinetics enhancement under nanoscale spatial confinement, Environmental Science & Technology 54 (17) (2020) 10868−10875.

[10] Z. Luo, M. Liu, D. Tang, Y. Xu, H. Ran, J. He, et al., High H_2O_2 selectivity and enhanced Fe^{2+} regeneration toward an effective electro-Fenton process based on a self-doped porous biochar cathode, Applied Catalysis B: Environmental 315 (2022) 121523.

[11] X. Shen, F. Xiao, H. Zhao, Y. Chen, C. Fang, R. Xiao, et al., In situ-formed PdFe nanoalloy and carbon defects in cathode for synergic reduction—oxidation of chlorinated pollutants in electro-Fenton process, Environmental Science & Technology 54 (7) (2020) 4564—4572.

[12] J. Li, C. Xiao, K. Wang, Y. Li, G. Zhang, Enhanced generation of reactive oxygen species under visible light irradiation by adjusting the exposed facet of $FeWO_4$ nanosheets to activate oxalic acid for organic pollutant removal and Cr (VI) reduction, Environmental Science & Technology 53 (18) (2019) 11023—11030.

[13] M. Liu, H. Xia, W. Yang, X. Liu, J. Xiang, X. Wang, et al., Novel Cu-Fe bi-metal oxide quantum dots coupled g-C_3N_4 nanosheets with H_2O_2 adsorption-activation trade-off for efficient photo-Fenton catalysis, Applied Catalysis B: Environmental 301 (2022) 120765.

[14] X. Chen, D. Vione, T. Borch, J. Wang, Y. Gao, Nano-MoO_2 activates peroxymonosulfate for the degradation of PAH derivatives, Water Research 192 (2021) 116834.

[15] Y. Chen, Y. Shao, O. Li, J. Liang, S. Tang, Z. Li, WS_2-cocatalyzed peroxymonosulfate activation via an enhanced Fe (III)/Fe (II) cycle toward efficient organic pollutant degradation, Chemical Engineering Journal 442 (2022) 135961.

[16] W. Wang, Y. Liu, Y. Yue, H. Wang, G. Cheng, C. Gao, et al., The confined interlayer growth of ultrathin two-dimensional Fe_3O_4 nanosheets with enriched oxygen vacancies for peroxymonosulfate activation, ACS Catalysis 11 (17) (2021) 11256—11265.

[17] Z. Li, B. Li, Y. Hu, X. Liao, H. Yu, C. Yu, Emerging ultrahigh-density single-atom catalysts for versatile heterogeneous catalysis applications: redefinition, recent progress, and challenges, Small Structures 3 (2022) 2200041.

[18] P. Duan, J. Pan, W. Du, Q. Yue, B. Gao, X. Xu, Activation of peroxymonosulfate via mediated electron transfer mechanism on single-atom Fe catalyst for effective organic pollutants removal, Applied Catalysis B: Environmental 299 (2021) 120714.

[19] Z. Wang, W. Wang, J. Wang, Y. Yuan, Q. Wu, H. Hu, High-valent iron-oxo species mediated cyclic oxidation through single-atom Fe-N_6 sites with high peroxymonosulfate utilization rate, Applied Catalysis B: Environmental 305 (2021) 121049.

[20] L.S. Zhang, X.H. Jiang, Z.A. Zhong, L. Tian, Q. Sun, Y.T. Cui, et al., Carbon nitride supported high-loading Fe single-atom catalyst for activation of peroxymonosulfate to generate $^1O_2$ with 100% selectivity, Angewandte Chemie International Edition 60 (40) (2021) 21751—21755.

[21] Y. Gao, T. Wu, C. Yang, C. Ma, Z. Zhao, Z. Wu, et al., Activity trends and mechanisms in peroxymonosulfate-assisted catalytic production of singlet oxygen over atomic metal-N-C catalysts, Angewandte Chemie International Edition 60 (41) (2021) 22513—22521.

[22] H. Wu, J. Yan, X. Xu, Q. Yuan, J. Wang, J. Cui, et al., Synergistic effects for boosted persulfate activation in a designed Fe—Cu dual-atom site catalyst, Chemical Engineering Journal 428 (2022) 132611.

PART 3

Application cases of nanomaterials in energy and environment fields

CHAPTER 19

3-D graphene nanosheets: recent progress in energy and environmental fields

19.1 Introduction

Graphene has many excellent properties and shows great application prospects in the fields of energy storage and conversion, environmental purification, and protection. The premise of these applications is to realize the macropreparation of graphene, and according to the needs of different applications, two-dimensional graphene can be assembled into graphene three-dimensional (3-D) macroscopic volume with specific macroscopic structure. Based on chemical stripping and chemical vapor deposition (CVD), several methods have been developed to prepare 3D graphene structures. The obtained 3D graphene has a unique network structure, ultra-high porosity and specific surface area, excellent electrical/thermal conductivity, and mechanical flexibility. The electrical conductivity of 3-D graphene network structures prepared by chemical stripping methods is often poor, because graphene oxide (GO) introduces a large number of structural defects in the redox process. The 3-D graphene grown directly by CVD method has higher electrical conductivity, but its yield is low due to the limitation of metal substrate surface area, which affects large-scale application [1]. Recently, our research group has reported the preparation of 3-D graphene materials (powder materials) with high conductivity (pyrolysis catalytic method from the ion-exchange resin), and the yield can reach the Kilogram level [2]. Currently, researchers have developed all kinds of mass preparation methods for 3-D graphene for the applications of energy storage and environmental purification. In order to commercialize 3-D graphene, it is also important that the manufacturing and mass production methods are simple, and that the geometry and chemistry can be designed flexibly [3].

19.2 Structural features of 3-D graphene nanosheets

Graphene is a new type of graphite carbon material with two-dimensional (2-D) structure. Its basic unit structure is usually formed by the regular accumulation of sp^2 hybrid carbon atoms in 2-D plane space [4]. Graphene materials show very clear application prospects in the field of energy and environmental technology, including electrocatalysis, electrochemical energy storage, solar cells, gas and ion adsorption, and so on [5]. Driven by strong π-π interaction and Van der Waals force, 2-D graphene nanosheets can be

Nanostructured Materials
ISBN 978-0-443-19256-2, https://doi.org/10.1016/B978-0-443-19256-2.00010-7

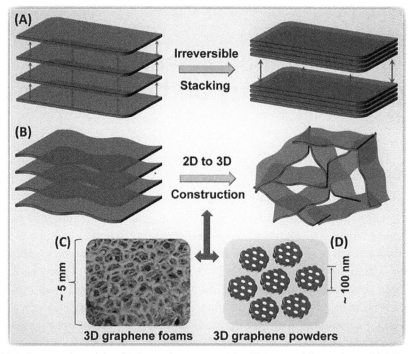

Figure 19.1 Structural models of 3-D graphene materials: (A) irreversible stacking, (B) 3-D construction, (C) 3-D graphene foams and (D) 3-D graphene powders [7].

irreversibly stacked when processed into powder materials, which reduces the available surface area and ion diffusion rate in applications, thus reducing the utilization of materials and corresponding properties [6]. The creation of 3-D graphene nanosheets new-style nanostructures with customized hierarchical nanosheets, including macroscopic 3-D foams and mesoscopic 3-D powders, can solve this challenge in both energy and environmental applications [7] (see Fig. 19.1 for details). These 3-D graphene nanosheets not only have the inherent properties of 2-D graphene nanosheets, but also provide some new collective physicochemical properties, such as high porosity, low density, large specific surface area, excellent mechanical properties, and good structural stability [8].

19.3 Preparation methods of 3-D graphene nanosheets

In order to expand the scope of 3-D carbon nanomaterials, we summarize the preparation methods of 3-D graphene nanosheets (including aerogel, foam, and powder) and generalized 3-D graphene-like porous carbon nanosheets. For the former, self-assembly and template catalytic growth are the most common methods, while for the latter, biomass-precursor pyrolysis, and organic-precursor pyrolysis are efficient methods.

19.3.1 Self-assembly method

The self-assembly method is usually a kind of "bottom–up" method for the preparation of nanomaterials. It is well known that in the field of colloidal chemistry, controlled colloidal aggregation and sedimentation can be initiated by changing the charging characteristics of colloidal particles by controlled electric bilayer thickness and Zeta potential (ζ) value (see Section 4.8.2 for details) [9]. Based on this principle, 3-D graphene materials can be prepared by self-assembly through the aggregation and precipitation of GO colloid. For example, the well-dispersed GO colloid can be deposited into a hydrogel with 3-D porous structure by hydrothermal [10] or template-assist [11] assembly, and then the 3-D porous graphene aerogel can be obtained by freeze drying and chemical/thermal reduction. The 3-D structure of graphene is often the result of the overlapping of many edges of graphene by physical and chemical actions (see Fig. 19.2A—C for details) [10]. The products prepared by this method often have high specific surface area and porosity. Unfortunately, this method uses the costly "GO" as raw material, and the process is relatively demanding.

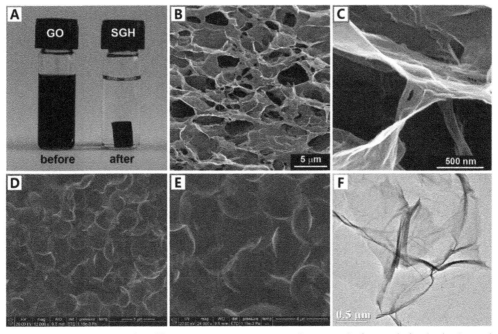

Figure 19.2 (A) Photographs of homogeneous GO aqueous dispersion before and after hydrothermal reduction and (B and C) SEM images of 3-D porous graphene aerogel [10]; (D and E) SEM images and (F) TEM image of 3-D porous graphene powder by template-assist assembly [11].

Our research group (Zesheng Li) has synthesized hollow hemispherical macroporous graphene-tungsten carbide-platinum (HMG-WC-Pt) 3-D nanocomposites by template-assisted assembly method with PS spheres preprepared template from GO (see Fig. 19.2D—F for details) [11]. Firstly, PS spheres, GO, and ammonium metatungstate (AMT) were uniformly mixed with distilled water to form mixed precursors (PS@ GO) before subsequent freeze drying. In the high-temperature treatment, PS spheres are decomposed into atmosphere containing carbon, and AMT reacts with carbon to form tungsten carbide (WC) nanoparticles to produce HMG-WC composites. Finally, HMG-WC-Pt nanostructures were formed on HMG-WC after loading Pt. It is obvious that PS sphere is the key template to form 3-D hollow hemispherical macroporous graphene structure. In addition to the PS sphere templates, silica templates, calcium carbonate, and sodium chloride templates are also widely used to prepare 3-D graphene materials, starting from GO precursor.

19.3.2 Template catalytic growth method

Based on the disadvantages of "GO" precursor method, such as high cost, complex production process, and unfavorable to mass production, let's take a further look at another technology: template catalytic growth (synchronous 3-D design and graphene growth strategy). Template catalysis is currently the most efficient method for the preparation of 3-D graphene structures [12]. This method usually uses 3-D structural porous metals as templates and catalysts to control the preparation of 3-D graphene structures. Typically, the nickel foam as a 3-D structure template and graphene growth catalyst, methane (CH_4) as precursor gas, the high-quality 3-D graphene foam (3-GF) can be prepared by chemical vapor deposition (CVD) technology at $1000^\circ C$ temperature. Under this condition, CH_4 can be decomposed into active carbon components and deposited on the 3-D nickel framework to form a continuous 3-D graphene foam product (or GF/ PDMS composite) (see Fig. 19.3A—C for details) [12]. The 3-D graphene essentially has a continuous structure, so it has very excellent conductivity and structural stability. The product also has interconnected macroporous network structure, which is very conducive to the diffusion of electrolyte ions (or other solution molecules) and greatly improves the electrochemical reaction kinetics and electrochemical performance (or the reaction rate of other-type applications) [13]. Because the pore structure of nickel foam is hundreds of microns, the porosity of graphene foam obtained is also hundreds of microns, resulting in low volume density. Therefore, it is the best choice to develop porous nickel with nanoporous structure as catalyst and template for preparing high-density 3-D graphene foam.

It is well known that under the catalytic promotion effect of transition metal elements (e.g., Fe, Co, Ni, Cu, etc.), extensive hydrocarbon carbon precursors (e.g., CH_4, $CH_2 = CH_2$, $CH \equiv CH$, etc.) can be transformed into graphene structures under specific temperature conditions ($600-1000^\circ C$), by a catalytic growth mechanism including

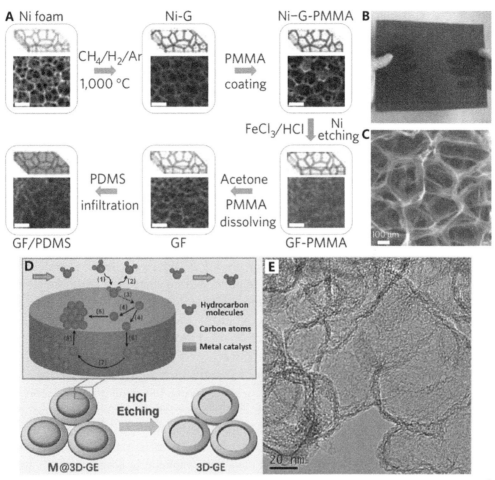

Figure 19.3 (A—C) Synthesis of a GF and integration with PDMS, photograph of a 170 × 220 mm² free-standing GF, and SEM image of GF [12]; (D and E) Mechanism schematic diagram of preparing 3-D graphene by chemical vapor deposition (CVD) [7].

adsorption, decomposition and precipitation steps [14]. The possible mechanism steps include: (1) Adsorption of carbon precursor on metal surface; (2) The carbon precursor returns to the gas phase; (3) Dehydrogenation and decomposition of carbon precursor into carbon atoms; (4) Migration of carbon atoms on the metal surface; (5) Carbon atoms nucleate directly on the metal surface and convert into graphene; (6) Carbon atoms dissolve into the metal at high temperature; (7) Diffusion and migration of carbon atoms in metal body; (8) Carbon atoms precipitate and nucleate on the surface to form graphene during cooling process (see Fig. 19.3D for details) [7]. Among them, steps (6—8) show the main mechanism of graphene catalytic growth (so-called "dissolution-precipitation" mechanism) [15]. At the stage of high-temperature decomposition, the concentration of carbon atoms on metal surface is much higher than that of metal body, so there is an obvious "concentration difference," which makes some carbon atoms dissolve into the metal, and carbon atoms interact with metal atoms to form C-M (M = Fe, Co, Ni, Cu, etc.) alloys. When the temperature drops, the solubility of carbon components in the metal decreases. At this time, the concentration of carbon atoms is much higher than the initial concentration of alloy formation. These excess carbon atoms will be precipitated on the metal surface in form of graphene. With the help of 3-D metal catalyst (i.e., 3-D template), well-formed 3-D porous graphene structure can be obtained (after removing the 3-D template by pickling) (see Fig. 19.3E for details) [7].

Generally, in the above "dissolution-precipitation" process, when the solubility of disordered carbon reaches saturation (for graphite, it is supersaturated at this time), part of the disordered carbon dissolved in the metal tends to precipitated into crystalline graphene with low energy level (amorphous carbon → alloyed carbon → crystalline graphene carbon). The reaction driving force of this process comes from the Gibbs free energy difference ($\triangle$ G) (thermodynamic factor) (see Section 4.2.1.5 for details) [16]. In particular, the preparation of graphene layer structure with controllable thickness (within 5 nm) can be successfully realized by adjusting the equilibrium relationship between carbon dissolution and graphene precipitation (phase equilibrium factor) (see Section 4.4.4 for details) and controlling the concentration of precursor gas, catalytic temperature and reaction time (kinetic factor) (see Section 4.3.2 for details) [17]. Recently, we have successfully prepared ultra-thin graphene hollow nanocages (with bagasse as precursor) through buried heat treatment technology (regulating the solubility of carbon atoms in metals in an atmosphere containing partial oxygen) and kinetic regulation (rapid and short-term heating heat treatment with nickel catalyst) [17].

In addition, chemical activation based on potassium hydroxide is one of the key strategies for de-graphitization and pore formation on the surface graphene-based materials [18]. In a sense, the chemical activation can controllably reduce the kinetics of graphitization process and prevent the formation of thick graphite layers. Based on this, our research group previously developed a synchronous graphitization-activation strategy and successfully prepared 3-D graphene powder materials [19]. This strategy takes cation exchange resin as the precursor, through ion exchange of nickel ions in nickel acetate and mixed potassium hydroxide, and then through high-temperature treatment and nickel catalysis to prepare thin-layer graphene nanosheets (see Fig. 19.4A for details). In the process of catalytic graphitization, the synchronously potassium hydroxide is introduced as a

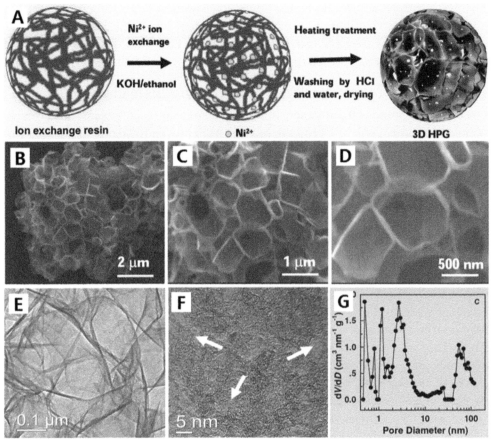

Figure 19.4 3-D porous graphene powder materials obtained by synchronous graphitization and activation: (A) synthesis schematic diagram, (B—D) SEM images, (E and F) TEM images, (G) pore size distribution [19].

pore-forming agent to activate and form pores (and also regulate the graphitization reaction kinetics in situ). Therefore, the synchronous design concept of ultra-thin graphitized structure (i.e., few-layer graphene) and high specific surface area (i.e., mesoporous graphene) is realized at the same time (as shown in Fig. 19.4B—G). The 3-D graphene powder has a good graphitization structure (crystal carbon structure), and its specific surface area is as high as $1810 \ m^2 \ g^{-1}$ (which is several times higher than that of the 3-D graphene aerogel [10] and 3-D graphene foam [12]). The 3-D graphene powder also has a high conductivity of up to $1000 \ S \ m^{-1}$ (2 times that of activated graphene [18]).

The 3-D graphene powder has unique structural advantages in electrochemical energy storage (such supercapacitors and lithium-ion batteries), where the hierarchical porous structure endows the electrode material with extremely high ionic diffusion kinetics, and the structure form of powder guaranteed high bulk density and bulk energy density [19].

19.3.3 Biomass or organic molecule precursor pyrolysis method

In all kinds of porous carbon materials, three-dimensional (3-D) graphene-like porous carbon nanosheets (3-D GPCNs) have recently been proven to be one of the advanced carbon materials. The 3-D GPCNs have highly 3-D network structure, high electrical conductivity, and good structural stability. The hierarchical porous structure of 3-D GPCNs can offer fast mass transport and efficient ion adsorption. Over the years, a variety of carbonaceous precursors have been selected for the design and synthesis of versatile 3-D GPCNs in the field of electrochemical energy storage. Among them, biomass precursor and molecular precursor are the two important categories, where schematic diagram for the formation of 3-D GPCN from the two precursors is vividly depicted in Fig. 19.5A [16]. As for the biomass precursors, pomelo peel, natural silk, salvia splenden, water lettuce, puffed rice, popcorn flower, shrimp shell, cattle bone, and so on have been proposed as potential precursors for 3-D GPCNs by pyrolysis, carbonization/graphitization, and/or chemical activation (see Fig. 19.5A left for details) [16]. Generally, the synchronous or subsequent process of chemical activation (e.g., KOH activation) can effectively increase the specific surface area of 3-D GPCN-based materials. Despite experiencing long-term development, unfortunately, there are still great challenges in satisfying several crucial requirements (e.g., product purity, dimensional controllability, and repeatability) of scientific research for biomass-based 3-D GPCNs. With this in mind, from a scientific perspective, looking for high-purity carbon precursors together with developing their controllable and repeatable synthesis routes is particularly significant and necessary.

Because of its extensive existence, diversity, and high purity, organic molecular precursor is an ideal precursor for the controllable preparation of carbon nanomaterials. Molecular precursor has become a preferred choice for the design of high-performance 3-D GPCNs in recent years, which includes the common water-soluble molecules of glucose, potassium citrate, resorcinol, oleic acid, polyvinylpyrrolidone, polyacrylamide, gelatin and metal-organic frameworks (see Fig. 19.5A right for details) [16]. For the purpose of building 3-D sheetlike and/or porous structures of 3-D GPCNs, suitable hard templates (pre-/posttemplates) are needed for these molecular precursors, where typical templates include NaCl micron cubes, $CaCO_3$ irregular particles, and g-C_3N_4 or GO nanosheets. Nevertheless, the 3-D GPCNs derived from molecular precursors are still faced with enormous challenges, such as complex synthesis procedures, high production cost, thickness nonuniformity, and low specific surface area. Consequently, it is extremely urgent to develop a straightforward and effective technique for

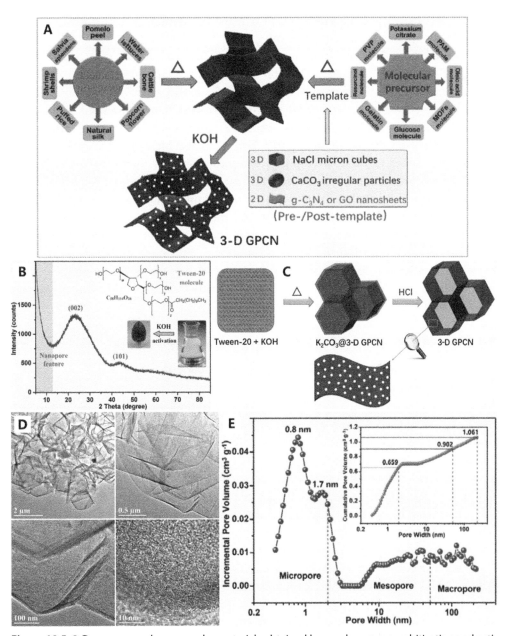

Figure 19.5 3-D porous graphene powder materials obtained by synchronous graphitization and activation: (A) synthesis schematic diagram, (B—D) SEM images, (E and F) TEM images, (G) pore size distribution [16].

production of high-performance 3-D GPCNs with ultrathin nanostructure (<10 nm) and high specific surface area (>2000 m^2 g^{-1}).

Recently, Li et al. reported a convenient and efficient one-pot KOH activation technology to synthesize a newly 3-D graphene-like porous carbon nanoflakes (i.e., 3-D GPCN) powders, by using the widely used surfactant (Tween-20) as carbon source (molecular precursor) (see Fig. 19.5B—E for details) [16]. The synthesized 3-D GPCN materials have good 3-D network structure composed of ultrathin nanosheets (8.5 nm), high specific surface area (2017.3 m^2 g^{-1}), and hierarchical porous structures (micropore, mesopore, and macropore). The proportion of micropores is as high as 62%, and the proportion of mesopores and macropores is 23% and 15%, respectively. The self-generated template (K$_2$CO$_3$) is an important guarantee to realize the good 3-D network structure of 3-D GPCN. At the same time, the one-pot buried-protection KOH activation technology is cheap and convenient, which has the vital significance of mass production and practical application. These results demonstrate that the present 3-D graphene-like carbon nanosheet network material is a promising electrode material for high-performance supercapacitors and other electrochemical energy storage applications [16].

19.4 Application progress of 3-D graphene nanosheets
19.4.1 Energy application of 3-D graphene nanosheets
19.4.1.1 Supercapacitor
In 2013, we report on a one-step ion-exchange/activation combination method using a metal ion-exchanged resin as a carbon precursor to prepare a novel 3-D hierarchical porous graphene-like (3-D HPG) materials [19]. The 3-D HPG material has an ultrahigh specific surface area and high C/O atomic ratio. The supercapacitor based on the 3D HPG material exhibited over 90% capacitance retention at the scan rate of 800 mV s^{-1} and an outstanding specific capacitance of 178 F g^{-1} at 1 A g^{-1} in an organic system, which is higher than those of typical carbon-based materials. The 3-D HPG contains: (1) Abundant micro- and mesopores which can provide high surface area, resulting in large capacitance; (2) Sub—micrometer sized macropores which can form ion-buffering reservoirs and provide short diffusion distance to the interior surfaces; (3) Interconnected micro-, meso-, and macropores which can provide fast ion channels to facilitate ion transport; (4) Graphene-like structure which provides excellent electrical conductivity and high electrochemical stability, resulting in high rate capability and high stability. The 3-D HPG architecture is not only useful for supercapacitors but also important for many other energy storage and catalytic applications [19].

Nitrogen doping structure can further improve the capacitor performance of 3-D graphene nanosheet materials. Li and coworkers reported an efficient synchronous graphitization-activation-doping method to synthesize 3-D N-doped activated graphene nanosheets (3-D NAGNs) powders with cheap ion exchange resin as carbon source and melamine as nitrogen source [20]. The 3-D NAGNs have a high specific surface area of $1815.6 \, m^2 \, g^{-1}$ and a moderate nitrogen content of 3.62 At %. The 3-D NAGNs electrode has good electrochemical performance in 6 M KOH aqueous electrolyte. The specific capacitance of 3-D NAGNs electrode is $383.2 \, F \, g^{-1}$ when the current density is $1.0 \, A \, g^{-1}$. Compared with the initial capacitance, the capacitance retention is 98% after 5000 cycles at a high current density of $10 \, A \, g^{-1}$. These excellent capacitance properties are attributed to the high specific surface area and good crystal structure of 3-D NAGNs, providing a large number of active sites and abundant N-doped sp^2 carbon structures.

Recently, we reported that three-dimensional activated carbon nanosheets (3-D ACNs) modified with graphitized carbon dots (GCDs) are proposed as a promising electrode material for the supercapacitor. The capacitive performances of the 3-D ACNs/GCDs electrode material are satisfactory, revealing a high specific capacitance ($202.9 \, F \, g^{-1}$ at $1 \, A \, g^{-1}$) and good rate performance ($144.2 \, F \, g^{-1}$ at $5 \, A \, g^{-1}$) [21]. As a promising supercapacitor electrode, a relatively high specific capacitance of $316.8 \, F \, g^{-1}$ at a current density of $1 \, A \, g^{-1}$, along with good cycling stability (with a 92.5% retention rate after 2000 cycles) is demonstrated for the as-prepared 3-D porous graphene powder electrode [16]. The 3-D graphene-like porous carbon nanosheet network material with high specific surface area exhibits ideal capacitive behavior indicating a promising electrode material for high-performance supercapacitors.

A composite consisting of well-dispersed and ultrafine Fe_2O_3 quantum dots anchored on a three-dimensional ultra-porous graphene-like framework (denoted as Fe_2O_3-QDs-3D GF) has been designed via a facile and scalable strategy by Li and coworkers [22]. The ultra-small-sized Fe_2O_3-QDs anchored on the 3D GF can endow the composite with a superior high surface area and enough active sites for electrochemical reactions, thus giving the composite a large specific capacitance. The as-prepared Fe_2O_3-QDs-3D GF electrode exhibited a high specific capacitance of $945 \, F \, g^{-1}$ at $1.0 \, A \, g^{-1}$ in a three-electrode system in $2.0 \, mol \, L^{-1}$ KOH aqueous solution. In addition, high-performance asymmetric supercapacitors have been fabricated with Fe_2O_3-QDs-3D GF as the anode and 3D HPG as the cathode, and they showed a very high energy density of $77.7 \, Wh \, kg^{-1}$ at a power density of $0.40 \, kW \, kg^{-1}$ and maximum power density of $492.3 \, kW \, kg^{-1}$, as well as excellent cycling stability.

19.4.1.2 Rechargeable batteries

In 2017, Li and coworkers successfully synthesize well-dispersed and ultrafine TiO_2-QDs, into the 3D porous graphene-like networks (TiO_2-QDs-3D GNs) with high-efficient electron and ion transport for lithium-ion battery (LIB) anodes [23]. The TiO_2-QDs-3D GNs hybrid electrode exhibited a high reversible capacity of $219 \, mA \, h \, g^{-1}$ after 100 cycles at $0.1 \, A \, g^{-1}$, accompanied by an ultrahigh-rate capability of $121 \, mA \, h \, g^{-1}$ and a super-long lifespan of 3000 cycles with $\sim 82.0\%$ capacity retention at 10 A g^{-1}. The integrated intercalation-based and interfacial lithium storage as well as the 3D fast electron/ion transfer of materials attributed to the excellent electrochemical performances. A rational design of MnO$_2$/3D porous graphene-like (PG) (denoted as 3D PG-Mn) composites also attributed extremely stable MnO$_2$ anode incorporated with 3D porous graphene-like networks for lithium-ion batteries [24]. A rational design and synthesis of sulfur-carbon nanocomposites by infiltrating S into 3-D graphene-like network with hierarchical pores has been achieved for the first time, and the resulting 3D GNs-S nanocomposite further showed a highly stable capacity and reversible high charge/discharge rate performance for lithium-sulfur battery [25]. It is worth mentioning that 3-D graphene network materials also show a positive promoting effect in the field of lead-acid batteries by Shen in 2021: the stereotaxically constructed graphene/nanolead (SCG-Pb) composites are synthesized by the electrodeposition method to enhance the high-rate (1C rate) battery cycle performance of lead-acid batteries for hybrid electric vehicles [26].

19.4.1.3 Electrocatalytic conversion

Recently, our research group proved that the three-dimensional mesoporous graphene conductive networks supporting bimetallic PtAg alloyed nanoparticles (PtAg/3DMGS) with a superior composited nanostructure can be fabricated as high-performance oxygen reduction reaction (ORR) electrocatalysts for fuel cells [27]. The combination of ultrafine PtAg NPs and 3DMGS conductive networks provides a relatively stable macroporous composite architecture, which offers convenient binary channels for both electron transport and ion diffusion. This promising PtAg/3DMGS composite material reveals an ultrahigh mass activity (at 0.9 V) of 392 mA mgPt^{-1}, which is nearly 4 times that of Pt/C (TKK) (102 mA mgPt^{-1}). After 1000 CV cycles, the retention rates of mass activity are 81.6% and 66.7% for PtAg/3DMGS and Pt/C (TKK), respectively. These results demonstrated that the PtAg/3DMGS composite material is a promising electrocatalyst with high catalytic activity and high stability for the ORR. The 3-D graphene materials can also be used as efficient catalytic materials (or carrier materials) for oxygen reduction and oxygen evolution reactions (ORR and OER) [28]. Recently, nickel/nickel oxide@ 3D dimensional hierarchical porous graphene (Ni-NiO@3DHPG) electrocatalysts were obtained from cation exchange resin, nickel acetate and cobalt nitrate as a source of carbon displayed onset potential, overpotential (10 mA cm^{-2}) and Tafel values of are 1.53 V, 1.64 V, and 55 mV dec^{-1} for OER and −0.18 V, −0.31 V, and 78 mV dec^{-1} for HER, respectively [29].

19.4.2 Environmental application of 3-D graphene nanosheets

19.4.2.1 Adsorbing purification

Due to the discharge of domestic sewage, industrial and agricultural wastewater, and crude oil leakage, more and more pollutants into the water body, damage the ecological environment, harm human health, so polluted wastewater purification treatment is urgently needed. The 3-D graphene functional material can remove heavy metal ions, organic pollutants (dyes, oil stains), antibiotics, alkanes, and other organic pollutants in water by electrostatic attraction, surface complexation, electroadsorption, and ion exchange and has certain recycling performance. It has been reported that the adsorption capacity of 3-D graphene is tens to hundreds of times that of traditional adsorption materials. The 3-D graphene shows a broader application prospect than traditional adsorption materials and 2-D graphene in water pollution treatment. The 3-D graphene nanosheets have the advantages of large specific surface area, good chemical stability, abundant oxygen-containing functional groups, strong modified ability, and easy to realize the solid-liquid separation in adsorbing purification [30].

19.4.2.2 Photocatalytic degradation

With its excellent performance, graphene can make up for many shortcomings of photocatalytic materials: (1) The ultra-high carrier migration rate of graphene at room temperature can promote the transport of photogenerated electrons, accelerate the separation of photogenerated electron-hole pairs, inhibit their recombination, and thus improve the quantum charge ratio of the material. (2) The composite of semiconductor photocatalytic materials and graphene can expand the optical absorption range and enhance the optical absorption intensity of the composite materials by forming the heterojunction interface. (3) In addition to the above effects, graphene can also be used as a support to make the photocatalyst disperse evenly and effectively inhibit its agglomeration, and inhibit photocorrosion of photocatalyst and so on [31]. The 2-D graphene was assembled into 3-D graphene and loaded with photoactive materials to prepare bulk composite photocatalysts, which can facilitate the separation and recycling of catalysts and liquids. In addition, the 3-D graphene, with its 3-D electron transport channels and multistage pore structure, is conducive to photocatalytic reactions, showing attractive applications in both energy and environmental aspects [32].

19.4.2.3 Advanced oxidation

Fenton-like reactions (including conventional Fenton, photo-Fenton, and electro-Fenton) are effective strategies for producing strong oxidative species that can be used to eliminate refractory organic pollutants in water. The 3-D graphene material (graphene aerogel), with unique π-π conjugated structure and properties, can be used for the preparation of heterogeneous catalysts in Fenton-like reactions, which contributes to the generation of more reactive species in Fenton-like reactions [33]. The system of peroxymonosulfate (PMS) activated by transition metal nanomaterials has also been widely investigated to degrade organic pollutants in water. The 3-D graphene material-supported metal nanomaterials, such as $CoFe_2O_4$ supported on N-doped 3D graphene aerogels ($CoFe_2O_4$/N-3DG), were developed for highly efficient BTA degradation with improved stability and recyclability. Particularly, multiple reactive oxygen species (ROS, •OH, SO_4^-•, O_2^-• and $^1O_2$) and direct electron transfer achieve effective degradation of BTA to smaller intermediates or mineralized to CO_2 [34]. The 3-D graphene-modified nanomaterials can accelerate the above-advanced oxidation reactions, so as to rapidly degrade organic pollutants adsorbed on the surface of nanomaterials.

19.5 Summary

In this chapter, we have discussed the structural features, preparation methods, energy and environmental applications, and typical case analysis of 3-D graphene nanosheet materials (including bulk material and powder material). The 3-D graphene materials can well maintain the high electrical conductivity, surface richness, and mechanical robustness of 2-D graphene, as well as the unique 2-D electronic behavior. In addition, continuous porosity and large curvature offer new features such as fast mass transfer, ample open space, mechanical flexibility, and adjustable electrical/ion conductivity. In particular, 3-D curvature provides a new degree of freedom for the catalytic and transport properties of graphene. The 3D graphene materials show fascinating application prospects and values in the fields of energy and environment.

Acknowledgments

This book was supported by National Natural Science Foundation of China (22078071, 22272034), Natural Science Foundation of Guangdong Province (2021A1515010125, 2020A1515010344), Maoming Science and Technology Project (mmkj2020032), Guangdong Province Universities and Colleges Pearl River Scholar Funded Scheme (2019), Guangdong Basic and Applied Basic Research Foundation (2019A1515011249, 2021A1515010305), Key Research Project of Natural Science of Guangdong Provincial Department of Education (2019KZDXM010), Environment and Energy Green Catalysis Innovation Team of Colleges and Universities of Guangdong Province (2022KCXTD019), the program for Innovative Research Team of Guangdong University of Petrochemical Technology.

References

[1]   Z. Chen, L. Jin, W. Hao, W. Ren, H.M. Cheng, Synthesis and applications of three-dimensional graphene network structures, Materials Today Nano 5 (2019) 100027.
[2]   B. Li, M. Yu, Z. Li, C. Yu, H. Wang, Q. Li, Constructing flexible all-solid-state supercapacitors from 3D nanosheets active bricks via 3D manufacturing technology: a perspective review, Advanced Functional Materials 32 (2022) 2201166.
[3]   J.H. Kim, J.M. Kim, G.W. Lee, G.H. Shim, S.T. Lim, K.M. Kim, et al., Advanced boiling—a scalable strategy for self-assembled three-dimensional graphene, ACS Nano 15 (2) (2021) 2839–2848.
[4]   Y. Zhu, S. Murali, W. Cai, X. Li, J.W. Suk, J.R. Potts, et al., Graphene and graphene oxide: synthesis, properties, and applications, Advanced Materials 22 (35) (2010) 3906–3924.
[5]   W. Ren, H.M. Cheng, The global growth of graphene, Nature Nanotechnology 9 (10) (2014) 726–730.

[6] J.Y. Lee, K.H. Lee, Y.J. Kim, J.S. Ha, S.S. Lee, J.G. Son, Sea-urchin-inspired 3D crumpled graphene balls using simultaneous etching and reduction process for high-density capacitive energy storage, Advanced Functional Materials 25 (23) (2015) 3606–3614.

[7] B. Li, Z. Li, Q. Pang, Q. Zhuang, J. Zhu, P. Tsiakaras, et al., Synthesis and characterization of activated 3D graphene via catalytic growth and chemical activation for electrochemical energy storage in supercapacitors, Electrochimica Acta 324 (2019) 134878.

[8] Z. Li, J. Lin, B. Li, C. Yu, H. Wang, Q. Li, Construction of heteroatom-doped and three-dimensional graphene materials for the applications in supercapacitors: a review, Journal of Energy Storage 44 (2021) 103437.

[9] H.J. Keh, T.H. Hsieh, Electrophoresis of a colloidal sphere in a spherical cavity with arbitrary zeta potential distributions and arbitrary double-layer thickness, Langmuir 24 (2) (2008) 390–398.

[10] Y. Xu, K. Sheng, C. Li, G. Shi, Self-assembled graphene hydrogel via a one-step hydrothermal process, ACS Nano 4 (7) (2010) 4324–4330.

[11] Z. Li, Z. Liu, B. Li, Z. Liu, D. Li, H. Wang, et al., Hollow hemisphere-shaped macroporous graphene/tungsten carbide/platinum nanocomposite as an efficient electrocatalyst for the oxygen reduction reaction, Electrochimica Acta 221 (2016) 31–40.

[12] Z. Chen, W. Ren, L. Gao, B. Liu, S. Pei, H.M. Cheng, Three-dimensional flexible and conductive interconnected graphene networks grown by chemical vapour deposition, Nature Materials 10 (6) (2011) 424–428.

[13] K. Chen, L. Shi, Y. Zhang, Z. Liu, Scalable chemical-vapour-deposition growth of three-dimensional graphene materials towards energy-related applications, Chemical Society Reviews 47 (9) (2018) 3018–3036.

[14] Z. Zou, B. Dai, Z. Liu, CVD process engineering for designed growth of graphene, Scientia Sinica Chimica 43 (2013) 1–17.

[15] L. Zhang, L. Zhang, J. Zhang, P. Xue, W. Hao, M. Shen, et al., In situ growth of three-dimensional graphene coatings on arbitrary-shaped micro/nano materials and its mechanism studies, Carbon 92 (2015) 84–95.

[16] Z. Li, L. Zhang, X. Chen, B. Li, H. Wang, Q. Li, Three-dimensional graphene-like porous carbon nanosheets derived from molecular precursor for high-performance supercapacitor application, Electrochimica Acta 296 (2019) 8–17.

[17] Z. Li, L. Zhang, B. Li, Z. Liu, Z. Liu, H. Wang, et al., Convenient and large-scale synthesis of hollow graphene-like nanocages for electrochemical supercapacitor application, Chemical Engineering Journal 313 (2017) 1242–1250.

[18] Y. Zhu, S. Murali, M.D. Stoller, K.J. Ganesh, W. Cai, P.J. Ferreira, et al., Carbon-based supercapacitors produced by activation of graphene, Science 332 (6037) (2011) 1537–1541.

[19] Y. Li, Z. Li, P.K. Shen, Simultaneous formation of ultrahigh surface area and three-dimensional hierarchical porous graphene-like networks for fast and highly stable supercapacitors, Advanced Materials 25 (17) (2013) 2474–2480.

[20] Z. Li, B. Li, Z. Liu, D. Li, H. Wang, Q. Li, One-pot construction of 3-D nitrogen-doped activated graphene-like nanosheets for high-performance supercapacitors, Electrochimica Acta 190 (2016) 378–387.

[21] B. Li, M. Yu, Z. Li, C. Yu, Q. Li, H. Wang, Three-dimensional activated carbon nanosheets modified by graphitized carbon dots: one-step alkali pyrolysis preparation and supercapacitor applications, Journal of Energy Storage 51 (2022) 104515.

[22] Y. Li, H. Zhang, S. Wang, Y. Lin, Y. Chen, Z. Shi, et al., Facile low-temperature synthesis of hematite quantum dots anchored on a three-dimensional ultra-porous graphene-like framework as advanced anode materials for asymmetric supercapacitors, Journal of Materials Chemistry A 4 (29) (2016) 11247–11255.

[23] Y. Li, C. Ou, Y. Huang, Y. Shen, N. Li, H. Zhang, Towards fast and ultralong-life Li-ion battery anodes: embedding ultradispersed TiO_2 quantum dots into three-dimensional porous graphene-like networks, Electrochimica Acta 246 (2017) 1183–1192.

[24] Y. Li, Q. Zhang, J. Zhu, X.L. Wei, P.K. Shen, An extremely stable MnO_2 anode incorporated with 3D porous graphene-like networks for lithium-ion batteries, Journal of Materials Chemistry A 2 (9) (2014) 3163–3168.

[25] Y. Li, Z. Li, Q. Zhang, P.K. Shen, Sulfur-infiltrated three-dimensional graphene-like material with hierarchical pores for highly stable lithium–sulfur batteries, Journal of Materials Chemistry A 2 (13) (2014) 4528–4533.

[26] Y. Zhang, A. Ali, J. Li, J. Xie, P.K. Shen, Stereotaxically constructed graphene/nano lead composite for enhanced cycling performance of lead-acid batteries, Journal of Energy Storage 35 (2021) 102192.

[27] Z. Li, Y. Li, C. He, P.K. Shen, Bimetallic PtAg alloyed nanoparticles and 3-D mesoporous graphene nanosheet hybrid architectures for advanced oxygen reduction reaction electrocatalysts, Journal of Materials Chemistry A 5 (44) (2017) 23158–23169.

[28] Z. Li, K. Xiao, C. Yu, H. Wang, Q. Li, Three-dimensional graphene-like carbon nanosheets coupled with MnCo-layered double hydroxides nanoflowers as efficient bifunctional oxygen electrocatalyst, International Journal of Hydrogen Energy 46 (69) (2021) 34239–34251.

[29] N. Ullah, W. Zhao, X. Lu, C.J. Oluigbo, S.A. Shah, M. Zhang, et al., In situ growth of M-MO (M = Ni, Co) in 3D graphene as a competent bifunctional electrocatalyst for OER and HER, Electrochimica Acta 298 (2019) 163–171.

[30] https://mp.weixin.qq.com/s/Ei4RcH0CFG-edUqKuRHVwQ.

[31] C. Yang, S. Shi, S. Hao, H. Chu, S. Dai, Graphene photocatalytic materials and their research progress in the field of environmental purification, Journal of Materials Engineering 48 (7) (2020) 1–13.

[32] X. Xie, N. Zhang, Z.R. Tang, Y.J. Xu, An adaptive geometry regulation strategy for 3D graphene materials: towards advanced hybrid photocatalysts, Chemical Science 9 (47) (2018) 8876–8882.

[33] L. Wang, Y. Zhang, J. Qian, Graphene aerogel-based catalysts in Fenton-like reactions for water decontamination: a short review, Chemical Engineering Journal Advances 8 (2021) 100171.

[34] X. Li, D. Zhang, Z. Liu, C. Lyu, S. Niu, Z. Dong, et al., Enhanced catalytic oxidation of benzotriazole via peroxymonosulfate activated by $CoFe_2O_4$ supported onto nitrogen-doped three-dimensional graphene aerogels, Chemical Engineering Journal 400 (2020) 125897.

CHAPTER 20

Hollow carbon nanocages: recent progress in energy and environment fields

20.1 Introduction

Carbon-based nanocages consist of sp^2 hybrid carbon shells with a hollow internal cavity, a high surface area with external surface defects, and a tunable electronic structure. In recent years, with the development of preparation methods, a large number of carbon-based nanocages with good structure and uniform size have been prepared (including amorphous carbon and graphited carbon nanocages). There are abundant channels (0.1–20 nm) connecting the inside and outside of the cage on the cage wall. In addition to the unique inner cavity and high specific surface, its interconnected skeleton and microporous, mesoporous, and macroporous hierarchical structure of carbon-based nanocages also facilitate the cooperative transport of charge/solution, which is widely used in energy storage, catalytic transformation, and other fields and has become an advanced platform material for energy chemistry and environmental science [1–3]. The mesoscopic and porous structure characteristics of carbon nanocages, design and preparation methods of carbon nanocages, the intrinsic properties of carbon nanocages, and the confined active species within carbon nanocages are reviewed in this chapter. The recent progress in supercapacitor, lithium-sulphury battery and lithium-ion battery, catalytic-related research is discussed, and the opportunities and challenges are prospected.

20.2 Structural features of hollow carbon nanocages

Hollow carbon nanocages are a new kind of 3-D nanostructured carbon material composed of curved carbon nanosheets with submicron gap space, and the carbon nanosheets are interconnected by graphene microcrystal as construction units. There are abundant sub–nanochannels (~ 1 nm) or specially designed nanopores (1–10 nm) connecting inside and outside on the shells of carbon nanocages. Different from other nanocarbon materials, this kind of new carbon nanocages material has integrated characteristics of the available inner cavity, coexistence of micropores, mesopores, and macropores, high specific surface area, easy doping, and modulation. Furthermore, the curved nanosheet structure of cage-like carbon nanomaterials could effectively reduce anisotropy due to the arch configuration of carbon layers, which can avoid interlayer slipping

Nanostructured Materials
ISBN 978-0-443-19256-2, https://doi.org/10.1016/B978-0-443-19256-2.00024-7

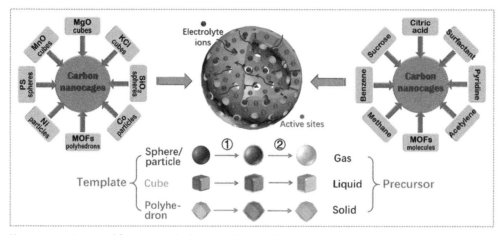

Figure 20.1 Structural features and schematic diagram for the formation of hollow carbon nanocages with diversified templates and precursors (step (1) is in situ carbon growth and step (2) is template removing) [3].

and ensure structural stability. Therefore, hollow carbon nanocages with favorable dimensional and porous structures can greatly promote the exchange and transfer of substances in liquid–solid and gas–solid environment, and effectively accommodate strain relaxation during application process, which has become a new platform for developing advanced energy and environmental functions (see Fig. 20.1 for details) [3].

20.3 Preparation methods of hollow carbon nanocages

Hollow carbon nanocages can be prepared by various synthetic approaches, including chemical vapor deposition (CVD) and hydrothermal synthesis methods. Among them, the template method has attracted great attention due to its advantages such as simple operation and low cost. The sphere/particle (PS sphere, SiO_2 sphere, and metal particle), cube (MgO, MnO, and KCl cubes), and polyhedron (MOFs) templates are the three important categories for the construction of homologous carbon nanocages, where the schematic diagram is vividly depicted in Fig. 20.1 [3]. On the basis of the different synthetic strategies (e.g., CVD, liquid-phase, and solid-phase synthesis), the precursors of carbon nanocages mainly include three types: gas-phase, liquid-phase, and solid-phase precursors. Numerous gas-phase precursors, including benzene vapor, acetylene, methane, and carbon monoxide, have been used for preparing carbon nanocages by rigorous CVD technique. On the other hand, liquid-phase (e.g., pyridine) and solid-phase (e.g., sucrose, citric acid, surfactant, and MOFs) precursors are often chosen for the catalytic preparation of graphitized carbon (GC) nanocages during liquid-phase and/or solid-phase synthesis (see Fig. 20.1 for details) [3].

Monodispersed carbon nanocages have many advantages, such as regular morphology, uniform diameter, good fluidity, high surface reactivity, and easy functionalization, which have high research and application values in the fields of electrocatalysis and electrochemical storage. In general, the amorphous carbon nanocages prepared by spherical colloid templates (e.g., PS spheres and SiO_2 spheres) have very high dispersity and good uniformity. The monodispersed graphene-like carbon nanocages can be also prepared by using pre-synthesized metallic particle templates (e.g., Ni nanoparticles). For example, uniform Ni nanoparticles (Ni-NPs) were synthesized by the reduction reaction of $NiCl_2 \cdot 6H_2O$, $N_2H_4 \cdot H_2O$ and NaOH, and then the graphene-like carbon layers were coated on the surface of Ni-NPs (with triethylene glycol as carbon source) by a successive carburization (refluxing at 220°C) and carbon-segregation (annealing at 500°C) process, and the well-shaped hollow graphene balls (HGBs) were obtained after etching Ni with 3M HCl solution (see Fig. 20.2A–C) [4].

The direct pyrolysis of nickel acetate and carbonaceous molecular precursors (citric acid) mixture at moderate temperatures (200–600°C) can produce highly homogenous, densely packed, interconnected graphene-like carbon nanocages with bilayer graphene shell (see Fig. 20.2D–F) [5]. These graphene-like carbon nanocages with their bilayer graphene structure showed unimodal pore size distribution of 2.5 nm and very high specific surface area of 1150 m^2/g (Fig. 20.2E and F). When sucrose is used as carbon source, unique carbon nanomesh constructed by interconnected densely packed carbon nanocages with ultrathin graphitic shells were obtained, which can be regarded as a 3-D conducting network for fast electron transport among these densely packed carbon nanocages, thus achieving better electrochemical kinetics to ensure excellent rate performance (Fig. 20.2G) [6].

Recently, out research group has proposed an efficient quasi-chemical vapor deposition (Q-CVD) strategy for the convenient synthesis of graphene-like hollow carbon nanocages (see Fig. 20.2H–K) [7]. Typically, low-cost bagasse as a carbon source was placed at the bottom of reaction crucible, and nickel acetate ss a catalyst precursor was placed at the top of reaction crucible for rapid heating treatment at 750°C for 15 min (see Fig. 5 H). The top black product is Ni@carbon nanocages, and the Ni is removed by acid treatment to obtain the final product. These carbon nanocages are about 200 nm in diameter, less than 10 nm in thickness, and rich in mesoporous structures on the surface (see Fig. 20.2I–K). This "solid-gas-solid" Q-CVD strategy is a high-efficiency and scalable production technique, which is superior to previous synthesis methods by direct mixing and pyrolysis of nickel acetate and carbon sources [4–6].

20.4 Application progress of hollow carbon nanocages

20.4.1 Energy application of hollow carbon nanocages

20.4.1.1 Supercapacitor

In 2017, we report on an efficient and scalable Q-CVD technique with Ni nanoparticle template to prepare hollow graphene-like nanocages for electrochemical supercapacitor application (see Fig. 20.3A–D) [7]. The hollow graphene-like nanocages have a hollow sphere morphology and nanoporous frameworks. The supercapacitive performances of the graphene-like electrode are investigated by cyclic voltammetry and charging-

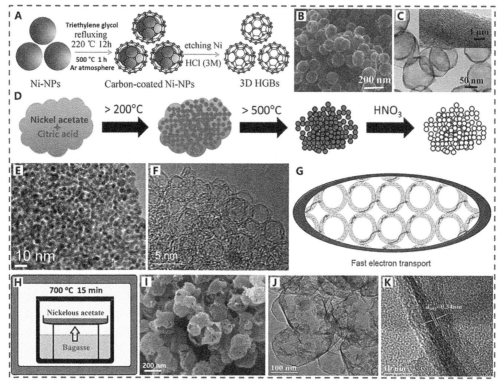

Figure 20.2 (A–C) Monodispersed graphene-like carbon nanocages [4], (D–F) graphene-like carbon nanocages with bilayer graphene shell [5], 3-D conducting network of densely packed carbon nanocages [6], Q-CVD synthesis of graphene-like hollow carbon nanocages [7].

discharging methods. When evaluated for supercapacitor electrode, relatively high specific capacitance of 165.7 F/g and 283.1 F/g are obtained at current density of 1 A/g in 1 M KOH and 1 M H$_2$SO$_4$ electrolytes, respectively. In addition, desirable rate performance and good cycling stability are also demonstrated for the hollow graphene-like nanocages.

In 2017, Hu and co-workers also developed an in-situ MgO template method to produce the carbon nanocages with unique cube-like morphology with optimized porous structures for ultrahigh-volumetric-performance supercapacitors [10]. The optimized carbon nanocage sample achieves a record-high stack volumetric energy density of

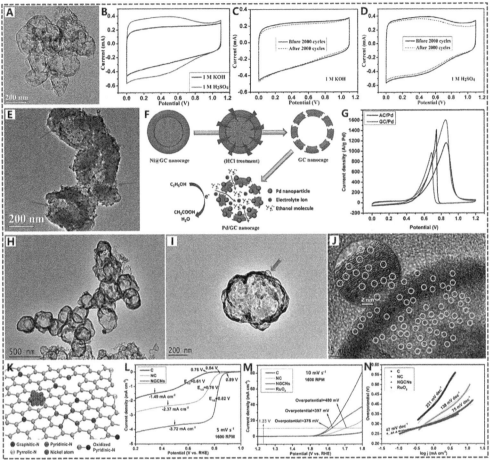

Figure 20.3 (A–D) Graphene-like hollow carbon nanocages for supercapacitor [7], (E–G) graphitized carbon nanocage/Pd electrocatalyst for ethanol oxidation reaction [8], (H–N) N-doped graphene-like carbon nanocages modified by Ni species for ORR and OER [9].

73 Wh/L in ionic liquid with superb power density and cycling stability. The large specific surface area, good mesoporosity, and regular structure are responsible for the excellent performances of carbon nanocages [11]. The microporosity-controlled and heteroatom-doped carbon nanocages prepared from the zeolitic imidazolate framework

(ZIF-8) template further demonstrated high energy and power density, and a long-term cycle ability is (75% capacitance retention after 20,000 cycles) when used in a symmetric and flexible all-solid-state-supercapacitor [12].

20.4.1.2 Rechargeable batteries

Novel hierarchical carbon nanocages (hCNCs) were proposed as high-rate anodes for Li- and Na-ion batteries by Hu [13]. The unique structure of the porous network for hCNCs greatly favors electrolyte penetration, ion diffusion, electron conduction, and structural stability, resulting in high-rate capability and excellent cyclability. For Li storage, the hCNCs electrode stored a high capacity of 970 mAh/g at a rate of 0.1 A/g and delivered a large specific power of 37 kW/kg and specific energy of 339 Wh/kg. For Na storage, the hCNC electrode reached a high capacity of $\sim$ 50 mAh/g even at a high rate of 10 A/g. Li and Fang also reported a Tin oxide coated with carbon nanocages ($SnO_2@$ carbon core-shell structure) as high-performance anodes for lithium-ion batteries [14]. More than 760 mAh/g of reversible discharge capacity was achieved at a current density of 300 mA/g, and above 85% retention can be obtained after 100 charge-discharge cycles. As an excellent sulfur carrier material, carbon nanocages are also widely used in lithium-sulfur batteries, which can greatly improve the electrical conductivity and electrochemical stability of sulfur electrodes [1−3].

20.4.1.3 Electrocatalytic conversion

Recently, our research group proved that GC nanocages were successfully prepared via a Ni catalysis-growth technology from Tween-80 molecule precursor, where the GC nanocages can be used as support for the construction of GC/Pd electrocatalyst toward ethanol oxidation reaction (see Fig. 20.3E−G) [8]. The GC/Pd electrocatalyst exhibits excellent electrocatalytic performance toward ethanol oxidation. The positive scanning peak current density of GC/Pd electrode is up to 1612 A/g/Pd in 1.0 mol/L NaOH + 1.0 mol/L ethanol electrolyte, which is much higher than those (500−1100 A/g/Pd) of traditional Pd electrodes supported with carbon nanotubes or graphene nanosheets. More recently, we further demonstrated that N-doped graphene-like carbon nanocages (NGCNs) modified by trace nickel (Ni) species (single atoms and clusters) showed much higher catalytic activity of ORR and OER than those of NC and pure C catalysts (see Fig. 20.3H−N) [9]. The synergistic effect between Ni single atoms and Ni clusters, or NGCNs and Ni atom can promote the catalytic activity of the NGCNs-supported atomized nickel catalyst by adjusting their electronic structures. The functionalized carbon nanocages (nonmetal doped or metal-loaded nanocages) are also widely studied in other electrocatalytic conversion fields [1−3].

20.4.2 Environmental application of hollow carbon nanocages

20.4.2.1 Adsorbing purification

The pollution of heavy metal ions in drinking water poses a great risk to human health. Carbon material adsorption is one of the effective methods to remove heavy metal ions in water. Holmes et al. prepared high-yield carbon nanocages with a specific surface area of 1175 m^2/g by supercritical fluid deposition and studied the ability of these high specific surface area carbon nanocages to adsorb pb^{2+} ions from simulated wastewater [15]. The study found that the level of Pb^{2+} removal by carbon nanocages was 11.1 mg/g, while the level of commercially available activated carbon was 7.6 mg/g. The kinetics of adsorption of metal ions by carbon nanocages and activated carbon conforms to the quasi-second-order kinetic model, and the rate coefficient (k_2) is 4.8×10^2 g/mg min. The magnetic carbon nanocages (Mag@CNCs) were further synthesized via a green one-step process using pine resin and iron nitrate salt as a carbon and iron source by Karakassides, which can be used as outstanding absorbents for As(III) removal from aqueous solutions [16]. The Mag@CNCs showed a total of 263.9 mg As(III)-uptake capacity per gram of material at pH $= 7$, which is a record sorption capacity value among all previously tested iron-based materials so far.

20.4.2.2 Photocatalytic degradation

Among the many catalyst structures, the hollow structure shows unique advantages in photocatalytic degradation. Hollow photocatalysts can effectively expose surface active sites by increasing the specific surface area, provide thin-wall porous structure to promote mass transfer process, enhance light scattering ability (multi-light reflection in cavity) to improve the utilization efficiency of light, and thus improve the photocatalytic performance of nanocage materials [17]. Although pure carbon materials have no photocatalytic activity, carbon nanocage-supported or carbon nanocage-integrated semiconductor catalysts can be widely used for photocatalytic degradation of pollutants in water. The semiconductor catalysts encapsulated in carbon nanocage materials can also exhibit the advantage of confinement catalysis effect, that is, a specific catalytic substrate or medium encapsulated into the carbon nanocages can cause the regional enhancement effect in some photocatalytic reactions [18].

20.4.2.3 Advanced oxidation

Recently, Wang et al. used in situ thermal conversion of Co-Fe Prussian blue analogs coated with polydopamine to prepare N-doped carbon nanocages-encapsulated carbon bubbles (CBs@NCCs) [19]. The unique hollow structure and appropriate nitrogen modification are of great significance to improve the activation performance of peroxymonosulfate (PMS). The evolution of free radicals showed that the sulfate radical (SO_4^-)

and singlet oxygen ($^1O_2$) is simultaneously responsible for the total elimination of MB in CBs@NCCs/PMS. The mixed Fe_xCo_y@C nanocages were systematically characterized and applied as effective catalysts to activate peroxymonosulfate (PMS) for the removal of bisphenol A (BPA) by Wang [20]. Through radical scavenger and EPR/DMPO experiments, SO_4^- radicals were proved to play a dominant role in the activation of PMS for BPA removal. The nitrogen-doped graphene shells were demonstrated to be effective in preventing the release of metal ions, thus resulting in better stability. In addition, carbon nanocages materials also have obvious stability advantages in the construction of Fenton and Fenton-like advanced oxidation systems.

20.5 Summary

In this chapter, we have discussed the structural features, preparation methods, energy and environmental applications, and typical case analysis of hollow carbon nanocages (including carbon nanocages and their composites). At present, the hot research directions in the field of carbon nanocages include (1) preparation method and batch technology of carbon nanocages; (2) construction of loaded (from high dispersion to single atom), domain-limited type catalysts with carbon nanocages as catalysts for energy electrocatalytic conversion (fuel cell electrocatalysis, water electrolysis electrocatalysis, other electrocatalysis, etc.); (3) carbon nanocages and composites used as electrode materials for energy storage (supercapacitors, lithium–sulfur batteries, lithium–ion batteries, etc.), (4) carbon nanocages and composites used as active materials for environmental remediation (adsorption, photocatalysis and other advanced oxidation). However, there are still many problems and challenges (such as pore size regulation and cost control) in the energy and environmental applications of carbon nanocages.

Acknowledgments

This book was supported by National Natural Science Foundation of China (22078071, 22272034), Natural Science Foundation of Guangdong Province (2021A1515010125, 2020A1515010344), Maoming Science and Technology Project (mmkj2020032), Guangdong Province Universities and Colleges Pearl River Scholar Funded Scheme (2019), Guangdong Basic and Applied Basic Research Foundation (2019A1515011249, 2021A1515010305), Key Research Project of Natural Science of Guangdong Provincial Department of Education (2019KZDXM010), Environment and Energy Green Catalysis Innovation Team of Colleges and Universities of Guangdong Province (2022KCXTD019), the program for Innovative Research Team of Guangdong University of Petrochemical Technology.

References

[1] Q. Wu, L. Yang, X. Wang, Z. Hu, Carbon-based nanocages: a new platform for advanced energy storage and conversion, Advanced Materials 32 (27) (2020) 1904177.
[2] Q. Wu, L. Yang, X. Wang, Z. Hu, Mesostructured carbon-based nanocages: an advanced platform for energy chemistry, Science China Chemistry 63 (5) (2020) 665–681.

[3] Z. Li, B. Li, C. Yu, H. Wang, Q. Li. Recent Progress of Hollow Carbon Nanocages: General Design Fundamentals and Diversified Electrochemical Applications, Advanced Science (2023) 2206605.

[4] H.Y. Yue, S.S. Song, S. Huang, X. Gao, B. Wang, E.H. Guan, X.R. Guo, Preparation of three-dimensional hollow graphene balls and simultaneous electrochemical determination of dopamine and uric acid, Journal of Materials Science: Materials in Electronics 29 (14) (2018) 12330−12339.

[5] D.A. Ziolkowska, J.D. Jangam, G. Rudakov, T.M. Paronyan, M. Akhtar, G.U. Sumanasekera, J.B. Jasinski, Simple synthesis of highly uniform bilayer-carbon nanocages, Carbon 115 (2017) 617−624.

[6] D. Wang, Y. Wang, H. Liu, W. Xu, L. Xu, Unusual carbon nanomesh constructed by interconnected carbon nanocages for ionic liquid-based supercapacitor with superior rate capability, Chemical Engineering Journal 342 (2018) 474−483.

[7] Z. Li, L. Zhang, B. Li, Z. Liu, Z. Liu, H. Wang, Q. Li, Convenient and large-scale synthesis of hollow graphene-like nanocages for electrochemical supercapacitor application, Chemical Engineering Journal 313 (2017) 1242−1250.

[8] Z. Li, L. Zhang, C. Yang, J. Chen, Z. Wang, L. Bao, P. Shen, Graphitized carbon nanocages/palladium nanoparticles: sustainable preparation and electrocatalytic performances towards ethanol oxidation reaction, International Journal of Hydrogen Energy 44 (12) (2019) 6172−6181.

[9] Mei Y., Z. Li, N-doped graphene-like carbon nanocages modified by trace nickel species for efficient ORR and OER bifunctional electrocatalyst.

[10] Y. Bu, T. Sun, Y. Cai, L. Du, O. Zhuo, L. Yang, Z. Hu, Compressing carbon nanocages by capillarity for optimizing porous structures toward ultrahigh-volumetric-performance supercapacitors, Advanced Materials 29 (24) (2017) 1700470.

[11] K. Xie, X. Qin, X. Wang, Y. Wang, H. Tao, Q. Wu, Z. Hu, Carbon nanocages as supercapacitor electrode materials, Advanced Materials 24 (3) (2012) 347−352.

[12] V.S. Kale, M. Hwang, H. Chang, J. Kang, S.I. Chae, Y. Jeon, T. Hyeon, Microporosity-controlled synthesis of heteroatom codoped carbon nanocages by wrap-bake-sublime approach for flexible all-solid-state-supercapacitors, Advanced Functional Materials 28 (37) (2018) 1803786.

[13] Z. Lyu, L. Yang, D. Xu, J. Zhao, H. Lai, Y. Jiang, Z. Hu, Hierarchical carbon nanocages as high-rate anodes for Li-and Na-ion batteries, Nano Research 8 (11) (2015) 3535−3543.

[14] X. Yu, S. Yang, B. Zhang, D. Shao, X. Dong, Y. Fang, H. Wang, Controlled synthesis of SnO2@carbon core-shell nanochains as high-performance anodes for lithium-ion batteries, Journal of Materials Chemistry 21 (33) (2011) 12295−12302.

[15] D.M. Burke, J.P. O'Byrne, P.G. Fleming, D. Borah, M.A. Morris, J.D. Holmes, Carbon nanocages as heavy metal ion adsorbents, Desalination 280 (1−3) (2011) 87−94.

[16] E. Petala, Y. Georgiou, V. Kostas, K. Dimos, M.A. Karakassides, Y. Deligiannakis, R. Zboril, Magnetic carbon nanocages: an advanced architecture with surface-and morphology-enhanced removal capacity for arsenites, ACS Sustainable Chemistry and Engineering 5 (7) (2017) 5782−5792.

[17] P. Zhang, X.F. Lu, D. Luan, X.W. Lou, Fabrication of heterostructured Fe_2TiO_5−TiO_2 nanocages with enhanced photoelectrochemical performance for solar energy conversion, Angewandte Chemie 132 (21) (2020) 8205−8209.

[18] H. Li, B. Chong, B. Xu, N. Wells, X. Yan, G. Yang, Nanoconfinement-induced conversion of water chemical adsorption properties in nanoporous photocatalysts to improve photocatalytic hydrogen evolution, ACS Catalysis 11 (22) (2021) 14076−14086.

[19] N. Wang, W. Ma, Z. Ren, L. Zhang, R. Qiang, K.Y.A. Lin, X. Han, Template synthesis of nitrogen-doped carbon nanocages−encapsulated carbon nanobubbles as catalyst for activation of peroxymonosulfate, Inorganic Chemistry Frontiers 5 (8) (2018) 1849−1860.

[20] X. Li, A.I. Rykov, B. Zhang, Y. Zhang, J. Wang, Graphene encapsulated Fe xCoy nanocages derived from metal−organic frameworks as efficient activators for peroxymonosulfate, Catalysis Science and Technology 6 (20) (2016) 7486−7494.

CHAPTER 21

Nanoporous-activated carbon: recent progress in energy and environment fields

21.1 Introduction

Nano-porous-activated carbon is a porous carbon material with controllable surface area and nano-porous structure. According to the pore structure, activated carbon can be divided into microporous activated carbon, mesoporous activated carbon, and macroporous activated carbon theoretically. In fact, the pore structure of activated carbon is often complex and hierarchical (mainly micro-pore and meso-pore structure, macropore is auxiliary). Nanostructured porous activated carbon has attracted extensive attention in the field of supercapacitors and lithium-sulfur battery due to its high specific surface area and high stability. One of our studies on the relationship between the electrochemical activity of the activated carbon electrode material and its electrical conductivity (increasing the graphited microcrystal and mesoporous structure) is helpful for its practical application in the field of energy storage [1]. Activated carbon is a kind of special carbon material, which has a good pore structure, large specific surface area, stability, adsorption performance, and renewability. Therefore, adsorption technology based on nano-porous-activated carbon has broad application prospects in the water treatment field and other environmental aspects [2]. Therefore, it is very important and necessary to summarize the structural characteristics and preparation methods of porous activated carbon in order to promote its application in energy chemistry and environmental science.

21.2 Structural features of nanoporous-activated carbon

Porous carbon materials have shown excellent performance in a variety of energy and environment-related applications. Over the past few decades, there has been a great deal of collaborative design and regulation of nano-porous carbon in terms of surface area, pore size, surface chemistry, and hybrid structure. Porous carbon materials have the advantages of high specific surface area, controllable physical and chemical properties, low price, and easy availability, showing great application prospects in energy storage and conversion, catalysis, adsorption and separation, and other fields. The structure—activity relationship between material structure and properties of porous carbon materials is an important research direction [3]. Hierarchical porous carbon contains pores of different

Nanostructured Materials
ISBN 978-0-443-19256-2, https://doi.org/10.1016/B978-0-443-19256-2.00035-1

sizes (from micro-pore, mesoporous to macro-pore), many of which are interconnected and assembled in a 3-D hierarchical structure. Generally, the existence of micro-pores provides a large surface area to enhance the charge storage capacity or ion/molecule adsorption capacity, while meso-pore and macro-pore can improve electrolyte or solution penetration and promote mass diffusion, so they have a very wide range of applications in electrochemical devices and environmental adsorption [4].

21.3 Preparation methods of nanoporous-activated carbon

Porous-activated carbon was prepared by differentiation activation and physical activation. Chemical activation, as the name implies, is a method of adding chemicals to raw materials and then heating them in an inert gas medium to carry out carbonization and activation simultaneously. Chemicals include zinc chloride, phosphoric acid, alkali, etc. The chemical activation method with alkaline activators such as potassium hydroxide (KOH) is notable (with advantage of high specific surface area and controllable pore size). The chemical activation method has three disadvantages: (1) it is very corrosive to equipment, (2) it pollutes the environment, (3) there are chemical activators left in activated carbon, and its application is limited. The physical activation method refers to high-temperature activation with carbon dioxide and water vapor activation, which has the advantage of environmental friendliness, but the disadvantage is low specific surface area. The preparation methods of porous carbon materials and the selection of precursors directly determine their properties and application ranges. In particular, the KOH chemical activation can be used to obtain hierarchical porous activated carbon by adjusting the proportion and temperature (see Fig. 21.1 for details) [5–7].

In our previous research work, for the first time, a new kind of "hierarchical porous active graphene carbon" was obtained by efficient ion exchange-graphitization/activation combined technology (see Fig. 21.1A and B for details) [5]. Typical preparation methods are as follows: Selection of cation exchange resin as the precursor, through the role exchange adsorption transition metal cation (Ni^{2+}), synchronous form homogeneous mixture by adding KOH as activator, the last under the high-temperature reaction (nickel catalyst to promote graphene layer formation, a simultaneous KOH for forming of hierarchical porous structure). According to IUPAC definition, the pores of a porous material can be classified into three groups: micropores ($d < 2$ nm), mesopores (2 nm $\leq d \leq 50$ nm), and macropores ($d > 50$ nm). We also reported that the hierarchical porous carbon microspheres achieved by KOH chemical activation of mesocarbon microbeads (MCMBs) showed high specific surface area (2890 m^2/g in BET method) (see Fig. 21.1C for details) [6]. It is well known that the micro-texture of MCMBs is global-type or Brooks–Taylor-type with regular lamellar structures, which favors the fabrication of porous activated carbon with high surface area and controllable porous structure by chemical activation. In the present study, KOH was used for

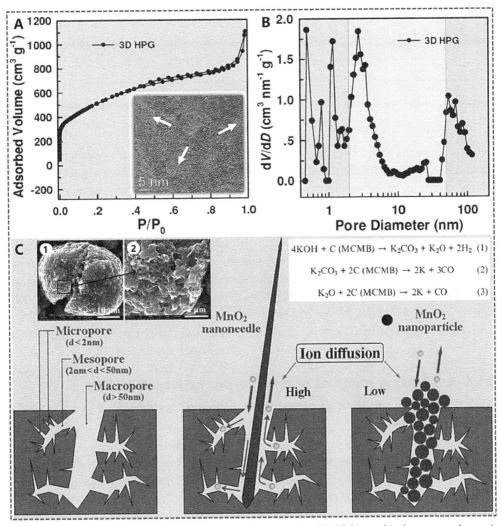

Figure 21.1 (A—B) hierarchical porous active graphene carbon [5], (C) hierarchical porous carbon microspheres [6] (the inset in C show KOH chemical activation reactions [7]).

activation of the MCMBs-the accepted reactions being as follows (see the inset in Fig. 21.1C for details) [7].

$$4KOH + C \text{ (MCMB)} \rightarrow K_2CO_3 + K_2O + 2H_2 \tag{21.1}$$

$$K_2CO_3 + 2C \text{ (MCMB)} \rightarrow 2K + 3CO \tag{21.2}$$

$$K_2O + 2C \text{ (MCMB)} \rightarrow 2K + CO \tag{21.3}$$

In addition to KOH chemical activation, our research group also developed an efficient CH_3COOLi esterification and Li_2CO_3 "posttemplet" technology, which resulted in the preparation of mesoporous carbon microspheres from hydrothermal carbon spheres (see Fig. 21.2A for details) [8]. The formation of mesopores might be attributed to the "posttemplet" role of Li_2CO_3 within the precursors, namely the Li_2CO_3 may act a "site-occupying" role for the formation of mesopores. Firstly, when the CH_3COOLi embedded into the hydrothermal carbon spheres, an acetic ester and lithium hydroxide might be produced by the esterification between CH_3COO^- and $-OH$ groups: $(R-OH)_n + nCH_3COOLi = nCH_3COOR + nLiOH$. Secondly, the LiOH can convert into Li_2CO_3 in subsequent high-temperature procedures. Finally, after washing wih dilute acid, these Li_2CO_3 were cleaned out from the carbonized framework of mesoporous carbon microspheres, resulting in their mesopore structures [8].

21.4 Application progress of nanoporous-activated carbon

21.4.1 Energy application of nanoporous-activated carbon

21.4.1.1 Supercapacitor

With the rapid development of electric vehicles and portable electronic devices, electric double-layer supercapacitors (EDLCs) have attracted wide attention for their high-power density and ultra-long cycle stability. Porous active carbon material is the most important electrode active material in commercial EDLCs, which is faced with high production cost, corrosion of production equipment, pollutant emission, and other problems. Therefore, it is of great significance to develop new synthetic strategies for porous carbon materials and pore-forming mechanisms under different strategies for reducing the cost of EDLCs and expanding the application field of EDLCs. The Li_2CO_3 "site-occupying" technology is an efficient and green preparation method for porous activated carbon microspheres (see Fig. 21.2A−C for details) [8]. The analysis results indicate that the porous carbon microspheres have a high specific surface area of 1163 m^2/g and a satisfactory small mesoporous texture (2−5 nm), with the mean pore size of 3.24 nm. The capacitive performances of the samples in 6 mol/L KOH aqueous electrolyte, have been tested by cyclic voltammetry, electrochemical impedance spectroscopy, and charge-discharge techniques. A specific capacitance of 171.5 F/g is obtained for the porous carbon microspheres via charge-discharge at a current density of 1 A/g. It also displayed a very high

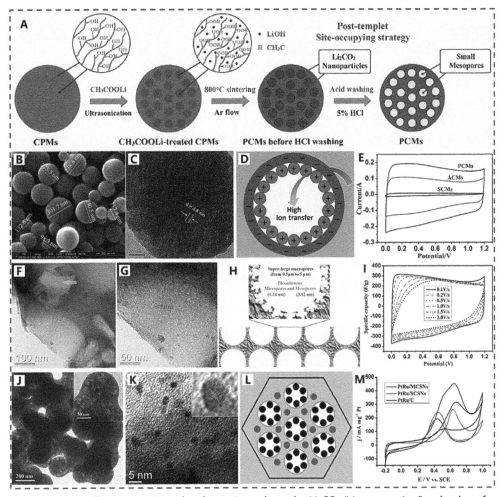

Figure 21.2 (A−E) porous activated carbon microspheres by Li$_2$CO$_3$ "site-occupying" technology for supercapacitors [8], (F−I) porous activated carbon foam by KOH chemical activation for supercapacitors [9], (J−M) mesoporous activated carbon nanochains-supported metal nanoparticles for electrocatalysis [10].

cycle stability of 97.8%, compared with the initial capacitance, after 1000 cycles at the high current density of 1000 mA/g (see Fig. 21.2D and E) [8].

Hierarchical porous structure can improve the migration of ions in the pores and enhance the EDLC. It has been proved that the hierarchical porous carbon materials with larger macropores, moderate mesopores, and abundant micropores, displayed significantly improved electrochemical performances relative to the single-pore-size porous carbon materials. Recently, we reported a simple and efficient buried activation technique to prepare a high-specific-surface-area carbon foam (3106.7 m^2/g), which possesses a unique hierarchical porous structure composed of super-large macropores (0.5–5 μm), bi-continuous large micropores (1.14 nm), and small mesopores (3.12 nm). The hierarchical porous structure allows rapid ion transport within the electrode, which endows the carbon foam with excellent supercapacitor performances. Ultrahigh specific capacitances of up to 364.2 F/g in KOH electrolyte and 413.6 F/g in H_2SO_4 electrolyte at a current density of 1 A/g are demonstrated for the hierarchical porous carbon foam (see Fig. 21.2F–I for details) [9]. The super-large macropores act as ion-buffering reservoirs and provide ultra-high ion diffusion rates for the electrolyte, which exhibits excellent ratio capacitance and power performance. The as-prepared electrode delivers extremely high energy densities of 72.8 and 82.72 Wh/kg at a power density of 600 W/kg in KOH and H_2SO_4 electrolytes, respectively.

21.4.1.2 Rechargeable batteries

Porous activated carbon has a wide range of applications in rechargeable batteries, such as lead-acid batteries (lead-carbon batteries with activated carbon) and lithium-sulfur batteries (activated carbon-sulfur composite electrodes). Special activated carbon (or special porous carbon) is added to the negative electrode of lead-acid battery, which solves the problem of sulfuric acid salting (lead sulfate crystalline particles grow up and lose the reversibility of charging and releasing), and prolonging the battery life for several times. In addition to the original safety, cheap, easy to regenerate, and other advantages, lead-carbon batteries should be the first choice for large-scale energy storage [11]. Sulfur is one of the most promising cathode materials for the next generation of batteries, but its application is severely restricted by the widespread polysulfide dissolution/shuttling phenomenon in sulfur REDOX chemistry. In order to provide electron and ion channels for sulfur positives, the authors permeated sulfur into the pores of activated carbon to form a nanocomposite electrode. In Li-sulfur batteries, even if all the porosity of activated carbon is filled by sulfur mass, the continuous dissolution of polysulfide can provide new space for ion transport to the active substance [12].

21.4.1.3 Electrocatalytic conversion

As the defect of porous activated carbon is a high-energy active site, it can have a strong interaction with the active metal components, which makes the distribution of the loaded metal particles more uniform and smaller in size, so as to improve the catalytic activity of the material. At the same time, this strong interaction makes the catalyst have better stability under working conditions [13]. The mesoporous structure of carbon material is conducive to anchoring metal nanoparticles and playing a limited catalytic role (see the confined effect in Section 3.7). Earlier, we prepared novel porous 1-D architectures, mesopore-functional carbon sphere nanochains (MCSNs) through a unique Li_2CO_3-molten salt strategy for electrocatalytic conversion (see Fig. 21.2J—M for details) [10]. The PtRu/MCSNs hybrid system, achieved by rational integration of 2.5 nm-size PtRu alloy NPs into the mesopores of MCSNs, was prepared. It is demonstrated that the PtRu/MCSN hybrid system exhibited superior catalytic properties toward methanol oxidation with specially enhanced catalytic activity and desirable stability. This can be ascribed to the functionalities of mesoporous carbon support, which affords more efficient electron transfer and better mass transport, maximizing the availability of nano-PtRu catalysts [10].

21.4.2 Environmental application of nanoporous-activated carbon
21.4.2.1 Adsorbing purification
The act of concentrating a solute onto a solid surface is called adsorption. The surface of actived carbon has an obvious adsorption effect. Activated carbon has surface energy, and its adsorption is caused by the force imbalance of carbon atoms on the surface of the hole wall, which leads to surface adsorption (see Section 4.7). In the process of wastewater treatment, porous activated carbon can play the role of deodorization, such as acetaldehyde, indole, etc., can be removed by physical adsorption method, and H_2S, thiols, etc., are further removed by the oxidation of active carbon surface. Activated carbon in the treatment of printing and dyeing wastewater also has extremely strong decolorization ability and adsorption capacity of heavy metal ions. There are different forms of activated carbon, which are granular and powdery in water treatment. Powdery activated carbon can be used in intermittent adsorption, that is, according to a certain proportion, the powdery activated carbon added to the treated water, mixed evenly, by precipitation or filtration of carbon, water separation, this method is also known as static adsorption. Granular activated carbon is often used for continuous adsorption. The treated water passes through the carbon adsorption bed to purify the water. This method is exactly the same as the fixed bed in form, also known as dynamic adsorption [14].

21.4.2.2 Photocatalytic degradation
At present, the combined technology of high surface area activated carbon adsorption and high-efficiency photocatalysis can effectively remove and mineralize refractory organic pollutants from industrial wastewater. In addition, the design of activated carbon-supported nanophotocatalyst and is an alternative solution strategy to improve the photocatalytic activity and stability. Activated carbon has an influence on the

structure and photocatalytic activity of photocatalyst. For example, the specific surface area and particle size of TiO_2 increased when different proportions of activated carbon were added during the preparation of TiO_2 photocatalyst. These TiO_2-activated carbon composite photocatalysts have high photocatalytic activity in UV-assisted degradation of Rhodamine B (RhB) in an aqueous solution [15].

21.4.2.3 Advanced oxidation

Advanced oxidation technologies are mainly divided into Fenton oxidation, photocatalytic oxidation, ozone oxidation, ultrasonic oxidation, wet oxidation, and supercritical water oxidation. Activated carbon adsorption method has the advantages of a stable concentration of organic matter and fast reaction speed. In recent years, activated carbon adsorption technology has been widely concerned in organic wastewater treatment. Fenton oxidation is simple, rapid, and does not require complex equipment, while the combination of activated carbon and Fenton oxidation can efficiently remove the harmful substances in wastewater. Activated carbon and other types of porous carbonaceous materials have been widely used as catalysts and supports (for activated transition metals or metal oxides) to promote the degradation of organic pollutants by the generation of hydroxyl radicals from H_2O_2 in Fenton advanced oxidation [16].

21.5 Summary

In this chapter, we have discussed the structural features, preparation methods, energy and environmental applications, and typical case analysis of porous activated carbon materials (activated carbon by KOH chemical activation and template synthesis). At present, the main research directions of porous active carbon materials in energy storage and conversion and environmental protection are as follows: (1) Preparation and application of hierarchical porous activated carbon with controllable and microporous/mesoporous/macroporous structures; (2) Preparation and application of porous activated carbon with ultra-high specific surface area (> 3000 m^2/g); (3) Preparation and application of porous activated carbon functionalized with surface groups and hybrid metal materials.

Acknowledgments

This book was supported by National Natural Science Foundation of China (22078071, 22272034), Natural Science Foundation of Guangdong Province (2021A1515010125, 2020A1515010344), Maoming Science and Technology Project (mmkj2020032), Guangdong Province Universities and Colleges Pearl River Scholar Funded Scheme (2019), Guangdong Basic and Applied Basic Research Foundation (2019A1515011249, 2021A1515010305), Key Research Project of Natural Science of Guangdong Provincial Department of Education (2019KZDXM010), Environment and Energy Green Catalysis Innovation Team of Colleges and Universities of Guangdong Province (2022KCXTD019), the program for Innovative Research Team of Guangdong University of Petrochemical Technology.

References

[1] M. Sevilla, R. Mokaya, Energy storage applications of activated carbons: supercapacitors and hydrogen storage, Energy and Environmental Science 7 (4) (2014) 1250−1280.

[2] T.J. Bandosz, Activated Carbon Surfaces in Environmental Remediation, Elsevier, 2006.

[3] T. Wang, H. Wang, Research progress on porous carbon materials, Scientia Sinica Chimica 49 (5) (2019) 729−740.

[4] Z. Li, L. Zhang, X. Chen, B. Li, H. Wang, Q. Li, Three-dimensional graphene-like porous carbon nanosheets derived from molecular precursor for high-performance supercapacitor application, Electrochimica Acta 296 (2019) 8−17.

[5] Y. Li, Z. Li, P.K. Shen, Simultaneous formation of ultrahigh surface area and three-dimensional hierarchical porous graphene-like networks for fast and highly stable supercapacitors, Advanced Materials 25 (17) (2013) 2474−2480.

[6] Z. Li, Q. Li, Y. Fang, H. Wang, Y. Li, X. Wang, Unique mesoporous carbon microsphere/1-D MnO_2-built composite architecture and their enhanced electrochemical capacitance performance, Journal of Materials Chemistry 21 (43) (2011) 17185−17192.

[7] H.Q. Wang, Z.S. Li, Y.G. Huang, Q.Y. Li, X.Y. Wang, A novel hybrid supercapacitor based on spherical activated carbon and spherical MnO_2 in a non-aqueous electrolyte, Journal of Materials Chemistry 20 (19) (2010) 3883−3889.

[8] Z. Li, D. Li, Z. Liu, B. Li, C. Ge, Y. Fang, Mesoporous carbon microspheres with high capacitive performances for supercapacitors, Electrochimica Acta 158 (2015) 237−245.

[9] Z. Li, X. Hu, D. Xiong, B. Li, H. Wang, Q. Li, Facile synthesis of bicontinuous microporous/mesoporous carbon foam with ultrahigh specific surface area for supercapacitor application, Electrochimica Acta 219 (2016) 339−349.

[10] P. Qi, Y. Siyuan, G. Chunyu, L. Yingju, L. Xiaotang, F. Yueping, Z. Liya, Mesopore-functional carbon sphere nanochains and their integration with alloy nanoparticles for enhanced electrochemical performances, Electrochimica Acta 114 (2013) 334−340.

[11] L. Wang, H. Zhang, W. Zhang, H. Guo, G. Cao, H. Zhao, Y. Yang, A new nano lead-doped mesoporous carbon composite as negative electrode additives for ultralong-cyclability lead-carbon batteries, Chemical Engineering Journal 337 (2018) 201−209.

[12] X. Wu, A. Markir, Y. Xu, E.C. Hu, K.T. Dai, C. Zhang, X. Ji, Rechargeable iron−sulfur battery without polysulfide shuttling, Advanced Energy Materials 9 (40) (2019) 1902422.

[13] X. Yan, Y. Jia, J. Chen, Z. Zhu, X. Yao, Defective-activated-carbon-supported Mn−Co nanoparticles as a highly efficient electrocatalyst for oxygen reduction, Advanced Materials 28 (39) (2016) 8771−8778.

[14] J.R. Perrich, Activated Carbon Adsorption for Wastewater Treatment, CRC press, 2018.

[15] M. Asiltürk, Ş. Şener, TiO2-activated carbon photocatalysts: preparation, characterization and photocatalytic activities, Chemical Engineering Journal 180 (2012) 354−363.

[16] S. Navalon, A. Dhakshinamoorthy, M. Alvaro, H. Garcia, Heterogeneous Fenton catalysts based on activated carbon and related materials, ChemSusChem 4 (12) (2011) 1712−1730.

CHAPTER 22

Nanomanganese oxides: recent progress in energy and environment fields

22.1 Introduction

Manganese oxides mainly include manganese monoxide (MnO), manganese dioxide (MnO_2), manganese trioxide (Mn_2O_3), manganese tetroxide (Mn_3O_4), and so on. Manganese dioxide, an inorganic compound with chemical formula MnO_2, is a black amorphous powder or black crystalline powder, which is insoluble in water. Manganese dioxide is used in the preparation of manganese salt, also used as oxidant, rust remover, and catalyst. Manganese dioxide nanomaterials include a variety of morphologies such as monodisperse nanoparticles, nanoflowers, nanofibers, nanowires, and nanorods. Manganese dioxide has become one of the alternative materials to replace precious metals as the electrode material of supercapacitors due to its cheap, easy to obtain, and environmentally friendly characteristics. Manganese dioxide with a high specific surface area is a novel pseudocapacitor material with a low price and similar electrochemical properties to Ruthenium oxide [1]. With the continuous development of new energy battery technology, the application of manganese oxide in the battery field has gradually expanded in recent years. For example, electrolytic manganese dioxide is the key material of lithium manganese battery, and manganese dioxide also has a place in Zinc-ion battery [2]. In addition, the nanomanganese dioxide has been widely used in environmental field because of its special characteristics of chemical oxidation and surface catalysis. The preparation method of nanomanganese dioxide material is simple, the raw material is cheap and easy to obtain, easy to operate, easy to control, good repeatability, and has no pollution, which is conducive to industrial production and energy-environmental applications [3].

22.2 Structural features of nanomanganese oxides

Manganese dioxide (MnO_2) is a kind of oxide with complex chemical structure. According to the different linkage ways of [MnO_6] octahedron in MnO_2 via sharing corners or edges, MnO_2 structure can be divided into three categories: one is chain or tunnel structure, such as α-MnO_2, β-MnO_2, γ-MnO_2, etc. The second type is lamellar structure, and δ-MnO_2 belongs to this category. The third class has a three-dimensional structure, such as λ-MnO_2. The MnO_2 has a variety of one-dimensional (1D) tunnel configuration

Nanostructured Materials
ISBN 978-0-443-19256-2, https://doi.org/10.1016/B978-0-443-19256-2.00012-0

of polycrystalline phase (in tunnel size of 0.3–0.7 nm) or 2D-layered configuration, widely used in ion transport and material separation (molecular sieve) and other fields. The α-MnO_2, β-MnO_2, and γ-MnO_2 possess 1D (1×1) (2×2), (1×1), and (1×1) (1×2) tunnel structures, respectively. The structure of ε-MnO_2 is similar to that of γ-MnO_2, but its manganese lattice points are highly disordered and its tunnel shape is irregular. δ-MnO_2 possesses 2D-layered structures formed by the common side of the $[MnO_6]$ octahedron; λ-MnO_2 is a typical spinel structure, which has a 3D (1×1) tunnel structure [3]. The (2×2) large tunnel of α-MnO_2 with a size of 0.46 nm can accommodate most metal cations (such as K^+, Ca^{2+}, Na^+, or Mg^{2+}) and water molecules. The (1×1) narrow tunnel of β-MnO_2 with a size of 0.19 nm can only accommodate small ions like H^+ or Li^+ and is not conducive to ion diffusion. The 2D layered δ-MnO_2 belongs to a typical monoclinic system and has a large interlayer distance of 0.7 nm, which can hold numbers of water molecules, metal cations, and other substances. The λ-MnO_2 has a typical 3D (1×1) tunnel structure which is conducive to electron transfer and widely used as electrocatalysis material. The schematic diagrams of the crystallographic structure and Thermodynamic morphology of the various types of MnO_2 are shown in Fig. 22.1 [4]. The complex and changeable crystal surface structure (including the atomic arrangement, unsaturated bond formation, defects, etc.) of MnO_2 nanomaterials has attracted extensive attention in the fields of energy storage and catalysis. The MnO_2 has abundant natural crystalline phases and is one of the most active candidates in the field of energy and environmental catalysis. However, the phase–activity relationship and the source of the catalytic activity of these MnO_2 remains ambiguous and controversial. Therefore, it is very important to study the six crystalline types MnO_2 (α, β, γ, δ, ε, and λ-MnO_2) to reveal the relationship between crystalline phase and catalytic activity [5].

22.3 Preparation methods of nanomanganese oxides

Manganese oxide nanomaterials have many specific properties, which have been widely used in the fields of electricity and catalysis, and their properties are largely affected by factors such as morphology, nanoscale, crystal structure, and crystallinity. Therefore, it is of great significance to study the controllable preparation of morphology and scale of manganese oxide nanomaterials. At present, the preparation methods of nanomanganese dioxide materials include hydrothermal method, coprecipitation method, solid phase method, and ultrasonic or microwave-assisted methods, etc. There are many methods to prepare nano-MnO_2, and different methods have their unique advantages and disadvantages. Thereinto, the hydrothermal and co-precipitation methods are widely used. By controlling different temperatures, different amounts of reactive substances, different pH values of solution, and different reaction times, nano-MnO_2 with different crystal types and morphologic features can be obtained [6].

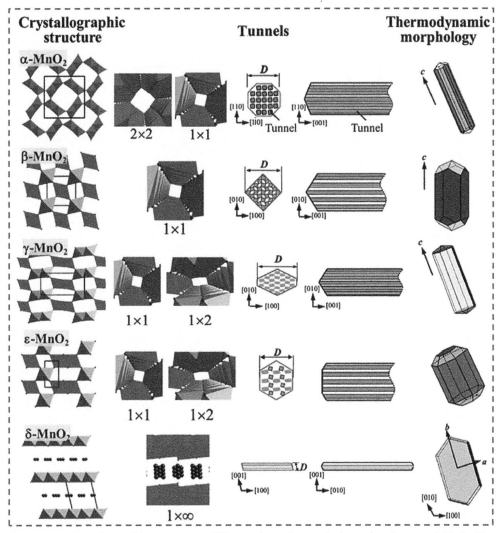

Figure 22.1 Crystallographic structure and Thermodynamic morphology of α-, β-, γ-, ε-, δ-MnO₂. The arrangement of tunnels in α-, β-, γ-, ε-MnO₂ is formed by stacking the tunnels along the axial-direction of the 1D morphology, while δ-MnO₂ is formed via stacking the 2D tunnels along the c-axis direction [4].

Different from the traditional hydrothermal synthesis of MnO_2, a novel two-step synthesis process was adopted in one of our previous works: 1) the ultrasonic chemical prereaction and 2) the hydrothermal synthesis of MnO_2 nanowire-spheres in acidic solution [7]. Sonochemistry is an effective method for fabricating nano-materials, and this technology was used to promote MnO_2 hydrothermal synthesis by enhancing mixing of reactants in the prereaction process. The 1-D MnO_2 nanostructures tend to form in acidic conditions, so HNO_3 was introduced as acid source in this study for the hydrothermal synthesis of MnO_2, in which Mn^{2+} could be easily oxidized into Mn^{4+} by ClO_3^- based on the following reaction:

$$Mn^{2+} + 2ClO_3^- + 4H^+ = MnO_2 + 2H_2O + Cl_2$$

It is clear that well-shaped MnO_2 nanowire spheres were formed effectively during the sonication-hydrothermal process. However, when the hydrothermal synthesis was performed in the absence of sonication prereaction, rod-like MnO_2 aggregations rather than nanowire-based MnO_2 were obtained. The result suggests that the sonochemistry prereaction contributes to the growth of a good 1-D nanostructure and well-distributed MnO_2 nanowire spheres [7].

22.4 Application progress of nanomanganese oxides

22.4.1 Energy application of nanomanganese oxides

22.4.1.1 Supercapacitor

Manganese dioxide (MnO_2) is an excellent material for supercapacitors, which has high theoretical capacitance ($1380\,F\,g^{-1}$), low material price, environment friendly and pollution-free characteristics. However, limited by poor ions ($10^{-13}\,S\,cm^{-1}$) and electronic conductivity (10^{-5}–$10^{-6}\,S\,cm^{-1}$), the actual specific capacitance of MnO_2 is often much lower than its theoretical specific capacity (only about 30% of theoretical capacitance), which greatly limits its practical application [8]. In addition, the active layer of MnO_2 electrode that can be used to store charge is only a very thin part of the surface, and most of the bulk phase MnO_2 cannot be effectively utilized. In order to solve this problem, the design of nanostructured MnO_2 has become a hot spot of researchers and industry attention (which can increase the effective utilization of electrodes). At present, MnO_2 nanostructure design (such as nanowires, nanorods, nanoneedles, nanosheets), effective combination with conductive substrates (carbon substrates or metallic network), defect construction, and metal doping technologies are comprehensively promoting and activating the intrinsic characteristics of MnO_2, and further improving their performances of electrode materials for supercapacitors (see Fig. 22.2 for details) [9–14].

The relevant findings showed that the MnO_2 can be used as the electrode of supercapacitor to exhibit considerable Faradaic pseudo-capacitance, which is closely related to the properties of electrolyte. For this reason, a lot of studies have been carried out on Faraday process in different media such as acid, alkaline and neutral electrolyte, and

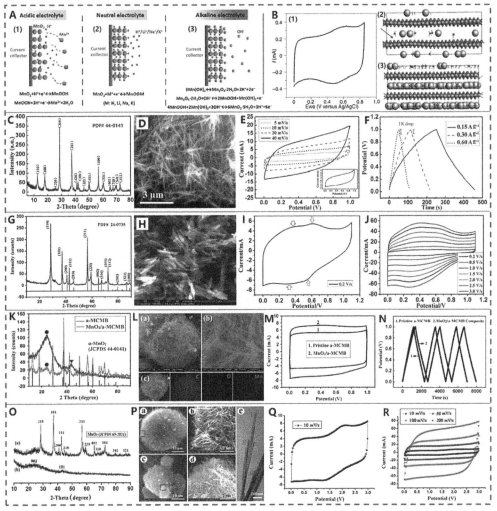

Figure 22.2 (A) Redox reaction and storage mechanism of MnO$_2$ in different electrolytes (acidic, neutral, and basic) [9]; (B) Pseudo-capacitance application and mechanism of birnessite (δ-MnO$_2$) [10]; (C—F) Pseudo-capacitance application of α-MnO$_2$ nanoneedles [11]); (G—J) Pseudo-capacitance application of β-MnO$_2$ nanorods [12]); (K—N) Pseudo-capacitance application of α-MnO$_2$ nanowires/a-MCMB [13]); (O—R) Pseudo-capacitance application of β-MnO$_2$ nanoneedles/a-MCMB [14]).

the energy storage mechanism derived from Faraday reaction has been gradually established, as shown in Fig. 22.2A [9]. In acidic electrolyte, the excessive protons may induce the reduction and dissolution of Mn from bulk MnO_2 ($MnO_2 + H^+ + e^- \rightarrow MnOOH$; $MnOOH + 3H^+ + e^- \rightarrow Mn^{2+} + 2H_2O$), leading to a poor stability and cycling performance. The electrochemical reactions in alkaline electrolyte were the following equations: $3Mn(OH)_2 \leftrightarrow Mn_3O_4 \cdot 2H_2O + 2H^+ + 2e^-$; $Mn_3O_4 \cdot 2H_2O + OH^- \leftrightarrow 2MnOOH + Mn(OH)_3 + e^-$; $4MnOOH + 2Mn(OH)_3 + 3OH^- \leftrightarrow 6MnO_2 \cdot 5H_2O + 3H^+ + 6e^-$. Fortunately, the mild and environmentally friendly neutral electrolyte can be used as an effective medium for sustainable and efficient energy storage. In the neutral electrolyte, the charge storage process and reaction mechanism of pseudo-capacitance are as follows:

$$(MnO_2)_{surface} + M^+ + e^- \leftrightarrow (MnOOM)_{surface} \text{ (M: H, Li, Na, K)}$$

Therefore, the capacitance value of MnO_2 is mainly derived from the contribution of surface-dependent redox reactions. Based on BET surface area, the theoretical capacitance of MnO_2 is only 110 $\mu F\ cm^{-2}$, which is much lower than the experimental results. Therefore, the insertion/deinsertion mechanism of alkali metal ions in the bulk phase of MnO_2 was proposed and determined as follows:

$$(MnO_2)bulk + M^+ + e^- \leftrightarrow (MnOOM)bulk \text{ (M: H, Li, Na, K)}$$

It is well known that the pseudo-capacitive behavior of MnO_2 is a surface reaction: only the surface or a very thin surface layer of the oxide can participate in this pseudo-capacitive reaction. The pseudo-capacitance of MnO_2 is based on the reversible redox process that takes place in the redox transition Mn^{4+} and Mn^{3+}. The generally accepted reactions for MnO_2 in Na_2SO_4 neutral aqueous electrolyteare as follows (the redox process is governed by the insertion and deinsertion of Na^+ into the porous nano-MnO_2 matrix) [8]:

$$MnO_2 + Na^+ + e^- \leftrightarrow MnOONa$$

$$(MnO_2)_{surface} + Na^+ + e^- \leftrightarrow (MnOO - Na^+)_{surface}$$

In an alkaline electrolyte (such as KOH), the charge storage process may be completed by the combination of the surface adsorption/desorption of ions from the electrolyte and proton insertion from water. This could be an interesting extension of the pseudo-capacitance of MnO_2 in aqueous solutions, and the possible reactions are as follows:

$$(MnO_2)_{surface} + K^+ + e^- \leftrightarrow (MnO_2 - K^+)_{surface}$$

$$MnO_2 + H_2O + e^- \leftrightarrow MnOOH + OH^-$$

$$MnO_a(OH)_b + nH^+ + ne^- \leftrightarrow MnO_{a-n}(OH)_{b+n}$$

When used for electrode materials, nanostructured metal oxides have been considered to be more beneficial to high capacitance than bulky ones due to their sufficiently high electrode surface area. This may indicate that electrolyte ions can effectively make contact with the active electrode materials in nanostructures. The porous structure of the nano-MnO_2 electrode here can significantly facilitate the penetration of alkali metal ions, thus resulting in a facile redox reaction and a fast charge/discharge in supercapacitor applications [8].

Birnessite (δ-MnO_2), a representative ceramic material containing a water layer, has been explored for energy storage applications. The δ-Mno_2 has a layered structure, and its charge storage mechanism is through the surface adsorption and intercalation process of metal cations (Na^+, K^+, H^+, etc.), which makes Mn(IV) and Mn(III) intertransform. Veronica Augustyn of North Carolina State University recently reported that interlayer limiting and hydration play a role in the charge storage of δ-MnO_2 materials. It is determined that the capacitive behavior of the δ-MnO_2 results from the cation embedding in the hydrated interlayer, where the presence of structural water increases the distance between the cation and the oxide. The significance of this work is that it provides a universal method to analyze the charging mechanism of pseudocapacitor materials. It is suggested that the spacing between ions and atoms of the laminates is the key to determine the charging and discharging of ions in the form of electrostatic adsorption or redox insertion (see Fig. 22.2B for details) [10].

Novel α-MnO_2 nanoneedles self-assembled micropowders were prepared by a simple one-step hydrothermal synthesis method from Mn^{7+} and Mn^{2+} in weak acidic condition. When evaluated for supercapacitor electrode, a desirable specific capacitance of 135 F g^{-1} is obtained at current density of 0.15 A g^{-1} in 1 M Na_2SO_4 aqueous solution (see Fig. 22.2C−F for details) [11]. Due to their unique crystallographic forms and self-assembled nanostructures, these newly synthesized α-MnO_2 micropowders showed a promising prospect for the technology application of supercapacitors. In addition, well-dispersed β-MnO_2 nanorods were prepared by a simple one-step hydrothermal synthesis method from Mn^{7+} and Mn^{2+} in strong acidic condition. When evaluated for supercapacitor electrode, a relatively high specific capacitance of 247.2 F g^{-1} is obtained at current density of 1 A g^{-1} in 1 mol/L KOH aqueous solution (see Fig. 22.2G−J for details) [12]. This is the first report on such well-controlled 1-D β-MnO_2 nanostructures for the cost-effective supercapacitor application in high capacitance and low material cost, although much attention has previously been paid to β-MnO_2 in various technical fields.

A α-MnO_2 nanowires/spherical activated carbon composite, namely α-MnO_2 nanowires growth onto the surface of activated mesocarbon microbeads (a-MCMB), was prepared by a simple hydrothermal synthesis method for supercapacitor application (see

Fig. 22.2K–N for details) [13]. The α-MnO$_2$ nanowires are found to be less than 50 nm in diameter and have a characteristic length of up to 2 μm. The novel α-MnO$_2$ nanowires/a-MCMB composite exhibited a specific capacitance of 357 F g^{-1} and good cycling stability in 1 M Na$_2$SO$_4$ aqueous neutral solution. A new class of micro-/nanocomposite architecture, characterized by vertically grown β-MnO$_2$ nanoneedles on high specific surface area a-MCMB for electrochemical capacitors in a nonaqueous electrolyte solution from 0.0 to 3.0 V (see Fig. 22.2O–R for details) [14]. The specific capacitances based on composite and MnO$_2$ nanoneedles have been calculated to be 226 and 547 F g^{-1}, respectively. It also demonstrated improved electrochemical properties with a high specific energy and energy density of 164 W h kg^{-1} and 25 kW h L^{-1}, respectively.

22.4.1.2 Rechargeable batteries

As a kind of cathode material for Zinc ion battery (ZIBs), MnO$_2$ materials have attracted extensive attention due to their low toxicity, low cost, diverse crystal structures, diverse energy storage mechanisms, and large theoretical capacity (308 mAh g^{-1}). Novel layered manganese dioxide nanodots (δ-MnO$_2$ NDs) were synthesized by simple redox reactions and used as positive electrodes in ZIBs for the first time [15]. Thanks to the layered structure and nanometer size, δ-MnO$_2$ NDs//Zn ZIBs has A specific capacity of 335 mAh g^{-1} at 0.1 A g^{-1} and exhibits excellent rate performance and stability. The MnO$_2$ of α, β, γ, or δ crystalline forms will undergo structural changes during cycle in ZIBs, and transform into layered MnO$_2$ phase with water molecules embedded in it. Large volume changes due to phase transition and hydration cation embedment will result in structure collapse and capacity decay. In order to solve this problem, Xia and Wang intercalated polyaniline (PANI) into the layered MnO$_2$ by the interface reaction method, which expanded the zinc storage channel of MnO$_2$ and effectively strengthened the extended layer structure, so as to effectively improve the zinc ion storage performance and structural stability of the material [16]. The ZIBs with this material as the positive electrode have excellent rate performance and cycle life. Especially when the active material utilization rate is up to 90% (~280 mAh g^{-1}), it can still maintain good cycle stability.

22.4.1.3 Electrocatalytic conversion

At present, there have been a large number of studies on Lithium-oxygen (Li-O$_2$) batteries MnO$_2$-based nonnoble metal cathode catalysts (ORR/OER). However, due to the poor catalytic conductivity of MnO$_2$, previous studies mainly focused on improving the conductivity of MnO$_2$ catalysts by introducing conductive substrates or doping Pd. Recently, Shahbazian-Yassar et al. synthesized β-MnO$_2$ crystals with a high proportion of {111} or {100} crystal planes and demonstrated the role of crystal plane regulation in modulating the catalytic activity of MnO$_2$ crystals in Li-O$_2$ cells [17]. Both the {100} and

{111} planes of β-MnO$_2$ crystal reduce the charge/discharge overpotential of Li-O$_2$ cell compared with the pure carbon cathode. The crystal surface engineering of MnO$_2$ crystal will bring more new discoveries for various energy storage devices and catalytic reactions. It is important to develop acid-stable electrocatalysts of OER for water decomposition. Recently, Lin group reported an electrocatalyst supported on α-MnO$_2$ with an array of Ru atoms (Ru/MnO$_2$) for OER, and then proposed a reaction mechanism involving only *O and *OH species as intermediates [18]. This mechanism allows direct O-O radical coupling to O$_2$ precipitate. The Ru/MnO$_2$ showed high activity (161 mV at 10 mA cm^{-2}) and excellent stability (little degradation after 200 h operation), making it one of the best performance acid-stable oxygen evolution reaction catalysts.

22.4.2 Environmental application of nanomanganese oxides

22.4.2.1 Adsorbing purification

In the application of removing heavy metal ions, manganese dioxide can effectively remove heavy metal ions by its oxidation and absorbability, as well as its surface binding effect. Hu et al. evaluated the ability of α-MnO$_2$ nanofibers (MO-2) to remove arsenite (As(III)) and arsenate (As(V)) experimentally and competatively. The maximum adsorption capacities of As(III) and As(V) for MO-2 were 117.72 mg g^{-1} and 60.19 mg g^{-1}, respectively, which were higher than those of α-MnO$_2$, β-MnO$_2$ and γ-MnO$_2$ reported in the literature. In particular, since the adsorption capacity of MO-2 for As(III) is much higher than that of As(V), it can be effectively applied to the removal of As(III) from groundwater without the need for preoxidation process. The fixed bed test showed that 800 mL of As(III) or 480 mL of As(V) contaminated water could be treated before the breakthrough, and only 12 mL of eluate could be used to effectively regenerate MO-2 (see Fig. 22.3A for details) [19]. According to density functional theory (DFT) calculations, the As(III) and As(V) form stable complexes on (100) and (110) of α-MnO$_2$. The adsorption kinetics of Pb(II) on β-MnO$_2$ can be well-fitted by a quasi-second-order rate equation. The thermodynamic parameters ΔH, ΔS, and ΔG were calculated according to the adsorption isotherm. The results showed that the adsorption of Pb(II) by β-MnO$_2$ was a spontaneous endothermic process. The adsorption of Pb(II) on β-MnO$_2$ is mainly due to surface complexation rather than ion exchange [25]. The Cr(VI) was also adsorbed on MnO$_2$ under environmentally relevant conditions. Both specific and nonspecific adsorption mechanisms may be involved, while the rate-control step involves intraparticle and film diffusion processes (Cr(VI) was strongly bound to MnO$_2$) [26].

22.4.2.2 Photocatalytic degradation

The freshly formed MnO$_2$ is used as a photocatalyst for the removal of multiple pollutants such as Nalidixic acid and Gefilozil. The freshly formed MnO$_2$ is flower-shaped β-MnO$_2$, which exhibits better multipollutant degradation efficiency due to its stronger pollutant adsorption capacity than commercial MnO$_2$. The reactive oxygen species in the

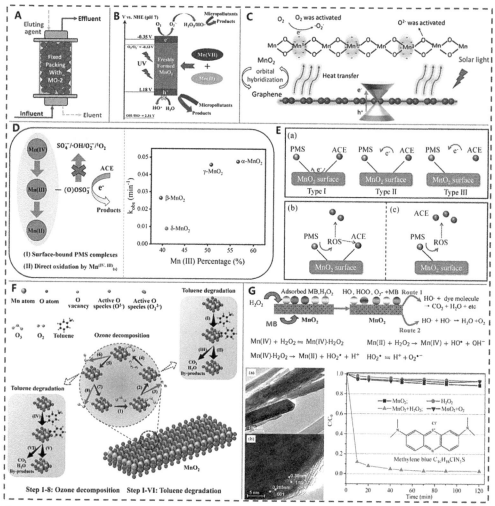

Figure 22.3 (A) MnO$_2$ fixed-bed adsorbing purification [19]; (B) UV/MnO$_2$ photocatalytic system [20]; (C) MnO$_2$/graphene photothermal system [21]); (D and E) MnO$_2$/PMS/ACE system [22]); (F) MnO$_2$-catalyzed ozonolysis of toluene [23]); (G) MnO$_2$ Fenton-like system [24]).

UV/MnO$_2$ photocatalytic system include hydroxyl, superoxide radical, and singlet oxygen. The only way for reactive oxygen species to be generated in this process is through the reaction between photogenerated electrons and oxygen (see Fig. 22.3B for details) [20]. The MnO$_2$/graphene composite was synthesized by a simple mechanochemical method. Under the light, the composite showed higher formaldehyde decomposition activity than MnO_2 or graphene alone. The enhanced activity is mainly due to the photothermal effect of graphene. The MnO_2 provides a reaction site for formaldehyde oxidation, and graphene transfers the transformed thermal energy to MnO_2. The temperature of MnO_2 increases and the surface lattice oxygen is activated. This work combines catalysts with photothermal materials and provides a new idea of using solar energy to improve thermal catalytic performance (see Fig. 22.3C for details) [21]. In addition, the interfacial hybridization also affects the electronic structure of MnO_2 and graphene, reduces the electron localization, and expands the π-conjugated system, which leads to the increase of surface charge density of MnO_2, promotes the activation of O_2 molecules, and produces more superoxide radicals. Both of them together improve the catalytic performance of the composite.

22.4.2.3 Advanced oxidation

Activation of persulfate by manganese oxides is an important process in environmental chemistry. Shen et al. used acetaminophen (ACE) as a model compound to investigate the degradation kinetics and oxidation mechanism of ACE by activated peroxymonosulfate (PMS) with different crystalline forms of MnO_2 (α-, β-, γ-, and δ-MnO_2). It is revealed that the degradation of ACE is dominated by the direct oxidation of surface-bonded PMS complex and surface manganese species (Mn (IV, III)). Among them, surface Mn (III) and associated oxygen vacancies are feasible sites for the formation of surface-bonded PMS complexes. In addition, the bonding configurations of PMS and ACE on the surface of MnO_2 were evaluated to distinguish the possible electron transfer processes (ETP) in the MnO_2/PMS/ACE system. Overall, this study may provide a deeper understanding of the mechanism of nonradical oxidation of PMS activated by different crystalline forms of MnO_2 (see Fig. 22.3D for details) [22].

The ETP can be divided into three categories: ACE and PMS are adsorbed on the surface of MnO_2, and the surface-bonded PMS complex formed by MnO_2 mediates electron transfer (type I) or adjacent electron transfer to oxidize ACE (type II); Only PMS are adsorbed on the surface of MnO_2 to form surface-bonded PMS complexes, which in turn degrade ACE by adjacent electron transfer (type III). Langmuir-Hinshelwood (L-H) and Eley-Rideal (E-R) models can be used to distinguish possible ETPs. For the L-H model, PMS and ACE were coadsorbed on the MnO_2 surface and thus could be used to determine type I and type II of ETP. In contrast, for the E-R model, only PMS are adsorbed on the MnO_2 surface and react directly with the unadsorbed ACE, which can be used to determine the type III ETP (see Fig. 22.3E for details) [22].

At present, phase engineering studies of nanomaterials show that crystal relative to MnO_2 nanocatalyst plays a crucial role in physicochemical properties, functions, and catalytic performance. Yang et al. successfully prepared α, β, γ, ε, λ, and δ-MnO_2 by simple hydrothermal method, calcination method, and combined hydrothermal calcination method, and revealed the relationship between crystalline phase and environmental catalytic activity. The order of their activities for ozonation-assisted catalytic oxidation of toluene at room temperature is $\delta\text{-MnO}_2 > \alpha\text{-MnO}_2 > \varepsilon\text{-MnO}_2 > \gamma\text{-MnO}_2 > \lambda\text{-MnO}_2 > \beta\text{-MnO}_2$. The $\delta\text{-MnO}_2$ exhibits the best catalytic activity due to the most abundant oxygen vacancies and the strongest oxygen species mobility. Further studies on specific oxygen species with toluene oxidation activity showed that the high catalytic activity of MnO_2 resulted from its abundant oxygen vacancies and strong oxygen species migration. The MnO_2-catalyzed ozonolysis of toluene involves two main reactions: ozonolysis (steps 1−8) and toluene degradation (steps I−IV), where the surface oxygen vacancy is the active center of O_3 adsorption and decomposition (see Fig. 22.3F for details) [23].

Under hydrothermal conditions, a series of $\beta\text{-MnO}_2$ nanorod catalysts were fabricated with different manganese precursors. The morphologies and crystallinity of MnO_2 were mainly determined by the hydrothermal time and temperature. The obtained $\beta\text{-MnO}_2$ nanorod catalysts were applied to degrade different dyes with high concentrations (methylene blue (MB), methyl orange (MO), rhodamine B (RB), and acid orange II (AOII)) in the presence of H_2O_2. High crystallinity and good morphology effectively promoted the catalytic performances. The catalytic mechanism was discussed and a Fenton-like reaction mechanism was proposed. The degradation proceeds by an adsorption-oxidation-desorption process. The first step in reactions is the adsorption of H_2O_2 over the surface of $\beta\text{-MnO}_2$ nanorods, which is followed by the decomposition of H_2O_2 into free radical species, such as $HO\bullet$, $O2\bullet^-$ or $HOO\bullet$ species. The free radical species ($HO\bullet$, $O2\bullet^-$) have high oxidative ability to decompose the adsorbed dye molecules to CO_2, H_2O, or other small molecules (see Fig. 22.3G for details) [24].

22.4.2.4 Thermal catalytic oxidation

Transition metal MnO_x oxides (such as Mn_2O_3, Mn_3O_4, and MnO_2) catalysts show good catalytic performance in the deep catalytic oxidation process of volatile organic pollutants (VOCs). In the process of VOCs catalytic oxidation, the high activity of oxide-based catalyst is mainly determined by morphology, surface area, oxygen vacancy, and surface composition [27]. In recent years, it has been proved that the construction of oxygen vacancy defects is an effective strategy for the synthesis of catalysts with outstanding catalytic activity, because the defective oxygen sites of catalysts facilitate the gas phase oxygen recruitment and efficient electron transfer in the catalytic process. The abundant oxygen vacancies in MnO_2 catalyst can significantly improve its redox capacity and thermal catalytic oxygen activation ability, enhance oxygen migration ability, and then generate more reactive oxygen species, which promotes C-H bond breaking and intermediate decomposition for VOCs oxidation [28]. The CO is a toxic and harmful gas, which can be effectively removed by thermal catalytic oxidation. MnO_2 polymorphs (α-, β-, and ε-MnO_2) were synthesized, and their chemical/physical properties for CO oxidation were systematically studied using multiple techniques. The β-MnO_2 shows the lowest energies for oxygen vacancy generation and excellent redox properties, exhibiting significant CO oxidation activity ($T_{90} = 75°C$) and excellent stability. The process of CO oxidation on β-MnO_2 is mainly MvK mechanism, that is, CO reacts with surface O to generate CO_2 and oxygen vacancies, and then O_2 fills the oxygen vacancies [29].

22.5 Summary

In this chapter, we have discussed the structural features, preparation methods, energy and environmental applications, and typical case analysis of nanomanganese oxides MnO_x (such as Mn_2O_3, Mn_3O_4, and MnO_2). As a case study, the structural features, crystalline types, and application of MnO_2 (α, β, γ, δ, ε, and λ-MnO_2) are summarized in detail. The crystalline types and nanostructures of MnO_2 are closely related to its surface catalytic and chemical properties. The preparation methods of nano-MnO_2 are various, among which hydrothermal synthesis and chemical codeposition are the most extensive. Nanometer MnO_2 can be used as active electrode materials in supercapacitors, Lithium manganese batters, Zinc ion batters, Lithium-oxygen batters, electrocatalytic hydrogen production, etc. Nanometer MnO_2 can be also used in adsorption applications and various environmental catalysis, such as photocatalytic degradation, Fenton catalysis persulfate activation, and so on. In terms of thermal catalysis, the research of MnO_2 mainly focuses on the catalysis of VOCs and CO.

Acknowledgments

This book was supported by National Natural Science Foundation of China (22078071, 2021A1515010305), Natural Science Foundation of Guangdong Province (2021A1515010125, 2020A1515010344), Maoming Science and Technology Project (mmkj2020032), Guangdong Province Universities and Colleges Pearl River Scholar Funded Scheme (2019), Guangdong Basic and Applied Basic Research Foundation (2019A1515011249, 2021A1515010305), Key Research Project of Natural Science of Guangdong Provincial Department of Education (2019KZDXM010), Environment and Energy Green Catalysis Innovation Team of Colleges and Universities of Guangdong Province (2022KCXTD019), the program for Innovative Research Team of Guangdong University of Petrochemical Technology.

References

[1] Q.Z. Zhang, D. Zhang, Z.C. Miao, X.L. Zhang, S.L. Chou, Research progress in MnO_2−carbon based supercapacitor electrode materials, Small 14 (24) (2018) 1702883.

[2] Y. Tang, S. Zheng, Y. Xu, X. Xiao, H. Xue, H. Pang, Advanced batteries based on manganese dioxide and its composites, Energy Storage Materials 12 (2018) 284−309.

[3] R. Yang, Y. Fan, R. Ye, Y. Tang, X. Cao, Z. Yin, et al., MnO_2-based materials for environmental applications, Advanced Materials 33 (9) (2021) 2004862.

[4] K. Chen, C. Sun, D. Xue, Morphology engineering of high performance binary oxide electrodes, Physical Chemistry Chemical Physics 17 (2) (2015) 732−750.

[5]   Y. Yuan, W. Yao, B.W. Byles, E. Pomerantseva, K. Amine, R. Shahbazian-Yassar, et al., Revealing the atomic structures of exposed lateral surfaces for polymorphic manganese dioxide nanowires, Small Structures 2 (3) (2021) 2000091.

[6]   H. Wang, Y. Song, X. Liu, S. Lu, C. Zhou, Y. Jin, et al., Preparation of anisotropic MnO_2 nanocatalysts for selective oxidation of benzyl alcohol and 5-hydroxymethylfurfural, Transactions of Tianjin University 26 (5) (2020) 382−390.

[7]   H.Q. Wang, Z.S. Li, Y.G. Huang, Q.Y. Li, X.Y. Wang, A novel hybrid supercapacitor based on spherical activated carbon and spherical MnO_2 in a non-aqueous electrolyte, Journal of Materials Chemistry 20 (19) (2010) 3883−3889.

[8]   H.Q. Wang, G.F. Yang, Q.Y. Li, X.X. Zhong, F.P. Wang, Z.S. Li, et al., Porous nano-MnO_2: large scale synthesis via a facile quick-redox procedure and application in a supercapacitor, New Journal of Chemistry 35 (2) (2011) 469−475.

[9]   W. Guo, C. Yu, S. Li, Z. Wang, J. Yu, H. Huang, et al., Strategies and insights towards the intrinsic capacitive properties of MnO_2 for supercapacitors: challenges and perspectives, Nano Energy 57 (2019) 459−472.

[10] S. Boyd, K. Ganeshan, W.Y. Tsai, T. Wu, S. Saeed, D.E. Jiang, et al., Effects of interlayer confinement and hydration on capacitive charge storage in birnessite, Nature Materials 20 (12) (2021) 1689−1694.

[11] Z. Li, Z. Liu, B. Li, D. Li, Q. Li, H. Wang, MnO_2 nanosilks self-assembled micropowders: facile one-step hydrothermal synthesis and their application as supercapacitor electrodes, Journal of the Taiwan Institute of Chemical Engineers 45 (6) (2014) 2995−2999.

[12] Z. Li, Z. Liu, B. Li, D. Li, Z. Liu, H. Wang, et al., Large area synthesis of well-dispersed β-MnO_2 nanorods and their electrochemical supercapacitive performances, Journal of the Taiwan Institute of Chemical Engineers 65 (2016) 544−551.

[13] Z. Li, Z. Liu, D. Li, B. Li, Q. Li, Y. Huang, et al., Facile synthesis of α-MnO_2 nanowires/spherical activated carbon composite for supercapacitor application in aqueous neutral electrolyte, Journal of Materials Science: Materials in Electronics 26 (1) (2015) 353−359.

[14] Z. Li, Q. Li, Y. Fang, H. Wang, Y. Li, X. Wang, Unique mesoporous carbon microsphere/1-D MnO_2-built composite architecture and their enhanced electrochemical capacitance performance, Journal of Materials Chemistry 21 (43) (2011) 17185−17192.

[15] H. Tang, W. Chen, N. Li, Z. Hu, L. Xiao, J. Xie, et al., Layered MnO_2 nanodots as high-rate and stable cathode materials for aqueous zinc-ion storage, Energy Storage Materials 48 (2022) 335−343.

[16] J. Huang, Z. Wang, M. Hou, X. Dong, Y. Liu, Y. Wang, et al., Polyaniline-intercalated manganese dioxide nanolayers as a high-performance cathode material for an aqueous zinc-ion battery, Nature Communications 9 (1) (2018) 1−8.

[17] W. Yao, Y. Yuan, G. Tan, C. Liu, M. Cheng, V. Yurkiv, et al., Tuning Li_2O_2 formation routes by facet engineering of MnO_2 cathode catalysts, Journal of the American Chemical Society 141 (32) (2019) 12832−12838.

[18] C. Lin, J.L. Li, X. Li, S. Yang, W. Luo, Y. Zhang, et al., In-situ reconstructed Ru atom array on α-MnO_2 with enhanced performance for acidic water oxidation, Nature Catalysis 4 (12) (2021) 1012−1023.

[19] J. Luo, X. Meng, J. Crittenden, J. Qu, C. Hu, H. Liu, et al., Arsenic adsorption on α-MnO_2 nanofibers and the significance of (1 0 0) facet as compared with (1 1 0), Chemical Engineering Journal 331 (2018) 492−500.

[20] W. Wei, A. Wang, K. Guo, S. He, A. Li, X. Kang, et al., Enhanced degradation of micropollutants by UV/freshly formed colloidal MnO_2: reactive species, kinetics and pathways, Applied Catalysis B: Environmental 313 (2022) 121441.

[21] J. Wang, G. Zhang, P. Zhang, Graphene-assisted photothermal effect on promoting catalytic activity of layered MnO_2 for gaseous formaldehyde oxidation, Applied Catalysis B: Environmental 239 (2018) 77−85.

[22] S. Shen, X. Zhou, Q. Zhao, W. Jiang, J. Wang, L. He, et al., Understanding the nonradical activation of peroxymonosulfate by different crystallographic MnO_2: the pivotal role of MnIII content on the surface, Journal of Hazardous Materials 439 (2022) 129613.

[23] R. Yang, Z. Guo, L. Cai, R. Zhu, Y. Fan, Y. Zhang, et al., Investigation into the phase—activity relationship of MnO_2 nanomaterials toward ozone-assisted catalytic oxidation of toluene, Small 17 (50) (2021) 2103052.

[24] C. Yu, G. Li, L. Wei, Q. Fan, Q. Shu, C.Y. Jimmy, Fabrication, characterization of β-MnO_2 micro-rod catalysts and their performance in rapid degradation of dyes of high concentration, Catalysis Today 224 (2014) 154—162.

[25] D. Zhao, X. Yang, H. Zhang, C. Chen, X. Wang, Effect of environmental conditions on Pb (II) adsorption on β-MnO_2, Chemical Engineering Journal 164 (1) (2010) 49—55.

[26] M. Gheju, I. Balcu, G. Mosoarca, Removal of Cr (VI) from aqueous solutions by adsorption on MnO_2, Journal of Hazardous Materials 310 (2016) 270—277.

[27] S. Mo, Q. Zhang, J. Li, Y. Sun, Q. Ren, S. Zou, et al., Highly efficient mesoporous MnO_2 catalysts for the total toluene oxidation: oxygen-vacancy defect engineering and involved intermediates using in situ DRIFTS, Applied Catalysis B: Environmental 264 (2020) 118464.

[28] S. Wu, H. Liu, Z. Huang, H. Xu, W. Shen, O-vacancy-rich porous MnO_2 nanosheets as highly efficient catalysts for propane catalytic oxidation, Applied Catalysis B: Environmental 312 (2022) 121387.

[29] F.X. Tian, H. Li, M. Zhu, W. Tu, D. Lin, Y.F. Han, Effect of MnO_2 polymorphs' structure on low-temperature catalytic oxidation: crystalline controlled oxygen vacancy formation, ACS Applied Materials & Interfaces 14 (16) (2022) 18525—18538.

CHAPTER 23

Nanostannic oxides: recent progress in energy and environment fields

23.1 Introduction

Tin-based oxides mainly include stannous oxide (SnO), tin dioxide (SnO_2), and tin trioxide (Sn_3O_4). Nanostructured SnO_2 powder is an important multifunctional nanomaterial with remarkable gas sensitivity, electroactivity, chemical stability, and excellent energy storage and catalytic properties. As a kind of basic functional material, it has a wide range of applications in electrochemical energy storage, surface catalysis, gas sensitivity, optical technology, and so on. Expressly, nanostructured SnO_2 powder has excellent activities for electrochemical lithium storage, electrocatalysis, and photocatalysis in energy and environment fields. Nano-SnO_2 is also an excellent transparent conductive material. It is the first transparent conductive material put into commercial use. In order to improve its conductivity and stability, it is often doped, such as Sb-doped SnO_2: F-doped SnO_2, etc [1]. The nanostructures and surface properties of SnO_2 nanomaterials prepared by different methods are different. The physical and chemical properties (such as optical, magnetic, electrical, etc.) of a material are closely related to its surface morphology, dimension, particle size, and surface defects. The physical and chemical properties of low-dimensional SnO_2 nanomaterials (such as nanochains and nanopolyhedras) are expected to be improved or exhibit new properties in energy and environment fields [2]. In this chapter, starting from the problems that need to be solved, the microstructure regulation of tin-based oxide materials is summarized, especially the preparation method of zero-dimensional SnO_2 quantum dots and carbon-based composite materials, and the preparation strategy of three-dimensional SnO_2 polyhedral (or SnO_2@C nanochain). The influence of special structures of tin-based oxides on the performances of solar cells, lithium-ion batteries, electrocatalysis, and various environmental catalysis was also discussed.

23.2 Structural features of nanostannic oxides

In different technical fields (such as solar cells, electrocatalysis, lithium-ion batteries), SnO_2 nanomaterials show different characteristics and structural dependence. In the field of solar cells, planar electrodes have been studied mainly by using SnO_2 electron transfer layer due to its many advantages, such as high electron mobility and good energy level arrangement with perovskites and electrodes [3]. Mobility is an important index to

Nanostructured Materials
ISBN 978-0-443-19256-2, https://doi.org/10.1016/B978-0-443-19256-2.00029-6

measure the performance of SnO_2 semiconductors, which is closely related to the speed of electron movement inside a substance. Tin and oxygen in SnO_2 are held together by ionic bonds. The researchers found that the mobility of electrons in the SnO_2 film is so high that it can be both conductive and transparent. In addition to photovoltaic solar cells, the transparent SnO_2 material could be used to enhance touch-screen displays (with greater accuracy and responsiveness) or more efficient light emitting diode lights [4]. In electrocatalysis, such as SnO_2—Pt electrocatalyst for methanol oxidation, the surface of oxide can adsorb a large number of oxygen-containing groups (such as hydroxyl), which is conducive to the further oxidation of C-containing intermediates in the process of methanol oxidation, so as to improve the anti-CO poisoning ability of Pt-based catalyst. At the same time, the addition of SnO_2 can promote the dispersion of Pt, increase the active site per unit mass of Pt, and reduce the preparation cost [5]. For lithium-ion batteries, Tin SnO_2 materials are often characterized by carbon-based composite structures (core shell or the three-dimensional structures): (1) the SnO_2@carrier material core-shell or three-dimensional framework structures can buffer huge volume change and improve the cycle performance and rate performance, (2) the various composite of SnO_2 and carbon materials can improve the conductivity of the electrode and make the SnO_2 material more stable [6].

23.3 Preparation methods of nanostannic oxides

It is well known that nanocrystalline SnO_2 possesses excellent characteristics such as a high gas sensitivity and a short response time. Since the properties of nanoscale materials are strongly dependent on their size and shape, it is extremely desirable to be able to achieve size and morphology control in a synthesis. Various structural and morphological forms of SnO_2 nanomaterials have been fabricated over the last two and 3 decades, including nanoparticles, nanowires, nanorods, nanotubes, nanocomposites, and mesoporous powders and thin films [7]. At present, wet chemical methods such as hydrothermal method, coprecipitation method, and sol-gel method are widely used to synthesize SnO_2 nanopowders. Thereinto, the hydrothermal method is an effective method to prepare oxide nanoparticles, which has the advantages of simple process, convenient operation, good repeatability, and easy production. Moreover, the prepared SnO_2 nanoparticles have high purity, uniform and fine particle size, and regular particle morphology. The pH value of reaction liquid and the proportion of reactants are the key factors for the hydrothermal synthesis of SnO_2 nanostructured materials.

Previously, our research group (Changlin Yu) reported a pH regulation strategy to prepare single-crystalline nanocubes of SnO_2 by oxidation of SnF_2 with $(NH_4)_2S_2O_8$ under proper hydrothermal conditions (see Fig. 23.1A—C for details) [8]. We describe for the first time a facile solution method for the synthesis of single-crystalline SnO_2 nanocubes with dimensions from 100 to 200 nm by an oriented attachment mechanism.

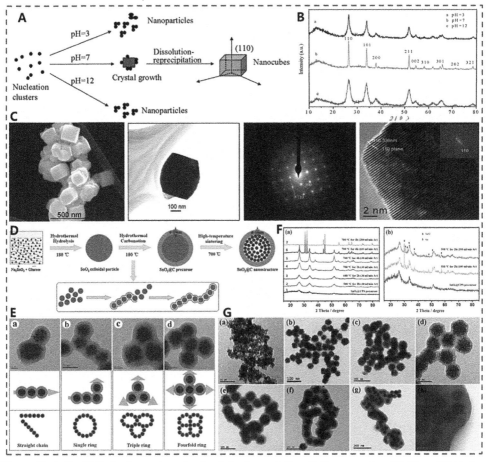

Figure 23.1 (A–C) Hydrothermal synthesis of single-crystalline SnO$_2$ nanocubes [8], (D and E) Hydrothermal synthesis of SnO$_2$@C nanochains [9], (F and G) Hydrothermal synthesis of SnO$_2$@C nanochains [10].

Compared with the conventional high-temperature method, this mild solution is more suitable for large-scale production of SnO$_2$ nanocrystals. The detailed synthesis procedure for the SnO$_2$ nanocrystals is described as follows. Three identical solutions were prepared by adding 1 mmol SnF$_2$ and 1 mmol (NH$_4$)$_2$S$_2$O$_8$ into 60 mL DI water under vigorous stirring for 0.5 h. The pH values of the solutions were found to be approximately 3. The pH values of two of the solutions were adjusted to 7 and 12 by adding appropriate amounts of a 4 mol/L NaOH solution. Then the solutions were placed in Teflon-lined stainless autoclaves and heated at 220°C for 36 h. The obtained SnO_2 nanocrystals were collected, washed three times with distilled water, and dried at 110°C for 12 h.

Meanwhile, our research group (Zesheng Li) presented a new 1-D SnO_2@C core-shell nanochains built 3-D superstructures by an easy hydrothermal and sintering continuous process, from low-cost starting materials of stannate and glucose (see Fig. 23.1D and E for details) [9]. The hydrothermal carbonation of glucose in this case is a halfway process (to form carbon-rich polysaccharide), so the subsequent sintering step is essential to the formation of veriest carbon layer. The adjacent SnO_2 nanocores were not in close contact within the chains and were covered by a thin layer of carbon, which appeared to bridge neighboring SnO_2 particles in the SnO_2@C core-shell nanochain. Li and co-workers further demonstrated the SnO_2 formation mechanism and the controlling factors of morphology and carbon layer thickness (see Fig. 23.1F and G for details) [10]. A low-flow-rate inert atmosphere strategy was demonstrated for the synthesis of perfect SnO_2@ carbon core-shell nanochains by carbonization of SnO_2@ carbon-rich polysaccharide precursor at a relatively high temperature. This strategy results in the thorough carbonization of polysaccharide while avoiding the carbothermal reduction of SnO_2 at 700°C. It has been investigated that a moderate carbon content contributes to the growth of nanochains, and the thickness of the carbon shell can be easily manipulated by varying the reactant ratio and hydrothermal treatment time in the precursor synthetic process.

23.4 Application progress of nanostannic oxides

23.4.1 Energy application of nanostannic oxides

23.4.1.1 Solar cells

The research on solar cells depends on semiconductors. In general, the more transparent color and the better conductivity, the better the performance of the semiconductor. Recently, researchers have found that SnO_2, which is transparent and conductive, is an excellent semiconductor material. The electron transport layer (ETL) with excellent performance (high transmittance, high electron migration, high stability, energy level matching, etc.) is of great significance for high-efficiency solar cell devices. In solar cells, the ETL plays a key role in the cell. Compared with other similar materials, SnO_2 has unique advantages such as low-temperature preparation and high electron extraction ability and has attracted great attention from the research community since it was first reported. The planar perovskite-type solar cells based on SnO_2 have simple structure, and the existing devices can achieve power conversion efficiency of more than 23%, which is comparable with the mesoporous TiO_2 devices. Nano-SnO_2 plays an important role in improving the performance of solar cells. Firstly, nano-SnO_2 has excellent photoelectric properties, such as large charge mobility, suitable band structure, and excellent chemical stability. Second, nano-SnO_2 can be prepared by a simple low-temperature method, which allows it to be used as flexible ETL in solar cells. Third, nano-SnO_2 has a larger band gap width and less damage to UV light, which can improve the stability of the device. These excellent properties of nano-SnO_2 have attracted more and more attention for solar cell scientific research and their commercial applications [11].

23.4.1.2 Rechargeable batteries

At present, the capacity of lithium battery electrode materials is difficult to break through. For example, commercial anode materials can only use low specific capacity carbon-based materials with a theoretical capacity of 372 mAh/g. Although experimental studies have shown that Si, Ge, Sn, and other elements as negative electrodes have the high specific capacity, they are limited by the rapid capacity decay after repeated use and are difficult to be applied in practice. In recent years, tin dioxide (SnO_2) anode material has attracted great attention because of its excellent cycling performance. Its theoretical capacity (783 mAh/g) has reached twice that of graphite anode. However, the existing SnO_2 and cathode materials cannot overcome the application bottleneck of volume expansion in the electrochemical process, and the cycle stability of lithium-ion batteries is difficult to meet the practical application requirements. Therefore, it is of great significance to develop new SnO_2-based lithium anode materials with high cycle stability and high capacity [12]. Nanosized S SnO_2/C composites have a number of advantages over raw tin oxide composites. On the one hand, the nano-scale size can not only reduce the absolute volume variation of SnO_2, but also shorten the diffusion length of ions and electrons, thus improving the structural stability and electrochemical kinetics of the nano-sized SnO_2 anode. On the other hand, the well-conducting flexible carbon not only improves the conductivity of the whole oxide electrode, but also buffers the volume change of tin oxides and finally improves the rate capacity and structural stability of tin oxides [13].

The above-mentioned 3-D superstructures made up of SnO_2@C core-shell nanochains exhibited desirable lithium storage properties as anode materials for lithium-ion batteries (see Fig. 23.2A and B for details) [9]. The SnO_2@C nanochain electrode exhibits a high capacity of 2076 mAh/g in the first cycle at a current density of 55 mA/g (1, 2, 3, 4 and 5 for 55, 110, 256, 552, and 1104 mA/g, respectively). At a very high current density of 1104 mA/g, the capacity is able to maintain more than 600 mAh/g. Furthermore, from the impedance spectra, it is found that the SnO_2@C nanochain electrode represents the capacitive performance before charge and discharge cycling. After several charge and discharge cycles, it tends to display the characteristics of a battery electrode. This is mainly due to the synergy between SnO_2 and carbon in SnO_2@C nanochains. Fig. 23.2C−E displays the TEM images and charge-discharge cycling performances of SnO_2@C nanochain before and after Li insertion cycling [10]. The

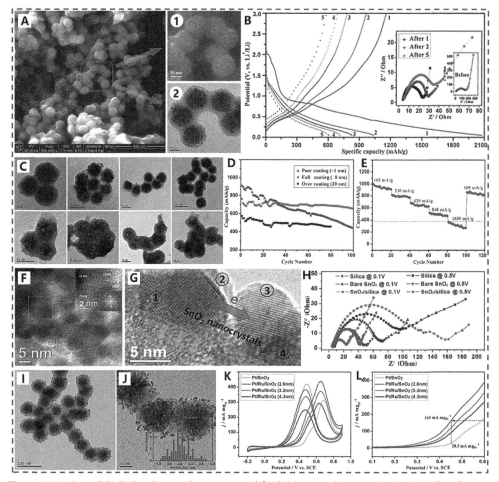

Figure 23.2 (A and B) SnO$_2$@C nanochains material for lithium-ion battery [9], (C—E) SnO$_2$@C nanochains material for lithium-ion battery [10], (F—H) SnO$_2$/silica material for lithium-ion battery [14], (I—L) SnO$_2$@C nanochains-supported PtRu alloy for electrocatalysis of methanol oxidation [15].

core-shell nanostructure of SnO$_2$@C (including tripod, hexagram, single chain, and branch chains) still maintains good shapes, demonstrating the physical buffer function of carbon shells to prevent the large volume change of SnO$_2$ anodes. The moderate carbon content contributes to the optimal electrochemical performances for desirable lithium storage capacity and long cycle life, due to the ideal SnO_2@carbon core-shell 1-D nanostructure.

We also reported close-packed SnO_2 nanocrystals anchored on amorphous silica as a stable anode material for lithium-ion battery (see Fig. 23.2F—H for details) [14]. The incorporating close-packed SnO_2 nanocrystals onto structurally stable silica matrix could offer desirable lithium storage capability and good electrochemical stability. The electrochemical performance of the SnO_2/silica composites shows a higher capacity and good cycle stability compared with that of the bare SnO_2 electrode. It is apparent that the close-packed SnO_2/silica sample has lower initial interfacial resistance and higher Li^+ ions transfer rate than the silica and bare SnO_2 samples. Generally, carbon has a conductivity advantage over silica which is more suitable for electrode material, while we find that close-packed SnO_2/silica sample shows an unexpected low resistance which is fairly close to those of the recently concerned SnO_2@carbon core-shell nanostructures [9,10]. It is believed that the good performance as a stable anode material originates from the unique structure of the close-packed nanocrystalline assemblies and the amorphous porous silica as inactive material to mediate the massive volume expansion and contraction of SnO_2 during lithiation and delithiation processes [14].

23.4.1.3 Electrocatalytic conversion

SnO_2 is a potential multifunctional electrocatalyst (or used as a cocatalytic component) (e.g., electrocatalysts of methanol oxidation reaction (MOR), carbon dioxide reduction reaction (CO_2RR), hydrogen evolution reaction (HER), etc.) due to its nontoxicity, abundant reserves and high catalytic activity [15—17]. In particular, the nano-SnO_2 can increase the surface area of electrocatalyst, expose more active sites, improve the electrolyte accessibility, and promote interfacial charge transfer with other active components. Recently, we reported the carbon-mediated synthesis of a ternary Pt—Ru—SnO_2 complex nano-necklace (a unique multicomponent 1-D hybrid architecture), which exhibited a superior electrocatalytic activity toward methanol oxidation (see Fig. 23.2I—L for details) [15]. For these hybrid systems, size-controlled PtRu alloys have been synthesized and uniformly dispersed on the surface of SnO_2@C nanochains. Electrochemistry analyses show that the resulting Pt—Ru—SnO_2 hybrid catalysts exhibit superior catalytic properties toward methanol oxidation, in terms of their specially enhanced catalytic activity and desirable stability. He et al. developed a series of Pd-supported SnO_2 nanosheet CO_2RR catalysts by photo deposition of Pd on the surface of SnO_2 nanosheets. The prepared catalyst exhibits an inhibited CO_2RR to HCOOH path due to the formation of the active Pd— SnO_2 interface, resulting in a Faraday efficiency of syngas close to 100% [16]. Recently, Feng and Sun synthesized Ru-doped single atom tin oxide nanoparticles on carbon support (Ru SAS-SnO_2/C) as a new basic HER electrocatalyst to regulate the strong interaction between Ru and OH_{ad}. The prepared Ru SAS-SnO_2/C catalyst had a low overpotential of 10 mV at a current density of

10 mA/cm and a Tafel slope of 25 mV/dec in 1.0 M KOH solution [17]. The SnO_2-based electrocatalysts can effectively improve the catalytic efficiency or selectivity of different types of reactions based on interfacial synergistic effects and electronic effects.

23.4.2 Environmental application of nanostannic oxides
23.4.2.1 Adsorbing purification
Adsorption technology based on nanooxide adsorbents is the method of choice for the removal of heavy metal ions due to its high surface area, smaller size, and enhanced reactivity during adsorbate/adsorbent interactions. Rehman et al. demonstrated that Pb^{2+} ions adsorbed in hydrated form through exchange reactions on the surface of SnO_2 [18]. The q_m and K_b values confirm better adsorption capacity and binding strength for Pb^{2+} ions as compared to the values reported in the literature. In addition, Naushad et al. synthesized a starch-based nanocomposite (starch/SnO_2) and used it as an effective adsorbent for the removal of Hg^{2+} from water [19]. Starch/SnO_2 nanocomposite has a good ability to remove Hg^{2+} in aqueous medium. The correlation coefficient of pseudo–second-order equation of adsorption kinetics was high (>0.998), and the Freundlich isotherm model was better than Langmuir model to fit the adsorption data. The feasibility of adsorption of Hg^{2+} on starch/SnO_2 nanocomposite was investigated by thermodynamics. The results showed that the adsorption was spontaneous chemisorption. Yan and coworkers reported that SnO_2 can adsorb O_2 to form O^{2-} on its surface which was beneficial for the oxidized mercury adsorption [20]. Moreover, SnO_2 exhibited high activity for Hg^0 oxidation when the temperature was higher than 250°C. The Hg-TPD results indicated that the mercury existed stronger binding state on the surface of $LaMnO_3$/SnO_2.

23.4.2.2 Photocatalytic degradation
The designing and developing novel photocatalysts with excellent photocatalytic activity and chemical stability are highly desirable for environment purification. The Sn_3O_4 is a novel, abundant, and environmental semiconductor with great potential and wide application for environmental purification. Particularly, the mixed-valence of Sn^{2+} and Sn^{4+} in Sn3O4 endues the desirable band structure, which favors more efficient light harvesting than other tin oxides with single valence state. Recently, we reported novel fluorine-doped Sn3O4 microspheres with excellent photocatalytic performances for Cr (VI) reduction and organic pollutant degradation under full spectrum light irradiation (see Fig. 23.3A−C for details) [21]. Comparing with Sn_3O_4, fluorine doping remarkably enhanced light harvesting, produced more electron-hole pairs, and promoted the separation of photoinduced electron-hole pairs, which reacted with dissolved O_2 and H_2O to produce more •O^{2-} and •OH radicals. Therefore, the F0.2-Sn3O4 degraded 90.24% of 10 ppm MO in a very short time of 2 min, while Sn3O4 and commercial TiO2 only degraded 9.93% and 1.79% of MO, respectively. Moreover, the F0.2-Sn3O4 reduced 94.95% of 10 ppm Cr (VI) in 12 min, which was 3.6, 10.2 and 64.5 times higher than that of Sn3O4 (25.83%), C3N4 (9.25%) and commercial TiO2 (1.47%), respectively.

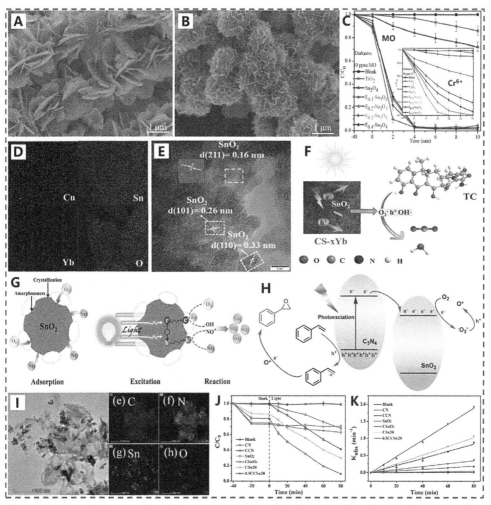

Figure 23.3 (A—C) Fluorine doped Sn_3O_4 microspheres for photocatalytic Cr (VI) reduction and MO degradation [21], (D—F) Cu, Yb co-doped SnO_2 for photocatalytic degradations of dyes and tetracycline [22], (G) crystalline/amorphous SnO_2 for photocatalytic NO oxidation [23], (H) g-C_3N_4/SnO_2 for photocatalytic purification [24], (I—K) g-C_3N_4/SnO_2 for photocatalytic purification [25].

Recently, we further exploited the Cu, Yb co-doped SnO_2 via one-step hydrothermal method, for the degradations of RhB, MO and tetracycline (TC) under simulated sunlight irradiation (see Fig. 23.3D−F for details) [22]. The effect of codoping on SnO_2 was understood by a series of characterizations, and the possible intensifying mechanism of photocatalytic degradation of pollutants was discussed. Benefiting from higher charge transfer rate, codoping of Cu and Yb into SnO_2 could achieve superior photocatalytic activities for the degradations of dyes and tetracycline. In addition, the photogenerated electrons were captured by the defective sites, and thus, it facilitated the efficient charge transfer over SnO_2. Zhang et al. prepared a kind of SnO_2 microspheres with crystalline/amorphous coexistence (with alternating crystalline bulges and amorphous pits) and excellent NO photocatalytic oxidation performances by a one-step hydrothermal method (see Fig. 23.3G for details) [23]. The oxygen vacancy defect in the amorphous region can reduce the band gap of the material, thus enlarging the light absorption range of the sample. In particular, this structure can distribute the chemisorption sites of NO and O_2 on crystalline bulges and amorphous pits, respectively, thus avoiding the competitive adsorption problem of NO and O_2 and improving the catalytic activity.

Duan's research group at Tsinghua university realized efficient photocatalytic epoxidation of styrene to oxidized styrene using g−C_3N_4−supported SnO_2 quantum dots heterojunction photocatalyst (see Fig. 23.3H for details) [24]. The photocatalytic epoxidation of styrene was coupled with the cyclo-amination reaction of epoxide, and high value-added β-amino alcohols were synthesized by cascade reaction. This work is of great significance for the selective synthesis of high value-added compounds by photocatalysis and the design of heterogeneous structural catalysts. The positive conduction band and valence band position of the wideband gap semiconductor SnO_2 can form a composite heterojunction catalyst with g–C_3N_4, which further facilitates electron-hole transport. Therefore, it is highly expected that the construction of SnO_2/g-C_3N_4 heterojunction can increase the charge separation and transfer ability, promote O_2 activation, and thus enhance the photocatalytic styrene epoxidation reaction.

Recently, Liu's research group selected g-C_3N_4, SnO_2, and carbon quantum dots (CDs) to construct a heterojunction photocatalyst with high visible light performance for degradation of PPCPs (Ninhydrin) (see Fig. 23.3I−Kfor details) [25]. The g-C_3N_4 has visible light effect, but its specific surface area is small, and the efficiency of photogenerated carrier separation is poor, while SnO_2 is a good electron acceptor with a large specific surface area. In addition, CDs have good water solubility, up-conversion photoluminescence behavior, and excellent photoelectron transfer to regulate g-C_3N_4/SnO_2 heterojunctions. The composite material can show stronger superoxide radical, hydroxyl radical, and singlet oxygen active species. Compared with single sample, the Ninhydrin photocatalytic degradation activity of CDs-modified g-C_3N_4/SnO_2 heterojunction photocatalyst is very significant, which is due to the optimizing of the photogenerated carrier separation efficiency of the composite heterojunction sample.

23.4.2.3 Thermal catalytic oxidation

The activation of Pt/SnO_2 catalyst for catalytic oxidation of volatile organic compounds (VOCs) has been demonstrated by Eguchi and coworkers in 2010 [26]. The catalytic combustion of toluene by SnO_2-supported noble metal catalysts (Pt/SnO_2, Pd/SnO_2, Ru/SnO_2, and Rh/SnO_2) was systematically studied. The results show that Pt/SnO_2 catalyst has the highest catalytic activity, which is due to the strengthening chemical interaction between Pt and Sn oxides. The thermal activation of Pd/CeO_2-SnO_2 catalysts for low-temperature CO oxidation was also demonstrated by Boronin and coworkers in 2020 [27]. It was revealed that calcination of Pd/CeO_2-SnO_2 catalysts at $800-1000\,°C$ induces significant growth of catalytic activity in CO oxidation at $T < 150°C$. The Pd/CeO_2-SnO_2 catalysts are further characterized by high water resistance in CO oxidation. A novel high-performance SnO_2 catalyst was prepared for high-performance oxidative desulfurization under mild conditions, where 99.8% sulfur removal rate and 14 reuse cycles can be achieved [28]. Lewis's acidity from Sn^{4+}/Sn^{2+} could be proved the catalytic sites of SnO_2 catalyst in oxidative desulfurization process. Proper heat treatment has a good effect on the specific surface area and acidic-site strength of the SnO_2 catalyst, so that the SnO_2 catalyst has good activity and reusability.

23.5 Summary

In this chapter, we have discussed the structural features, preparation methods, energy and environmental applications, and typical case analysis of nanostannic oxides (such as Sn_3O_4 and SnO_2). Low-dimensional nano-SnO_2 can be prepared by hydrothermal synthesis, which shows a unique electronic structure and excellent functional properties. The SnO_2 material can be used as transparent ETL for photovoltaic solar cells, which can achieve power conversion efficiency of more than 23%. The SnO_2 anode material has attracted great attention from lithium-ion battery because of its high theoretical capacity (783 mAh/g) and excellent cycling performance. The SnO_2 is also a multifunctional electrocatalyst material for MOR), CO_2RR, HER, etc., due to its nontoxicity, abundant reserves, and high catalytic activity. The SnO_2 material can be used in adsorbing purification of heavy metal ion, photocatalytic degradation of organic pollutants, thermal catalytic oxidation of VOCs, CO oxidation, and oxidative desulfurization. To sum up, the nanostannic oxides are promising energy and environmental materials with wide resources and low price, which has application prospects for mass production and scale application.

Acknowledgments

This book was supported by National Natural Science Foundation of China (22078071, 22272034), Natural Science Foundation of Guangdong Province (2021A1515010125, 2020A1515010344), Maoming Science and Technology Project (mmkj2020032), Guangdong Province Universities and Colleges Pearl River Scholar Funded Scheme (2019), Guangdong Basic and Applied Basic Research Foundation

(2019A1515011249, 2021A1515010305), Key Research Project of Natural Science of Guangdong Provincial Department of Education (2019KZDXM010), Environment and Energy Green Catalysis Innovation Team of Colleges and Universities of Guangdong Province (2022KCXTD019), the program for Innovative Research Team of Guangdong University of Petrochemical Technology.

References

[1] H. Kim, R.C.Y. Auyeung, A. Piqué, Transparent conducting F-doped SnO_2 thin films grown by pulsed laser deposition, Thin Solid Films 516 (15) (2008) 5052−5056.

[2] C. Kim, M. Noh, M. Choi, J. Cho, B. Park, Critical size of a nano SnO_2 electrode for Li-secondary battery, Chemistry of Materials 17 (12) (2005) 3297−3301.

[3] H. Min, D.Y. Lee, J. Kim, G. Kim, K.S. Lee, J. Kim, S. Il Seok, Perovskite solar cells with atomically coherent interlayers on SnO_2 electrodes, Nature 598 (7881) (2021) 444−450.

[4] S.S. Lekshmy, G.P. Daniel, K. Joy, Microstructure and physical properties of sol gel derived SnO_2: Sb thin films for optoelectronic applications, Applied Surface Science 274 (2013) 95−100.

[5] S. Wu, J. Liu, D. Liang, H. Sun, Y. Ye, Z. Tian, C. Liang, Photo-excited in situ loading of Pt clusters onto rGO immobilized SnO_2 with excellent catalytic performance toward methanol oxidation, Nano Energy 26 (2016) 699−707.

[6] L.I.A.N.G. Jumei, G.U.O. Yumeng, W.A.N.G. Mingxuan, X.I.L.I. Dege, Z.H.A.N.G. Lijuan, Recent research progress of tin oxide as anode materials for sodium-ion batteries, Energy Storage Science and Technology 8 (5) (2019) 813.

[7] J.S. Chen, X.W. Lou, SnO_2-based nanomaterials: synthesis and application in lithium-ion batteries, Small 9 (11) (2013) 1877−1893.

[8] C. Yu, C.Y. Jimmy, F. Wang, H. Wen, Y. Tang, Growth of single-crystalline SnO_2 nanocubes via a hydrothermal route, CrystEngComm 12 (2) (2010) 341−343.

[9] B. Zhang, X. Yu, C. Ge, X. Dong, Y. Fang, Z. Li, H. Wang, Novel 3-D superstructures made up of SnO_2@ C core-shell nanochains for energy storage applications, Chemical Communications 46 (48) (2010) 9188−9190.

[10] X. Yu, S. Yang, B. Zhang, D. Shao, X. Dong, Y. Fang, H. Wang, Controlled synthesis of SnO_2@ carbon core-shell nanochains as high-performance anodes for lithium-ion batteries, Journal of Materials Chemistry 21 (33) (2011) 12295−12302.

[11] K. Deng, Q. Chen, L. Li, Modification engineering in SnO_2 electron transport layer toward perovskite solar cells: efficiency and stability, Advanced Functional Materials 30 (46) (2020) 2004209.

[12] W. Dong, J. Xu, C. Wang, Y. Lu, X. Liu, X. Wang, F. Huang, A robust and conductive black tin oxide nanostructure makes efficient lithium-ion batteries possible, Advanced Materials 29 (24) (2017) 1700136.

[13] X.W. Lou, D. Deng, J.Y. Lee, L.A. Archer, Preparation of SnO_2/carbon composite hollow spheres and their lithium storage properties, Chemistry of Materials 20 (20) (2008) 6562−6566.

[14] J. Cai, Z. Li, S. Yao, H. Meng, P.K. Shen, Z. Wei, Close-packed SnO2 nanocrystals anchored on amorphous silica as a stable anode material for lithium-ion battery, Electrochimica Acta 74 (2012) 182−188.

[15] S. Yang, C. Zhao, C. Ge, X. Dong, X. Liu, Y. Liu, Z. Li, Ternary Pt−Ru−SnO_2 hybrid architectures: unique carbon-mediated 1-D configuration and their electrocatalytic activity to methanol oxidation, Journal of Materials Chemistry 22 (15) (2012) 7104−7107.

[16] H. He, D. Xia, X. Yu, J. Wu, Y. Wang, L. Wang, Y.N. Liu, Pd-SnO_2 interface enables synthesis of syngas with controllable H_2/CO ratios by electrocatalytic reduction of CO_2, Applied Catalysis B: Environmental 312 (2022) 121392.

[17] J. Zhang, G. Chen, Q. Liu, C. Fan, D. Sun, Y. Tang, X. Feng, Competitive adsorption: reducing the poisoning effect of adsorbed hydroxyl on Ru single-atom site with SnO_2 for efficient hydrogen evolution, Angewandte Chemie 134 (2022).

[18] M.U. Rehman, W. Rehman, M. Waseem, S. Hussain, S. Haq, M.A.U. Rehman, Adsorption mechanism of Pb^{2+} ions by Fe_3O_4, SnO_2, and TiO_2 nanoparticles, Environmental Science and Pollution Research 26 (19) (2019) 19968–19981.

[19] M. Naushad, T. Ahamad, G. Sharma, H. Ala'a, A.B. Albadarin, M.M. Alam, A.A. Ghfar, Synthesis and characterization of a new starch/SnO_2 nanocomposite for efficient adsorption of toxic Hg2+ metal ion, Chemical Engineering Journal 300 (2016) 306–316.

[20] H. Xu, Z. Qu, S. Zhao, D. Yue, W. Huang, N. Yan, Enhancement of heterogeneous oxidation and adsorption of Hg^0 in a wide temperature window using SnO_2 supported $LaMnO_3$ perovskite oxide, Chemical Engineering Journal 292 (2016) 123–129.

[21] D. Zeng, C. Yu, Q. Fan, J. Zeng, L. Wei, Z. Li, H. Ji, Theoretical and experimental research of novel fluorine doped hierarchical Sn_3O_4 microspheres with excellent photocatalytic performance for removal of Cr(VI) and organic pollutants, Chemical Engineering Journal 391 (2020) 123607.

[22] Z. Yu, R. Liang, M. Zhou, K. Yang, P. Mu, K. Lu, C. Yu, Steering oxygen vacancies for the enhanced photocatalytic degradations of dyes and tetracycline over Cu, Yb co-doped SnO_2 with efficient charge separation and transfer, Journal of the Taiwan Institute of Chemical Engineers 133 (2022) 104249.

[23] L. Zhang, R. Tong, S.E. Shirsath, Y. Yang, G. Dong, The crystalline/amorphous stacking structure of SnO_2 microspheres for excellent NO photocatalytic performance, Journal of Materials Chemistry A 9 (8) (2021) 5000–5006.

[24] M. Li, L. Ma, L. Luo, Y. Liu, M. Xu, H. Zhou, H. Duan, Efficient photocatalytic epoxidation of styrene over a quantum-sized SnO_2 on carbon nitride as a heterostructured catalyst, Applied Catalysis B: Environmental 309 (2022) 121268.

[25] D. Li, J. Huang, R. Li, P. Chen, D. Chen, M. Cai, G. Liu, Synthesis of a carbon dots modified g-C_3N_4/SnO_2 Z-scheme photocatalyst with superior photocatalytic activity for PPCPs degradation under visible light irradiation, Journal of Hazardous Materials 401 (2021) 123257.

[26] N. Kamiuchi, T. Mitsui, N. Yamaguchi, H. Muroyama, T. Matsui, R. Kikuchi, K. Eguchi, Activation of Pt/SnO_2 catalyst for catalytic oxidation of volatile organic compounds, Catalysis Today 157 (1–4) (2010) 415–419.

[27] E.M. Slavinskaya, A.V. Zadesenets, O.A. Stonkus, A.I. Stadnichenko, A.V. Shchukarev, Y.V. Shubin, A.I. Boronin, Thermal activation of Pd/CeO_2-SnO_2 catalysts for low-temperature CO oxidation, Applied Catalysis B: Environmental 277 (2020) 119275.

[28] A. Liu, M. Zhu, B. Dai, A novel high-performance SnO_2 catalyst for oxidative desulfurization under mild conditions, Applied Catalysis A: General 583 (2019) 117134.

CHAPTER 24

Nanonickel sulfides: recent progress in energy and environment fields

24.1 Introduction

Due to its adjustable composition and excellent electrochemical performances, nickel-based sulfur compounds (such as Ni_3S_2, NiS_2, NiS) with nanostructures have been widely paid attention to in recent years because, which have broad application prospects as photovoltaic cells, catalytic hydrogen production, supercapacitors, lithium-ion batteries, and sodium ion batteries. Because of its room temperature resistivity of about 1.2×10^4 Ω cm, Ni_3S_2 can transport electrons more efficiently than other nickel sulfides, so it is considered as a potential material for electrocatalytic water decomposition, supercapacitor and lithium-ion batteries [1]. Some research progress of Ni_3S_2 has been made in photocatalysis, electrochemical oxidation process, and so on. Ni_3S_2 has attracted the attention of researchers mainly because of its following advantages: (1) nickel and sulfur as reaction raw materials are rich in content, low in price, and low in production cost; (2) Ni_3S_2 is easy to generate, so it is relatively simple to synthesize nanoscale or micron scale nickel sulfide; (3) Ni_3S_2 has relatively high electrochemical activity when used as electrode material [2]. The Ni_3S_2 micro-/nanostructures have attracted much attention due to their low cost and superior physical and chemical properties, which also make them a favorable competitor for a new generation of energy and environmental materials. However, due to the complexity of Ni_3S_2 micro- or nano-structures, there are still great challenges in the preparation of pure and satisfying Ni_3S_2 micro-/nano-structures [3]. At present, how to combine various modification methods skillfully and apply the as-prepared excellent materials in practical production will become the focus of research workers. The batch preparation and practical application will also be another innovative development direction for micro/nano-Ni_3S_2 materials in the future.

24.2 Structural features of nanonickel sulfides

In nature, nickel ore mainly exists in two forms: laterite nickel ore and nickel sulfide ore. Domestic nickel ore is mainly nickel sulfide, mostly used in the production of pure nickel. Fig. 24.1A shows the crystal structure of different forms of nickel sulfide (such as Ni_3S_2, NiS_2, NiS) [4]. The Ni_3S_2 has better electrochemical performance than NiS and NiS_2 in fully electrolyzed water device, which is comparable to the noble metal catalyst. Experimental and theoretical results show that the remarkable catalytic performance

Nanostructured Materials
ISBN 978-0-443-19256-2, https://doi.org/10.1016/B978-0-443-19256-2.00034-X

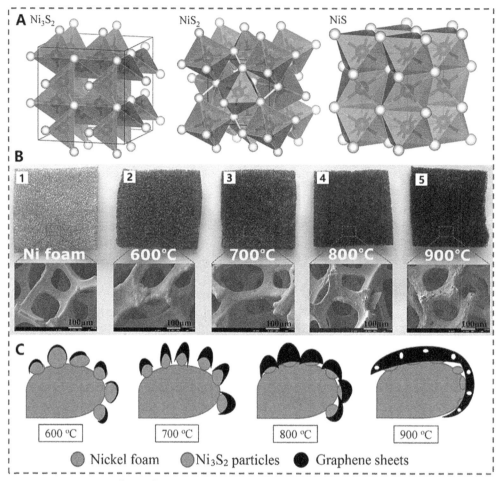

Figure 24.1 (A) Crystallographic structure of Ni_3S_2 [4] and (B–C) Ni foam-supported graphene@Ni_3S_2 [5].

of Ni_3S_2 can be attributed to its inherent metal conductivity, abundant active centers, and optimal Gibbs free energy [6]. From powder synthesis to substrate (such as Ni foam) growth, the electrochemical performance of the Ni_3S_2 free-standing electrode has been greatly improved, so that the goal of its commercial production is no longer impossible (see Fig. 24.1B and C) [5]. In addition, the nano-electrode material will inevitably bring some negative effects, such as the capacity of the nano-electrode material will decay with the increase of the number of cycles, and has a low vibration density, etc. These problems are often not conducive to its practical application without special treatment. So, researchers have used a series of methods to optimize the properties of electrode materials. At present, there are three main modification methods [7]: (1) Adjust the morphology and size of the material by adjusting the parameters in the synthesis process to find the electrode structure with the best performance; (2) The electrode material itself was doped with positive and anion ions to improve its conductance and activity; (3) It is mixed with other oxides or sulfides, and the synergistic effect between them is used to optimize the performance, or the electrode material is coated and modified, mainly including carbon material, organic polymer, and solid electrolyte, so as to improve the performance of the entire electrode structure.

24.3 Preparation methods of nanonickel sulfides

At present, the construction of Ni_3S_2 micro- and nanostructures and the preparation of nano-powder have been studied to a certain extent. The chemical vapor deposition (CVD), electrodeposition, hydrothermal, or solvothermal methods are mainly used in the experimental preparation of Ni_3S_2 micro- and nanostructures. According to the different requirements of material composition and morphology, the synthesis methods of Ni_3S_2 are quite different and the primary methods include as follows: (1) Hydrothermal/solvothermal synthesis. This method has the advantages of high purity, simple operation, and easy control of the morphology and structure of Ni_3S_2. (2) Electrochemical synthesis. This method is always operated at normal temperature and pressure, so it is easy to obtain an excellent grown layer of Ni_3S_2 on carrier. (3) CVD synthesis. High-purity and high-activity nanostructures of Ni_3S_2 can be prepared by this method owing to its controllable gas–solid conversion process. Researchers can choose reasonable synthesis methods according to different conditions and purposes.

Recently, we developed a new-fashioned Ni_3S_2@3-D graphene nanosheets (Ni_3S_2@3-D GNs) free-standing electrode as efficient OER catalysts via a facile one-pot CVD technique with Ni foam as catalytic skeleton and thiourea resin as carbon/sulfur precursors (see Fig. 24.1B and C for details) [5]. Among all Ni_3S_2@3-D GNs samples synthesized at different temperatures (600°C, 700°C, 800°C, and 900°C), the Ni_3S_2@3-D GNs sample synthesized at 900°C shows the good nanostructure and optimized catalytic performances. At present, many works have been done to optimize the electrochemical properties of Ni_3S_2 nanomaterials by adjusting the synthesis parameters. The structure and size of Ni_3S_2 nanomaterials can be optimized by adjusting different parameters, such as synthesis temperature, synthesis time, type and content of nickel source and sulfur source, solvent composition, the proportion of different components, and different deposition conditions.

Particularly, through the relationship between different morphology sizes and different properties, we can deeply understand the microstructure structure-activity relationship. Rational construction of active materials with hierarchical structure is a feasible and effective strategy to achieve super physicochemical properties. For example, the nanorods array synthesized on nickel foam with hydrogen peroxide as inducer can not only serve as the main channel of charge transport, but also support the growth of active materials, and the exposed active part can also participate in the electrochemical energy storage process [7]. In short, the nanostructure optimization of Ni_3S_2, such as low-dimensional nanoscale morphology and multi-component interface structure, can change the geometric and electronic structure of active materials.

24.4 Application progress of nanonickel sulfides

24.4.1 Energy application of nanonickel sulfides

24.4.1.1 Supercapacitor

Due to their special electronic effects (e.g., low electronegativity and favorable bonding model) and sequent high performances, transition metal sulfides-based materials (e.g., nickel sulfides and cobalt sulfides) in recent years have attracted great attention in electrochemical supercapacitor energy storage. Recently, we developed a new 3-D graphene nanosheets/Ni_3S_2 nanoparticles (3-D GNs/Ni_3S_2 NPs) composite for supercapacitor application, synthesized by a one-pot quasi-chemical vapor deposition (Q-CVD) technique with nickel acetate and thiourea resin as precursors (see Fig. 24.2 for details) [8]. This Q-CVD technique is proved to be a simple and effective synthesis strategy for the synchronous construction of Ni_3S_2 and graphene composite nanomaterials as electrodes for high-performance supercapacitor applications. The 3-D GNs/Ni_3S_2 NPs composite manifests the following structural features and advantages: (1) The 3-D construction of graphene can effectively prevent the accumulation of graphene sheets and Ni_3S_2 particles, which maintains a high surface area and high conductivity for the composite; (2) The Ni_3S_2 component was devised to be nanoscale and dispersed into the porous network of graphene, which provides a dual channel for the high-efficiency electron transport and ion diffusion; (3) The 3-D GNs/Ni_3S_2 NPs composite electrode demonstrated a high capacitance and an outstanding electrochemical stability for the application of supercapacitors. As a promising supercapacitor electrode, a relatively high specific capacitance of 652.5 F/g at 1 A/g in 1 mol/L KOH aqueous solution, along with good cycling stability (with a 93% retention rate after 2000 cycles) was demonstrated for the 3-D GNs/Ni_3S_2 NPs composite electrode [8].

Properly designed self-supporting Ni_3S_2 nanosheet arrays can be used to design advanced supercapacitors with ultra-high energy densities. By controlling the nanostructure of the active substance and modifying its chemical components, Chen et al. successfully prepared self-supported Ni_3S_2 nanosheet arrays grown directly on Ni foam by hydrothermal sulfide treatment for high-performance asymmetric capacitors [9]. The Ni_3S_2 array material exhibited a reversible capacity of up to 1000 F/g at a very high current density of 50 A/g in a three-electrode system, and no significant exhaustion was

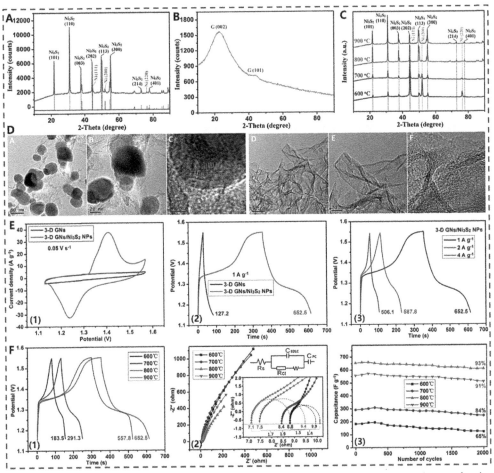

Figure 24.2 The preparation of 3-D GNs/Ni$_3$S$_2$ NPs composite electrode by Q-CVD technique for the application of supercapacitors [8].

observed after 20,000 cycles. Subsequently, the material exhibited an energy density of up to 202 W/h/kg in an asymmetric capacitor composed of Ni$_3$S$_2$ array and activated carbon. Recently, Xu and Liu's group also developed a one-step electrodeposition method to prepare Ni$_3$S$_2$ nanosheet array supercapacitor electrodes [10]. The interconnection of Ni$_3$S$_2$ nanosheets can provide a fast channel for electron conduction, which is conducive to the transport of electrons and ions and provides a wealth of pseudocapacitance reaction sites. These results indicate that the electrode materials of Ni_3S_2 supercapacitors have broad application prospects. The strategy of controlling Ni_3S_2 loading by electrodeposition can provide a new idea for the preparation of electrode materials.

24.4.1.2 Rechargeable batteries

The react-induced charge storage mechanism of transition metal sulfides has attracted much attention in the design of high-capacity electrodes for lithium-ion batteries. Yao et al. reported a simple one-step CVD method to prepare single-crystal Ni_3S_2 nanowire coated with nitrogen-doped carbon (NC) (i.e., Ni_3S_2@NC core@shell array) [11]. Thanks to the excellent structural stability and electronic conductivity of the NC housing, the Ni_3S_2 nanowire can accommodate large volume expansion during cycling, resulting in excellent high-rate capacity (470 mAh/g at 0.05 A/g) and excellent cycling stability (capacity retention of 91% after 100 cycles at 1 A/g). In addition, the reaction mechanism of Ni_3S_2@NC during the charging and discharging process was investigated by means of transmission electron microscopy, X-ray diffraction, and Raman spectroscopy. The product after delithiation is composed of Ni_3S_2 and sulfur, indicating that the electrode capacity comes from the conversion reaction between Ni_3S_2 and sulfur and Li_2S. Lee and colleagues have also fabricated a high-performance Ni_3S_2 Li-ion battery electrode formed by Ni_3S_2 on a metal nickel nanoparticle supported by a vertical carbon nanotube (VCN) skeleton (i.e., Ni_3S_2/Ni@VCN) [12]. The Ni_3S_2/Ni@VCN electrode has excellent lithium storage capacity with high reversible capacity (1113 mAh/g after 100 cycles of 100 mA/g) and good long-term cycling stability (770 mAh/g after 500 cycles of 200 mA/g). The obtained Ni_3S_2/Ni@VCN electrode is one of the electrodes with the best lithium-ion storage performance in the Ni_3S_2 type anode material. Recently, Yu et al. encapsulated the Ni_3S_2–Co_9S_8 heterostructure with an open nanocage structure in reduced graphene oxide (i.e., Ni–Co–S@rGO cage) as the negative electrode of a potassium ion battery [13]. The hollow Ni–Co–S@rGO nanocages with large surface area, abundant heterogeneous interfaces, and unique open nanocages structure can reduce K^+ diffusion length and facilitate reaction kinetics.

24.4.1.3 Electrocatalytic conversion

The electrocatalytic performances of nickel sulfide nanostructured materials are affected by particle size, shape, dimension, etc. How to effectively and controllably synthesize nano-catalysts with specific morphology has become a challenging task in the field of nanoscience. In order to improve the water electrolysis performance of a single Ni_3S_2 catalyst, our research group adopted three kinds of nanomorphology designs (Ni_3S_2 nanoparticles (Fig. 24.3A–B) [5], Ni_3S_2 nanocubes (Fig. 24.3C–E) [14] and Ni_3S_2 nanowires (Fig. 24.3F–K) [15]). The Ni_3S_2 nanoparticles have general catalytic activity (OER

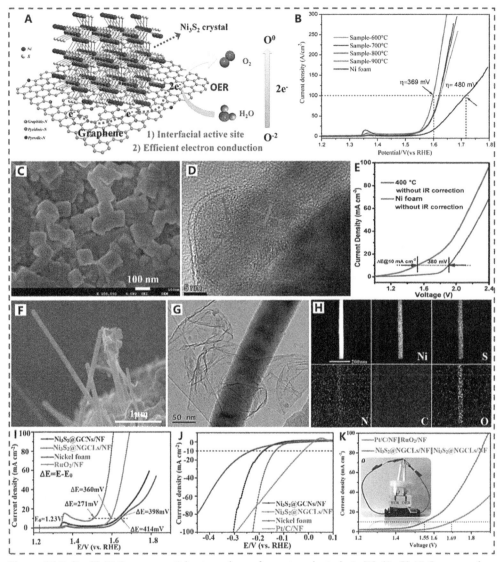

Figure 24.3 (A—B) Ni₃S₂ nanoparticles@graphene for water electrolysis [5], (A—B) Ni₃S₂ nanocubes @graphene for water electrolysis [14], (A—B) Ni₃S₂ nanowires @graphene for water electrolysis [15].

and HER overpotentials are 305 and 158 mV at 10 mA/cm^2). The catalytic activity of Ni$_3$S$_2$ nanowires was significantly increased (OER and HER overpotential were 271 and 132 mV at 10 mA/cm^2). The Ni$_3$S$_2$ nanocubes have a polyhedral structure, and its catalytic activity is much better than that of other samples (OER and HER overpotentials are 238 and 100 mV at 10 mA/cm^2).

We prepared the coaxial one-dimensional structure of Ni$_3$S$_2$ nanowires@graphene carbon layer (Fig. 24.3C—E) [14] and the polyhedral nanostructure of Ni$_3$S$_2$ nanocubes@graphene graphene carbon layer (Fig. 24.3F—K) [15] by reasonable design. The results show that the interface structure coated with graphene carbon layer can not only reflect the high catalytic activity of the interface material (the voltage reaching the current density of 10 mA/cm^2 in full electrolytic test is: Ni$_3$S$_2$ nanowires@ graphene (1.55 V), Ni$_3$S$_2$ nanocubes@ graphene (1.53 V), single Ni$_3$S$_2$ (1.79 V)). At the same time, due to the special ultra-thin carbon coating, the Ni$_3$S$_2$ component is protected during the catalytic process, and the catalytic stability is greatly improved (the stability of Ni$_3$S$_2$ nanowires and nanocubes is up to 32 and 70 h). Nitrogen-doped graphene (or nitrogen-doped Ni$_3$S$_2$) changes the crystal and electronic structure of Ni$_3$S$_2$, resulting in a significant increase in the catalytic activity of the composite. At the same time, the structural stability, electronic conductivity, and catalytic kinetics of this series of composite catalysts were significantly improved due to the support effect of carbon support.

Electrochemical upgrading of raw ethanol into value-added chemicals holds promise for sustainable societies. Zhang et al. synthesized defective Ni$_3$S$_2$ nanowires that exhibited high activity for the electrochemical oxidation of ethanol to acetate (selectivity for acetate formation was approximately 99%) [16]. The Ni$_3$S$_2$ nanowire is formed by directional attachment mechanism, which introduces abundant defects in the growth process. For the ethanol electrooxidation, a low starting potential of 1.31 V and high mass activity of 8716 mA/mg Ni at 1.5 V was achieved using the as-synthesized Ni$_3$S$_2$ nanowires, which were superior to Ni(OH) nanowires and Ni$_3$S$_2$ nanoparticles. Electrooxidation of organic compounds instead of oxygen evolution is considered as a promising method to improve the energy conversion efficiency of electrolytic water decomposition. Wang et al. reported a self-supported Co-doped Ni$_3$S$_2$ nonelectrocatalyst (written as Co$_x$NiS@NF) on a nickel foam substrate, which was also used as an electrocatalyst for the oxidation of 5-hydroxymethylfurfural (HMF) in alkaline aqueous solution [17]. Only 1.04 V is needed to achieve the current density of 10 mA/cm^2 of HMF oxidation, which is 430 mV lower than that of OER. The catalyst can facilitate H$_2$ production at an industrial level by combining a conventional HER cathode process with HMFOR.

24.4.2 Environmental application of nanonickel sulfides
24.4.2.1 Photocatalytic environmental application
Photocatalytic decomposition of water is one of the most promising approaches for clean and renewable solar-hydrogen conversion. Yang and coworkers have implemented a

highly enhanced photocatalytic H_2 production system using CdS nanoparticles modified on spiny Ni_3S_2 nanowires (NWs) as light-driven photocatalysts [18]. The photocatalyst was prepared by coprecipitation, in which spiny Ni nanowires were used as starting materials for spiny Ni_3S_2 nanowires. The Ni_3S_2/CdS photocatalyst shows reduced photoluminescence peak intensity, which means that the Ni_3S_2 nanowires play a role in electron collection and transport, which inhibits the photoluminescence of CdS. Their findings highlight the potential application of Ni_3S_2/CdS hybrid structures in the field of energy conversion for visible light photocatalytic hydrogen production. Hierarchical layered Ni_3S_2-graphene hybrid composites were synthesized by a facile microwave-assisted method for efficient photocatalytic reduction of Cr(VI) by Hu and coworkers [19]. This high catalytic performance (reduction rate of Cr(VI) reached more than 90% in 180 min) is attributed to its efficient charge separation and more active sites due to the integration effect and good interfacial contact between Ni_3S_2 and graphene.

24.4.2.2 Electrocatalytic environmental application

Urea electrolysis is a cost-effective method for urea-rich wastewater degradation to achieve a pollution-free environment. Yin reported the Ni_3S_2/Ni heterostructure nano-belt arrays supported on nickel foam (Ni_3S_2/Ni/NF) for accelerating the urea oxidation reaction and hydrogen evolution reaction (HER) [20]. Meanwhile, the overall urea oxidation driven by Ni_3S_2/Ni/NF only needs 1.36 V to achieve 10 mA/cm^2, and it can remain at 100 mA/cm^2 for 60 h without obvious activity attenuation. This work thus provides a feasible and cost-effective strategy for urea-rich wastewater degradation and hydrogen production. The Ni@Ni_3S_2/CNTs nanostructured electrodes can be used for hydrogen production (cathode) in saline with low energy consumption and removal of ethanolamine contaminants (anode) [21]. Combined with the experimental results and density functional theory, the adsorption of electrolyte ions and ethanolamine molecules can cooperatively regulate the adsorption/desorption characteristics of the catalytic active site on the surface of Ni@Ni_3S_2/CNTs, so as to ensure the long-term stable electrocatalytic oxidation degradation of ethanolamine pollutants in saline, and at the same time, hydrogen production with low energy consumption.

24.4.2.3 Thermocatalytic environmental application

Bimetallic iron-nickel sulfide can activate peroxydisulfate to produce sulfate radical and hydroxyl radicals, which play a major role in the oxidative dechlorination and degradation of chlorinated organic pollutants due to their strong oxidizing property [22]. The Cl^- abscised from chlorinated organic pollutants during the dechlorination can turn into the chlorine radicals and enhance the degradation and cause further mineralization of intermediate products. The self-supporting cobalt-doped nickel sulfide nanosheet arrays synthesized in situ on nickel foam can be used as recyclable and integrated catalysts for peroxymono-sulfate (PMS) activation [23]. This integrated catalyst is more practical in water treatment due to its separable and recyclable properties. The thermocatalytic degradation performance of levofloxacin hydrochloride (LFX) by this free-standing catalyst was comparable to that of most powder catalysts.

24.5 Summary

In this chapter, we have discussed the structural features, preparation methods, energy and environmental applications, and typical case analysis of nanonickel sulfides (mainly Ni_3S_2). Energy applications of nanonickel sulfides include supercapacitors, lithium-ion batteries, and electrocatalytic conversion. The environmental applications of nanonickel sulfides include photocatalysis, electrocatalysis, and thermal catalysis. With the introduction of nanotechnology, the performance of Ni_3S_2 material for energy material and environmental material has been greatly improved. However, the most Ni_3S_2 nanostructures are still 1 nm wire, rod, and two-dimensional nanosheet powder structures. In the long-time practical application of Ni_3S_2, these nanostructures are prone to self-agglomerate due to their large surface energy and low mechanical stability, resulting in the reduction of the active specific surface area of the electrode. To solve this problem, in addition to traditional modification methods such as composite carbon materials, it is a promising method to select appropriate loading substrates (such as nickel foam) to improve the physical and chemical properties of Ni_3S_2 nanostructures from the perspective of 3D electrode structure design and modification.

Acknowledgments

This book was supported by National Natural Science Foundation of China (22078071, 22272034), Natural Science Foundation of Guangdong Province (2021A1515010125, 2020A1515010344), Maoming Science and Technology Project (mmkj2020032), Guangdong Province Universities and Colleges Pearl River Scholar Funded Scheme (2019), Guangdong Basic and Applied Basic Research Foundation (2019A1515011249, 2021A1515010305), Key Research Project of Natural Science of Guangdong Provincial Department of Education (2019KZDXM010), Environment and Energy Green Catalysis Innovation Team of Colleges and Universities of Guangdong Province (2022KCXTD019), the program for Innovative Research Team of Guangdong University of Petrochemical Technology.

References

[1] X. Song, X. Li, Z. Bai, B. Yan, D. Li, X. Sun, Morphology-dependent performance of nanostructured Ni_3S_2/Ni anode electrodes for high performance sodium ion batteries, Nano Energy 26 (2016) 533–540.

[2] Y. Zhao, J. You, L. Wang, W. Bao, R. Yao, Recent advances in Ni_3S_2-based electrocatalysts for oxygen evolution reaction, International Journal of Hydrogen Energy 46 (79) (2021) 39146–39182.

[3] Y. Yao, J. He, L. Ma, J. Wang, L. Peng, X. Zhu, M. Qu, Self-supported Co_9S_8-Ni_3S_2-CNTs/NF electrode with superwetting multistage micro-nano structure for efficient bifunctional overall water splitting, Journal of Colloid and Interface Science 616 (2022) 287–297.

[4] B. Li, The Transition Metal Sulfide/nano Carbon Interface Structure Design and Electrolysis Catalytic Properties Control, (Doctoral dissertation, guangxi university), 2021.

[5] B. Li, Z. Li, F. He, Q. Pang, P. Shen, One-pot preparation of $Ni_3S_2@$ 3-D graphene free-standing electrode by simple Q-CVD method for efficient oxygen evolution reaction, International Journal of Hydrogen Energy 44 (59) (2019) 30806−30819.

[6] X. Zheng, X. Han, Y. Zhang, J. Wang, C. Zhong, Y. Deng, W. Hu, Controllable synthesis of nickel sulfide nanocatalysts and their phase-dependent performance for overall water splitting, Nanoscale 11 (12) (2019) 5646−5654.

[7] Y. Yan, B.Y. Xia, B. Zhao, et al., A review on noble-metal-free bifunctional heterogeneous catalysts for overall electrochemical water splitting [J], Journal of Materials Chemistry A 4 (45) (2016) 17587−17603.

[8] Z. Li, B. Li, C. Liao, Z. Liu, D. Li, H. Wang, Q. Li, One-pot construction of 3-D graphene nanosheets/Ni_3S_2 nanoparticles composite for high-performance supercapacitors, Electrochimica Acta 253 (2017) 344−356.

[9] J.S. Chen, C. Guan, Y. Gui, D.J. Blackwood, Rational design of self-supported Ni_3S_2 nanosheets array for advanced asymmetric supercapacitor with a superior energy density, ACS Applied Materials and Interfaces 9 (1) (2017) 496−504.

[10] J. Xu, Y. Sun, M. Lu, L. Wang, J. Zhang, X. Liu, One-step electrodeposition fabrication of Ni_3S_2 nanosheet arrays on Ni foam as an advanced electrode for asymmetric supercapacitors, Science China Materials 62 (5) (2019) 699−710.

[11] Z. Yao, L. Zhou, H. Yin, X. Wang, D. Xie, X. Xia, J. Tu, Enhanced Li-storage of Ni_3S_2 nanowire arrays with N-doped carbon coating synthesized by one-step CVD process and investigated via ex situ TEM, Small 15 (49) (2019) 1904433.

[12] N.M. Santhosh, N. Shaji, P. Stražar, G. Filipič, J. Zavašnik, C.W. Ho, U. Cvelbar, Advancing Li-ion storage performance with hybrid vertical carbon/Ni_3S_2-based electrodes, Journal of Energy Chemistry 67 (2022) 8−18.

[13] S. Zhang, F. Ling, L. Wang, R. Xu, M. Ma, X. Cheng, Y. Yu, An open-ended Ni_3S_2−Co_9S_8 heterostructures nanocage anode with enhanced reaction kinetics for superior potassium-ion batteries, Advanced Materials 34 (18) (2022) 2201420.

[14] B. Li, Z. Li, Q. Pang, Controllable preparation of N-doped Ni_3S_2 nanocubes@ N-doped graphene-like carbon layers for highly active electrocatalytic overall water splitting, Electrochimica Acta 399 (2021) 139408.

[15] B. Li, Z. Li, Q. Pang, J.Z. Zhang, Core/shell cable-like Ni_3S_2 nanowires/N-doped graphene-like carbon layers as composite electrocatalyst for overall electrocatalytic water splitting, Chemical Engineering Journal 401 (2020) 126045.

[16] Y. Zhang, W. Zhu, J. Fang, et al., Defective Ni_3S_2 nanowires as highly active electrocatalysts for ethanol oxidative upgrading[J], Journal of Energy Chemistry 103 (2021) 4044−4098.

[17] Y. Sun, J. Wang, Y. Qi, W. Li, C. Wang, Efficient electrooxidation of 5-hydroxymethylfurfural using Co-doped Ni_3S_2 catalyst: promising for H_2 production under industrial-level current density, Advanced Science (2022) 2200957.

[18] S. Yang, H. Guan, Y. Zhang, et al., CdS@ Ni_3S_2 for efficient and stable photo-assisted electrochemical (P-EC) overall water splitting[J], Chemical Engineering Journal 405 (2021) 126231.

[19] P. Hu, X. Liu, B. Liu, L. Li, W. Qin, H. Yu, M. Wang, Hierarchical layered Ni_3S_2-graphene hybrid composites for efficient photocatalytic reduction of Cr (VI), Journal of Colloid and Interface Science 496 (2017) 254−260.

[20] X. Zhuo, W. Jiang, G. Qian, J. Chen, T. Yu, L. Luo, S. Yin, Ni_3S_2/Ni heterostructure nanobelt arrays as bifunctional catalysts for urea-rich wastewater degradation, ACS Applied Materials and Interfaces 13 (30) (2021) 35709−35718.

[21] B. Zhao, J. Liu, R. Feng, L. Wang, J. Zhang, J.L. Luo, X.Z. Fu, Less-energy consumed hydrogen evolution coupled with electrocatalytic removal of ethanolamine pollutant in saline water over Ni@ Ni_3S_2/CNT nano-heterostructured electrocatalysts, Small Methods 6 (3) (2022) 2101195.

[22] X. Yan, D. Yue, C. Guo, S. Wang, X. Qian, Y. Zhao, Effective removal of chlorinated organic pollutants by bimetallic iron-nickel sulfide activation of peroxydisulfate, Chinese Chemical Letters 31 (6) (2020) 1535–1539.

[23] L. Jiang, Z. Wei, Y. Ding, Y. Ma, X. Fu, J. Sun, J. Wang, In-situ synthesis of self-standing cobalt-doped nickel sulfide nanoarray as a recyclable and integrated catalyst for peroxymonosulfate activation, Applied Catalysis B: Environmental 307 (2022) 121184.

CHAPTER 25

Nano-tungsten carbides: recent progress in energy and environment fields

25.1 Introduction

Tungsten carbides mainly include tungsten carbide (WC), di-tungsten carbide (W_2C), carbon–deficient tungsten carbide (WC_{1-x}), cobalt tungsten carbide (Co_3W_3C) and so on. Tungsten carbide is a compound made of tungsten and carbon. The molecular formula is WC with a molecular weight of 195.85. It is a black hexagonal crystal with metallic luster and similar hardness to diamond. WC is widely used in national defense, chemical industry, electronic industry, mechanical tools, and surface coating. WC has the characteristics of high hardness, good wear resistance, good fracture resistance, and high strength at high temperature. It is a good conductor of electricity and heat. WC has similar surface electronic structure to Pt, good electrical conductivity, and acid resistance, which is widely used in thermal catalysis, electrocatalysis, and even photocatalysis [1]. WC was first used as a thermal catalyst for the isomerization of alkanes, showing comparable catalytic activity with Pt. WC also has high catalytic activity in hydrogenation of ethane and corn straw, reforming of methane and cellulose, decomposition of methanol, dehydrogenation of butane, and hydrodechlorination of Freon. In electrochemical studies, WC exhibits limited oxygen reduction activity only in alkaline solutions. The catalytic activity of WC for hydrogen oxidation is 1/100,000th that of Pt catalyst. The catalytic activity of WC on methanol oxidation is not so bad (electronegative WC can adsorb hydrogen in methanol to improve the activity). It is noteworthy that WC has a synergistic effect with Pt or Pd in electrocatalysis, that is, WC can improve the electrocatalytic activity of noble metal catalysts as an electrocatalyst additive [2]. However, up to now there is still a big gap for the catalytic activity between the WC and noble metal Pt. How to improve the Pt-like catalytic performance of WC has become a difficult problem for scientists.

25.2 Structural features of nano tungsten carbides

Tungsten carbide (WC) is an interstitial compound filled with C atoms in W crystal. As a covalent compound, it has high strength and rigidity, as an ionic crystal, it has high melting point, as a transition metal, it has high electromagnetic performance, and as a catalyst, it has platinum-like electronic structure and synergistic catalytic properties. In 2011, Professor

Nanostructured Materials
ISBN 978-0-443-19256-2, https://doi.org/10.1016/B978-0-443-19256-2.00021-1

P.K. Shen explained the origin of the "synergistic effect" of WC through theoretical calculation (see Fig. 25.1 for details) [3]. The results show that the synergistic effect of WC on Pt is mainly based on the enhancement induced by the "strong electron donor" characteristic of WC. Fig. 25.1 shows the structure and surface electrostatic potential of various catalysts: (a) Pt_9 cluster, (b) WC and (c) Pt_7/WC. Firstly, Fig. 25.1A,B show the structure and surface electrostatic potential of single Pt and WC, respectively. It can be seen that their electron densities are highly concentrated in the red central atomic region, indicating that both of them have "strong electron donor" characteristics. It is worth noting that the W cluster has higher electron density around it, which means that W has stronger "strong electron donor" ability than Pt. Second, Fig. 25.1C shows the structure and surface electrostatic potential of Pt/WC. When Pt is deposited into the WC-based carrier, the electron density is all transferred to the Pt atom and no longer appears around the W atom. After calculation, the electron density of Pt in Pt/WC composite structure is as high as $-3.758\ e^{-2}$, which is twice as high as that of single Pt ($-1.364\ e^{-2}$). This result can be interpreted as the "strong electron donor" characteristic of WC base carrier

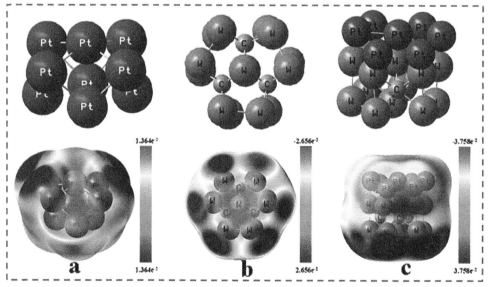

Figure 25.1 Structure and surface electrostatic potential of catalyst: (A) Pt_9 cluster, (B) WC, and (C) Pt_7/WC [3].

gives higher electron density of Pt cluster. Consistent with the results of many previous studies, the changes of Pt electronic structure (including core-shell structure and alloy structure) often lead to higher catalytic activity of the catalysts [4].

25.3 Preparation methods of nano tungsten carbides

Tungsten carbide (WC) is a widely used engineering material which is usually prepared by high-temperature solid phase synthesis. A new mechanism for synthesizing nano-scaled WC at ultralow temperature has been discovered by Shen and coworkers [2]. The novel formation mechanism is based on an ion-exchange resin as a carbon source to locally anchor the W and Fe species (AMT as W source and $K_4[Fe(CN)_6]$ as graphitization catalyst precursor and reactant). As an intermediate, $FeWO_4$ can be formed at lower temperature (865−800°C), which can be directly converted into WC along with the carbonization of resin. The size of WC can be less than 2 nm. This discovery opens a novel route to synthesize valuable WC and other carbides in a cost-efficient way. As a co-catalyst component, WC can help to enhance the catalytic performances of noble metal catalysts by so-called synergistic effect. The catalytic reaction is influenced by the mass diffusion kinetics of actual electrodes. Based on this, we recently reported the high-temperature solid phase synthesis of a new hollow hemisphere-shaped macroporous graphene/tungsten carbide/platinum (HMG/WC/Pt) composite as an efficient electrocatalyst for the ORR of fuel cell. There are several obvious structural advantages for HMG/WC/Pt: (1) Hollow hemisphere-shaped graphene with a unique macroporous structure is proposed as support material of ORR electrocatalysts, which provides a favorable pore structure for enhancing mass transfer in the catalytic reaction process; (2) Ultrafine WC nanoparticles surrounded by ultrafine Pt nanoparticles are designed on the surface of graphene, where the potential synergistic effect between WC and Pt can lead to greatly enhanced ORR catalytic performances for this composite electrocatalyst (see Fig. 25.2A,E for details) [5].

Although carbide-promoted noble-metal catalysts are widely reported, the carbide-promoted non−noble-metal catalysts are rarely reported. We synthesized a novel bimetallic carbide enhanced N and P co-doped graphite nanocomposite (Co_3W_3C/NPG) and we examined its electrochemical properties (see Fig. 25.2F−J for details) [6]. The results demonstrate that this hybrid electrocatalyst shows high catalytic activity and long-term stability for ORR in acidic medium. The ion-exchange resins are polymers composed of high molecular weight polyelectrolyte that can exchange their mobile ions with targeted ions from the surrounding medium. The ion exchange is a reversible chemical reaction wherein an ion from a solution is exchanged by a similarly charged ion attached to an immobile solid particle. During the ion exchange process, ion diffuses from the solution to the surface of resin, further diffuses into the resin to ionic groups, and exchanges with them. The Co_3W_3C/NPG nanocomposites were synthesized by an efficient high-temperature treatment assisted by ion-exchange procedure.

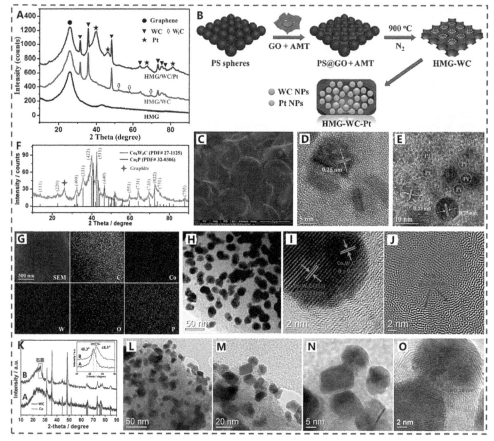

Figure 25.2 Preparation of nano-WC materials: (A—E) HMG/WC/Pt ORR electrocatalyst [5], (F—J) Co₃W₃C/GC ORR electrocatalyst [6] and (K—O) N-dopped WC ORR electrocatalyst [4].

Recently, we have developed an extremely simple and efficient systematic "booster/self-doped nitrogen" technique for the synthesis of N–WC/GC composite nanomaterials. In the process of heating, the Co catalytic graphitization and the self-doped nitrogen were achieved by adopting the system autopressurization (resin decomposition gas) technology (see Fig. 25.2K—O for details) [4]. The specific process is as follows: the anion exchange resin (D301), ammonium metapungstate ($(NH_4)_6H_2W_{12}O_{40}$), sodium cobalt nitrite ($Na_3[Co(NO_2)_6]$) are dissolved in distilled water and treated with ion exchange under stirring. The resin-metal ion complex was placed in the tube furnace for high-temperature heat treatment. During the heating process, the discharge rate of the gas outlet was controlled to ensure that the internal pressure of the tube furnace was between 0.10 and 0.15 mpa. In the process of carbonization, $[H_2W_{12}O_{40}]^{3+}$ reacts with carbon to turn into WC, and $[Co(NO_2)_6]^{3-}$ is reduced by carbon to Co nanoparticles and catalyzes graphitization under a certain pressure. At the same time, the nitrogen in the amino group realizes the nitrogen doping of WC. Finally, after removing cobalt, nitrogen-doped tungsten carbide/graphitized carbon complex (N-WC/GC) can be obtained.

25.4 Application progress of nano-tungsten carbides

25.4.1 Energy application of nano-tungsten carbides

25.4.1.1 Electrocatalytic oxygen reduction

As a "cooperative component" with relatively stable physical and chemical properties, tungsten carbide (WC) has attracted extensive attention and has been successfully applied in the design of high-performance low platinum ORR electrocatalysts. It was Professor P.K. Shen of Sun Yat-sen University who first proposed WC as a cocatalyst for fuel cells. Professor P.K. Shen found that tungsten oxide (WO_3) had an obvious synergistic enhancement effect on PT–based electrocatalyst when he was studying in Britain in 1994. After returning to China, after unremitting efforts, he took the lead in putting forward WC-enhanced Pt electrocatalyst in 2005. Under the "synergistic effect" of WC, the Pt/C electrocatalyst enhanced by WC can significantly reduce the over-potential of oxygen reduction and can reduce the dosage of Pt by 2/3 under the same performance as Pt/C, and the stability of WC is higher than WO_3. This work has attracted worldwide attention, and subsequently the research reports of carbide-enhanced noble metal electrocatalysts have mushroomed, including other carbides such as molybdenum carbide and vanadium carbide co-catalysts have also been discovered [4]. In the last 10 years, Shen and Li's group devoted themselves to the study of tungsten carbides (WC and Co_3W_3C)-promoted Pt or Pd ORR electrocatalyst (carbide-based "synergistic effect" electrocatalyst in acidic electrolyte solution) (see Fig. 25.3 for details) [7–10].

Recently, He and Shen utilized large-surface-area graphene as a support to load high-density WC and Pt NPs, which showed high activity and high stability for ORR in 0.1 M $HClO_4$ (see Fig. 25.3A–C) [7]. A microwave-assisted method was used to synthesize truncated hexagonal pyramid (THP) WC with 5 nm in size on graphene ($WC_{THP}/$G) firstly, and then the Pt NPs on $WC_{THP}/$G composite with close-contact Pt-WC interfaces were prepared by a chemical adsorption/reduction method (see Fig. 25.3A). The Pt-$WC_{THP}/$G showed a much higher ORR onset potential (1.052 vs. 0.993 V), half-wave potential (0.942 vs. 0.900 V), and mass activity (528 vs. 137 mA/mg/Pt) compared with commercial Pt/C (see Fig. 25.3B and C). The enhancement of ORR activity on Pt-$WC_{THP}/$G is mainly due to the synergistic effect between Pt and WC, which correlates with the change of the Pt surface d-band center caused by the electron metal support

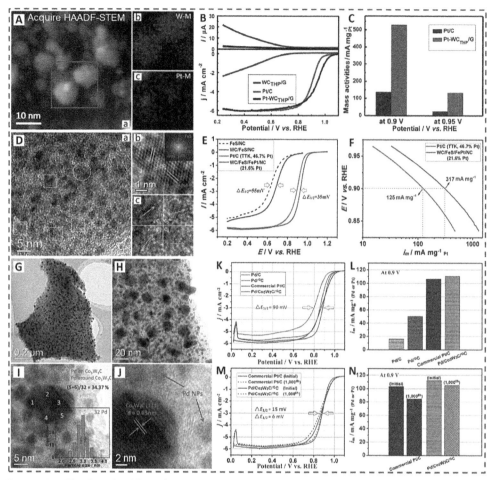

Figure 25.3 The Pt-WC$_{THP}$/G catalyst [7]: (A) HAADF-STEM images and (B and C) ORR electrochemical performances; the WC/FeS/FePt/NC catalyst [8]: (D) TEM images and (E and F) ORR electrochemical performances; the Pd/Co$_3$W$_3$C/GC catalyst [9]: (G—J) TEM images and (K—N) ORR electrochemical performances. These images and content are from one of our recently-reported review papers [10].

interaction (EMSI) on Pt-WC interface. The EMSI can also increase the binding energy of oxygen on Pt-WC$_{THP}$/G, thereby enhancing its ORR catalytic activity.

The development of multicomponent hybrid catalysts offers great promise to enhance catalytic performance for the ORR. Recently, Li and coworkers reported a quaternary hybrid material composed of WC, FeS, FePt alloy, and N–doped carbon (NC), i.e., WC/FeS/FePt/NC hybrid architecture, as a high-performance electrocatalyst for the ORR (see Fig. 25.3D—F) [8]. Due to the efficient ternary promoting effects from WC, FeS, and NC, the FePt alloy electrocatalyst exhibits an excellent mass activity of 317 mA/mg/Pt, which is much higher than that of Pt/C catalyst (125 mA/mg/Pt) (see Fig. 25.3E and F). Moreover, superior durability of the WC/FeS/FePt/NC is also demonstrated for the ORR in an acidic electrolyte (0.1 M $HClO_4$). This hybrid catalyst has three structural advantages over previous reports: (1) Ultrafine 1-D WC nanorods are prepared by FeS-regulated strategy; (2) FePt alloy is formed by in-situ transform on FeS without external Fe source; (3) The multiple synergistic effects on FePt alloy might be in operation relying on WC, FeS and NC components.

Pt-free electrocatalysts based on Pd have been proposed as promising candidates for ORR in acidic electrolyte, due to the inherent catalytic activity and lower cost of Pd than Pt. Recently, Li and coworkers synthesized high-performance Pd electrocatalyst ($Pd/Co_3W_3C/GC$) for ORR, which is synergistically enhanced by Co_3W_3C and graphitic carbon (see Fig. 25.3G—N) [9]. The GC nanosheet is uniformly decorated by the ultrahigh-density and well-proportioned Co_3W_3C NPs ($\sim$ 20 nm) and Pd NPs ($\sim$ 3 nm) (see Fig. 25.3G and H). The Pd NPs are deposited not only onto the carbon substrate but also onto Co_3W_3C, indicating a strong interaction between the Co_3W_3C and Pd NPs (see Fig. 25.3I and J). It is estimated that more than 30% of Pd NPs were deposited on onto or closely around the Co_3W_3C, which provides a necessary condition for interface synergistic effect. Due to the synergistic effects of Co_3W_3C and acceleration by GC, the $Pd/Co_3W_3C/GC$ electrocatalyst showed much higher activity than that of Pd/GC and Pd/C in a 0.1 M $HClO_4$ electrolyte, and mass activity of $Pd/Co_3W_3C/GC$ (110 mA/mg/Pd) was comparable to that of the commercial Pt/C (107 mA/mg/Pt) (see Fig. 25.3K and L). After 1000 cycles, a high activity retention of 93% was achieved for $Pd/Co_3W_3C/GC$, which was higher than that of commercial Pt/C at 82% (see Fig. 25.3M and N). These excellent properties make it a highly active and stable Pt-free acidic ORR electrocatalyst.

25.4.1.2 Electrocatalytic methanol oxidation

A ternary electrocatalyst consisting of small-sized and contacting Pt-WC nanostructures on graphene was designed as a highly efficient anode catalyst for direct methanol fuel cells (DMFCs) [11]. Compared to Pt/graphene and commercial catalysts, the Pt-WC/graphene electrocatalyst exhibits higher mass activity and stability due to its superior synergistic effect, highly dispersed, well-crystallized catalyst particles, and the combined functions of the three constituents (Pt, WC, and graphene). The synergistic effect between Pt and WC is beneficial for methanol electro-oxidation and makes Pt-WC catalyst a promising anode candidate for the DMFCs. However, the synergistic effect between Pt and WC is still a controversial issue for the methanol electro-oxidation reaction. Recently,

Zhou and coworkers demonstrated that the hydrogen overflow effect and bifunctional mechanism are responsible for the outstanding electrochemical properties of Pt–WC/C catalyst [12]. Furthermore, benefiting from the unique double-layer structure of ionic liquids (ILs), the Pt–WC/C catalyst exhibits an excellent cycling life toward methanol oxidation reaction. This study provides new insights into the development of WC-promoted Pt electrocatalyst and ionic liquids in the field of fuel cells.

25.4.1.3 Electrocatalytic water splitting

Recently, Han et al. reported a nitrogen–doped tungsten carbide (WC) nanoarray electrode, which has high stability and hydrogen evolution activity, and can efficiently drive the oxygen evolution reaction in acids [13]. Nitrogen doping and nanoarray structure accelerate the release of hydrogen from the electrode and achieves a current density of -200 mA/cm at a potential of -190 mV. Under acidic conditions (0.5 M sulfuric acid), the initial potential of nitrogen-doped tungsten carbide nanoarray for oxygen evolution is about 1.4 V, which is better than most other water-cracking catalysts. Harnisch et al. also demonstrated that WC is a promising electrocatalyst for hydrogen evolution reactions in neutral electrolytes [14]. The mixed catalysts with different components of WC, W_2C, W, and WO_2 have been systematically studied. The results show that the performance of the catalyst is proportional to the content of WC, while W_2C, W, and WO_2 have little effect. The relationship between the content of WC and the electrocatalytic activity indicates that the hydrogen evolution and oxidation on WC are related to the preferential formation of similar surface sites on WC.

25.4.2 Environmental application of nano-tungsten carbides

25.4.2.1 Photocatalytic oxidation of water

Tungsten carbide exhibits platinum-like behavior, which makes it an interesting potential substitute for noble metals in photocatalytic environmental applications. The phase-controlled synthesis of tungsten carbide nanoparticles (W_2C or WC) from the nano-confinement of a mesoporous polymer graphitic C_3N_4 (mpg-C_3N_4) reactive template is demonstrated for photocatalytic oxidation of water (hydrogen evolution and water oxidation reactions) (see Fig. 25.4A for details) [15]. Tungsten carbide is an effective co-catalyst for photocatalytic overall water splitting and give H_2 and O_2 in a stoichiometric ratio from H_2O decomposition when supported on a Na-doped $SrTiO_3$ photocatalyst. Previously, Li and coworkers also proved that earth-abundant WC nanoparticles can be used as an active noble-metal-free co-catalyst for highly boosted photocatalytic H_2 production over g-C_3N_4 nanosheets under visible light [18]. The availability of low-cost noble-metal-free photocatalyst is vital for sustainable and large-scale hydrogen production. Recently, Zhou and coworkers reported that the N-doped-carbon coated Co_3W_3C nanocrystallines (NC—Co_3W_3C), can be used as a novel co-catalyst, when anchored onto g-C_3N_4, forming a (NC—Co_3W_3C@g-C_3N_4) composite photocatalyst

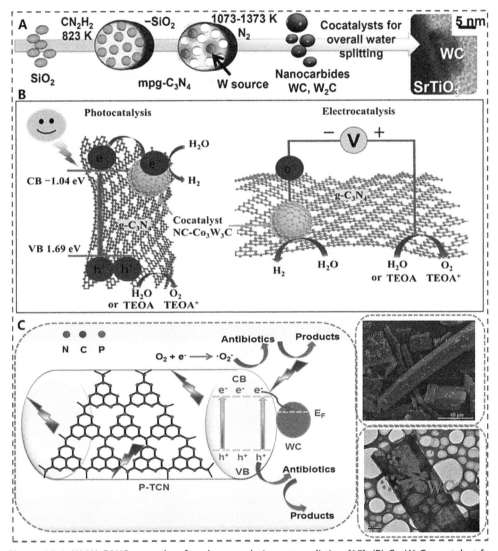

Figure 25.4 (A) W_2C/WC cocatalyst for photocatalytic water splitting [15]; (B) Co_3W_3C cocatalyst for photocatalytic water splitting [16]; (C) WC cocatalyst for photocatalytic degradation of antibiotics [17].

for application in photocatalytic hydrogen production (see Fig. 25.4B for details) [16]. Under visible light irradiation, the NC-Co$_3$W$_3$C@g-C$_3$N$_4$ photocatalyst shows a remarkable hydrogen production rate of 1332 μmol/h/g, achieving 148 times higher than pristine g-C$_3$N$_4$ photocatalyst and 89% as high as Pt/g-C$_3$N$_4$ photocatalyst. The high photocatalytic efficiency could be attributed to the boosted light absorption and accelerated photocatalytic kinetic that resulted from the enhanced conductivity and the suitable H adsorption-free energy introduced by the Co$_3$W$_3$C.

25.4.2.2 Photocatalytic degradation of organics

In general, photocatalytic decomposition of water to produce green hydrogen can be regarded as an environmental catalytic application, while photocatalytic degradation of water organic pollutants is more of an environmental catalytic application [19]. Song et al. used heterogeneous interface engineering technology to prepare a W$_2$C/W$_2$N@ g-C$_3$N$_4$ Schottky heterojunction, which can effectively enhance the absorption of visible light and inhibit charge recombination. Its rich heterogeneous interface and active sites together lead to excellent photocatalytic performances for the synchronous photocatalytic hydrogen production and photocatalytic removal of 4-nitrophenol (4-NP) [20]. The dramatically reduced concentration of 4-NP was attributed to the simultaneous hydrogenation-based reduction of 4-NP to 4-aminophenol and the photooxidation of 4-NP. Zhang et al. synthesized a novel P-doped hollow tube g-C$_3$N$_4$/tungsten carbide (P-TCN/WC) photocatalyst for the degradation of tetracycline (TC) and ciprofloxacin (CIP), two typical antibiotics, under visible light irradiation (see Fig. 25.4C for details) [17]. The photocatalytic activity of 8% P-TCN/WC is best, in 120 min 93.76% TC and 76.21% of CIP can be decomposed. The enhanced photocatalytic activity is due to the expansion of light absorption and the reduction of carrier recombination. The P-doping and WC loading enlarged the optical absorption of P-TCN/WC in the whole visible spectral range. Meanwhile, the hollow tubular morphology of P-TCN/WC boosted the utilization of light.

25.5 Summary

In this chapter, we have discussed the structural features, preparation methods, energy and environmental applications, and typical case analysis of nano-tungsten carbides (such as WC, W$_2$C, and Co$_3$W$_3$C). Nanostructured WC has high platinum-like catalytic properties and is a class of promising heterogeneous catalysts or co-catalysts (such as thermocatalysis, electrocatalysis, and photocatalysis). The energy applications of nano-tungsten carbides mainly include electrocatalytic oxygen reduction, electrocatalytic methanol oxidation, and electrocatalytic water splitting. The environmental applications of nano-tungsten carbides include photocatalytic oxidation of water and photocatalytic degradation of organics. In particular, we emphasize the modification strategies of electric- or photocatalysts of tungsten carbides with heterostructure and element doping. The enhancement of catalytic activity of tungsten carbides can be demonstrated from the perspectives of nanostructure dispersion, electrical conductivity, and surface electronic structure regulation.

Acknowledgments

This book was supported by National Natural Science Foundation of China (22078071, 22272034), Natural Science Foundation of Guangdong Province (2021A1515010125, 2020A1515010344), Maoming Science and Technology Project (mmkj2020032), Guangdong Province Universities and Colleges Pearl River Scholar Funded Scheme (2019), Guangdong Basic and Applied Basic Research Foundation (2019A1515011249, 2021A1515010305), Key Research Project of Natural Science of Guangdong Provincial Department of Education (2019KZDXM010), Environment and Energy Green Catalysis Innovation Team of Colleges and Universities of Guangdong Province (2022KCXTD019), the program for Innovative Research Team of Guangdong University of Petrochemical Technology.

References

[1]   R.B. Levy, M. Boudart, Platinum-like behavior of tungsten carbide in surface catalysis, Science 181 (4099) (1973) 547−549.

[2]   Z. Yan, M. Cai, P.K. Shen, Nanosized tungsten carbide synthesized by a novel route at low temperature for high performance electrocatalysis, Scientific Reports 3 (1) (2013) 1−7.

[3]   G. Cui, P.K. Shen, H. Meng, J. Zhao, G. Wu, Tungsten carbide as supports for Pt electrocatalysts with improved CO tolerance in methanol oxidation, Journal of Power Sources 196 (15) (2011) 6125−6130.

[4]   Z. Li, The Advanced Oxygen Reduction Reaction Catalyst for Proton Exchange Membrane Fuel Cell (Doctoral Dissertation, Sun Yat-Sen University), 2013.

[5]   Z. Li, Z. Liu, B. Li, Z. Liu, D. Li, H. Wang, Q. Li, Hollow hemisphere-shaped macroporous graphene/tungsten carbide/platinum nanocomposite as an efficient electrocatalyst for the oxygen reduction reaction, Electrochimica Acta 221 (2016) 31−40.

[6]   B. Li, J. Zhou, L. Zhang, Z. Li, Bimetallic carbide of Co_3W_3C enhanced non-noble-metal catalysts with high activity and stability for acidic oxygen reduction reaction, RSC Advances 8 (22) (2018) 12292−12299.

[7]   C. He, P.K. Shen, Pt loaded on truncated hexagonal pyramid WC/graphene for oxygen reduction reaction, Nano Energy 8 (2014) 52−61.

[8]   Z. Li, B. Li, Z. Liu, Z. Liu, D. Li, A tungsten carbide/iron sulfide/FePt nanocomposite supported on nitrogen-doped carbon as an efficient electrocatalyst for oxygen reduction reaction, RSC Advances 5 (128) (2015) 106245−106251.

[9]   Z. Li, S. Ji, B.G. Pollet, P.K. Shen, A Co_3W_3C promoted Pd catalyst exhibiting competitive performance over Pt/C catalysts towards the oxygen reduction reaction, Chemical Communications 50 (5) (2014) 566−568.

[10] Z. Li, B. Li, Y. Hu, S. Wang, C. Yu, Highly-dispersed and high-metal-density electrocatalysts on carbon supports for the oxygen reduction reaction: from nanoparticles to atomic-level architectures, Materials Advances 3 (2) (2022) 779−809.

[11] R. Wang, Y. Xie, K. Shi, J. Wang, C. Tian, P. Shen, H. Fu, Small-sized and contacting Pt−WC nanostructures on graphene as highly efficient anode catalysts for direct methanol fuel cells, Chemistry−A European Journal 18 (24) (2012) 7443−7451.

[12] Y. Zhou, X. Li, C. Yu, X. Hu, Y. Yin, S. Guo, S. Zhong, Synergistic and durable Pt-WC catalyst for methanol electro-oxidation in ionic liquid aqueous solution, ACS Applied Energy Materials 2 (12) (2019) 8459−8463.

[13] N. Han, K.R. Yang, Z. Lu, Y. Li, W. Xu, T. Gao, X. Sun, Nitrogen-doped tungsten carbide nano-array as an efficient bifunctional electrocatalyst for water splitting in acid, Nature Communications 9 (1) (2018) 1–10.

[14] F. Harnisch, G. Sievers, U. Schröder, Tungsten carbide as electrocatalyst for the hydrogen evolution reaction in pH neutral electrolyte solutions, Applied Catalysis B: Environmental 89 (3–4) (2009) 455–458.

[15] A.T. Garcia-Esparza, D. Cha, Y. Ou, J. Kubota, K. Domen, K. Takanabe, Tungsten carbide nano-particles as efficient cocatalysts for photocatalytic overall water splitting, ChemSusChem 6 (1) (2013) 168–181.

[16] X. Zhou, J. Luo, B. Jin, Z. Wu, S. Yang, S. Zhang, X. Zhou, Sustainable synthesis of low-cost nitro-gen-doped-carbon coated $Co_3W_3C@$ $g-C_3N_4$ composite photocatalyst for efficient hydrogen evolution, Chemical Engineering Journal 426 (2021) 131208.

[17] Y. Zhang, M. Zhang, L. Tang, J. Wang, Y. Zhu, C. Feng, Y. Hu, Platinum like cocatalysts tungsten carbide loaded hollow tubular $g-C_3N_4$ achieving effective space separation of carriers to degrade antibiotics, Chemical Engineering Journal 391 (2020) 123487.

[18] K. He, J. Xie, Z. Yang, R. Shen, Y. Fang, S. Ma, X. Li, Earth-abundant WC nanoparticles as an active noble-metal-free co-catalyst for the highly boosted photocatalytic H_2 production over $g-C_3N_4$ nano-sheets under visible light, Catalysis Science and Technology 7 (5) (2017) 1193–1202.

[19] W. Zhao, Z. Chen, X. Yang, X. Qian, C. Liu, D. Zhou, Y.S. Ok, Recent advances in photocatalytic hydrogen evolution with high-performance catalysts without precious metals, Renewable and Sus-tainable Energy Reviews 132 (2020) 110040.

[20] T. Song, X. Zhang, P. Yang, Interface engineering of W_2C/W_2N co-catalyst on $g-C_3N_4$ nanosheets for boosted H_2 evolution and 4-nitrophenol removal, Environmental Science: Nano 9 (5) (2022) 1888–1899.

CHAPTER 26

Nanopolyaniline: recent progress in energy and environment fields

26.1 Introduction

Conductive polymers are a class of multifunctional materials with great application prospects, mainly including polyaniline, polythiophene, and polypyrrole. These conductive polymers have similar electrical properties as inorganic materials such as semiconductors and metals. Among them, the polyaniline (PANI) has unique acid-doped/alkali-doped regulated electrical, electrochemical, and optical properties. Polyaniline is a kind of long-chain conjugated polymer whose main chain consists of two units of p-phenylenediamine and quinone diamine [1]. Although it existed as "aniline black" as early as the mid-19th century and was widely used in the dye industry, it was not until the early 20th century that people began to understand polyaniline deeply, since Green and Fritzsche studied the molecular structure of polyaniline. In 1985, MacDiarmid and his collaborators reported the protonic acid doping of polyaniline, which led to the rapid research and application of this conductive polymer material. In 2017, Richard B. Kaner et al. from the University of California discussed the physical and chemical properties of conductive polyaniline nanofibers in detail, introduced the synthesis methods of nanostructured polyaniline, and described their applications in electrochemical energy, sensors, environment, and other fields by their properties [2]. At present, the conductive polyaniline nanomaterials have been found to have high conductivity, good environmental stability, simple synthesis method, and the doping degree can also be controlled, which has become a multidisciplinary frontier research field, such as polymer chemistry, physical chemistry, inorganic chemistry, and material science. Combined with the latest research status, we briefly described the structure, doping properties of nanostructured polyaniline, and introduced the energy and environmental applications of nanostructured polyaniline in detail.

26.2 Structural features of nano polyaniline

Mac Diarmid and Heeger won the Nobel Prize in Chemistry in 2000 for their discovery of conductive polymers. It is worth mentioning that Mr. Yong Cao has made a landmark contribution to the molding of conductive polyaniline, and the results of his cooperation with Mr. Heeger are still widely used in academia and industry today. In China, a team led by Mr. Fusong Wang from Changchun Institute of Applied Chemistry, Chinese Academy of Sciences was the first to carry out polyaniline research (the related work

Nanostructured Materials
ISBN 978-0-443-19256-2, https://doi.org/10.1016/B978-0-443-19256-2.00016-8

has lasted for more than 30 years). Hitherto, scientists not only realized the simple water-system processing of conductive polyaniline, but also explored the two intrinsic properties of conductivity and doping/reverse doping (oxidation/reduction) reversibility of polyaniline, and actively promoted its application in metal corrosion, antistatic, electrode materials for storage batteries, and other fields. The molecular structure of polyaniline is closely related to its physical and chemical properties. The structure of the intrinsic state of polyaniline was obtained, and the comprehensive structural analysis of the doped state of polyaniline was also achieved, which elaborated the relationship between the structure of polyaniline and its conductive and redox properties [3].

The redox state and doping mechanism of conductive polymers have received much attention. Good stability, redox chemistry, unique dopant/dedopant properties, and excellent electrical conductivity make it the best choice among conductive polymers. The initial and continuing academic interest in polyaniline, in contrast to other conducting materials, especially conjugated polymers, is mainly due to its unique redox state and doping mechanism. For polyaniline, there are three main oxidation states: Leucoemeraldine (fully reduced), Emeraldine (half-oxidized), and Pernigraniline (fully oxidized) as shown in Fig. 26.1 [2], where the different oxidation states have different structures and exhibit different properties. Actually, the oxidation states of polyaniline are not completely different, since any degree of oxidation can occur along the polyaniline chain. Under controlled conditions, the oxidation process can produce an intermediate semi-oxidized state, Protoemeraldine, located between the Leucoemeraldine and Emeraldine; or Nigraniline, located between Emeraldine and Pernigraniline. Structurally, the differences between the oxidation states are primarily determined by the number of quinoid and benzenoid units in the polyaniline as labeled in Fig. 26.1.

26.3 Preparation methods of nanopolyaniline

At present, the main methods for preparing polyaniline include chemical oxidation polymerization, electrochemical polymerization, radiation synthesis, and acoustic chemical polymerization. These chemical processes are complex and produce large amounts of organic waste. Nanoconductive polyaniline can be successfully prepared by both chemical and electrochemical synthesis methods [2]. The chemical oxidation polymerization of polyaniline is usually done by oxidizing aniline monomer under acidic conditions. Protic acid is an important factor affecting the oxidative polymerization of aniline. It mainly plays two roles: providing the pH value required by the reaction medium and entering the polyaniline skeleton in the form of dopant to give it certain electrical conductivity. The polymerization can be simultaneously doped in situ: both polymerization and doping are completed simultaneously. Commonly used oxidants are hydrogen peroxide, dichromate, persulfate, and so on. Chemical synthesis methods mainly include various soft and hard template methods and non-template synthesis methods. Worth pointing out that interfacial polymerization is a new and simple template synthesis and

Figure 26.1 (A) Each of the five polyaniline oxidation states shown on top can be interconverted by either oxidation (electron removals) or reduction (electron addition) as indicated. (B) The undoped emeraldine base can be doped with an acid to yield the conductive emeraldine salt structure as shown at thebottom [2].

fast mixing reaction method, which can obtain morphology-controllable and high-quality polyaniline nanostructures, such as carbon-supported array architecture of polyaniline nanofibers [4]. In recent years, free-standing polyaniline nanofibers based on electrospinning technology have attracted much attention because of their industrial production advantages and unique and excellent performances. It is well known that such polyaniline nanofibers are prepared from precursor polymer solutions by electrospinning, which is a direct and simple method to utilize strong electrostatic fields [5].

26.4 Application progress of nanopolyaniline

26.4.1 Energy application of nanopolyaniline

26.4.1.1 Supercapacitor

Among various electrode materials used in electrochemical supercapacitors, polyaniline (PANI) has attracted extensive attention due to its low cost, good environmental stability, fast, and reversible doping/dedoping kinetic process. The unique doping mechanism of PANI brings high charge density, so PANI has high specific capacitance. Recently, Bai et al. reported a simple and controllable method for the preparation of molecularly homogeneous PANI/RGO composite gel, which consists of two continuous self-assembly processes, namely, the two-dimensional assembly of polyaniline on GO sheets in water/N-methyl-2-pyrrolidone mixture solvent. And 3D reduction-assembly of the obtained PANI/GO complexes. The prepared PANI/RGO composite gel has a three-dimensional porous network structure composed of reduced GO sheets. When the content of PANI is up to 80wt%, the distribution of single molecule level can still be basically maintained in the composite. Due to this favorable microstructure, the composite exhibits a high specific capacitance of 808 F g^{-1} at a current density of 53.33A g^{-1}, as well as excellent rate performances [6]. In recent years, our research group has also been committed to the preparation of nano polyaniline and the performance of supercapacitors. The main direction of these studies work is focused on the effects of different oxidants (different crystalline manganese dioxide) and different carbon carriers (graphene hollow spheres, carbon nanospheres, etc.) on the nanostructures and electrochemical properties of polyaniline electrode materials (see Fig. Fig. 26.2 for details) [7–9].

The different crystalline oxidants, α-Manganese dioxide (α-MnO_2) and β-MnO_2, have been prepared by a simple one-step hydrothermal synthesis method. Polyaniline (PANI)/carbon black composites were further synthesized in acidic medium by an in-situ polymerization method using α-MnO_2, β-MnO_2, and ammonium peroxydisulfate (APS) as chemical oxidant (see Fig. 26.2A–E for details) [7]. The PANI/carbon black composite (PANI/C-2) prepared using β-MnO_2 as oxidant shows significantly better specific capacity performance compared with those prepared using α-MnO_2 (PANI/C-1) and APS as oxidant (PANI/C). The redox reaction between ANI and MnO_2 can happen in the form of galvanic cell reaction. In this galvanic cell reaction, The MnO_2 meets with H^+ ion, picks up electrons, and is reduced to water-soluble Mn^{2+}

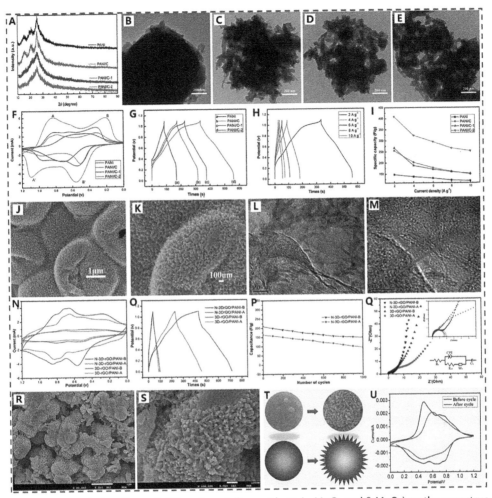

Figure 26.2 (A—I) The effects of different crystalline oxidants (α-MnO₂ and β-MnO₂) on the nanostructures and electrochemical properties of polyaniline [7]; (J—Q) the effects graphene hollow spheres on the nanostructures and electrochemical properties of polyaniline [8]; (R—U) the effects of carbon nanospheres on the nanostructures and electrochemical properties of polyaniline [9].

ion on cathode (see Equ. (1)). The ANI monomer loses electrons and is oxidatively polymerized to PANI on anode (see Equ. (2)).

$$MnO_2 + 4H^+ + 2e^- \rightarrow Mn^{2+} + 2H_2O \tag{1}$$

$$n \text{ Aniline} \rightarrow PANI + ke^- \tag{2}$$

The mechanism of β-MnO$_2$ in giving better specific capacity than α-MnO$_2$ can be explained by the unique crystallographic structure and oxidation properties of β-MnO$_2$. The interaction with carbon black could provide high electrical conductivity of PANI/carbon black composite. The specific capacitance of PANI/C-2 (409.5 F g^{-1}) is more than that of PANI/C-1 (267.3 F g^{-1}), PANI/C (254.7 F g^{-1}), and PANI (147.2 F g^{-1}) (see Fig. 26.2F−I for details) [7]. Therefore, the β-MnO$_2$ is a good oxidant for the polymerization of ANI and is significant for the development of high-performance PANI-based materials for supercapacitors.

A facile strategy for the fabrication of a nitrogen-doped 3D reduced graphene oxide (N-3D-rGO) macroporous structure (i.e., hollow sphere structure) is proposed by our group. Using β-MnO$_2$ as the oxidant, the as-prepared N-3D-rGO hollow sphere was then composited with polyaniline (PANI) ultrathin nanowires by the interface in-situ polymerization synthesis method (denoted as N-3D-rGO/PANI-B) (see Fig. 26.2J−M for details) [8]. The N-3D-rGO/PANI-B composite has a better specific capacity than the composites prepared with 3D-rGO as the support material and peroxydisulfate as the oxidant. The specific capacitance reached up to 282 F g^{-1} at 1 A g^{-1} with a retention rate of 64.5% as the current density varied from 1 A g^{-1}−8 A g^{-1}. The composite exhibits both excellent stability and high electrical conductivity (see Fig. 26.2N−Q for details). This superior performance is attributed to the nitrogen-doped hollow sphere structure of graphene and the ultrathin nanowires of PANI by efficient oxidation of β-MnO$_2$. The N-3D-rGO/PANI-B composite material prepared in this study is a promising electrode material for high-performance supercapacitors.

The conductive polyaniline (PANI)/porous carbon microspheres (PCMs) composites were also synthesized by simple solution polymerization using PCMs as support (see Fig. 26.2R−U for details) [9] The results showed that carbon carriers (PCMs) played an important role in regulating the morphology and structure of PANI. In PANI/PCMs composites, small and uniform PANI nanofibers were grown on the surface of PCMs, while the original PANI only formed micrometer fibers. The PANI/PCMs composites showed excellent capacitance performance in 1M H$_2$SO$_4$ aqueous electrolyte. When the current density is 1 A g^{-1}, the maximum specific capacitance of PANI/PCMs composites is 242.5 F g^{-1}, which is much higher than that of original PANI (135.2 F g^{-1}) and PCMs (37.2 F g^{-1}). In short, the PANI nanofibers provide abundant active sites that interact with porous carbon support and improve synergistic effects and the electrochemical performance of the nanocomposites.

26.4.1.2 Rechargeable batteries

Polyaniline (PANI) is often used in alkaline metal ion batteries with organic electrolytes. When applied to water system electrolyte, PANI needs a high concentration of hydrogen ions to promote its redox reaction, but the strong acid environment has a strong corrosion effect on zinc metal. Sun et al. prepared a sulfonic acid group doped PANI (PANI-S) for the positive electrode of zinc ion batteries. Since the pKa value of m-aminobenzenesulfonic acid is 3.7, which is less than the pH of zinc sulfate solution (4.2), $-SO_3H$ group is ionized, so the SO_3-functional group can ensure a higher hydrogen ion concentration around the polymer skeleton, and finally make PANI-S have a better zinc storage performance [10]. The PANI intercalated V_2O_5 material exhibits abundant mesoporous structure and excellent electrical conductivity. However, due to the complex energy storage mechanism of the material, it has not been applied in the field of zinc electricity. Zhang et al. successfully synthesized V_2O_5 nanosheets intercalated with PANI, and the specific capacity was as high as 372 mAh g^{-1}, and the cycle stability was superior. The intercalated polyaniline effectively widens the crystal plane spacing of V_2O_5 and thus accommodates more zinc ions without phase transition [11]. Cao et al. also obtained a MnO_2-PANI composite network zinc ion battery material with long cycle life and high-rate performance by polymerizing PANI protective layer on MnO_2 in situ through interface control engineering. The PANI protective layer obtained by in situ polymerization on the surface of MnO_2 not only effectively improves the conductivity of MnO_2, but also provides more ion adsorption sites to improve the specific capacity and rate performance, and also stabilizes the structure of MnO_2 to improve the cycle stability [12].

26.4.1.3 Electrocatalytic conversion

Polyaniline (PANI) is considered as a promising electrocatalytic reaction material due to its excellent chemical durability, high conductivity, and strong adsorption capacity of reactants. Recently, Li et al. synthesized a polyaniline/cobalt phosphide hybrid nanowires (PANI/CoP) electrocatalyst, which was as effective as Pt-based catalyst in catalyzing hydrogen evolution reaction (HER) [13]. This is because PANI can effectively capture H^+ from the hydronium ion $[H(H_2O)_6]^+$, forming a protonated amine group with a higher positive charge density than the hydronium ion, which can be more easily electro reduced. As a low-cost electrocatalyst, the PANI/CoP showed excellent catalytic properties for hydrogen evolution in acidic solutions, such as ultra-high catalytic activity, small Tafel slope, and excellent stability. Wang et al. effectively regulated the interface electronic structure and the adsorption strength (ΔG *H) of intermediate *H at the N site of PANI, based on the interfacial d-π electron coupling interaction between different metal oxides (such as WO_3, $W_{18}O_{49}$, and MoO_3) and PANI [14]. When WO_3 interacts with PANI, the ΔG *H can be effectively optimized close to the optimal value of 0. Therefore, the WO_3/PANI composite catalyst shows excellent performance of electrocatalytic hydrogen evolution and the lowest overpotential (74 mV) at 10 mA cm^{-2}.

26.4.2 Environmental application of nanopolyaniline
26.4.2.1 Adsorbing purification
Researchers from the Institute of Solids of Hefei Institute of Chinese Academy of Sciences have carried out a systematic study on the preparation and application of polyaniline, deeply explored the application of polyaniline in the removal of Cr(VI) from wastewater, and made a series of progress [15]. In series of studies, different morphologies of polyaniline nanostructure were synthesized under acidic and alkaline conditions, and these polyaniline nanostructures were used in the field of wastewater treatment with a good ability to remove Cr(VI) from water. Furthermore, by loading polyaniline on the modified fiber ball of macroscopic size, it can effectively remove Cr(VI) and avoid the secondary pollution problem in the process of removing Cr(VI), which lays a foundation for realizing its industrial application. Combined with unique redox properties and reversible doping, the application of polyaniline micro-/nanostructures with different morphologies in wastewater treatment was discussed.

When 1-D polyaniline nanowires/tubes were used to remove Cr(VI) from water, it was found that Cr(VI) in water was reduced to Cr(III) by polyaniline, and the reduced Cr(III) could also be adsorbed by polyaniline. At the same time, PANI will be oxidized by Cr(VI), from doped intermediate oxidation state (veridimide salt) to complete oxidation state (polyp-phenimide), and the oxidized polyp-phenimide can still be transformed into veridimide salt after acid treatment, and the morphology of PANI does not change significantly [16]. Due to its nanometer scale of PANI nanowires/tubes, centrifuge or filter processing is needed to realize reutilization, which is not only easy to cause secondary pollution, also increased the processing costs, not conducive to large-scale industrialized application. In view of this, the researchers used chemical oxidation polymerization to prepare the macroscopic size fiber ball loaded polyaniline (PANI/M-FB) composite, which effectively solved the secondary pollution problem caused by nanoscale polyaniline (see Fig. 26.3A−C for details) [17]. At the same time, the composite has a high removal capacity of Cr(VI), and the preparation process is simple, low cost, can be recycled, and has great potential for industrial application.

Liao's team used a two-step strategy of in situ cross-linking and acid-induced in situ polymerization to prepare a controllable PANI/CNF composite nanofiber aerogel adsorbent composed of PANI nanofiber and cellulose nanofiber (CNF) supramolecular self-assembly. The results show that PANI/CNF aerogel has good compressive mechanical properties and excellent adsorption properties. In addition, based on the property that PANI can activate persulfate to degrade pollutants by advanced oxidation, the team used perdisulfide (PDS) process for the first time to realize the green regeneration of PANI/CNF adsorbents and the cooperative degradation of pollutants (see Fig. 26.3D−E

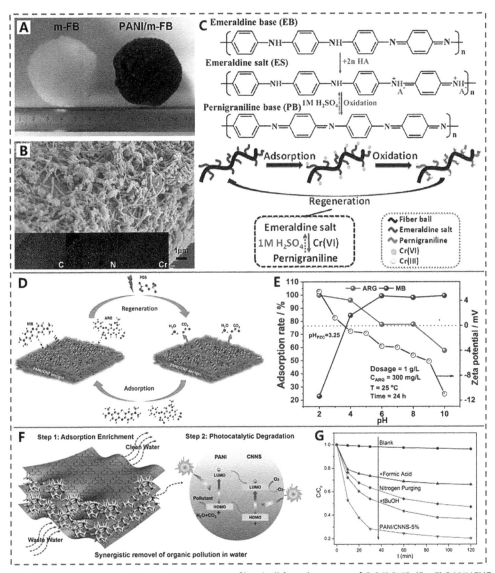

Figure 26.3 (A—C) Polyaniline macroscopic size fiber ball for adsorption of Cr(VI) [17]; (D—E) PANI/CNF composite nanofiber aerogel for adsorption and PDS degradation of organic dyes [18]; (F—G) PANI/CNNS composite hydrogels for photocatalytic degradation of pollutants [19]).

for details) [18]. The adsorption behavior of anionic dye ARG and cationic dye MB on PANI/CNF aerogel was studied by batch static adsorption experiment. The optimal adsorption dosage ($1g L^{-1}$), the optimal pH (ARG and MB 2 and 10), and the maximum Langmuir adsorption capacity of ARG and MB (600.7 and 1369.6 mg g^{-1}, respectively) were determined, indicating the potential application of PANI/CNF aerogel adsorbent in the removal of ionic pollutants.

26.4.2.2 Photocatalytic degradation

Photocatalysis, as a green and environmental protection technology, is widely used in the field of energy conversion and environmental purification. Zhu et al. stripped bulk carbon nitride into a few layers of carbon nitride nanosheets (CNNS) by thermal etching method, and then constructed PANI/CNNS composite hydrogels by in situ polymerization (see Fig. 26.3F—G for details) [19]. PANI hydrogel is composed of coral-like nanofibers and intercalated between the layers of CNNs to form a sandwich structure, which can not only prevent the aggregation of CNNs, but also prevent the loss of CNNs with water. It has the advantages of easy separation and easy recovery. In particular, the introduction of PANI can enhance the absorption of visible light region in the catalytic system, which is beneficial to light capture and thus increases the utilization efficiency of sunlight. When PANI was introduced into the system, the fluorescence of PANI decreased obviously, which indicated that the photogenerated carrier recombination was inhibited and the carrier lifetime was prolonged, thus benefiting the photocatalytic reaction. At the same time, there is π-π interaction between carbon nitride and PANI, which can effectively improve the separation efficiency of electrons and holes and photocatalytic degradation activity [19].

26.4.2.3 Electrochemical oxidation

The mass transfer of pollutants to the anode surface is often an important factor affecting the efficiency of electrochemical oxidation of organic wastewater. Based on the form of magnetic assembly electrode (MAE), Fe_3O_4/polyaniline (PANI) nano-magnetic particles with good adsorption performance were magnetically loaded on the surface of Ti/SB-SnO_2 electrode to form the so-called 2.5D Ti/Sb—SnO_2/PANI electrode [20]. This electrode is actually a smart combination of adsorbent and electrocatalyst, which can enrich the pollutants on the surface of the anode in the electrochemical oxidation treatment of organic wastewater, so as to effectively solve the mass transfer limitation problem and improve the treatment efficiency. In terms of organic elimination and solution biodegradability enhancement, the 2.5D Ti/Sb—SnO_2/PANI showed a boosted 30%—60% oxidation efficiency on two typical bio-refractory targets, i.e., Acid Red G and lignosulphonate. The adsorption capacity of the fixed PANI adsorbent on the 2D surface of Ti/Sb—SnO_2 by magnetic force was inferior to the dispersed 3D assembled granules. Therefore, the specific adsorption-oxidation effectiveness was obviously dependent on the loading amount of magnetic adsorbent (i.e., Fe_3O_4/PANI nanoparticles).

26.5 Summary

In this chapter, we have discussed the structural features, preparation methods, energy and environmental applications, and typical case analysis of nanopolyaniline (nano-PANI). Polyaniline is a kind of conductive polymer with broad application prospects. It not only has unique proton doping ability, oxidation-reduction ability, adjustable electrical conductivity, abundant adsorption active sites, strengthening chemical, and environmental stability, but also has low raw material and a simple synthesis process. Therefore, the preparation and properties of nano PANI have become a research hotspot in the field of conductive polymers, which shows broad application prospects in electrochemical energy storage (supercapacitors and zinc-ion batteries) and conversion (electrocatalytic hydrogen production), removal of dyes and heavy metal ions by adsorption purification, photocatalytic degradation, and electrochemical oxidation. With the deepening of the research, the conductivity and electronic characteristics of nano-PANI are constantly improved and optimized, and the application fields are constantly expanded.

Acknowledgments

This book was supported by National Natural Science Foundation of China (22078071, 22272034), Natural Science Foundation of Guangdong Province (2021A1515010125, 2020A1515010344), Maoming Science and Technology Project (mmkj2020032), Guangdong Province Universities and Colleges Pearl River Scholar Funded Scheme (2019), Guangdong Basic and Applied Basic Research Foundation (2019A1515011249, 2021A1515010305), Key Research Project of Natural Science of Guangdong Provincial Department of Education (2019KZDXM010), Environment and Energy Green Catalysis Innovation Team of Colleges and Universities of Guangdong Province (2022KCXTD019), the program for Innovative Research Team of Guangdong University of Petrochemical Technology.

References

[1]   S. Bhadra, D. Khastgir, N.K. Singha, J.H. Lee, Progress in preparation, processing and applications of polyaniline, Progress in Polymer Science 34 (8) (2009) 783−810.
[2]   C.O. Baker, X. Huang, W. Nelson, R.B. Kaner, Polyaniline nanofibers: broadening applications for conducting polymers, Chemical Society Reviews 46 (5) (2017) 1510−1525.
[3]   X. Wang, Polyaniline Preparation and Applied, Science Press, 2019.
[4]   H.P. Cong, X.C. Ren, P. Wang, S.H. Yu, Flexible graphene−polyaniline composite paper for high-performance supercapacitor, Energy and Environmental Science 6 (4) (2013) 1185−1191.
[5]   C. Bavatharani, E. Muthusankar, S.M. Wabaidur, Z.A. Alothman, K.M. Alsheetan, M. mana AL-Anazy, D. Ragupathy, Electrospinning technique for production of polyaniline nanocomposites/nanofibres for multi-functional applications: a review, Synthetic Metals 271 (2021) 116609.
[6]   J. Wu, J. Wang, X. Huang, H. Bai, A self-assembly route to porous polyaniline/reduced graphene oxide composite materials with molecular-level uniformity for high-performance supercapacitors, Energy and Environmental Science 11 (5) (2018) 1280−1286.

[7]   Z. Liu, Z. Li, D. Li, X. Yin, Z. Liu, Use of manganese dioxide as oxidant in polymerization of aniline on carbon black for supercapacitor performance, High Performance Polymers 28 (10) (2016) 1105−1113.

[8]   Z. Liu, D. Li, Z. Li, Z. Liu, Z. Zhang, Nitrogen-doped 3D reduced graphene oxide/polyaniline composite as active material for supercapacitor electrodes, Applied Surface Science 422 (2017) 339−347.

[9]   B. Li, Z. Li, L. Zhang, Z. Liu, D. Xiong, D. Li, Facile synthesis of polyaniline nanofibers/porous carbon microspheres composite for high performance supercapacitors, Journal of the Taiwan Institute of Chemical Engineers 81 (2017) 465−471.

[10] H.Y. Shi, Y.J. Ye, K. Liu, Y. Song, X. Sun, A long-cycle-life self-doped polyaniline cathode for rechargeable aqueous zinc batteries, Angewandte Chemie 130 (50) (2018) 16597−16601.

[11] S. Chen, K. Li, K.S. Hui, J. Zhang, Regulation of lamellar structure of vanadium oxide via polyaniline intercalation for high-performance aqueous zinc-ion battery, Advanced Functional Materials 30 (43) (2020) 2003890.

[12] P. Ruan, X. Xu, X. Gao, J. Feng, L. Yu, Y. Cai, X. Cao, Achieving long-cycle-life Zn-ion batteries through interfacial engineering of MnO_2-polyaniline hybrid networks, Sustainable Materials and Technologies 28 (2021) e00254.

[13] J.X. Feng, S.Y. Tong, Y.X. Tong, G.R. Li, Pt-like hydrogen evolution electrocatalysis on PANI/CoP hybrid nanowires by weakening the shackles of hydrogen ions on the surfaces of catalysts, Journal of the American Chemical Society 140 (15) (2018) 5118−5126.

[14] Z.F. Huang, J. Song, Y. Du, S. Dou, L. Sun, W. Chen, X. Wang, Optimizing interfacial electronic coupling with metal oxide to activate inert polyaniline for superior electrocatalytic hydrogen generation, Carbon Energy 1 (1) (2019) 77−84.

[15] https://mp.weixin.qq.com/s/c-7pEpsKLbKWTwMtZflikA.

[16] X. Guo, G.T. Fei, H. Su, L. De Zhang, High-performance and reproducible polyaniline nanowire/tubes for removal of Cr(VI) in aqueous solution, The Journal of Physical Chemistry C 115 (5) (2011) 1608−1613.

[17] X.L. Ma, G.T. Fei, S.H. Xu, Synthesis of polyaniline coating on the modified fiber ball and application for Cr (VI) removal, Nanoscale Research Letters 16 (1) (2021) 1−12.

[18] W. Lyu, J. Li, L. Zheng, H. Liu, J. Chen, W. Zhang, Y. Liao, Fabrication of 3D compressible polyaniline/cellulose nanofiber aerogel for highly efficient removal of organic pollutants and its environmental-friendly regeneration by peroxydisulfate process, Chemical Engineering Journal 414 (2021) 128931.

[19] W. Jiang, W. Luo, R. Zong, W. Yao, Z. Li, Y. Zhu, Polyaniline/carbon nitride nanosheets composite hydrogel: a separation-free and high-efficient photocatalyst with 3D hierarchical structure, Small 12 (32) (2016) 4370−4378.

[20] D. Shao, W. Lyu, J. Cui, X. Zhang, Y. Zhang, G. Tan, W. Yan, Polyaniline nanoparticles magnetically coated Ti/Sb−SnO_2 electrode as a flexible and efficient electrocatalyst for boosted electrooxidation of biorefractory wastewater, Chemosphere 241 (2020) 125103.

CHAPTER 27

Nanographitic carbon nitride: recent progress in energy and environmental fields

27.1 Introduction

Organic polymer semiconductor is an ideal candidate material for photocatalysis due to its abundant raw materials, low price, simple preparation process, and convenience in molecular design. Its band gap width is generally between 1.5 and 3.0 eV, which can well absorb visible light and even near-infrared light. In recent years, a kind of nonmetallic organic polymer semiconductor material, graphitic carbon nitride (g-C_3N_4) is widely concerned, due to its narrow band gap ($E_g = 2.66$ eV), strong response to visible light, and the advantages of high chemical stability, easy modification, high photocatalytic performance, low price, low toxicity and environmental protection, etc. It has attracted extensive attention in the field of photocatalysis (expressly, it is known as the "Holy Grail photocatalyst") [1]. Although g-C_3N_4 has many advantages, it also has some disadvantages: small specific surface area; the band gap width is relatively large, and the range of response to visible light is narrow; the separation of photogenerated electrons and holes is not high and they are easy to recombine. In order to improve the photocatalytic performance of g-C_3N_4, researchers have conducted a large number of studies on improving the photocatalytic activity of g-C_3N_4 by modification, which can be divided into the following three directions [2]: (1) Design the structure of nano-g-C_3N_4 to improve the specific surface area of the material; (2) The band gap width of g-C_3N_4 was reduced by doping to improve its response range to visible light; (3) g-C_3N_4 and other semiconductor photocatalyst were combined to form a heterojunction photocatalyst to improve the separation efficiency of photogenerated electrons and holes. In the past 2 decades, g-C_3N_4 has been widely used in the fields of photocatalysis, electrocatalysis and thermal catalysis, involving the energy production and conversion, as well as environmental protection and purification aspects.

27.2 Structural features of nanographitic carbon nitride

Polymer semiconductor C_3N_4 has five kinds of structure, they are α phase, β phase, cubic phase, quasi-cubic phase, and graphitic phase. Among them, the graphitic phase C_3N_4 (i.e., g-C_3N_4) has the most stable structure, which has a graphite-like layered structure

Nanostructured Materials
ISBN 978-0-443-19256-2, https://doi.org/10.1016/B978-0-443-19256-2.00032-6

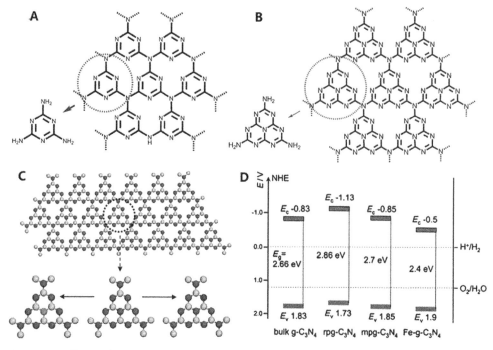

Figure 27.1 Chemical structure diagram of g-C$_3$N$_4$: s-Triazine (A) and tri-s-Triazine (B) as molecular tectons; (B) substitutional N atom at different periodic sites by P or S atom. C yellow, N red, P or S green (site 1), P or S blue (site 2); Electronic band structures (HOMO and LUMO) of different g-C$_3$N$_4$ solids [3]. For interpretation of the references to color in this figure legend, please refer online version of this title.

and contains two allotrophes (s–Triazine (A) and tri-s–Triazine (B) as structural units) (see Fig. 27.1A and B for details) [3]. The two allotropes have different stability due to the different positions and sizes of nitrogenous pores (with six-nitrogen or nine-nitrogen pores). Density functional theory calculation showed that the nine-nitrogen-pore g-C$_3$N$_4$, which is connected by tri-s–Triazine as structural units, has the best stability. Therefore, the g-C$_3$N$_4$ used in recent studies is all of this structure in Fig. 27.1B. The C and N atoms of g-C$_3$N$_4$ have lone pair electrons in the pz orbital, which can interact to form a large π bond similar to the benzene ring, and form a highly delocalized conjugate system by sp2 hybridization (that is, conjugated polymer). Heteroatomic (such as P and S) doping of g-C$_3$N$_4$ by postfunctionalization can regulate the electronic structure and catalytic properties of materials. The structural details on the incorporation of P or S into the C/N framework can be obtained with XPS and XANES spectroscopy, which suggested that C-P or C-S bonds formed in g-C$_3$N$_4$ by substituting P or S for lattice nitrogen (see Fig. 27.1C for details) [3]. Heteroatomic doping (with C or N vacancy) also modified the surface area and the morphology of g-C$_3$N$_4$, which is as such relevant for catalytic applications. The suitable electronic band structure makes g-C$_3$N$_4$ a promising candidate for many solar energy converting systems. Basically, the electronic band structures of g-C$_3$N$_4$ could be tuned by modification of the nanomorphology or doping, which makes the improvement in photocurrent possible (see Fig. 27.1D for details) [3]. Mesoporous polymeric g-C$_3$N$_4$ (mpg-C$_3$N$_4$) can in principle enhance the light-harvesting ability owing to its large surface area and multiple scattering effects and therefore showed an increase in photocurrent. Other modifications, including protonation (e.g., rpg-C$_3$N$_4$) and doping (e.g., Fe-C$_3$N$_4$), can also increase the photocurrent and visible-light catalytic activity.

27.3 Preparation methods of nanographitic carbon nitride

No natural g-C$_3$N$_4$ crystals have been found in nature. Therefore, g-C$_3$N$_4$ is mainly derived from experimental synthesis. Under certain reaction conditions, simple or mixed g-C$_3$N$_4$ can be obtained by selecting appropriate carbon and nitrogen sources. Commonly used reactants are melamine, melamine chlorine, melamine, dicyandiamine, urea, thiourea, etc. At present, the commonly used preparation methods mainly include high-temperature and high-pressure synthesis method, physical and chemical vapor deposition method, electrochemical deposition method, solvothermal polymerization method, pyrolysis organic matter method, and so on. Among them, thermal polymerization can easily adjust the structure of g-C$_3$N$_4$ by adding other substances or changing the reaction conditions, so as to improve the photocatalytic performance of g-C$_3$N$_4$. Therefore, thermal polymerization (with temperature from 450 to 650°C) is the most commonly used synthesis method of g-C$_3$N$_4$ (see Fig. 27.2 for details) [4].

Recently, our research group reported that g-C$_3$N$_4$ was synthesized in one-step by thermal polycondensation of melamine at different temperatures (450, 500, 550, 600, and 650°C) [5]. Generally, above 390°C, the structure of melamine begins to rearrange, resulting in the formation of the 3-s-triazine structural unit, and when the temperature reaches 520°C, the 3-s-triazine structural unit is further polycondensation to form g-C$_3$N$_4$. Moreover, compared to the primary stage (450°C) and the intermediate stage (500 and 550°C), the g-C$_3$N$_4$ synthesized at the advanced stage (600 and 650°C) had not only the strongest absorption of visible light but also the narrowest band gap, enabling controllable adjustment of the band structure of catalysts. Meanwhile, for the photodegradation of 2-naphthol, g-C$_3$N$_4$ synthesized at 600°C performed the best with a rate constant of 1.949 h^{-1} for the first-order kinetic model, which was 2.67 times that of the catalyst synthesized at 450°C. In general, heat treatment temperature is a key parameter to regulate the structures (crystal and electronic structures) and photocatalytic properties of carbon nitride nanomaterials.

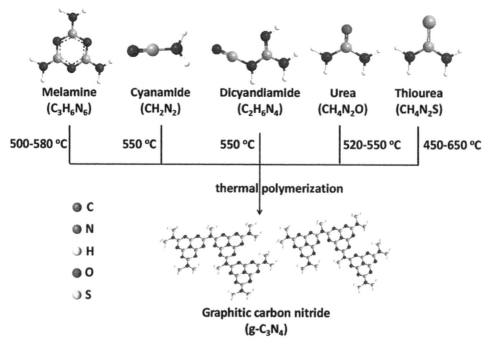

Figure 27.2 Schematic diagram of preparation of g-C₃N₄ with different precursors [4].

Nanostructured dimension design can effectively improve the specific surface area and catalytic performance of g-C₃N₄ materials, such as 0-D quantum dots, 1-D nanofibers, 2-D nanosheets, 3-D nanosheets, porous nanosheets, and hollow nanospheres (see Fig. 27.3 for details) [6–15]. Because g-C₃N₄ is a typical layered material, 2-D nanosheets are the most common nanostructures, which can be made from bulk materials by thermal stripping. Recently, we successfully prepared ultrathin porous g-C₃N₄ nanosheets (∼30 nm) by air oxidation using urea as a precursor (see Fig. 27.3A—D) [6]. This nanosheet can be further converted into a 3-D P-doped g-C₃N₄ nanosheet by postdoping method. Moreover, using melamine as a precursor and sodium dihydrogen phosphate as P source, 3-D P-doped g-C₃N₄ nanosheet can be also prepared by synchronous heat treatment (see Fig. 27.3E—H) [7]. It is worth mentioning that the P doping process (postdoping) is conducive to the transformation of 2-D g-C₃N₄ nanosheet structure to 3-D nanosheet structure. The 3-D g-C₃N₄ nanosheet structure can be prepared by

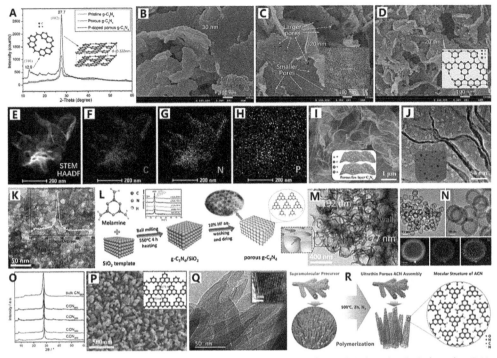

Figure 27.3 (A—D) Ultrathin 2-D or 3-D P-doped g-C_3N_4 nanosheets [6], (E—H) 3-D P-doped g-C_3N_4 nanosheet [7], (I and J) template-free mesoporous g-C_3N_4 nanosheets [8], (K) SiO_2-template mesoporous g-C_3N_4 nanosheets [9], (L and M) macroporous g-C_3N_4 [10], (N) hollow spheres g-C_3N_4 [11], (O—Q) crystalline g-C_3N_4 nanofibers [12—14], (R) mesoporous g-C_3N_4 nanofibers [15].

simultaneous thermal condensation polymerization and phosphorus doping. At the same time, phosphorus doping can lead to rich carbon defects for 3-D g-C_3N_4 nanosheet, which is beneficial to improve the specific surface area and the number of active sites of catalytic materials [7].

Homogeneous and small mesoporous structures (2—50 nm) can effectively improve the specific surface area and ion diffusion kinetics of the photocatalytic materials. Through precise molecular intercalation and thermal-induced exfoliation treatment, ultrathin g-C_3N_4 nanosheets with uniform mesoporous structure (10—20 nm) can be prepared under controllable condition (see Fig. 27.3I and J) [8]. Obviously, the released gas and volume shrinkage of precursor during the thermal polycondensation process would create many pores on the layers, finally producing porous few-layer g-C_3N_4. In addition, silica (SiO_2) nanoparticles can be used as templates to prepare mesoporous g-C_3N_4 materials with a single pore size (about 15 nm) (see Fig. 27.3K) [9]. When SiO_2 nanospheres or polystyrene (PS) nanospheres are used as templates, the 3-D macroporous g-C_3N_4 materials (see Fig. 27.3L and M) [10] and hollow spheres g-C_3N_4 materials (see Fig. 27.3N) [11] can be obtained. Generally, the macroporous or hollow nanostructures can promote light reflection and improve light energy utilization. The 1-D crystalline g-C_3N_4 nanofibers can be obtained by using LiCl-KCl as eutectic mixture through high-temperature solution to mediate the polymerization process (see Fig. 27.3O–Q) [12–14]. In addition, the 1-D mesoporous g-C_3N_4 nanofibers can be fabricated based on the pyrolysis of an asymmetric supramolecular precursor came from L-arginine and melamine (see Fig. 27.3R) [15]. The controllable preparation of g-C_3N_4 nanostructures with different dimensions has been realized, which lays the material foundation for the optimization of catalytic performances.

27.4 Application progress of nanographitic carbon nitride

27.4.1 Energy application of nanographitic carbon nitride

27.4.1.1 Electrocatalytic conversion

As an electrocatalyst, the catalytic activity of g-C_3N_4 results from the changes in electronic structure caused by vacancies, doping, intrinsic defects, and edge modifications on g-C_3N_4. The combination of the above methods will cause different electronic structure changes, so that multifunctional electrocatalysts can be constructed. The thin porous structure makes g-C_3N_4 nanosheets easy to be modified, doped, and defects introduced, which can change the electronic structure, thereby improving the catalytic activity of reaction centers and introducing more active centers [16]. For example, g-C_3N_4 has great potential in oxygen reduction reaction (ORR) due to its high N content and considerable stability and low cost in acid/alkaline environments. In 2009, Lyth reported that the catalytic activity of g-C_3N_4 in ORR was superior to that of pure carbon materials. However, the current density is still relatively low, which is related to the low surface area of bulk g-C_3N_4. Moreover, the poor conductivity will inevitably affect the electron transfer and the performance of g-C_3N_4 in ORR [17]. Combining the g-C_3N_4 with conductive carbon or metal materials to improve its conductivity and form hybrid structures can greatly improve its electrocatalytic performances for different electrocatalytic applications (such as reduction of CO_2, water splitting for H_2 evolution and fuel cell electrocatalysis).

More recently, our group report a novel graphitic carbon nitride/graphite carbon/palladium nanocomposite (Pd@g-C_3N_4/GC) as an efficient fuel cell electrocatalyst for the ethanol electro-oxidation (see Fig. 27.4A–K for details) [18]. To the best of our knowledge, this is the first report about the g-C_3N_4-promote Pd electrocatalyst for the application of ethanol electro-oxidation. For this composite system, several features have become apparent over previous reports: (i) The graphite carbon support with

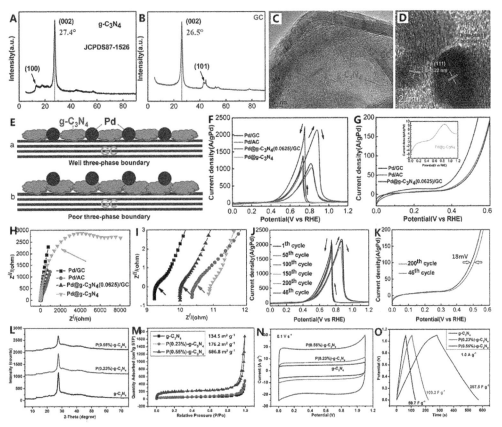

Figure 27.4 (A−K) Pd@g-C₃N₄/GC for ethanol electro-oxidation of fuel cell [18]; (B) P-doped g-C₃N₄ nanosheets for electrochemical supercapacitors [19].

nanosheet-like structure is prepared by a cost-effective low-temperature catalytic route from inexpensive ion-exchange resin; (ii) The ultra-thin g-C₃N₄ "nano-islands" (∼5 nm) is successfully deposited on the surface of graphite carbon (GC) support, which is expressly favorable for the electron transfer and ion diffusion of electrolyte; (iii) The electron-coupling effect between g-C₃N₄ and GC can promote the fixation of Pd nano-particles on to the support; (iv) The pyridine-type nitrogen-rich structure units of g-C₃N₄ can induce a large amount of electrochemical active points when interacted with the Pd nanoparticles by systematic effect. With these merits, we investigated that the ethanol oxidation reaction electrocatalyst with excellent performances (including high oxidation activity and stability) could be designed based on the $Pd@g-C_3N_4/GC$ composite architectures.

27.4.1.2 Supercapacitor

As a structural analogous of graphite with aromatic tri-s-Triazine structural units, $g-C_3N_4$ has attracted and opened a new arena in energy storage and conversion of supercapacitors owing to its nitrogen-rich framework, metal-free characteristic, earth abundance, and environmental friendliness in the last 10 years [20]. At present, the applications of $g-C_3N_4$ in supercapacitors are mainly to enhance the ultracapacitor performance of interface structures through coupling with transition metal oxides/hydroxides, metal sulfides, or conductive polymers. The nano-$g-C_3N_4$ can increase the surface area, the number of active sites, and the diffusion kinetics of inserted/deinserted ions at the electrode-electrolyte interface, and further promote the Faraday reaction of the binary composite interface structures. It is noteworthy that the design of highly conductive $g-C_3N_4$-based nonmetallic electrode materials, such as carbon/$g-C_3N_4$ composites and doped $g-C_3N_4$ materials, can effectively improve the conductivity and capacitance.

The low electrical conductivity (less than 1 S cm^{-1}) of $g-C_3N_4$ limits its application in supercapacitors energy storage. An ultrathin $g-C_3N_4$ composite nanosheet ($g-C_3N_4$/graphene/$g-C_3N_4$ sandwich structure) was prepared by the van der Waals epitaxy strategy with graphene as template, which showed ultrahigh electrical conductivity (12.2 S cm^{-1}), narrow pore size distribution (5.3 nm), and large specific surface area (724.9 m^2 g^{-1}) [21]. The ultrathin two-dimensional structure of the sandwich provides a large number of channels and active sites for efficient ion transport and storage, while the graphene layer in the middle acts as a microcurrent collector. The composite exhibits extremely high capacitive energy storage capacity and ultra-high energy density, as well as excellent electrochemical stability and physical flexibility. Our latest research shows that the specific surface area and conductivity of phosphorus (P)-doped $g-C_3N_4$ material is obviously increased than pristine $g-C_3N_4$. The maximum specific surface area of P(0.55%)-$g-C_3N_4$ is 686.8 m^2 g^{-1}. The P-doped sample showed a specific capacitance of 267.5 F g^{-1} at a constant current at a current density of 1.0 A g^{-1}, and 207.3 F g^{-1} at 10.0 A g^{-1}. After 2000 cyclic charging and discharging tests, the capacitance retention rate of the material can reach 87.73%. Therefore, the P-doped $g-C_3N_4$ shows good electrochemical performance for the energy storage of supercapacitors (see Fig. 27.4L–O for details) [19].

27.4.1.3 Rechargeable batteries

The electrode design principle that relates the physicochemical properties of $g-C_3N_4$ nanosheets to the target function can more pertinently exert the characteristics and utility of $g-C_3N_4$ in electrochemical systems of rechargeable batteries. For example, because $g-C_3N_4$ is porous and easily modified by functional groups, it is suitable for the adsorption of lithium polysulfide in Li-sulfur batteries. Moreover, the high N content and stable chemistry character are suitable for protecting the separator in lithium metal batteries [16]. Researchers from Tianjin University of Technology and Central Michigan University used magnesium thermal denitrification technology to reduce the nitrogen content of g-C_3N_4 and introduce nitrogen defects. As the negative electrode of Li-ion battery, this N-deficient g-C_3N_4 still had good battery capacity (2753 mAh g^{-1} at 0.1 A g^{-1}) and cycle stability after 300 cycles [22]. The porous structure of N-deficient g-C_3N_4 has a high specific surface area, which can increase the electrode/electrolyte contact area and shorten the ion diffusion distance to promote the addition of lithium ions. In particular, the formation of nitrogen defects and hanging bonds around N-dopants can enhance the mobility of Li and the embedding ability of Li.

27.4.2 Environmental application of nanographitic carbon nitride

27.4.2.1 Photocatalytic degradation

For the g-C_3N_4 photocatalytic system, the improved performance is usually attributed to high electron/hole separation rates or sufficient reaction sites. While these statements are true, the mechanism discussion is not specific enough and quantitative analysis is often lacking. Some advanced characterization instruments and theoretical calculations are required. In addition, some physicochemical properties (photoelectricity and piezoelectricity) of g-C_3N_4 nanosheets are encouraged to be coupled with light to play a role of one plus one more than two [16]. In the last 10 years, our research group (Zesheng Li and Changlin Yu) has been engaged in photocatalytic degradation performance and degradation mechanism of organic pollutants with a series of g-C_3N_4 catalytic materials. These research works principally include the photocatalytic degradation of organic dyes and antibiotics by doping-structured g-C_3N_4 and g-C_3N_4-based heterojunction materials (see Fig. 27.5 for details) [6,23–26].

In 2016, an efficient "in situ growth" strategy was developed to create the g-C_3N_4 nanosheets (NSs) and CdS nanorods (NRs) 1-D/2-D hybrid architectures, i.e., the CdS NRs/g-C_3N_4 NSs nanocomposites, from cadmium-containing carbon nitride nanosheets (Cd/g-C_3N_4) compounds. This novel polymer/semiconductor 1-D/2-D hybrid architecture demonstrated a very high photoelectrochemical response under visible light irradiation. The CdS NRs/g-C_3N_4 NSs electrode displays the largest photocurrent (about 100 μA cm^{-2}), which is about 30 times compared with that of pristine g-C_3N_4 electrode (about 3.5 μA cm^{-2}). The elevated photoelectrochemical performances are originated from the direct physical and electronic contact between the interfaces of the two semiconductor nanomaterials. The high-efficiency charge-transfer processes between CdS NRs and g-C_3N_4 NSs polymers have been demonstrated after being activated by visible light (see Fig. 27.5A–C for details) [23].

In 2014, a novel hybrid architecture made up of BiPO$_4$ nanorods and mesoporous g-C_3N_4 (namely BiPO$_4$/mg-C_3N_4) was synthesized as a heterojunction photocatalyst for

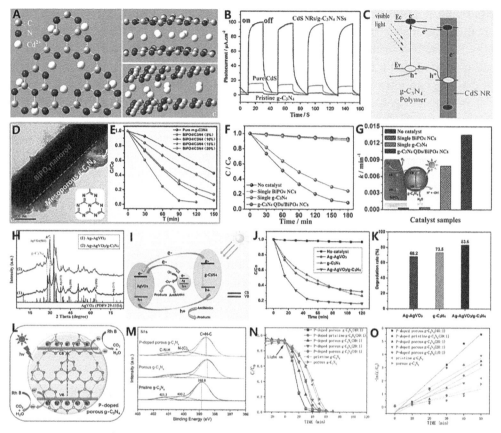

Figure 27.5 (A–C) CdS NRs/g-C$_3$N$_4$ NSs heterojunction [23]; (D and E) BiPO$_4$ nanorods/mg-C$_3$N$_4$ heterojunction [24]; (F and G) g-C$_3$N$_4$ QDs/BiPO$_4$ NCs heterojunction [25]; (H–K) Ag-AgVO$_3$/g-C$_3$N$_4$ heterojunction [26]; (L–O) 3-D P-doped porous g-C$_3$N$_4$ nanosheets [6]).

environmental application. The photocatalytic activity of the BiPO$_4$/mg-C$_3$N$_4$ photocatalyst for degradation of Methyl Orange (MO) dye has been significantly improved under visible-light irradiation. The optimum photocatalytic activity of BiPO$_4$/mg-C$_3$N$_4$ with BiPO$_4$ weight ratio of 15% is above 2.5 times as high as that of single mg-C$_3$N$_4$. The enhanced photocatalytic activity comes from the high migration efficiency of photoinduced electrons on the interface of mg-C$_3$N$_4$ and BiPO$_4$ (see Fig. 27.5D and E for details) [24]. In 2014, a novel composite architecture made up of g-C$_3$N$_4$ quantum dots/BiPO$_4$ nanocrystals was also synthesized as a visible light-induced photocatalyst for efficient degradation of MO. The decolorization rate can reach 92% for the g-C$_3$N$_4$ QDs/BiPO$_4$ NCs, while that of single g-C$_3$N$_4$ was only about 75%. The photocatalytic activity on the base of g-C$_3$N$_4$ QDs in g-C$_3$N$_4$ QDs/BiPO$_4$ NCs can be estimated to be 13.5 times as high as that of single g-C$_3$N$_4$ (see Fig. 27.5F and G for details) [25].

In 2019, the degradation of tetracycline antibiotic by silver vanadate (AgVO$_3$), g-C$_3$N$_4$, and their composite (Ag-AgVO$_3$/g-C$_3$N$_4$) was studied by visible light photocatalysis. Nanorod-like AgVO$_3$ was synthesized by hydrothermal method. The gap between nanorods is reduced by adding spinning g-C$_3$N$_4$, and the photocatalytic performance of the composite is stronger than that of a single material. The reaction rate constants of Ag-AgVO$_3$/g-C$_3$N$_4$ composites were 0.0298 min^{-1}, 2.4 and 2.0 times that of g-C$_3$N$_4$ (0.0125 min^{-1}) and AgVO$_3$ (0.0152 min^{-1}), respectively. At 120 min, the degradation rate of the Ag-AgVO$_3$/g-C$_3$N$_4$ composites reached 83.6%. The excellent photo-catalytic degradation performance is mainly due to the enhancement of optical absorption, adsorption capacity, and effective separation efficiency of photo-generated carriers due to the heterojunction effect (see Fig. 27.5H−K for details) [26].

In 2020, we further prove that the three-dimensional P-doped porous g-C$_3$N$_4$ nanosheets can be used as an efficient metal-free photocatalyst for visible-light photocatalytic degradation of Rhodamine B (RhB) model pollutant. Abundant in-plane mesopores (from 2 to 50 nm), high specific surface area (202.9 cm^2 g^{-1}), and desirable P content (0.87%) were obtained for this 3-D P-doped porous g-C$_3$N$_4$ nanosheets. The P-doped porous g-C$_3$N$_4$ photocatalyst showed much-enhanced visible-light photocatalytic activity, with RhB degradation ratio of 99.5% and a kinetic reaction rate constant of 0.120 min^{-1}, compared to the doped-free porous g-C$_3$N$_4$ nanosheets (58.2% and 0.031 min^{-1}). The mesoporous structure and high P doping endowed the g-C$_3$N$_4$ photocatalyst with abundant active sites, high conductivity, and efficient separation of photo-produced electron-hole pairs (see Fig. 27.5L−O for details) [6].

27.4.2.2 Photocatalytic conversion

The g-C$_3$N$_4$ has a moderate band gap (2.66 eV) and suitable conduction band (CB, −1.3 eV) and valence band (VB, +1.4 eV) positions, which can be used in photocatalytic water decomposition and carbon dioxide reduction. In photocatalytic carbon dioxide reduction, g-C$_3$N$_4$ nanosheets showed high selectivity for CH$_4$ under UV-visible light, while bulk g-C$_3$N$_4$ tended to produce CH$_3$CHO. The protonated porous g-C$_3$N$_4$ nanosheet exposes more active catalytic sites and cross−plane diffusion channels, which are conducive to mass and charge transfer. The surface amine functionalized g-C$_3$N$_4$ nanosheets provide abundant catalytic sites for CO$_2$ adsorption and reduction and enhance the redox capacity of charge carriers [16]. Due to the quantum size effect, the positions of CB and VB of g-C$_3$N$_4$ move in opposite directions, resulting in an increase in the band gap of g-C$_3$N$_4$ nanosheets. The widening of the band gap makes g-C$_3$N$_4$ have a more negative conduction band position (stronger reduction potential) (see Fig. 27.1D for details) [3]. The self-doping (carbon, nitrogen), heteroatom (oxygen, sulfur, phosphorus, halogen) doping, crystal defect introduction, heterojunction construction, surface functionalization. and other modification strategies of g-C_3N_4 can give it stronger visible light response and higher charge carrier concentration for photocatalytic conversion [27].

27.5 Summary

In this chapter, we have discussed the structural features, preparation methods, energy and environmental applications, and typical case analysis of nanographitic carbon nitride (nano-g-C_3N_4). The g-C_3N_4 has attracted great attention in the field of energy storage and conversion as well as environmental catalysis due to its unique layered structure, tunable band gap, nonmetallic properties, high physicochemical stability, and easy availability. Nano-g-C_3N_4 has a short charge/mass transfer path, abundant reaction sites and easy functionalization, which is conducive to optimize its performance in different fields. We focus on the rational design and preparation of g-C_3N_4 low-dimensional, porous and hollow nanostructures and their diverse applications for energy and the environment, including electrochemical applications such as fuel cell electrocatalysis, supercapacitors, batteries, as well as photocatalytic applications such as photocatalytic degradation and photocatalytic conversion. Overall, nanoscale g-C_3N_4 is a versatile heterogeneous catalytic material for energy and environmental applications.

Acknowledgments

This book was supported by National Natural Science Foundation of China (22078071, 22272034), Natural Science Foundation of Guangdong Province (2021A1515010125, 2020A1515010344), Maoming Science and Technology Project (mmkj2020032), Guangdong Province Universities and Colleges Pearl River Scholar Funded Scheme (2019), Guangdong Basic and Applied Basic Research Foundation (2019A1515011249, 2021A1515010305), Key Research Project of Natural Science of Guangdong Provincial Department of Education (2019KZDXM010), Environment and Energy Green Catalysis Innovation Team of Colleges and Universities of Guangdong Province (2022KCXTD019), the program for Innovative Research Team of Guangdong University of Petrochemical Technology.

References

[1] X. Wang, K. Maeda, A. Thomas, K. Takanabe, G. Xin, J.M. Carlsson, et al., A metal-free polymeric photocatalyst for hydrogen production from water under visible light, Nature Materials 8 (1) (2009) 76–80.

[2] W.J. Ong, L.L. Tan, Y.H. Ng, S.T. Yong, S.P. Chai, Graphitic carbon nitride (g-C_3N_4)-based photocatalysts for artificial photosynthesis and environmental remediation: are we a step closer to achieving sustainability? Chemical Reviews 116 (12) (2016) 7159–7329.

[3] Y. Wang, X. Wang, M. Antonietti, Polymeric graphitic carbon nitride as a heterogeneous organocatalyst: from photochemistry to multipurpose catalysis to sustainable chemistry, Angewandte Chemie International Edition 51 (1) (2012) 68–89.

[4] B. He, M. Feng, X. Chen, J. Sun, Multidimensional (0D-3D) functional nanocarbon: promising material to strengthen the photocatalytic activity of graphitic carbon nitride, Green Energy & Environment 6 (6) (2021) 823—845.

[5] Y. Lan, Z. Li, D. Li, G. Yan, Z. Yang, S. Guo, Graphitic carbon nitride synthesized at different temperatures for enhanced visible-light photodegradation of 2-naphthol, Applied Surface Science 467 (2019) 411—422.

[6] Z. Li, Q. Chen, Q. Lin, Y. Chen, X. Liao, H. Yu, et al., Three-dimensional P-doped porous g-C$_3$N$_4$ nanosheets as an efficient metal-free photocatalyst for visible-light photocatalytic degradation of Rhodamine B model pollutant, Journal of the Taiwan Institute of Chemical Engineers 114 (2020) 249—262.

[7] Q. Lin, Z. Li, T. Lin, B. Li, X. Liao, H. Yu, et al., Controlled preparation of P-doped g-C$_3$N$_4$ nanosheets for efficient photocatalytic hydrogen production, Chinese Journal of Chemical Engineering 28 (10) (2020) 2677—2688.

[8] Y. Xiao, G. Tian, W. Li, Y. Xie, B. Jiang, C. Tian, et al., Molecule self-assembly synthesis of porous few-layer carbon nitride for highly efficient photoredox catalysis, Journal of the American Chemical Society 141 (6) (2019) 2508—2515.

[9] S. Yang, W. Zhou, C. Ge, X. Liu, Y. Fang, Z. Li, Mesoporous polymeric semiconductor materials of graphitic-C$_3$N$_4$: general and efficient synthesis and their integration with synergistic AgBr NPs for enhanced photocatalytic performances, RSC Advances 3 (16) (2013) 5631—5638.

[10] W. Chen, M. Liu, X. Li, L. Mao, Synthesis of 3D mesoporous g-C$_3$N$_4$ for efficient overall water splitting under a Z-scheme photocatalytic system, Applied Surface Science 512 (2020) 145782.

[11] D. Zheng, C. Huang, X. Wang, Post-annealing reinforced hollow carbon nitride nanospheres for hydrogen photosynthesis, Nanoscale 7 (2) (2015) 465—470.

[12] L. Lin, W. Ren, C. Wang, A.M. Asiri, J. Zhang, X. Wang, Crystalline carbon nitride semiconductors prepared at different temperatures for photocatalytic hydrogen production, Applied Catalysis B: Environmental 231 (2018) 234—241.

[13] M.J. Bojdys, J.O. Müller, M. Antonietti, A. Thomas, Ionothermal synthesis of crystalline, condensed, graphitic carbon nitride, Chemistry—A European Journal 14 (27) (2008) 8177—8182.

[14] L. Cheng, X. Yue, L. Wang, D. Zhang, P. Zhang, J. Fan, et al., Dual-single-atom tailoring with bifunctional integration for high-performance CO$_2$ photoreduction, Advanced Materials 33 (49) (2021) 2105135.

[15] B. Wu, L. Zhang, B. Jiang, Q. Li, C. Tian, Y. Xie, et al., Ultrathin porous carbon nitride bundles with an adjustable energy band structure toward simultaneous solar photocatalytic water splitting and selective phenylcarbinol oxidation, Angewandte Chemie International Edition 60 (9) (2021) 4815—4822.

[16] Y. Wang, L. Liu, T. Ma, Y. Zhang, H. Huang, 2D graphitic carbon nitride for energy conversion and storage, Advanced Functional Materials 31 (34) (2021) 2102540.

[17] Y. Zheng, Y. Jiao, J. Chen, J. Liu, J. Liang, A. Du, et al., Nanoporous graphitic-C$_3$N$_4$@carbon metal-free electrocatalysts for highly efficient oxygen reduction, Journal of the American Chemical Society 133 (50) (2011) 20116—20119.

[18] Z. Li, R. Lin, Z. Liu, D. Li, H. Wang, Q. Li, Novel graphitic carbon nitride/graphite carbon/palladium nanocomposite as a high-performance electrocatalyst for the ethanol oxidation reaction, Electrochimica Acta 191 (2016) 606—615.

[19] R. Chen, Z. Li, Preparation and Electrochemical Capacitance Performance of Phosphorus-Doped Three-Dimensional Carbon Nitride Nanosheets, Undergraduate Graduation Thesis, 2021.

[20] M.G. Ashritha, K. Hareesh, A review on graphitic carbon nitride based binary nanocomposites as supercapacitors, Journal of Energy Storage 32 (2020) 101840.

[21] C. Lu, Y. Yang, X. Chen, Ultra-thin conductive graphitic carbon nitride assembly through van der Waals epitaxy toward high-energy-density flexible supercapacitors, Nano Letters 19 (6) (2019) 4103—4111.

[22] J. Chen, Z. Mao, L. Zhang, D. Wang, R. Xu, L. Bie, et al., Nitrogen-deficient graphitic carbon nitride with enhanced performance for lithium ion battery anodes, ACS Nano 11 (12) (2017) 12650—12657.

[23] Z. Li, Z. Liu, B. Li, D. Li, C. Ge, Y. Fang, Novel CdS nanorods/g-C$_3$N$_4$ nanosheets 1-D/2-D hybrid architectures: an in situ growth route and excellent visible light photoelectrochemical performances, Journal of Materials Science: Materials in Electronics 27 (3) (2016) 2904—2913.

[24] Z. Li, S. Yang, J. Zhou, D. Li, X. Zhou, C. Ge, et al., Novel mesoporous g-C_3N_4 and $BiPO_4$ nano-rods hybrid architectures and their enhanced visible-light-driven photocatalytic performances, Chemical Engineering Journal 241 (2014) 344—351.

[25] Z. Li, B. Li, S. Peng, D. Li, S. Yang, Y. Fang, Novel visible light-induced gC_3N_4 quantum dot/$BiPO_4$ nanocrystal composite photocatalysts for efficient degradation of methyl orange, RSC Advances 4 (66) (2014) 35144—35148.

[26] D. Chen, B. Li, Q. Pu, X. Chen, G. Wen, Z. Li, Preparation of Ag-$AgVO_3$/g-C_3N_4 composite photo-catalyst and degradation characteristics of antibiotics, Journal of Hazardous Materials 373 (2019) 303—312.

[27] P. Xia, B. Zhu, J. Yu, S. Cao, M. Jaroniec, Ultra-thin nanosheet assemblies of graphitic carbon nitride for enhanced photocatalytic CO_2 reduction, Journal of Materials Chemistry A 5 (7) (2017) 3230—3238.

CHAPTER 28

Nano Bi-based oxometallates: recent progress in energy and environmental fields

28.1 Introduction

Photocatalytic oxidation technology has attracted much attention for its rapid and effective degradation of organic pollutants in a mild environment with solar energy. At present, the inorganic semiconductor photocatalysis represented by TiO_2 has some scientific and technical difficulties, such as low quantum efficiency, low solar energy utilization rate (can only absorb UV light of less than 5% of sunlight), low selectivity, poor stability, and so on [1]. In order to solve these problems, a key research direction is to develop new efficient "visible light" responsive inorganic semiconductor photocatalysts. Bismuth (Bi)-based oxometallates have attracted wide attention due to their unique electronic structure, excellent absorption capacity of visible light, high stability, and efficient degradation of refractory organic pollutants, which has become one hot spot in the research of new semiconductor photocatalysis [2]. The common Bi-based oxometallates semiconductor photocatalysts include bismuth phosphate ($BiPO_4$), bismuth tungstate (Bi_2WO_6), bismuth molybdate (Bi_2MoO_6), vanadate ($BiVO_4$), bismuth oxycarbonate ($Bi_2O_2CO_3$), and so on. Bismuth-based catalysts (e.g., Bi_2WO_6 and $Bi_2O_2CO_3$) also show excellent catalytic activity in the field of electrocatalysis (e.g., electrocatalytic CO_2 reduction and nitrogen reduction), and Bi-O hybrid structures can achieve excellent activity and selectivity over a wide voltage range (e.g., electrocatalytic CO_2 reduction to HCOOH) [3]. The Bi-based oxometallates show attractive application prospects in both photocatalytic oxidation degradation and electrocatalytic energy conversion. The rational design of nanostructures, vacancy defects, and heterojunction structures can further improve the catalytic activity of the Bi-based oxometallates materials. The structural feature and preparation strategies of Bi-based catalysts, and their electrocatalysis and photocatalysis applications were summarized.

28.2 Structural features of nano Bi-based oxometallates

Different Bi-based oxometallates have a different crystal structure, electronic structure, and light properties. $BiPO_4$ has high electron-hole separation rate and high photocatalytic activity, but its wide band gap can only have a certain response under ultraviolet conditions, which greatly hindrance the utilization of sunlight. The band gap width of

Nanostructured Materials
ISBN 978-0-443-19256-2, https://doi.org/10.1016/B978-0-443-19256-2.00005-3

457

Bi_2WO_6 is less than 3.0 eV, the conduction band is formed by W5d, and the valence band is formed by Bi 6s and O 2p hybrid orbitals. Bi_2WO_6 has high oxidation and charge mobility, which makes it a promising visible light catalyst. The crystal structure of Bi_2MoO_6 is similar to that of Bi_2WO_6, and Bi_2MoO_6 shows good photocatalytic performance under visible light. $BiVO_4$ has attracted extensive attention from scholars and has been applied to the degradation of pollutants, photolysis of aquatic oxygen, etc., mainly because its bandgap width is about 2.4 eV, and it is a stable, nontoxic, and visible light-responsive semiconductor photocatalytic material [4].

From the electronic structure viewpoint, the hybridization of Bi 6s and O 2p orbitals may enlarge the boundary of the valence band and increase the divergence of valence band for Bi-based oxometallates. These characteristics contribute to the separation and movement of electron-hole pairs in the photocatalytic process and lead to the catalytic activity of bismuth compounds under visible light. For example, Bi_2WO_6 is one simplest aurivillius layered oxometallates composed of Bi_2O_2 layers and WO_6 octahedral layers. Compared with other types of Bi compounds, its reaction site is on the surface and edge, and photocatalysis excites valence band electrons to migrate to the conduction band, and then the reaction takes place on this surface to consume photogenerated holes. The band gap width of Bi_2WO_6 decreases with the increase of valence band potential after hybridization of Bi 6s and O 2p orbitals ($E_g = 2.75$ eV), which shows obvious photocatalytic activity under visible-light irradiation (see Fig. 28.1A for details) [5].

In order to improve the visible light response and promote the photocatalytic activity of Bi-based oxometallates, the heteroatom doping, oxygen vacancy (OV) design, and heterostructure construction are three efficient methods. Rare earth ions doping is an efficient strategy to improve the photocatalytic property of bismuth-based photocatalysts. Our previous research indicated that doping of Eu^{3+} induced the formation of $BiVO_4$ microspheres and the phase transformation of $BiVO_4$. The Gd^{3+} doped Bi_2WO_6 photocatalyst can improve photocatalytic activity due to the electron shallow-trapping mechanism for the efficient separation of electron and hole pairs. Our recent investigations showed that the doping of Gd^{3+} into Bi_2MoO_6 can obviously enhance visible light harvesting and promote the separation of photogenerated electrons and holes. The doping of Eu^{3+} into Bi_2MoO_6 crystals induced a distortion of Bi_2MoO_6 lattice and a decrease in crystalline grain size. The Eu^{3+} doping also reduced the energy gap of Bi_2MoO_6 and increased its UV-Vis light absorption (see Fig. 28.1B for details) [6].

For most metal-oxide semiconductors with wide band gaps, the introduction of OV can greatly expand the optical absorption and narrow the band gap width. In addition, oxygen vacancies can effectively prevent the recombination of photogenerated electrons and holes and act as the active center of the reaction [9]. Different from metal oxides whose valence band is composed of O 2p orbitals, the valence band of Bi-based semiconductor is generally composed of O 2p and Bi 6s hybrid orbitals, which will cause the band gap to decrease. The introduction of OV can adjust the band structure of Bi-based

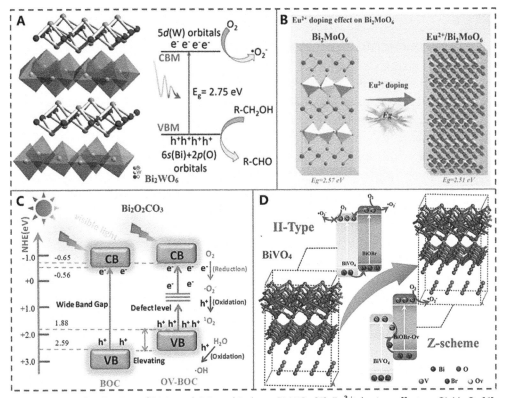

Figure 28.1 Hybridization of Bi 6s and O 2p orbitals on Bi_2WO_6 [5], Eu^{3+} doping effect on Bi_2MoO_6 [6], Oxygen vacancy (OV) regulation of $Bi_2O_2CO_3$ [7], heterostructure construction based on $BiVO_4$ [8].

oxometallates more effectively, so as to make better use of solar energy. OV can be constructed on the bulk phase or surface of different types of photocatalysts to enhance their light harvesting, charge carrier migration efficiency, and surface catalysis process, so as to achieve efficient solar energy conversion. For example, $Bi_2O_2CO_3$ with OV is used in a variety of photocatalytic reactions, including pollutant purification, water decomposition, NO oxidation, CO_2 reduction, nitrogen fixation, and organic synthesis (see Fig. 28.1C for details) [7].

So far, the construction of heterojunctions (type I, type II, and Z schemes) can significantly improve carrier separation and transport and is considered to be an effective method to inhibit carrier recombination. Inspired by natural photosynthesis, the researchers designed a Z–scheme heterojunction, which was proven to achieve efficient charge separation and retain photogenerated holes and electrons with high oxidation/reduction potentials [10]. Wang's team synthesized the $BiVO_4/BiOBr$ heterojunction using a simple method. During the preparation process, the content of OV in BiOBr is changed, and then the relative positions of BiOBr and $BiVO_4$ Fermi levels are regulated, and the photogenerated carrier transport path is transformed from II-type to Z–scheme. The photocatalytic degradation performance of $BiVO_4/BiOBr$-OV (BVB-OV) was significantly improved under the combined action of oxygen vacancies and Z-scheme heterojunctions (see Fig. 28.1D for details) [8]. This work provides insights and guidance for OV coordination interface charge transfer pathways.

In recent years, our research group has designed a series of Bi-based oxometallates/g-C_3N_4 conjugated polymer composites to increase the photocatalytic activity and structural stability of the heterojunction materials to varying degrees [11–13]. The incorporation of conjugated polymer can enable the composite to absorb the whole UV-Vis light. Some polar groups (−C=N, −NH, etc.) in g–C_3N_4 conjugated polymer have certain chemical bonds with oxometallates, which is beneficial to the effective separation of photogenerated charge and improve its catalytic performance. These composite catalysts are all deep mineralization catalysts, which can destroy most of the structure of organic pollutants molecules in a very short time. The h_{VB}^+, •OH, and O_2^- produced in the photocatalytic process have the strongest oxidation ability and can react with organic pollutants to realize the mineralization and degradation of molecules into nontoxic inorganic substances and they have good stability performances.

28.3 Preparation methods of nano Bi-based oxometallates

Up to now, Bi-based oxometallates have been synthesized by various methods, such as sol-gel method, co-precipitation method, solvothermal method and hydrothermal process. The hydrothermal method has the following advantages: (1) The reaction and crystal growth can be effectively controlled by controlling the composition, volume fraction, pH value, and reaction temperature of solution; (2) The crystallization process of hydrothermal synthesis makes the product have high purity, the reaction process is relatively simple, and does not require complex equipment; (3) The product synthesized by hydrothermal method has controllable crystal defects, good orientation, high crystallinity, excellent catalytic performance, and high stability. Our group focused on the crystal structure regulation of Bi-based oxometallates and prepared favorable crystal phase structures through controlled hydrothermal synthesis strategies, such as $BiVO_4$ with monoclinic schewolframite structure, Bi_2WO_6 with layered Aurivillius structure and $BiPO_4$ with hexagonic phase structure. In field of photocatalysis, the self-assembly of Bi-based oxometallates with multiscale 3-D hierarchical nanostructures (such as flower-like and spherical nanostructures) by using nanoparticles, nanowires, and nanosheets can significantly improve their quantum efficiency and enhance the photocatalytic activity [14].

Our colleagues have recently carried out the design and preparation of "g-C$_3$N$_4$ conjugated polymer/Bi-based oxometallates" heterojunction photocatalysts: multi-scale heterojunction nanostructures are synthesized by growing Bi-based oxometallates nanocrystals on the g-C$_3$N$_4$ porous networks. The Bi-based oxometallates nanocrystals anchored to the pore network of g-C$_3$N$_4$ can effectively prevent detachment and agglomeration, thus improving the stability of the catalytic system (as shown in Fig. 28.2A). The conjugate delocalization effect and porous limiting effect of g-C$_3$N$_4$ were used to strengthen the interface contact between porous support and foreign components, and a multi-scale heterojunction photochemical catalytic material with high activity and stability was formed. Particularly, the core-shell heterostructures may be generated, where the 3-D porous network of g-C$_3$N$_4$ forms a complete coating structure for the corresponding nanoparticles, nanorods, and nanosheets of Bi-based oxometallates (as shown in Fig. 28.2B). Due to the high permeability of macroporous g-C$_3$N$_4$, sunlight can penetrate into the interface of conjugated polymer/oxometallates, ensuring high catalytic activity, and the coating structure can greatly improve the stability of the heterojunction catalyst [16].

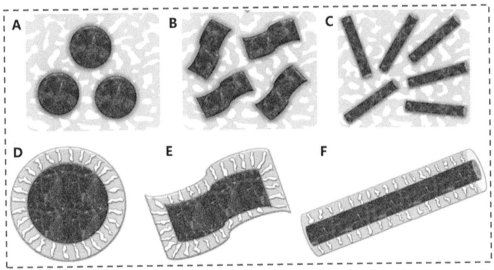

Figure 28.2 g-C$_3$N$_4$ conjugated polymer/Bi-based oxometallates" heterojunction photocatalysts: (A) multiscale heterojunction nanostructures, (B) core-shell heterojunction nanostructures [15].

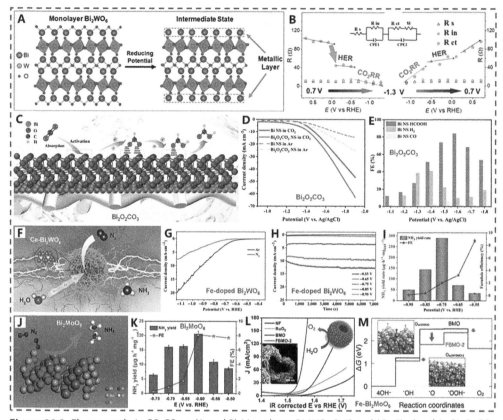

Figure 28.3 Electrocatalytic CO_2RR on (A and B) Monolayer Bi_2WO_6 [15] and (C–E) ultrathin $Bi_2O_2CO_3$ [17]; Electrocatalytic NRR on (F) Ce-doped Bi_2WO_6 [18], (G–I) Fe-doped Bi_2WO_6 [19] and (J and K) Bi_2MoO_6 [20]; Electrocatalytic OER on (L and M) Bi_2MoO_6 [21].

28.4 Application progress of nano Bi-based oxometallates

28.4.1 Energy application of nano Bi-based oxometallates

28.4.1.1 Electrocatalytic energy conversion

Electrocatalytic conversion of carbon dioxide (CO_2) into high-value fuels and chemical feedstocks is a promising solution for achieving carbon neutrality. For bismuth and its oxide CO_2RR electrocatalysts, Bi is the active site of carbon dioxide reduction, and significant surface Bi exposure is the basis of satisfying performance. Bi_2WO_6 and other Bi-based oxometallates semiconductors are commonly used in photocatalytic processes, where the position of the Fermi level, which is closely related to the morphology and structure of the semiconductor, is the determining factor. For the first time, Liu et al. reported that semiconductor monolayer Bi_2WO_6 can also be used for efficient electrocatalytic conversion of CO_2 to formic acid, with properties comparable to bismuth, which is in marked contrast to photocatalyzed or thermocatalyzed products (see Fig. 28.3A and B for details) [15]. The unprecedented "metal intermediate surface state" in Bi_2WO_6 rationalizes the unique formic acid pathway in electrocatalysis, which provides unique insights into the electrocatalytic CO_2RR for Bi-based oxometallates.

Bi-based catalysts show excellent catalytic activity for HCOOH in electrocatalytic CO_2RR. However, the Bi-based catalysts are difficult to achieve excellent activity and selectivity in a wide voltage range. The Bi-O structure in Bi_2O_3 is favorable for electrocatalytic reduction of CO_2 to HCOOH. The oxygen content and Bi-O bond coordination number of $Bi_2O_2CO_3$ are higher than those of Bi_2O_3, so the content of Bi-O structure in $Bi_2O_2CO_3$ is higher. Th $Bi_2O_2CO_3$ in rich Bi-O structure can efficiently convert CO_2 to HCOOH. An ultrathin $Bi_2O_2CO_3$ nanosheet flower-like catalyst with abundant Bi-O structure was prepared in situ on carbon paper by Wang et al., which showed excellent performance in electrocatalytic reduction of CO_2 to HCOOH (see Fig. 28.3C−E for details) [17]. In a wide voltage window (from −1.5 to −1.8 V), the Faraday efficiency (FE) of HCOOH can reach about 90%. The excellent CO_2RR performance can be attributed to its rich Bi-O structure, which is conducive to enhance the adsorption of CO_2^* and $OCHO^*$ intermediates, effectively inhibiting hydrogen evolution.

Electrochemical nitrogen reduction reaction (NRR) is a promising method for ammonia synthesis. However, electrochemical NRR processes remain a great challenge in achieving high NH_3 yields and FE due to extremely strong $N \equiv N$ bonds and competitive hydrogen evolution reactions (HER). The Bi-based or W-based catalysts have been used for electrocatalytic NRR due to their low HER activity. Recently, Yang et al. developed a simple scheme to introduce and tune crystal defects in the host lattice of Bi_2WO_6 nanoflower by adjusting the amount of Ce doping. The NH_3 yield at −0.20 V is 22.5 $\mu g\ h^{-1}\ mg^{-1}$cat., and Faradaic efficiency is as high as 15.9% for Ce-doped Bi_2WO_6. The density functional theory calculation showed that the introduction of crystal defects in Bi_2WO_6 can enhance the adsorption and activation of N_2, significantly increasing the activity of NRR (see Fig. 28.3F for details) [18].

Recently, Dong and coworkers achieved ultra-high electrocatalytic NH_3 yield on Fe-doped Bi_2WO_6 catalyst by a simple iron doping regulating strategy. The Fe-doped Bi_2WO_6 catalyst achieves an NH_3 production rate of 289 $\mu g\ h^{-1}\ mg_{cat}^{-1}$ in 0.05 M H_2SO_4 electrolyte at −0.75 V, which is far beyond the best performance of Fe-based and Bi-based electrocatalysts. In addition, the Fe-doped Bi_2WO_6 electrocatalyst also showed durable electrocatalytic stability. The excellent catalytic performance is mainly attributed to the effective inhibition of HER, the synergistic interaction between

Bi and Fe, and the acceleration of the overall electron transfer rate and catalytic NRR reaction kinetics by Fe doping. In addition, the Fe-doped Bi_2WO_6 electrocatalyst showed durable stability (see Fig. 28.3G—I for details) [19]. In addition, Dong and co-workers proved that hollow Bi_2MoO_6 spheres are an efficient NRR electrocatalyst with good selectivity. At -0.6 V, the FE and yield of the catalyst are 8.17% and 20.46 $\mu g\ h^{-1}\ mg_{cat}^{-1}$, respectively. At the same time, the hollow Bi_2MoO_6 spheres also show good electrochemical performance and structural durability (see Fig. 28.3J and K for details) [20].

It is very important to develop an efficient and stable anodic oxygen evolution reaction (OER) electrocatalyst is essential for achieving water-splitting hydrogen production applications. Iron-promoted bismuth molybdate (Fe-Bi_2MoO_6) with hollow sphere morphology can be used as an excellent electrocatalyst for the OER in alkaline media due to its special normal phase layered structure and hollow sphere morphology. The strain and dislocation in the crystal structure of Bi_2MoO_6 doped with iron were investigated. The presence of optimal amounts of iron and the resulting oxygen vacancies proved to be beneficial for OER. The best iron-promoted Bi_2MoO_6 catalyst has an overpotential value of 286 mV at 10 mA cm^{-2} current density, and the Tafel slope of OER is only 44 mV dec^{-1}. Density-functional theory calculations showed that iron incorporation can reduce the energy barrier by facilitating the adsorption of OER intermediates, most notably oxygen adsorption (see Fig. 28.3L and M for details) [21].

28.4.1.2 Electrochemical energy storage

Bismuth oxygen-containing compounds, such as Bi_2O_3, $BiMoO_6$, $BiMnO_2$, $BiFe_2O_3$, BiV_2O_5, etc., are a general electrode material for supercapacitor applications, due to their low cost, chemical stability, mechanical robustness, natural abundance, ecological environmental protection, quasi-Faradic redox reactions and the availability of a variety of structures and forms [22]. Recently, Yu et al. synthesized the flowerlike bismuth molybdate (Bi_2MoO_6) hollow microspheres via a facile hydrothermal method for high-performance supercapacitors. The material characterization suggests that this Bi_2MoO_6 possesses numerous mesopores as well as a high specific surface area. The electrochemical characterization suggests that as supercapacitor electrode material the Bi_2MoO_6 hollow microspheres demonstrate a high specific capacitance (182 F g^{-1} at current densities of 1 A g^{-1}) as well as excellent rate property (retaining 80% of the capacitance at a current density of 5 A g^{-1}) and cyclic stability [23].

28.4.2 Environmental application of nano Bi-based oxometallates

28.4.2.1 Photocatalytic oxidative degradation

In recent years, our research group (Zesheng Li and Changlin Yu) has developed several Bi-based oxometallates catalytic systems (such as $BiPO_4$, Bi_2WO_6, Bi_2MoO_6, and $Bi_2O_2CO_3$) for photocatalytic degradation of various organic pollutants (antibiotics and organic dyes), via the 3-D nanostructure, doping, vacancy, and heterojunction multi-directional design strategies (see Fig. 28.4 for details) [6,11–13,24–29]. The 3-D nanostructure design is beneficial to the utilization of sunlight, the doping structure can effectively regulate the valence band structure, the vacancy design can achieve rich active sites for adsorption, and the heterojunction structure engineering is mainly designed to promote the transfer and separation of photogenerated carriers. Based on these principles, a variety of efficient visible light Bi-based oxometallates nano-structured materials has been successfully designed and prepared by our group.

Due to $BiPO_4$ photocatalyst having a rather wide band gap (3.7 eV), the application of $BiPO_4$ was still limited to ultraviolet visible light that is less than 4% of solar irradiance at the Earth's surface. The g-C_3N_4 as one commonly available and promising photoca-talyst with visible light response possesses particular superiority for photo-degradation environment application. In 2014, we reported novel hybrid architectures of $BiPO_4$ and mesoporous g-C_3N_4 (termed as $BiPO_4$/mg-C_3N_4) as a composite photocatalyst for visible light environmental application [11]. This $BiPO_4$/mg-C_3N_4 hetero-structured photocatalysts were synthesis via the insitu growth of $BiPO_4$ nanorods (NRs) within the mesoporous g-C_3N_4. This novel composite photocatalysts of $BiPO_4$ nanorods covered with mesoporous g-C_3N_4 exhibit significantly enhanced visible-light-driven photocatalytic activity for degradation of methyl orange (MO) Dye. It is demonstrated that the enhanced photoactivity of the $BiPO_4$/mg-C_3N_4 catalyst results from the high migration efficiency of photoinduced electron-hole pairs (see Fig. 28.4A for details) [11].

Bi_2WO_6 is a typical n-type semiconductor with a relatively small band-gap energy (2.6–2.8 eV), which allows it to be excited under visible light. However, the recombi-nation rate of photoexcited carriers in the original Bi_2WO_6 is high, and the photocata-lytic activity is low. Recently, a series of novel Sm^{3+}/Bi_2WO_6 nanosheets with superior visible-light photocatalytic performances were successfully fabricated by Yu and co-workers [24]. The doping of Sm^{3+} ions into Bi_2WO_6 caused the lattice contraction of crystal, which brought about the enhancement of specific surface area and surface −OH groups. Moreover, the Sm^{3+} doping strengthened visible light absorption associ-ated with OV. The OV generated by the substitution of Bi^{3+} with Sm^{3+} acted as the positive charge centers to trap the electrons, and consequently increased the life of photo-generated charge carriers. The obtained Sm^{3+}/Bi_2WO_6 nanosheets were used to degrade different azo dyes, e.g., rhodamine B (RhB), methylene blue (MB), MO, and acid orange II (AO-II) (see Fig. 28.4B for details) [24].

The band position change caused by quantum effect will change the absorption of light and the photocatalytic oxidation ability of semiconductor with 3-D hierarchical mi-cro/nano-structures (HMNSs). For these 3-D nanostructures, the spatial motion path of charge carriers is not only conducive to the effective separation of photogenerated electron-hole pairs but also endows the 3-D nanomaterials with strong redox ability.

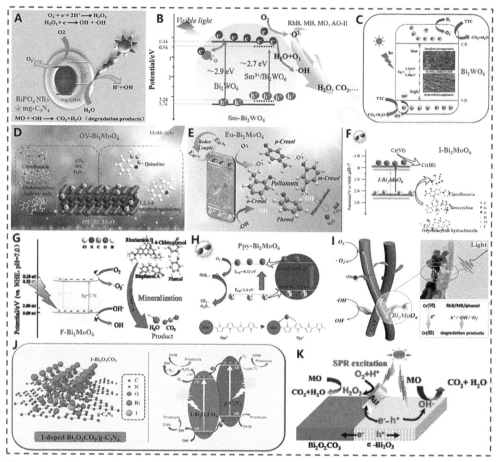

Figure 28.4 Photocatalytic degradation on different Bi-based oxometallates: (A) BiPO$_4$/mg-C$_3$N$_4$ [11]; (B) Sm^{3+}/Bi$_2$WO$_6$ [24] (C) 3-D HMNSs Bi$_2$WO$_6$ [12]) (D) OV-Bi$_2$MoO$_6$ [25]) (E) Eu-doped Bi$_2$MoO$_6$ [6]) (F) I-doped Bi$_2$MoO$_6$ [26]); (G) F-doped Bi$_2$MoO$_6$ [27]; (H) Ppy/Bi$_2$MoO$_6$ [28]; (I) CDs/Bi$_2$MoO$_6$/GNFs [29]; (J) Bi$_2$O$_2$CO$_3$/g-C$_3$N$_4$ [13]; (K) α-Bi$_2$O$_3$/Bi$_2$O$_2$CO$_3$ promoted with Au [30].

More recently, a series of Bi_2WO_6 3-D HMNSs photocatalysts with adjustable band structures are successfully prepared by Li and co-workers [12]. The band gap energies (Eg) of Bi_2WO_6-1#, 2#, 3#, 4#, and 5# were 2.54, 2.88, 2.93, 2.93, and 2.98 eV. The Eg of Bi_2WO_6-1# is smaller than theoretical value of Bi_2WO_6, which is due to the quantum effect of its small nanocrystals. With the increase of nanocrystals and oriented arrangement, the increase of E_g of Bi_2WO_6-4# and 5# may be attributed to the ensemble effect of these 3-D self-assemble structures (see Fig. 28.4C for details) [12].

Bi_2MoO_6 is a member of the Aurivillius family and has attracted considerable attention, but limited photocatalytic properties limit its potential applications. Recently, we developed Bi_2MoO_6 nanocrystals with tunable oxygen vacancy (OV) by a simple, low-cost solvothermal approach [25]. With the introduction of OV, the optical absorption of Bi_2MoO_6 expands and the band gap narrows. The OV not only led to the appearance of defect bands in the forbidden band but also lead to a slight upward shift of the maximum valence band, which promotes the migration of photogenerated holes. The OV can also act as electron acceptors, trapping photoexcited electrons, and reducing electron-hole recombination. At the same time, The OV can help to capture oxygen molecule, which reacts with photogenerated electrons to generate superoxide radical ($\cdot O_2^-$), thus significantly promoting photocatalytic performances. Therefore, the Bi_2MoO_6 containing OV (OV-Bi_2MoO_6) has good photocatalytic performance for the degradation of antibiotics (see Fig. 28.4D for details) [25].

Volatile phenolic substances are the main source of industrial environmental pollution due to their high risk and high toxicity. To remove volatile phenols, a powerful rare earth Eu^{3+}-doped Bi_2MoO_6 nanosheet photocatalyst was developed by a hydrothermal-calcination process from our group in 2021 [6]. The effect of rare earth Eu^{3+} ions doping on the physical structure and photocatalytic performance of Bi_2MoO_6 in degradation of some volatile phenols, e.g., phenol, 2-methyl phenol, 3-methyl phenol, and 4-methyl phenol were explored. With an optimum concentration of Eu^{3+}, the Eu^{3+}/Bi_2MoO_6 exhibited superior photocatalytic performance for removing four volatile phenols. The Eu^{3+} doping of Bi_2MoO_6 results in lattice distortion of Bi_2MoO_6 and grain size decrease. Doping of Eu^{3+} reduces the energy gap of Bi_2MoO_6 and increases its UV–Vis optical absorption. In addition, the doped Eu^{3+} can act as an electron trap to reduce the recombination rate of e^-/h^+ (see Fig. 28.4E for details) [6].

Doping of nonmetallic elements on Bi_2MoO_6 is another simple method to effectively enhance its photocatalytic activity. In 2020, we reported I-doped Bi_2MoO_6 microspheres with distinct performance for removing antibiotics and Cr(VI) under visible light illumination [26]. After I doping, the specific surface area of Bi_2MoO_6 was obviously increased, which contributed to the enhanced adsorption for antibiotics and Cr(VI) in water. The I^- doping resulted in that the potential of CB and VB over I-Bi_2MoO_6 is more negative than pure Bi_2MoO_6. The E (IO_3^-/I^-) = 1.085 V is much more negative than the top of the valence band of I-Bi_2MoO_6 (2.418 V), so we can expect that I^- is efficiently oxidized to IO_3^- by holes. The doped I^- in the lattice of Bi_2MoO_6 became carrier capture center, which enhanced the separation of photogenerated electron and hole pairs, promoted the utilization efficiency of carriers, and greatly improve the photocatalytic performances (see Fig. 28.4F for details) [26].

In 2017, we demonstrated that fluorinated Bi_2MoO_6 nanocrystals (F–Bi_2MoO_6) exhibited efficient photocatalytic performance for the removal of organic pollutants, e.g., bisphenol A, 4-chlorophenol phenol, and Rhodamine B dye [27]. The substitution of F^- anions for the host O_2^- anions induced the lattice shrinkage, a decrease in crystal size and an increase in crystallinity. Moreover, the oxygen vacancies in F–Bi_2MoO_6 and F^- adsorbed over the catalyst surface could withdraw the photoexcited electrons, largely boosting the separation of photoexcited electron-hole pairs. F-doping led to more positive potential of VB over F–Bi_2MoO_6, which improved the oxidation ability of holes in the valence band. F–Bi_2MoO_6 displayed a large enhancement in degradation efficiency compared with pure Bi_2MoO_6. These results provide an instructive guidance for developing nontoxic and efficient visible-light-driven Bi_2MoO_6 photocatalysts for the removal of organic pollutants in water (see Fig. 28.4G for details) [27].

The construction of Bi_2MoO_6-based heterojunction with the help of conductive materials (such as conductive polymers [28] and nano-carbon materials [29]) can effectively improve the activity and efficiency of photocatalysis. By adjusting the content of polypyrrole (Ppy), a series of Ppy/Bi_2MoO_6 microsphere photocatalysts was prepared by Yu [28]. The introduction of Ppy was beneficial to the increase of crystallinity and specific surface area of Bi_2MoO_6. The Ppy/Bi_2MoO_6 microspheres photocatalyst showed an enhanced migration rate of photo-generated carriers and improved utilization efficiency of photogenerated carriers compared with pure Bi_2MoO_6. Therefore, the Ppy/Bi_2MoO_6 microspheres photocatalyst showed excellent visible-light-driven photocatalytic performance for the degradation of high-concentrated organic dyes (RhB) and the mixed dyes of (RhB and MO) (see Fig. 28.4H for details) [28].

Novel ternary carbon quantum dots (CDs)/Bi_2MoO_6 (BMO)/graphitic carbon nanofibers (GNFs) composites (CDs/BMO/GNFs) were further prepared and studied for use as visible-light-driven photocatalysts by Yu [29]. The CDs-decorated BMO particles were anchored on the surfaces of GNFs to form heterojunctions, which showed superior photocatalytic performance for the degradation of three different organics, including Rhodamine B (RhB), methylene blue (MB) and phenol, as well as the reduction of a heavy metal ion Cr(VI). The superior photocatalytic performance was attributed to the synergistic effects between ternary components (CDs, BMO and GNFs) and heterojunctions, resulting in an efficient spatial separation of the photogenerated electrons and holes. A catalytic mechanism was proposed that the photogenerated electrons (e^-), or •OH, and O_2^- radicals contributed to the photocatalytic Cr(VI) reduction or organics oxidation, which was supported by the radical quenching experiment and electron spin resonance analysis (see Fig. 28.4I for details) [29].

As a "sillén" phase oxide, the bismutite ($Bi_2O_2CO_3$) is composed of alternating $[Bi_2O_2]^{2+}$ layers and CO_3^{2-} layers, with the plane of the $[Bi_2O_2]^{2+}$ layer orthogonal to the plane of the CO_3^{2-} group. Although $Bi_2O_2CO_3$ exhibits the high photocatalytic activity under ultraviolet light, the wide bandgap (3.0–3.5 eV) limits its visible-light harvesting, and the fast recombination rate of charge carriers greatly reduces its photocatalytic efficiency. Recently, we synthesized the I-$Bi_2O_2CO_3$/g-C_3N_4 heterojunctions consisting of g-C_3N_4 and iodine (I)-doped $Bi_2O_2CO_3$ components with much-enhanced photodegradation activity of 1,5-dihydroxynaphthalene under visible light [13]. The activity enhancement was due to the double mechanism of heterojunction construction (promoted the separation of photoinduced carriers) and iodine doping (tuned the bandgap for sufficient visible-light harvesting). This study provides a rational approach for enhancing the visible-light activity of wide-bandgap $Bi_2O_2CO_3$, and reveals a new perspective on the removal mechanism of organic pollutants (see Fig. 28.4J for details) [13].

To explore the property relationship between Bi-based semiconductor and plasmonic noble metals is important for developing highly efficient visible light-driven photocatalyst. Previously, we synthesized α-Bi_2O_3/$Bi_2O_2CO_3$ bi-phasic heterostructures. Then, plasmonic Au nanospheres or nanorods were loaded onto α-Bi_2O_3/$Bi_2O_2CO_3$ heterostructure [30]. Compared to pristine α-Bi_2O_3/$Bi_2O_2CO_3$ heterostructures, loading of Au nanospheres brought $\sim$4 times increase in activity and Au nanorods 5–11 times depending on nanorods size. The significant boosting of activity is attributed to the large enhancement of charge separation by the formation of α-Bi_2O_3/$Bi_2O_2CO_3$ interface and more production of •OH radicals by Au nanospheres or Au nanorods. The surface plasmon resonance absorption of these Au nanostructures on the α-Bi_2O_3/$Bi_2O_2CO_3$ heterostructures could also have a significant contribution to the activities due to their strong plasmonic near-fields (see Fig. 28.4K for details) [30].

28.4.2.2 Photocatalytic green production

Bismuth-based oxometallates (Bi_2WO_6, $BiVO_4$, and Others) are always considered the best visible-light photocatalysts for oxygen production from water. However, they failed to photocatalytic reduction of water to produce hydrogen, due to their lower conduction band made up of Bi 6p and O 2p (not satisfying the reduction potential of H^+ to H_2) [31]. In recent years, there have been some reports that modified bismuth-based oxometallates can achieve visible light photocatalytic hydrogen production, mainly including energy band engineering and Z-scheme system for overall water splitting. These strategies can modulate the levels of the conduction and valence bands of Bi-based oxometallates photocatalysts, meeting the potential requirements of reduction and oxidation of water at the same time. For example, the ultrathin monoclinic $BiVO_4$ nanosheets-based Z-scheme overall water splitting system under visible light has been successfully constructed by Liu and coworkers [32]. This newly Z-scheme photocatalytic system presented high

H_2 and O_2 evolution rates (16.7 and 8.0 μmol h^{-1}) with an apparent quantum yield of 1.88% (420 nm) and good photocatalytic stability.

28.5 Summary

In this chapter, we have discussed the structural features, preparation methods, energy and environmental applications, and typical case analysis of nano Bi-based oxometallates (such as $BiPO_4$, Bi_2WO_6, Bi_2MoO_6, $BiVO_4$, and $Bi_2O_2CO_3$). The Bi-based electrocatalyst has attracted wide attention due to unique geometric structures, tunable electronic structure, and decent catalytic activity for electrocatalytic energy conversion (such as CO_2RR, NRR and OER) and electrochemical energy storage (supercapacitor). Solar-driven photocatalytic technology based on Bi-based oxometallates (Bi_2WO_6, Bi_2MoO_6, $BiVO_4$, and $Bi_2O_2CO_3$) is regarded as an extremely attractive solution to environmental remediation and energy conversion under visible light radiation. Although Bi-based oxometallates can be used as independent photocatalysts or electrocatalyst for environmental purification and energy development, their efficiency is not ideal. Therefore, aiming the practical engineering applications, many efforts need to be made to enhance their photocatalytic or electrocatalytic performances in the next decade.

Acknowledgments

This book was supported by National Natural Science Foundation of China (22078071, 22272034), Natural Science Foundation of Guangdong Province (2021A1515010125, 2020A1515010344), Maoming Science and Technology Project (mmkj2020032), Guangdong Province Universities and Colleges Pearl River Scholar Funded Scheme (2019), Guangdong Basic and Applied Basic Research Foundation (2019A1515011249, 2021A1515010305), Key Research Project of Natural Science of Guangdong Provincial Department of Education (2019KZDXM010), Environment and Energy Green Catalysis Innovation Team of Colleges and Universities of Guangdong Province (2022KCXTD019), the program for Innovative Research Team of Guangdong University of Petrochemical Technology.

References

[1] N. Serpone, A.V. Emeline, Semiconductor photocatalysis: past, present, and future outlook, The Journal of Physical Chemistry Letters 3 (5) (2012) 673–677.
[2] Q. Chen, X. Cheng, H. Long, Y. Rao, A short review on recent progress of Bi/semiconductor photocatalysts: the role of Bi metal, Chinese Chemical Letters 31 (10) (2020) 2583–2590.
[3] D. Xia, H. Yu, H. Xie, P. Huang, R. Menzel, M.M. Titirici, et al., Recent progress of Bi-based electrocatalysts for electrocatalytic CO_2 reduction, Nanoscale 14 (22) (2022) 7957–7973.
[4] S. Cao, P. Zhou, J. Yu, Recent advances in visible light Bi-based photocatalysts, Chinese Journal of Catalysis 35 (7) (2014) 989–1007.
[5] L. Zhang, Y. Li, Q. Li, J. Fan, S.A.C. Carabineiro, K. Lv, Recent advances on Bismuth-based photocatalysts: strategies and mechanisms, Chemical Engineering Journal 419 (2021) 129484.
[6] X. Liu, W. Zhou, F. Li, C. Yu, Eu^{3+} doped Bi_2MoO_6 nanosheets fabricated via hydrothermal-calcination route and their superior performance for aqueous volatile phenols removal, Journal of the Taiwan Institute of Chemical Engineers 125 (2021) 276–284.

[7]   H. Liu, P. Chen, X. Yuan, Y. Zhang, H. Huang, F. Dong, Pivotal roles of artificial oxygen vacancies in enhancing photocatalytic activity and selectivity on $Bi_2O_2CO_3$ nanosheets, Chinese Journal of Catalysis 40 (5) (2019) 620−630.

[8]   C. Liu, S. Mao, M. Shi, X. Hong, D. Wang, F. Wang, et al., Enhanced photocatalytic degradation performance of $BiVO_4/BiOBr$ through combining Fermi level alteration and oxygen defect engineering, Chemical Engineering Journal 449 (2022) 137757.

[9]   L. Hao, H. Huang, Y. Zhang, T. Ma, Oxygen vacant semiconductor photocatalysts, Advanced Functional Materials 31 (25) (2021) 2100919.

[10] K. Yang, X. Li, C. Yu, D. Zeng, F. Chen, K. Zhang, et al., Review on heterophase/homophase junctions for efficient photocatalysis: the case of phase transition construction, Chinese Journal of Catalysis 40 (6) (2019) 796−818.

[11] Z. Li, S. Yang, J. Zhou, D. Li, X. Zhou, C. Ge, et al., Novel mesoporous $g-C_3N_4$ and $BiPO_4$ nanorods hybrid architectures and their enhanced visible-light-driven photocatalytic performances, Chemical Engineering Journal 241 (2014) 344−351.

[12] Z. Li, B. Li, S. Peng, D. Li, S. Yang, Y. Fang, Novel visible light-induced $g-C_3N_4$ quantum dot/$BiPO_4$ nanocrystal composite photocatalysts for efficient degradation of methyl orange, RSC Advances 4 (66) (2014) 35144−35148.

[13] Y. Lan, Z. Li, W. Xie, D. Li, G. Yan, S. Guo, et al., In situ fabrication of I-doped $Bi_2O_2CO_3/g-C_3N_4$ heterojunctions for enhanced photodegradation activity under visible light, Journal of Hazardous Materials 385 (2020) 121622.

[14] Z. Li, M. Luo, B. Li, Q. Lin, X. Liao, H. Yu, et al., 3-D hierarchical micro/nano-structures of porous Bi_2WO_6: controlled hydrothermal synthesis and enhanced photocatalytic performances, Microporous and Mesoporous Materials 313 (2021) 110830.

[15] S. Liu, C. Wang, J. Wu, B. Tian, Y. Sun, Y. Lv, et al., Efficient CO_2 electroreduction with a monolayer Bi_2WO_6 through a metallic intermediate surface state, ACS Catalysis 11 (20) (2021) 12476−12484.

[16] https://kd.nsfc.gov.cn/finalDetails?id=72dcc9c17e503110252599460bdf4d42.

[17] Y. Wang, B. Wang, W. Jiang, Z. Liu, J. Zhang, L. Gao, et al., Sub-2 nm ultra-thin $Bi_2O_2CO_3$ nanosheets with abundant Bi-O structures toward formic acid electrosynthesis over a wide potential window, Nano Research 15 (4) (2022) 2919−2927.

[18] X. Yang, Y. Ma, Y. Liu, K. Wang, Y. Wang, M. Liu, et al., Defect-induced Ce-doped Bi_2WO_6 for efficient electrocatalytic N_2 reduction, ACS Applied Materials & Interfaces 13 (17) (2021) 19864−19872.

[19] Y. Liu, L. Huang, Y. Fang, X. Zhu, S. Dong, Achieving ultrahigh electrocatalytic NH_3 yield rate on Fe-doped Bi_2WO_6 electrocatalyst, Nano Research 14 (8) (2021) 2711−2716.

[20] Z. Xing, W. Kong, T. Wu, H. Xie, T. Wang, Y. Luo, et al., Hollow Bi_2MoO_6 sphere effectively catalyzes the ambient electroreduction of N_2 to NH_3, ACS Sustainable Chemistry & Engineering 7 (15) (2019) 12692−12696.

[21] S. Khatun, K. Shimizu, S. Singha, R. Saha, S. Watanabe, P. Roy, Defect enriched hierarchical iron promoted Bi_2MoO_6 hollow spheres as efficient electrocatalyst for water oxidation, Chemical Engineering Journal 426 (2021) 131884.

[22] N.M. Shinde, P.V. Shinde, R.S. Mane, K.H. Kim, Solution-method processed Bi-type nanoelectrode materials for supercapacitor applications: a review, Renewable and Sustainable Energy Reviews 135 (2021) 110084.

[23] T. Yu, Z. Li, S. Chen, Y. Ding, W. Chen, X. Liu, et al., Facile synthesis of flowerlike Bi_2MoO_6 hollow microspheres for high-performance supercapacitors, ACS Sustainable Chemistry & Engineering 6 (6) (2018) 7355−7361.

[24] Z. Liu, X. Liu, L. Wei, C. Yu, J. Yi, H. Ji, Regulate the crystal and optoelectronic properties of Bi_2WO_6 nanosheet crystals by Sm^{3+} doping for superior visible-light-driven photocatalytic performance, Applied Surface Science 508 (2020) 145309.

[25] Z. Liu, J. Tian, C. Yu, Q. Fan, X. Liu, Solvothermal fabrication of Bi_2MoO_6 nanocrystals with tunable oxygen vacancies and excellent photocatalytic oxidation performance in quinoline production and antibiotics degradation, Chinese Journal of Catalysis 43 (2) (2022) 472−484.

[26] Z. Liu, X. Liu, C. Yu, L. Wei, H. Ji, Fabrication and characterization of I doped Bi_2MoO_6 micro-spheres with distinct performance for removing antibiotics and Cr (VI) under visible light illumination, Separation and Purification Technology 247 (2020) 116951.

[27] C. Yu, Z. Wu, R. Liu, D.D. Dionysiou, K. Yang, C. Wang, et al., Novel fluorinated Bi_2MoO_6 nano-crystals for efficient photocatalytic removal of water organic pollutants under different light source illumination, Applied Catalysis B: Environmental 209 (2017) 1−11.

[28] H. Sun, Z. Liu, X. Liu, C. Yu, L. Wei, Preparation and characterization of Ppy/Bi_2MoO_6 micro-spheres with highly photocatalytic performance for removal of high-concentrated organic dyes, Materials Today Sustainability 19 (2022) 100154.

[29] W. Huang, S. Wang, Q. Zhou, X. Liu, X. Chen, K. Yang, et al., Constructing novel ternary com-posites of carbon quantum dots/Bi_2MoO_6/graphitic nanofibers with tunable band structure and boosted photocatalytic activity, Separation and Purification Technology 217 (2019) 195−205.

[30] C. Yu, W. Zhou, L. Zhu, G. Li, K. Yang, R. Jin, Integrating plasmonic Au nanorods with dendritic like α-Bi_2O_3/$Bi_2O_2CO_3$ heterostructures for superior visible-light-driven photocatalysis, Applied Catalysis B: Environmental 184 (2016) 1−11.

[31] W. Fang, W. Shangguan, A review on bismuth-based composite oxides for photocatalytic hydrogen generation, International Journal of Hydrogen Energy 44 (2) (2019) 895−912.

[32] C. Dong, S. Lu, S. Yao, R. Ge, Z. Wang, Z. Wang, et al., Colloidal synthesis of ultrathin monoclinic $BiVO_4$ nanosheets for Z-scheme overall water splitting under visible light, ACS Catalysis 8 (9) (2018) 8649−8658.

CHAPTER 29

Nano Ag-based heterojunctions: recent progress in energy and environmental fields

29.1 Introduction

Photocatalysis, as green and environmentally friendly technology, has attracted much attention in pollutant degradation due to its efficient degradation rate. In the last 2 decades, many studies found that most of the Ag-based semiconductors (e.g., Ag_2S, AgX (Cl, Br, I), Ag_2O, $AgVO_3$, Ag_2CrO_4, Ag_2CO_3, and Ag_3PO_4) could exhibit strong visible light absorption and obvious visible light catalytic activity due to their narrow band gap energy [1]. Most Ag-based semiconductors could exhibit high initial photocatalytic activity, while they easily suffer from poor stability because of photochemical corrosion. Design heterojunction, increasing specific surface area, controlling crystal facets, and producing plasmonic effects were effective strategies to improve the photocatalytic performance of Ag-based photocatalysts. In one of our previous reviews, the design of typical Ag-based heterojunction photocatalysts (including simple Ag-based heterojunctions, Ag-based solid solution heterojunctions, carbon materials–coupled Ag-based semiconductors, etc.) and their applications in decomposing the typical organic pollutants have been summarized and analyzed [2]. Moreover, combining the superior conductive properties of carbon materials (e.g., carbon quantum dots, carbon nano-tube, carbon nanofibers, graphene) and metal or metallic compound materials, some Ag-based semiconductors (such as Ag_2S and Ag_2O) could produce excellent electrochemical catalytic performances for energy production and conversion. The rational design of heterojunction structures, composite nanostructures, and vacancy defects can further improve the catalytic activity of the Ag-based semiconductor materials. In this chapter, the structural features and preparation strategies of Ag-based heterojunction nanocatalysts, and their electrocatalysis and photocatalysis applications in energy and environmental fields are especially summarized.

29.2 Structural features of nano-Ag-based semiconductors

Nowadays, there are different kinds of reported Ag-based semiconductors, e.g., simple Ag-based compounds (Ag_2O, Ag_2S, AgX(Cl, Br, I)), complex compounds (Ag_2CO_3, Ag_3PO_4), Ag-based solid solution ($AgVO_3$, Ag_2CrO_4, $AgAlO_2$), etc. The band gap energy (Eg), the potentials of the conduction band (CB), and valence band (VB) of some

Nanostructured Materials
ISBN 978-0-443-19256-2, https://doi.org/10.1016/B978-0-443-19256-2.00022-3

Table 29.1 Band structures of Ag-based semiconductors.

Compounds	E_g(eV)	E_{VB} (eV)	E_{CB} (eV)
Ag_2O	1.20	1.40	0.20
Ag_2S	0.92	0.92	0
Ag_2CO_3	2.30	2.67	0.37
Ag_3PO_4	2.36−2.42	2.87($E_g = 2.42$)	0.45
$AgVO_3$	2.15	2.41	0.26
Ag_2CrO_4	1.80	2.27	0.47
$AgCl$	2.07	2.61	0.54
$AgBr$	2.60	2.60	0
AgI	2.80	2.38	−0.42

typical Ag-based semiconductors are listed in Table 29.1 [2−4]. Generally, all these Ag-based semiconductors are responsive to the visible light irradiation due to their small band gap energy (<3.0 eV). Even less band gap energies (<2.2 eV) were observed over AgCl (∼2.07 eV), Ag_2O (∼1.20 eV), Ag_2S (∼0.92 eV), $AgVO_3$ (∼2.15 eV), and Ag_2CrO_4 (∼1.80 eV). It should be noted that the photocatalytic performances of Ag-based semiconductors are affected not only by its band gap, but also by their composition, crystal structure, morphology, etc. Particularly, due to their strong visible light absorption, great efforts have been devoted to the design, preparation, characterization, and application of Ag-based heterojunction photocatalysts (such as Ag-based semiconductors and conjugated polymer g-C_3N_4 Z-scheme heterojunction).

29.3 Preparation methods of Ag-based heterojunctions

The presence of the phase junction is an effective way to promote photocatalytic activity by increasing the separation efficiency of the electron-hole pairs. Accordingly, extensive research has been conducted on the design of Ag-based heterojunction photocatalysts to improve their charge transfer properties and efficiencies. Numerous techniques have been developed to establish Ag-based heterojunction photocatalysts using facile, low-cost, and energy-efficient methods, such as hydrothermal/solvothermal methods, electrochemical deposition, chemical bath deposition, sol-gel processes, and chemical precipitation. The photocatalytic properties of the Ag-based heterojunction interface determine the resistance of electron transfer. The ohmic contact can change the path of electron transfer by optimizing the preparation or treatment conditions. The in-situ phase transformation (such as chemical solution–phase transitions and calcination-induced phase transitions) is facile, low-cost, and energy-efficient technique to structure low-resistance Ag-based heterojunction (such as Ag_2O−Ag_2CO_3 heterojunction) with a close interface and high catalytic performance [5].

29.4 Application progress of nano Ag-based heterojunctions

29.4.1 Energy application of nano Ag-based heterojunctions

29.4.1.1 Electrocatalytic energy conversion

Heterogeneous interface design can effectively optimize the electronic structure at the interface of material and further regulate the adsorption behavior of substrate. In addition, the heterogeneous structure can provide a large number of active sites, which play a unique advantage in many electrocatalytic energy conversion reactions, such as electrocatalytic water splitting to produce hydrogen. Xu et al. developed a nonequivalent cation exchange strategy to fabricate a layered porous Ag/Ag_2S heterostructure hollow network, based on the CoS hollow polyhedron derived from metal-organic framework (MOF) (see Fig. 29.1A—C for details) [6]. The chemical valence mismatch between Co^+/Co^{3+} and Ag^+ changes the original coordination mode of Co node and reassembles the coordination bond heterostructure of Ag/Ag_2S. Due to coordination loss and in-situ epitaxial growth of metallic Ag, the Ag/Ag_2S heterostructure has abundant S vacancies and lattice strains. The rich defects and intrinsic stresses of Ag-based heterostructure can effectively optimize its electronic structure and the adsorption energy of hydrogen, so as to achieve efficient electrocatalytic hydrogen production.

Of all the metals, silver (Ag) has the highest conductivity (6.30×10^7 S m^{-1} at 20°C), and it should be a good choice for increasing the conductivity and intrinsic activity of oxide-based electrocatalysts. Tuysuz et al. have significantly improved the performance of oxygen evolution reaction (OER) of mesoporous Co_3O_4 electrocatalysts through the coupling of silver species (forming Co_3O_4/Ag_2O—Ag heterostructures) (see Fig. 29.1D—F for details) [7]. Silver exists in the form of metal Ag particles and well-dispersed Ag_2O clusters within the mesostructured of Co_3O_4. For electrocatalytic OER, the benefits of this synergy are twofold: the highly conductive metal Ag improves the charge transfer capacity of the electrocatalyst, while the ultra-small Ag_2O cluster provides the absorption of Fe impurities as active centers from KOH electrolyte and increases the catalytic efficiency of the Co-Ag oxide heterostructure.

The AgP_2 is a promising electrocatalytic material for CO_2 reduction reaction (CO_2RR). Li et al. prepared monodisperse AgP_2 nanocrystals by colloidal synthesis and used them for high CO_2RR electrocatalysis (see Fig. 29.1G—H for details) [8]. Compared with Ag catalyst, the overpotential of CO produced by CO_2RR catalyzed by AgP_2 nanocrystals is reduced by 0.3 V, and the maximum Faradaic efficiency is 82%, and the ratio of $CO:H_2$ can be adjusted in the range of 1:3—5:1. The calculation proved the key role of alloying P in the low overpotential and high tunable syngas ratio of AgP_2: the $\Delta G H^*$ values of three P active sites on high exponential surface AgP_2 (211) were −0.360, −0.436 and −0.486 eV, respectively. The strong adsorption of H^* on P will not only inhibit the HER reaction rate but also the adsorbed H^* may be transferred to the adsorbed carbon on silver to promote hydrogenation reaction.

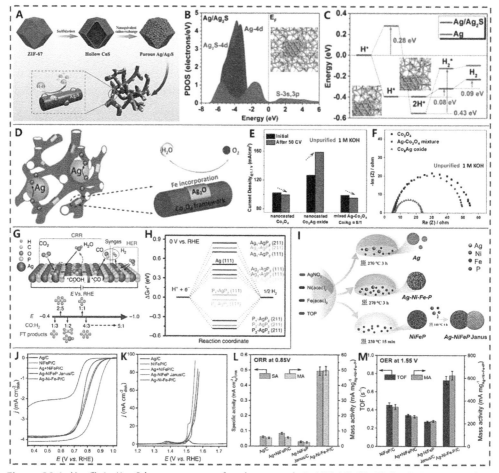

Figure 29.1 (A–C) Ag/Ag$_2$S heterostructure for electrocatalytic HER [6]; (D–F) Co$_3$O$_4$/Ag$_2$O–Ag heterostructure for electrocatalytic OER [7]; (G–H) monodisperse AgP$_2$ nanocrystals for electrocatalytic CO$_2$RR [8]; (I–M) Ag–Ni–Fe–P nanoparticles for electrocatalytic ORR and OER [9].

Multimetallic phosphide nanoparticles offer the possibility of integrating multiple catalytic functions of different elements into a single nanoparticle. Xu et al. successfully obtained Ag-based multimetallic phosphide nanoparticles through solution phase chemistry, demonstrating excellent catalytic activity of bifunctional oxygen reduction and evolution reaction (ORR and OER) (see Fig. 29.1I–M for details) [9].

The ORR activity of the obtained Ag—Ni—Fe—P nanoparticle was comparable to that of commercial Pt/C, and the OER activity was superior to that of commercial IrO$_2$. The enhanced ORR activity was attributed to enriched double Ag—Ni, Fe sites, while the specific OER activity resulted from the Ag-facilitated electron tuning effect of oxidized Ni—Fe—P. The Zn-air battery based on Ag—Ni—Fe—P/C heterostructure has high performance and good recyclability. These results indicate that multi-metallic phosphide nanoparticles have a promising application in multifunctional electrocatalysis.

29.4.1.2 Electrochemical energy storage

Silver zinc (Ag—Zn) battery is a promising power supply for portable devices due to its high energy density, stable output voltage, and environmental friendliness. At present, the controllable fabrication of Ag nanostructures (such as nanowires) and heterogeneous structures (such as carbon cloth-Ag nanowires) are the main means to design high-performance Ag—Zn batteries [10]. Ag-based materials with high conductivity, excellent lipophilicity, and excellent mechanical stability have also attracted extensive attention as additives for lithium metal batteries. The introduction of Ag-based nanostructures on lithium anode can inhibit the dendrite growth and stabilize the solid electrolyte interface, which can greatly improve the safety and stability of lithium metal battery [11]. In conclusion, silver-based nanomaterials and their composites are promising functional materials for electrochemical energy storage.

29.4.2 Environmental application of nano-Ag-based heterojunctions
29.4.2.1 Photocatalytic oxidative degradation

In the last decade, our research group has been devoted to the design of Ag-based materials and heterojunction materials for photocatalytic pollutant degradation applications. The main Ag-based materials include AgCl, AgBr, Ag$_2$O, AgVO$_3$, Ag$_2$CO$_3$, Ag$_2$CrO$_4$, and Ag$_3$PO$_4$, as well as their heterojunction materials with carbon nitride g-C$_3$N$_4$ [12—17]. Due to the favorable band structure of Ag-based semiconductor nanocrystals and the efficient charge transfer of polymer g—C$_3$N$_4$—based heterojunction, the visible light performances of these heterojunction materials for the reduction of heavy metal ion (such as Cr(VI)) and oxidation degradation of organic pollutants (including antibiotics and organic dyes) has been greatly improved.

Recently, we designed a novel g—C$_3$N$_4$—Ag/AgCl nanoparticle heterojunction (g-C$_3$N$_4$/DE-Ag/AgCl) photocatalyst supported by microdisk-like diatomite (DE) for efficient visible light Cr(VI) reduction applications (see Fig. 29.2A for details) [12]. The g-C$_3$N$_4$/DE provides a large number of supporting sites for uniformly dispersed Ag/AgCl NPs, which effectively inhibits Ag/AgCl NPs agglomeration. The introduction of Ag/AgCl NPs can enhance the visible light response due to the surface plasmon resonance (SPR) effect of Ag. The complex interface of g-C$_3$N$_4$/DE and Ag/AgCl can accelerate the transfer and separation of photoelectrons. Previously, we also designed a

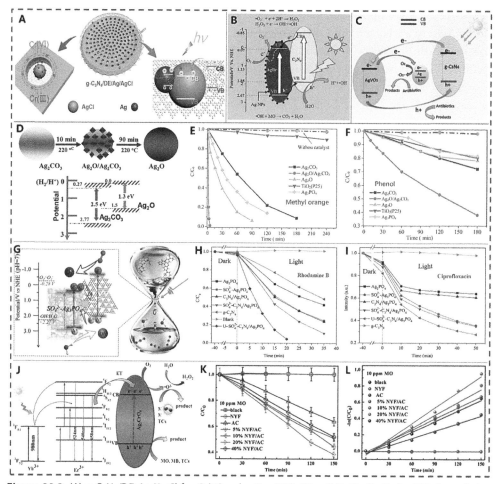

Figure 29.2 (A) g-C₃N₄/DE-Ag/AgCl for Cr(VI) reduction [12]; (B) g-C₃N₄/Ag/AgBr for MO degradation [13]; (C) Ag—AgVO₃/g-C₃N₄ for antibiotics degradation [14]; (D—F) Ag₂O/Ag₂CO₃ for MO and phenol degradation [15]; (G—I) SO₄²⁻ doped Ag₃PO₄/g-C₃N₄ for Rh B and ciprofloxacin degradation [16]; (J—L) NaYF₄:Yb³⁺, Er³⁺/Ag₂CrO₄ for MO degradation [17].

mesoporous g—C₃N₄—supported Ag/AgBr NPs with excellent visible-light-driven photocatalytic activity for degradation of Methyl Orange (MO) (see Fig. 29.2B for details) [13]. The reasonable SPR effect, band gap matching, and interfacial charge transfer guarantee the high performance of these g-C₃N₄/Ag/AgX heterojunction materials.

The preparation of $Ag-AgVO_3/g-C_3N_4$ heterojunction composite photocatalyst and the degradation characteristics of antibiotics under visible light were further reported by our group in 2019 (see Fig. 29.2C for details) [14]. Under the irradiation of visible light, both $g-C_3N_4$ and $AgVO_3$ excitation generate photo-generated electron-hole pairs, the conduction band (CB) level of $g-C_3N_4$ is -1.2 eV and the CB level of $AgVO_3$ is 0.26 eV. Obviously, the CB level of $g-C_3N_4$ is lower, so the photo-generated electrons excited by $g-C_3N_4$ will to the CB of $AgVO_3$. Since Ag has excellent electrical conductivity and large electronic storage capacity, excessive photo-generated electrons in the CB of $AgVO_3$ will be transferred to the Ag, avoiding the reduction of $AgVO_3$ and ensuring the stability of the catalyst. And the VB of $AgVO_3$ will produce photo-generated holes which are then transferred to the VB of $g-C_3N_4$. The oxygen radical $\cdot O_2{}^-$, which will form hydroxyl radical $\cdot OH$, coupled with the holes (h^+) can decompose the antibiotics into corresponding degradation products.

The Ag-based heterojunction photocatalytic materials can also be designed as one Ag-based semiconductor coupled with another Ag-based semiconductor. The following is a typical example of Ag_2O/Ag_2CO_3 heterojunction photocatalyst (see Fig. 29.2D for details) that is fabricated by a facile calcination phase transformation route [2,15]. In the process of calcination, the Ag_2CO_3 surface first breaks down into Ag_2O and the generated Ag_2O coat over the surface of Ag_2CO_3, producing core@shell-like $Ag_2CO_3@Ag_2O$ heterojunction. The band gap energies of Ag_2CO_3 and Ag_2O were 2.5 and 1.3 eV, respectively; the potentials of Ag_2CO_3 VB and CB were 2.77 and 0.27 eV, respectively; the potentials of Ag_2O VB and CB were 1.5 and 0.2 eV. The formation of well-defined heterojunction between Ag_2O and Ag_2CO_3 can effectively facilitate the charge transfer between them and suppresses the recombination of photogenerated electrons and holes, resulting in extremely high photocatalytic activity and stability in degradation of methyl orange and phenol (see Fig. 29.2E and F) [15].

Among numerous visible-light-driven materials, Ag_3PO_4 received considerable attention for high photo-oxidative capabilities. However, Ag_3PO_4 encounters poor stability because of photo corrosion, which largely limits its application. To resolve the photo corrosion, one effect method is the construction of the heterojunction which could effectively enhance the separation of photogenerated electron-hole pairs and improve the photocatalytic activity and stability. Inspired by previous investigations, we utilized ultrasonic assistant method to prepare the $SO_4{}^{2-}$ doped $Ag_3PO_4/g-C_3N_4$ composite heterojunction. The CB of $SO_4{}^{2-}$ doped Ag_3PO_4 composite was shifted to lower energy regions, which resulted in high oxidizability. The close contact heterojunction interface can improve the separation efficiency of photoinduced e^-/h^+, which gives rise to more OH^- and $\cdot O_2{}^-$ radicals to participate in the photocatalytic reaction. Therefore, the $SO_4{}^{2-}$ doped $Ag_3PO_4/g-C_3N_4$ shows excellent photocatalytic performances for the degradation Rhodamine B and ciprofloxacin (see Fig. 29.2G–I for details) [16].

Due to its small band gap energy (~ 1.80 eV), Ag_2CrO_4 has become a promising visible-light-responsive photocatalyst. Its stronger absorption for visible light region can contribute to excellent photocatalytic activity. However, various defects, such as self-photocorrosion and rapid recombination of photogenerated carries, inhibit its widespread practical application. More recently, we reported a new-style $NaYF_4$: Yb^{3+}, Er^{3+}/Ag_2CrO_4 (NYF/AC) heterojunction photocatalyst, which exhibited excellent photocatalytic performances than single Ag_2CrO_4 for the H_2O_2 production and disposals of pollutants, such as methyl orange (MO), methylene blue (MB), rhodamine B (RhB), and tetracycline (TCs) (see Fig. 29.2J—L for details) [17]. The $NaYF_4$: Yb^{3+}, Er^{3+} can convert near-infrared (NIR) light to visible light via upconversion process, while the heterojunction interface can endow with efficient charge transfer and separation. So, the degradation rates on MO over 20% NYF/AC could be enhanced 6.5 times and 1.7 times compared with bare AC under NIR light and visible light irradiation, respectively.

29.4.2.2 Photocatalytic green production

The construction of Ag-based heterostructures for photocatalytic applications is one of the most promising means to solve these environmental and energy problems. Ag-based material has good visible light absorption, quantum efficiency, excellent electrical conductivity, and photo-electrochemical activity. The structure and photocatalytic properties of Ag-based heterojunctions (including semiconductor heterojunctions, Schottky heterojunctions, and Z-type heterojunctions) with fast charge separation routes and strong photostability have attracted interest in photocatalytic energy conversion for practical applications (e.g., photochemical water splitting, CO_2 conversion, and N_2 fixation) [18]. For example, the Ag_2S/Ag/Ag_3VO_4 ternary heterojunction system displayed a higher photocatalytic H_2 evolution activity than that of pure Ag_3VO_4, Ag_2S, and their binary composites under visible light irradiation, due to the improved visible light absorption and effective charge separation [19]. The high-efficiency photocatalytic heterojunctions containing plasma Ag are particularly suitable for the carbon dioxide reduction to methane (CH_4), methanol (CH_3OH), and other chemicals, due to the SPR promotion mechanism of Ag (improved charge separation and light responsiveness) [20].

29.5 Summary

In this chapter, we have discussed the structural features, preparation methods, energy and environmental applications, and typical case analysis of nano Ag-based heterojunctions (such as heterojunctions of Ag_2S, AgX (Cl, Br, I), Ag_2O, $AgVO_3$, Ag_2CrO_4, Ag_2CO_3, and Ag_3PO_4). It is very vital in expanding light absorption range of Ag-based heterostructures (such as type-II heterojunctions and Z-scheme heterojunctions). Band-gap engineering is also important for Ag-based photocatalytic heterostructures, in both green productions of energy (such as water splitting, CO_2 conversion, and N_2 fixation) and environmental photocatalytic applications (including reduction and degradation). Some Ag-based heterojunction or nanostructure (Ag_2S, Ag_2O, and Ag-based phosphides) materials are also widely used in electrocatalytic energy conversion and electrochemical energy storage. In conclusion, Ag-based heterojunction nanomaterials have a wide range of applications in energy and environmental fields, including photocatalysis and electrocatalysis energy conversion and energy storage.

Acknowledgments

This book was supported by National Natural Science Foundation of China (22078071, 22272034), Natural Science Foundation of Guangdong Province (2021A1515010125, 2020A1515010344), Maoming Science and Technology Project (mmkj2020032), Guangdong Province Universities and Colleges Pearl River Scholar Funded Scheme (2019), Guangdong Basic and Applied Basic Research Foundation (2019A1515011249, 2021A1515010305), Key Research Project of Natural Science of Guangdong Provincial Department of Education (2019KZDXM010), Environment and Energy Green Catalysis Innovation Team of Colleges and Universities of Guangdong Province (2022KCXTD019), the program for Innovative Research Team of Guangdong University of Petrochemical Technology.

References

[1] G. Li, Y. Wang, L. Mao, Recent progress in highly efficient Ag-based visible-light photocatalysts, RSC Advances 4 (96) (2014) 53649−53661.

[2] J. Li, W. Fang, C. Yu, W. Zhou, Y. Xie, Ag-based semiconductor photocatalysts in environmental purification, Applied Surface Science 358 (2015) 46−56.

[3] Z. Liu, Y. Liu, X. Sun, H. Ji, W. Liu, Z. Cai, Construction of Z-scheme Ag/AgVO$_3$/carbon-rich g-C$_3$N$_4$ heterojunction for enhanced photocatalytic degradation of sulfamethiadiazole: DFT calculation and mechanism study, Chemical Engineering Journal 433 (2022) 133604.

[4] D. Xu, B. Cheng, W. Wang, C. Jiang, J. Yu, Ag$_2$CrO$_4$/g-C$_3$N$_4$/graphene oxide ternary nanocomposite Z-scheme photocatalyst with enhanced CO$_2$ reduction activity, Applied Catalysis B: Environmental 231 (2018) 368−380.

[5] K. Yang, X. Li, C. Yu, D. Zeng, F. Chen, K. Zhang, H. Ji, Review on heterophase/homophase junctions for efficient photocatalysis: the case of phase transition construction, Chinese Journal of Catalysis 40 (6) (2019) 796−818.

[6] H. Xu, X. Niu, Z. Liu, M. Sun, Z. Liu, Z. Tian, C.H. Yan, Highly controllable hierarchically porous Ag/Ag$_2$S heterostructure by cation exchange for efficient hydrogen evolution, Small 17 (44) (2021) 2103064.

[7] M. Yu, G.H. Moon, R.G. Castillo, S. DeBeer, C. Weidenthaler, H. Tüysüz, Dual role of silver moieties coupled with ordered mesoporous cobalt oxide towards electrocatalytic oxygen evolution reaction, Angewandte Chemie 132 (38) (2020) 16687−16695.

[8] H. Li, P. Wen, D.S. Itanze, Z.D. Hood, X. Ma, M. Kim, S.M. Geyer, Colloidal silver diphosphide (AgP$_2$) nanocrystals as low overpotential catalysts for CO$_2$ reduction to tunable syngas, Nature Communications 10 (1) (2019) 1−10.

[9] Z. Xu, X. Zhang, X. Wang, J. Fang, Y. Zhang, X. Liu, Z. Zhuang, Synthesis of Ag−Ni−Fe−P multi-elemental nanoparticles as bifunctional oxygen reduction/evolution reaction electrocatalysts, ACS Nano 15 (4) (2021) 7131−7138.

[10] C. Li, Q. Zhang, J. Sun, T. Li, S. E, Z. Zhu, Y. Yao, High-performance quasi-solid-state flexible aqueous rechargeable Ag−Zn battery based on metal−organic framework-derived Ag nanowires, ACS Energy Letters 3 (11) (2018) 2761−2768.

[11] Z. Liu, S. Ha, Y. Liu, F. Wang, F. Tao, B. Xu, H. Li, Application of Ag-based materials in high-performance lithium metal anode: a review, Journal of Materials Science and Technology 133 (2023) 165−182.

[12] H. He, J. Li, C. Yu, Z. Luo, Surface decoration of microdisk-like g-C_3N_4/diatomite with Ag/AgCl nanoparticles for application in Cr (VI) reduction, Sustainable Materials and Technologies 22 (2019) e00127.

[13] S. Yang, W. Zhou, C. Ge, X. Liu, Y. Fang, Z. Li, Mesoporous polymeric semiconductor materials of graphitic-C_3N_4: general and efficient synthesis and their integration with synergistic AgBr NPs for enhanced photocatalytic performances, RSC Advances 3 (16) (2013) 5631−5638.

[14] D. Chen, B. Li, Q. Pu, X. Chen, G. Wen, Z. Li, Preparation of Ag-$AgVO_3$/g-C_3N_4 composite photo-catalyst and degradation characteristics of antibiotics, Journal of Hazardous Materials 373 (2019) 303−312.

[15] C. Yu, G. Li, S. Kumar, K. Yang, R. Jin, Phase transformation synthesis of novel Ag_2O/Ag_2CO_3 heterostructures with high visible light efficiency in photocatalytic degradation of pollutants, Advanced Materials 26 (6) (2014) 892−898.

[16] Z. Liu, J. Tian, C. Yu, Q. Fan, X. Liu, K. Yang, H. Ji, Ultrasonic fabrication of SO_4^{2-} doped g-C_3N_4/Ag_3PO_4 composite applied for effective removal of dyestuffs and antibiotics, Materials Chemistry and Physics 240 (2020) 122206.

[17] K. Zhang, M. Zhou, C. Yu, K. Yang, X. Li, S. Yang, W. Huang, Enhanced visible−NIR-driven photocatalytic activities over $NaYF_4$: Yb^{3+}, Er^{3+}/Ag_2CrO_4 composite, Journal of Materials Science 55 (24) (2020) 10435−10452.

[18] G. Li, C. Yang, Q. He, J. Liu, Ag-based photocatalytic heterostructures: construction and photocatalytic energy conversion application, Journal of Environmental Chemical Engineering (2022) 107374.

[19] J.Y. Do, R.K. Chava, Y.I. Kim, D.W. Cho, M. Kang, Fabrication of Ag based ternary nanocomposite system for visible-light photocatalytic hydrogen evolution reaction, Applied Surface Science 494 (2019) 886−894.

[20] G.V. Belessiotis, A.G. Kontos, Plasmonic silver (Ag)-based photocatalysts for H_2 production and CO_2 conversion: review, analysis and perspectives, Renewable Energy 195 (2022) 497−515.

CHAPTER 30

Nanolayered double hydroxides: recent progress in energy and environmental fields

30.1 Introduction

Layered double hydroxides (LDHs) are a class of two-dimensional metal hydroxides (layered anionic compound) composed of two metal (M^{3+}/M^{2+}) elements. The structure of the main lamina and the anions between the lamina overlaps with each other is similar to that of the brucite (lamina is octahedral MO_6 with common edges, and metal ions occupy the center of the octahedron). Due to its low price, simple synthesis method, composition (type and proportion of metal ions on the lamina, type of anion between the lamina, etc.) easy to adjust, structure (layer number, layer spacing, etc.) easy to cut, and easy to combine with other materials to achieve functional advantages, etc., LDHs have shown promising application prospects in electrochemical energy conversion and energy storage such as electrocatalysis, supercapacitors, and secondary batteries [1]. The electronic structure of the active metal can be effectively adjusted by adjusting the ratio of M^{3+}/M^{2+}, which is characterized by the adjustable cation ratio of layered bimetallic hydroxides. By regulating the types of metal ions in LDHs laminates, the band absorption migration to visible light and even infrared light can be effectively regulated after metal-metal charge transfer. Therefore, at present, LDHs have shown superior tunability in photocatalytic water splitting, reduction of CO_2, and photocatalytic degradation [2]. Due to abundant defects and a large number of coordination unsaturated sites, monolayer LDHs are an ideal material platform to explore the correlation between atomic environment, electronic structure, and intrinsic catalytic properties. However, monolayer LDHs dispersed in solution usually aggregates or reaccumulates easily, requiring highly polar solvents or excessive surfactants to ensure stable dispersion of monolayer LDHs materials, which will inevitably block the surface-active sites for different catalytic reactions [3].

30.2 Structural features of nanolayered double hydroxides

LDHs are a class of 2-D anionic compounds, which consist of a main layer of positively charged $M(OH)_6$ octahedron and interlayers of anionic layers to stabilize the layered structure and form a sandwich layered structure (see Fig. 30.1A for details) [4]. The general formula of LDHs is $[M^{2+}_{1-x}M^{3+}_x(OH)_2]^{z+}A^{n-}_{z/n}\cdot mH_2O$, where M^{2+} and M^{3+} are

Nanostructured Materials
ISBN 978-0-443-19256-2, https://doi.org/10.1016/B978-0-443-19256-2.00025-9

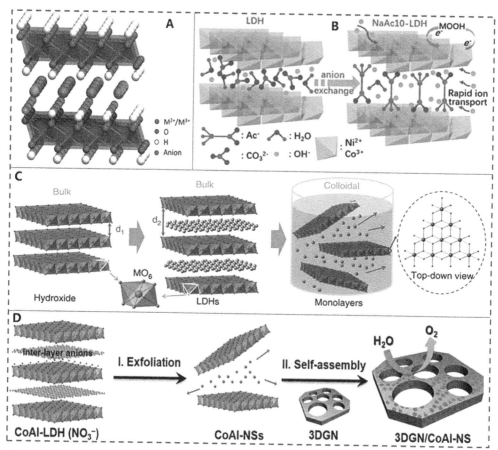

Figure 30.1 Typical crystal structure of LDHs [4], anion exchange process of LDHs [5], building the monolayer structure of LDHs [6], constructing carbon matrix composite of LDHs [7].

divalent (e.g., Mg^{2+}, Zn^{2+}, Ni^{2+}, Co^{2+}) and trivalent (e.g., Al^{3+}, Ga^{3+}, Fe^{3+}, Mn^{3+}) metal cations, respectively. $z = M^{3+}/(M^{2+}+M^{3+})$ represents the surface valence of LDHs determined by the ratio of two metal cations. A^{n-} is the interlayer exchangeable anion (such as CO_3^{2-}, NO_3^-, Cl^-, SO_4^{2-} and RCO^{2-}), which can compensate the positive charge on LDHs layer and maintain charge balance of LDHs. The interlayer distance of LDHs can be controlled by exchanging different anions, and then the physico-chemical properties can be controlled. For example, the interlayer distance of LDHs nanosheets can be expanded from 0.8 to 0.94 nm by exchanging CO_3^{2-} with acetate Ac^- (see Fig. 30.1B for details) [5]. The increasing interlayer distance is beneficial to accelerate the electron transport and solution penetration in reactions. When the concentration of Ac^- is much higher than the concentration of CO_3^{2-}, high concentration of Ac^- can replace the CO_3^{2-} in the LDHs interlayer. It is helpful to synthesize functional nanomaterials with excellent physicochemical properties by integrating unique layered structure and interlayer anion exchange characteristics of LDHs. Due to the flexible and adjustable structure of LDHs, such as the number of layers, variable metal types, variable interlayer distance and interlayer anions, as well as the arrangement of specific metals in LDHs layers, LDHs-based nanomaterials have great prospects in adsorption, catalysis, energy storage, and other applications.

LDHs are composed of positively charged (M^{2+}, M^{3+}) $(OH)_6$ octahedral main lamellae and negatively charged anions and water molecules interlayer, and their active sites mainly exist in the active metal ions on the lamellae. However, when LDHs is used as a catalyst, its biggest deficiency lies in the stacked layered structure, which makes its active site cannot be fully utilized. And the low electrical conductivity of LDHs is not conducive to the electron transfer between catalyst and reactant (or product). So, during the design of LDHs catalyst, the overall performances of the catalyst can be improved from three aspects: (1) Changing the metal ion species and proportion of LDHs to regulate the electronic structure of active sites; (2) Building the monolayer structure to improve material utilization and surface activity (see Fig. 30.1C for details) [6]; (3) Constructing carbon matrix composites to improve the electrical conductivity and electrochemical performances (see Fig. 30.1D for details) [7].

30.3 Preparation methods of nanolayered double hydroxides

The preparation methods of LDHs often include coprecipitation, hydrothermal synthesis, electrochemical deposition, and monolayer stripping [8]. (1) Coprecipitation method: according to the pH conditions required by the coprecipitation of the metal used, the pH value of the solution is finally maintained at the value of the metal coprecipitation by adjusting the pH range of the solution during the preparation process. (2) Hydrothermal synthesis method: it is the mixed solution to be reacted in the reactor device, the reactor is heated to high temperature and high pressure under the condition of reaction, this method is simple and easy to operate. (3) Electrochemical deposition method: when the anion in the metal ion salt solution is reduced at the cathode, OH− will be generated at the cathode, so that the metal ions will coprecipitate at the cathode. In general, the timing current method is used to control the voltage and the time of electrolysis to obtain the target product. (4) Stripping method: to prepare monolayer or ultrathin LDHs nanosheets, stripping method is an effective method to destroy the anions between the layers. Stripping method has wet stripping method and stripping peel method. By creating an ideal interlayer environment, the wet stripping method enables large interlayer ions to enter the interlayer, and then adds solvents or dispersants to promote LDHs stratification with a large number of solvents or dispersants. The dry stripping method is to destroy the ionic and hydrogen bonds of LDHs through Ar plasma corrosion, destroy normal charge balance and positive charge separation between main layers, and finally achieve the monolayer LDHs.

30.4 Application progress of nanolayered double hydroxides

30.4.1 Energy application of nanolayered double hydroxides

30.4.1.1 Electrocatalytic water splitting

In recent years, LDHs have been widely used as oxygen evolution reaction (OER) and hydrogen evolution reaction (HER) electrocatalysts in water splitting, due to their high catalytic activity and stability in the alkaline solution [9]. Han et al. used one-step electrodeposition method to prepare graphene oxide (GO)/NiFe-LDHs, which had good electronic interaction and excellent catalytic performance (at 10 and 100 mA cm^{-2}, the overpotential of HER and OER were 119, 210 mV and 285, 303 mV, respectively) [10]. At the same time, only 1.48 V voltage is required to drive entire water splitting at 10 mA cm^{-2}, which is lower than most advanced electrocatalysts. Shen et al. also prepared reduced graphene oxide (rGO) by electrochemical reduction method as an intermediate layer between nickel foam (NF) substrate and NiCo-LDHs for the OER application [11]. The NF/rGO/NiCo-LDHs composite exhibited remarkable OER catalytic performance, with an overpotential of only 60 mV at 10 mA cm^{-2}, much lower than that of the electrocatalyst without an rGO intermediate layer (78 mV).

NiCo-LDHs are one of the most effective OER electrocatalysts, while it is still necessary to improve the lower conductivity and limited active sites of LDHs. Recently, we designed and prepared novel flower-like 3D hetero-electrocatalysts of NiCo-LDHs nanosheets incorporated with silver (Ag) nanoclusters on a Ni foam (labeled as Ag@ NiCo-LDH/NF) by a one-pot hydrothermal method (see Fig. 30.2A and B for details) [12]. We also conducted experimental and theoretical investigations to demonstrate the excellent electrocatalytic performances of the Ag@NiCo-LDH/NF hetero-electrocatalysts for OERs and the underlying mechanism (see Fig. 30.2C—H for details). The electrocatalysts show a low overpotential of 262 mV at 10 mA cm^{-2}, and even exhibit low overpotentials of 300 mV at 50 mA cm^{-2} and 324 mV at 100 mA cm^{-2}, and a small Tafel slope of 41 mV dec^{-1} as well as excellent durability for 80 h for OER in 1.0 M KOH. The excellent performances are attributed to the synergistic effects between Ag nanoclusters and LDHs (improving the electrical conductivity by Ag doping and modulating intrinsic properties by oxygen vacancy designing).

30.4.1.2 Electrocatalytic oxygen reduction

LDHs also show excellent catalytic performance and attractive prospects in oxygen reduction reaction (ORR) for fuel cell and metal air cell applications. Zhan et al. prepared NiFe

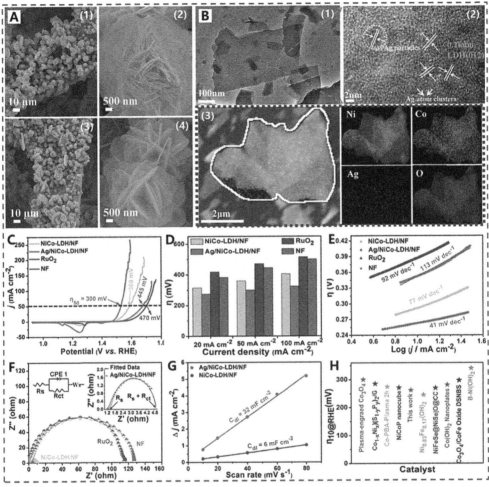

Figure 30.2 Hydrothermal preparation and OER performances of Ag@NiCo-LDH/NF [12]: (A) SEM images; (B) TEM images; (C—H) OER performances.

LDHs/nitrogen-doped reduced graphene oxide (NiFe-LDHs/NrGO) mesoporous nanospheres by a one-pot solvothermal reaction for ORR application [13]. The composite material has the potential to be a new type of nonnoble metal bifunctional catalyst because of its excellent performance. The ORR activity of NiFe-LDHs/NrGO was better than that of NiFe-LDHs and NiFe-LDHs/rGO. The ORR results show that the

NiFe/LDHs/NrGO hybrid system has perfect 4e mechanism and has better durability and methanol resistance than the 20% Pt/C catalyst with 0.1 mol L^{-1} KOH. Su and coworkers reported NiRu-LDHs nanosheets decorated with Ag nanoparticles for ORR application, which interestingly induce their multivacancies associated with catalytic site activity and populations [14]. The superb ORR performance of Ag NP/NiRu-LDHs can be ascribed to the multivacancies' mutual benefits of synergistic effect between metal LDHs and Ag nanoparticles, and increased accessible active sites.

More recently, we reported novel 3-D active carbon nanosheets (AGC)/MnCo-LDHs nanoflowers (AGC/MnCo-LDHs) nanocomposite as high-performance electrode material for ORR application (see Fig. 30.3 for details) [15]. In order to solve the problems of poor conductivity and agglomeration of LDHs materials, a two-step synthesis method was used in this study to build 3-D nanocomposites. Firstly, AGC were synthesized by using ion exchange resin as carbon source, nickel acetate as precursor of graphitization catalyst and potassium hydroxide as activator. Then, MnCo-LDHs rose-like 3-D nanosheets were loaded on to AGC by solvothermal synthesis from cobalt nitrate and manganese acetate. The AGC/MnCo-LDHs nanocomposites showed superior electrochemical performances for ORR (with a higher on-set potential of 0.765 V and better stability) than single AGC and MnCo-LDHs. The favorable 3-D porous architecture (fast ion diffusion) of MnCo-LDHs and carrier effect of AGC (high electron conductivity) were the key contributing factors for the excellent performances.

30.4.1.3 Electrochemical energy storage

LDHs are considered as a promising electrode material for supercapacitors due to their controllable composition, designable function, and high theoretical capacity. Qi et al. used nickel-copper—coated industrial polyester conductive fiber (PCF) as a flexible flow collector, coated graphene oxide (GO) on the surface of the PCF and then electrodeposited NiCo-LDHs on the GO. The PCF/GO/NiCo-LDHs electrode showed excellent electrochemical performance, the capacitance reached 1220.5 F g^{-1} at 1 A g^{-1}, and maintained 84.1% after 5000 cycles at 8 A g^{-1} [16]. Xuan et al. prepared a hybrid structure of MnCo-LDHs with reduced graphene oxide (MnCo-LDHs/rGO) and $NiCo_2S_4$ (NCS) by a two-step process. The resulted composite showed excellent specific capacitance (1446.5 C g^{-1} at 1 A g^{-1}) and excellent cycle life (98% capacitance maintained after 5000 cycles at 10 A g^{-1}). An energy density of 55.8 Wh kg^{-1} was obtained for the supercapacitor assembled with composite materials and activated carbon electrodes at 856.2 W kg^{-1} [17]. Increasing interlayer distance is an important strategy to improve the capacitance performance of LDHs by large size anion intercalation. After H_2BDC intercalation, the layer spacing of CoNi-LDHs can be greatly increased, which has the advantage of large specific surface area of materials, so it is very conducive to obtain outstanding specific capacitance and ratio performance.

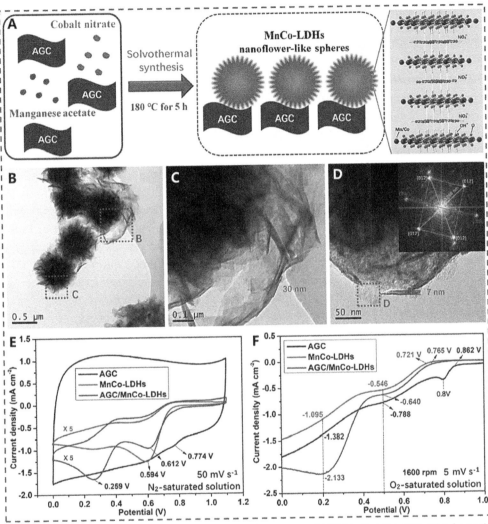

Figure 30.3 Solvothermal preparation and ORR performances of AGC/MnCo-LDHs [15]: (A) Schematic diagram; (B–D) TEM images; (E and F) ORR performances.

The sample with the largest layer spacing can exhibit an excellent specific capacitance of up to 229 mAh g^{-1} at 1 A g^{-1} current density [18].

30.4.2 Environmental application of nanolayered double hydroxides
30.4.2.1 Adsorbing purification

Heavy metal wastewater treatment is still an important worldwide problem. Compared with other water treatment methods, adsorption has the advantages of low cost, easy operation, simple design and so on. Traditional adsorbents, such as molecular sieve, activated carbon for heavy metal ion adsorption demonstrate low selectivity and poor affinity. Sulfide can be used as adsorbent design because of its strong coordination bond with heavy metals. The polysulfide anion $[S_x]^{2-}$ intercalated into LDHs has a good affinity for heavy metal ions. However, $[S_x]^{2-}$ is easily oxidized to sulfate ions [19]. Recently, Professor Shulan Ma et al. from Beijing Normal University prepared a new type of LDHs adsorbent. Different from conventional hydrotalcite, the prepared LDHs anion is MoS_4^{2-}. Researchers used MoS_4^{2-} anion to replace the NO_3^- anion of MgAl-LDHs to obtain MgAl-MoS_4^{2-}-LDHs, which has excellent adsorption performance for heavy metal cations and oxic acid anions. For different concentrations of heavy metal ions, the removal effect can reach the discharge standard, which provides a new path for adsorbent design (see Fig. 30.4A and B for details) [20]. According to the above work, Zhuqi Chen research group in Huazhong University of Science and Technology has also done related research on the adsorption of heavy metal ions by Mn-MoS_4^{2-}-LDHs [25] and Fe-MoS_4^{2-}-LDHs [26], respectively. More interestingly, LDH layers offer protective space for intercalated MoS_4^{2-} anions against oxidation under ambient environments, and facilitate Mn-MoS_4 or Fe-MoS_4 with the advantage of easy storage and application over other adsorbents. These features provide Mn-MoS_4 or Fe-MoS_4 with enormous adsorption capacity, good reusability, and excellent selectivity even in the presence of huge concentration of heavy metal ions.

According to Lewis acid-base theory, sulfide as a soft base has a high affinity with soft acid heavy metal ions. $Mo_3S_{13}^{2-}$ is a molybdenum sulfide composed of various types of sulfur atoms located at the edge. However, the $(NH_4)_2Mo_3S_{13}$ crystal has a low solubility in water and its adsorption site cannot be effectively exposed, which weakens its trapping ability. Recently, Shulan Ma et al. inserted the $Mo_3S_{13}^{2-}$ anion into MgAl LDHs to obtain Mo_3S_{13}-LDHs and demonstrated its superadsorption capacity for heavy metal ions (see Fig. 30.4C for details) [21]. The as-prepared Mo_3S_{13}-LDHs have high adsorption capacity and selectivity for Ag^+ ($q_mAg = 1073$ mg g^{-1}) and Hg^{2+} ($q_mHg = 594$ mg g^{-1}). Most importantly, the Mo_3S_{13}-LDHs can capture Ag^+ in two ways: (a) using its sulfide complexation property to precipitate Ag^+ to generate Ag_2S and (b) using the reduction of S_2^{2-} and Mo^{4-} in $Mo_3S_{13}^{2-}$ to reduce Ag^+ to banded silver (Ag^0). Therefore, the Mo_3S_{13}-LDHs are a promising material for silver extraction from copper rich minerals and the capture of highly toxic Hg^{2+} from polluted water.

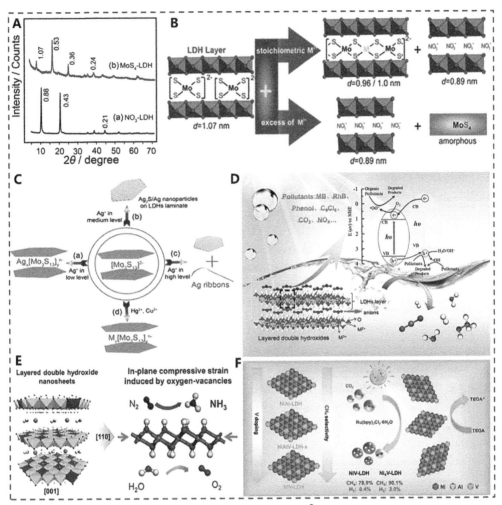

Figure 30.4 (A and B) Adsorbing purification by MgAl-MoS$_4$$^{2-}$-LDHs adsorbent [20], (C) adsorbing purification by Mo$_3$S$_{13}$-LDHs adsorbent [21], (D) Photocatalytic degradation of organic pollutants by LDHs [22], (E) CuCr-LDHs for photocatalytic NRR [23], (F) V-doped NiAl-LDHs for photocatalytic CO$_2$RR [24].

30.4.2.2 Photocatalytic degradation

LDHs and their heterojunctions are promising photocatalysts which have been widely used in the photodegradation of various organic pollutants. Recently Zhang et al. reviewed the recent progress of LDHs-based materials for photodegradation of organic pollutants driven by visible light, focusing on the control of their morphology, composition, and electronic properties, as well as the mechanistic understanding of photocatalytic processes (see Fig. 30.4D for details) [22]. LDHs photocatalysts can be divided into five categories: LDHs-derived metal oxides, supported LDHs, intercalated LDHs, modified LDHs, and LDHs with unique structures (such as core-shell LDHs). Target organic pollutants can be divided into four categories: azo dyes, phenols, persistent organic pollutants and other types of organic pollutants. The main factors of degradation performances of LDHs-based photocatalysts include interface characteristics of LDHs-based heterojunction and adsorption effect organic molecules. For example, Jo et al. fabricated a novel ternary heterojunction of $CoAl-LDHs/g-C_3N_4/rGO$, which showed outstanding photocatalytic performances for the degradation of Congo red and tetracycline pollutants [27]. The significant improvement of photocatalytic performance and good stability of the triplet heterojunction are mainly due to the huge close contact interface created by the special 2D/2D/2D arrangement between the components $CoAl-LDHs$, $g-C_3N_4$, and rGO, which accelerates the interfacial charge transfer process under visible light irradiation.

30.4.2.3 Photocatalytic green production

LDHs-based photocatalysts or heterojunction are also used for photocatalytic green production, such hydrogen production from water, ammonia synthesis from nitrogen, and preparation of chemicals from CO_2. For example, Ramireddy et al. prepared a strongly coupled triplet heterojunction photocatalyst by introducing reduced graphene oxide (rGO) and NiFe layered double hydroxides (NiFe-LDHs) on the surface of lanthanum titanate (LTO) [28]. Even without Pt cocatalyst, the synthesized rGO/LTO/NiFe-LDHs composite photocatalyst has obvious photocatalytic hydrogen evolution activity under simulated light. The enhanced photocatalytic activity was attributed to the effective charge transfer at the rGO/LTO heterojunction interface and the enhanced hole trapping ability of the NiFe-LDHs cocatalyst at the LTO/NiFe-LDHs interface, respectively. These interface properties can effectively prolong the lifetime of photogenerated electron-hole pairs and improve the electron density for visible light driven photocatalytic hydrogen production.

The industry of reducing nitrogen (N_2) from the air to synthetic ammonia plays an important role in the national economy. Tierui Zhang's group successfully prepared a series of $M^{II}M^{III}-LDH$ (M^{II} = Mg, Zn, Ni, Cu; M^{III} = Al, Cr) nanosheet photocatalyst for ammonia synthesis from N_2 and water under visible light (see Fig. 30.4E for details) [23]. Due to the oxygen-rich defects, obvious structural distortion and compression strain, the adsorption of N_2 molecules on catalyst and the transfer efficiency of visible-light-generated electron from LDHs photocatalyst to N_2 are enhanced, which promotes the efficient synthesis of NH_3 (especially the CuCr-LDHs nanosheet can still achieve 0.10% quantum yield at 500 nm). This work shows that the reduction in N_2 to NH_3 based on LDHs is an extremely promising new approach under normal temperature and pressure, visible light, or direct solar radiation.

Photocatalytic CO_2 reduction to convert CO_2 into high-value fuel is an effective way to reduce greenhouse gas emissions and alleviate the energy crisis. Recently, Yufei Song et al. based on density functional theory calculation found that the electronic structure of Ni-based LDHs and the adsorption behavior of CO_2RR intermediates on its surface could be greatly optimized by V incorporation (see Fig. 30.4F for details) [24]. Therefore, the researchers introduced V into NiAl-LDHs and synthesized a series of monolayers of LDHs with different V/Al ratios. The results of CO_2RR experiment show that V incorporation has a significant effect on the performance: under visible light irradiation, with the increase in V content, the CH_4 selectivity was also significantly improved, while H_2 production was significantly decreased (V-doped NiAl-LDHs showed a high CH_4 selectivity of 78.9% and C-containing product selectivity of 99.6%, while H_2 release was inhibited to only 0.4%). Overall, this work provides an effective strategy to develop LDHs-based photocatalysts with high CH_4 selectivity and electron-hole pair separation efficiency by multivalent transition metal modulation.

30.5 Summary

In this chapter, we have discussed the structural features, preparation methods, energy and environmental applications, and typical case analysis of nanolayered double hydroxides (LDHs) (such as NiFe, NiCo, MnCo, NiAl, CoAl, MgAl, and CuCr LDHs). Among many 2D materials, LDHs, as a kind of intercalated structure materials, exhibit unique advantages in the fields of energy storage and catalysis due to their highly adjustable types and proportions of laminar metal elements and interlaminar anions. The LDHs still have some shortcomings such as low electrical conductivity and poor structural stability. In order to solve these problems, more active sites can be effectively exposed by adjusting the local nano structure (such as stripping and anion exchange), adding defect and heteroatom doping, so as to improve the electrical conductivity or photogenerated electron transport efficiency of LDHs-based catalysts and promote their intrinsic activity and structural stability for electrocatalysis or photocatalysis. The LDHs have also become an attractive option for the removal of heavy metal ions from water due to their good hydrophilicity and high anion exchange capacity.

Acknowledgments

This book was supported by National Natural Science Foundation of China (22078071, 22272034), Natural Science Foundation of Guangdong Province (2021A1515010125, 2020A1515010344), Maoming Science and Technology Project (mmkj2020032), Guangdong Province Universities and Colleges Pearl River Scholar Funded Scheme (2019), Guangdong Basic and Applied Basic Research Foundation (2019A1515011249, 2021A1515010305), Key Research Project of Natural Science of Guangdong Provincial Department of Education (2019KZDXM010), Environment and Energy Green Catalysis Innovation Team of Colleges and Universities of Guangdong Province (2022KCXTD019), the program for Innovative Research Team of Guangdong University of Petrochemical Technology.

References

[1]   C. Tan, X. Cao, X.J. Wu, Q. He, J. Yang, X. Zhang, et al., Recent advances in ultrathin two-dimensional nanomaterials, Chemical Reviews 117 (9) (2017) 6225–6331.

[2]   X. Bian, S. Zhang, Y. Zhao, R. Shi, T. Zhang, Layered double hydroxide-based photocatalytic materials toward renewable solar fuels production, InfoMat 3 (7) (2021) 719–738.

[3]   J. Kang, X. Qiu, Q. Hu, J. Zhong, X. Gao, R. Huang, et al., Valence oscillation and dynamic active sites in monolayer NiCo hydroxides for water oxidation, Nature Catalysis 4 (12) (2021) 1050–1058.

[4]   J. Yu, B.R. Martin, A. Clearfield, Z. Luo, L. Sun, One-step direct synthesis of layered double hydroxide single-layer nanosheets, Nanoscale 7 (21) (2015) 9448–9451.

[5]   Q. Pan, F. Zheng, D. Deng, B. Chen, Y. Wang, Interlayer spacing regulation of NiCo-LDH nanosheets with ultrahigh specific capacity for battery-type supercapacitors, ACS Applied Materials & Interfaces 13 (47) (2021) 56692–56703.

[6]   F. Song, X. Hu, Exfoliation of layered double hydroxides for enhanced oxygen evolution catalysis, Nature Communications 5 (1) (2014) 1–9.

[7]   J. Ping, Y. Wang, Q. Lu, B. Chen, J. Chen, Y. Huang, et al., Self-assembly of single-layer CoAl-layered double hydroxide nanosheets on 3D graphene network used as highly efficient electrocatalyst for oxygen evolution reaction, Advanced Materials 28 (35) (2016) 7640–7645.

[8]   Q. Ma, Preparation and Performance of High-Performance Nickel-Cobalt Layered Double Hydroxide Nanoarray Oxygen Evolution Catalyst, Master's Thesis, Guangxi University, 2020.

[9]   S. Anantharaj, K. Karthick, S. Kundu, Evolution of layered double hydroxides (LDH) as high performance water oxidation electrocatalysts: a review with insights on structure, activity and mechanism, Materials Today Energy 6 (2017) 1–26.

[10] X. Han, N. Suo, C. Chen, Z. Lin, Z. Dou, X. He, et al., Graphene oxide guiding the constructing of nickel-iron layered double hydroxides arrays as a desirable bifunctional electrocatalyst for HER and OER, International Journal of Hydrogen Energy 44 (57) (2019) 29876–29888.

[11] Y. Shen, K. Dastafkan, Q. Sun, L. Wang, Y. Ma, Z. Wang, et al., Improved electrochemical performance of nickel-cobalt hydroxides by electrodeposition of interlayered reduced graphene oxide, International Journal of Hydrogen Energy 44 (7) (2019) 3658–3667.

[12] B. Chu, Q. Ma, Z. Li, B. Li, F. Huang, Q. Pang, et al., Design and preparation of three-dimensional hetero-electrocatalysts of NiCo-layered double hydroxide nanosheets incorporated with silver nanoclusters for enhanced oxygen evolution reactions, Nanoscale 13 (25) (2021) 11150–11160.

[13] T. Zhan, X. Liu, S. Lu, W. Hou, Nitrogen doped NiFe layered double hydroxide/reduced graphene oxide mesoporous nanosphere as an effective bifunctional electrocatalyst for oxygen reduction and evolution reactions, Applied Catalysis B: Environmental 205 (2017) 551–558.

[14] S.A. Chala, M.C. Tsai, W.N. Su, K.B. Ibrahim, A.D. Duma, M.H. Yeh, et al., Site activity and population engineering of NiRu-layered double hydroxide nanosheets decorated with silver nanoparticles for oxygen evolution and reduction reactions, ACS Catalysis 9 (1) (2018) 117–129.

[15] Z. Li, K. Xiao, C. Yu, H. Wang, Q. Li, Three-dimensional graphene-like carbon nanosheets coupled with MnCo-layered double hydroxides nanoflowers as efficient bifunctional oxygen electrocatalyst, International Journal of Hydrogen Energy 46 (69) (2021) 34239–34251.

[16] J. Qi, Y. Chen, Q. Li, Y. Sui, Y. He, Q. Meng, et al., Hierarchical NiCo layered double hydroxide on reduced graphene oxide-coated commercial conductive textile for flexible high-performance asymmetric supercapacitors, Journal of Power Sources 445 (2020) 227342.

[17] H. Xuan, Y. Guan, X. Han, X. Liang, Z. Xie, P. Han, et al., Hierarchical MnCo-LDH/rGO@NiCo$_2$S$_4$ heterostructures on Ni foam with enhanced electrochemical properties for battery-supercapacitors, Electrochimica Acta 335 (2020) 135691.

[18] C. Cao, F. Liang, W. Zhang, H. Liu, H. Liu, H. Zhang, et al., Commercialization-driven electrodes design for lithium batteries: basic guidance, opportunities, and perspectives, Small 17 (43) (2021) 2102233.

[19] S. Ma, L. Huang, L. Ma, Y. Shim, S.M. Islam, P. Wang, et al., Efficient uranium capture by polysulfide/layered double hydroxide composites, Journal of the American Chemical Society 137 (10) (2015) 3670−3677.

[20] L. Ma, Q. Wang, S.M. Islam, Y. Liu, S. Ma, M.G. Kanatzidis, Highly selective and efficient removal of heavy metals by layered double hydroxide intercalated with the MoS$_4{}^{2-}$ ion, Journal of the American Chemical Society 138 (8) (2016) 2858−2866.

[21] L. Yang, L. Xie, M. Chu, H. Wang, M. Yuan, Z. Yu, et al., Mo$_3$S$_{13}{}^{2-}$ intercalated layered double hydroxide: highly selective removal of heavy metals and simultaneous reduction of Ag$^+$ ions to metallic Ag^0 ribbons, Angewandte Chemie 134 (1) (2022) e202112511.

[22] G. Zhang, X. Zhang, Y. Meng, G. Pan, Z. Ni, S. Xia, Layered double hydroxides-based photocatalysts and visible-light driven photodegradation of organic pollutants: a review, Chemical Engineering Journal 392 (2020) 123684.

[23] Y. Zhao, Y. Zhao, G.I. Waterhouse, L. Zheng, X. Cao, F. Teng, et al., Layered-double-hydroxide nanosheets as efficient visible-light-driven photocatalysts for dinitrogen fixation, Advanced Materials 29 (42) (2017) 1703828.

[24] S. Yu, L. Tan, S. Bai, C. Ning, G. Liu, H. Wang, et al., Rational regulation of electronic structure in layered double hydroxide via vanadium incorporation to trigger highly selective CO$_2$ photoreduction to CH$_4$, Small 18 (2022) e2202334.

[25] J. Ali, H. Wang, J. Ifthikar, A. Khan, T. Wang, K. Zhan, et al., Efficient, stable and selective adsorption of heavy metals by thio-functionalized layered double hydroxide in diverse types of water, Chemical Engineering Journal 332 (2018) 387−397.

[26] A. Jawad, Z. Liao, Z. Zhou, A. Khan, T. Wang, J. Ifthikar, et al., Fe-MoS4: an effective and stable LDH-based adsorbent for selective removal of heavy metals, ACS Applied Materials & Interfaces 9 (34) (2017) 28451−28463.

[27] W.K. Jo, S. Tonda, Novel CoAl-LDH/g-C$_3$N$_4$/RGO ternary heterojunction with notable 2D/2D/2D configuration for highly efficient visible-light-induced photocatalytic elimination of dye and antibiotic pollutants, Journal of Hazardous Materials 368 (2019) 778−787.

[28] R. Boppella, C.H. Choi, J. Moon, D.H. Kim, Spatial charge separation on strongly coupled 2D-hybrid of rGO/La$_2$Ti$_2$O$_7$/NiFe-LDH heterostructures for highly efficient noble metal free photocatalytic hydrogen generation, Applied Catalysis B: Environmental 239 (2018) 178−186.

CHAPTER 31

Nano-noble metal catalysts: recent progress in energy and environmental fields

31.1 Introduction

Noble metals include gold (Au), silver (Ag), platinum (Pt), palladium (Pd), ruthenium (Ru), rhodium (Rh), osmium (Os), and iridium (Ir), which are important components of nonferrous metals. Nanomaterials refer to materials at the nanometer level on the one-dimensional or multidimensional scale, such as nanoparticles, nanowires, nano-sheets, and nano-frames. Noble metal nanomaterials refer to the use of nanotechnology to develop and produce noble metal products, resulting in the new materials containing noble metals in size of below 100 nm (or even in 1—5 nm nanophase) [1]. Noble metal nanomaterials, including noble metal elemental materials, noble metal compound materials, noble metal film materials, and other major types. Among them, noble metal elemental materials and compound materials, which can be divided into loaded type and non-loaded type, are the most industrial applications of noble metal nanomaterials. Nano-precious metal catalysts are widely used in industry, covering electronics, chemical, energy, metallurgy, environment, and other industries. Noble metal nanostructured materials (most commonly Pt and Pd nanostructures) can be used as efficient nanostructured electrocatalysts, which are widely used to catalyze various electrochemical reactions, such as oxygen reduction reaction (ORR), oxygen evolution reaction, hydrogen evolution reaction, alcohol oxidation reaction (AOR), formic acid oxidation reaction (FAOR), and carbon dioxide reduction reaction (CO_2RR) (see Chapter 13) [2]. Noble metal nanocrystals can also be used as co-catalytic components of photocatalytic reactions to promote photogenerated electron transfer and charge separation and ultimately improve the efficiency of photocatalysis. Noble metal nanomaterials also have a broad application basis and prospects in thermal catalytic energy conversion and environmental protection fields.

31.2 Structural features of nano-noble metal catalysts

The controlled synthesis of noble metal nanocrystals with specific shapes can not only change their original physical and chemical properties but also broaden their applications in many fields. The activity of noble metal catalysts depends to a large extent on the interaction of surface atoms with the intermediates involved in the rate-determining step. The strength of the interaction can be optimized by adjusting the surface atomic and electronic

Nanostructured Materials
ISBN 978-0-443-19256-2, https://doi.org/10.1016/B978-0-443-19256-2.00027-2

structure of the catalyst. The electronic structure of noble metal surface is ultimately determined by its atomic geometric shape. Geometric control is expected to improve the application potential of catalytic system. In addition, nanocrystals in the same crystal plane can still exhibit different catalytic activities due to the effects of twin defects and surface strain. The size of nanocrystalline can also affect the surface structure of noble metal, for example, by influencing the content of atoms located at the vertex and edge to regulate the coordination number of surface atoms (see Section 3.2.3). From the above, it can be seen that the surface structure of noble metal catalysts is closely related to the catalytic activity. The surface structure of noble metal catalysts is determined by many factors, including shape, crystal plane, size, defect, and crystal structures [3].

31.3 Preparation methods of nano-noble metal catalysts

It is very important to understand the growth process of nanocrystals for the synthesis of specific shape noble metal catalysts. The preparation of nanocrystals in general can be divided into physical method and chemical method. The main steps of crystal growth during liquid-phase chemical synthesis include atom formation (from precursor to atom), uniform nucleation, and growth (controlled by thermodynamics and kinetics). As capping agents play a crucial role in controlling the shape of noble metal nanocrystals, they are widely used in nanocrystals synthesis. Thermodynamically speaking, the role of capping agents is to selectively stabilize specific crystalline surfaces of nanocrystals by changing the surface free energy. Kinetically, chemisorbed capping agents on the crystal surface can act as physical barriers to hinder the deposition of atoms on the crystal surface, thus affecting the synthesis of nanocrystals [3]. For Pt-based and Pd-based nanostructures, the 1-D nanowires and 3-D nanoframes are the two kinds of popular noble metal nanostructures, which are widely used in the fields of electrocatalytic energy conversion and even environmental catalysis (see Fig. 31.1 for details) [4–8].

A number of efforts have focused on novel Pt nanowires with high surface area and high catalytic activity. However, the majority of these novel Pt nanowires are obtained using either hard templates such as anodic aluminum oxide or soft templates such as organic surfactants. Sun and Dodelet reported on the template-free synthesis of Pt nanowires at room temperature via the reduction of hexachloroplatinic acid (H_2PtCl_6) by formic acid (HCOOH) [9]. Recently, Meng et al. reported a detailed investigation of the template-free synthesis of Pt nanowires via the chemical reduction of Pt salt precursors with formic acid (see Fig. 31.1A for details) [4]. The results indicate that both the oxidation state of Pt in the salt and the pH value of the aqueous solution comprising the platinum salt and formic acid are critical factors for the formation of Pt nanowires. Nanowires are obtained from platinum atoms in a + IV oxidation state, with ligating chloride anions (H_2PtCl_6 and K_2PtCl_6) or non-ligating chloride anions ($PtCl_4$). Increasing the pH of the reaction solution led to a reduction in the length of Pt nanowires. Adjusting the pH value in range 2–3 led to the formation of loose web-like nanowires with a smaller diameter.

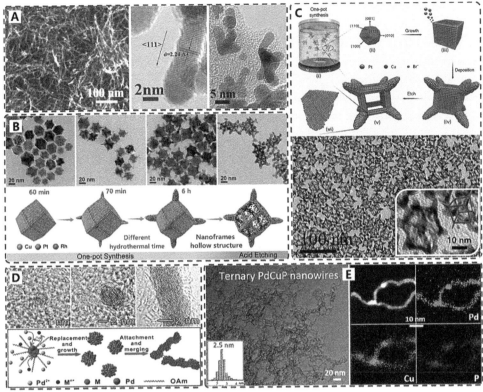

Figure 31.1 (A) Template-free synthesis of Pt nanowires [4]; one-pot solvothermal and acid etching synthesis of (B) Pt−Cu−Rh nanoframes [5] and (C) Pt−Cu nanoframes [6]; (D) OAm-ligand and M-core induced synthesis of PdM alloy nanowires [7]); (E) surfactant-directed synthesis of PdCuP nanowires [8].

A variety of hollow noble-metal nanostructures have been reported, such as nano-shells, nano-boxes, nano-cages, and nano-frames. The nano-frame structure is only composed of edges and angles, which maintain the same morphology as solid 3-D nanocrystals. This results in a highly open, 3-D structure compared to other hollow nanocrystals of the same size. The open structure can enable the catalytic reaction to occur on the inner surface of these nano-frame catalysts and improve the use efficiency of noble metals [10]. Recently, Shen and colleagues reported that the vertex-type-selective growth of Pt−Cu−Rh nano-horns on a central nanocrystal can be constructed via a one-pot solvothermal synthesis, and hollow Pt—Cu—Rh nano-frames can be obtained by subsequent acid etching (see Fig. 31.1B for details) [5]. The hollow Pt—Cu—Rh nano-frames are composed of a Rh-decorated Pt—Cu rhombic dodecahedral nano-cage and six Pt—Cu—Rh nano-horns protruding from {100} vertices of rhombic dodecahedron. Shen also reported the facile synthesis of novel Pt—Cu octopod nano-frame architectures that have 3D catalytic surfaces with beneficial high-index facets (HIF), and the atomic-level engineering of various nano-frame architectures based on a similar recipe (see Fig. 31.1C for details) [6]. The reliable synthesis recipes, facile synthesis procedure, and sophisticated nano-frame architectures provide a path toward mass producing novel catalysts for a wide range of applications.

The Pd-based 1-D nanowires are also considered as one of promising catalytic materials in energy-related application fields due to their unique properties. Recently, Jin and colleagues designed an efficient oleamine-ascorbic acid (OAm-AA) reaction system to induce the bottom-up growth of a series of amorphous PdM alloy 1-D nanowires (M = Fe, Co, Ni, and Cu), by using amorphous non-noble metal (M) nuclei as templates (see Fig. 31.1D for details) [7]. The large-scale preparation of ultrathin PdM amorphous alloy nanowires ($\sim$ 5 nm in diameter) can be realized by introducing palladium atom via replacement reaction at low temperature using the amorphous OAm-ligand M core as inducer. Lv et al. also developed a facile surfactant-directed aqueous synthetic strategy to fabricate 1-D ternary PdCuP alloy ultrathin nanowires ($\sim$ 2.5 nm in diameter) under ambient conditions (see Fig. 31.1E for details) [8]. NaH_2PO_2 is used as a reducing agent for the co-reduction of Pd and Cu precursors and a P source of phosphorization (i.e., amorphization) simultaneously, where the amorphous P with disordered lattices was uniformly dispersed on the PdCuP phosphide alloy nanowires. Particularly, the amphiphilic dioctadecyldimethylammonium chloride (DODAC) surfactant confining template plays a key role in the bottom-up anisotropic growth of ultralong PdCuP nanowires.

31.4 Application progress of nano-noble metal catalysts

31.4.1 Energy application of nano-noble metal catalysts

31.4.1.1 Pt-based nanostructures for electrocatalysis

Platinum (Pt)-group noble metals are the most effective electrocatalysts to facilitate both methanol oxidation reaction (MOR) and ORR for acidic DMFCs. The tunable catalytic activities of Pt electrocatalysts by designing favorable morphologies and structures have been demonstrated. Particularly, Pt nanoflowers with highly branched morphologies have been proposed to be one of the desirable architectures that are promising for reaching an optimized activity and stability [11]. In 2013, we presented a new carbon-supported Pt nanoflowers with rational 3-D structures for electrocatalysis MOR applications, synthesized by a straightforward galvanic battery reaction approach (see Fig. 31.2A—D for details) [12]. For these 3-D Pt nanoflowers, three features become apparent over previous

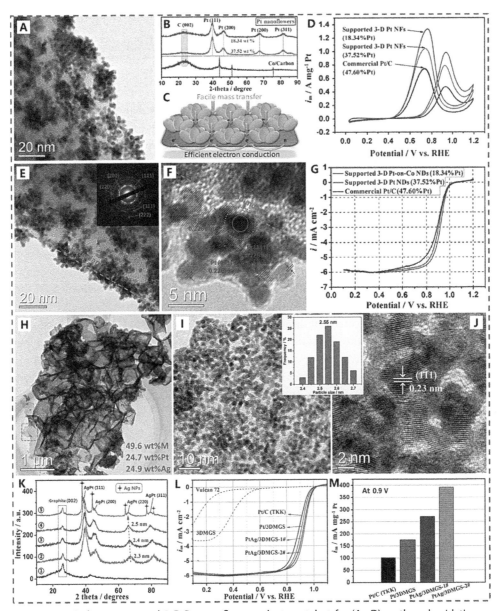

Figure 31.2 Carbon-supported 3-D Pt nanoflowers electrocatalyst for (A—D) methanol oxidation reaction (MOR) [12] and (E—G) oxygen reduction reaction (ORR) [13]; (H—M) 3-D mesoporous graphene networks-supported high-metal-density AgPt alloy electrocatalyst for ORR [14].

reports: (i) carbon-supported mode imparts satisfactory framework stability for Pt nano-structures, (ii) 3-D Pt configuration allows a facile mass transfer, and (iii) good contact be-tween Pt component and carbon results in an efficient electron conduction. With these merits, we demonstrated that the MOR electrocatalysts with high activity (982 mA/mg/Pt at forward peak potential) and desirable durability can be designed on the basis of the novel supported 3-D Pt nanostructures. On the other hand, this 3-D Pt nano-flowers can be also used as highly active catalyst for the ORR, showing a much higher activity with the maximal Pt-mass activity of 251 mA/mg/Pt at 0.9 V (vs. RHE) than commercial Pt/C (122 mA/mg/Pt) (see Fig. 31.2E—G for details) [13]. These excellent MOR and ORR electrocatalytic performances demonstrated that the carbon-supported 3-D Pt nanoflowers are a promising candidate for fuel cell applications.

The 3-D mesoporous graphene networks supported bimetallic PtAg alloyed nano-particles (i.e., PtAg/3DMGS) with a superior stereo nanostructure have been fabricated latterly as advanced ORR electrocatalysts by our group (see Fig. 31.2H—M for details) [14]. The unique architecture of 3D porous graphene exhibits a high surface area (1382 m^2/g), a well-defined mesoporous structure (an average pore size of 3.28 nm), as well as an excellent electronic conductivity (1350 S/m). High-density and ultrafine PtAg NPs ($\sim$ 2.5 nm) were well dispersed on the surface of 3DMGS. The combination of ultrafine PtAg NPs and 3DMGS provides a relatively stable architecture with binary channels for both electron transport and ion diffusion. This PtAg/3DMGS material showed an ultrahigh mass activity (at 0.9 V) of 392 mA/mg/Pt, which is nearly 4 times that of Pt/C (TKK) (102 mA/mg/Pt). After 1000 CV cycles, the retention rates of mass activity are 81.6% and 66.7% for PtAg/3DMGS and Pt/C, respectively. These results demonstrated that the PtAg/3DMGS material is a promising electrocatalyst with high catalytic activity and high stability for the ORR.

For the Pt nanowires synthesized by chemical reduction of Pt salt precursors with for-mic acid (see Fig. 31.1A) [4], the optimized synthesis conditions are selected for investi-gating the kinetics of the ORR of such nanowires in a fuel cell. The ORR mass activity of the Pt nanowires is 130 A/g/Pt at 0.9 V iR-free potential, which is greatly higher than that of commercial Pt/C catalysts tested in the same conditions. The higher mass activity is explained based on a higher surface-specific activity. Accelerated degradation tests indi-cate that Pt nanowires supported on carbon are as stable as Pt nanoparticles supported on carbon in fuel cell applications. In addition, the Pt—Cu—Rh nanoframes (see Fig. 31.1B) [5] and Pt—Cu nanoframes (see Fig. 31.1C) [6] also showed excellent electrocatalytic performances for ethanol oxidation reaction (EOR) and ORR, respectively. Impres-sively, the Pt—Cu—Rh nano-frames exhibited 8.1 times higher specific and 6.8 times higher mass activity toward the EOR under acidic conditions than commercial Pt/C catalyst. And the PtCu nano-frames achieved 20-fold enhancement in mass activity (3260 mA/mg/Pt) for ORR under acidic conditions compared to the commercial Pt/C catalyst.

31.4.1.2 Pd-based nanostructures for electrocatalysis

Palladium (Pd)-group noble metals are also the most effective electrocatalysts to facilitate both EOR and ORR for alkaline DMFCs. Many studies have shown that Pd showed higher electrocatalytic activity than Pt in the alkaline environment for ethanol oxidation, suggesting that Pd is of more research value and application prospects. The structural properties of carbon support materials are closely related to the catalytic performances of Pd electrocatalysts. As competent catalyst support for fuel cells, the following conditions are required: (i) excellent electrical conductivity to facilitate the electron transfer; (ii) high surface area to improve the dispersion of the Pd catalyst on the surface; (iii) excellent stability and good corrosion resistance. In 2019, a new-style graphitized carbon (GC) support material with nanocages morphology was designed and synthesized by using Tween-80 as raw material, Ni (nickel acetate) as catalyst to catalyze the formation of GC, and KOH as activator to increase the specific surface area of GC. The GC nanocages are used as support for the further construction of GC/Pd electrocatalyst, and the catalytic activity of GC/Pd catalyst for EOR was studied, which manifested high anodic peak current and good stability (see Fig. 31.3A–C for details) [15]. The positive scanning peak current density of GC/Pd electrode is up to 1612 A/g/Pd in 1.0 M NaOH and 1.0 M ethanol electrolyte, which is much higher than those (500–1100 A/g/Pd) of traditional Pd electrodes supported with carbon nanotubes or graphene nanosheets.

Cobalt hexacyanocobaltate ($Co_3[Co(CN)_6]_2$) is a typical Prussian blue analog (PBA) with chemical formula of $M^{II}{}_3[M^{III}(CN)_6]_2$ (M^{II} = Co, Cu, Fe, Mn, Ni; M^{III} = Co, Fe), which includes two different valence states of cobalt (Co^{2+} and Co^{3+}) and universal cyanide-group (-C≡N-) where cyanide group act as bridges between the transition metal ions (M^{II}-C≡N-M^{III}). In 2022, a newly graphite carbon/Prussian blue analogue/palladium (GC/PBA/Pd) synergistic-effect electrocatalyst for EOR were developed, with Co-based PBA ($Co_3[Co(CN)_6]_2$) as a co-catalyst (see Fig. 31.3D–H for details) [16]. The $Co_3(Co(CN)_6)_2$ nanoparticles were highly dispersed and inlaid on surface of GC with Pd nanoparticles around them, showing outstanding structural stability. The $GC/Co_3(Co(CN)_6)_2/Pd$ electrocatalyst exhibits greatly enhanced electrocatalytic activity toward EOR with a maximum mass activity of 2644 A/g/Pd GC/Pd, which is more than double that of GC/Pd electrocatalyst (1249 A/g). The redox activity and coordinating properties of PBA may facilitate the electron transfer and the oxidative removal of intermediate products, thereby resulting in superior electrochemical activity and stability.

Previously, a bimetallic carbide (Co_3W_3C)-promoted Pd electrocatalyst with competitive performance over Pt/C electrocatalyst toward ORR in acidic media has been demonstrated by our group (see Fig. 31.3I–L for details) [17]. The synergistically enhanced Pd electrocatalyst ($Pd/Co_3W_3C/GC$) was synthesized by homogeneous deposition of small Pd nanoparticles onto the Co_3W_3C/graphitized carbon (GC) support material. The unique carbide-promoted Pt-free Pd electrocatalyst exhibited very high

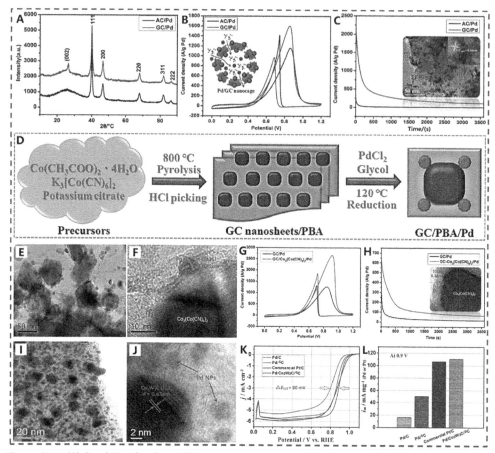

Figure 31.3 (A) Graphitized carbon (GC) nanocages-supported Pd electrocatalyst for EOR [15]; (B) GC/Co₃(Co(CN)₆)₂ (PBA)/Pd synergistic interfacial electrocatalyst for EOR [16]; (C) Pd/Co₃W₃C/GC synergistic interfacial electrocatalyst for ORR [17].

activity and stability toward the ORR, which is comparable to that of the commercial Pt/C catalysts (47.6% Pt, TKK, Japan) in a 0.1 M HClO₄ electrolyte. The mass activities at 0.9 V of these catalysts were determined, and were found to be in the following order: Pd/Co₃W₃C/GC (110 mA/mg/Pd) > commercial Pt/C (107 mA/mg/Pt) > Pd/GC (54 mA/mg/Pd) > Pd/C (16 mA/mg/Pd). Most importantly, the mass activity of Pd/Co₃W₃C/GC at 0.9 V was almost 7 times higher than that of Pd/C, exhibiting comparable performances to the commercial Pt/C catalyst in acidic media.

For the previously introduced PdM alloy nanowires (see Fig. 31.1D) [7], remarkable catalytic activity for FAOR has been demonstrated. The mass activity and area activity of PdCu alloy nanowires reached 2.93 A/mg/Pd and 5.33 mA/cm^2, respectively, with the highest record for Pd-based FAOR catalysts. The calculations show that the amorphous atomic structures can effectively activate the stable C—H bond, thus significantly promoting the dissociation of formic acid (HCOOH), and ultimately enhancing the reactivity for FOR. The PdCuP nanowires (see Fig. 31.1E) [8] also revealed outstanding catalytic activity for EOR. Compared with Pd and PdCu nanowires, the ultrathin ternary PdCuP nanowires demonstrated significantly improved mass activity of 6.7 A/mg/Pd for EOR. Due to the favorable synergy of ultrathin 1-D nanostructure and ternary composition, the electronic state of PdCuP nanowires is changed and the removal of toxic intermediates is promoted.

31.4.2 Environmental application of nanonoble metal catalysts

31.4.2.1 Nanonoble metal for photocatalysis

In order to produce photocatalysts that work efficiently in visible light, many plasmonic photocatalysts have been generated, that is, noble metal (such as Au and Ag) nanoparticles deposited on the surface of polar semiconductor or insulator particles. In the noble metal-semiconductor composite photocatalysts, noble metal nanoparticles are the main components for visible light capturing due to their surface plasmon resonance, and the metal-semiconductor interface effectively separates photogenerated electrons and holes [18]. In fact, the research of solar-powered multiphase photocatalysis based on surface plasmon resonance has made rapid progress and may open up a potential technological pathway for green energy production and environmental remediation. Noble metal plasma photocatalysts are widely used in the mineralization of organic pollutants, air purification, organic synthesis, and water cracking. The in-depth study of surface plasmon resonance-mediated photocatalysis has not only influenced the basic science of multiphase photocatalysis but also produced a new concept [19].

31.4.2.2 Nanonoble metal for thermocatalysis

Most volatile organic compounds (VOCs) are harmful to the atmosphere and human health. Several technologies have been developed to reduce VOC emissions, among which catalytic oxidation (or catalytic combustion) based on thermocatalysis is particularly suitable for the treatment of highly diluted VOCs. The development of precious metals (Au, Pt, Pd) supported by transition metal oxides (CeO_2 and Fe_3O_4) as VOCs oxidation catalysts has been widely reported in the literature, and the research field has been very active [20]. Among these catalysts, porous catalysts have attracted much attention, whose performance is better than bulk catalysts. The synthesis of ordered mesoporous and macroporous metal oxide-supported noble metal catalysts with excellent catalytic oxidation performances for VOCs has been developed rapidly. This excellent catalytic performance is due to their high surface area, high concentration of adsorbed oxygen, low-temperature reduction, strong interaction between noble metal and support, highly dispersed noble metal nanoparticles, and unique porous structures [21]. Besides, the Pt, Pd, and Ru-based nanoparticles were proved to be highly efficient catalysts for the removal of CO via the CO preferential oxidation (CO-PROX) reaction, which can be used to purify hydrogen-rich feed gas for proton exchange membrane fuel cells (PEMFC) [22].

31.5 Summary

In this chapter, we have discussed the structural features, preparation methods, energy and environmental applications, and typical case analysis of nanonoble metal catalysts (such as Pt, Pd, Au, Ag, and so on). Platinum group metals (Pt and Pd) play an important role in the field of electrocatalysis. Many nanostructured electrocatalysts have been developed by designing single crystals, alloying, surface defects, etc. One-dimensional platinum group nanowires and three-dimensional platinum group nanoframes are two typical noble metal nanostructures, which have unique nanoadvantages and electronic structures. Noble metal-based 3-D nanoflowers and synergistic interfacial catalysts are also very popular. These nanostructures show excellent performances in electrocatalytic ORR, MOR, EOR, and FAOR, due to their high surface area and well-catalytic reactivity. Noble metal nanocatalysts also show a wide range of application prospects in the field of photocatalysis (such as plasmonic photocatalysts with Au and Ag) and thermocatalysis (such as VOCs catalytic oxidation).

Acknowledgments

This book was supported by National Natural Science Foundation of China (22078071, 22272034), Natural Science Foundation of Guangdong Province (2021A1515010125, 2020A1515010344), Maoming Science and Technology Project (mmkj2020032), Guangdong Province Universities and Colleges Pearl River Scholar Funded Scheme (2019), Guangdong Basic and Applied Basic Research Foundation (2019A1515011249, 2021A1515010305), Key Research Project of Natural Science of Guangdong Provincial Department of Education (2019KZDXM010), Environment and Energy Green Catalysis Innovation Team of Colleges and Universities of Guangdong Province (2022KCXTD019), the program for Innovative Research Team of Guangdong University of Petrochemical Technology.

References

[1] https://mp.weixin.qq.com/s/N2-rAT2gVrxYCThW7E53Ew.
[2] Z. Li, B. Li, M. Yu, C. Yu, P. Shen, Amorphous metallic ultrathin nanostructures: a latent ultra-high-density atomic-level catalyst for electrochemical energy conversion, International Journal of Hydrogen Energy 47 (63) (2022) 26956—26977.
[3] Y. Shi, Z. Lyu, M. Zhao, R. Chen, Q.N. Nguyen, Y. Xia, Noble-metal nanocrystals with controlled shapes for catalytic and electrocatalytic applications, Chemical Reviews 121 (2) (2020) 649—735.
[4] H. Meng, Y. Zhan, D. Zeng, X. Zhang, G. Zhang, F. Jaouen, Factors influencing the growth of Pt nanowires via chemical self-Assembly and their fuel cell performance, Small 11 (27) (2015) 3377—3386.

[5]   K. Wang, H. Du, R. Sriphathoorat, P.K. Shen, Vertex-type engineering of Pt–Cu–Rh heteroge-
      neous nanocages for highly efficient ethanol electrooxidation, Advanced Materials 30 (45) (2018)
      1804074.
[6]   S. Luo, M. Tang, P.K. Shen, S. Ye, Atomic-scale preparation of octopod nanoframes with high-index
      facets as highly active and stable catalysts, Advanced Materials 29 (8) (2017) 201601687.
[7]   W. Wang, T. He, X. Yang, Y. Liu, C. Wang, J. Li, M. Jin, General synthesis of amorphous PdM
      (M= Cu, Fe, Co, Ni) alloy nanowires for boosting HCOOH dehydrogenation, Nano Letters 21
      (8) (2021) 3458–3464.
[8]   H. Lv, L. Sun, D. Xu, Y. Ma, B. Liu, When ternary PdCuP alloys meet ultrathin nanowires: synergic
      boosting of catalytic performance in ethanol electrooxidation, Applied Catalysis B: Environmental 253
      (2019) 271–277.
[9]   S.H. Sun, D.Q. Yang, D. Villers, G.X. Zhang, E. Sacher, J.P. Dodelet, Template-and surfactant-free
      room temperature synthesis of self-assembled 3D Pt nanoflowers from single-crystal nanowires,
      Advanced Materials 20 (3) (2008) 571–574.
[10] X. Wang, A. Ruditskiy, Y. Xia, Rational design and synthesis of noble-metal nanoframes for catalytic
      and photonic applications, National Science Review 3 (4) (2016) 520–533.
[11] B. Lim, Y. Xia, Metal nanocrystals with highly branched morphologies, Angewandte Chemie Inter-
      national Edition 50 (1) (2011) 76–85.
[12] Z. Li, S. Ji, B.G. Pollet, P.K. Shen, Supported 3-D Pt nanostructures: the straightforward synthesis and
      enhanced electrochemical performance for methanol oxidation in an acidic medium, Journal of Nano-
      particle Research 15 (10) (2013) 1–6.
[13] Z. Li, C. He, M. Cai, S. Kang, P.K. Shen, A strategy for easy synthesis of carbon supported Co@ Pt
      core–shell configuration as highly active catalyst for oxygen reduction reaction, International Journal
      of Hydrogen Energy 37 (19) (2012) 14152–14160.
[14] Z. Li, Y. Li, C. He, P.K. Shen, Bimetallic PtAg alloyed nanoparticles and 3-D mesoporous graphene
      nanosheet hybrid architectures for advanced oxygen reduction reaction electrocatalysts, Journal of Ma-
      terials Chemistry A 5 (44) (2017) 23158–23169.
[15] Z. Li, L. Zhang, C. Yang, J. Chen, Z. Wang, L. Bao, P. Shen, Graphitized carbon nanocages/palla-
      dium nanoparticles: Sustainable preparation and electrocatalytic performances towards ethanol oxida-
      tion reaction, International Journal of Hydrogen Energy 44 (12) (2019) 6172–6181.
[16] M. Yu, Z. Li, H. Shi, S. Lin, X. Zhang, F. Mo, D. Liang, Preparation of graphite carbon/Prussian blue
      analogue/palladium (GC/PBA/Pd) synergistic-effect electrocatalyst with high activity for ethanol
      oxidation reaction, International Journal of Hydrogen Energy 47 (10) (2022) 6721–6733.
[17] Z. Li, S. Ji, B.G. Pollet, P.K. Shen, A Co_3W_3C promoted Pd catalyst exhibiting competitive perfor-
      mance over Pt/C catalysts towards the oxygen reduction reaction, Chemical Communications 50 (5)
      (2014) 566–568.
[18] P. Wang, B. Huang, Y. Dai, M.H. Whangbo, Plasmonic photocatalysts: harvesting visible light with
      noble metal nanoparticles, Physical Chemistry Chemical Physics 14 (28) (2012) 9813–9825.
[19] X. Zhou, G. Liu, J. Yu, W. Fan, Surface plasmon resonance-mediated photocatalysis by noble metal-
      based composites under visible light, Journal of Materials Chemistry 22 (40) (2012) 21337–21354.
[20] L.F. Liotta, Catalytic oxidation of volatile organic compounds on supported noble metals, Applied
      Catalysis B: Environmental 100 (3–4) (2010) 403–412.
[21] Y. Liu, J. Deng, S. Xie, Z. Wang, H. Dai, Catalytic removal of volatile organic compounds using or-
      dered porous transition metal oxide and supported noble metal catalysts, Chinese Journal of Catalysis
      37 (8) (2016) 1193–1205.
[22] I. Rosso, C. Galletti, G. Saracco, E. Garrone, V. Specchia, Development of A zeolites-supported no-
      ble-metal catalysts for CO preferential oxidation: H_2 gas purification for fuel cell, Applied Catalysis B:
      Environmental 48 (3) (2004) 195–203.

CHAPTER 32

Atomically dispersed catalysts: recent progress in energy and environmental fields

32.1 Introduction

Faced with the energy crisis and environmental pollution caused by the depletion of non-renewable fossil fuels, there is an urgent need to develop efficient technologies for chemical and energy conversion. However, most advanced technologies rely on various catalytic processes (e.g., thermocatalysis, electrocatalysis and photocatalysis) [1]. Therefore, it is very important to design efficient catalysts with high selectivity and rapid reaction rate. Since the concept of single-atom catalysis was proposed in 2011, single-atom catalysts (SACs) have become a new research frontier in the field of materials science and catalysis due to the good stability and recyclability of heterogeneous catalysts, as well as the excellent activity and selectivity of homogeneous catalysts [2]. In particular, the SACs with nearly 100% atomic utilization can provide a perfect research platform and have made encouraging advances in catalysis and energy conversion and utilization. Essentially, the SACs belong to a new type of sub−nanostructured (~ 0.2 nm) catalytic material, and their active sites need to be distributed on the surface of appropriate carriers (including metallic carriers and non-metallic carriers) [3]. Atomically dispersed catalysts (ADCs) refer to the diversified sub−nanostructured catalysts (including SACs, dual-atom catalysts (DAC), triple-atom catalysts (TAC), and so on). In these ADCs, the metal atoms are uniformly dispersed on the surface of carriers to the greatest extent, which has unparalleled electronic structure and geometric configuration, and show excellent catalytic performances in many energy and environment-related applications [4]. The ADCs demonstrated broad application prospects in the fields of energy conversion and environmental catalysis, such as fuel cells, electric or photocatalytic decomposition of water, photocatalytic degradation of organic matter, and catalytic carbon monoxide oxidation, etc.

32.2 Structural features of atomically dispersed catalysts

After the concept of SACs was proposed by Zhang and co-workers [5], several different atomic-level catalysts were further defined later, including single-atom alloy catalysts (SAACs) [6], DACs [7], TACs [8], fully exposed cluster catalysts (FECCs) [9], single-atom layer catalysts (SALCs) [10], atomic-site ensemble catalysts (ECs) [11] and ultra-high-density atomic foam catalysts (AFCs) [12] (see Fig. 32.1 for details).

Nanostructured Materials
ISBN 978-0-443-19256-2, https://doi.org/10.1016/B978-0-443-19256-2.00002-8

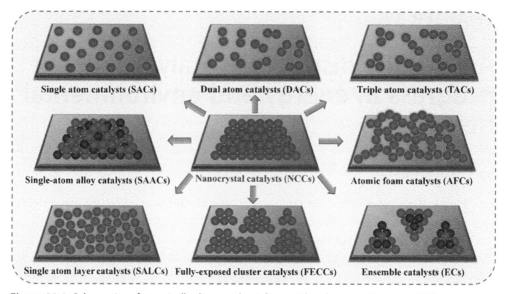

Figure 32.1 Schematics of atomically dispersed catalysts with sub–nanostructures [12].

Among them, SACs, DACs, TACs, SAACs, SALCs, and AFCs have no metallic bond or less metallic bond for their active metal species, all of which can be classified as ADCs. These ADCs often exhibit the maximum atomic utilization and more excellent catalytic characteristics than nanocrystal catalysts. The FECCs and ECs have quite a few metallic bonds for their active metal species, which can exhibit synergistic interactions between metal atoms and overall catalytic effects. In this chapter, we focus on the structural characteristics and catalytic applications of SACs or DACs.

At present, the hotspot directions of SACs include the following: coordination engineering (including the first coordination and adjacent environment), support engineering (nanostructure design and defect structure regulation), dynamic catalytic structures (dynamic change and plasticity of metal atoms in catalytic reaction process), batch preparation (such as gram-level and kilogram-level preparation), and ultra-high content (limit loading on differentiated supports and site density effect of metal atoms). Particularly, the coordination engineering (such as coordination atoms and coordination numbers) and support engineering (such as defect structures of metallic supports (metal oxides or sulfides) or non-metallic supports (graphene or carbon nitride)) are the two most fundamental directions for the design of SACs with well-defined catalytic sites and excellent catalytic performances [13].

Graphene is a 2-D carbon material with unique electronic properties, which makes it an excellent support material for SACs. Depending on the conditions of the graphene support, the interaction between metal single atoms and the graphene support can be divided into embedded type (for raw or defective graphene) (including a monovacancy with three carbon atoms (MV-C_3), a divacancy with four carbon atoms (DV-C_4)) and inserted type (for doped defective graphene) (including four pyridine N atoms (pyridine-N_4), and four pyrrole N atoms (pyrrole-N_4)) (see Fig. 32.2A for details) [14]. In terms of structure and properties, the catalytic activity of graphene-based SACs can be attributed to the strong electronic interactions between the d orbital of metal atoms and the p orbital of coordinated nonmetallic atoms (usually C, N, O, B, P, etc.). Thus, the catalytic activity is closely related to the discrete quantum states of metallic single atoms and their local chemical coordination environment, including the coordination number and type of neighbor atoms, such as the famous "M-N_4" centers (see Fig. 32.2B for details) [15] and the asymmetrical "M-N_3P_1" centers (see Fig. 32.2C for details) [16].

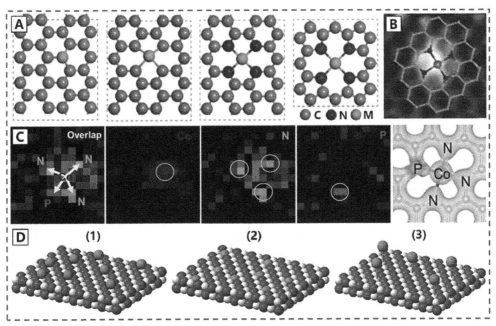

Figure 32.2 Structure types of graphene-supported SACs [14]; famous "M-N_4" centers [15]; asymmetrical "M-N_3P_1" centers [16]; structure types of metallic compounds-supported SACs [17].

Metallic compounds (e.g., transition metal oxides, sulfides, and carbides)-supported SACs is a kind of very important catalyst material for heterogeneous catalysis, in which the synergistic effect can be demonstrated between metallic supports and metal single atoms. Currently, the approaches for dispersing metal single atoms on metallic supports include the following three categories: (1) interacting with surface anchoring sites, (2) substituting surface atoms into lattice matrix, and (3) coordinating with organic bridging ligands (see Fig. 32.2D for details) [17]. The in-depth insight into metal-support interaction for metallic compound-supported SACs is especially important for the controlled synthesis of high-atom-density SACs (i.e., the AFCs) with good stability and unique electronic structures. In order to realize the high metal loading of metallic compound-supported AFCs, engineering of vacancy defect sites in supports and strong metal-support interaction (SMSI) have been introduced. The defects, vacancies, and unsaturated sites in metallic compounds play important roles in maintaining the high dispersion of single atoms. Particularly, the cation vacancy defect strategy based on metallic compound supports (i.e., substituting support metal atoms in lattice matrix by active metal single atoms) is a preferential strategy for constructing high-performance supported SACs [18].

The synchrotron X-ray absorption spectroscopy (XAS) can provide valuable information about the coordination environment and the chemical state of the detected SACs. The XAS spectrum consists of two regions: Extended X-ray absorption fine structure (EXAFS) and X-ray absorption near edge structure (XANES). Spherical aberration-corrected transmission electron microscopy (AC-TEM) is a state-of-the-art analytical instrument to demonstrate the atomic structures of SACs (see Section 6.6 for atomic structure characterization methods).

32.3 Preparation methods of atomically dispersed catalysts

32.3.1 Preparation of carbon (graphene)-supported SACs

In recent years, various synthetic methods have been developed for the preparation of carbon (graphene)-supported SACs, mainly including physical methods (such as atomic layer deposition, ALD) and chemical methods (such as chemical co-deposition and chemical vapor deposition). Although they have their own advantages, the physical method, however, faces shortcomings such as low output, complex equipment, and high cost, which hinder its wide application. The chemical synthesis is also complicated and sensitive, so it is also difficult to scale up production. Recently, the directly conversion of metal nanoparticles (or bulk metal) into SACs by high-temperature heat treatment is considered a promising strategy, which further promoted the batch preparation of SACs from cheap and easily available bulk metal materials. These direct heat conversion synthetic routes refer to thermal emitting or called gas migration (with the principle of metal solid volatilization) (see Fig. 32.3A–I for details) [19–22].

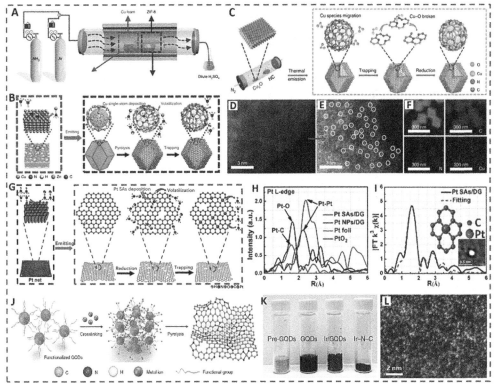

Figure 32.3 Gas migration synthesis of (A–B) Cu_1/N–C SACs from Cu foam [19], (C–F) Cu_1/N–C SACs from Cu_2O powder [20], (G–I) Pt_1/defective graphene SACs [21]; (J–L) crosslinking and pyrolysis synthesis of Ir_1/NC SACs supported on graphene quantum dots [22].

The gas migration strategy was proposed for the first time to prepare Cu SACs on a large scale (more than 1 g in yield) from massive Cu foam by Wu and Li' groups (see Fig. 32.3A and B) [19]. The Cu foam and the zeolite imidazole ester framework material (ZIF-8) are used as metal and carbon precursors. The ammonia can coordinate with Cu atom from Cu foam to generate volatile $Cu(NH_3)_x$, and then $Cu(NH_3)_x$ is transported to the surface of nitrogen-rich carbon derived from pyrolysis of ZIF-8, and finally $Cu(NH_3)_x$ is captured by the nitrogen-rich carbon to produce Cu–SAs/N–C single-atom catalysts. Besides, Wu et al. further reported a more feasible and versatile gas migration strategy for the synthesis of single-atom Cu on nitrogen-doped carbon

(Cu—SAs/N—C) catalysts from cuprous oxide (Cu$_2$O) precursor without NH$_3$ (see Fig. 32.3C—F) [20]. Commercial Cu$_2$O powder will sublimate into flowing steam when it is close to the melting temperature (1270—1500K), and then can be migrated, trapped, and reduced by defect-rich NC (from metal-organic frameworks, MOFs) to form a separate Cu SACs. Recently, Duan and co-workers used a simple thermal emitting strategy to directly synthesize Pt SACs from bulk Pt nets with the assistant of NH$_3$ (see Fig. 32.3G—I) [21]. The NH$_3$ from the pyrolysis of dicyandiamide can coordinate with Pt atoms by strong coordination, and form volatile Pt(NH$_3$)$_x$, which can be easily anchored on the surface of defective graphene support.

Generally, the carbon-supported atomically dispersed catalysts are composed of graphene skeleton and N-coordinated metal atoms. The graphene-skeleton materials (e.g., carbon black, carbon nanotubes, graphene quantum dots (GQDs), and pyrolysis-derived carbon) with covalent bonds have unique physical and chemical properties, including the controllable size and porosity, high surface area, high stability, and abundant vacancy defects. Recently, Xia et al. reported a universal crosslinking and pyrolysis method for the synthesis of high-loading transition metal SACs, such as 40 wt.% (3.8 at. %) Ir SACs supported on GQDs (with M-N$_4$ moieties) (see Fig. 32.3J—L) [22]. When organic amines are modified on the surface of GQDs, the transition metals in solution are uniformly dispersed and limited on the surface by strong chelation/coordination between organic amines and metal cations. This strong surface ligands interaction improves the connection of GQDs, forms Ir^{3+}/GQDs-NH$_2$ mixed layered micron-sized aerogel structure during freeze-drying, and then the pyrolysis in ammonia atmosphere is carried out to obtain high-density ($\sim$5 atoms nm^{-2}) Ir$_1$/NC SACs.

32.3.2 Preparation of carbon nitride (g—C$_3$N$_4$)—supported SACs

The graphitic carbon nitride (i.e., g-C$_3$N$_4$) has a graphite-like layered structure and a stable crystallographic structure (tri-s-triazineas as structural units) (see Section 27.2 for details). The nine-nitrogen pore of g-C$_3$N$_4$ is connected by three groups of tri-s-triazine structural units and has the best structural stability in lots of carbon nitride structures. The nine-nitrogen pore of g-C$_3$N$_4$ can be used as an effective space to accommodate single metal atoms, providing a unique environment for the design of g—C$_3$N$_4$—supported SACs. For the g—C$_3$N$_4$—based SACs, four coordination moieties are usually presented, namely, the M-N$_2$, M-N$_4$, and M-N$_6$ moieties in nine-nitrogen pore of g-C$_3$N$_4$, as well as the M-N$_3$ moiety with the substitution of carbon atoms on the deficient g-C$_3$N$_4$ (see Fig. 32.4 for details) [24—29].

In 2020, Capobianco et al. investigated the Cu-doped g-C$_3$N$_4$ (Cu-g-C$_3$N$_4$) and demonstrated via XRE and EXAFS that Cu$^+$ incorporates as an individual ion (single atom structure with M-N$_2$ coordination moiety) (see Fig. 32.4A—D) [24]. The single Cu atoms doping reduces the interlayer distance of g-C$_3$N$_4$ by approximately 0.02 Å and also reduces the peak FWHM by nearly 20%. The M-N$_2$ coordination moiety in

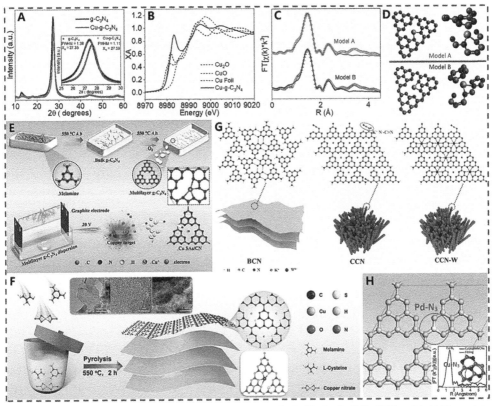

Figure 32.4 (A—D) Cu$_1$/g-C$_3$N$_4$ SACs with M-N$_2$ moiety [24], (E) Cu$_1$/g-C$_3$N$_4$ SACs with M-N$_4$ moiety [25], (F) Cu$_1$/g-C$_3$N$_4$ SACs with M-N$_4$ moiety and C—S—C group [26]; (G) W$_1$/g-C$_3$N$_4$ SACs with M-N$_6$ moiety [27]; (H) Pd$_1$/g-C$_3$N$_4$ SACs with M-N$_3$ moiety [28] and Cu$_1$/g-C$_3$N$_4$ SACs with M-N$_3$ moiety [29].

nine-nitrogen pore of g-C$_3$N$_4$ consists of two potential models: model A and model B based on the reported X-ray crystal structures. Despite its low coordination number of 2, the Cu single atoms in Cu-g-C$_3$N$_4$ evidently do not have any neighboring atoms besides small C and N atoms in g-C$_3$N$_4$.

Recently, Professor Guowei Yang of Sun Yat-sen University and Professor Lei Zheng of Southern Medical University prepared g-C$_3$N$_4$ anchored with Cu SAs by using pyrolysis of melamine and electrochemical deposition method of metal precursor. The calculation based on density functional theory shows that the active center of Cu SAs/CN is Cu—N$_4$ moiety within the nine-nitrogen pore of g-C$_3$N$_4$ (see Fig. 32.4E) [25].

The anchoring of atomically dispersed Cu atoms will lead to an electron transition through the Cu atom to the linked N atoms. Such a charge transfer channel from Cu—N$_4$ coordination moiety can effectively improve the charge mobility of g-C$_3$N$_4$ in an actual reaction environment. Previously, Wang et al. reported the preparation of diatomic site catalysts by a simple synchronous pyrolysis strategy, consisting of Cu—N$_4$ moiety and C—S—C active groups decorated on g-C$_3$N$_4$ (Cu$_1$/g-C$_3$N$_4$ SACs with M-N$_4$ moiety and C—S—C groups) (see Fig. 32.4F) [26]. The two atomic sites can greatly improve the separation efficiency of photogenerated charge carriers due to the electron acceptor and donor roles of Cu SAs and S atoms. Specifically, the Cu—N$_4$ moiety directly captures photogenerated electrons, while the S atoms carry photogenerated holes, which cooperatively promote the separation of photogenerated carriers, resulting in enhanced photocatalytic activity.

Crystalline g-C$_3$N$_4$ (CCN) has attracted much attention, but due to the lack of a suitable active site, its photocatalytic efficiency and selectivity are still not ideal. Professor Shengwei Liu and colleagues at Sun Yat-sen University recently reported the construction of a tungsten (W)-doped crystalline form of CCN (CCN—W) by forming W—N$_6$ moiety at the cavity position of adjacent tri-s-triazine units (see Fig. 32.4G) [27]. With the help of solvothermal treatment, W^{6+} doped crystalline carbon nitride (CCN—W) nanorods, including W—N$_6$ bonding, were prepared using prefabricated CCN as the carrier and W(CO)$_6$ as the metal source. The W—N$_6$ moiety in CCN—W is formed by coordinating the lone pair electron of N 2p at the cavity position with the vacant orbital of the W^{6+} ion. The electron storage capability of W^{6+} is conducive to the capture and accumulation of photoelectrons in W—N$_6$ moiety, which inhibits the charge recombination and improves photocatalytic performances.

In the absence of C defects, the above studies indicate that metal single atoms usually form M-N$_6$, M-N$_4$, M-N$_2$ coordination moieties with N in the nine-nitrogen pores within g-C$_3$N$_4$. But what about the coordination situation in the C-deficient g-C$_3$N$_4$ condition? For the Pd$_1$/g-C$_3$N$_4$ SACs with C defects, the enchenting position of single atom Pd was changed, from the nine-nitrogen pore to the C-defect site (see Fig. 32.4H) [28]. The unique Pd—N$_3$ structure is formed by coordinating with the surrounding unsaturated N. Further theoretical calculations show that single-atom Pd is more likely to "take root" at the C defect in thermodynamics when the C defect exists. Similarly, Cu—N$_3$ structure can be formed at deficient carbon nitride frameworks (see the inset of Fig. 32.4H) [29]. These special deficients g—C$_3$N$_4$—based SACs with M-N$_3$ coordination structures showed excellent photocatalytic and electrocatalytic performances, due to their densely colonized isolated sites and unique coordination structures.

32.3.3 Preparation of metallic compound-supported SACs

The isolated atoms dispersed on the metallic compounds are usually stabilized by various defects of supports. Mass production of SACs with high metal loading and thermal stability remains a huge challenge because it is difficult to produce high-density defects on supports. Significantly, the isolated single metal atoms can be stabilized by strong covalent metal-support interaction (CMSI) (not depending on the support defects), by trapping metal atoms that have been deposited or vaporized from metal oxides during high-temperature calcination. Since 2011, Zhang, Li, and Liu jointly reported Pt_1/FeO_x SACs for the first time [5], Zhang's team is committed to developing metallic compounds-supported SACs (the CMSI effect can occur in these supported SACs system) (see Fig. 32.5A—J for details) [30,31].

Recently, Zhang and co-workers reported that high-concentration isolated Pt atoms can be stabilized on low-surface-area Fe_2O_3 support by CMSI effect, which belongs to a typical support defect-free thermally stable SACs (see Fig. 32.5A—C for details) [30].

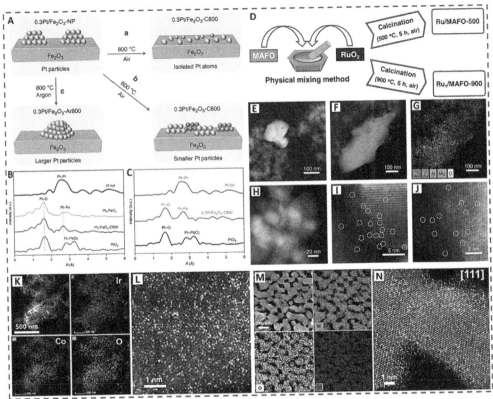

Figure 32.5 (A—C) Pt_1/Fe_2O_3 SACs by CMSI [30], (D—J) $Ru_1/MAFO$ SACs by CMSI [31], (K and L) Ir_1/CoO_x SACs by CMSI [32], and (M and N) Ir_1/NiO SACs by vacancy defect anchoring [23].

The experimental results show that Pt SACs can be obtained by calcination of Pt nano-particles supported on Fe_2O_3 under $800°C$ in air atmosphere. A strong $Pt-Fe_2O_3$ inter-action is proved to be raised from covalent bonding interaction, which inhibits migration and reunion of isolated Pt atoms. The PtO_2 units evaporated from Pt NPs at $800°C$ calcination, the reducible iron oxide is capable to trap Pt atoms by forming $Pt-O-Fe$ covalent bond. More recently, Zhang and co-workers further reported a batch prepara-tion strategy (more than 10 g in yield) for producing thermally stable Ru SACs from commercial RuO_2 powder, by the "physical mixing and high-temperature method" with $MgAl_{1.2}Fe_{0.8}O_4$ (MAFO) support (see Fig. 32.5D−J for details) [31]. The re-searchers have achieved the goal of dispersing submicron RuO_2 powder into Ru single atoms on the MAFO support at high temperature with the help of a strong CMSI effect.

Recently, Gu and co-workers reported that high-concentration Ir_1/CoO_x SACs can be designed by in situ deposition on amorphous CoO_x nanosheets by the strategy of interacting with surface anchoring sites (see Fig. 32.5K and L for details) [32]. The results show that Ir single atoms are supported on CoO_x via interacting with the rich interfacial oxygen bound on CoO_x, and the $Ir-O-Co$ structure significantly improves the stability of Ir single atoms. More recently, Gu and co-workers further reported a simple and effi-cient immersing and heating method to produce Ir_1/NiO SACs with ultra-high Ir loading, which enables an unprecedented loading (~ 18 wt.%) of Ir single atoms on nanoporous NiO support (see Fig. 32.5M and N for details) [23]. The Ir single atom syn-thesized by this method is located on the surface of NiO support, and the Ir atoms are occupied with the vacancy of Ni atoms. In general, metal-oxygen covalent coordination (M_1-O-M structure) and metal cation vacancy anchoring are the two most accepted for-mation principles in the design of metal oxides-supported SACs.

32.4 Application progress of atomically dispersed catalysts

At first, the invention and application of SACs were limited to the field of thermal catalysis (thermocatalysis), such as catalytic oxidation reactions, selective hydrogena-tion reactions, carbon-carbon (or carbon-nitrogen) coupling reactions, and other reactions (see Fig. 32.6A for details) [33]. Currently, the energy and environmental-related applications of atomically dispersed catalysts (such as single atom and diatomic catalysts) have pervaded thermocatalysis, electrocatalysis, photocatalysis, and other fields (see Fig. 32.6B for details) [34]. For the bimetallic SACs or diatomic catalysts (DACs), their additional two-site synergistic catalytic effects (synergistic adsorption and electron interaction) make them show unprecedented scientific fascination and bright applica-tion prospects for the three major heterogeneous catalytic fields (see Fig. 32.6C−F for details) [35−37].

32.4.1 Electrocatalytic energy conversion

The SACs are widely used to catalyze various electrochemical reactions, such as oxygen reduction reaction (ORR), oxygen evolution reaction (OER), hydrogen evolution

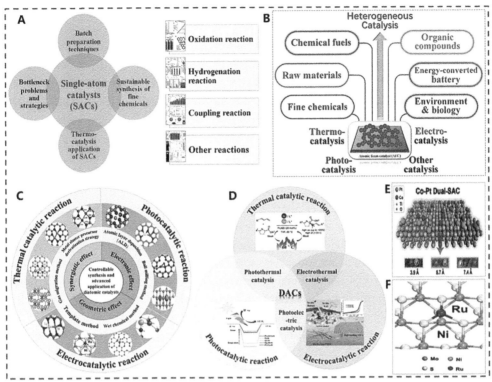

Figure 32.6 (A) SACs for the applications of thermocatalysis [33], (B) SACs for the applications of thermocatalysis, electrocatalysis, photocatalysis, and other fields [34], (C and D) DACs for the applications of three major heterogeneous catalytic fields [35], (E) Co-Pt dual SACs [36], and (F) Ni–Ru DACs [37].

reaction (HER), alcohol oxidation reaction (AOR), formic acid oxidation reaction (FAOR), and carbon dioxide reduction reaction (CO_2RR) [34]. These reactions are mainly related to energy and environmental applications such as fuel cells, hydrogen production from water decomposition, and carbon dioxide emission reduction. Electrocatalyst for ORR is crucial for a variety of renewable energy applications (e.g., proton exchange membrane fuel cells, PEMFCs). The synthesis of highly dispersed and highly active ORR electrocatalysts (e.g., nanoscale and atom-level structures) on carbon supports with strong durability is extremely desirable but remains challenging. Aside from manipulating the geometric and electronic structures of active metal sites, another key challenge is the development of strategies for preparing high-metal-density SACs, thus rendering the atom-level ORR electrocatalysts dramatically reactive, selective, and stable compared to their nanoscale counterparts [38].

Because ORR activity is controlled by kinetics and mass transfer process, in order to better mass diffusion, optimizing pore structure of catalyst can effectively affect the ORR activity. The rapid transfer of O_2 from the bulk solution to active center is a key step to provide high current density. Recently, Feng and co-workers designed a novel N-doped hierarchical micro/meso-porous carbon (NHPC)-supported Fe—N—C SACs with dense available FeN_4 species by Zn-mediated silica-template strategy, and it is applied to high-performance alkaline ORR (see Fig. 32.7A—E for details) [39]. The Fe—NHPC SACs showed unprecedented high ORR activity in 0.1 M KOH electrolyte, and the half-wave potential was 0.93 V, which is much better than Pt/C catalyst (0.82 V) and commercial Fe—N—C catalyst (0.85 V) (see Fig. 32.7F) [40]. This work opens a new way to improve the density and accessibility of FeN_4 species and develop high-performance Fe—N—C ORR catalysts. To sum up, the design of mesoporous carbon and high metal loading provide a double guarantee for the high-performance SACs.

When the density of single-atom active sites increases to a certain extent, the distance between single atoms will become very small, and the interaction between adjacent active sites becomes a key factor affecting intrinsic activity. Recently, Yu and Xiao studied and revealed the origin of the enhancement of ORR activity (in 0.1 M KOH electrolyte) of isolated Fe—N_4 SACs with the different distances between inter-sites at the sub—nanometer level, by integrating the experimental and theoretical methods (see Fig. 32.7G—K) [41]. The atomically-dispersed Fe—N_4 sites with controllable density and various distance of sites (d_{site}) are prepared on the N-doped carbon substrate via the hydrogel anchoring strategy. When the d_{site} is controlled at 0.5—2.6 nm, favorable Fe—N_4 moieties are obtained without Fe clusters or nanoparticles. When the d_{site} is less than 1.2 nm, the strong interaction between adjacent Fe—N_4 sites changes the electronic structure and improves the inherent activity of ORR. This distance-dependent enhanced activity can keep until the d_{site} is close to 0.7 nm, when the d_{site} is further reduced, the ORR activity decreases slightly. This study detailly determined the kinetic behavior of a single active site and the site distance effect of adjacent metal atoms, which provides an important opportunity to understand the inherent catalytic behavior of carbon-supported SACs.

Electrocatalyst for OER is also crucial for a variety of renewable energy applications (e.g., hydrogen production by overall water splitting and various metal-air batteries). The newly emerging amorphous metallic ultrathin nanostructured materials (AMUNMs) usually have single or few-atom-layer thickness, disordered metal atom arrangement, abundant vacancy (or micropores), and intensively exposed atomic construction. A new notion of ultra-high-density atomic-level catalysts (UHD ALCs) has been proposed to describe the AMUNMs catalysts [42]. Particularly, some AMUNMs can be used as a unique free-standing atomic-level system without supports for OER and a novel single-atom-layer system for HER and overall water splitting (see Fig. 32.8 for details) [10,43].

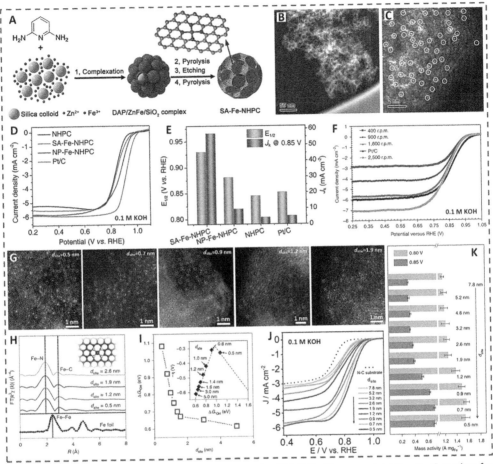

Figure 32.7 (A−E) NHPC-supported Fe−N−C SACs for ORR [39], (F) commercial Fe−N−C catalyst for ORR [40], (G−K) Fe−N$_4$ SACs with a controllable distance of sites for ORR [41].

Recently, Hong et al. proposed a general synthesis method for the preparation of an atomic-level Ir-based amorphous metal nanosheets with a thickness of less than 10 nm by directly annealing the mixture of acetylacetone metal salt and alkali metal salt in air, as an outstanding electrocatalyst OER under acidic media (see Fig. 32.8A−H) [43]. The atomic structure (abundant Ir−C/O coordination moiety and less Ir−Ir metallic bond)

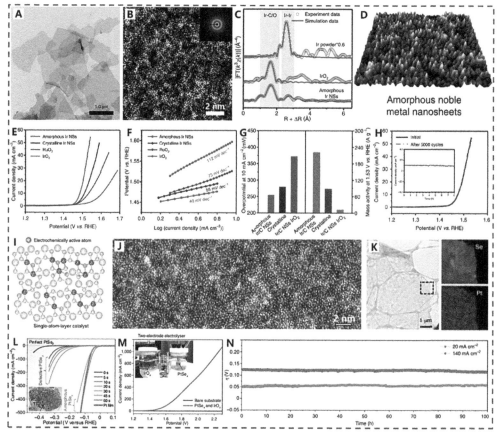

Figure 32.8 (A–H) Free-standing atomic-level Ir-based AMUNMs nanosheets for OER [43], (I–N) single-atom-layer PtSe$_x$-based AMUNMs nanosheets for overall water splitting [10].

of this amorphous Ir-based nanosheet has been proved. In 0.1 M HClO$_4$ solution, low overpotential (255 mV at 10 mA cm^{-2}), minimal Tafel slope (40 mV dec^{-1}), and very high mass activity (221.8 A g^{-1} at an overpotential of 300 mV under 1.53 V) are also proved. More recently, He et al. demonstrated the fabrication of wafer-sized amorphous PtSe$_x$ SALCs on SiO$_2$ by low-temperature amorphization strategy, which realized a single atom layer Pt-based catalyst with high atomic utilization ($\sim$26 wt.%) for efficient

HER catalysis and overall water splitting (see Fig. 32.8I–N) [10]. The $PtSe_x$ SALCs showed excellent HER catalytic performance (on-set potential of 0 V, Tafel slope of 39 mV dec^{-1}), which was comparable to commercial Pt catalyst. In addition, the high performance (200 mA cm^{-2} at 1.72 V) and super durability (100 h) of the wafer grade $PtSe_x$ are further demonstrated in the two-electrode electrolytic cell.

As mentioned above, Lei et al. produced a bimetallic atomic catalyst in which the dual atom Ru and Ni were co-modified on MoS_2 (Ru_1Ni_1–MoS_2 DACs) (see Fig. 32.6F for details) [37]. The experimental results and theoretical calculations show that a single Ru atom is anchored by a single Ni atom with strong electronegativity. In addition, due to the synergistic effect of taking the S atom bonded with Ni as a hydrogen receptor and the Ru as a hydroxyl receptor, the intermediate energy barrier in the hydrolysis separation step is effectively reduced. Therefore, the as-prepared Ru_1Ni_1–MoS_2 DACs exhibited an ultra-low overpotential of 32 mV at 10 mA cm^{-2}, a corresponding Tafel slope of 41 mV dec^{-1}, and negligible current decay over 20 h for HER, well beyond that of Ru_1–MoS_2 and Ni_1–MoS_2 SACs. Compared with SACs, DACs, while maintaining highly efficient atom utilization and excellent selectivity, can further enhance the catalytic activity of catalysts greatly due to the dual-site synergistic effect.

32.4.2 Photocatalytic degradation and energy production

Different from the nanomaterials, metal single atoms loaded on the semiconductors can achieve the maximum utilization of metal atoms and greatly promote the separation of photo-induced electron-hole pair (the isolated metal sites can be used as electron pumps to speed up electron-hole separation), thus improving the intrinsic activity of respective catalytic sites on single-atom interfacial photocatalysis [34]. The SACs photocatalysis also plays a role in the photocatalytic oxidative degradation of organic pollutants, especially the high-density SACs may affect the catalytic efficiency and mechanism. The g-C_3N_4 (visible light absorption) and metal oxides (e.g., Fe_3O_4 or ZnO semiconductor) with good band gap properties, have been used in the photocatalytic degradation of pollutants. The synergistic effects between single atoms (e.g., Fe, Co, Mo, W, and Au) and the above supports can effectively improve the capturing capacity of visible light, the binding energy with oxygen, and the charge separation behavior, thus promoting the surface reactions of catalytic oxidation (see Fig. 32.9 for details) [44–48].

In 2018, Guo and co-workers reported a g–C_3N_4–supported single atom Fe catalyst (FeN_x/g-C_3N_4) with a high density (~6 atoms cm^{-2}) and ultrahigh iron loading (18.2 wt.%) for the efficient degradation (by photo-Fenton reaction) of several typical organic dyes (methylene blue (MB), methyl orange (MO), rhodamine B (RhB) and phenol) with the addition of H_2O_2 under visible light irradiation (see Fig. 32.9A–C) [44]. The dense Fe(II)-N_x active sites on g-C_3N_4 can rapidly activate H_2O_2 to generate HO• and trigger high photo-Fenton catalytic activities under visible light. Besides, the carbon dots-supported single atom Co catalyst (Co_1/NC) with a high atom density

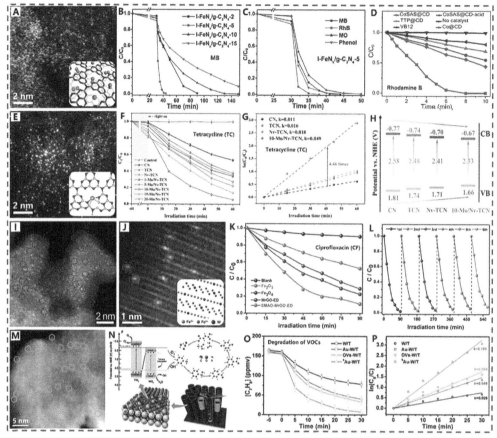

Figure 32.9 (A—C) FeN$_x$/g-C$_3$N$_4$ for organic dyes degradation [44], (D) Co$_1$/NC for organic dyes degradation [45]. (E—H) Mo/NV-g-C$_3$N$_4$ for tetracycline degradation [46], (I—L) W$_1$V$_1$ SMAO-Fe$_3$O$_4$ for antibiotic residues degradation [47], (M—P) Au single atom-dispersed WO$_3$/TiO$_2$ for VOCs oxidation [48].

($\sim$10 atoms nm^{-2}) also showed the high removal efficiency (in O$_2$ bubbling) of RhB of 100% in 10 min under visible light (see Fig. 32.9D) [45]. Recently, Zeng and co-workers reported an effective photocatalyst (Mo/NV-TCN) for the degradation of tetracycline, prepared by constructing high-site-density Mo species ($\sim$4 atoms nm^{-2}) on the nitrogen-vacancy (NV) tubular porous g-C$_3$N$_4$ (TCN) (see Fig. 32.9E—H) [46].

In latest 2022, Sui et al. reported a novel W$_1$V$_1$ (W—O$_3$/V—O$_{2.5}$) single metal atom oxide (SMAO)-Fe$_3$O$_4$ catalyst for highly efficient photocatalytic degradation of antibiotic residues (ciprofloxacin and ibuprofen) (see Fig. 32.9I—L) [47]. The W and V elements in the catalyst are anchored on the surface of Fe_3O_4 in the form of SMAO, and W element occupied the position of Fe^{2+} in Fe_3O_4, which greatly enhanced the separation ability of photo-electron-hole pair and improved the band gap of catalyst. Single-atom photocatalysis is also a promising technique for the oxidation of volatile organic compounds (VOCs). Zhang and co-workers reported a gold-loaded (Au) atom-dispersed WO_3/TiO_2 nanotube arrays for the photo-oxidation of Toluene (see Fig. 32.9M—P) [48]. The anchoring of high-density Au single atoms (Au atoms are anchored by O vacancies WO_3) greatly enhanced charge transfer of WO_3/TiO_2, reduced electron-hole recombination, and promoted toluene adsorption and oxidation.

As described previously, Li and Zhou developed a novel Co-O—Pt dimer-based DACs on the surface of titanium dioxide (TiO_2) to improve the photocatalytic efficiency for hydrogen production (see Fig. 32.6E for details) [36]. These Co-Pt dimerization sites were derived from high-density Pt single atoms and Co single atoms randomly anchored to the TiO_2 support. The excellent photocatalytic hydrogen production performance stems from the oxygen-coordinated Co-O—Pt dimer coupling, which can mutually optimize the electronic states at Pt and Co sites, thus weakening the H* bond. As a result, photocatalytic hydrogen production rate of 43.467 mmol $g^{-1}h^{-1}$, and the external quantum efficiency of 83.4% are acquired at the same time. This non-bonded dimerization site strategy and the oxygen-mediated mechanism provide great opportunities for greatly improving catalytic efficiency and developing novel catalysts.

32.4.3 Thermocatalytic energy production and purification

Highly-dispersed SACs have been proved to be effective in thermocatalysis for chemical energy production (such as hydrogen production by water-gas shift (WGS) reaction) and energy purification (such as preferential oxidation (PROX) of carbon monoxide (CO) in hydrogen feedstock), due to their special "electronic/geometric structures" and abundant "isolated active sites" multiple advantages [34]. Carbon monoxide and hydrogen are both flammable gases, and such mixture is well known in the industry as "water gas," where the water-gas shift (WGS) reaction (CO + H_2O(vapor)$\rightarrow CO_2+H_2$, $\Delta H = -41.2$ kJ mol^{-1}) is one of the key strategies for industrial production of high purity hydrogen. On the other hand, due to the easy CO poisoning of Pt metal, the removal of CO from hydrogen is important when Pt metal is used as catalyst in fuel cells, where the hydrogen purification by PROX of CO becomes crucial (via the reaction of CO+1/ $2O_2 \rightarrow CO_2$). Noble metal SACs have emerged as a class of promising catalysts have attracted great interests in PROX of CO, due to their high activity, selectivity, and stability.

Recently, He and Ji developed a dry ball milling method for the mass production of Au_1/CeO_2 SACs in large batch (above 1 kg each batch. The as-prepared Au_1/CeO_2 SAC demonstrated high activity, selectivity, and stability for PROX at 120°C, where

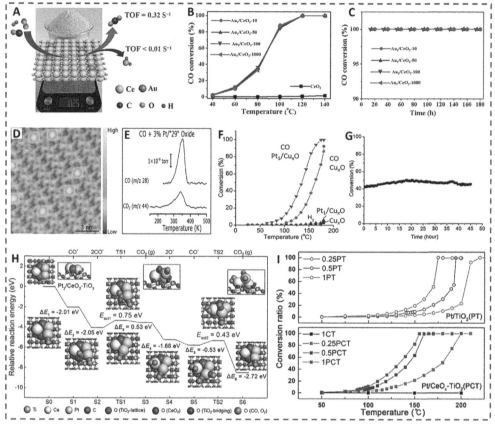

Figure 32.10 (A–C) Au$_1$/CeO$_2$ SACs for PROX of CO [49]; (D–G) Pt$_1$/Cu$_x$O SACs for PROX of CO [50]; (H and I) Pt$_2$/CeO$_x$-TiO$_2$ DACs for PROX of CO [51].

the TOFs for conversion of CO to CO$_2$ can reach 0.32 s^{-1} (while the TOFs for H$_2$ oxidation is < 0.01 s^{-1}) (see Fig. 32.10A–C for details) [49]. The outstanding catalytic performance was largely due to the strong occupying of Au$_1$ into the Ce vacancies of CeO$_2$ and thus coordinated with oxygen ions of CeO$_2$ to form highly stable M$_1$-O$_x$ entity for PROX. More recently, Liu et al. reported that the atomically dispersed Pt atoms in the surface of Cu_xO (i.e., Pt_1/Cu_xO SACs) are active for CO oxidation but do not catalyze H_2 oxidation (i.e., Pt_1/Cu_xO SACs are active for PROX reaction) (see Fig. 32.10D–G) [50]. The Pt_1/Cu_xO model surfaces enable low-temperature CO oxidation via a Mars-van Krevelen mechanism, in which the oxygen for CO oxidation is supplied by the "29" oxides. The Pt_1/Cu_xO demonstrated excellent selectivity for CO PROX (reach 100% CO conversion at 170 °C), and showed excellent stability of 45 h.

Recently, by manipulating the chemical nature of multi-component interfaces, Kim and co-workers synthesized CO-tolerant dense Pt dual-atoms (DAs) stabilized at the CeO_x-TiO_2 interfaces (i.e., Pt_2/CeO_x-TiO_2 DACs), which demonstrated ultrahigh reactivity for the CO oxidation reaction by the interface-mediated reaction mechanism (see Fig. 32.10H and I) [51]. The addition of 1 wt.% of Ce to TiO_2 particles created the specific CeO_x-TiO_2 interface (CeO_x clusters on TiO_2 (101) plane), which can stabilize Pt-DAs by strong electronic metal-support interactions (EMSI) (the electron donation from Pt to oxides). The CeO_x-TiO_2 hybrid-oxide support can provide strong binding sites and reactive oxygen species for Pt-DAs to form rich M_1-O_x entities and activate the Mars-van Krevelen (MvK) mechanism (protecting Pt atoms from CO-poisoning). Different amounts of Pt were impregnated on the CeO_x-TiO_2 hybrid-oxide support (denote as nPCT, where n = 0.25, 0.5, and 1.0 wt%). Clearly, the nPCT catalysts oxidize CO more actively than the nPT (without CeO_x) for all Pt-loadings, in which the 1PCT reached 100% CO conversion at 150 °C. This study presents a novel design strategy of Pt DACs by atomically precise interface engineering toward efficient CO-PROX reaction.

Moreover, Ma, Zhou, and Shi jointly reported a novel interfacial catalytic material of high-density, atomically dispersed Pt-based catalyst (high-density mixed structure of Pt_1 single sites and sub-nano Pt_n clusters) stabilized on α-MoC support (Pt_1-Pt_n)/α-MoC), which can be used to efficiently catalyze the activation of H_2O and CO into H_2 by WGS reaction [52]. It was found that the Pt species on α-MoC particles evolved from atomically-dispersed Pt species (Pt_1) (0.02 wt.% Pt) to coexist of Pt_1 and Pt clusters (Pt_n) (2 wt.% Pt) with the increase of Pt loading, and the structure of high-density Pt species remained stable in the catalytic reaction. The high-density 2 wt.% (Pt_1-Pt_n)/α-MoC quasi-AFCs are the first to achieve efficient WGS reaction for H_2 production in the ultra-wide temperature range of 40°C to 400°C, breaking through the limitations of existing catalysts in the high and narrow operating temperature range and greatly improving the reaction activity (100% CO conversion at 100°C) of α-MoC-based catalysts (much better than 0.2 wt.% Pt_1/α-MoC and 2 wt.% Au/α-MoC). This study breaks through the temperature limit of current carbon monoxide and water reforming technology for hydrogen production, providing a new technology choice for promoting the hydrogen economy.

32.5 Summary

In this chapter, we have discussed the structural features, preparation methods, energy and environmental applications, and typical case analysis of ADCs (focus on the SACs and DACs). Structural properties and preparation methods of carbon (graphene)-supported SACs, carbon nitride ($g-C_3N_4$)−supported SACs and metallic compounds (e.g., transition metal oxides, sulfides, and carbides)-supported SACs are systematically summarized. Graphene is an excellent support material of SACs, where "M-N_4" centers are formed on defective graphene. Metal-oxygen covalent coordination and metal cation vacancy anchoring are the two most accepted formation principles in the design of metal oxides-supported SACs. The atomically dispersed catalysts (SACs or DACs) have demonstrated extensive energy and environmental-related applications, including hydrogen energy production, chemical energy conversion, and pollutant degradation by means of thermocatalysis, electrocatalysis, and/or photocatalysis.

Acknowledgments

This book was supported by National Natural Science Foundation of China (22078071, 22272034), Natural Science Foundation of Guangdong Province (2021A1515010125, 2020A1515010344), Maoming Science and Technology Project (mmkj2020032), Guangdong Province Universities and Colleges Pearl River Scholar Funded Scheme (2019), Guangdong Basic and Applied Basic Research Foundation (2019A1515011249, 2021A1515010305), Key Research Project of Natural Science of Guangdong Provincial Department of Education (2019KZDXM010), Environment and Energy Green Catalysis Innovation Team of Colleges and Universities of Guangdong Province (2022KCXTD019), the program for Innovative Research Team of Guangdong University of Petrochemical Technology.

References

[1] L. Wang, D. Wang, Y. Li, Single-atom catalysis for carbon neutrality, Carbon Energy (2022), https://doi.org/10.1002/cey2.194.

[2] F. Zhang, Y. Zhu, Q. Lin, L. Zhang, X. Zhang, H. Wang, Noble-metal single-atoms in thermocatalysis, electrocatalysis, and photocatalysis, Energy and Environmental Science 14 (5) (2021) 2954−3009.

[3] R. Li, L. Luo, X. Ma, W. Wu, M. Wang, J. Zeng, Single atoms supported on metal oxides for energy catalysis, Journal of Materials Chemistry A 10 (2022) 5717−5742.

[4] X. Sui, L. Zhang, J. Li, K. Doyle-Davis, R. Li, Z. Wang, X. Sun, Advanced support materials and interactions for atomically dispersed noble-metal catalysts: from support effects to design strategies, Advanced Energy Materials 12 (1) (2022) 2102556.

[5] B. Qiao, A. Wang, X. Yang, L.F. Allard, Z. Jiang, Y. Cui, T. Zhang, Single-atom catalysis of CO oxidation using Pt1/FeOx, Nature Chemistry 3 (8) (2011) 634−641.

[6] R.T. Hannagan, G. Giannakakis, M. Flytzani-Stephanopoulos, E.C.H. Sykes, Single-atom alloy catalysis, Chemical Reviews 120 (21) (2020) 12044−12088.

[7] R. Li, D. Wang, Superiority of dual-atom catalysts in electrocatalysis: one step further than single-atom catalysts, Advanced Energy Materials 12 (9) (2022) 2103564.

[8] J. Gu, M. Jian, L. Huang, Z. Sun, A. Li, Y. Pan, J. Lu, Synergizing metal−support interactions and spatial confinement boosts dynamics of atomic nickel for hydrogenations, Nature Nanotechnology 16 (10) (2021) 1141−1149.

[9]   M. Peng, C. Dong, R. Gao, D. Xiao, H. Liu, D. Ma, Fully exposed cluster catalyst (FECC): toward rich surface sites and full atom utilization efficiency, ACS Central Science 7 (2) (2020) 262−273.

[10]   Y. He, L. Liu, C. Zhu, S. Guo, P. Golani, B. Koo, Z. Liu, Amorphizing noble metal chalcogenide catalysts at the single-layer limit towards hydrogen production, Nature Catalysis 5 (3) (2022) 212−221.

[11]   H. Jeong, O. Kwon, B.S. Kim, J. Bae, S. Shin, H.E. Kim, H. Lee, Highly durable metal ensemble catalysts with full dispersion for automotive applications beyond single-atom catalysts, Nature Catalysis 3 (4) (2020) 368−375.

[12]   Z. Li, B. Li, Y. Hu, C. Yu, Atomic-structured Metal Catalysts (Beyond Single Atom Catalysts): Design Fundamentals and Versatile Applications, 2023.

[13]   H.Y. Zhuo, X. Zhang, J.X. Liang, Q. Yu, H. Xiao, J. Li, Theoretical understandings of graphene-based metal single-atom catalysts: stability and catalytic performance, Chemical Reviews 120 (21) (2020) 12315−12341.

[14]   H. Xu, D. Cheng, D. Cao, X.C. Zeng, A universal principle for a rational design of single-atom electrocatalysts, Nature Catalysis 1 (5) (2018) 339−348.

[15]   D. Deng, X. Chen, L. Yu, X. Wu, Q. Liu, Y. Liu, X. Bao, A single iron site confined in a graphene matrix for the catalytic oxidation of benzene at room temperature, Science Advances 1 (11) (2015) e1500462.

[16]   H. Jin, P. Li, P. Cui, J. Shi, W. Zhou, X. Yu, C. Cao, Unprecedentedly high activity and selectivity for hydrogenation of nitroarenes with single atomic Co_1-N_3P_1 sites, Nature Communications 13 (1) (2022) 1−9.

[17]   C. Gao, J. Low, R. Long, T. Kong, J. Zhu, Y. Xiong, Heterogeneous single-atom photocatalysts: fundamentals and applications, Chemical Reviews 120 (21) (2020) 12175−12216.

[18]   X. Hai, S. Xi, S. Mitchell, K. Harrath, H. Xu, D.F. Akl, J. Lu, Scalable two-step annealing method for preparing ultra-high-density single-atom catalyst libraries, Nature Nanotechnology 17 (2) (2022) 174−181.

[19]   Y. Qu, Z. Li, W. Chen, Y. Lin, T. Yuan, Z. Yang, Y. Li, Direct transformation of bulk copper into copper single sites via emitting and trapping of atoms, Nature Catalysis 1 (10) (2018) 781−786.

[20]   Z. Yang, B. Chen, W. Chen, Y. Qu, F. Zhou, C. Zhao, Y. Wu, Directly transforming copper (I) oxide bulk into isolated single-atom copper sites catalyst through gas-transport approach, Nature Communications 10 (1) (2019) 1−7.

[21]   Y. Qu, B. Chen, Z. Li, X. Duan, L. Wang, Y. Lin, Y. Li, Thermal emitting strategy to synthesize atomically dispersed Pt metal sites from bulk Pt metal, Journal of the American Chemical Society 141 (11) (2019) 4505−4509.

[22]   C. Xia, Y. Qiu, Y. Xia, P. Zhu, G. King, X. Zhang, H. Wang, General synthesis of single-atom catalysts with high metal loading using graphene quantum dots, Nature Chemistry 13 (9) (2021) 887−894.

[23]   Q. Wang, X. Huang, Z.L. Zhao, M. Wang, B. Xiang, J. Li, M. Gu, Ultrahigh-loading of Ir single atoms on NiO matrix to dramatically enhance oxygen evolution reaction, Journal of the American Chemical Society 142 (16) (2020) 7425−7433.

[24]   M.D. Capobianco, B. Pattengale, J. Neu, C.A. Schmuttenmaer, Single copper atoms enhance photoconductivity in g-C_3N_4, The Journal of Physical Chemistry Letters 11 (20) (2020) 8873−8879.

[25]   Y. Chen, H. Zou, B. Yan, X. Wu, W. Cao, Y. Qian, G. Yang, Atomically dispersed Cu nanozyme with intensive ascorbate peroxidase mimic activity capable of alleviating ROS-mediated oxidation damage, Advanced Science 9 (5) (2022) 2103977.

[26]   G. Wang, R. Huang, J. Zhang, J. Mao, D. Wang, Y. Li, Synergistic modulation of the separation of photo-generated carriers via engineering of dual atomic sites for promoting photocatalytic performance, Advanced Materials 33 (52) (2021) 2105904.

[27]   Y. Liang, X. Wu, X. Liu, C. Li, S. Liu, Recovering solar fuels from photocatalytic CO_2 reduction over W^{6+}-incorporated crystalline g-C_3N_4 nanorods by synergetic modulation of active centers, Applied Catalysis B: Environmental 304 (2022) 120978.

[28]   G. Liu, Y. Huang, H. Lv, H. Wang, Y. Zeng, M. Yuan, C. Wang, Confining single-atom Pd on g-C_3N_4 with carbon vacancies towards enhanced photocatalytic NO conversion, Applied Catalysis B: Environmental 284 (2021) 119683.

[29] N.K. Wagh, S.S. Shinde, C.H. Lee, J.Y. Jung, D.H. Kim, S.H. Kim, J.H. Lee, Densely colonized isolated Cu-N single sites for efficient bifunctional electrocatalysts and rechargeable advanced Zn-air batteries, Applied Catalysis B: Environmental 268 (2020) 118746.

[30] R. Lang, W. Xi, J.C. Liu, Y.T. Cui, T. Li, A.F. Lee, T. Zhang, Non defect-stabilized thermally stable single-atom catalyst, Nature Communications 10 (1) (2019) 1−10.

[31] K. Liu, X. Zhao, G. Ren, T. Yang, Y. Ren, A.F. Lee, T. Zhang, Strong metal-support interaction promoted scalable production of thermally stable single-atom catalysts, Nature Communications 11 (1) (2020) 1−9.

[32] C. Cai, M. Wang, S. Han, Q. Wang, Q. Zhang, Y. Zhu, M. Gu, Ultrahigh oxygen evolution reaction activity achieved using Ir single atoms on amorphous CoOx nanosheets, ACS Catalysis 11 (1) (2020) 123−130.

[33] Y. Hu, H. Li, Z.S. Li, B. Li, S. Wang, Y. Yao, Progress in batch preparation of single-atom catalysts and application in sustainable synthesis of fine chemicals, Green Chemistry 23 (2021) 8754−8794.

[34] Z. Li, B. Li, Y. Hu, X. Liao, H. Yu, C. Yu, Emerging ultrahigh-density single-atom catalysts for versatile heterogeneous catalysis applications: redefinition, recent progress, and challenges, Small Structures (2022) 2200041.

[35] Y. Hu, Z. Li, B. Li, C. Yu, Recent progress of diatomic catalysts: general design fundamentals and diversified catalytic applications, Small (2022) 202203589.

[36] C. Wang, K. Wang, Y. Feng, C. Li, X. Zhou, L. Gan, X. Han, Co and Pt dual-single-atoms with oxygen-coordinated Co−O−Pt dimer sites for ultrahigh photocatalytic hydrogen evolution efficiency, Advanced Materials 33 (13) (2021) 2003327.

[37] J. Ge, D. Zhang, Y. Qin, T. Dou, M. Jiang, F. Zhang, X. Lei, Dual-metallic single Ru and Ni atoms decoration of MoS$_2$ for high-efficiency hydrogen production, Applied Catalysis B:Environmental 298 (2021) 120557.

[38] Z. Li, B. Li, Y. Hu, S. Wang, C. Yu, Highly-dispersed and high-metal-density electrocatalysts on carbon supports for the oxygen reduction reaction: from nanoparticles to atomic-level architectures, Materials Advances 3 (2) (2022) 779−809.

[39] G. Chen, P. Liu, Z. Liao, F. Sun, Y. He, H. Zhong, X. Feng, Zinc-mediated template synthesis of Fe-N-C electrocatalysts with densely accessible Fe-Nx active sites for efficient oxygen reduction, Advanced Materials 32 (8) (2020) 1907399.

[40] H. Adabi, A. Shakouri, N. Ul Hassan, J.R. Varcoe, B. Zulevi, A. Serov, W.E. Mustain, High-performing commercial Fe−N−C cathode electrocatalyst for anion-exchange membrane fuel cells, Nature Energy 6 (2021) 834−843.

[41] Z. Jin, P. Li, Y. Meng, Z. Fang, D. Xiao, G. Yu, Understanding the inter-site distance effect in single-atom catalysts for oxygen electroreduction, Nature Catalysis 4 (2021) 615−622.

[42] Z. Li, B. Li, M. Yu, C. Yu, P. Shen, Amorphous metallic ultrathin nanostructures: a latent ultra-high-density atomic-level catalyst for electrochemical energy conversion, International Journal of Hydrogen Energy 47 (2022) 26956−26977.

[43] G. Wu, X. Zheng, P. Cui, H. Jiang, X. Wang, Y. Qu, Y. Li, A general synthesis approach for amorphous noble metal nanosheets, Nature Communications 10 (1) (2019) 1−8.

[44] S. An, G. Zhang, T. Wang, W. Zhang, K. Li, C. Song, X. Guo, High-density ultra-small clusters and single-atom Fe sites embedded in graphitic carbon nitride (g-C$_3$N$_4$) for highly efficient catalytic advanced oxidation processes, ACS Nano 12 (9) (2018) 9441−9450.

[45] Q. Wang, J. Li, X. Tu, H. Liu, M. Shu, R. Si, R. Li, Single atomically anchored cobalt on carbon quantum dots as efficient photocatalysts for visible light-promoted oxidation reactions, Chemistry of Materials 32 (2) (2019) 734−743.

[46] C. Zhang, D. Qin, Y. Zhou, F. Qin, H. Wang, W. Wang, G. Zeng, Dual optimization approach to Mo single atom dispersed g-C$_3$N$_4$ photocatalyst: morphology and defect evolution, Applied Catalysis B: Environmental 303 (2022) 120904.

[47] K. Selvakumar, Y. Wang, Y. Lu, B. Tian, Z. Zhang, J. Hu, M. Sui, Single metal atom oxide anchored Fe$_3$O$_4$-ED-rGO for highly efficient photodecomposition of antibiotic residues under visible light illumination, Applied Catalysis B: Environmental 300 (2022) 120740.

[48] X. Wang, H. Pan, M. Sun, Y. Zhang, Au single atom-anchored WO_3/TiO_2 nanotubes for the photo-catalytic degradation of volatile organic compounds, Journal of Materials Chemistry A 10 (11) (2022) 6078−6085.

[49] T. Gan, Q. He, H. Zhang, H. Xiao, Y. Liu, Y. Zhang, H. Ji, Unveiling the kilogram-scale gold single-atom catalysts via ball milling for preferential oxidation of CO in excess hydrogen, Chemical Engineering Journal 389 (2020) 124490.

[50] J. Liu, A.J. Hensley, G. Giannakakis, A.J. Therrien, A. Sukkar, A.C. Schilling, E.C.H. Sykes, Developing single-site Pt catalysts for the preferential oxidation of CO: a surface science and first principles-guided approach, Applied Catalysis B: Environmental 284 (2021) 119716.

[51] M. Yoo, Y.S. Yu, H. Ha, S. Lee, J.S. Choi, S. Oh, H.Y. Kim, A tailored oxide interface creates dense Pt single-atom catalysts with high catalytic activity, Energy and Environmental Science 13 (4) (2020) 1231−1239.

[52] X. Zhang, M. Zhang, Y. Deng, M. Xu, L. Artiglia, W. Wen, D. Ma, A stable low-temperature H_2-production catalyst by crowding Pt on α-MoC, Nature 589 (7842) (2021) 396−401.

PART 4

Opportunities, challenges, and future outlooks

CHAPTER 33

Opportunities

Nanostructured materials with multiple nano-effects and structure—activity relationship will provide completely new functions that are different from traditional materials, thus generating new research directions and application mechanisms in various fields of science and technology. The revolution of nanoscience and nanotechnology will produce a profound impact on the chemical industry, energy industry, environment industry, and other related industries. These technological breakthroughs will completely change the way of human existence, and the economic value it brings is incalculable. The application of nanotechnology in energy and environmental industries will become a major cornerstone and driving force for the growth and development of green energy economy and the improvement of human living environment in the 21st century. In conclusion, in the last 30 years and into the future, nanomaterials and nanotechnology are offering continuous power and new opportunities for scientific exploration and technological innovation in the field of energy and environment.

In the era of continuous development of technology, the scale of matter studied by people is also constantly shrinking: from millimeters, to micrometers, and to nanometers. At the nanoscale, many matters exhibit particular properties different from macroscopic ones, marking humanity's ability to modify nature at the microscopic level (a collection of atoms/molecules). In field of metal materials, the structural transformation of metal foam materials from macroscopic and mesoscopic horizon to microscopic horizon has been quietly occurring since the appearance of 3-D atomic-level materials [1]. Taking Ni foam as an example, conventional macroscopic Ni foam material is structured with approximately 100-micron nickel matrix as the building units (see Fig. 33.1A) [2], and mesoscopic Ni foam material is composed of sub-1-micron nickel matrix as the building units (see Fig. 33.1B and C) [3,4]. From a typical ultra-high-density Ni single-atom catalyst (SAC) on carbon nanotubes (see Fig. 33.1D and E) [5], one can find that this 3-D atomic-level material shows partial linear tri/four-atoms and trigonometric tri-atoms (Fig. 33.1D), while most Ni atoms (about 0.2 nm) are isolated by support' atoms (C and N atoms) (Fig. 33.1E). The same results can be seen in nickel-copper bimetallic 3-D atomic-level material on graphitic carbon nitride, where the linear Cu—Ni—Cu (with bridging O atoms) tri-atom stereo structures are formed (Fig. 33.1F) [6]. The paradigm of 3-D metal atomic foam materials (3-D AFMs) is of great significance in both material science and nanoscience, by which the traditional metal micro/nano-materials have entered the atomic structure era.

Nanostructured Materials
ISBN 978-0-443-19256-2, https://doi.org/10.1016/B978-0-443-19256-2.00007-7

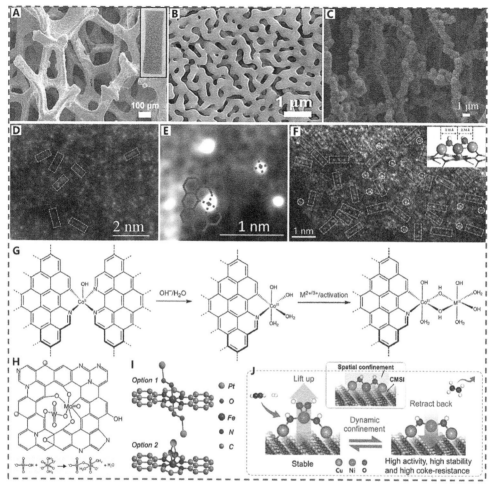

Figure 33.1 Typical 3-D Ni foam architectures: (A) Macroscopic [2], (B, C) mesoscopic [3,4], and (D—F) microscopic structures [5,6]; metal molecular groups graft (or oxygen bridging) strategy of 3-D atomic construction of AFMs: (G, H) MM' dual atom stereo-structures [7,8], (I) double O-bridging MM' or MM'M dual/triple atom stereo structures [9], (J) single O-bridging MM'M triple atom stereo structure [6]. (The above images and analysis are from one of our recent review papers [1]).

Once the dense-site 3-D atomic construction of AFMs is formed, the stereoscopic effect (enhancement effect by 3-D atomic construction) in atomic catalytic behavior may occur for these unique sub—nanostructured materials [1]. The formation of 3-D atomic construction of AFMs depends on three aspects: (1) molecular-level 3-D support materials (directly deriving 3-D atomic construction), (2) abundant coordinated molecular functional groups (coupled with support self-assembly or self-sacrifice process), and (3) metal molecular graft functional groups (multi-metal atoms is bridged by non-metallic atoms) (see Fig. 33.1G—J for details) [7—9]. Metal molecular graft (Fig. 33.1G and H) [7,8] and oxygen atom (or—OH group) bridging (Fig. 33.1I and J) [6,9] belong to the sophisticated 3-D atomic manipulation on the surface or defect edges of specific nanostructured supports. The most noteworthy feature is that these bridging atoms have very high plasticity (the lift-up and retract-back effect of middle active M' atom) in the dynamic catalytic process (Fig. 33.1J) [6], which may be an inherent property and attractiveness of 3-D atomic construction AFMs catalysts. For 3-D bridging AFMs in particular, the dynamic catalysis and stereoscopic effect are likely to be their unique characteristics (influence on catalytic mechanism and stability). It is believed that more and more structural functionalities and advantageous features of AFMs will be discovered one by one during the preparation and application process in the near future.

Hitherto, the metal foam materials can be divided into atomic foam materials (coordinated or bridged 3-D metal atoms on carriers), nano-foam materials (e.g., nano-metal aerogel), and block foam materials (e.g., metal Ni foam), by identifying building units under the microscopic, mesoscopic, and macroscopic horizons. The supported metal atomic foam catalysts (AFCs) have characteristics of atomically dispersed structure, ultrahigh site density (corresponding to upper-limit metal loading), stereoscopic or 3-D atomic architecture, and other expected advantages. The AFCs are likely to fill the gap between SACs and nanocrystal catalysts, which have the advantages of both catalysts and exhibit additional features such as dense site effect, synergistic effect, and stereoscopic effect in versatile heterogeneous catalysis applications [1]. In summary, in the field of heterogeneous catalysis, the construction of high-density metal AFCs based on nanostructured carrier materials is a major opportunity in the design of high-performance sub—nanostructured catalysts.

There is no doubt that the exploration and application of nanostructured materials and atomic-structured materials have become a hot spot at present. And the basic research and the application research appear a new situation of parallel development. Globally, the economic benefits created by nanomaterials (or sub—nanomaterials) and their corresponding products in the international market are growing at an annual rate of more than 15%. At the same time, the basic research of nanomaterials (or atomic materials) has become increasingly in-depth and systematic, and the theoretical research on the formation factors, active sites, and stabilization mechanisms of nano-functional structures (or atomic coordination structures) has also been developed and improved. At present, the research objects of nanoscience mainly focus on nano-array system, mesoporous system, hollow system, and heterojunction system. In particular, the characterization of the atomic structure on the surface of nanomaterials, the in situ transition from nanoparticles to atomically dispersed materials, and the interaction between atomic metals and nano-carriers have become the focus of recent research. To sum up, the transition from nanomaterials (1−100 nm) to sub−nanomaterials (0.1 ~ 1 nm) presents unprecedented new and key opportunities in the field of energy and environmental science and technology [10].

33.1 Summary

In this chapter, we have discussed the importance and opportunity of nanomaterials and sub−nanomaterials. At present, material science is shifting from the era of mesoscopic nanostructures to the era of microscopic atomic structures. The parallel development of nanostructured materials and atomic-structured materials has brought new impetus to the technological innovation of energy and environmental disciplines. Since various dimensions of nanomaterials have been discovered, people are increasingly aware of the extremely high application value of nanomaterials. However, the exploration of nano/atomic technology is still in its infancy. How to control the production cost cheaply and how to control the synthesis method to obtain the desired properties are many problems that need to be solved urgently.

Acknowledgments

This book was supported by National Natural Science Foundation of China (22078071, 22272034), Natural Science Foundation of Guangdong Province (2021A1515010125, 2020A1515010344), Maoming Science and Technology Project (mmkj2020032), Guangdong Province Universities and Colleges Pearl River Scholar Funded Scheme (2019), Guangdong Basic and Applied Basic Research Foundation (2019A1515011249, 2021A1515010305), Key Research Project of Natural Science of Guangdong Provincial Department of Education (2019KZDXM010), Environment and Energy Green Catalysis Innovation Team of Colleges and Universities of Guangdong Province (2022KCXTD019), the program for Innovative Research Team of Guangdong University of Petrochemical Technology.

References

[1]   Z. Li, B. Li, Y. Hu, X. Liao, H. Yu, C. Yu, Emerging ultrahigh-density single-atom catalysts for versatile heterogeneous catalysis applications: redefinition, recent progress, and challenges, Small Structures (2022) 2200041.

[2]   N.K. Chaudhari, H. Jin, B. Kim, K. Lee, Nanostructured materials on 3D nickel foam as electrocatalysts for water splitting, Nanoscale 9 (34) (2017) 12231−12247.

[3]   X. Guo, J. Han, P. Liu, Y. Ito, A. Hirata, M. Chen, Graphene@Nanoporous nickel cathode for Li-O$_2$ batteries, ChemNanoMat 2 (3) (2016) 176−181.

[4]   L. Li, X. Liu, C. Liu, H. Wan, J. Zhang, P. Liang, H. Wang, Ultra-long life nickel nanowires@ nickel-cobalt hydroxide nanoarrays composite pseudocapacitive electrode: construction and activation mechanism, Electrochimica Acta 259 (2018) 303−312.

[5]   Y. Cheng, S. Zhao, B. Johannessen, J.P. Veder, M. Saunders, M.R. Rowles, S.P. Jiang, Atomically dispersed transition metals on carbon nanotubes with ultrahigh loading for selective electrochemical carbon dioxide reduction, Advanced Materials 30 (13) (2018) 1706287.

[6]   J. Gu, M. Jian, L. Huang, Z. Sun, A. Li, Y. Pan, J. Lu, Synergizing metal—support interactions and spatial confinement boosts dynamics of atomic nickel for hydrogenations, Nature Nanotechnology 16 (10) (2021) 1141—1149.

[7]   L. Bai, C.S. Hsu, D.T. Alexander, H.M. Chen, X. Hu, Double-atom catalysts as a molecular platform for heterogeneous oxygen evolution electrocatalysis, Nature Energy (2021) 1—13.

[8]   Y. Yang, Y. Qian, H. Li, Z. Zhang, Y. Mu, D. Do, X. Fan, O-coordinated W-Mo dual-atom catalyst for pH-universal electrocatalytic hydrogen evolution, Science Advances 6 (23) (2020) eaba6586.

[9]   X. Zeng, J. Shui, X. Liu, Q. Liu, Y. Li, J. Shang, R. Yu, Single-atom to single-atom grafting of Pt_1 onto Fe-N_4 center: Pt_1@Fe-N-C multifunctional electrocatalyst with significantly enhanced properties, Advanced Energy Materials 8 (1) (2018) 1701345.

[10] Z. Li, B. Li, Y. Hu, S. Wang, C. Yu, Highly-dispersed and high-metal-density electrocatalysts on carbon supports for the oxygen reduction reaction: from nanoparticles to atomic-level architectures, Materials Advances 3 (2) (2022) 779—809.

CHAPTER 34

Challenges

At present, an important trend in the research of nanomaterial fabrication technology is to strengthen the research of microscopic control engineering, which includes the microscopic control of particle size, surface shape, and microstructure. Because of the concurrence of small size effect, surface effect, and quantum size effect on nanomaterial, it is difficult to distinguish the level of their contribution to a material. Whether these effects are beneficial or detrimental is difficult to judge. This not only brings difficulties to the interpretation of some phenomena, but also brings disadvantages to the design of new nanostructured materials. How to control the influence of these nanoscale effects on the properties of nanomaterials and how to control the effect level of each nanoscale effect on the structure and properties of nanomaterials is an urgent problem to be solved in microscopic control engineering [1].

How to process nanomaterials is also a big challenge for the application of engineering technology. The treatment of nanomaterials is mainly divided into two aspects: (1) From the perspective of safety, how to deal with nanometer powder safely will be the challenge we face (such as the flammability and oxidation of nanomaterials, etc.). (2) From the perspective of transfer, it is a challenge to transfer nanomaterials from the site of growth (usually the substrate) to the site of application (usually the nanomaterials need to be integrated into the device to be prepared). Some of the unique characteristics of nanomaterials may be lost in the process of nanomaterial handling (preservation and transfer) if improper conditions occur. Therefore, from the perspective of device application of nanotechnology, the following three aspects need to be paid special attention: preservation and transfer process of nanomaterials [2].

Despite its basic achievements, nanotechnology is experiencing a major hurdle. This is because translating scientific findings published in research journals into actual industrial applications remains a major challenge (i.e., the dilemma of mass production of nanomaterials). The problem is multifaceted. First, the material's characteristics change when scaled up, just as they do when scaled down to the nanoscale. Second, the industry is hesitant to develop new large-scale nanomaterial manufacturing technologies unless substantial profits are made. These dilemmas are particularly important in applied science, where there is a gap between laboratory and industrial-scale research. The transfer of nanomaterials from the laboratory to the industrial environment (i.e., the scale-up production) should follow carefully verified procedures to ensure that cost-effective nanomaterials can be produced [3].

Nanostructured Materials
ISBN 978-0-443-19256-2, https://doi.org/10.1016/B978-0-443-19256-2.00014-4

There are also some challenges in the application of nanomaterials to the field of energy storage, mainly due to the side reactions on the electrode surface caused by the huge specific surface area of nanomaterials, such as irreversible effects in the first cycle. The huge surface area of nanomaterials is conducive to the contact reaction of substances and the formation of SEI film, but it will also cause the significant irreversible capacity of the first cycle and the occurrence of side reactions. The reaction between electrode and electrolyte surface is also a field that needs to be further studied [4]. On the other hand, nanomaterials also face some challenges in the field of environmental purification, mainly including the recycling problem of nano-powder materials, secondary pollution possibility, and environmental-ecological risk of nanomaterials. Designing controllable, smarter nanostructures, and developing nanomaterial with complementary functions and recyclability are feasible solutions. The safety evaluation of nanomaterials is undoubted of great social value and will affect the further reliable application of nanomaterials in both energy and environment fields [5].

The evolution from nanostructured materials to atomic-structured materials is an important advancement for nanoscience and nanotechnology. However, the challenges in the designs and applications of atomically dispersed materials (such as single-atom catalysts (SACs) on nano-carriers) will be more severe. As presented in a review paper of our group, the structural effects of ultra-high-density SACs, or atomic foam catalyst (AFCs), include three aspects: (1) dense site effect, (2) synergistic effect, and (3) stereoscopic effect, which make the AFCs have unique functionalities in many heterogeneous catalytic fields. Nevertheless, the AFCs still face many scientific and technological challenges in both preparation and application. The main challenges may come from the following four aspects: (1) coordinated and electronic structures, (2) pore structure and mass transfer, (3) dynamic catalysis and structural stability, (4) batch preparation and industrial evaluation (see Fig. 34.1 for details) [6].

(I) **Coordinated and electronic structures:** The geometric coordination environment and electronic structure of central metal atoms in SACs (especially for AFCs) are very important to the catalytic characteristics for the heterogeneous catalysis (based on the intrinsic structure-performance relationship and metal-support interaction) [7]. However, in the current reports, a large proportion of high-density SACs fail to achieve the single-site design (in non-uniform coordination moiety), which will inevitably bring obstruction to the later regulation of geometric/electronic structures and study of single-site catalysis mechanism.

(II) **Pore structure and mass transfer:** Although high-loading SACs may have better overall activity, the mass transfer of reactants, products and intermediates are still worthy of in-depth study. Designing porous structure of support materials can improve the actual utilization of sites and promote catalytic efficiency [8]. However, most of the high-density SACs have ignored the design of porous support materials, only using the easily stacked nano-sheets, large-volume, and dense polymer

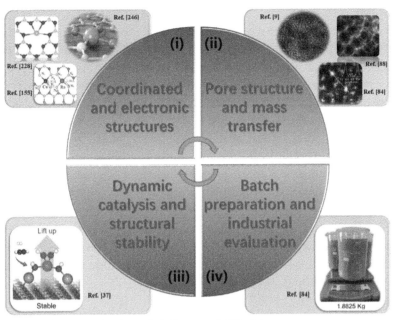

Figure 34.1 Scientific and technological challenges of AFCs [6].

or metallic compounds as support materials. The accessible rate of metal sites is far from 100% in reaction solutions due to poor mass transfer.

(III) Dynamic catalysis and structural stability: The catalytic mechanism based on the dynamic change of active sites (or coordination structures) has become a hot topic at present. The progress of dynamic catalysis provides new ideas and opportunities for revealing the black box of catalytic electron cycle and developing efficient SACs [9]. However, the relationship between atom density and dynamic catalysis has not been reported for the ultra-high-density SACs. The highly-dense sites and complex coordination structures are likely to bring extra difficulties and new challenges to the exploration of dynamic mechanism and structural stability, despite under current state-of-the-art in situ or operando analysis technologies.

(III) Batch preparation and industrial evaluation: It is very important to develop a general batch preparation strategy and production technology for promoting the industrial application in heterogeneous catalysis of ultra-high-density SACs [10].

However, only one report has achieved the general and batch preparation of ultra-high-density SACs, while this method belongs to the wet chemical method which still faces many technical challenges in real industrial production (such as equipment capacity, time and space yield, and reaction economy). On the other hand, AFCs lack catalytic efficiency and practical level evaluation under industrial conditions of the device or conditions. Frankly speaking, the mass production and industrial evaluation of ultra-high-density SACs (i.e., AFCs) still have a long way to go.

For ultra-high-density single atomic materials, the above four problems are very obvious, which have become the biggest bottleneck for the development of high-performance atomic-structured materials. Admittedly, for the current nanostructured materials or sub—nanostructured materials, it is still the most critical challenge to understand the co-ordination structures and electronic structures of metal atoms on the surface of materials. The pore structure and mass diffusion of nanomaterials are the most direct factors affecting the related properties of both energy and environmental applications. Besides, structural stability and mass production are still technical difficulties in the design and application of most nanomaterials.

34.1 Summary

In this chapter, we have discussed the problems and challenges of nanomaterials and sub—nanomaterials (including atomic-structured materials). Distinguishing the contribution level of various nano-effects independently on a nanomaterial and systematically evaluating structure—activity relationship are still challenging problems for microscopic control engineering. How to process (preservation and transfer) nanomaterials is also a big challenge for the application of engineering technology. Translating scientific findings into industrial applications remains a major challenge due to the gap between laboratory and industrial-scale environments. There are also some challenges in the application of nanomaterials to the field of energy storage and environmental purification. The challenges in the designs and applications of atomically dispersed materials (such as SACs on nano-carriers) will be more severe.

Acknowledgments

This book was supported by National Natural Science Foundation of China (22078071, 22272034), Natural Science Foundation of Guangdong Province (2021A1515010125, 2020A1515010344), Maoming Science and Technology Project (mmkj2020032), Guangdong Province Universities and Colleges Pearl River Scholar Funded Scheme (2019), Guangdong Basic and Applied Basic Research Foundation (2019A1515011249, 2021A1515010305), Key Research Project of Natural Science of Guangdong Provincial Department of Education (2019KZDXM010), Environment and Energy Green Catalysis Innovation Team of Colleges and Universities of Guangdong Province (2022KCXTD019), the program for Innovative Research Team of Guangdong University of Petrochemical Technology.

References

[1] https://mp.weixin.qq.com/s/e76b_ZCovHeeel_hyyJIvA.

[2] https://mp.weixin.qq.com/s/erNmUladChzoJuiCyGKOmQ.

[3] https://mp.weixin.qq.com/s/0ljNcxQagBKfucuThIjCFw.

[4] E. Pomerantseva, F. Bonaccorso, X. Feng, Y. Cui, Y. Gogotsi, Energy storage: the future enabled by nanomaterials, Science 366 (6468) (2019) eaan8285.

[5] B. Fadeel, L. Farcal, B. Hardy, S. Vázquez-Campos, D. Hristozov, A. Marcomini, K. Savolainen, Advanced tools for the safety assessment of nanomaterials, Nature Nanotechnology 13 (7) (2018) 537−543.

[6] Z. Li, B. Li, Y. Hu, X. Liao, H. Yu, C. Yu, Emerging ultrahigh-density single-atom catalysts for versatile heterogeneous catalysis applications: redefinition, recent progress, and challenges, Small Structures (2022) 2200041.

[7] S. Ji, B. Jiang, H. Hao, Y. Chen, J. Dong, Y. Mao, Y. Li, Matching the kinetics of natural enzymes with a single-atom iron nanozyme, Nature Catalysis 4 (5) (2021) 407−417.

[8] Y. Guo, F. Liu, L. Feng, X. Wang, X. Zhang, J. Liang, Single Co atoms anchored on nitrogen-doped hierarchically ordered porous carbon for selective hydrogenation of quinolines and efficient oxygen reduction, Chemical Engineering Journal 429 (2022) 132150.

[9] J. Gu, M. Jian, L. Huang, Z. Sun, A. Li, Y. Pan, J. Lu, Synergizing metal−support interactions and spatial confinement boosts dynamics of atomic nickel for hydrogenations, Nature Nanotechnology 16 (10) (2021) 1141−1149.

[10] X. Hai, S. Xi, S. Mitchell, K. Harrath, H. Xu, D.F. Akl, J. Lu, Scalable two-step annealing method for preparing ultra-high-density single-atom catalyst libraries, Nature Nanotechnology 17 (2) (2022) 174−181.

CHAPTER 35

Future outlooks

Nanomaterials industry, new energy industry, and environmental materials industry, as three emerging industries in the 21st century, have a bright future. Nanomaterials have been widely used in various fields due to their unique structure and physicochemical properties. Since the emergence of the words "carbon dioxide peak emission" and "carbon neutrality" in 2020, the development of the field of new energy and environmental materials has received higher attention worldwide [1]. Now the nanomaterials industry has been making steady progress: in the last 20 years, nanoscience has brought many disciplines together in a way that hadn't been seen before, but nanoscience has done that. If these three emerging fields can be more widely combined, with the unique advantages of nanomaterials, there will be a lot of new energy products and environmental materials to be developed. This will help us achieve the goal of "carbon neutrality" faster, improve the Earth's environment, and contribute to the sustainable development of energy science and technology.

Taking catalysis as an example, we can find that catalytic materials have undergone the evolution from micrometer structure to nanostructure and even the current atomic structure. At the beginning of the 20th century, the surface catalysis of metal materials had been widely used in industry. In the 1990s, people realized a new understanding of catalysis from the perspective of nanometer: size effect, crystal plane effect, defect effect, composition effect, synergistic effect, electron effect (at nanolevel), etc. In recent 10 years (after the discovery of single-atom catalysis in 2011) and in the future, we need to deeply understand catalysis from the atomic perspective: single atomic sites, coordination structures, hybrid orbitals, dynamic catalysis, electronic effects (at atomic level), etc [2]. Whether it is thermocatalysis, photocatalysis, or electrocatalysis, whether it is energy application or environmental application, nanomaterials are undergoing the transition from the nano-level age to the atomic-level age. Or in a long period of time, nanostructured materials and atomic-structured materials will go hand in hand and complement each other in scientific research and technological applications.

It is worth noting that there is an inextricably linked relationship between nanostructured materials and atomic-structured materials: (1) The atomic-structured materials often exist independently without nano-carrier materials, and the activity of nanomaterials can be greatly increased because of the single-atom active centers on their surface [3]; (2) Elemental metal nanoparticles and higher state metal active centers can be thermodynamically interconverted on a specific carrier under oxidizing and reducing gas conditions [4]. Encouragingly, a new-type amorphous metallic ultrathin nanostructured

Nanostructured Materials
ISBN 978-0-443-19256-2, https://doi.org/10.1016/B978-0-443-19256-2.00009-0

materials (AMUNMs) can be regarded as a latent ultra-high-density atomic-level catalysts (UHD ALCs) free-standing system (including 0-D, 1-D, and 2-D ultrathin nanostructures) for versatile electrochemical conversion applications [5]. The ultrathin nanostructures (single or few-atom-layer thickness), long-range disordered atomic arrangement (abundant vacancy or micropores), and abundant metal-nonmetal coordination structures (ultra-high-density atomic structures), endowed the AMUNMs with high atom utilization rate, high catalytic efficiency, and stability.

Admittedly, the structural transformation from nanostructured materials (such as the AMUNMs) to atomic-structured materials (such as the UHD ALCs) involves the regulation of mesoscopic nanostructures and the optimization of microscopic atomic structures, which needs to balance multiple relationships to achieve perfect results. It is indeed a meaningful work to carry out the research on "material design" and "structure-activity relationship" at mesoscopic nanoscale and microscopic atomic scale and deepen the understanding of the activity and stability of these atomic-level catalytic materials. The "vacancy and porous structures," "atomic-coordination structures," and "electronic structures" of the amorphous catalytic materials are very important to the catalytic performances. Therefore, we suggest to conduct causal analysis on the structural transformation from AMUNMs to UHD ALCs and their catalytic efficiency and carry out research on "structure—activity relationship" (i.e., the relationship between the catalytic efficiency and vacancy-atomic-electronic multiple structures), so as to realize the functional regulation of UHD ALCs with high catalytic activity and stability, and comprehensively obtain the scientific theory and design principles of catalytic materials for both energy and environmental applications (as shown in Fig. 35.1) [5].

Ultrathin nanostructures and amorphous structure can provide abundant active sites for catalytic reaction, and the high activity of AMUNMs may be attributed to the independent atomic structure of metal sites, metal-nonmetal coordination structure, or high-density vacancy structure. However, in the final analysis, the high activity originates from the change in electronic structure of the metal sites and the surrounding environment. Electronic state control is the core issue of catalysis, which determines the charge transfer behavior of reaction and improves the catalytic efficiency. Therefore, we propose to explore the atomic and electronic structures of AMUNMs by means of advanced technologies. In addition to conventional structural characterization (X-ray Diffraction (XRD) and X-ray photoelectron spectroscopy (XPS)), more advanced techniques need to be introduced to analyze the atomic structures (atomic phase and planar distribution) and electronic structures (electronic states and atom coordination) of AMUNMs. The above-mentioned atomic-resolved AC HAADF-STEM and EXAFS are naturally the preferred techniques. Due to the progress of the data acquisition method (2-D atom image at different tilting angles) and reconstruction algorithms (Fourier transform cycle), the atomic-resolution electron tomography (AET) technology makes it possible to accurately characterize the 3-D atom coordinates of AMUNMs. Besides, the in situ

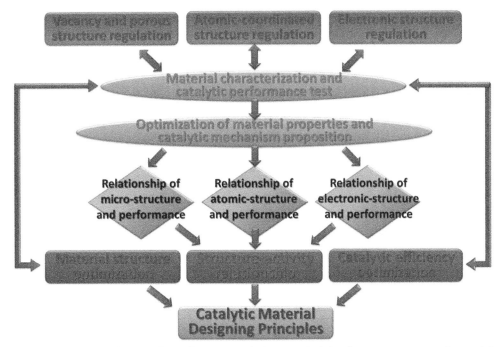

Figure 35.1 Proposed research roadmap toward design principles from nanostructured materials (such as the AMUNMs) to atomic-structured materials (such as the UHD ALCs) [5].

structural analysis under operando electrochemical conditions (e.g., operando XAFS) can be used to explore the dynamic atom reconstruction of AMUNMs [5].

Nanomaterials prepared by conventional methods (such as nitrogen-doped carbon or carbon-supported metal catalysts) may have many monatomic active centers (residual metal species or implied single-atom species). But these invisible single atoms, and not just the visible nanoparticles, may actually be at work, which I not visible under ordinary high-resolution transmission electron microscopy [6]. How to deal with this problem is worth thinking, and we suggest that appropriate manpower and resources can be invested to reevaluate these nano–atomic structural materials. In order to better solve the problem of active sites, the techniques that need to be vigorously developed include (1) in situ characterization: which can be used to explore the actual active sites and obtain a deeper understanding of catalytic reaction mechanism. (2) Density functional theory (DFT): that can be used to predict which component or which interface on nanomaterial is the real catalytic active center. (3) Controllable synthetic technology: that can be used to control the coordination structure and site density of catalytic centers [7].

In the two disciplines of nano-energy materials and nano-environmental materials, the current scientific workers often face the following great problems: (1) where do you find your research inspiration and (2) where do you find opportunity in your fields. Professor Yi Cui at Stanford University offers the following advices: We should start from the end of the application, such as the problem of energy or environmental systems, to find inspiration for our scientific research. Working backward from the end of tapplication to the material design reveals a lot of new directions and new ideas. From the perspective of solving practical problems, to the system level to find problems and solutions to the problems. In the past 20—30 years, the energy structure of the whole society has also changed a lot, among which electricity has become cheaper and cheaper. Electronics has become a very cheap "chemical raw material", that can also be said to be an "energy material." Therefore, starting from electronics, new chemical fuel can be synthesized and the storage energy can be used for electric vehicles or energy-chemical industry. The connection between the entire energy industry and chemical industry or maybe a new opportunity for nano-energy and environmental fields [8].

35.1 Summary

In this chapter, we have discussed the prospect and future outlooks of nanomaterials and sub—nanomaterials (including atomic-structured materials). The emergence of new concepts of "carbon dioxide peak emission" and "carbon neutrality" may accelerate the development of new energy and environmental nanomaterials. Catalytic materials have undergone the evolution from micrometer structure to nanostructure and even the atomic structure. Nanostructured materials and atomic-structured materials will go hand in hand and complement each other in scientific research and technological applications. A new-type amorphous metallic ultrathin nanostructured materials (AMUNMs) can be regarded as a latent ultra-high-density atomic-level catalysts (UHD ALCs) freestanding system. We propose to explore the atomic and electronic structures of nano-atomic materials by means of advanced technologies, such as AC HAADF-STEM, EXAFS, AET, in situ characterization, and DFT calculation.

Acknowledgments

This book was supported by National Natural Science Foundation of China (22078071, 22272034), Natural Science Foundation of Guangdong Province (2021A1515010125, 2020A1515010344), Maoming Science and Technology Project (mmkj2020032), Guangdong Province Universities and Colleges Pearl River Scholar Funded Scheme (2019), Guangdong Basic and Applied Basic Research Foundation (2019A1515011249, 2021A1515010305), Key Research Project of Natural Science of Guangdong Provincial Department of Education (2019KZDXM010), Environment and Energy Green Catalysis Innovation Team of Colleges and Universities of Guangdong Province (2022KCXTD019), the program for Innovative Research Team of Guangdong University of Petrochemical Technology.

References

[1] https://mp.weixin.qq.com/s/A5DiPHw8JSEekNyn_y_gHw.

[2] Z. Li, S. Ji, Y. Liu, X. Cao, S. Tian, Y. Chen, Y. Li, Well-defined materials for heterogeneous catalysis: from nanoparticles to isolated single-atom sites, Chemical Reviews 120 (2) (2019) 623—682.

[3] Z. Li, B. Li, Y. Hu, X. Liao, H. Yu, C. Yu, Emerging ultrahigh-density single-atom catalysts for versatile heterogeneous catalysis applications: redefinition, recent progress, and challenges, Small Structures 3 (6) (2022) 2200041.

[4] S. Wei, A. Li, J.C. Liu, Z. Li, W. Chen, Y. Gong, Y. Li, Direct observation of noble metal nanoparticles transforming to thermally stable single atoms, Nature Nanotechnology 13 (9) (2018) 856—861.

[5] Z. Li, B. Li, M. Yu, C. Yu, P. Shen, Amorphous metallic ultrathin nanostructures: a latent ultra-high-density atomic-level catalyst for electrochemical energy conversion, International Journal of Hydrogen Energy 47 (2022) 26956—26977.

[6] Z. Li, B. Li, Y. Hu, S. Wang, C. Yu, Highly-dispersed and high-metal-density electrocatalysts on carbon supports for the oxygen reduction reaction: from nanoparticles to atomic-level architectures, Materials Advances 3 (2) (2022) 779—809.

[7] https://mp.weixin.qq.com/s/i10m7XoG_gM93X23YmnawQ.

[8] https://mp.weixin.qq.com/s/hSpHxuwwa_nI_Wv2OCmwnw.

Index

CPI Antony Rowe
Eastbourne, UK
September 08, 2023